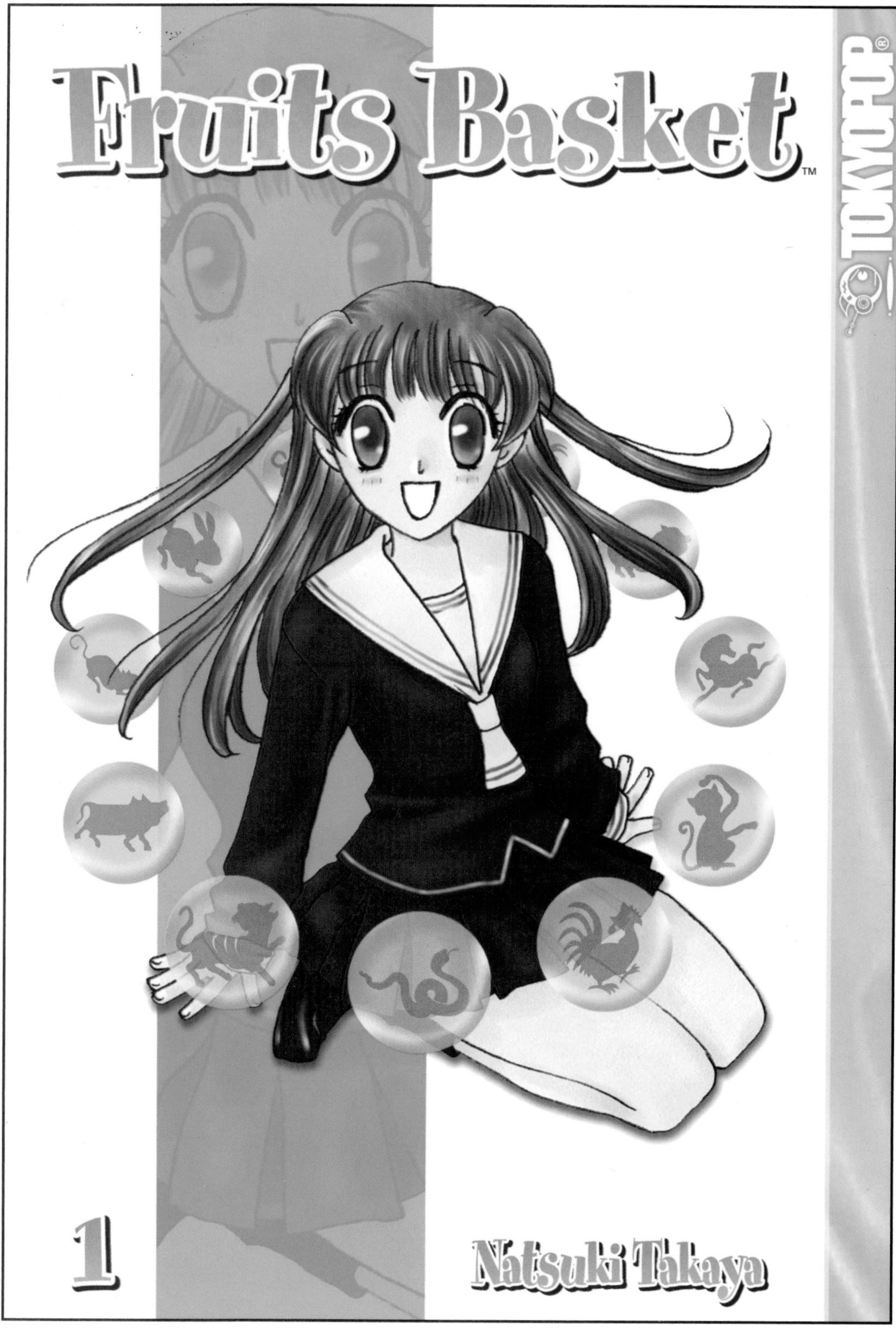
Fruits Basket™
TOKYOPOP®
1
Natsuki Takaya

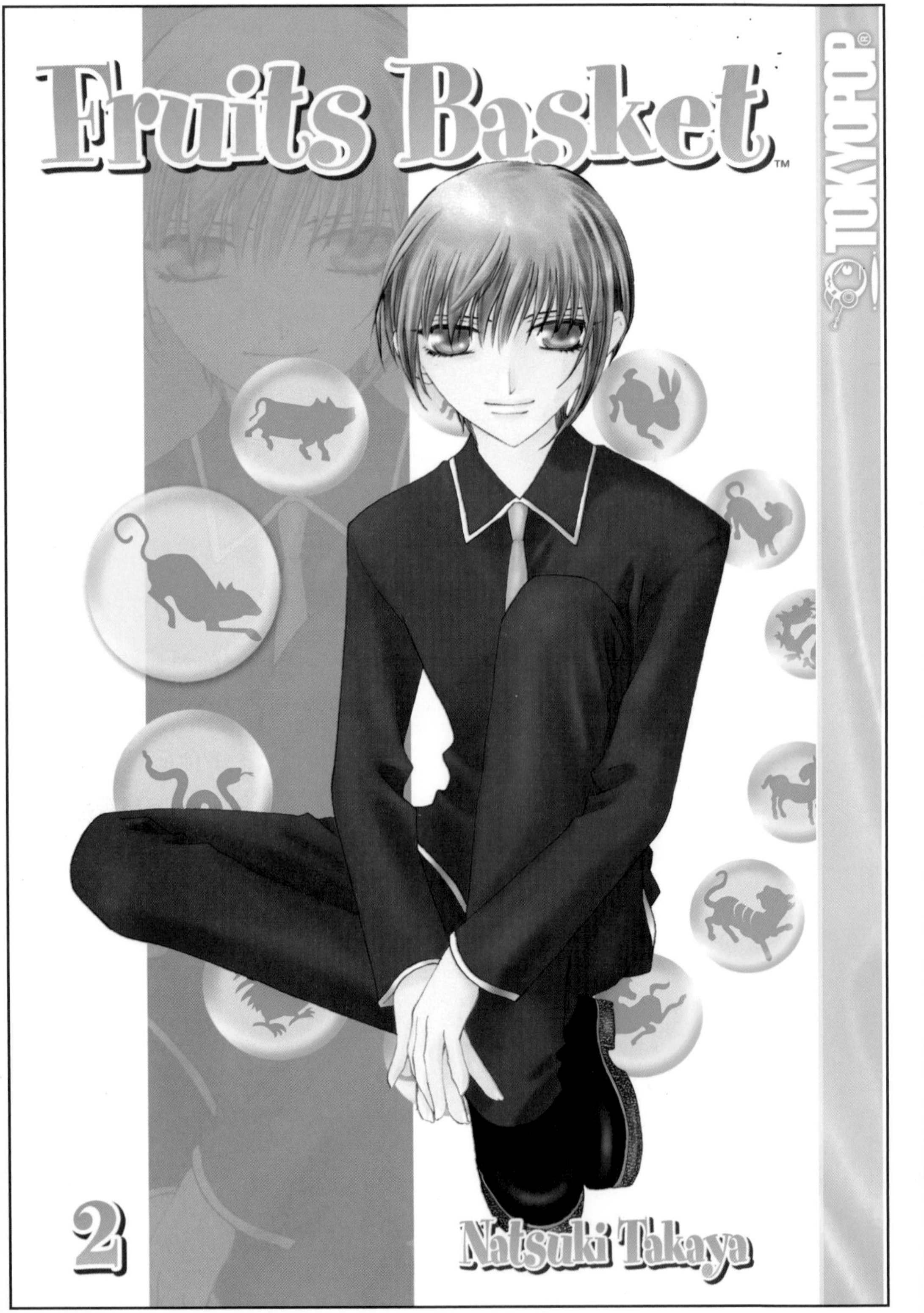
Fruits Basket™
TOKYOPOP
2
Natsuki Takaya

You Like Us!
You Really, Really Like Us!

Showcasing the very best manga and anime to make its way to North America, the inaugural "American Anime Awards" took place at the historic New Yorker hotel during New York Comic-Con on a chilly February night in The Big Apple. After more than 43,000 fans cast their votes online, the winner for "Best Manga" was chosen. And the winner is... The Departed. Oops, wrong ceremony! The winner is... Fruits Basket! TOKYPOP would like to take this opportunity to thank all of our loyal fans, mobilized through www.tokyopop.com, for voting Takaya-sensei's #1 shojo manga into the Winners Circle!

Fruits Basket
Ultimate Edition

Foreword
From Lianne Sentar, Current Fruits Basket Rewriter!

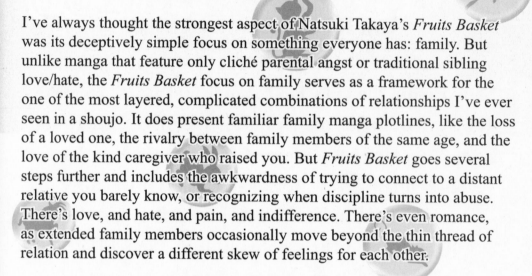

I've always thought the strongest aspect of Natsuki Takaya's *Fruits Basket* was its deceptively simple focus on something everyone has: family. But unlike manga that feature only cliché parental angst or traditional sibling love/hate, the *Fruits Basket* focus on family serves as a framework for the one of the most layered, complicated combinations of relationships I've ever seen in a shoujo. It does present familiar family manga plotlines, like the loss of a loved one, the rivalry between family members of the same age, and the love of the kind caregiver who raised you. But *Fruits Basket* goes several steps further and includes the awkwardness of trying to connect to a distant relative you barely know, or recognizing when discipline turns into abuse. There's love, and hate, and pain, and indifference. There's even romance, as extended family members occasionally move beyond the thin thread of relation and discover a different skew of feelings for each other.

The theme of family is present on every page of *Fruits Basket*. The sprawling Sohma family is joined by the orphaned Tohru and the makeshift family she's created with her friends--not unlike the nuclear family her own mother began when her parents abandoned her. Families--formed through blood, marriage, or even just shared feelings--are the only units in *Fruits Basket*. Not a single character is completely alone.

Since every person on earth has had or will have a family, *Fruits Basket* strikes a chord in readers around the world. Takaya-sensei's work and its universal themes have tied together countless readers around the globe and given them a connection to each other they can use to start a relationship; any reader who's met another *Fruits Basket* fan on the bus or online can attest to that. Thus, true to its nature, *Fruits Basket* has managed to spawn its own massive family. And with each new reader, the *Fruits Basket* family grows.

~ Lianne Sentar, July 2007

Fruits Basket™

Volume 1

Natsuki Takaya

Fruits Basket Ultimate Edition Volume 1
Created by Natsuki Takaya

Translation - Alethea & Athena Nibley
English Adaptation - Kelly Sue DeConnick & Jake Forbes
Copy Editor - Carol Fox & Kathy Schilling
Retouch and Lettering - James Lee & Yoohae Yang
Production Artists - Lucas Rivera & Skooter
Graphic Designer - Jennifer Carbajal

Editor - Paul Morrissey
Digital Imaging Manager - Chris Buford
Pre-Production Supervisor - Erika Terriquez
Production Manager - Elisabeth Brizzi
Managing Editor - Vy Nguyen
Creative Director - Anne Marie Horne
Editor-in-Chief - Rob Tokar
Publisher - Mike Kiley
President and C.O.O. - John Parker
C.E.O. and Chief Creative Officer - Stuart Levy

A  Manga

TOKYOPOP and 🐭 are trademarks or registered trademarks of TOKYOPOP Inc.

TOKYOPOP Inc.
5900 Wilshire Blvd. Suite 2000
Los Angeles, CA 90036

E-mail: info@TOKYOPOP.com
Come visit us online at www.TOKYOPOP.com

ISBN: 978-1-4278-0689-5

First TOKYOPOP printing: October 2007
10 9 8 7 6 5 4 3 2 1
Printed in the USA

Fruits Basket™

Volume 1

Table of Contents

Fruits Basket ™

What exactly is *Fruits Basket?* It doesn't fit into the ordinary manga categories, but then, it's not an ordinary manga. Take two parts drama, one part comedy, add a spoonful of romance and a pinch of magic and you're partway there, but…something about *Fruits Basket* is special. What that special ingredient is, you'll have to discover for yourself. But to help you get started, here's a brief history of the series.

Natsuki Takaya's *Fruits Basket* (or *"Furuba"* as it's known to fans) began its life in the pages of *Hana to Yume* magazine, the shojo manga anthology from Japanese publisher Hakusensha that is also home to *Kare Kano* and *Angel Sanctuary*. This wasn't the first time Takaya-sensei worked with the publisher. Since the early '90s she has created a steady flow of series and short stories for Hakusensha's various anthologies. Her two biggest pre-Fruits series were Ge-neimusou, a dark fantasy romance, and *Tsubasa O Motsu Mono (Those with Wings)*, a story about an orphaned thief in a totalitarian future. When *Fruits Basket* premiered in 1999, it took Takaya-sensei to new levels of success.

2001 was a big year for *Furuba*. The series became a huge fan-favorite in Japan, jumping to the top of manga sales. Takaya-sensei won one of the manga world's highest recognitions, the prestigious Kodansha Manga Award (she won for Sho-jo manga the same year Ken Akamatsu won the shonen award for *Love Hina!*). And beginning that summer, Hakusensha and TV Tokyo teamed up to turn *Fruits Basket* into a 26 episode anime series.

An established hit in Japan, *"Furuba* fever" quickly spread throughout the American fan community. In 2002 the anime was released in English by FUNimation (see the interview with voice actress Laura Bailey at the back of the book!), but for several years the manga remained in limbo. We conducted a poll on TOKYOPOP.com in which fans could send in their wish list of manga series they'd like to see translated. *Fruits Basket* didn't just top the poll—it DOMINATED. Now, at long last, the English manga is here!

TOKYOPOP's presentation of *Fruits Basket* is published in the original right-to-left format with original sound effects retained to preserve the art. Also retained are "honorifics," the suffixes used with characters names. At the back of each book you'll find bonus features and exclusive interviews—look for some big surprises in the books to come! Future volumes will also include a special Reader Feedback section with letters, fan art and more. Please send us your pictures, questions, poetry, or whatever Furuba inspires you to send and we'll try to include it!

Fruits Basket Fan Mail
c/o TOKYOPOP
5900 Wilshire Blvd.
Suite 2000
Los Angeles, CA 90036

We look forward to hearing from you, and we hope you'll enjoy the #1 most wanted manga in America!

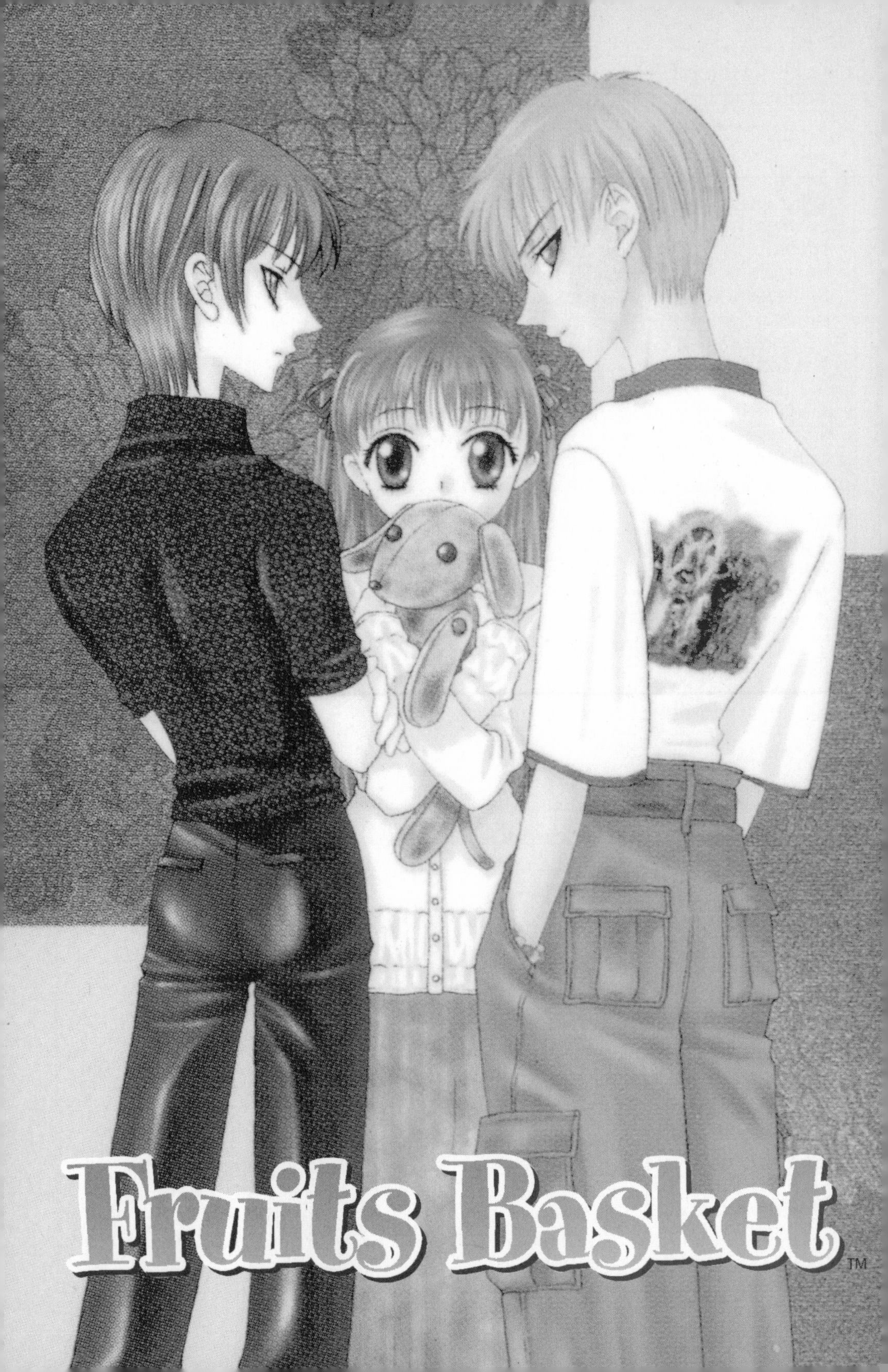
Fruits Basket™

Omake Theater 1: Life in the Sohma Household, pre- Tohru

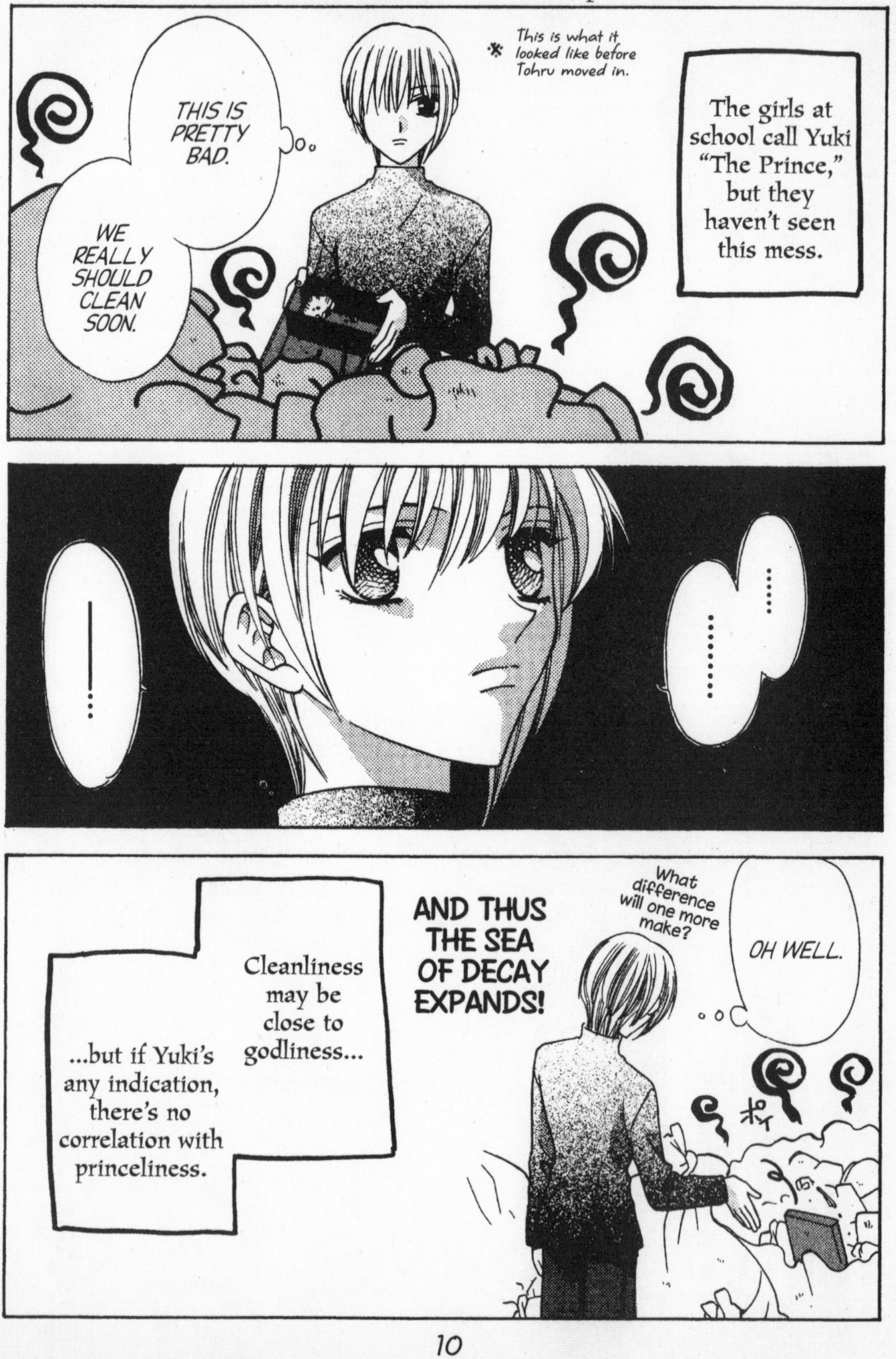

* This is what it looked like before Tohru moved in.
The girls at school call Yuki "The Prince," but they haven't seen this mess.
THIS IS PRETTY BAD.
WE REALLY SHOULD CLEAN SOON.
......
......
—......
What difference will one more make?
OH WELL.
ポイ
AND THUS THE SEA OF DECAY EXPANDS!
Cleanliness may be close to godliness...
...but if Yuki's any indication, there's no correlation with princeliness.

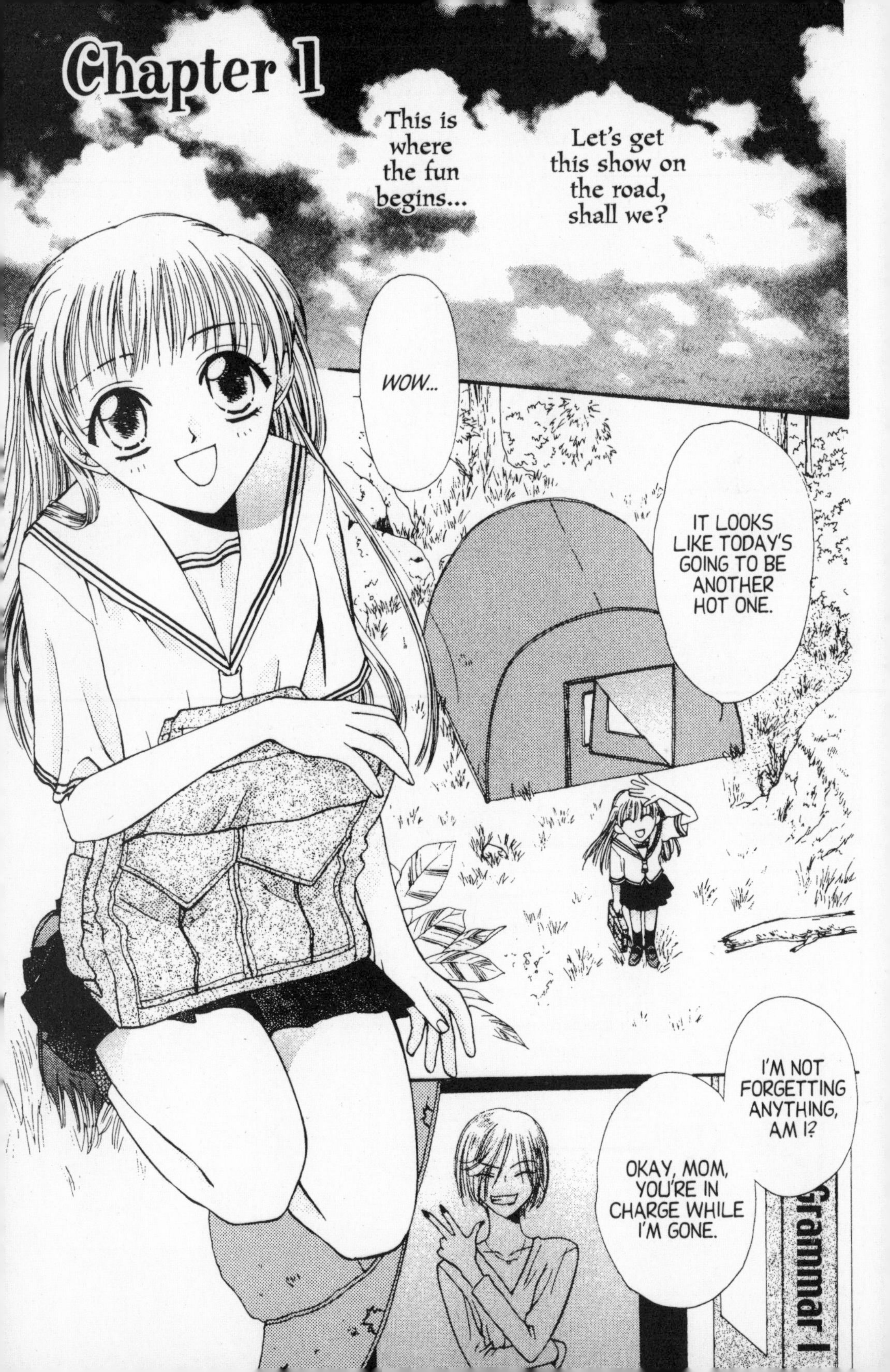
Chapter 1
Let's get this show on the road, shall we?
This is where the fun begins...
WOW...
IT LOOKS LIKE TODAY'S GOING TO BE ANOTHER HOT ONE.
I'M NOT FORGETTING ANYTHING, AM I?
OKAY, MOM, YOU'RE IN CHARGE WHILE I'M GONE.
Grammar 1

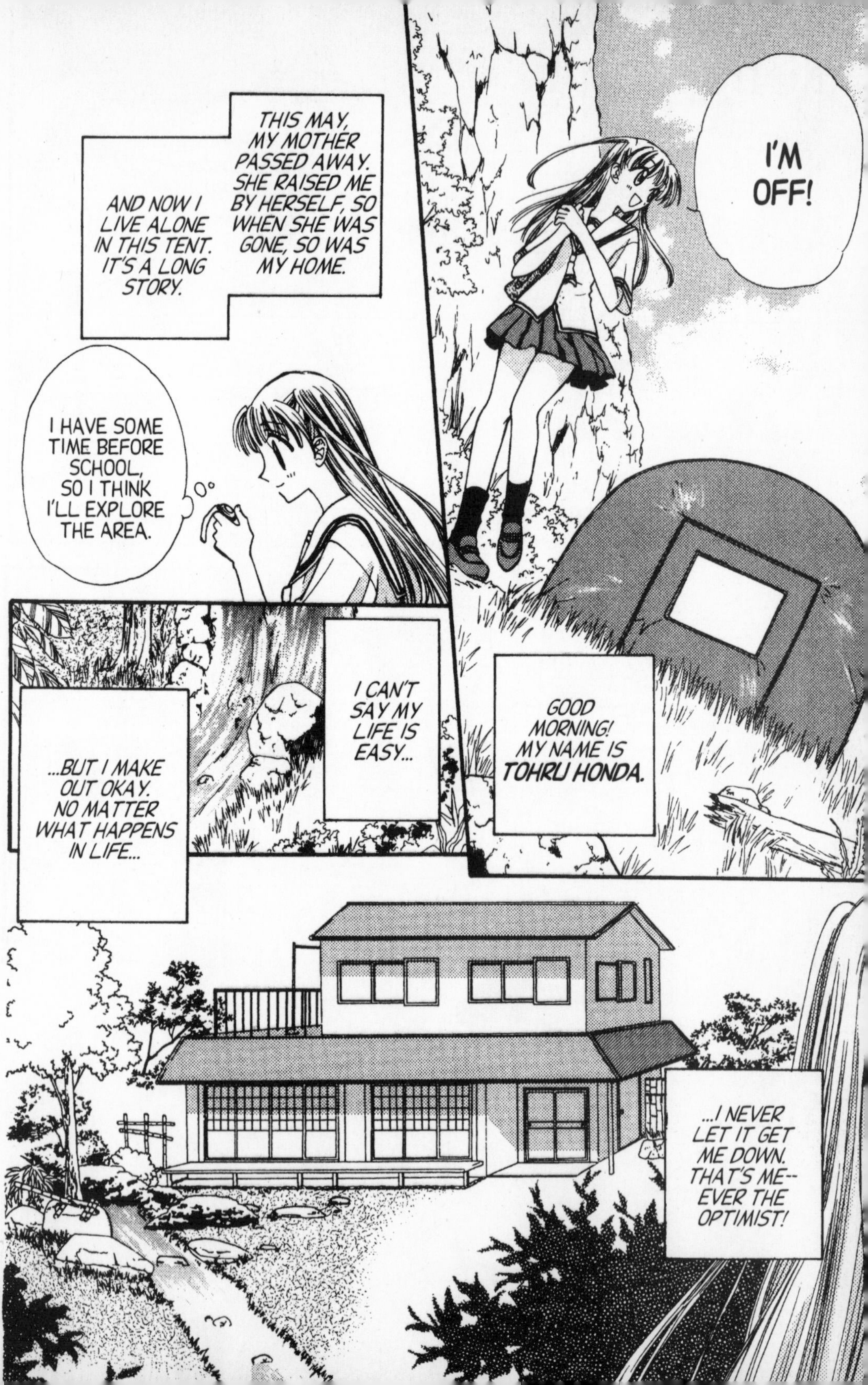
I'M OFF!
GOOD MORNING! MY NAME IS TOHRU HONDA.
THIS MAY, MY MOTHER PASSED AWAY. SHE RAISED ME BY HERSELF, SO WHEN SHE WAS GONE, SO WAS MY HOME.
AND NOW I LIVE ALONE IN THIS TENT. IT'S A LONG STORY.
I HAVE SOME TIME BEFORE SCHOOL, SO I THINK I'LL EXPLORE THE AREA.
I CAN'T SAY MY LIFE IS EASY...
...BUT I MAKE OUT OKAY. NO MATTER WHAT HAPPENS IN LIFE...
...I NEVER LET IT GET ME DOWN. THAT'S ME-- EVER THE OPTIMIST!

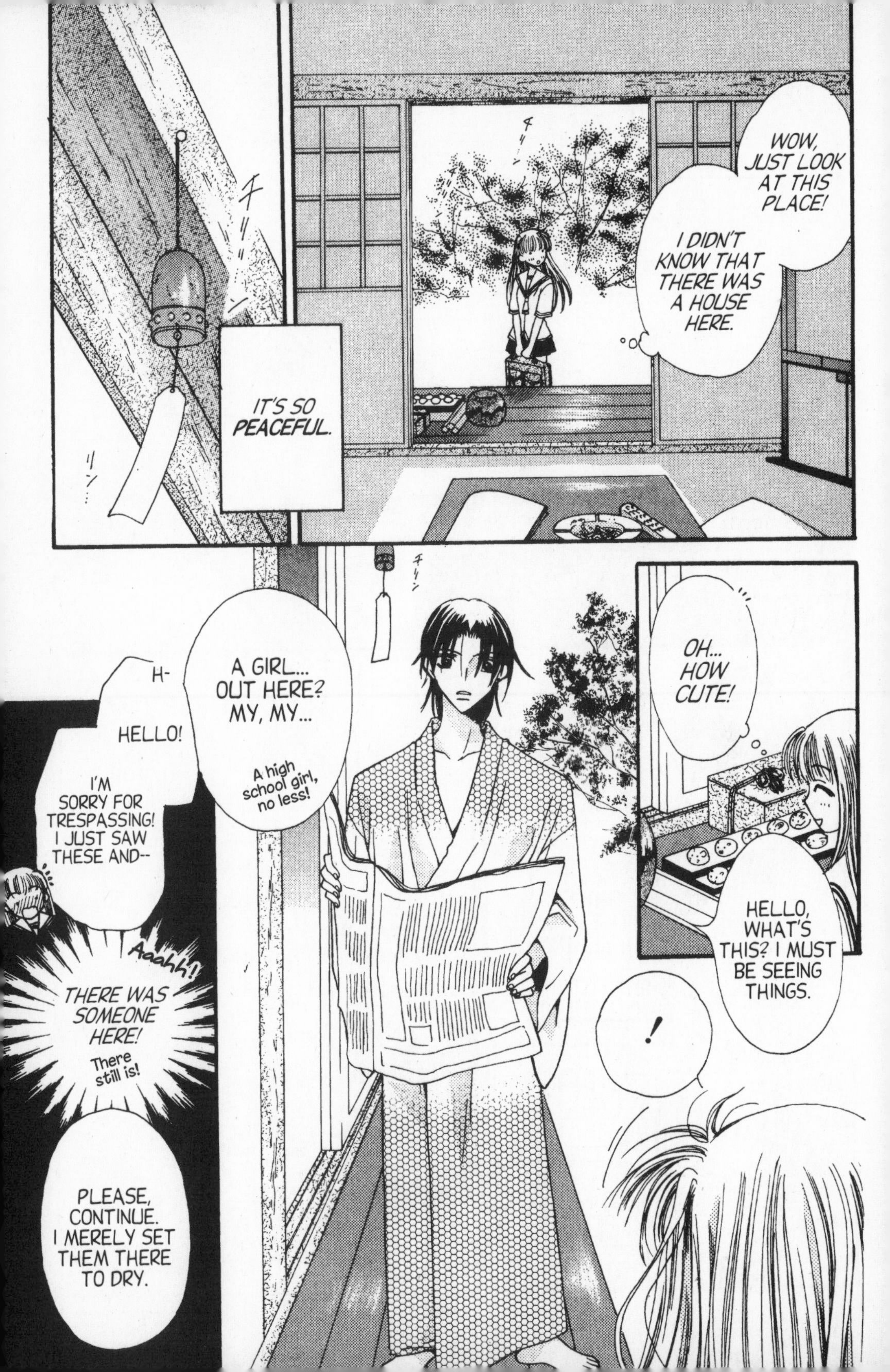
WOW, JUST LOOK AT THIS PLACE!
I DIDN'T KNOW THAT THERE WAS A HOUSE HERE.
IT'S SO PEACEFUL.
OH... HOW CUTE!
HELLO, WHAT'S THIS? I MUST BE SEEING THINGS.
!
A GIRL... OUT HERE? MY, MY...
A high school girl, no less!
H-
HELLO!
I'M SORRY FOR TRESPASSING! I JUST SAW THESE AND--
Aaahh!
THERE WAS SOMEONE HERE!
There still is!
PLEASE, CONTINUE. I MERELY SET THEM THERE TO DRY.

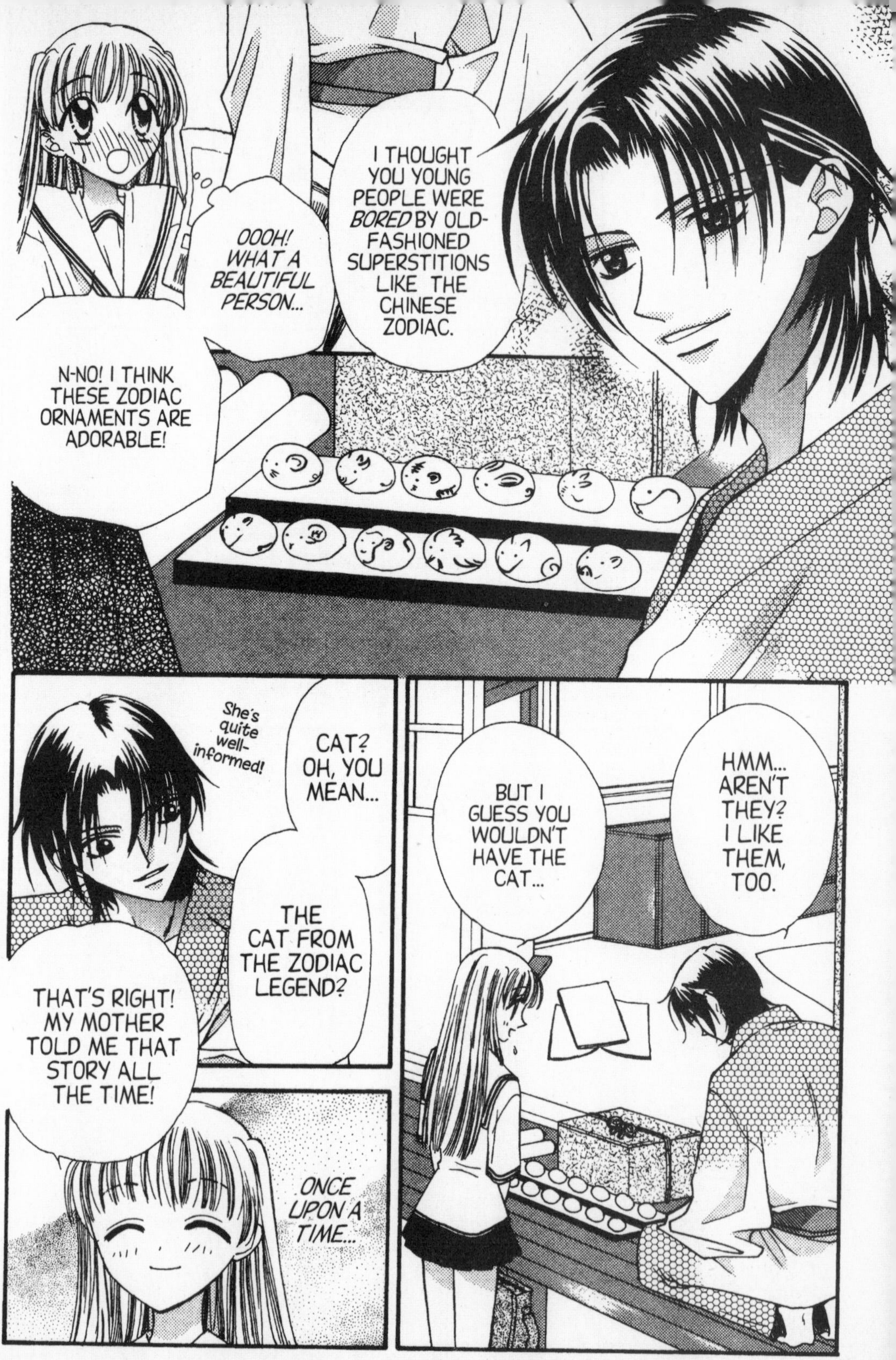
I THOUGHT YOU YOUNG PEOPLE WERE BORED BY OLD-FASHIONED SUPERSTITIONS LIKE THE CHINESE ZODIAC.
OOOH! WHAT A BEAUTIFUL PERSON...
N-NO! I THINK THESE ZODIAC ORNAMENTS ARE ADORABLE!
HMM... AREN'T THEY? I LIKE THEM, TOO.
BUT I GUESS YOU WOULDN'T HAVE THE CAT...
CAT? OH, YOU MEAN...
She's quite well-informed!
THE CAT FROM THE ZODIAC LEGEND?
THAT'S RIGHT! MY MOTHER TOLD ME THAT STORY ALL THE TIME!
ONCE UPON A TIME...

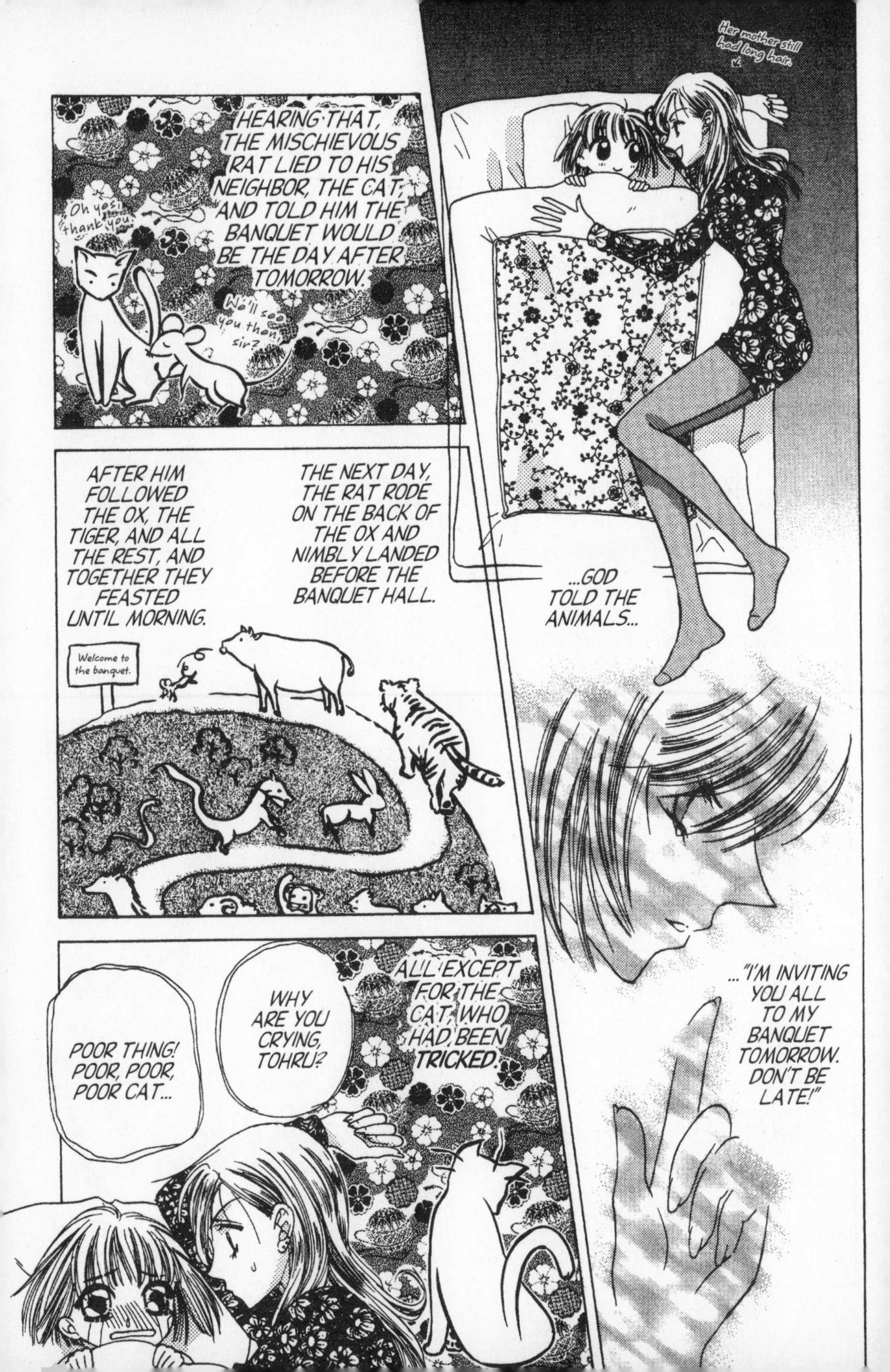
Her mother still had long hair.
...GOD TOLD THE ANIMALS...
..."I'M INVITING YOU ALL TO MY BANQUET TOMORROW. DON'T BE LATE!"
HEARING THAT, THE MISCHIEVOUS RAT LIED TO HIS NEIGHBOR, THE CAT, AND TOLD HIM THE BANQUET WOULD BE THE DAY AFTER TOMORROW.
Oh yes, thank you.
We'll see you then, sir.
THE NEXT DAY, THE RAT RODE ON THE BACK OF THE OX AND NIMBLY LANDED BEFORE THE BANQUET HALL.
AFTER HIM FOLLOWED THE OX, THE TIGER, AND ALL THE REST, AND TOGETHER THEY FEASTED UNTIL MORNING.
Welcome to the banquet.
ALL EXCEPT FOR THE CAT, WHO HAD BEEN TRICKED.
WHY ARE YOU CRYING, TOHRU?
POOR THING! POOR, POOR, POOR CAT...

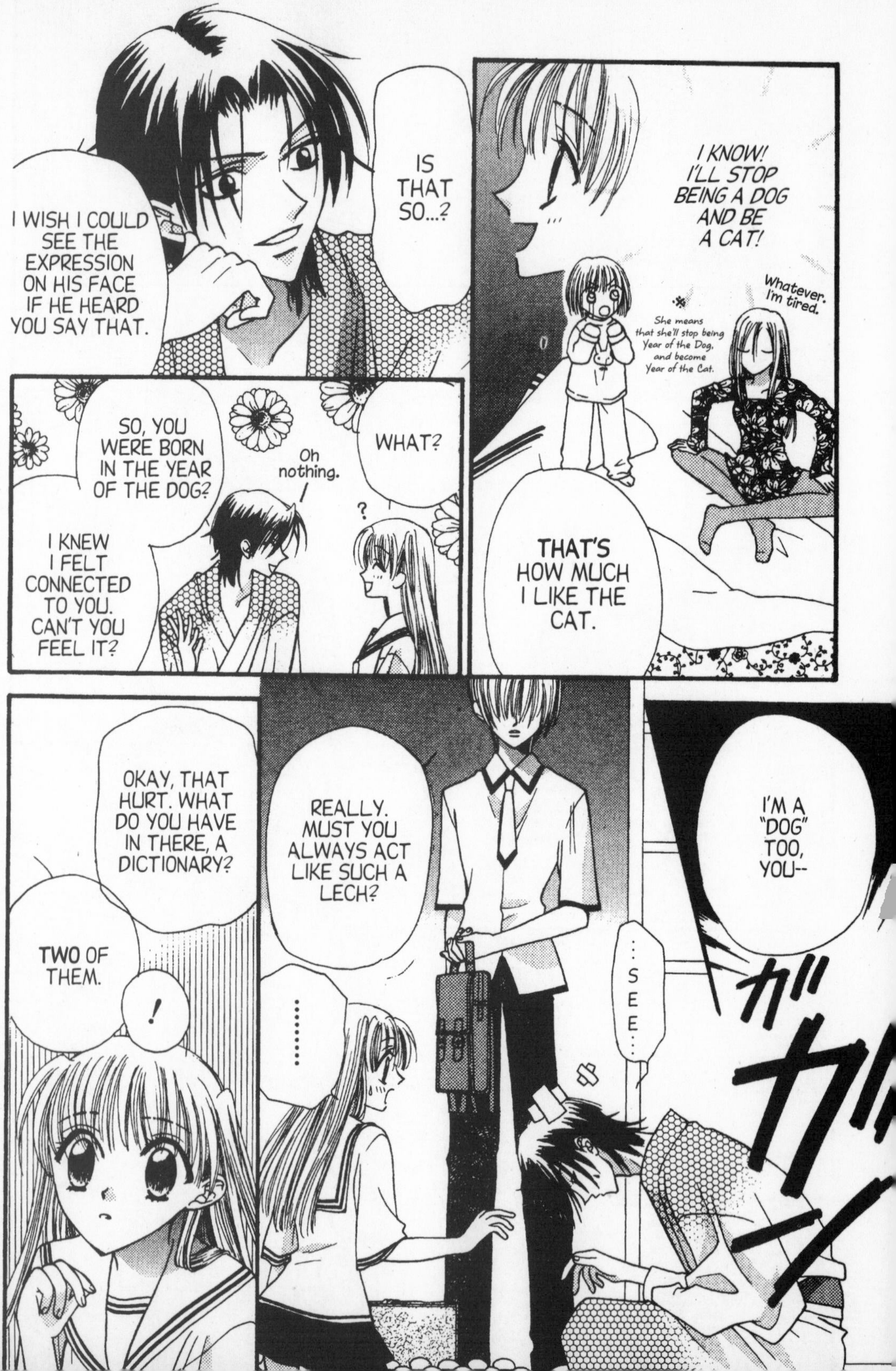
I KNOW! I'LL STOP BEING A DOG AND BE A CAT!
Whatever. I'm tired.
※ She means that she'll stop being Year of the Dog, and become Year of the Cat.
THAT'S HOW MUCH I LIKE THE CAT.
IS THAT SO...?
I WISH I COULD SEE THE EXPRESSION ON HIS FACE IF HE HEARD YOU SAY THAT.
WHAT?
SO, YOU WERE BORN IN THE YEAR OF THE DOG?
Oh nothing.
?
I KNEW I FELT CONNECTED TO YOU. CAN'T YOU FEEL IT?
I'M A "DOG" TOO, YOU--
ガ
...SEE...
REALLY. MUST YOU ALWAYS ACT LIKE SUCH A LECH?
....
OKAY, THAT HURT. WHAT DO YOU HAVE IN THERE, A DICTIONARY?
TWO OF THEM.
!

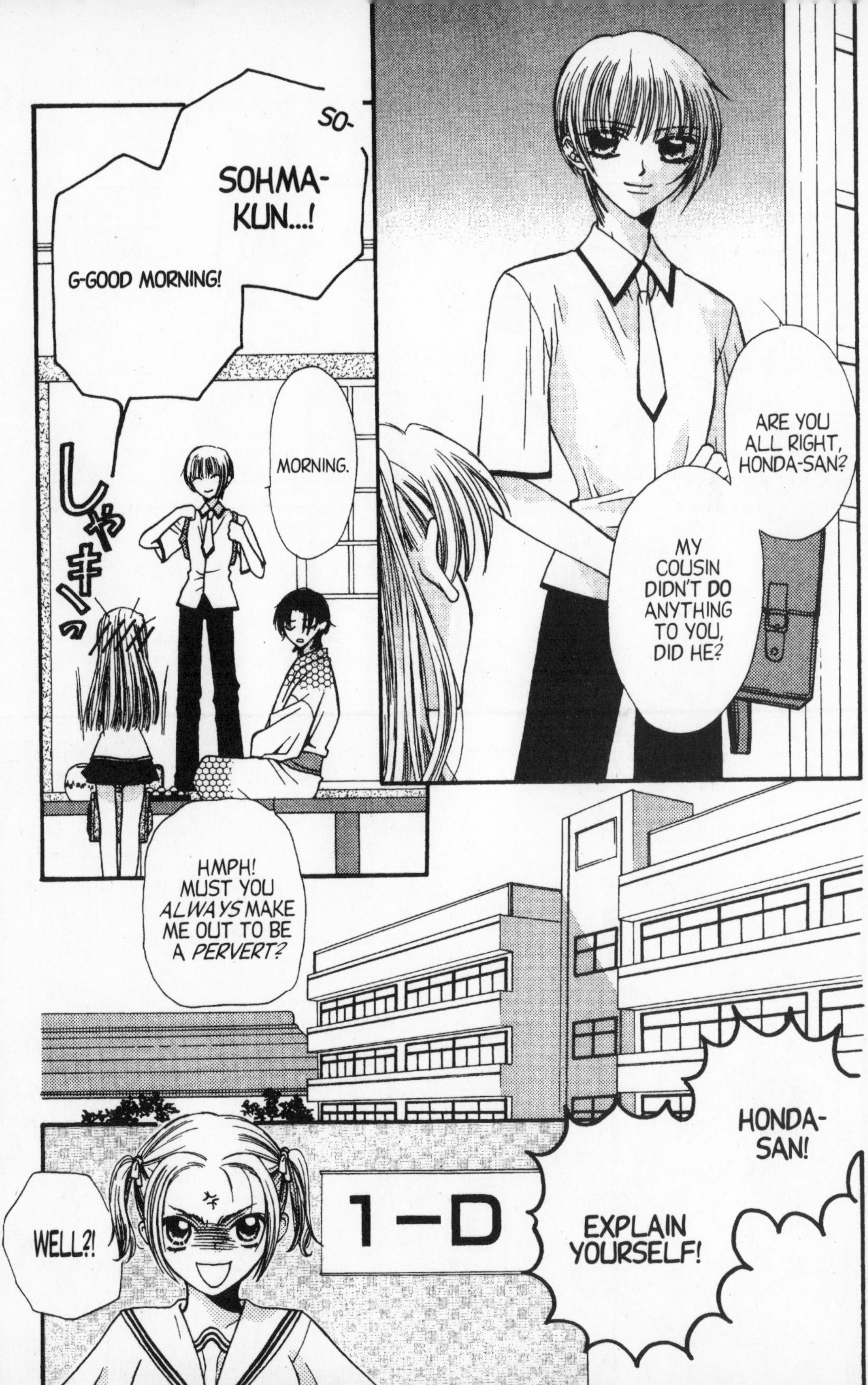
ARE YOU ALL RIGHT, HONDA-SAN?
MY COUSIN DIDN'T DO ANYTHING TO YOU, DID HE?
SO-
SOHMA-KUN...!
G-GOOD MORNING!
しゃキーっ
MORNING.
HMPH! MUST YOU *ALWAYS* MAKE ME OUT TO BE A *PERVERT*?
HONDA-SAN!
EXPLAIN YOURSELF!
1-D
WELL?!

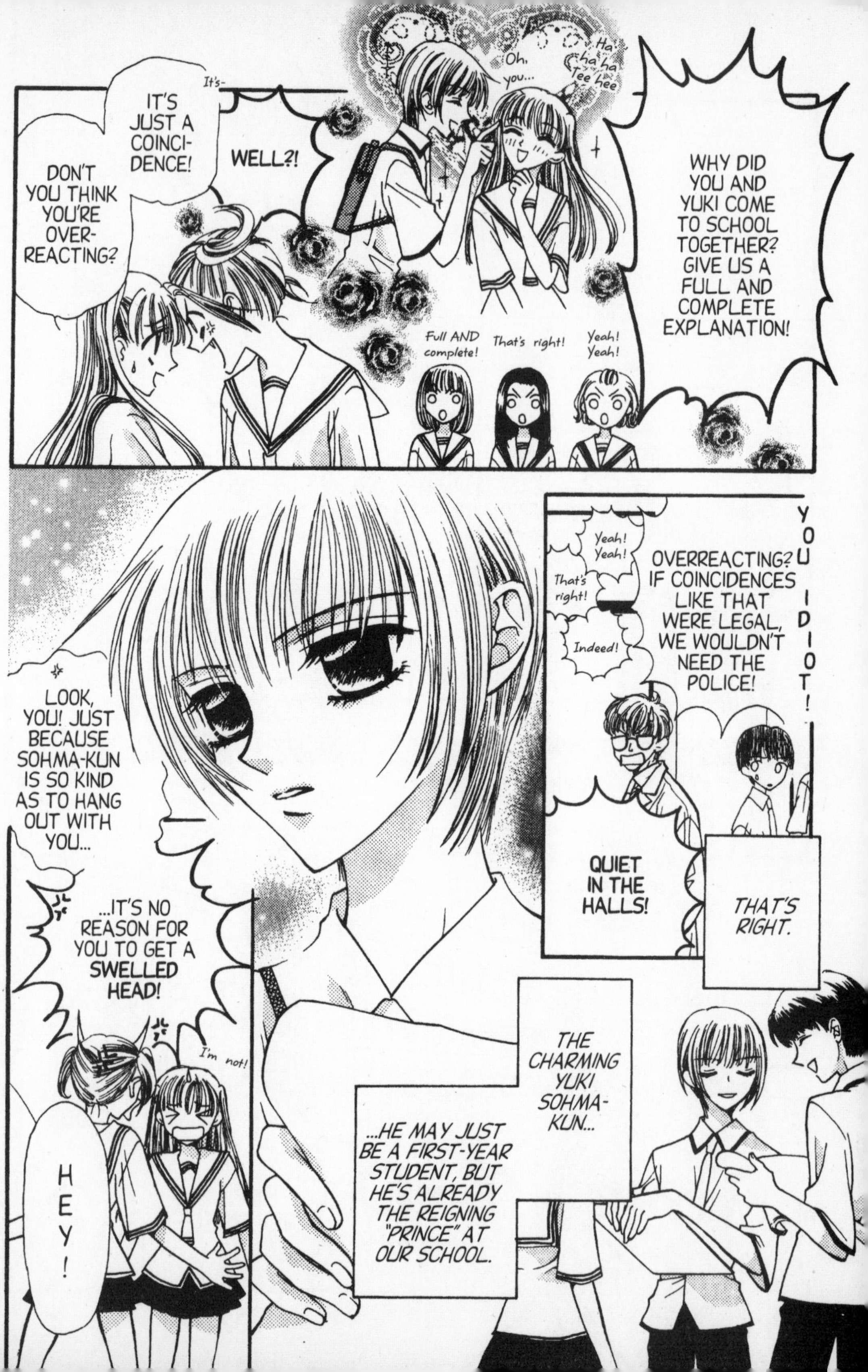

WHY DID YOU AND YUKI COME TO SCHOOL TOGETHER? GIVE US A FULL AND COMPLETE EXPLANATION!
Yeah! Yeah!
That's right!
Full AND complete!
Ha ha ha Tee hee
Oh, you...
WELL?!
It's-
IT'S JUST A COINCIDENCE!
DON'T YOU THINK YOU'RE OVER-REACTING?
YOU IDIOT!
OVERREACTING? IF COINCIDENCES LIKE THAT WERE LEGAL, WE WOULDN'T NEED THE POLICE!
Yeah! Yeah!
That's right!
Indeed!
THAT'S RIGHT.
QUIET IN THE HALLS!
LOOK, YOU! JUST BECAUSE SOHMA-KUN IS SO KIND AS TO HANG OUT WITH YOU...
...IT'S NO REASON FOR YOU TO GET A SWELLED HEAD!
I'm not!
HEY!
THE CHARMING YUKI SOHMA-KUN...
...HE MAY JUST BE A FIRST-YEAR STUDENT, BUT HE'S ALREADY THE REIGNING "PRINCE" AT OUR SCHOOL.

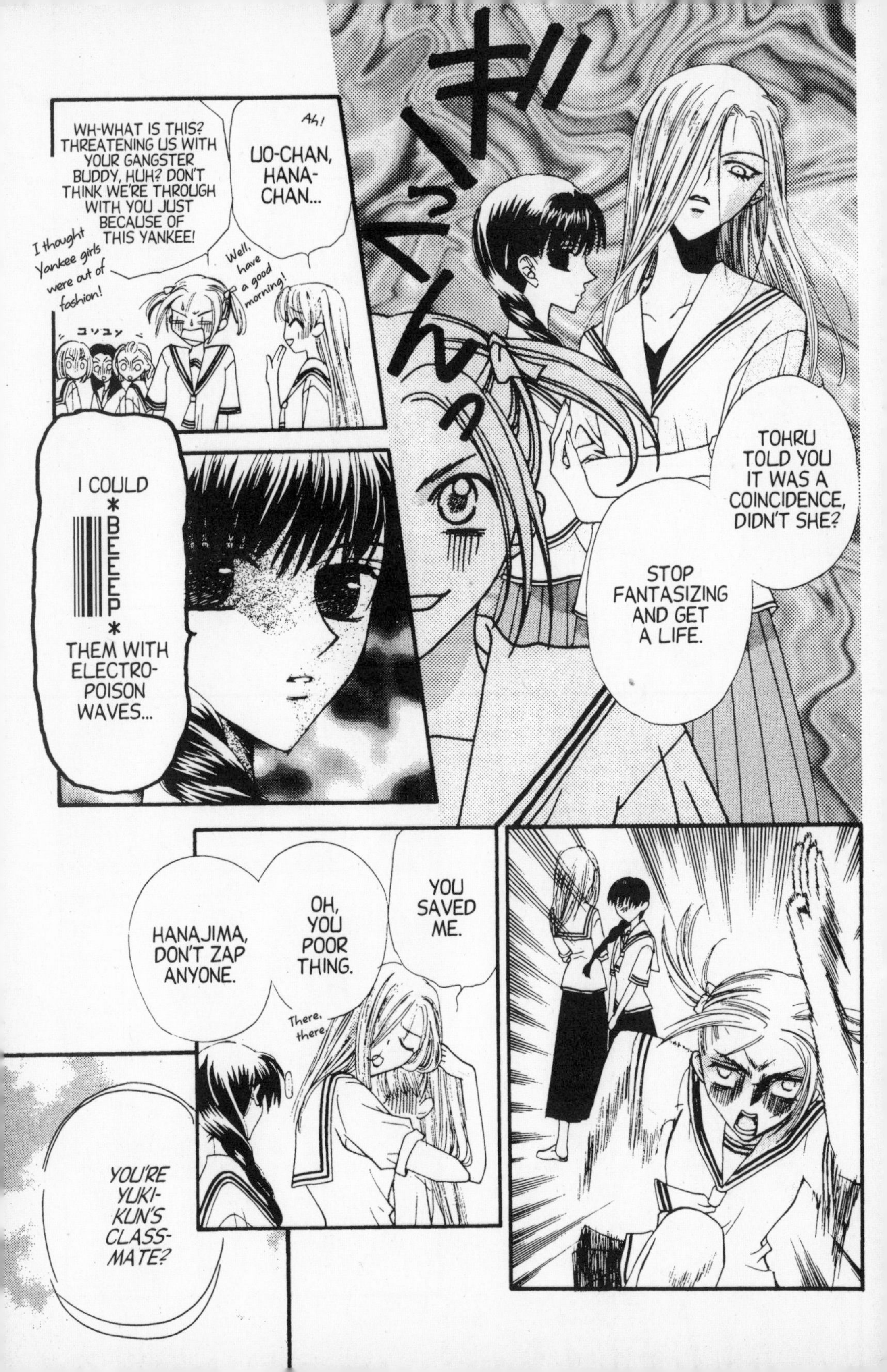
TOHRU TOLD YOU IT WAS A COINCIDENCE, DIDN'T SHE?
STOP FANTASIZING AND GET A LIFE.
Ah!
UO-CHAN, HANA-CHAN...
WH-WHAT IS THIS? THREATENING US WITH YOUR GANGSTER BUDDY, HUH? DON'T THINK WE'RE THROUGH WITH YOU JUST BECAUSE OF THIS YANKEE!
Well, have a good morning!
I thought Yankee girls were out of fashion!
I COULD *BEEEP* THEM WITH ELECTRO-POISON WAVES...
YOU SAVED ME.
OH, YOU POOR THING.
HANAJIMA, DON'T ZAP ANYONE.
There, there.
YOU'RE YUKI-KUN'S CLASSMATE?

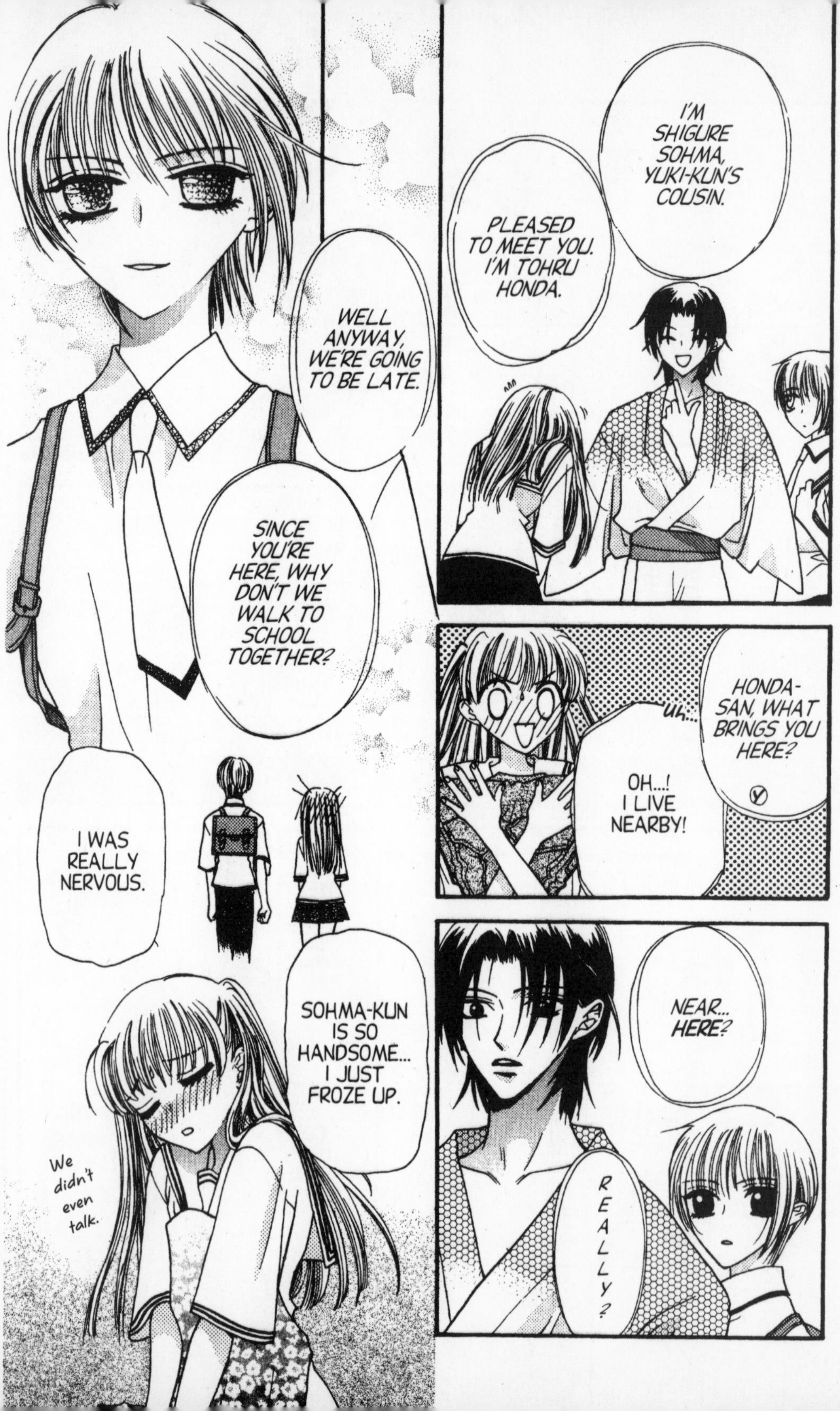
I'M SHIGURE SOHMA, YUKI-KUN'S COUSIN.
PLEASED TO MEET YOU. I'M TOHRU HONDA.
HONDA-SAN, WHAT BRINGS YOU HERE?
uh...
OH...! I LIVE NEARBY!
NEAR... HERE?
REALLY?
WELL ANYWAY, WE'RE GOING TO BE LATE.
SINCE YOU'RE HERE, WHY DON'T WE WALK TO SCHOOL TOGETHER?
I WAS REALLY NERVOUS.
SOHMA-KUN IS SO HANDSOME... I JUST FROZE UP.
We didn't even talk.

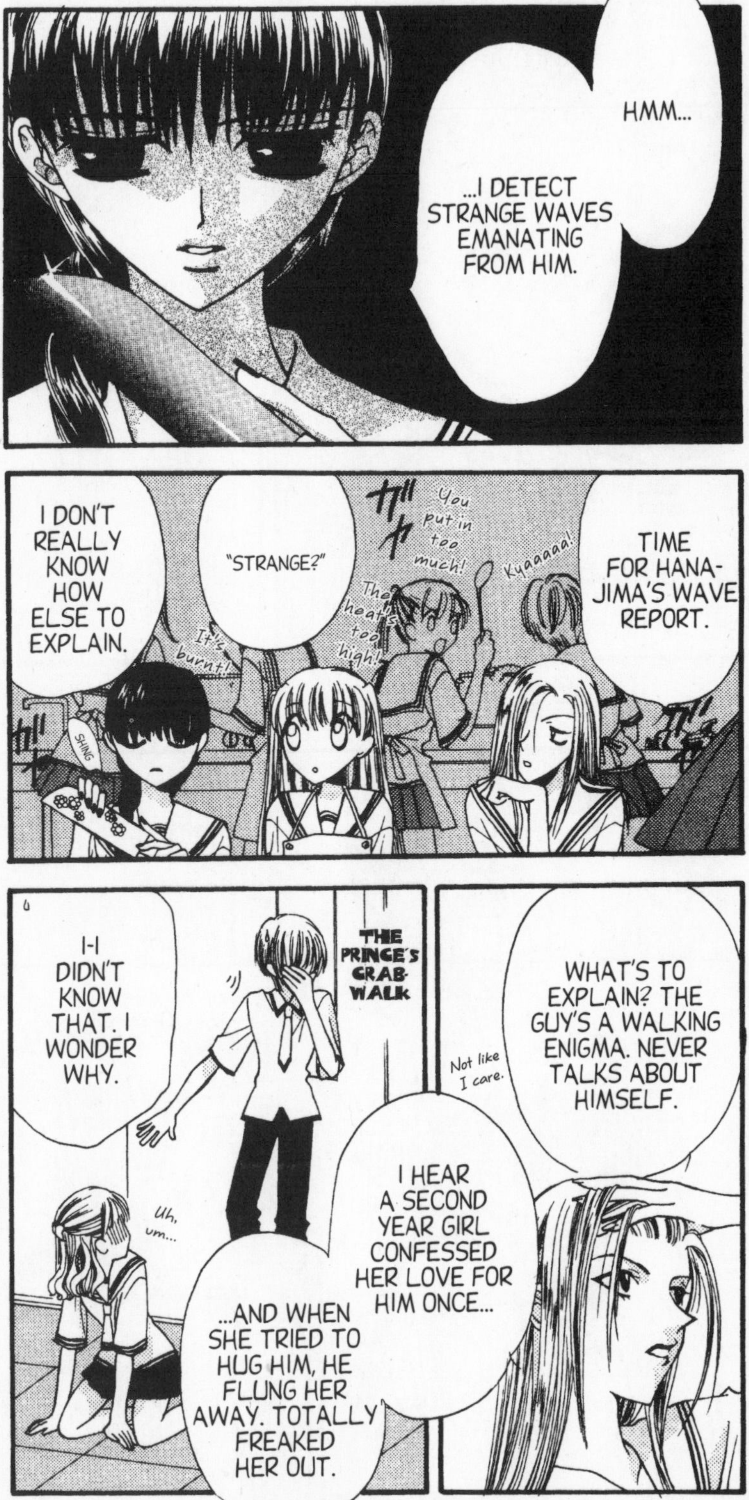
HMM...
...I DETECT STRANGE WAVES EMANATING FROM HIM.
TIME FOR HANA-JIMA'S WAVE REPORT.
Kyaaaaa!
You put in too much!
The heat's too high!
It's burnt!
"STRANGE?"
I DON'T REALLY KNOW HOW ELSE TO EXPLAIN.
SHING
WHAT'S TO EXPLAIN? THE GUY'S A WALKING ENIGMA. NEVER TALKS ABOUT HIMSELF.
Not like I care.
I HEAR A SECOND YEAR GIRL CONFESSED HER LOVE FOR HIM ONCE...
...AND WHEN SHE TRIED TO HUG HIM, HE FLUNG HER AWAY. TOTALLY FREAKED HER OUT.
THE PRINCE'S CRAB-WALK
I-I DIDN'T KNOW THAT. I WONDER WHY.
Uh, um...

Fruits Basket Number 1:

Hello!
Nice to meet you, I'm Takaya. To those of you who have been waiting--and to those of you who haven't been waiting, too--I am proud to present Fruits Basket Volume 1. It's a new world, different from my last manga, "Tsubasa," but I think you'll find similarities, too. (Because I'm drawing all the people, basically. Even if the details are different, I am still me!) But if there were any parts in "Tsubasa" that were weird or confusing to you, I blame my lack of sleep. Ah, sleep. I remember sleep. Maybe I should try that again one day...? In the meantime, please enjoy Fruits Basket Vol. 1!

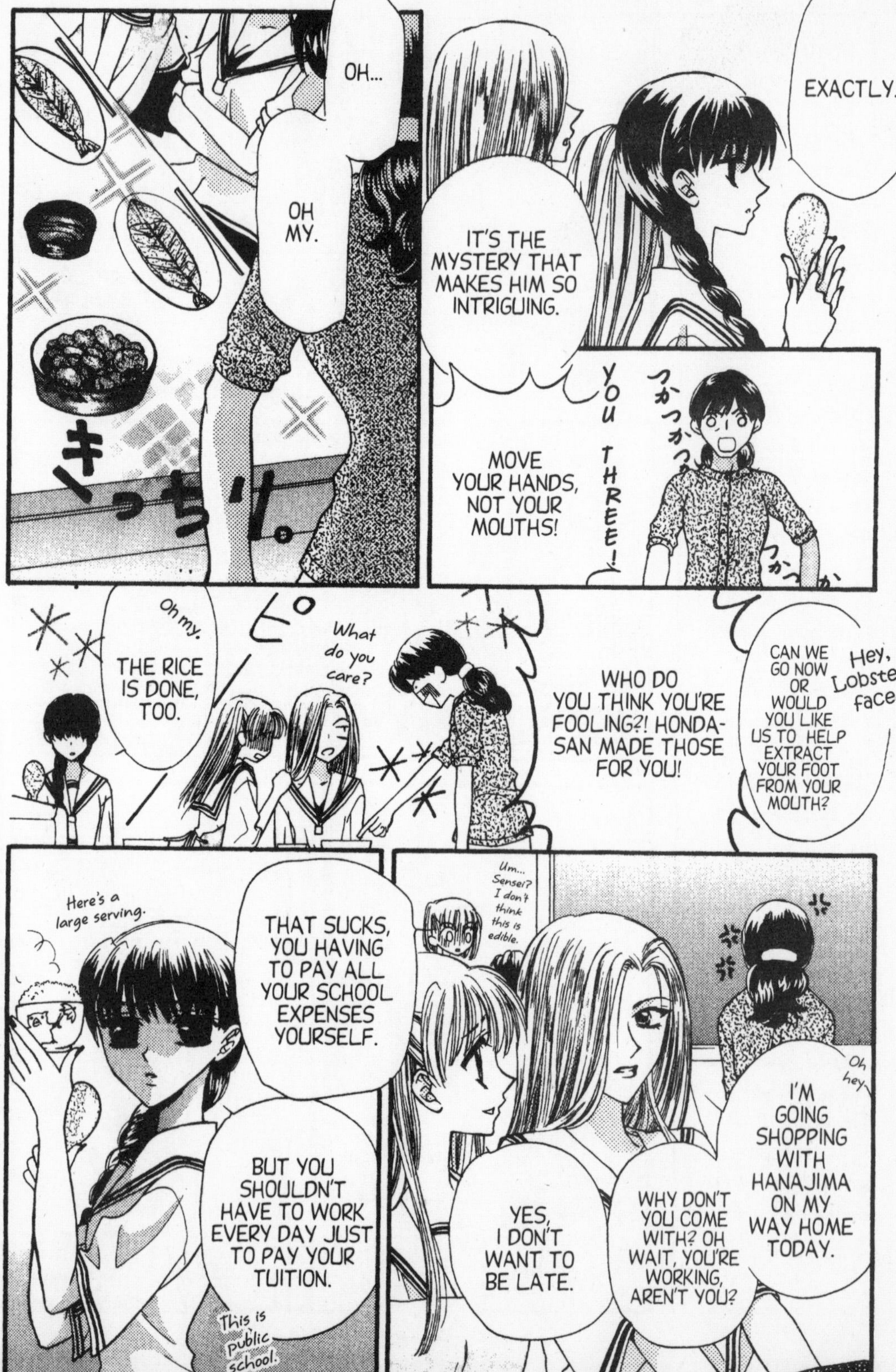
EXACTLY.
IT'S THE MYSTERY THAT MAKES HIM SO INTRIGUING.
YOU THREE!
つかつかつ
MOVE YOUR HANDS, NOT YOUR MOUTHS!
つかつか
OH...
OH MY.
きっちり。
Hey, Lobster face.
CAN WE GO NOW OR WOULD YOU LIKE US TO HELP EXTRACT YOUR FOOT FROM YOUR MOUTH?
WHO DO YOU THINK YOU'RE FOOLING?! HONDA-SAN MADE THOSE FOR YOU!
What do you care?
ピ
Oh my.
THE RICE IS DONE, TOO.
Oh hey
I'M GOING SHOPPING WITH HANAJIMA ON MY WAY HOME TODAY.
WHY DON'T YOU COME WITH? OH WAIT, YOU'RE WORKING, AREN'T YOU?
YES, I DON'T WANT TO BE LATE.
Um... Sensei? I don't think this is edible.
THAT SUCKS, YOU HAVING TO PAY ALL YOUR SCHOOL EXPENSES YOURSELF.
Here's a large serving.
BUT YOU SHOULDN'T HAVE TO WORK EVERY DAY JUST TO PAY YOUR TUITION.
This is public school.

The Yankee has a soft spot for her friends.

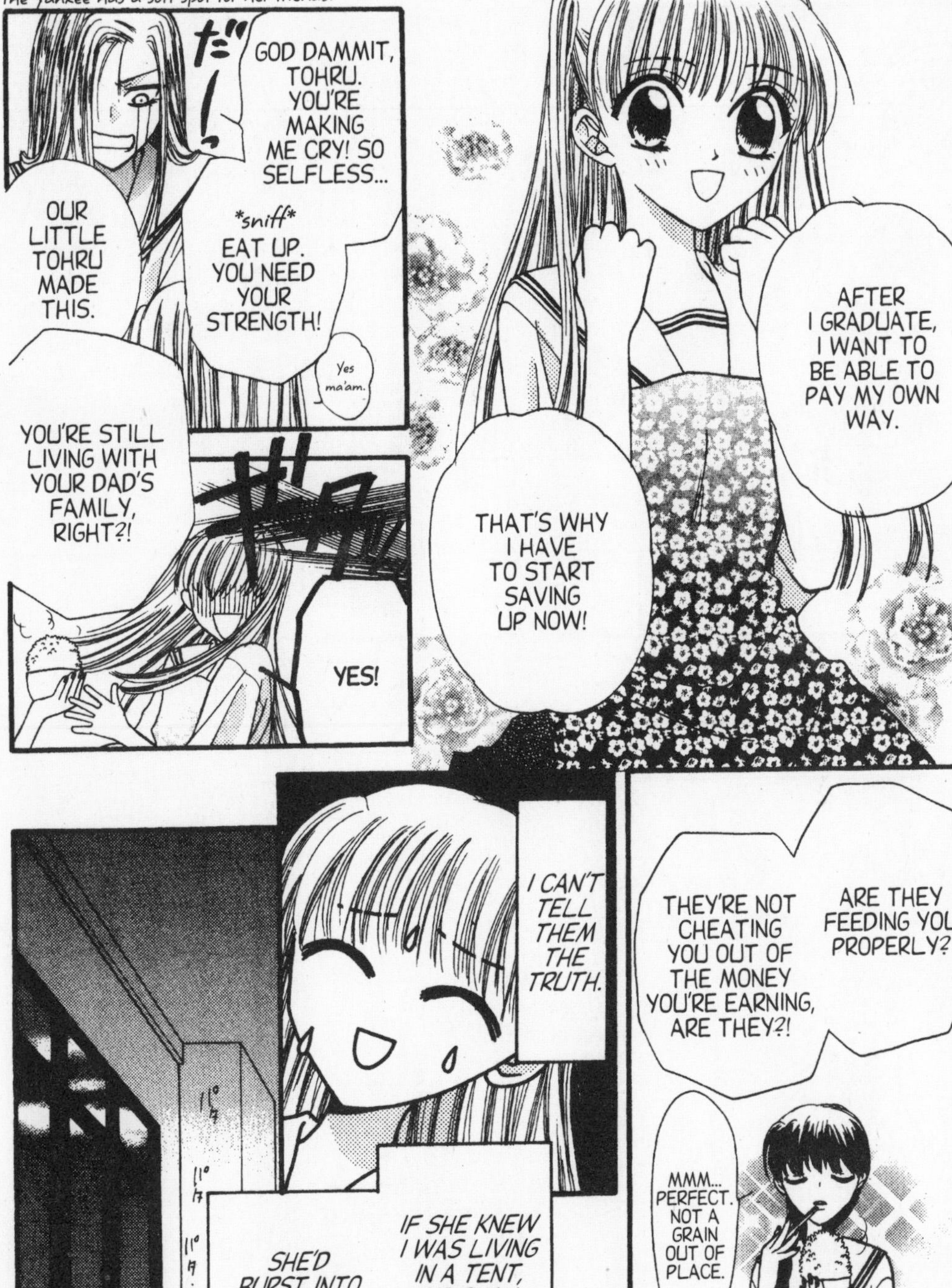
AFTER I GRADUATE, I WANT TO BE ABLE TO PAY MY OWN WAY.
THAT'S WHY I HAVE TO START SAVING UP NOW!
GOD DAMMIT, TOHRU. YOU'RE MAKING ME CRY! SO SELFLESS...
sniff EAT UP. YOU NEED YOUR STRENGTH!
OUR LITTLE TOHRU MADE THIS.
Yes ma'am.
YOU'RE STILL LIVING WITH YOUR DAD'S FAMILY, RIGHT?!
YES!
ARE THEY FEEDING YOU PROPERLY?
THEY'RE NOT CHEATING YOU OUT OF THE MONEY YOU'RE EARNING, ARE THEY?!
MMM... PERFECT. NOT A GRAIN OUT OF PLACE.
I CAN'T TELL THEM THE TRUTH.
IF SHE KNEW I WAS LIVING IN A TENT, UO-CHAN WOULD BE OUTRAGED.
SHE'D BURST INTO GRANDPA'S HOUSE ON HER MOTORCYCLE!

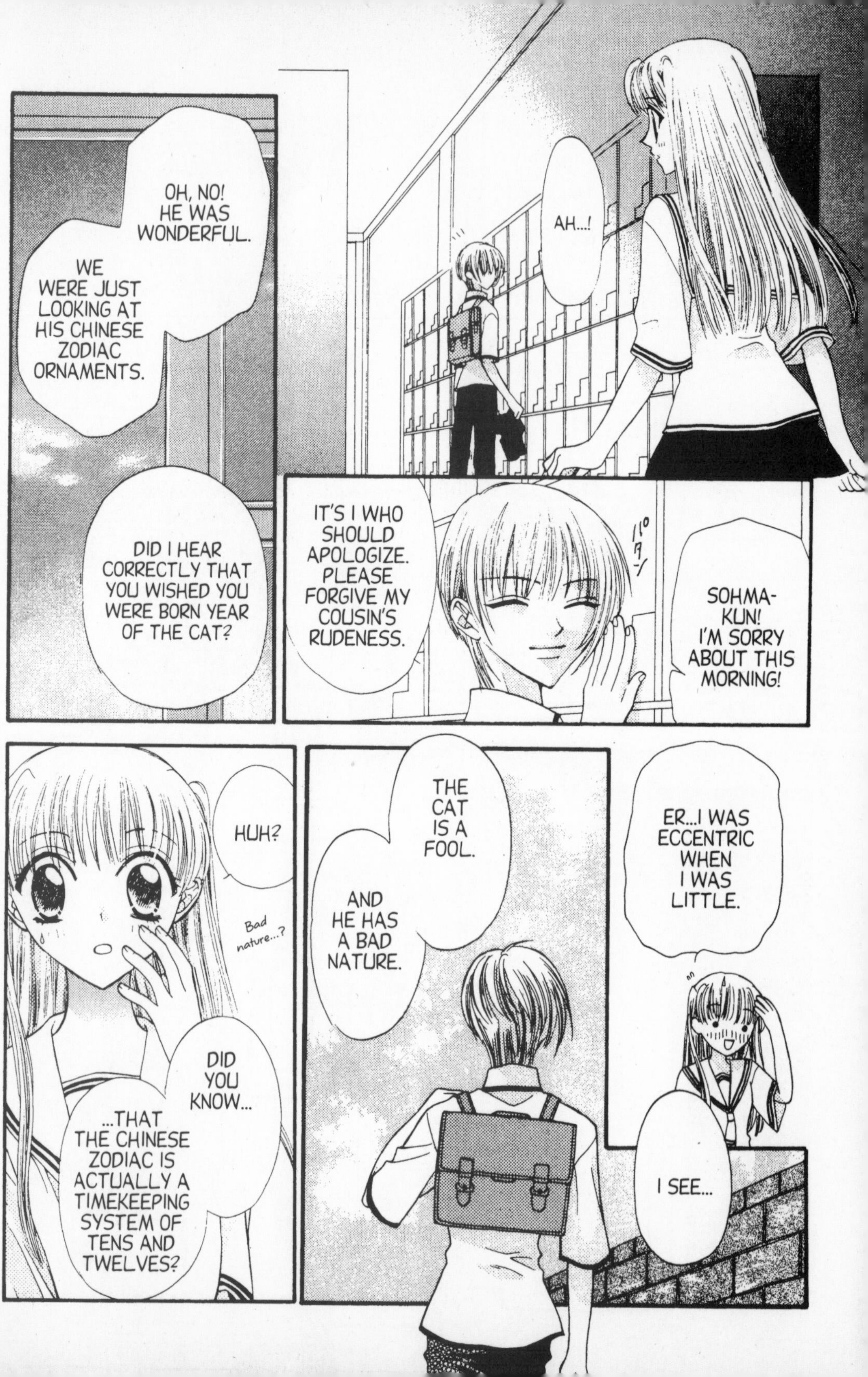
AH...!
SOHMA-KUN! I'M SORRY ABOUT THIS MORNING!
IT'S I WHO SHOULD APOLOGIZE. PLEASE FORGIVE MY COUSIN'S RUDENESS.
OH, NO! HE WAS WONDERFUL.
WE WERE JUST LOOKING AT HIS CHINESE ZODIAC ORNAMENTS.
DID I HEAR CORRECTLY THAT YOU WISHED YOU WERE BORN YEAR OF THE CAT?
ER...I WAS ECCENTRIC WHEN I WAS LITTLE.
I SEE...
THE CAT IS A FOOL.
AND HE HAS A BAD NATURE.
HUH?
Bad nature...?
DID YOU KNOW...
...THAT THE CHINESE ZODIAC IS ACTUALLY A TIMEKEEPING SYSTEM OF TENS AND TWELVES?

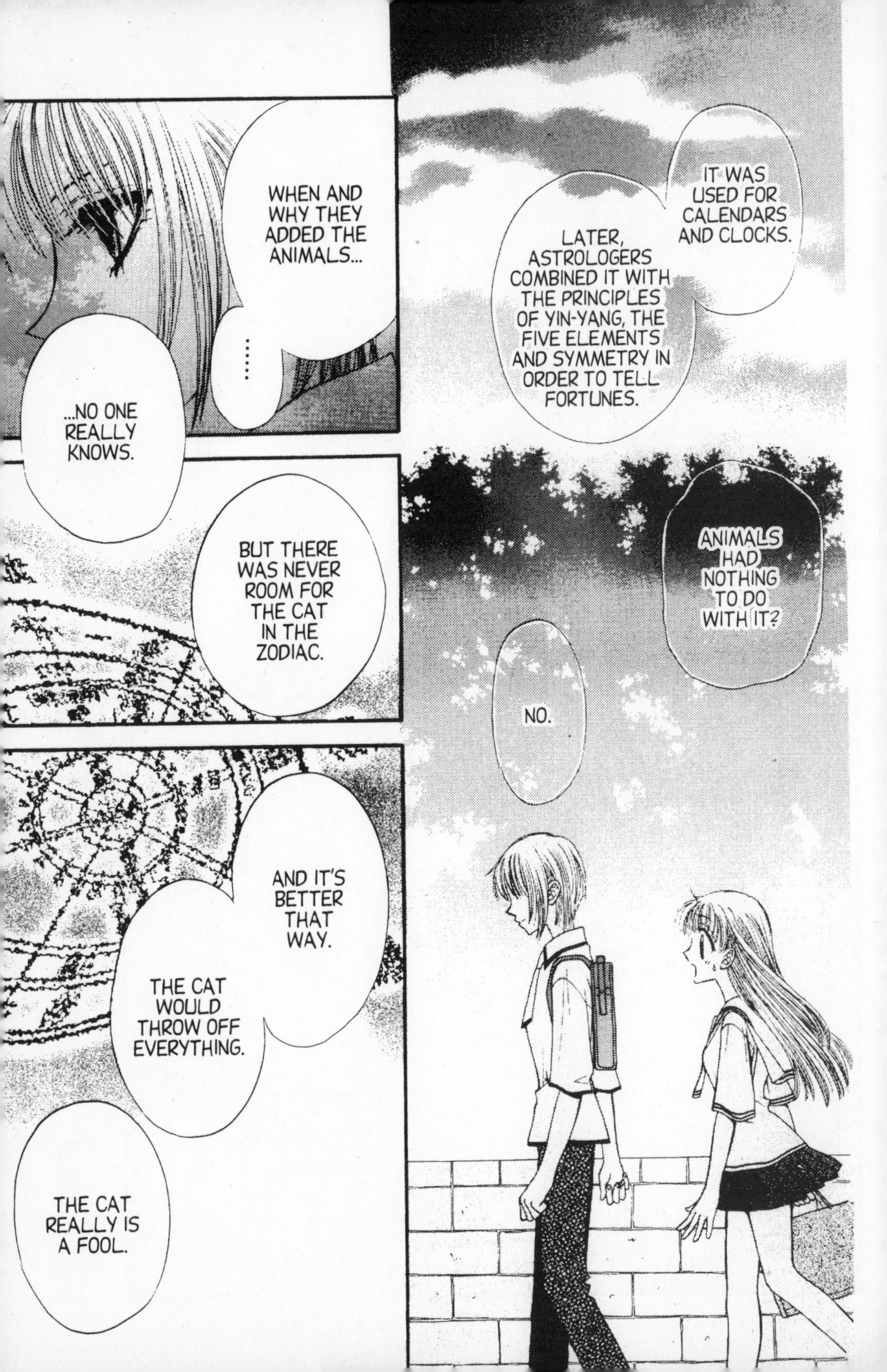
IT WAS USED FOR CALENDARS AND CLOCKS.
LATER, ASTROLOGERS COMBINED IT WITH THE PRINCIPLES OF YIN-YANG, THE FIVE ELEMENTS AND SYMMETRY IN ORDER TO TELL FORTUNES.
WHEN AND WHY THEY ADDED THE ANIMALS...
......
...NO ONE REALLY KNOWS.
ANIMALS HAD NOTHING TO DO WITH IT?
NO.
BUT THERE WAS NEVER ROOM FOR THE CAT IN THE ZODIAC.
AND IT'S BETTER THAT WAY.
THE CAT WOULD THROW OFF EVERYTHING.
THE CAT REALLY IS A FOOL.

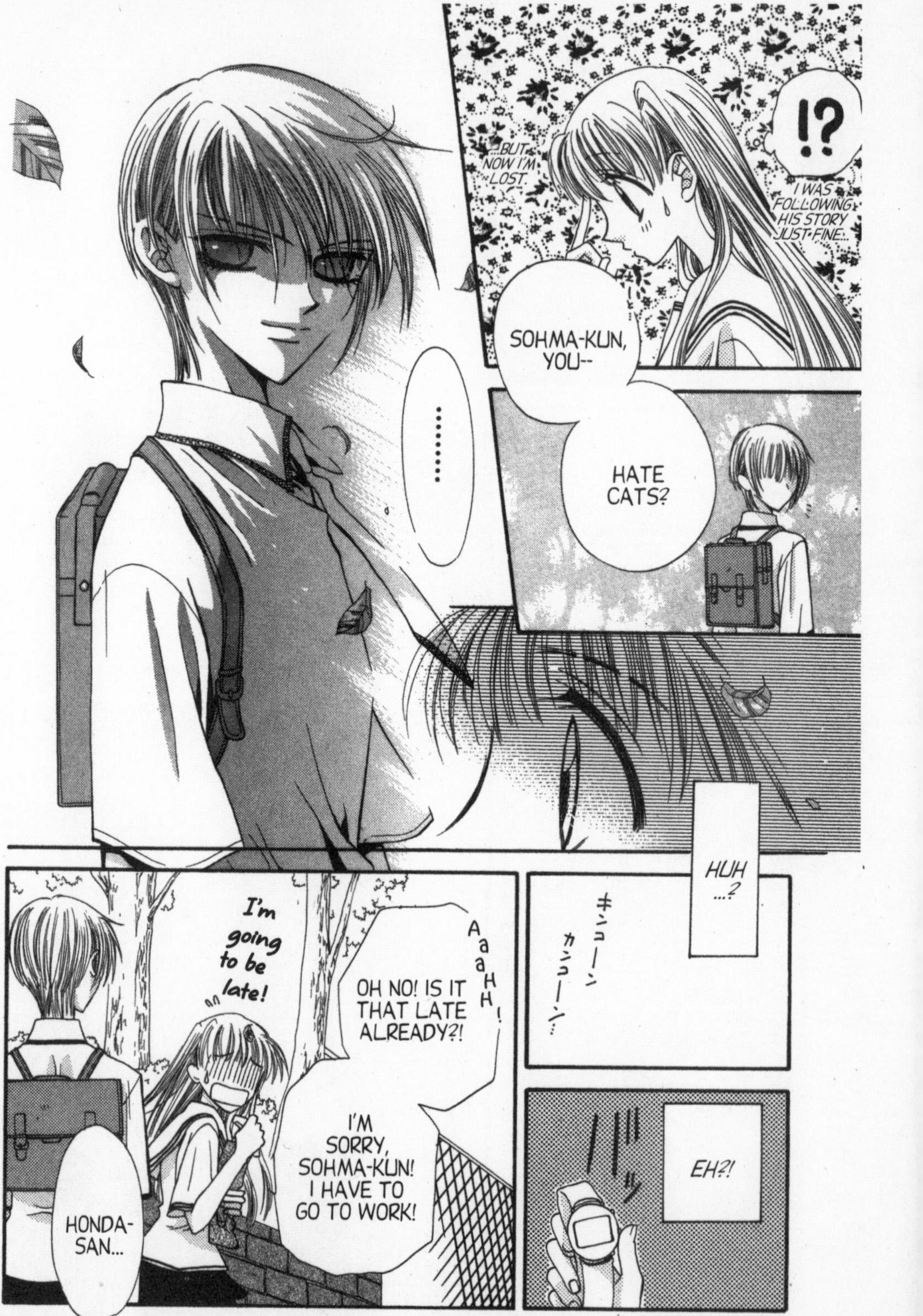
!?
I WAS FOLLOWING HIS STORY JUST FINE...
...BUT NOW I'M LOST.
SOHMA-KUN, YOU--
HATE CATS?
......
HUH...?
キンコーン
カンコーン...
EH?!
AaaHH!
OH NO! IS IT THAT LATE ALREADY?!
I'm going to be late!
I'M SORRY, SOHMA-KUN! I HAVE TO GO TO WORK!
HONDA-SAN...

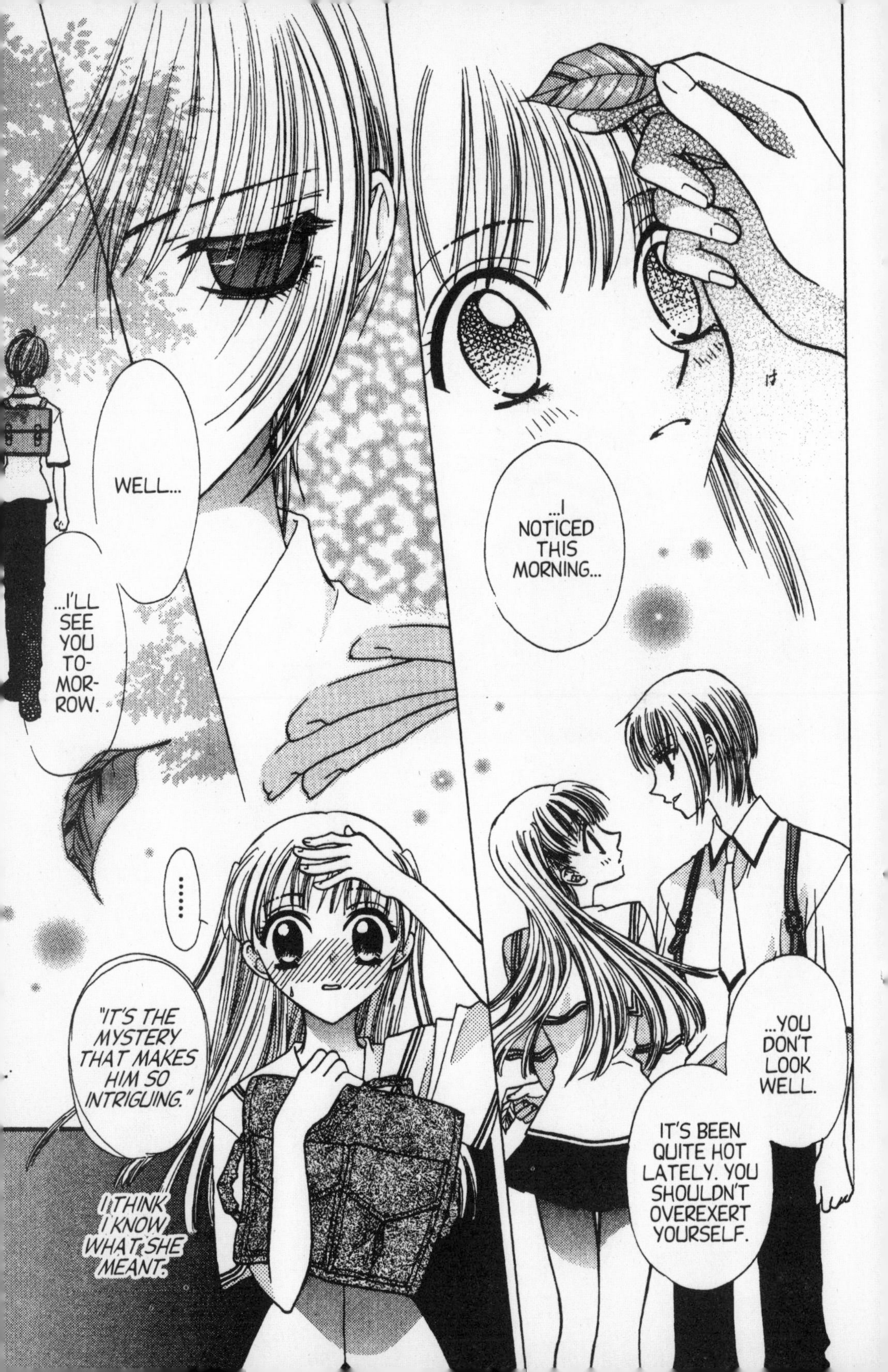
は
...I NOTICED THIS MORNING...
...YOU DON'T LOOK WELL.
IT'S BEEN QUITE HOT LATELY. YOU SHOULDN'T OVEREXERT YOURSELF.
WELL...
...I'LL SEE YOU TO-MOR-ROW.
......
"IT'S THE MYSTERY THAT MAKES HIM SO INTRIGUING."
I THINK I KNOW WHAT SHE MEANT.

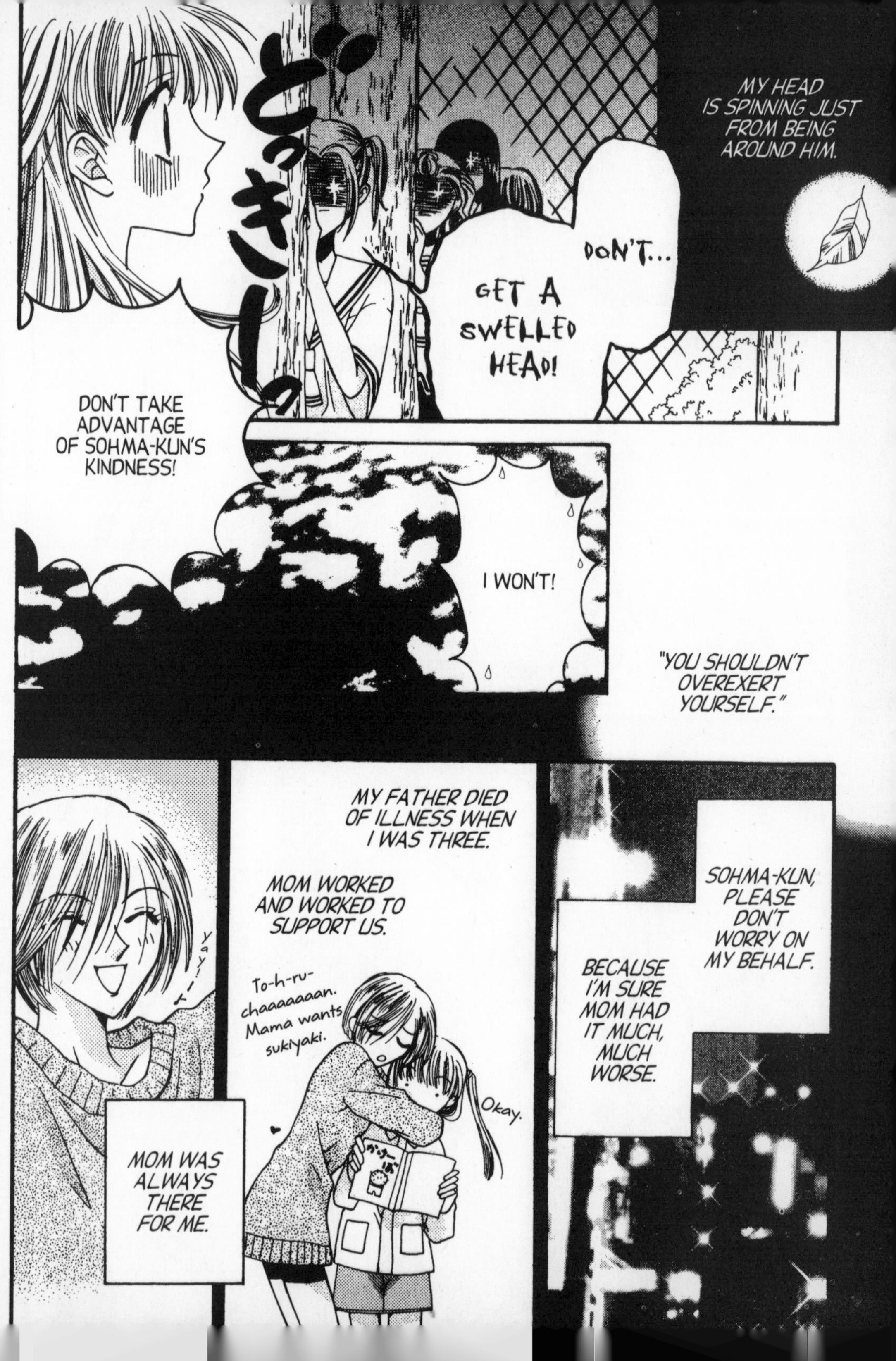
MY HEAD IS SPINNING JUST FROM BEING AROUND HIM.
どっきーっ
DON'T...
GET A SWELLED HEAD!
DON'T TAKE ADVANTAGE OF SOHMA-KUN'S KINDNESS!
I WON'T!
"YOU SHOULDN'T OVEREXERT YOURSELF."
SOHMA-KUN, PLEASE DON'T WORRY ON MY BEHALF.
BECAUSE I'M SURE MOM HAD IT MUCH, MUCH WORSE.
MY FATHER DIED OF ILLNESS WHEN I WAS THREE.
MOM WORKED AND WORKED TO SUPPORT US.
To-h-ru-chaaaaaaan. Mama wants sukiyaki.
Okay.
Yay!!
MOM WAS ALWAYS THERE FOR ME.

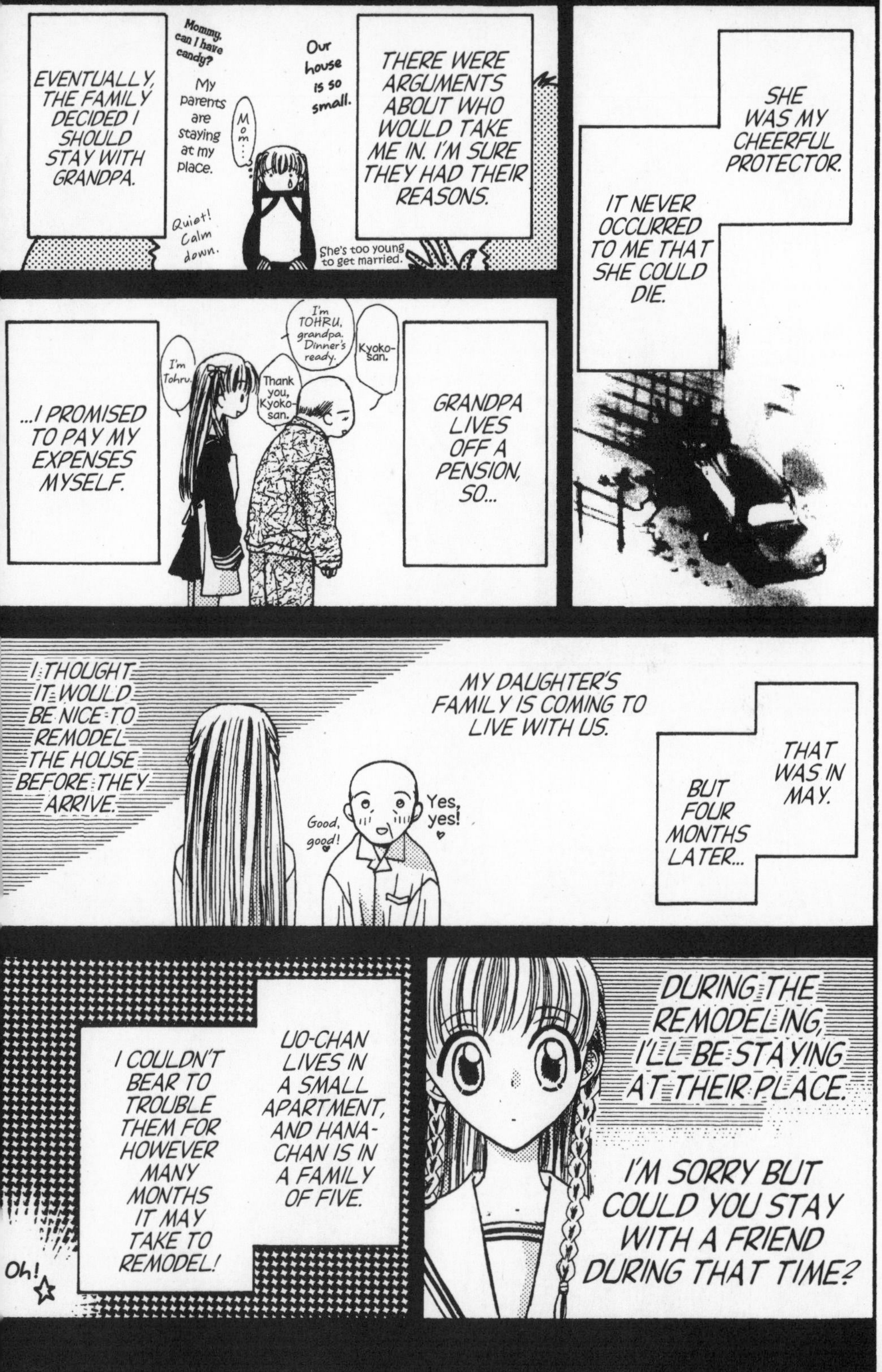
SHE WAS MY CHEERFUL PROTECTOR.
IT NEVER OCCURRED TO ME THAT SHE COULD DIE.
THERE WERE ARGUMENTS ABOUT WHO WOULD TAKE ME IN. I'M SURE THEY HAD THEIR REASONS.
Our house is so small.
She's too young to get married.
Mom...
Mommy, can I have candy?
My parents are staying at my place.
Quiet! Calm down.
EVENTUALLY, THE FAMILY DECIDED I SHOULD STAY WITH GRANDPA.
GRANDPA LIVES OFF A PENSION, SO...
Kyoko-san.
I'm TOHRU, grandpa. Dinner's ready.
Thank you, Kyoko-san.
I'm Tohru.
...I PROMISED TO PAY MY EXPENSES MYSELF.
THAT WAS IN MAY.
BUT FOUR MONTHS LATER...
MY DAUGHTER'S FAMILY IS COMING TO LIVE WITH US.
Yes, yes!
Good, good!
I THOUGHT IT WOULD BE NICE TO REMODEL THE HOUSE BEFORE THEY ARRIVE.
DURING THE REMODELING, I'LL BE STAYING AT THEIR PLACE.
I'M SORRY BUT COULD YOU STAY WITH A FRIEND DURING THAT TIME?
UO-CHAN LIVES IN A SMALL APARTMENT, AND HANA-CHAN IS IN A FAMILY OF FIVE.
I COULDN'T BEAR TO TROUBLE THEM FOR HOWEVER MANY MONTHS IT MAY TAKE TO REMODEL!
Oh!

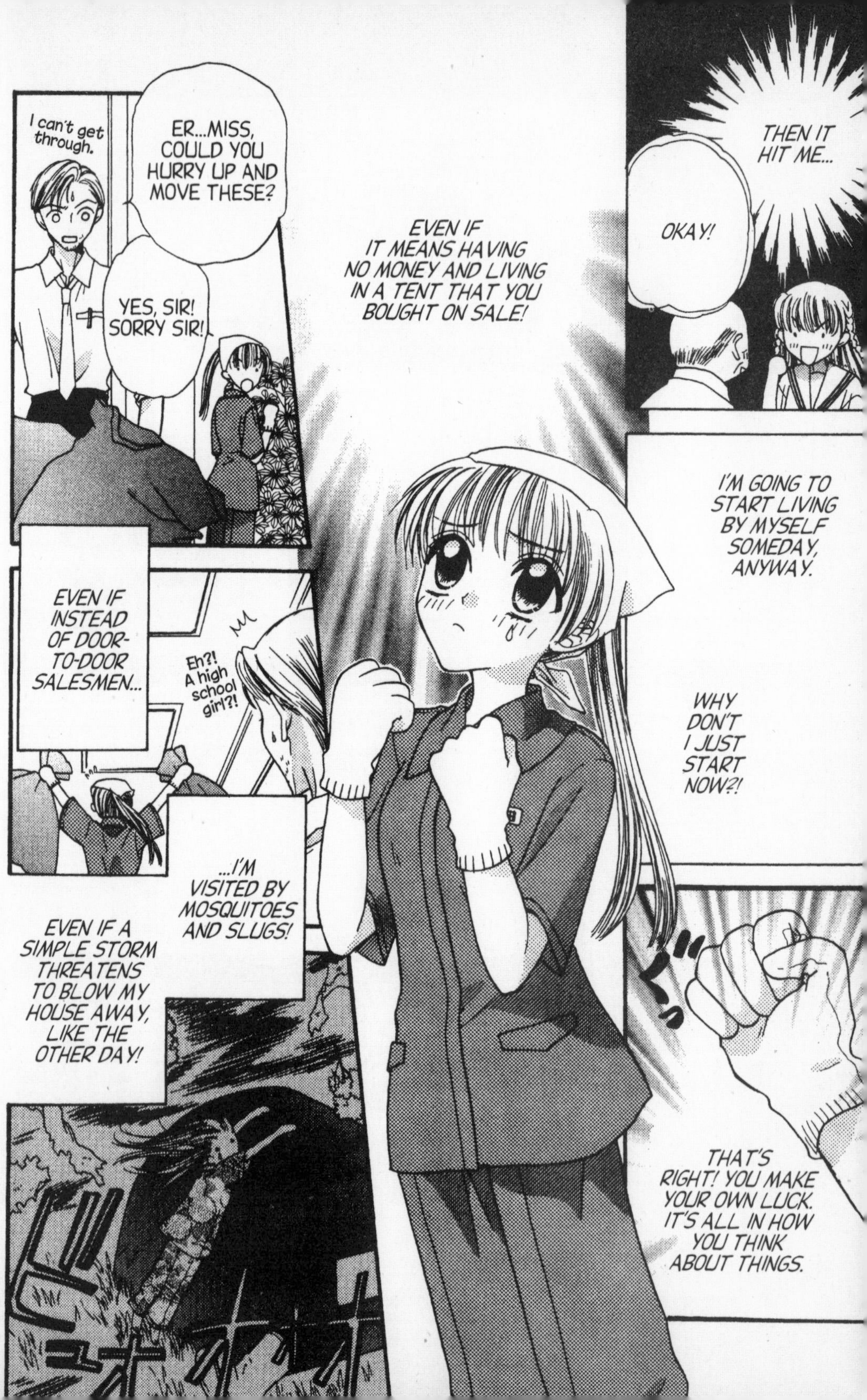

THEN IT HIT ME...
OKAY!
I'M GOING TO START LIVING BY MYSELF SOMEDAY, ANYWAY.
WHY DON'T I JUST START NOW?!
THAT'S RIGHT! YOU MAKE YOUR OWN LUCK. IT'S ALL IN HOW YOU THINK ABOUT THINGS.
I can't get through.
ER...MISS, COULD YOU HURRY UP AND MOVE THESE?
YES, SIR! SORRY SIR!
EVEN IF IT MEANS HAVING NO MONEY AND LIVING IN A TENT THAT YOU BOUGHT ON SALE!
EVEN IF INSTEAD OF DOOR-TO-DOOR SALESMEN...
Eh?! A high school girl?!
...I'M VISITED BY MOSQUITOES AND SLUGS!
EVEN IF A SIMPLE STORM THREATENS TO BLOW MY HOUSE AWAY, LIKE THE OTHER DAY!

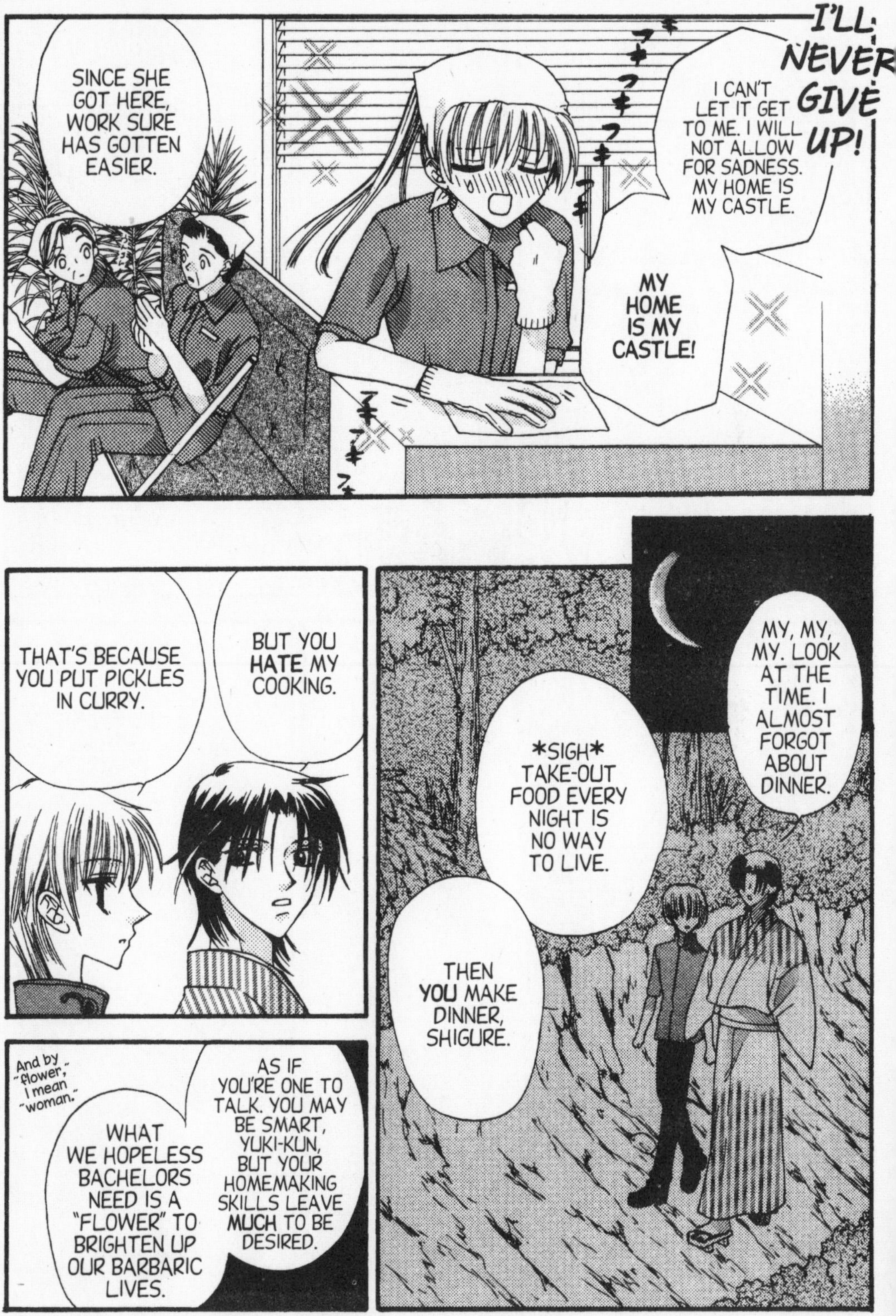
I'LL NEVER GIVE UP!
I CAN'T LET IT GET TO ME. I WILL NOT ALLOW FOR SADNESS. MY HOME IS MY CASTLE.
SINCE SHE GOT HERE, WORK SURE HAS GOTTEN EASIER.
MY HOME IS MY CASTLE!
MY, MY, MY. LOOK AT THE TIME. I ALMOST FORGOT ABOUT DINNER.
SIGH TAKE-OUT FOOD EVERY NIGHT IS NO WAY TO LIVE.
THEN YOU MAKE DINNER, SHIGURE.
BUT YOU HATE MY COOKING.
THAT'S BECAUSE YOU PUT PICKLES IN CURRY.
AS IF YOU'RE ONE TO TALK. YOU MAY BE SMART, YUKI-KUN, BUT YOUR HOMEMAKING SKILLS LEAVE MUCH TO BE DESIRED.
WHAT WE HOPELESS BACHELORS NEED IS A "FLOWER" TO BRIGHTEN UP OUR BARBARIC LIVES.
And by "flower," I mean "woman."

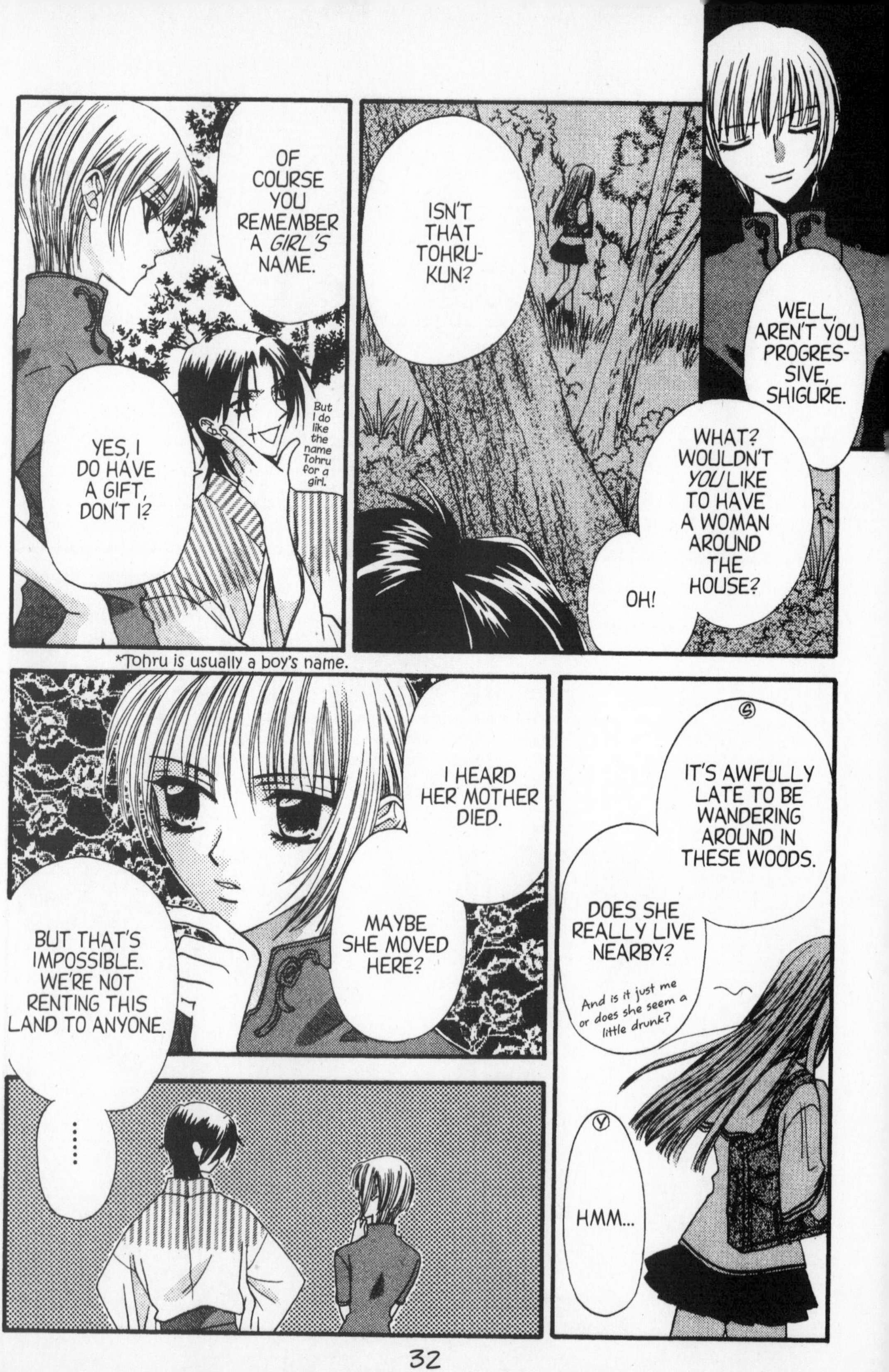
WELL, AREN'T YOU PROGRESSIVE, SHIGURE.
WHAT? WOULDN'T *YOU* LIKE TO HAVE A WOMAN AROUND THE HOUSE?
OH!
ISN'T THAT TOHRU-KUN?
OF COURSE YOU REMEMBER A *GIRL'S* NAME.
YES, I DO HAVE A GIFT, DON'T I?
But I do like the name Tohru for a girl.
*Tohru is usually a boy's name.
IT'S AWFULLY LATE TO BE WANDERING AROUND IN THESE WOODS.
DOES SHE REALLY LIVE NEARBY?
And is it just me or does she seem a little drunk?
HMM...
I HEARD HER MOTHER DIED.
MAYBE SHE MOVED HERE?
BUT THAT'S IMPOSSIBLE. WE'RE NOT RENTING THIS LAND TO ANYONE.
......

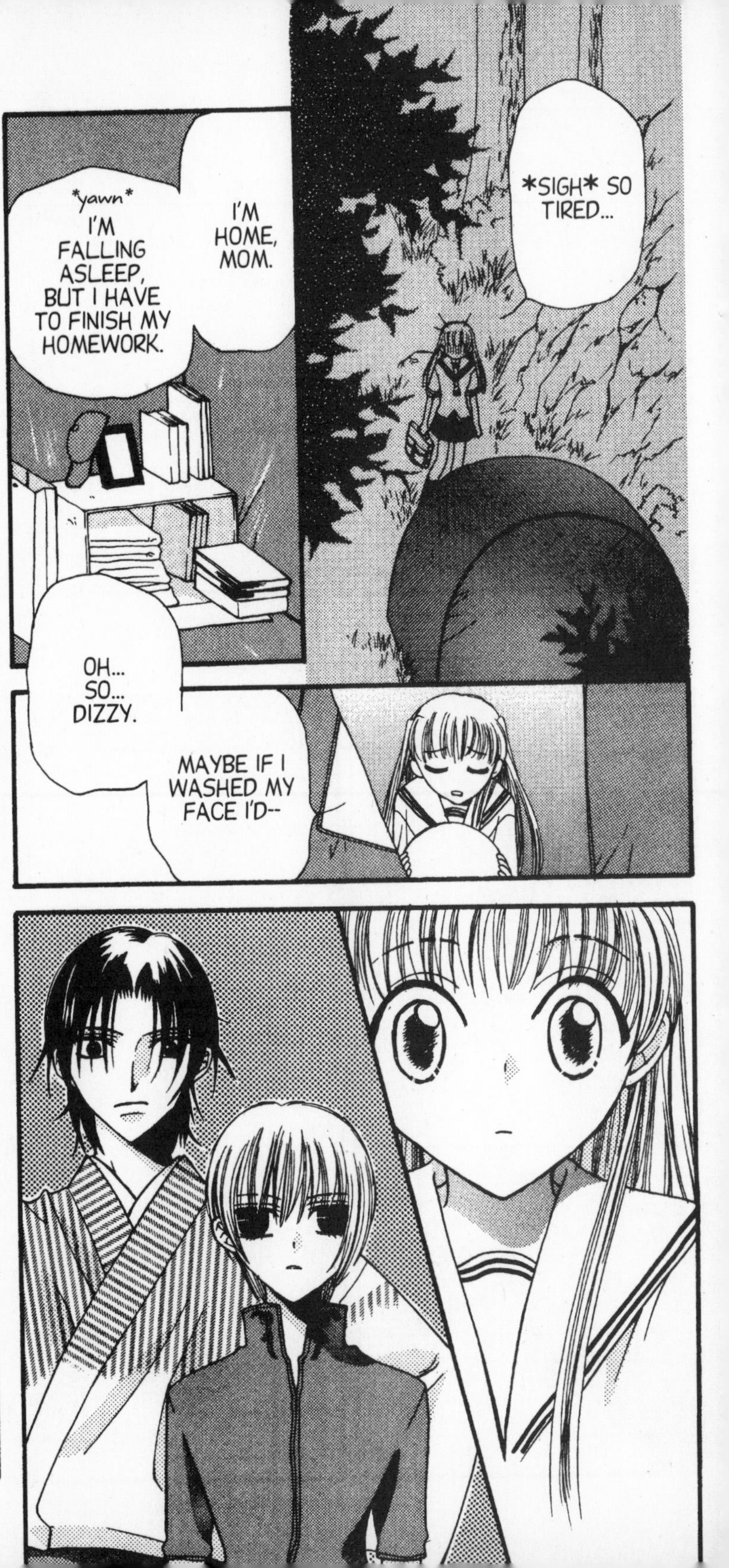
SIGH SO TIRED...
I'M HOME, MOM.
yawn I'M FALLING ASLEEP, BUT I HAVE TO FINISH MY HOMEWORK.
OH... SO... DIZZY.
MAYBE IF I WASHED MY FACE I'D--

Number 2:

I get mail from people who started with "Furuba" asking me to introduce myself, so here I go: Natsuki Takaya (pen name)/ July 7th/Cancer/ Blood type A/ Tokyo (I moved)/ left-handed. People say that left-handers are natural students—not me! I couldn't study. I didn't ever feel like it, and when I did study, my grades stayed the same anyway. I like games and music and I'm not that interested in talking about myself. It's way more fun to talk about my favorite things and favorite characters. Like, "Pikachu is adorable!" (Ha ha!)

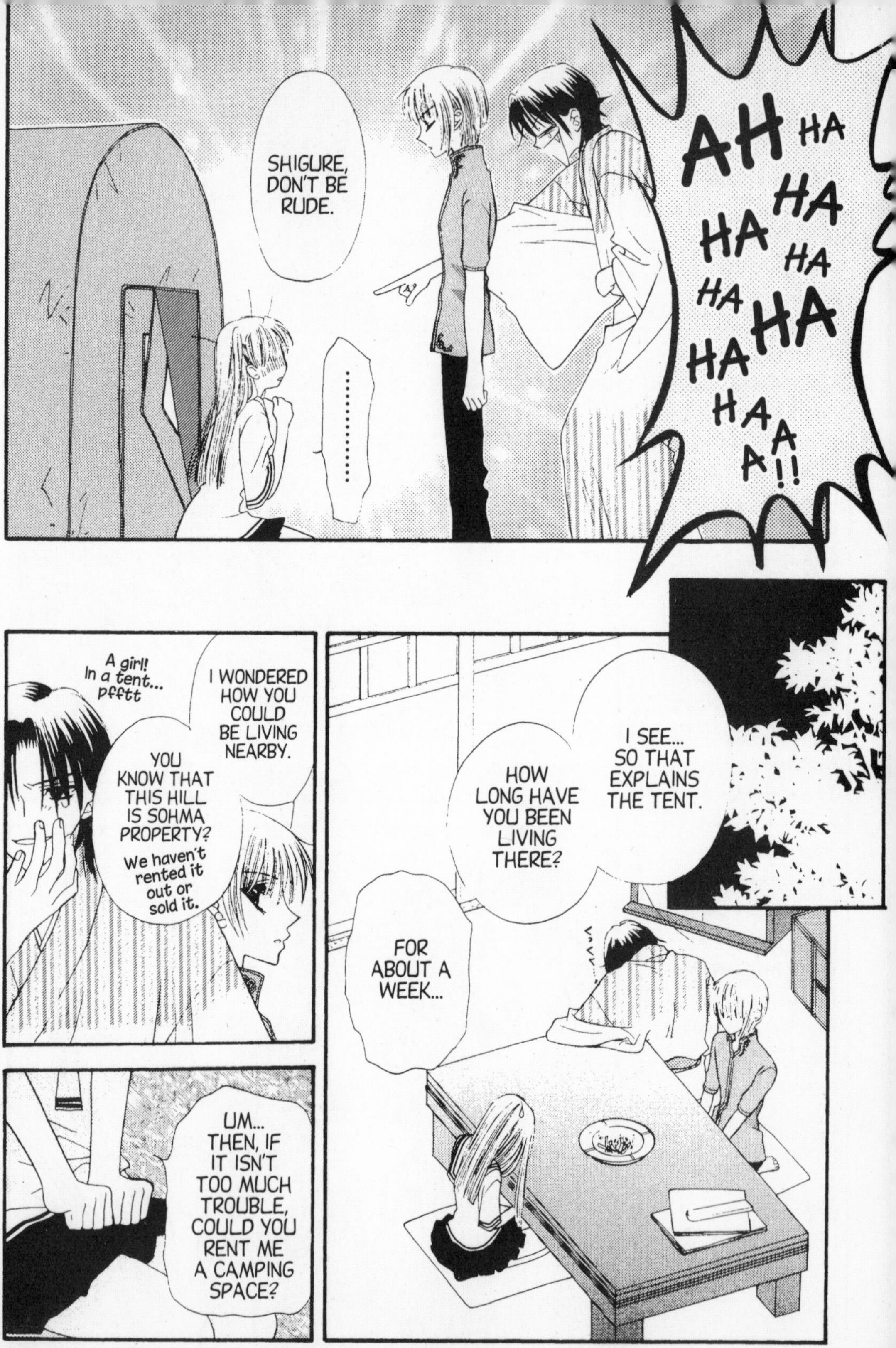
AH HA HA HA HA HA HA HA HAAA!!
SHIGURE, DON'T BE RUDE.
......
I SEE... SO THAT EXPLAINS THE TENT.
HOW LONG HAVE YOU BEEN LIVING THERE?
FOR ABOUT A WEEK...
I WONDERED HOW YOU COULD BE LIVING NEARBY.
A girl! In a tent... pfftt
YOU KNOW THAT THIS HILL IS SOHMA PROPERTY?
We haven't rented it out or sold it.
UM... THEN, IF IT ISN'T TOO MUCH TROUBLE, COULD YOU RENT ME A CAMPING SPACE?

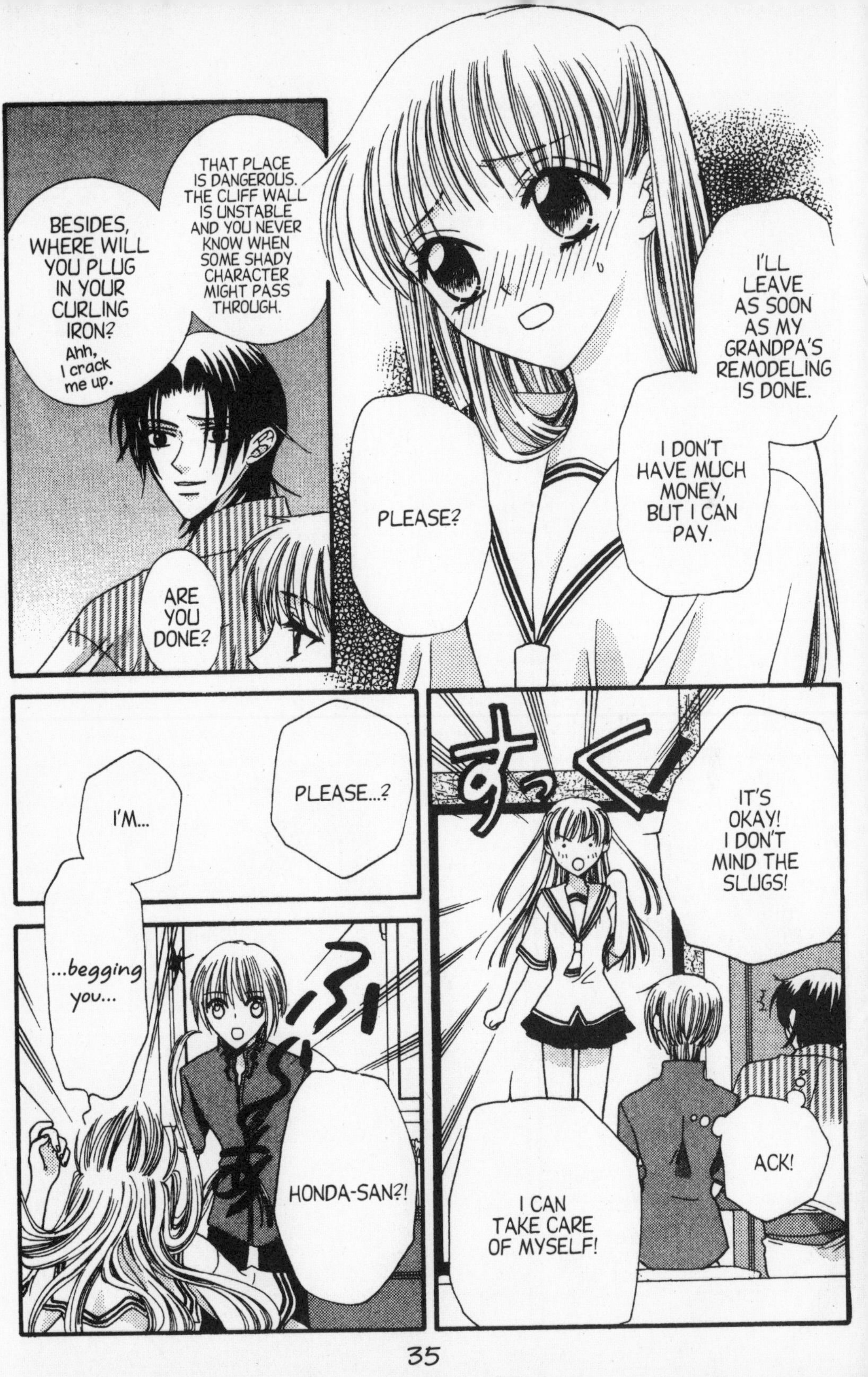
I'LL LEAVE AS SOON AS MY GRANDPA'S REMODELING IS DONE.
I DON'T HAVE MUCH MONEY, BUT I CAN PAY.
PLEASE?
THAT PLACE IS DANGEROUS. THE CLIFF WALL IS UNSTABLE AND YOU NEVER KNOW WHEN SOME SHADY CHARACTER MIGHT PASS THROUGH.
BESIDES, WHERE WILL YOU PLUG IN YOUR CURLING IRON?
Ahh, I crack me up.
ARE YOU DONE?
すっく
IT'S OKAY! I DON'T MIND THE SLUGS!
ACK!
I CAN TAKE CARE OF MYSELF!
PLEASE...?
I'M...
...begging you...
HONDA-SAN?!

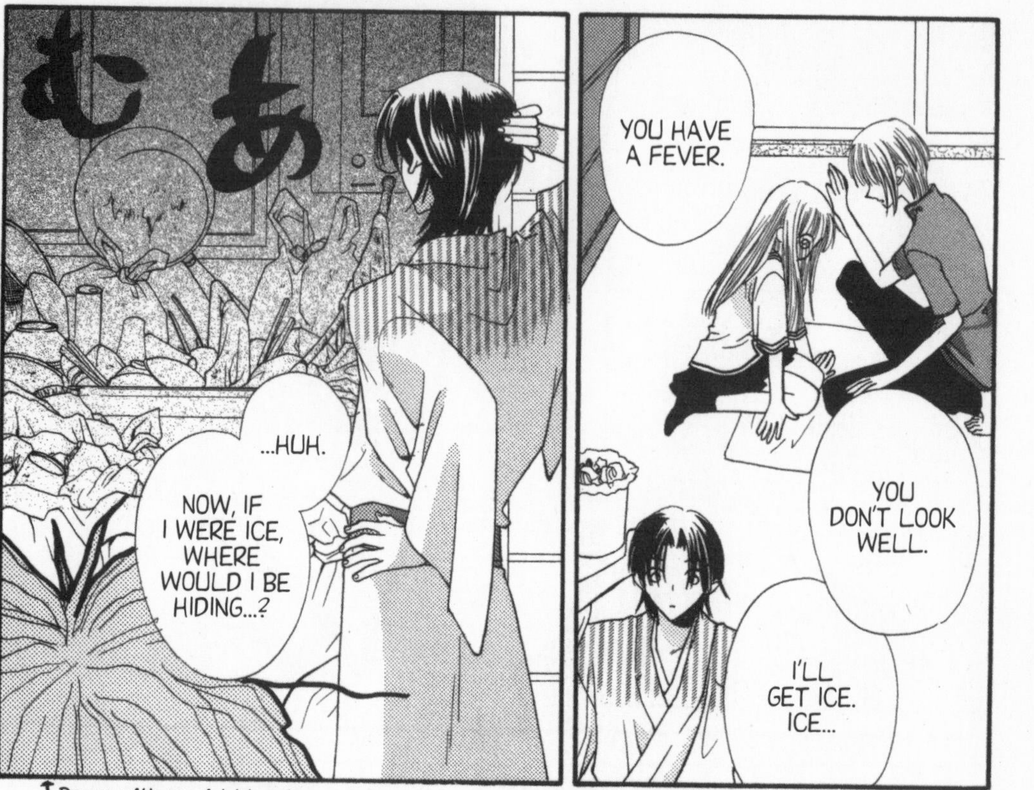
YOU HAVE A FEVER.
YOU DON'T LOOK WELL.
I'LL GET ICE. ICE...
むあ
...HUH.
NOW, IF I WERE ICE, WHERE WOULD I BE HIDING...?

↑ Drawn with my right hand.

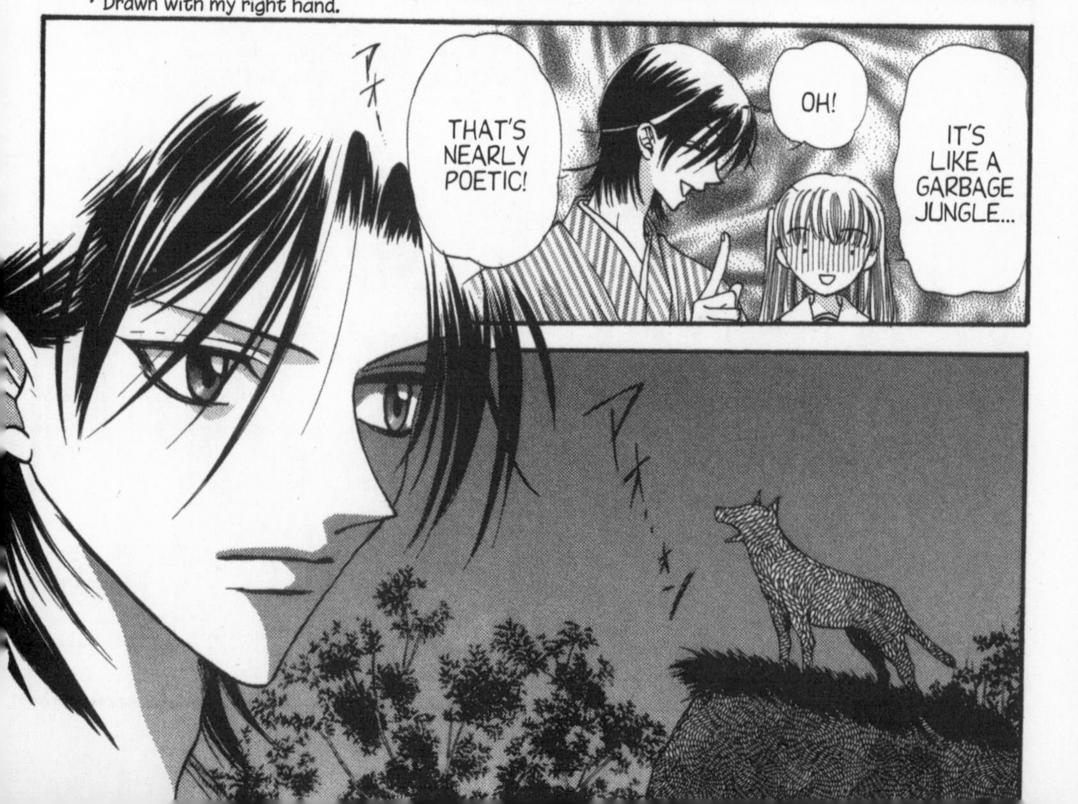
IT'S LIKE A GARBAGE JUNGLE...
OH!
THAT'S NEARLY POETIC!

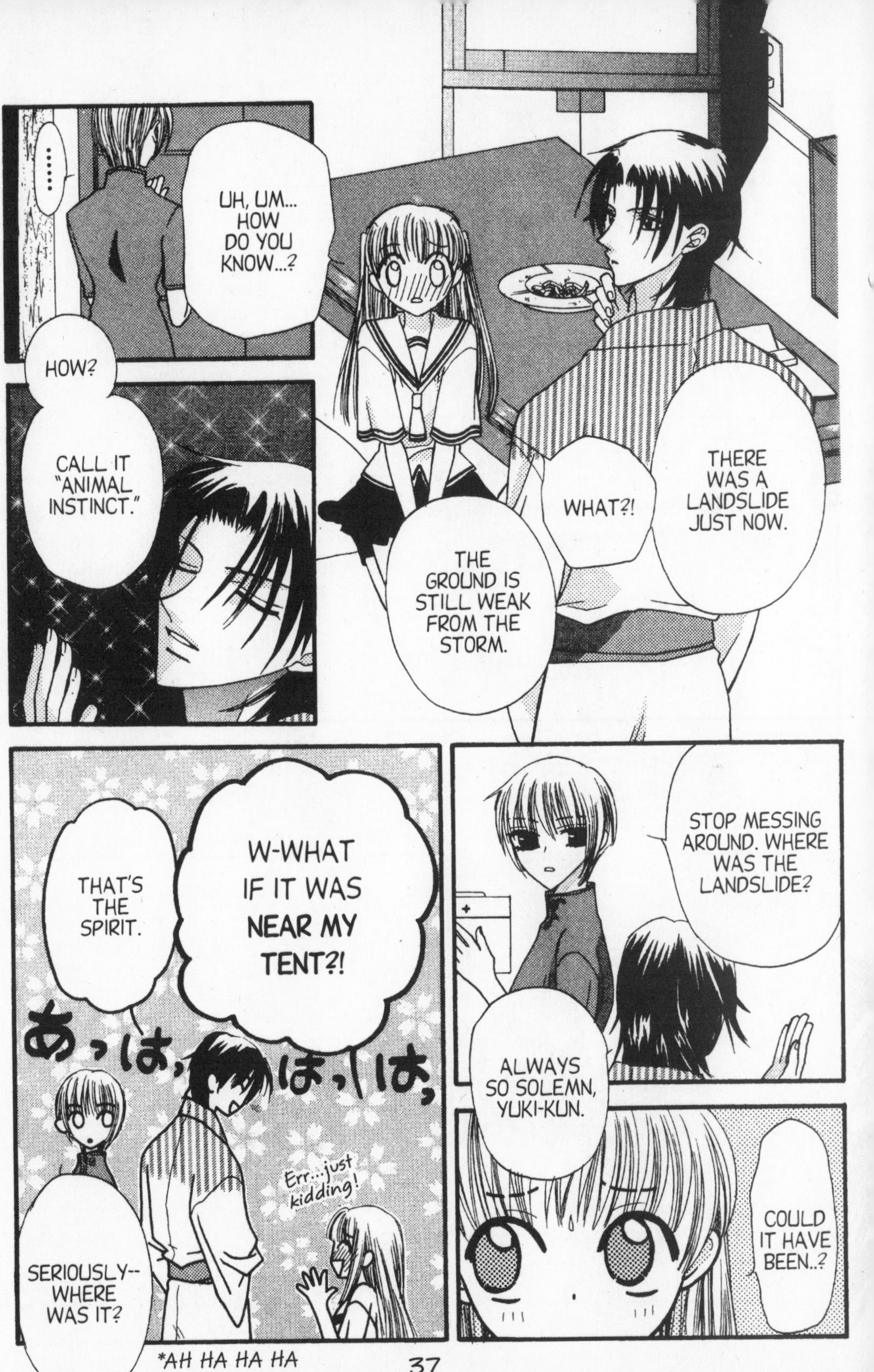
THERE WAS A LANDSLIDE JUST NOW.
WHAT?!
THE GROUND IS STILL WEAK FROM THE STORM.
......
UH, UM... HOW DO YOU KNOW...?
HOW?
CALL IT "ANIMAL INSTINCT."
STOP MESSING AROUND. WHERE WAS THE LANDSLIDE?
ALWAYS SO SOLEMN, YUKI-KUN.
COULD IT HAVE BEEN...?
W-WHAT IF IT WAS **NEAR MY TENT**?!
THAT'S THE SPIRIT.
あっは、はっは、
Err...just kidding!
SERIOUSLY-- WHERE WAS IT?

*AH HA HA HA

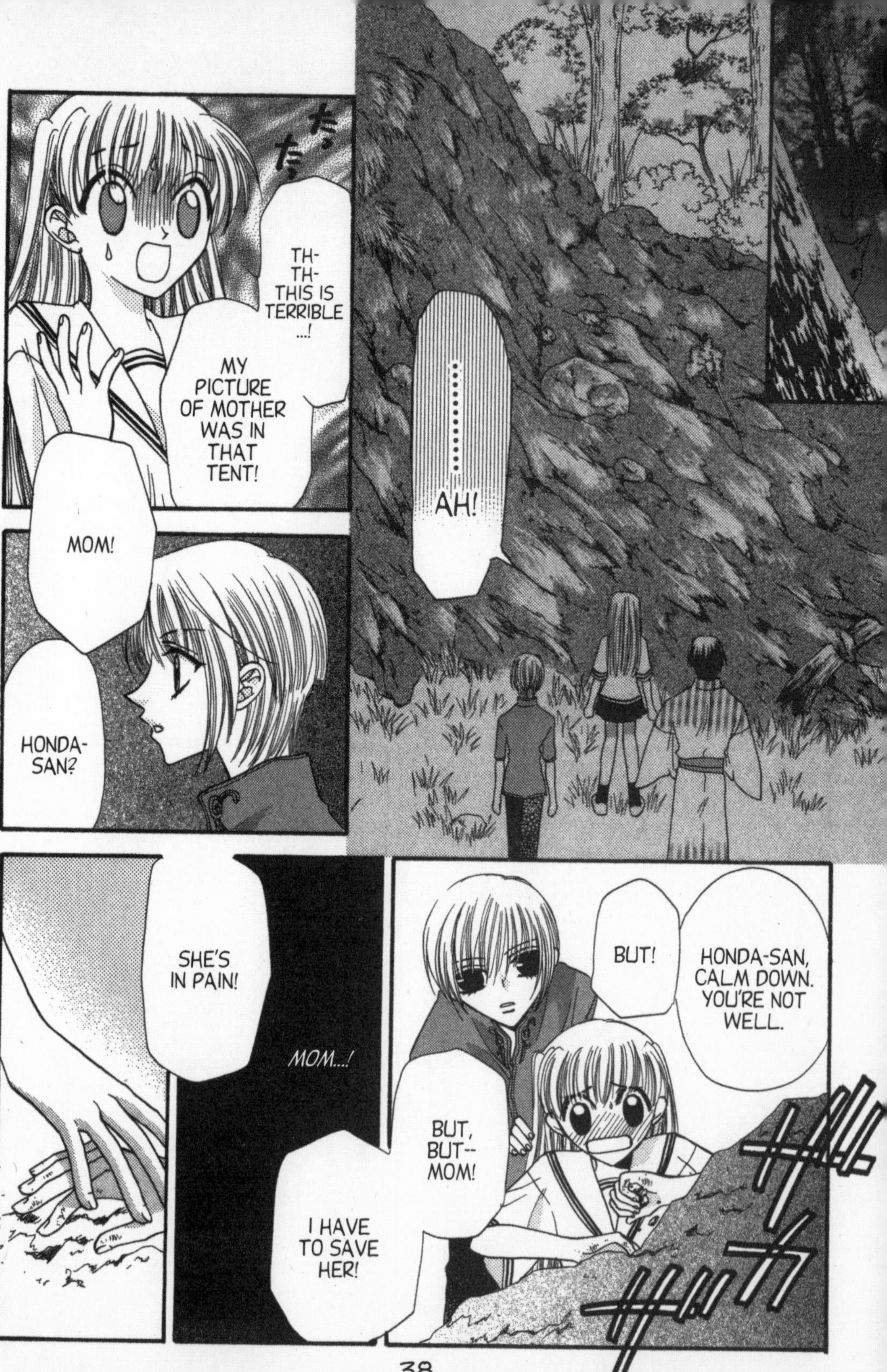
......
AH!
たっ たっ
TH-TH-THIS IS TERRIBLE ...!
MY PICTURE OF MOTHER WAS IN THAT TENT!
MOM!
HONDA-SAN?
HONDA-SAN, CALM DOWN. YOU'RE NOT WELL.
BUT!
BUT, BUT-- MOM!
I HAVE TO SAVE HER!
SHE'S IN PAIN!
MOM...!

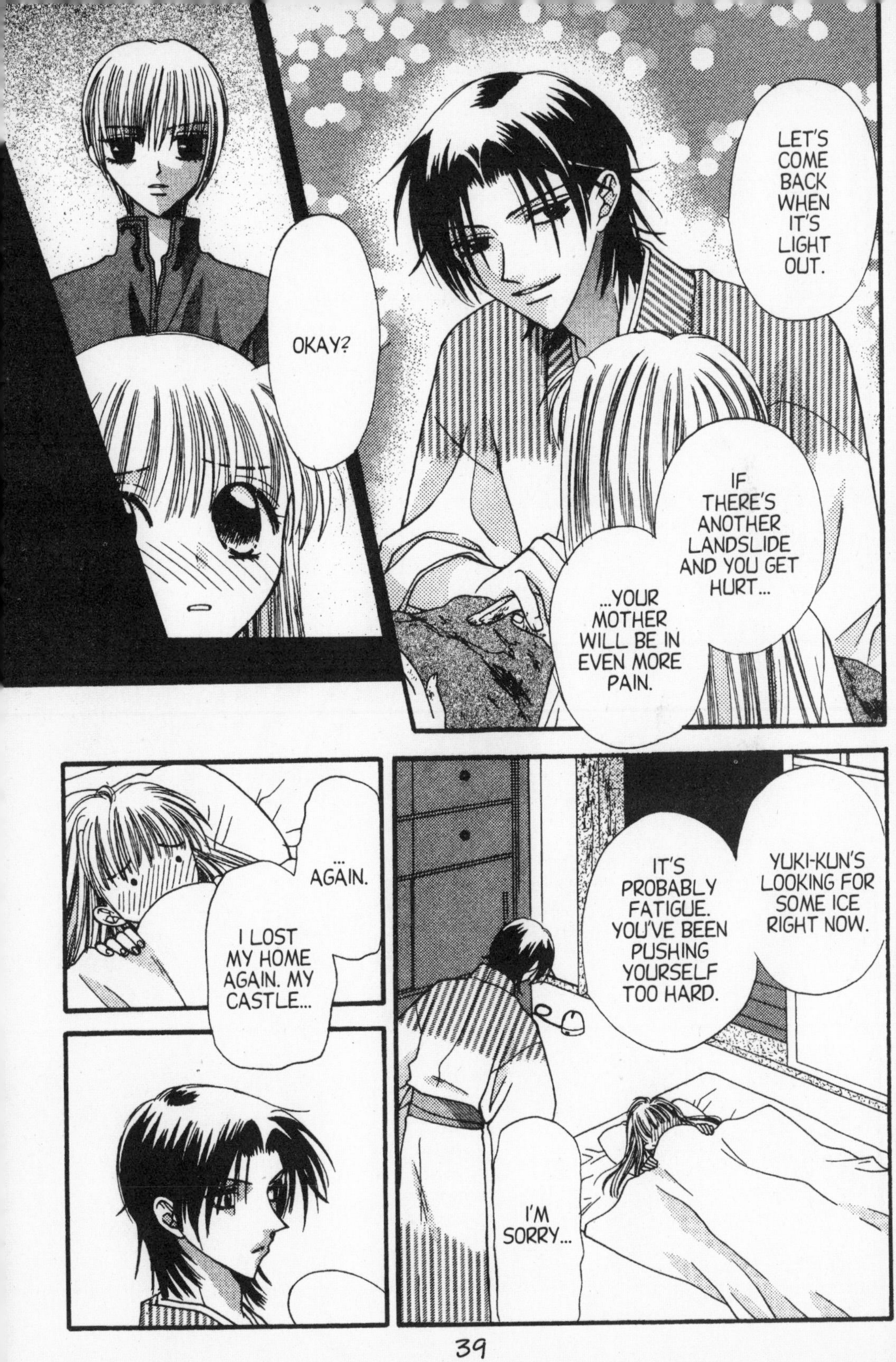
LET'S COME BACK WHEN IT'S LIGHT OUT.
IF THERE'S ANOTHER LANDSLIDE AND YOU GET HURT...
...YOUR MOTHER WILL BE IN EVEN MORE PAIN.
OKAY?
YUKI-KUN'S LOOKING FOR SOME ICE RIGHT NOW.
IT'S PROBABLY FATIGUE. YOU'VE BEEN PUSHING YOURSELF TOO HARD.
I'M SORRY...
...AGAIN.
I LOST MY HOME AGAIN. MY CASTLE...

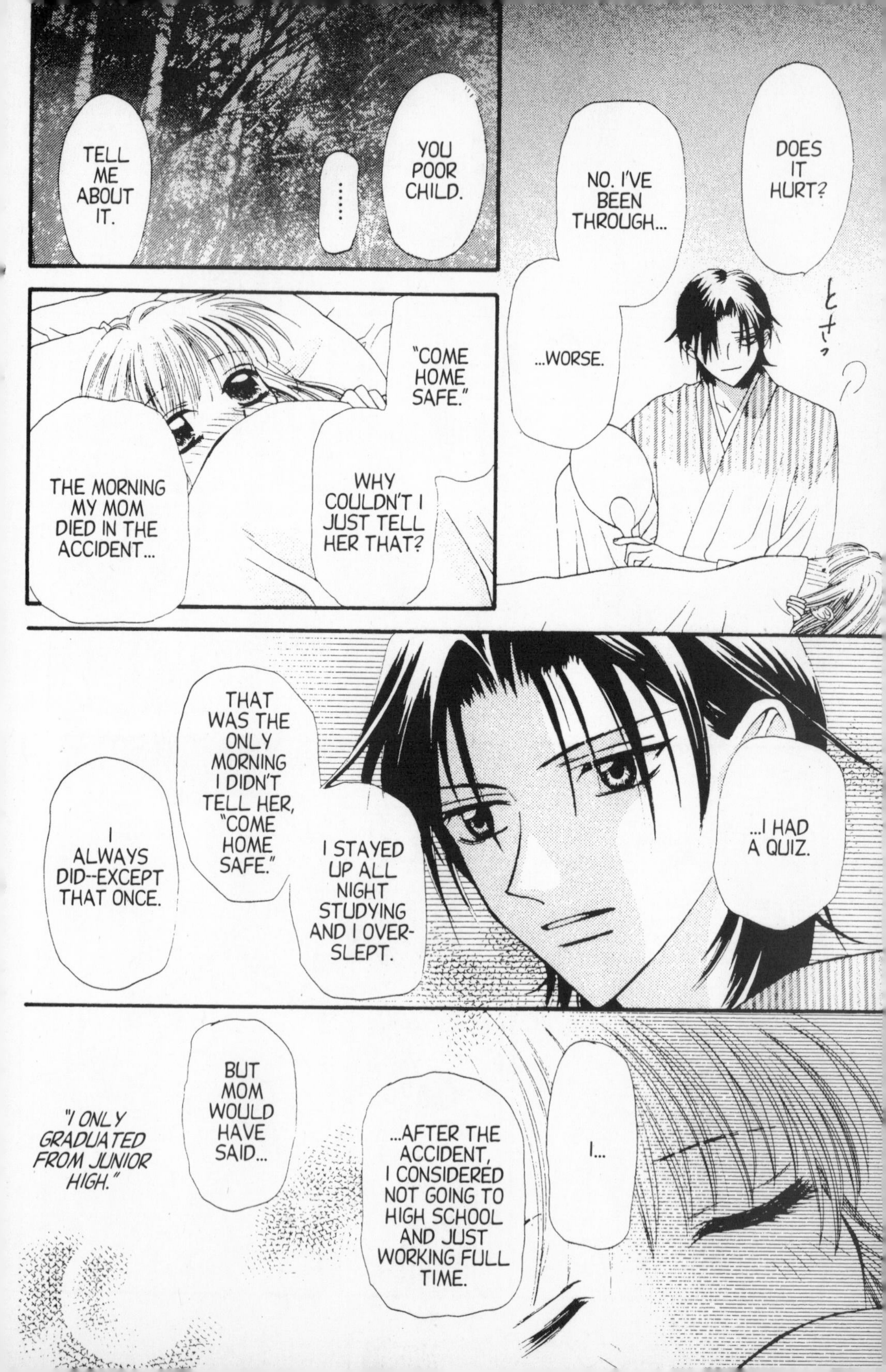
DOES IT HURT?
とさっ
NO. I'VE BEEN THROUGH...
...WORSE.
YOU POOR CHILD.
......
TELL ME ABOUT IT.
"COME HOME SAFE."
WHY COULDN'T I JUST TELL HER THAT?
THE MORNING MY MOM DIED IN THE ACCIDENT...
...I HAD A QUIZ.
I STAYED UP ALL NIGHT STUDYING AND I OVER-SLEPT.
THAT WAS THE ONLY MORNING I DIDN'T TELL HER, "COME HOME SAFE."
I ALWAYS DID--EXCEPT THAT ONCE.
I...
...AFTER THE ACCIDENT, I CONSIDERED NOT GOING TO HIGH SCHOOL AND JUST WORKING FULL TIME.
BUT MOM WOULD HAVE SAID...
"I ONLY GRADUATED FROM JUNIOR HIGH."

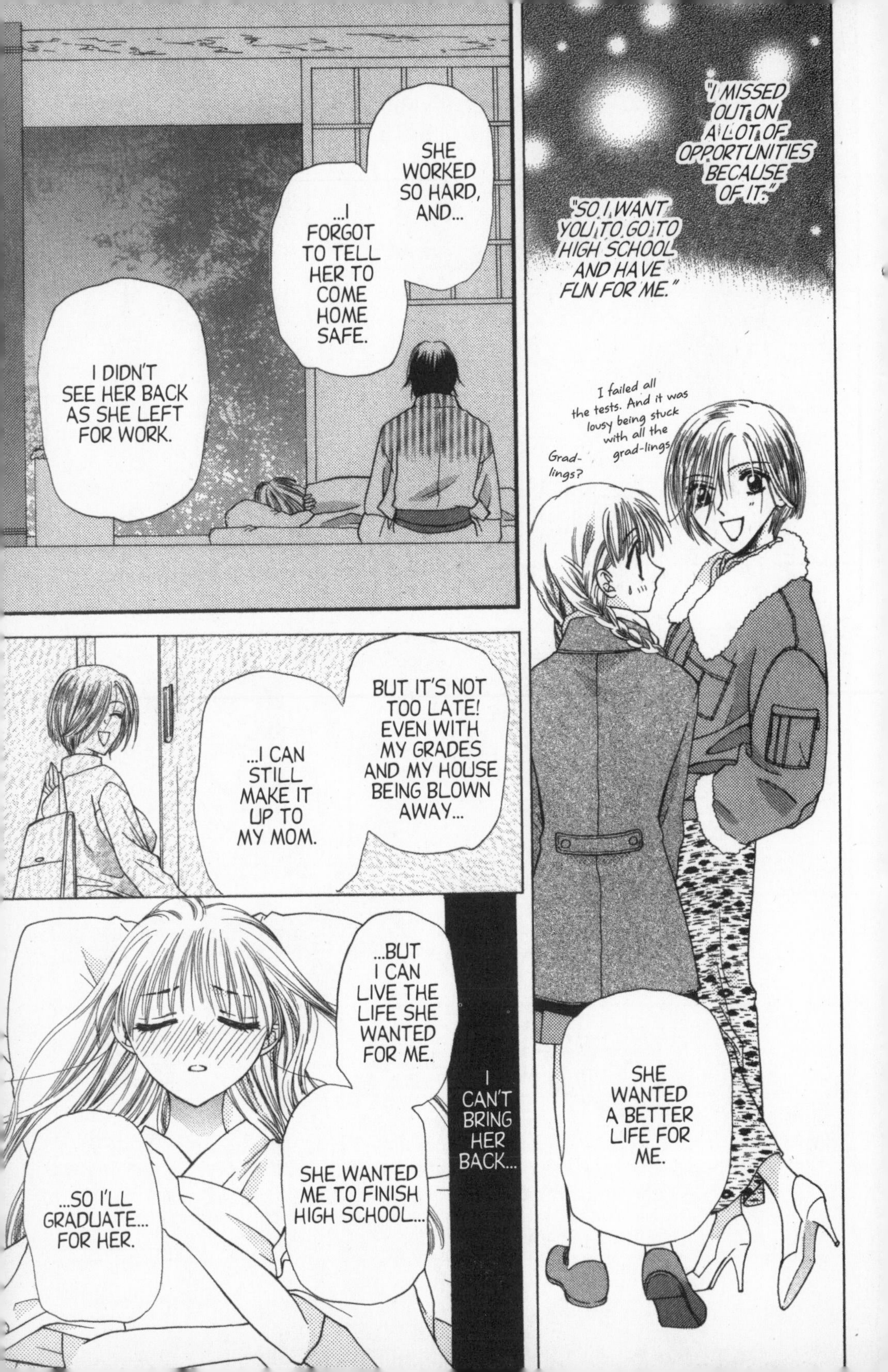
"I MISSED OUT ON A LOT OF OPPORTUNITIES BECAUSE OF IT."
"SO I WANT YOU TO GO TO HIGH SCHOOL AND HAVE FUN FOR ME."
I failed all the tests. And it was lousy being stuck with all the grad-lings.
Grad-lings?
SHE WANTED A BETTER LIFE FOR ME.
SHE WORKED SO HARD, AND...
...I FORGOT TO TELL HER TO COME HOME SAFE.
I DIDN'T SEE HER BACK AS SHE LEFT FOR WORK.
BUT IT'S NOT TOO LATE! EVEN WITH MY GRADES AND MY HOUSE BEING BLOWN AWAY...
...I CAN STILL MAKE IT UP TO MY MOM.
I CAN'T BRING HER BACK...
...BUT I CAN LIVE THE LIFE SHE WANTED FOR ME.
SHE WANTED ME TO FINISH HIGH SCHOOL...
...SO I'LL GRADUATE... FOR HER.

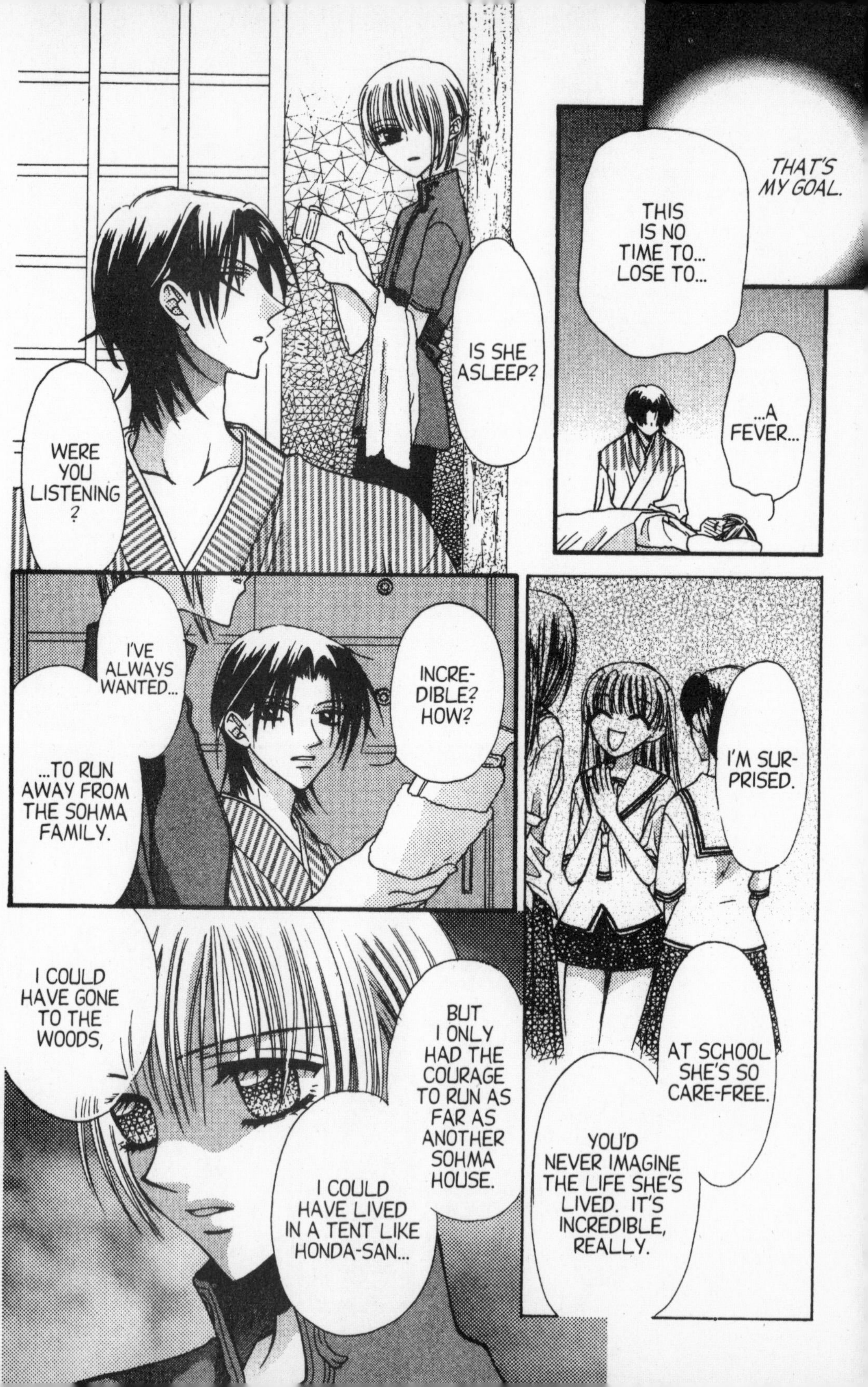
THAT'S MY GOAL.
THIS IS NO TIME TO... LOSE TO...
...A FEVER...
IS SHE ASLEEP?
WERE YOU LISTENING?
I'M SUR-PRISED.
AT SCHOOL SHE'S SO CARE-FREE.
YOU'D NEVER IMAGINE THE LIFE SHE'S LIVED. IT'S INCREDIBLE, REALLY.
INCRE-DIBLE? HOW?
I'VE ALWAYS WANTED...
...TO RUN AWAY FROM THE SOHMA FAMILY.
I COULD HAVE GONE TO THE WOODS,
I COULD HAVE LIVED IN A TENT LIKE HONDA-SAN...
BUT I ONLY HAD THE COURAGE TO RUN AS FAR AS ANOTHER SOHMA HOUSE.

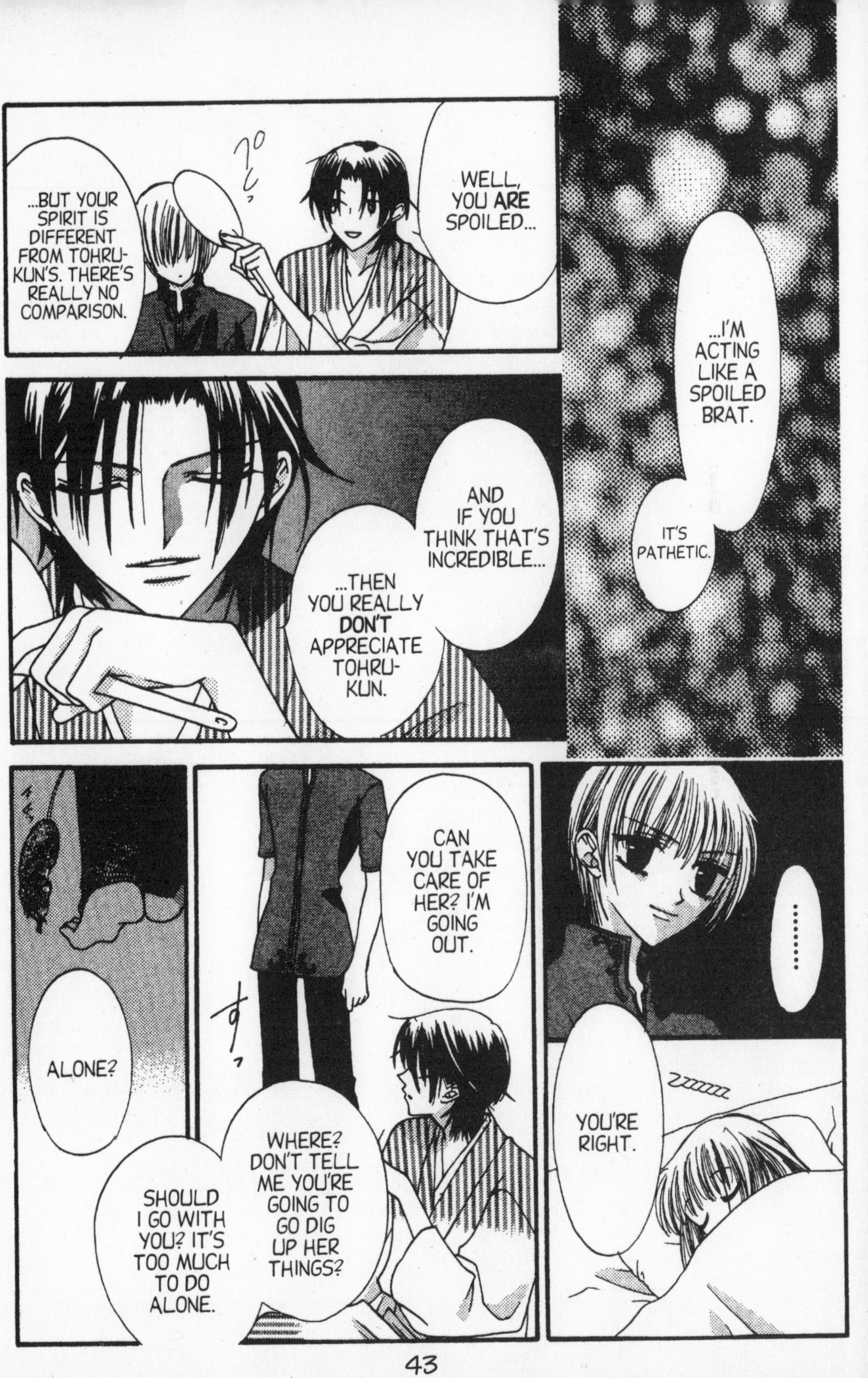
...I'M ACTING LIKE A SPOILED BRAT.
IT'S PATHETIC.
WELL, YOU **ARE** SPOILED...
...BUT YOUR SPIRIT IS DIFFERENT FROM TOHRU-KUN'S. THERE'S REALLY NO COMPARISON.
AND IF YOU THINK THAT'S INCREDIBLE...
...THEN YOU REALLY **DON'T** APPRECIATE TOHRU-KUN.
......
ZZZZZZ
YOU'RE RIGHT.
CAN YOU TAKE CARE OF HER? I'M GOING OUT.
WHERE? DON'T TELL ME YOU'RE GOING TO GO DIG UP HER THINGS?
ALONE?
SHOULD I GO WITH YOU? IT'S TOO MUCH TO DO ALONE.

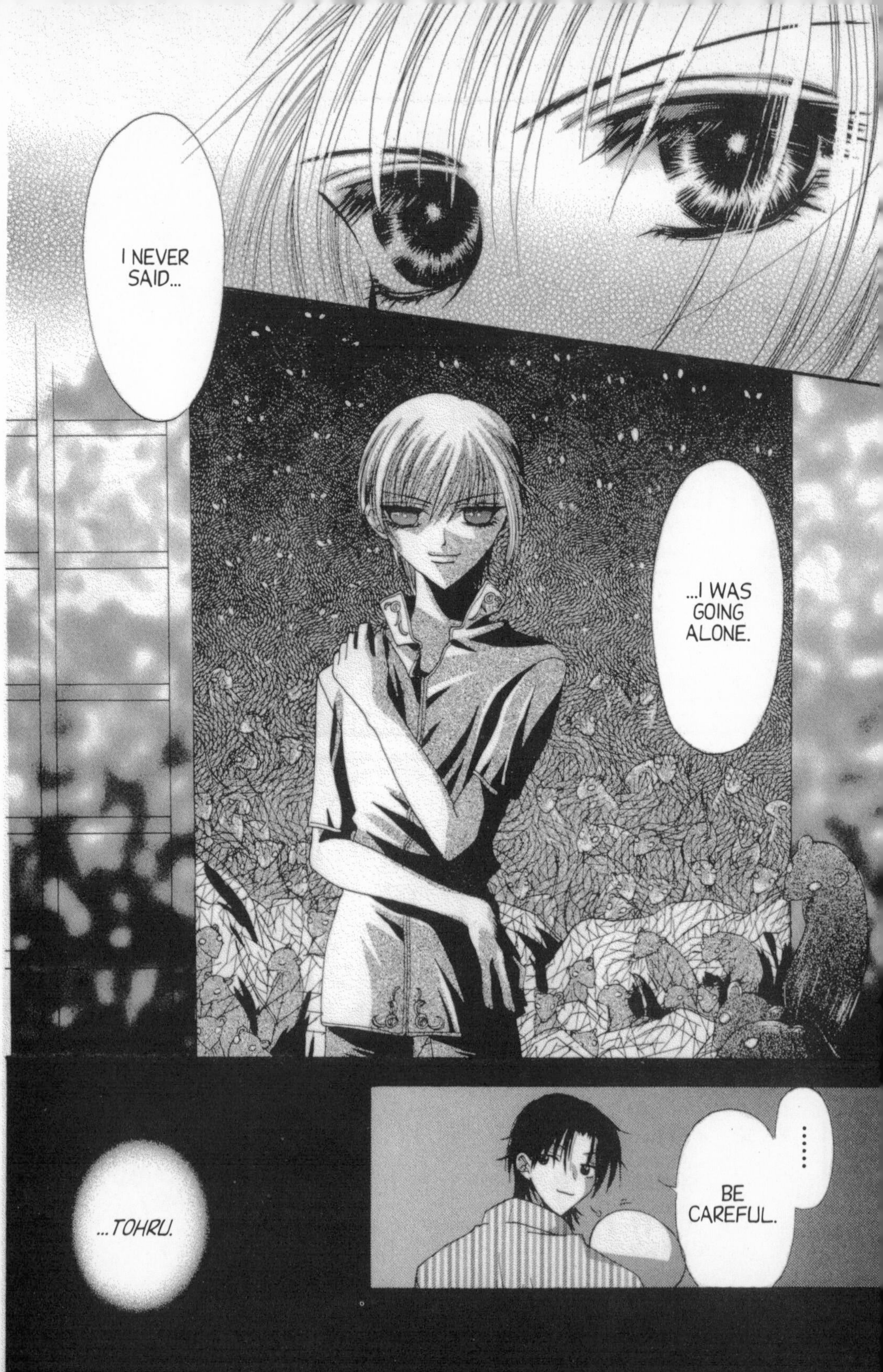
I NEVER SAID...
...I WAS GOING ALONE.
......
BE CAREFUL.
...TOHRU.

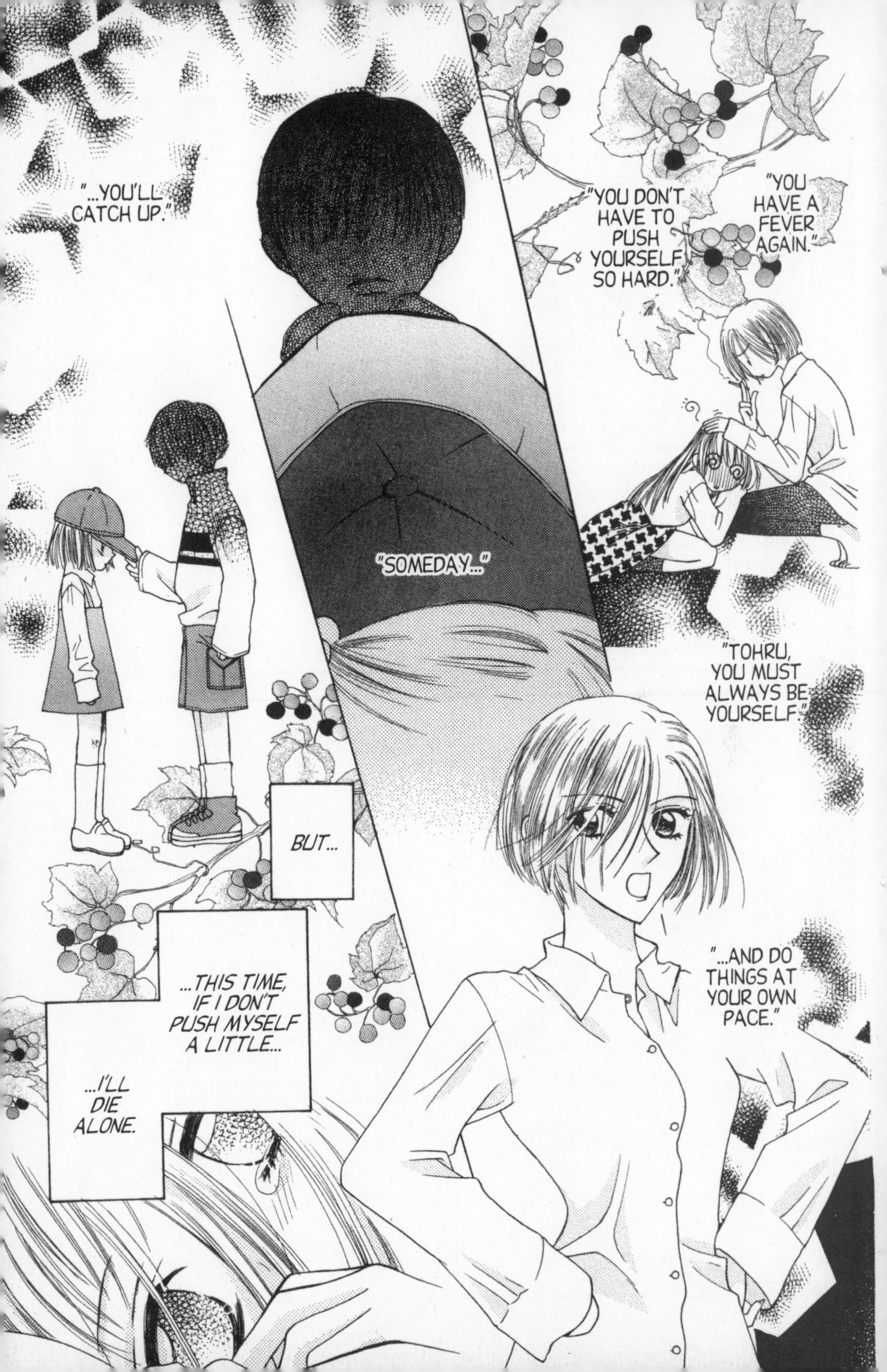
"YOU HAVE A FEVER AGAIN."
"YOU DON'T HAVE TO PUSH YOURSELF SO HARD."
"TOHRU, YOU MUST ALWAYS BE YOURSELF."
"...AND DO THINGS AT YOUR OWN PACE."
"SOMEDAY..."
"...YOU'LL CATCH UP."
BUT...
...THIS TIME, IF I DON'T PUSH MYSELF A LITTLE...
...I'LL DIE ALONE.

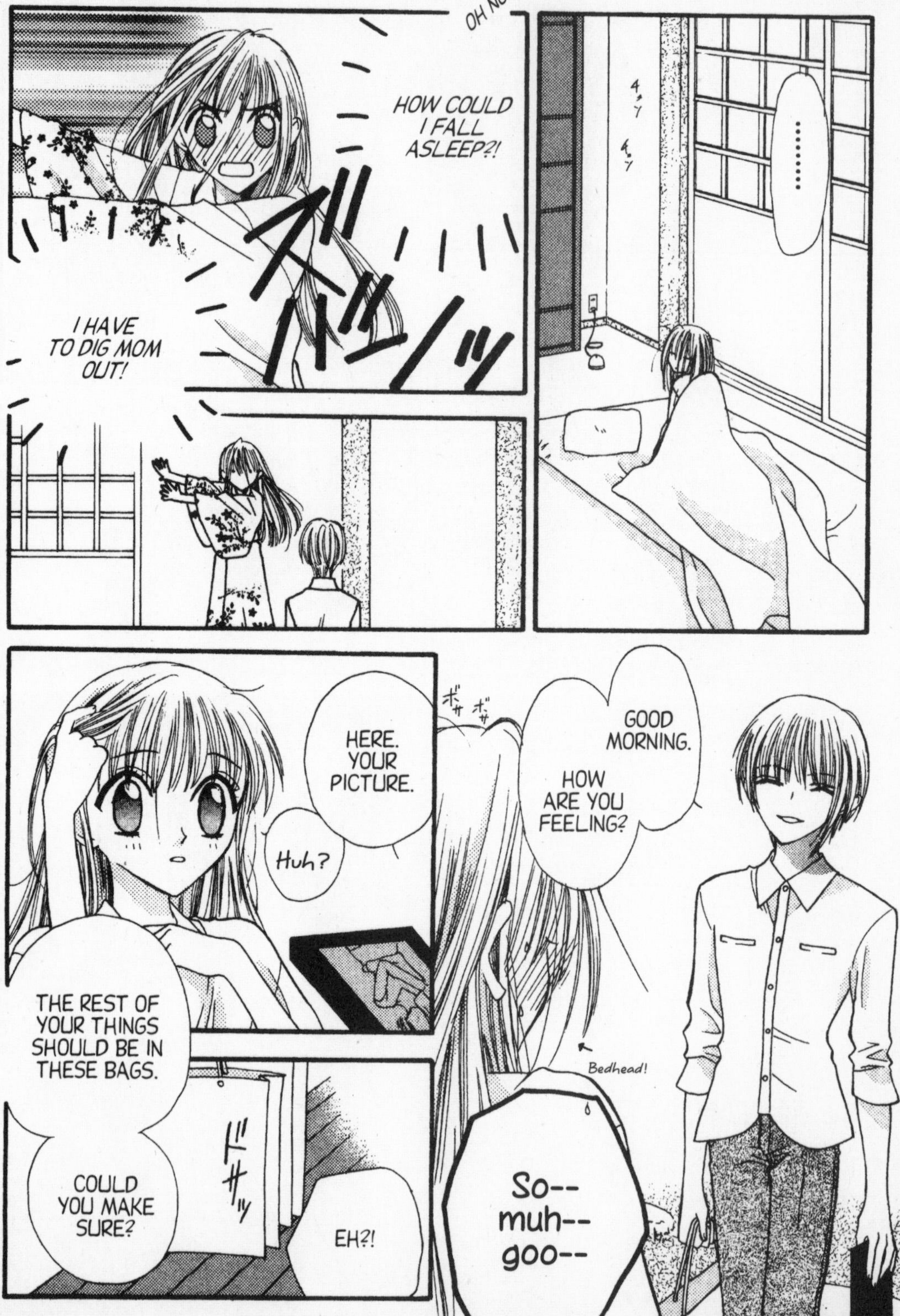

......
OH NO!
HOW COULD I FALL ASLEEP?!
I HAVE TO DIG MOM OUT!
GOOD MORNING.
HOW ARE YOU FEELING?
Bedhead!
So-- muh-- goo--
*Sohma-kun, um, good morning.
HERE. YOUR PICTURE.
Huh?
THE REST OF YOUR THINGS SHOULD BE IN THESE BAGS.
COULD YOU MAKE SURE?
EH?!

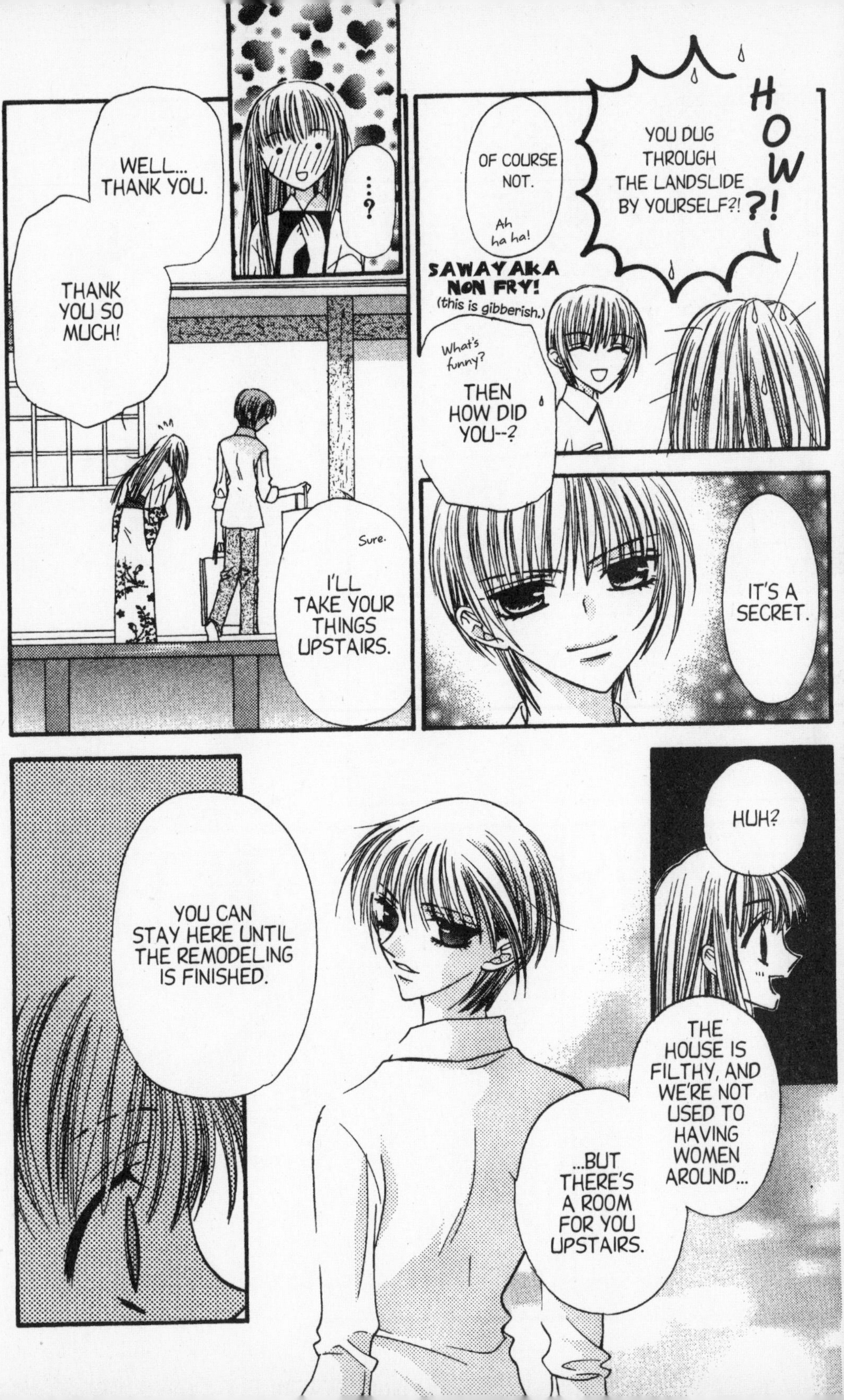
HOW?!
YOU DUG THROUGH THE LANDSLIDE BY YOURSELF?!
OF COURSE NOT.
Ah ha ha!
SAWAYAKA NON FRY!
(this is gibberish.)
What's funny?
THEN HOW DID YOU--?
IT'S A SECRET.
...?
WELL... THANK YOU.
THANK YOU SO MUCH!
Sure.
I'LL TAKE YOUR THINGS UPSTAIRS.
HUH?
YOU CAN STAY HERE UNTIL THE REMODELING IS FINISHED.
THE HOUSE IS FILTHY, AND WE'RE NOT USED TO HAVING WOMEN AROUND...
...BUT THERE'S A ROOM FOR YOU UPSTAIRS.

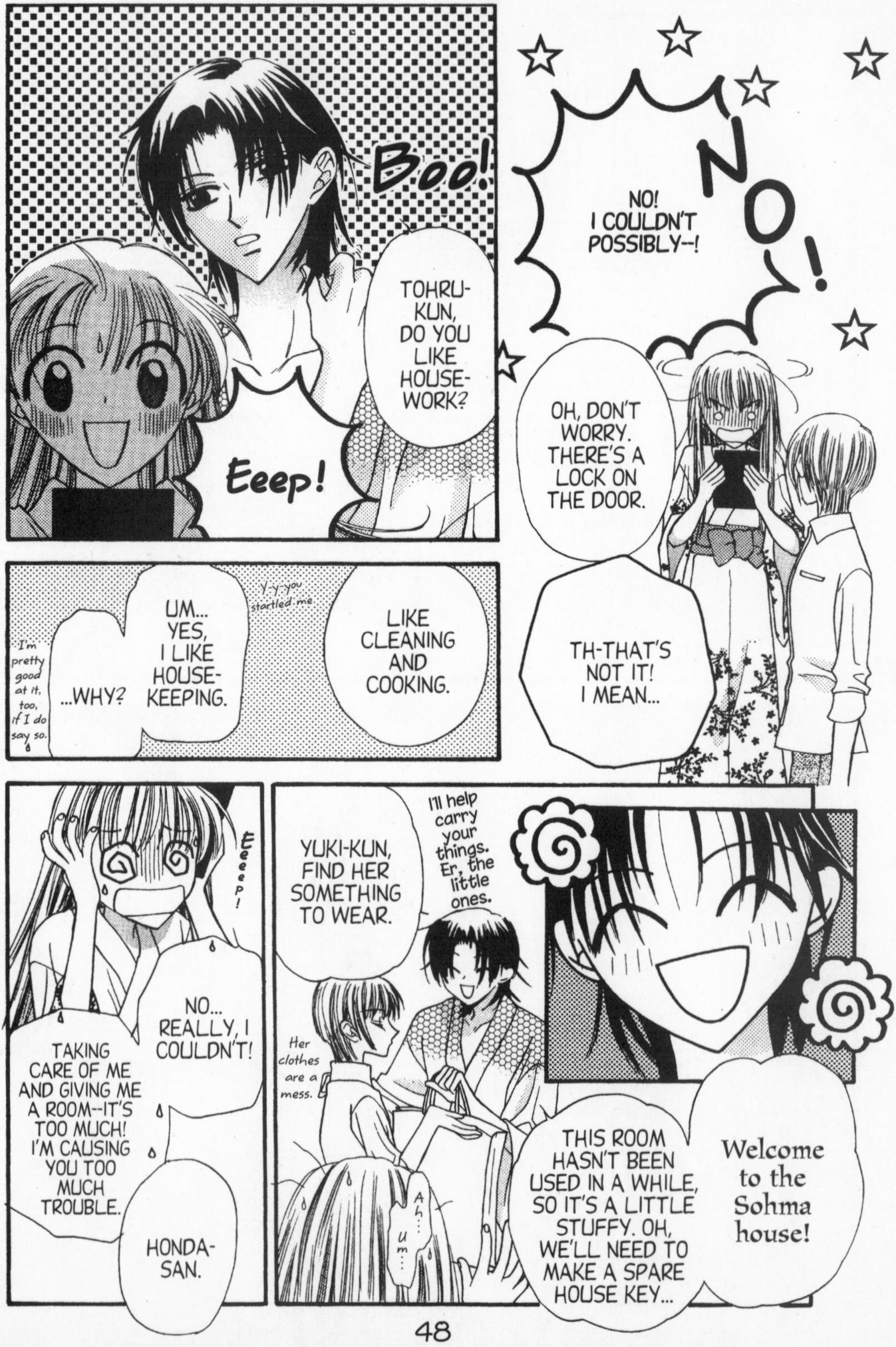
NO!
NO! I COULDN'T POSSIBLY--!
OH, DON'T WORRY. THERE'S A LOCK ON THE DOOR.
TH-THAT'S NOT IT! I MEAN...
Boo!
TOHRU-KUN, DO YOU LIKE HOUSE-WORK?
Eeep!
LIKE CLEANING AND COOKING.
Y-y-you startled me
UM... YES, I LIKE HOUSE-KEEPING.
...WHY?
I'm pretty good at it, too, if I do say so.
Welcome to the Sohma house!
THIS ROOM HASN'T BEEN USED IN A WHILE, SO IT'S A LITTLE STUFFY. OH, WE'LL NEED TO MAKE A SPARE HOUSE KEY...
I'll help carry your things. Er, the little ones.
YUKI-KUN, FIND HER SOMETHING TO WEAR.
Her clothes are a mess.
Ah... um...
Eeeep!
NO... REALLY, I COULDN'T!
TAKING CARE OF ME AND GIVING ME A ROOM--IT'S TOO MUCH! I'M CAUSING YOU TOO MUCH TROUBLE.
HONDA-SAN.

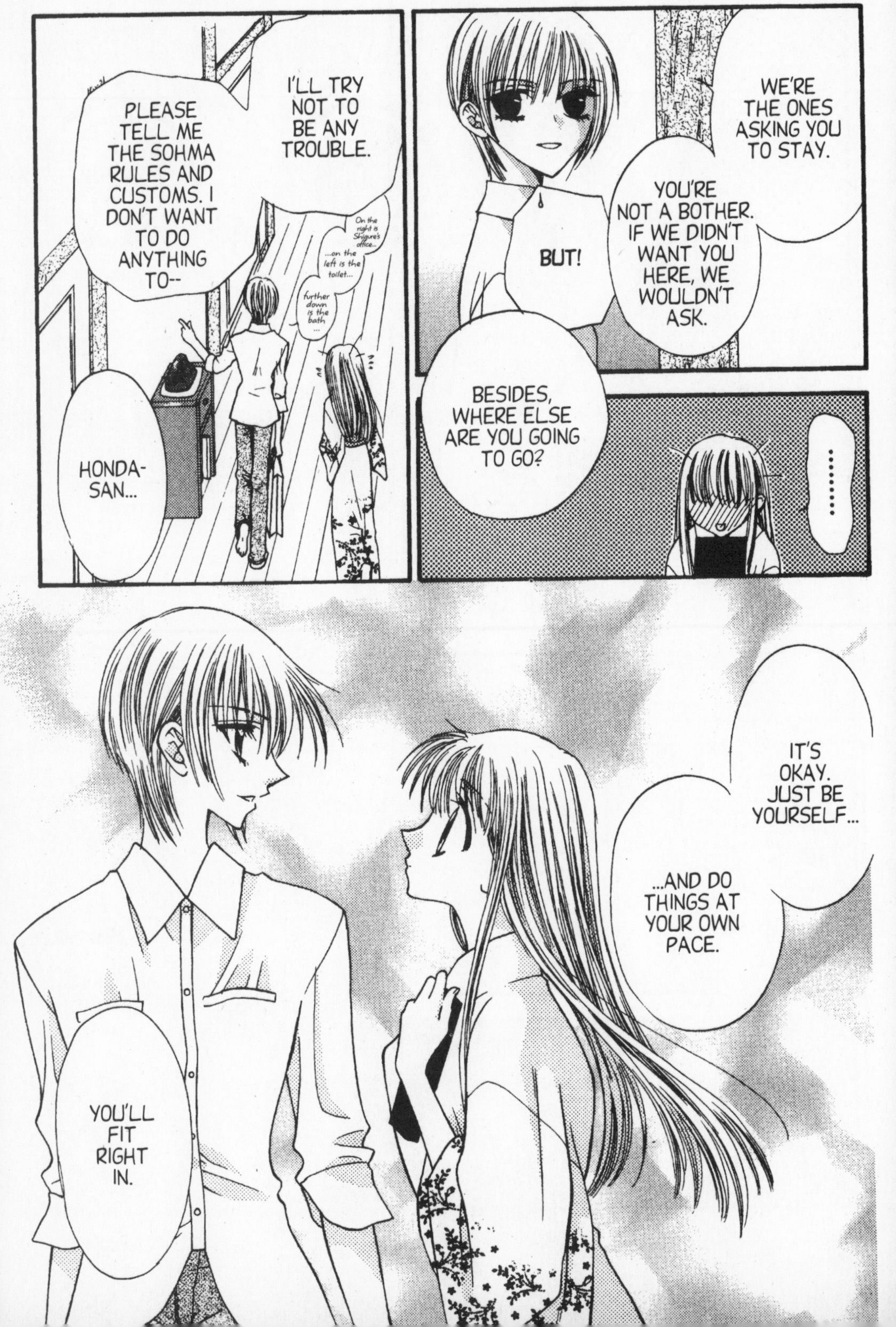
WE'RE THE ONES ASKING YOU TO STAY.
YOU'RE NOT A BOTHER. IF WE DIDN'T WANT YOU HERE, WE WOULDN'T ASK.
BUT!
BESIDES, WHERE ELSE ARE YOU GOING TO GO?
....
I'LL TRY NOT TO BE ANY TROUBLE.
PLEASE TELL ME THE SOHMA RULES AND CUSTOMS. I DON'T WANT TO DO ANYTHING TO--
On the right is Shigure's office...
...on the left is the toilet...
further down is the bath...
HONDA-SAN...
IT'S OKAY. JUST BE YOURSELF...
...AND DO THINGS AT YOUR OWN PACE.
YOU'LL FIT RIGHT IN.

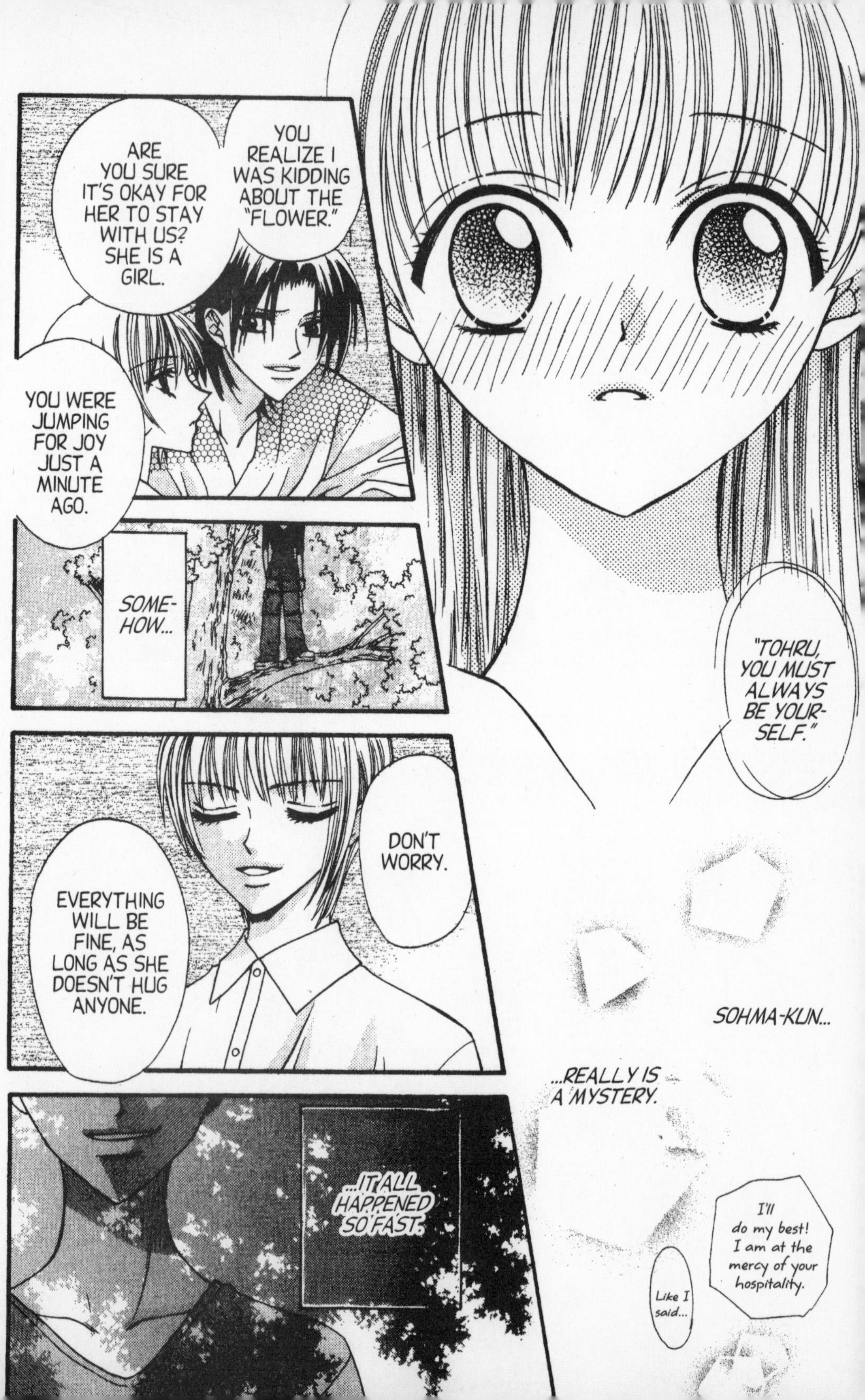
"TOHRU, YOU MUST ALWAYS BE YOURSELF."
SOHMA-KUN...
...REALLY IS A MYSTERY.
I'll do my best! I am at the mercy of your hospitality.
Like I said...
YOU REALIZE I WAS KIDDING ABOUT THE "FLOWER."
ARE YOU SURE IT'S OKAY FOR HER TO STAY WITH US? SHE IS A GIRL.
YOU WERE JUMPING FOR JOY JUST A MINUTE AGO.
SOME-HOW...
DON'T WORRY.
EVERYTHING WILL BE FINE, AS LONG AS SHE DOESN'T HUG ANYONE.
...IT ALL HAPPENED SO FAST.

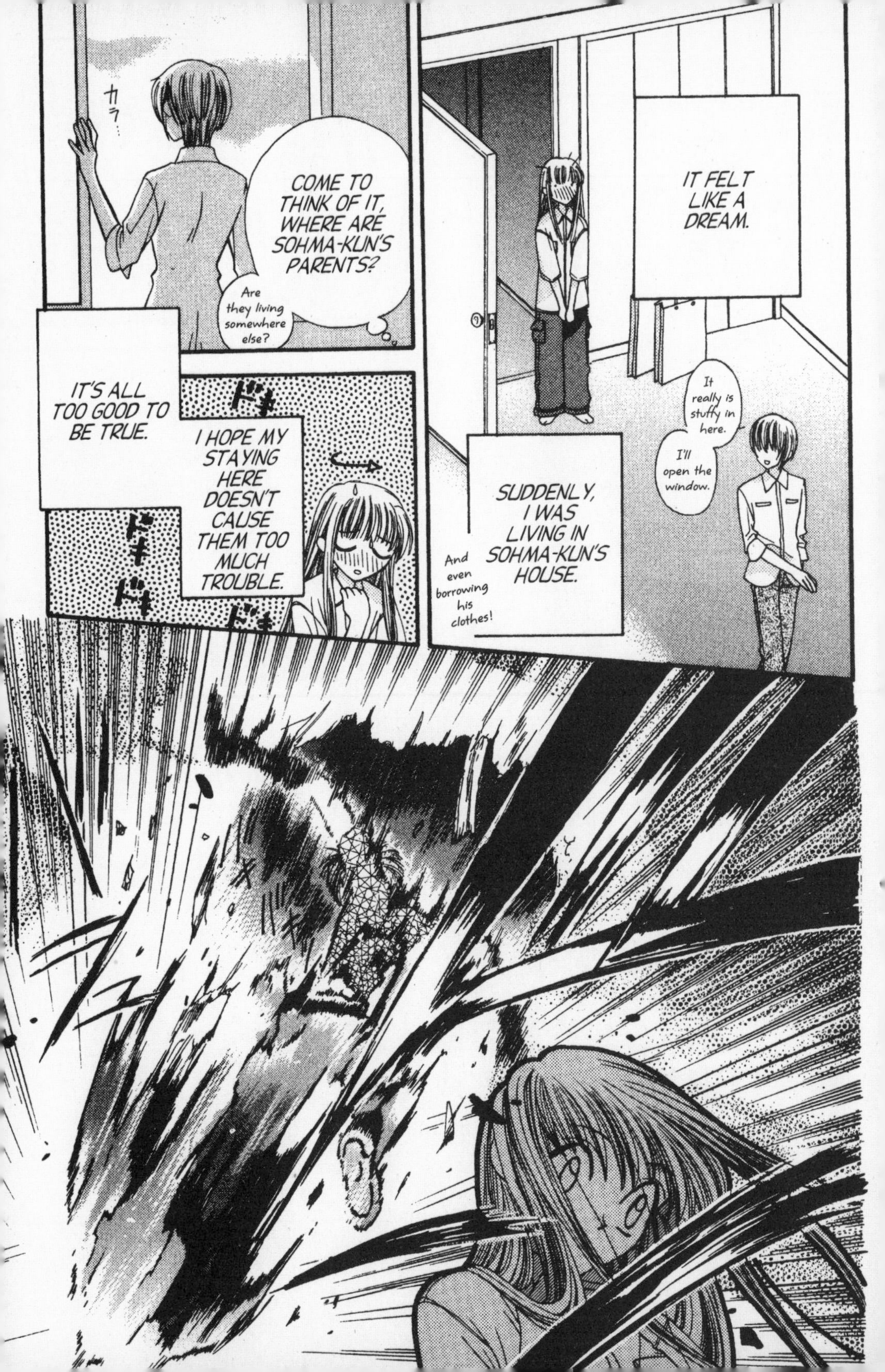
IT FELT LIKE A DREAM.
It really is stuffy in here.
I'll open the window.
SUDDENLY, I WAS LIVING IN SOHMA-KUN'S HOUSE.
And even borrowing his clothes!
カラ…
COME TO THINK OF IT, WHERE ARE SOHMA-KUN'S PARENTS?
Are they living somewhere else?
ドキ
IT'S ALL TOO GOOD TO BE TRUE.
I HOPE MY STAYING HERE DOESN'T CAUSE THEM TOO MUCH TROUBLE.
ドキ ドキ ドキ ドキ

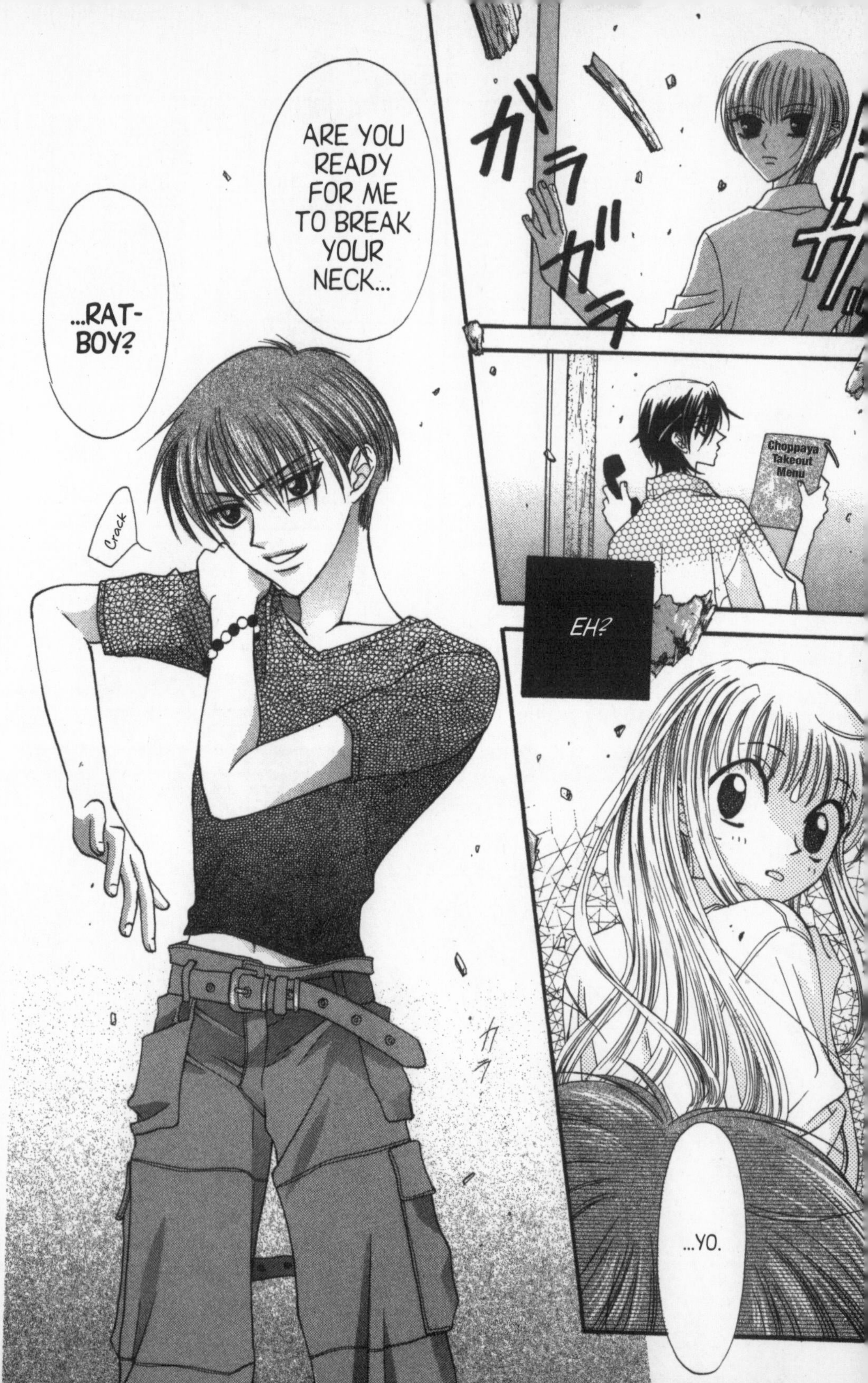
ガラガラ
Choppaya Takeout Menu
EH?
...YO.
ARE YOU READY FOR ME TO BREAK YOUR NECK...
...RAT-BOY?
Crack
カラ

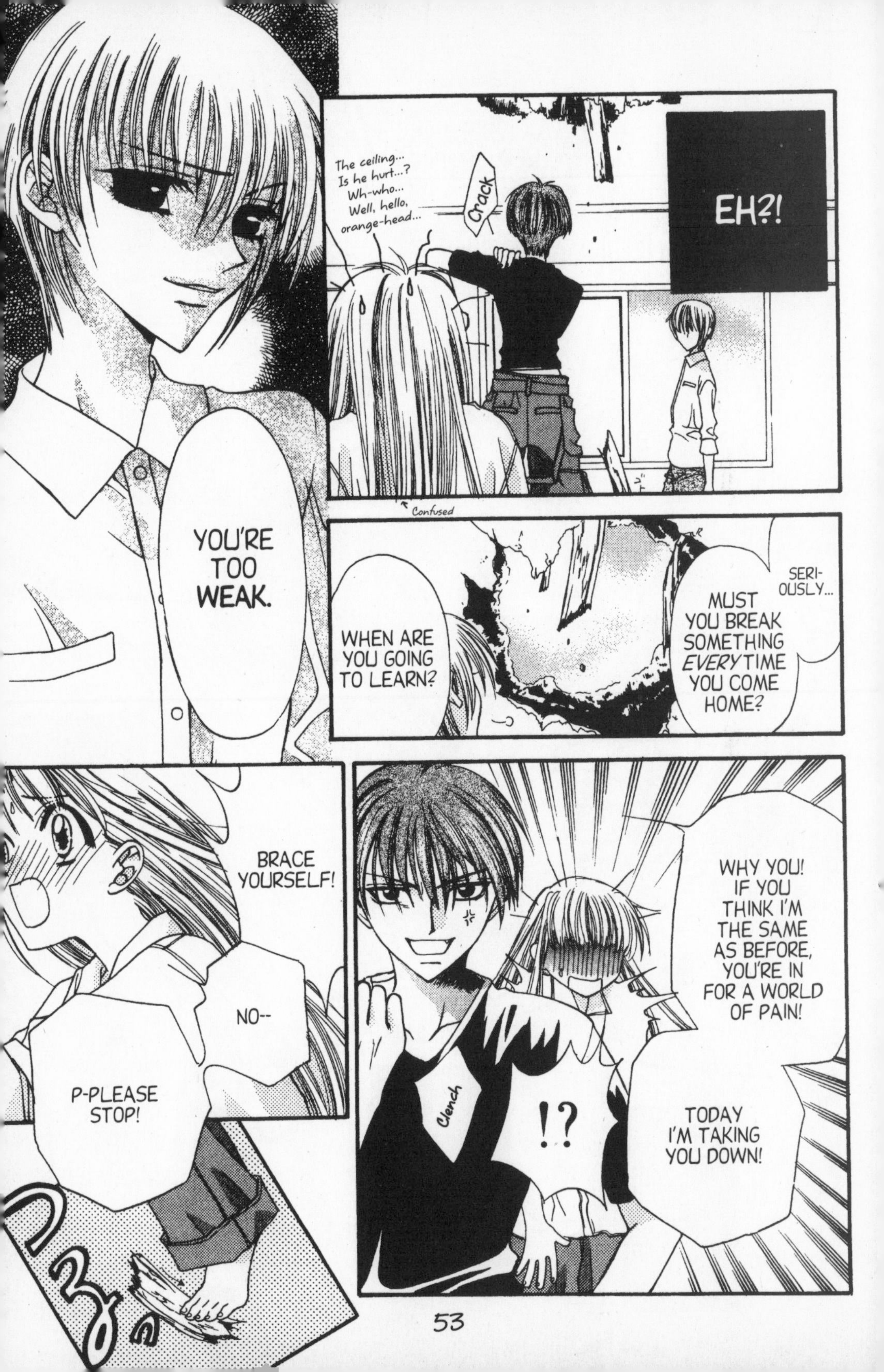
EH?!
The ceiling...
Is he hurt...?
Wh-who...
Well, hello, orange-head...
Crack
Confused
SERIOUSLY...
MUST YOU BREAK SOMETHING *EVERY* TIME YOU COME HOME?
WHEN ARE YOU GOING TO LEARN?
YOU'RE TOO **WEAK.**
WHY YOU! IF YOU THINK I'M THE SAME AS BEFORE, YOU'RE IN FOR A WORLD OF PAIN!
TODAY I'M TAKING YOU DOWN!
!?
Clench
BRACE YOURSELF!
NO--
P-PLEASE STOP!

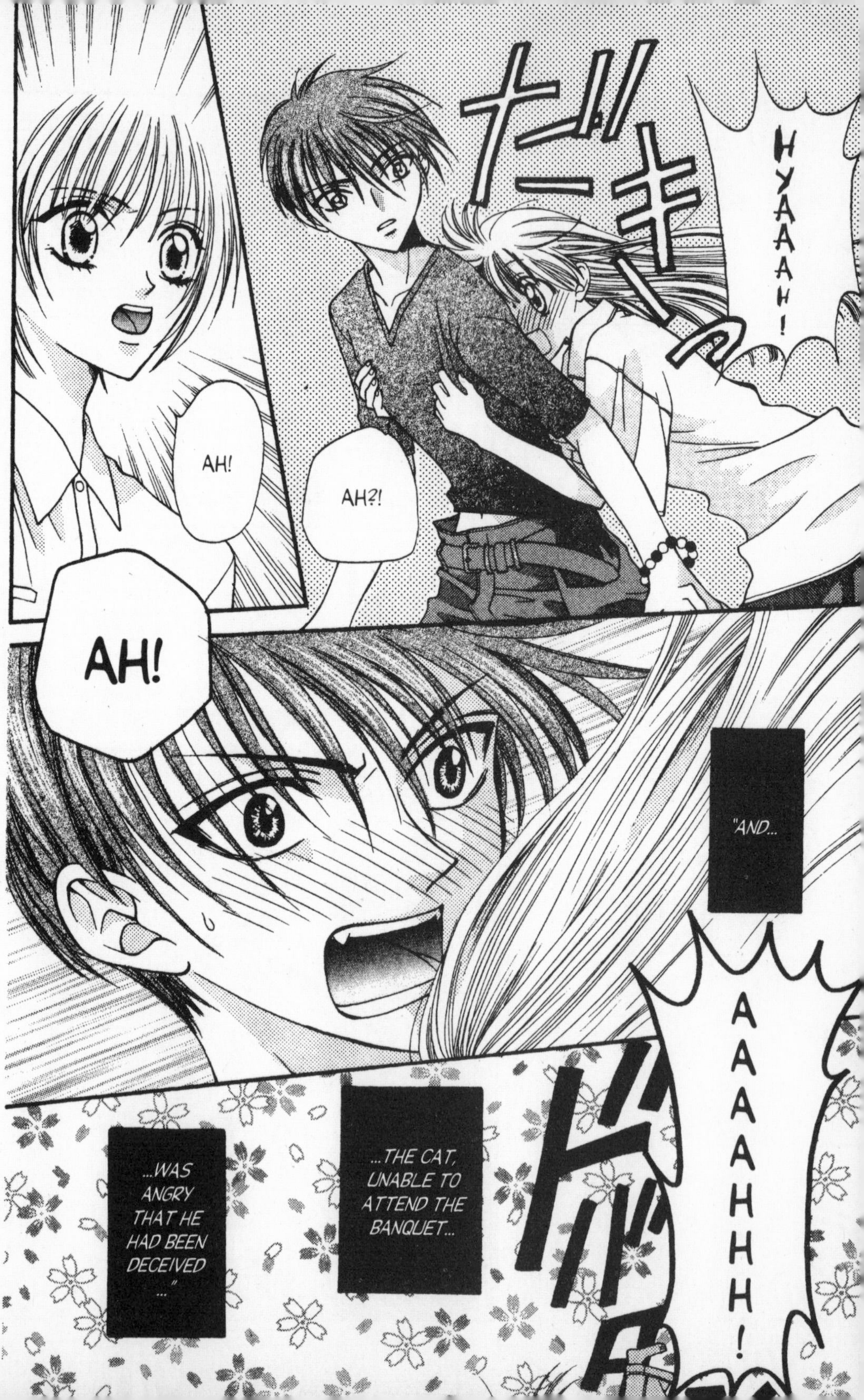
HYAAAAH!
AH?!
AH!
"AND...
AH!
AAAAAHHH!
...THE CAT, UNABLE TO ATTEND THE BANQUET...
...WAS ANGRY THAT HE HAD BEEN DECEIVED..."

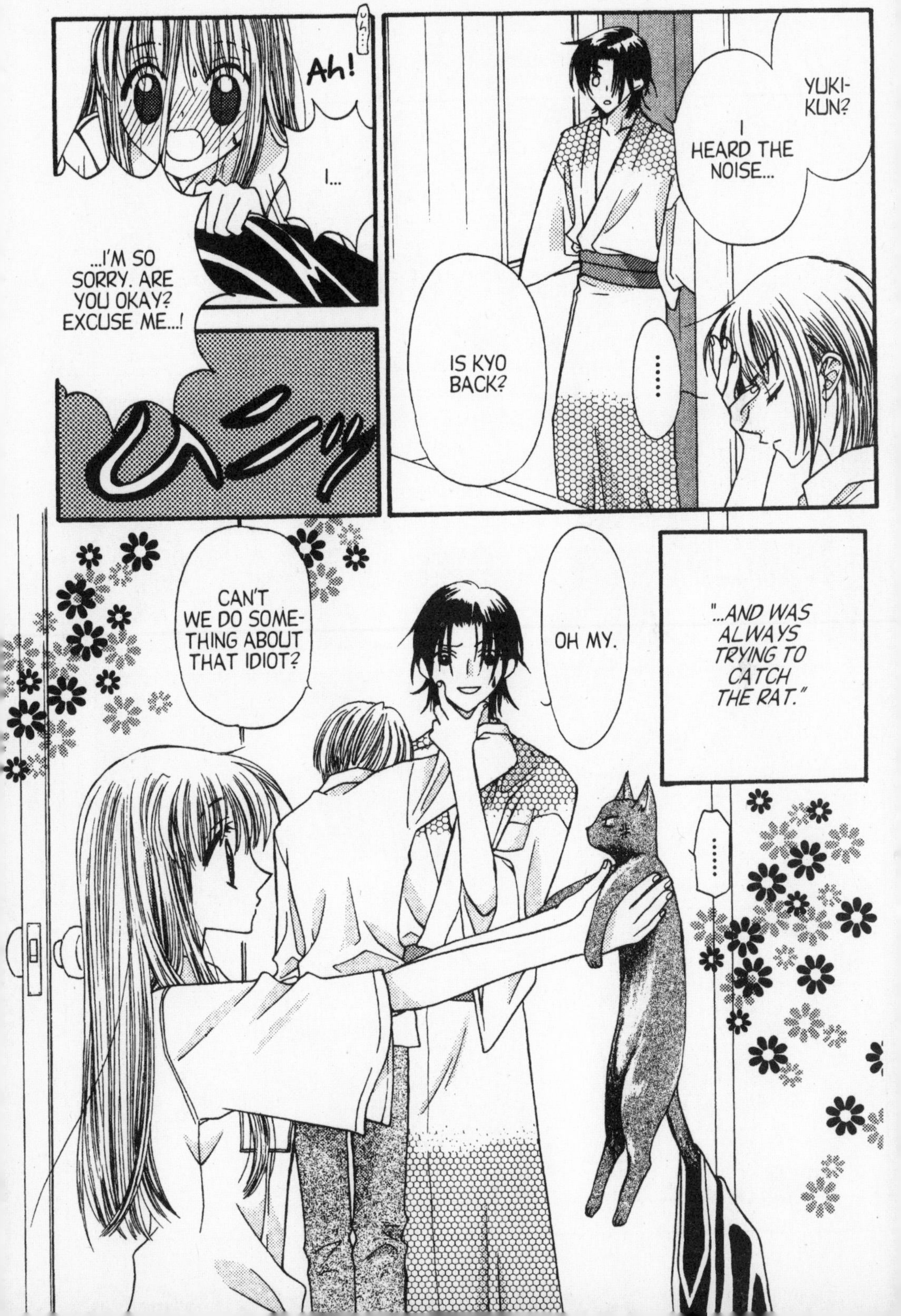
YUKI-KUN?
I HEARD THE NOISE...
......
IS KYO BACK?
Ah!
I...
...I'M SO SORRY. ARE YOU OKAY? EXCUSE ME...!
ひ〜ッ
"...AND WAS ALWAYS TRYING TO CATCH THE RAT."
......
OH MY.
CAN'T WE DO SOMETHING ABOUT THAT IDIOT?

Omake Theater 2: It's part of his charm.

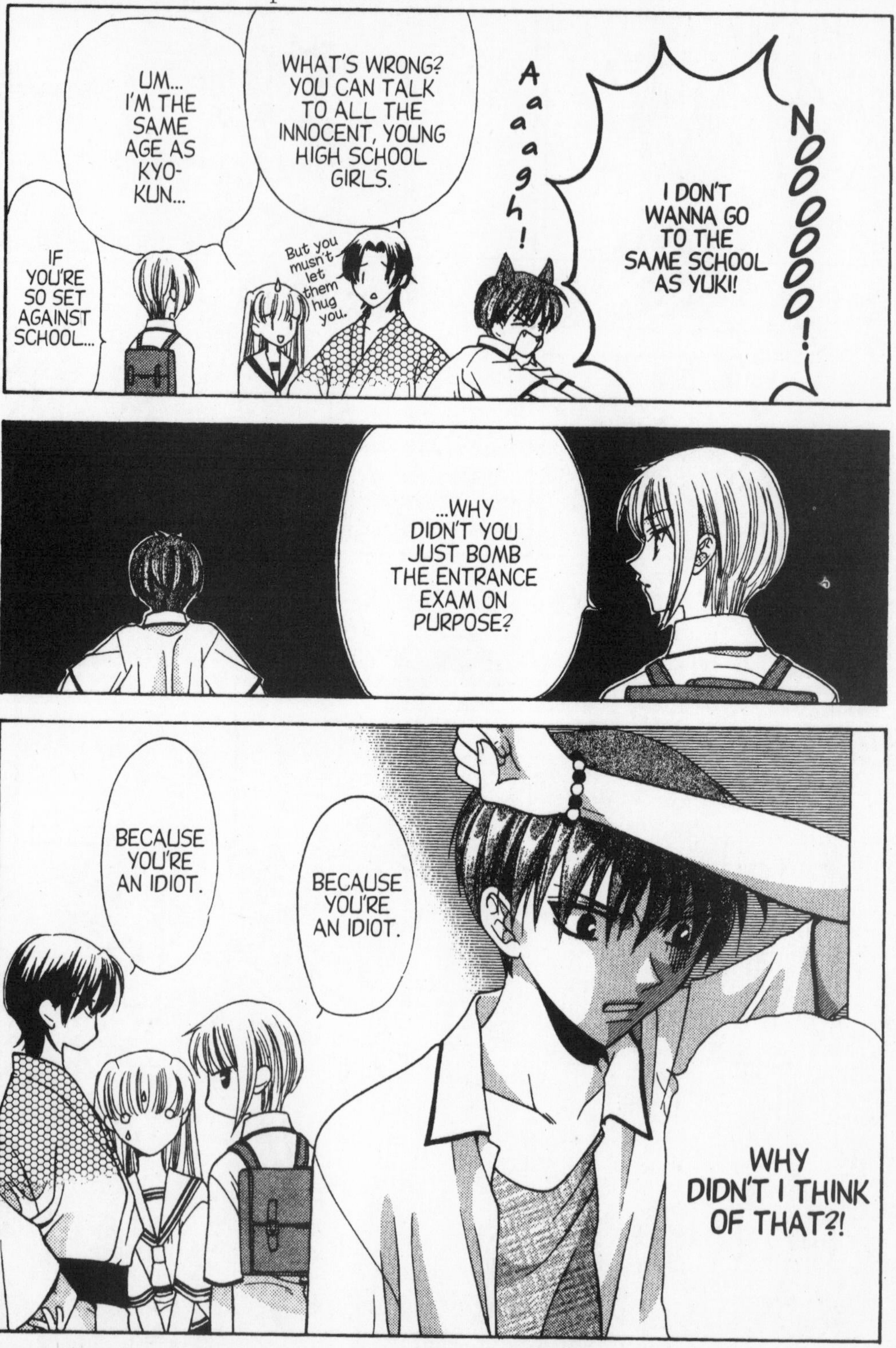
NOOOOOOO!!
I DON'T WANNA GO TO THE SAME SCHOOL AS YUKI!
Aaaaagh!
WHAT'S WRONG? YOU CAN TALK TO ALL THE INNOCENT, YOUNG HIGH SCHOOL GIRLS.
But you musn't let them hug you.
UM... I'M THE SAME AGE AS KYO-KUN...
IF YOU'RE SO SET AGAINST SCHOOL...
...WHY DIDN'T YOU JUST BOMB THE ENTRANCE EXAM ON PURPOSE?
WHY DIDN'T I THINK OF THAT?!
BECAUSE YOU'RE AN IDIOT.
BECAUSE YOU'RE AN IDIOT.

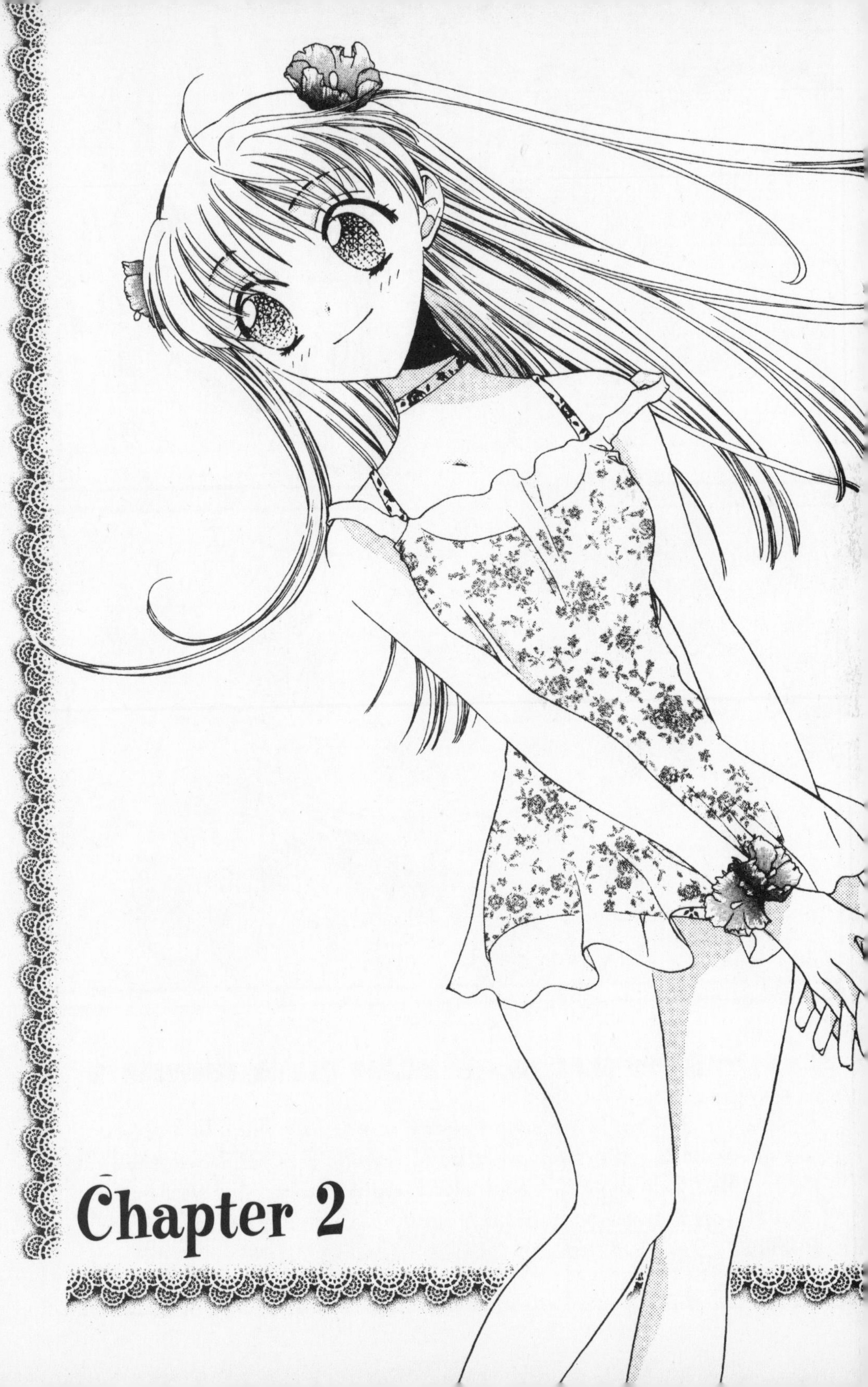

Chapter 2

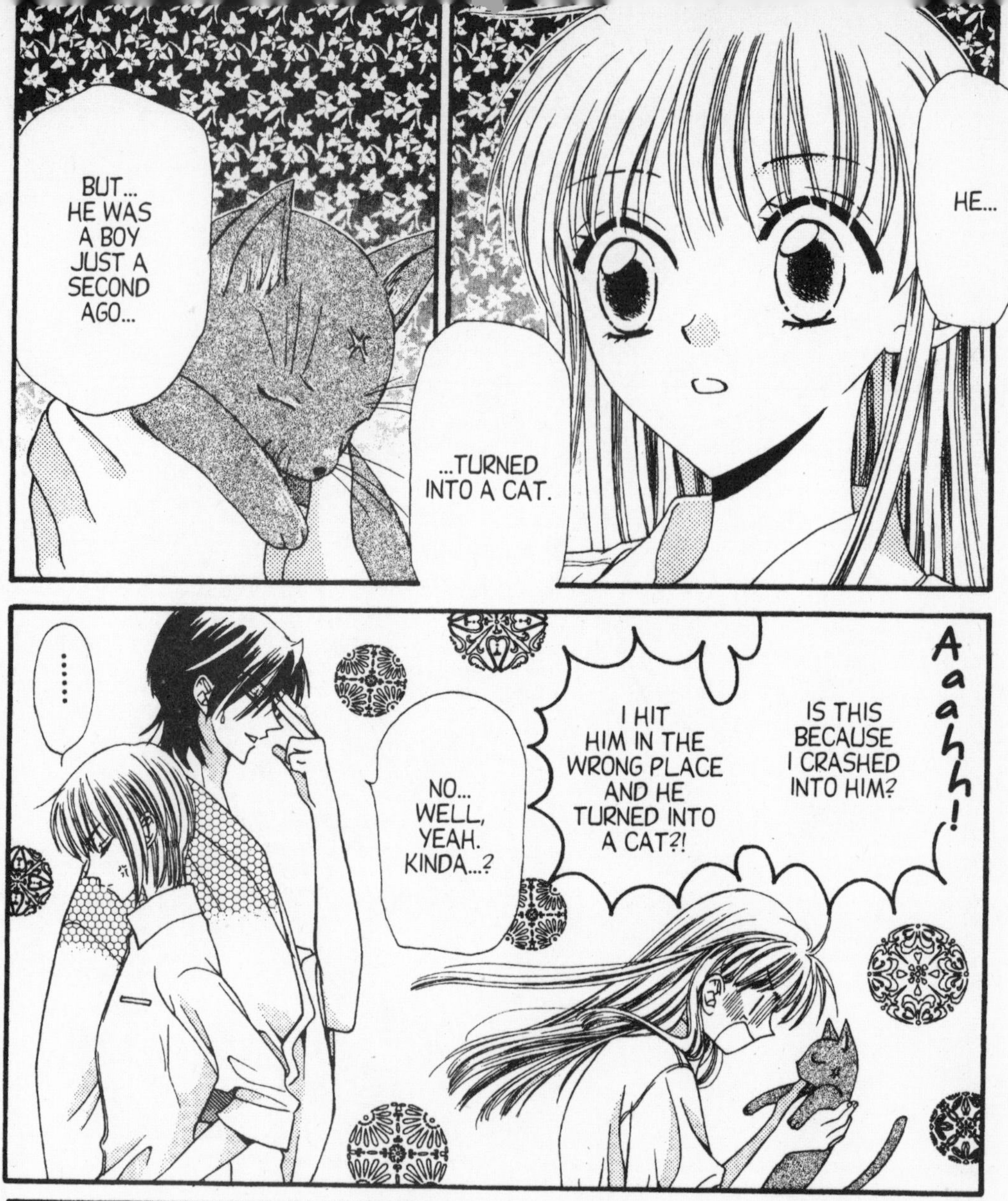
HE...
...TURNED INTO A CAT.
BUT... HE WAS A BOY JUST A SECOND AGO...
Aaahh!
IS THIS BECAUSE I CRASHED INTO HIM?
I HIT HIM IN THE WRONG PLACE AND HE TURNED INTO A CAT?!
NO... WELL, YEAH. KINDA...?
......

ULTRA SPECIAL BLAH BLAH BLAH, NUMBER 1:

I got a letter from some smart aleck reminding me, "Didn't you say you wouldn't use English titles?" Well... I guess I did say that... And, actually, this book did have a Japanese title at first. But things happened (nothing really big) and it became "Fruits Basket." Sometimes that's just how it works.

Number 3:

Now I'm going to talk about games. I once wrote that I wouldn't play Sakura Wars 2... well, I played it. And...
IT WAS AWESOME!
I'm hooked. Seriously, it's really good. And I ended up playing the first one, too (because I was so obsessed). It's weird that I'm more into SW2 than some of the games **I** worked on!

(Of course, **I** do all the best endings.)

It's also weird that K-chan (who has been a Sakura Wars fan from the beginning of time and is in love with Ren and Ohgami-san) and I are now having success with those two characters' storylines.

K-chan: thank you always for everything!

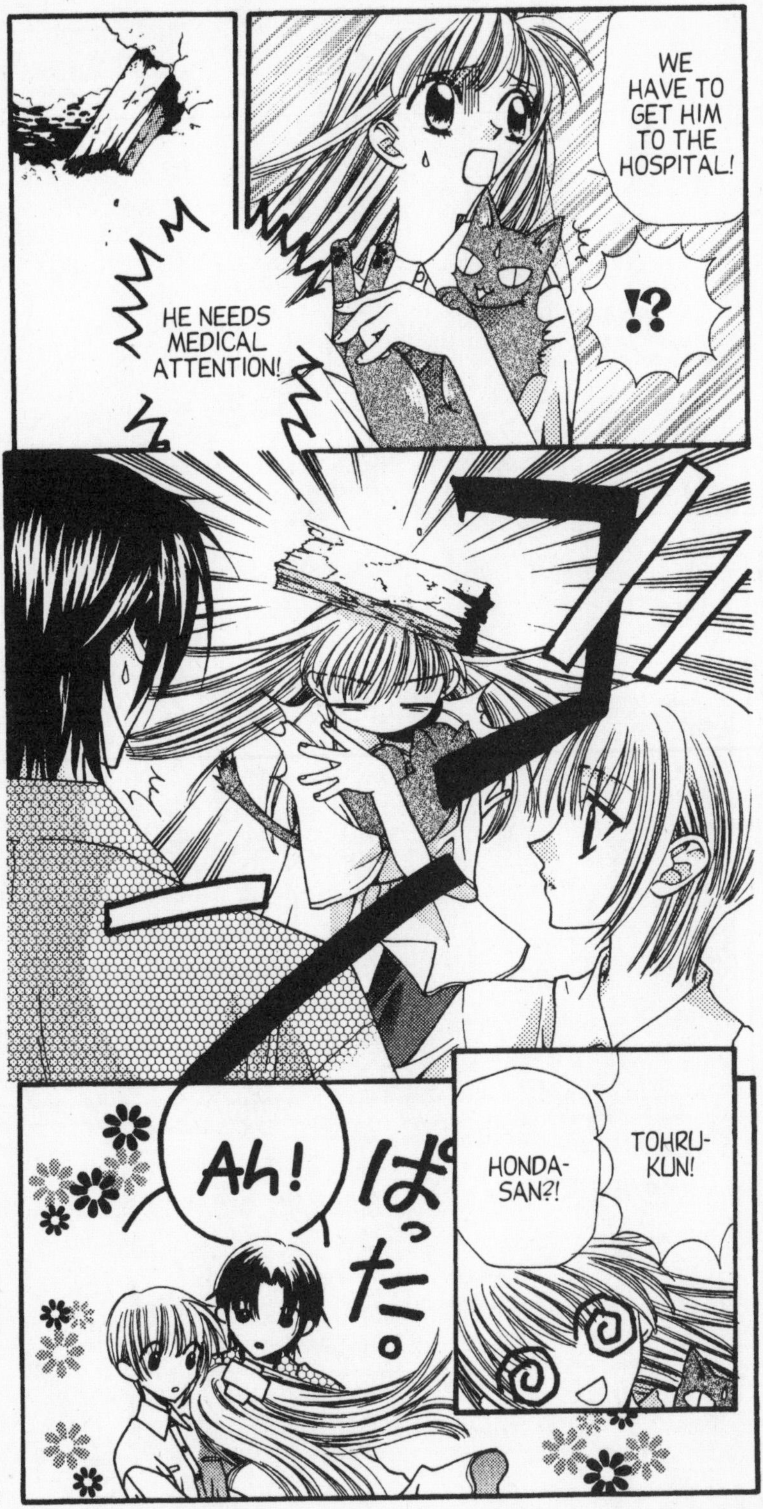
WE HAVE TO GET HIM TO THE HOSPITAL!
!?
HE NEEDS MEDICAL ATTENTION!
TOHRU-KUN!
HONDA-SAN?!
Ah!
ぱった。

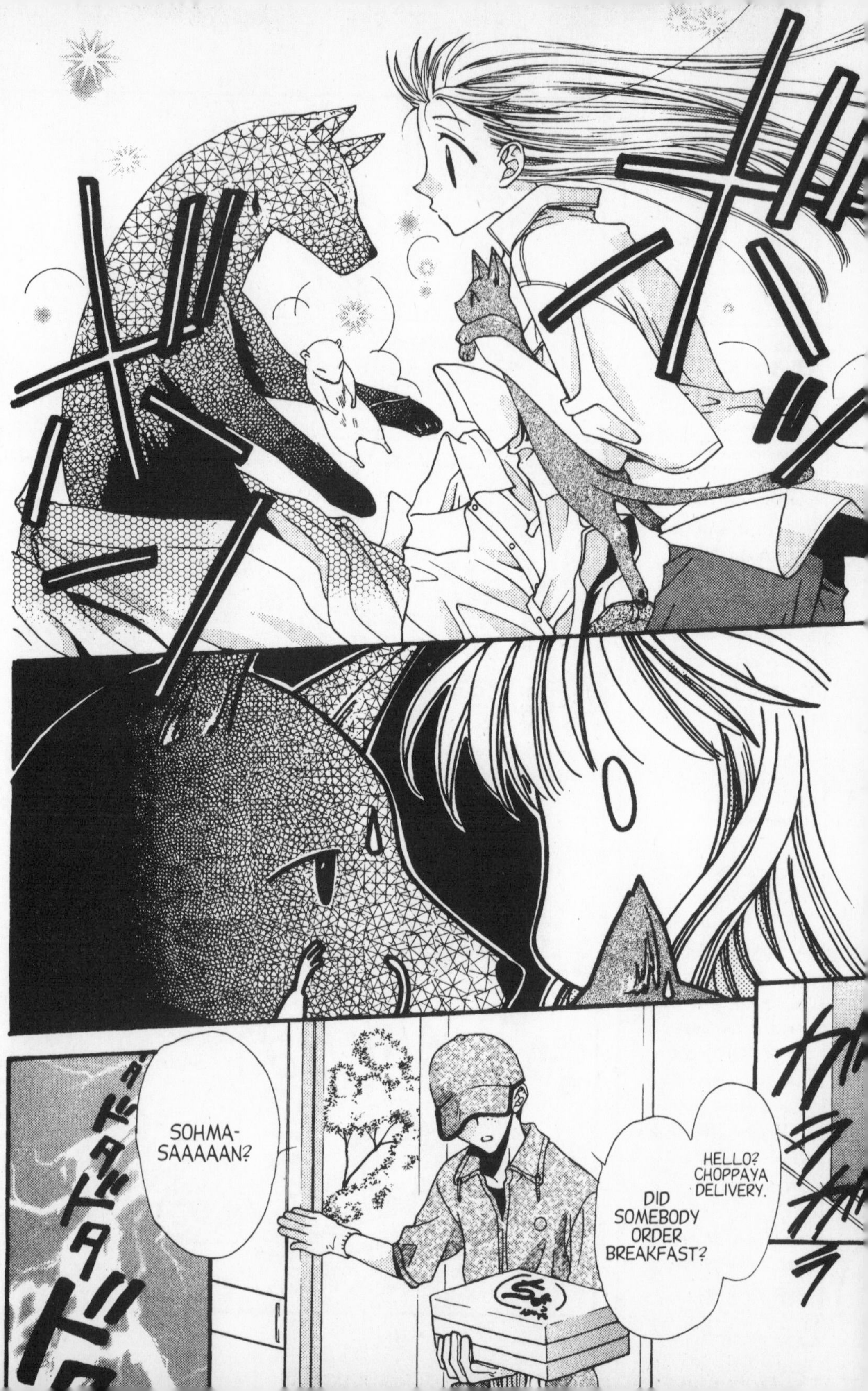
HELLO? CHOPPAYA DELIVERY.
DID SOMEBODY ORDER BREAKFAST?
SOHMA-SAAAAAN?

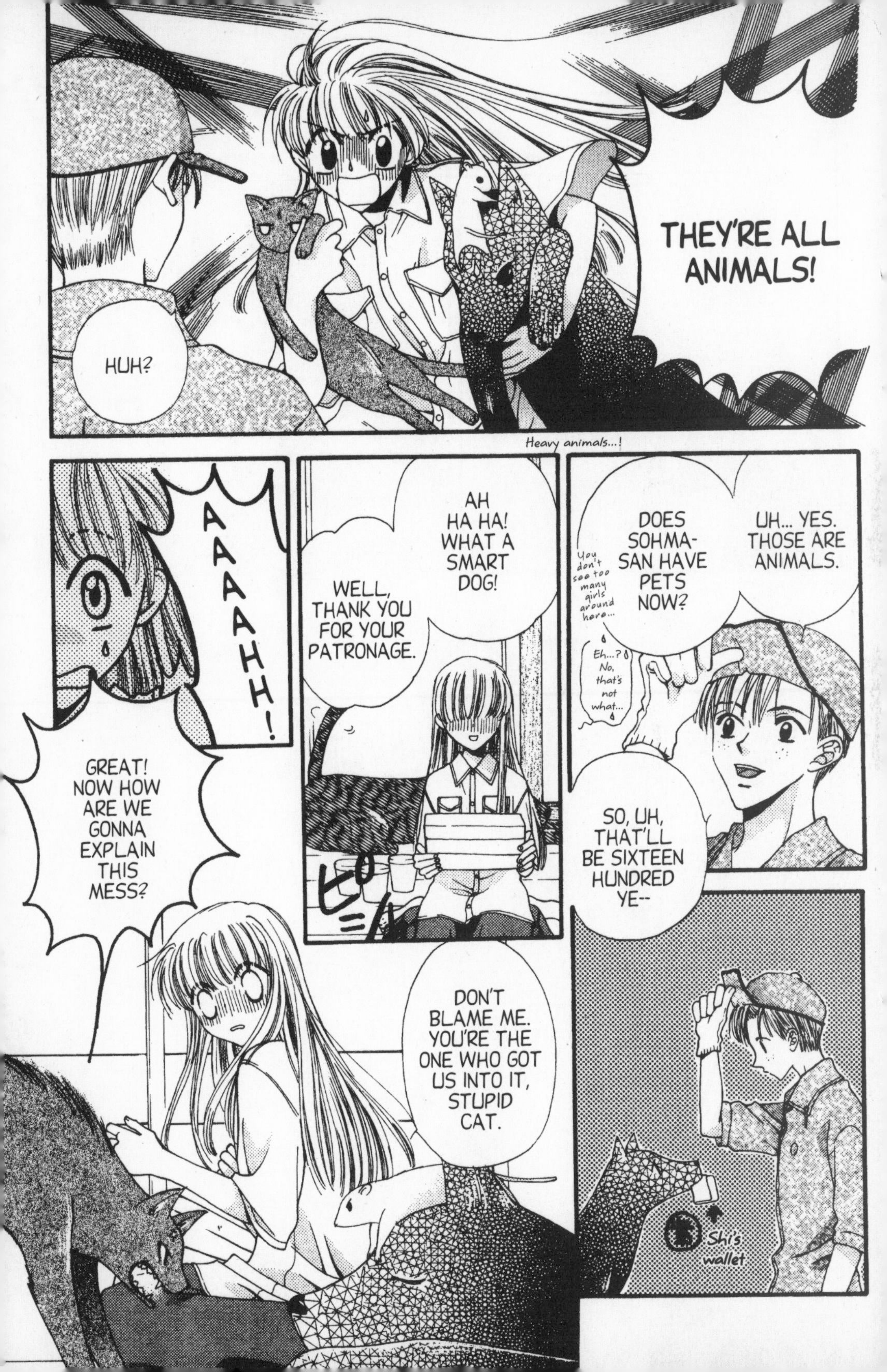
THEY'RE ALL ANIMALS!
HUH?
Heavy animals...!
DOES SOHMA-SAN HAVE PETS NOW?
UH... YES. THOSE ARE ANIMALS.
You don't see too many girls around here...
Eh...? No, that's not what...
SO, UH, THAT'LL BE SIXTEEN HUNDRED YE--
AH HA HA! WHAT A SMART DOG!
WELL, THANK YOU FOR YOUR PATRONAGE.
AAAAAHH!
Shi's wallet
GREAT! NOW HOW ARE WE GONNA EXPLAIN THIS MESS?
DON'T BLAME ME. YOU'RE THE ONE WHO GOT US INTO IT, STUPID CAT.

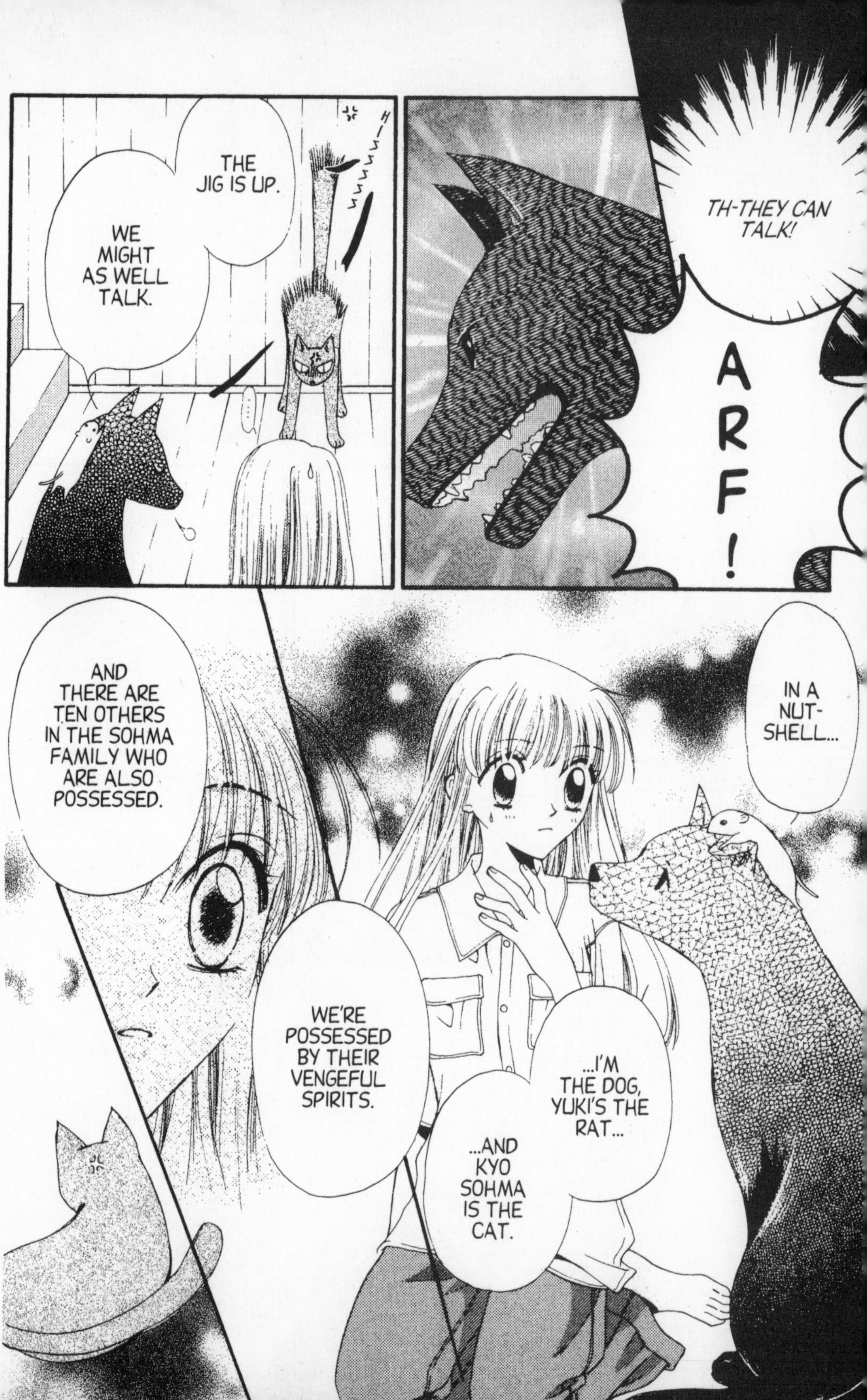
TH-THEY CAN TALK!
ARF!
THE JIG IS UP.
WE MIGHT AS WELL TALK.
IN A NUT-SHELL...
...I'M THE DOG, YUKI'S THE RAT...
...AND KYO SOHMA IS THE CAT.
WE'RE POSSESSED BY THEIR VENGEFUL SPIRITS.
AND THERE ARE TEN OTHERS IN THE SOHMA FAMILY WHO ARE ALSO POSSESSED.

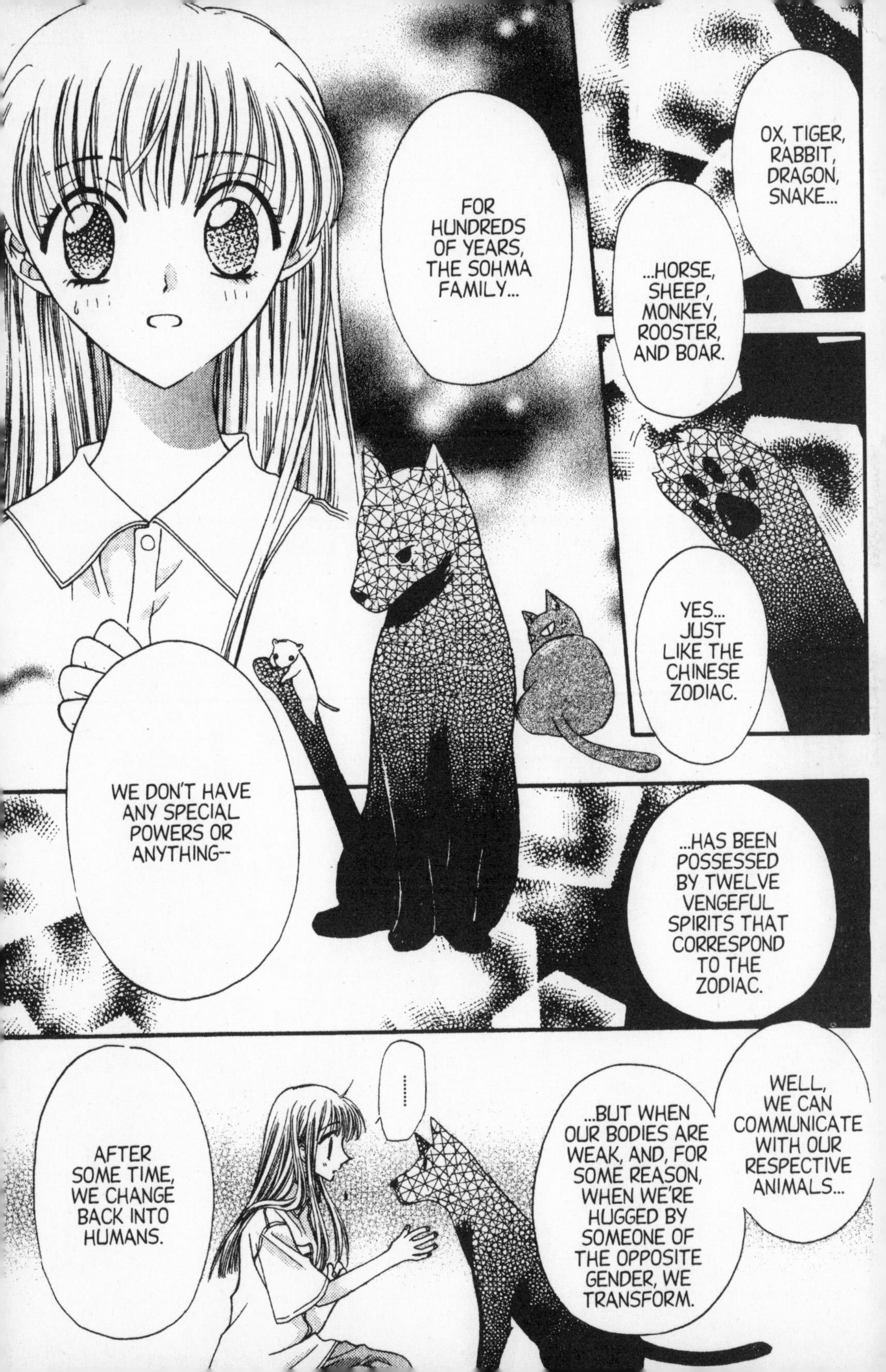
FOR HUNDREDS OF YEARS, THE SOHMA FAMILY...
...HAS BEEN POSSESSED BY TWELVE VENGEFUL SPIRITS THAT CORRESPOND TO THE ZODIAC.
OX, TIGER, RABBIT, DRAGON, SNAKE...
...HORSE, SHEEP, MONKEY, ROOSTER, AND BOAR.
YES... JUST LIKE THE CHINESE ZODIAC.
WE DON'T HAVE ANY SPECIAL POWERS OR ANYTHING--
WELL, WE CAN COMMUNICATE WITH OUR RESPECTIVE ANIMALS...
...BUT WHEN OUR BODIES ARE WEAK, AND, FOR SOME REASON, WHEN WE'RE HUGGED BY SOMEONE OF THE OPPOSITE GENDER, WE TRANSFORM.
......
AFTER SOME TIME, WE CHANGE BACK INTO HUMANS.

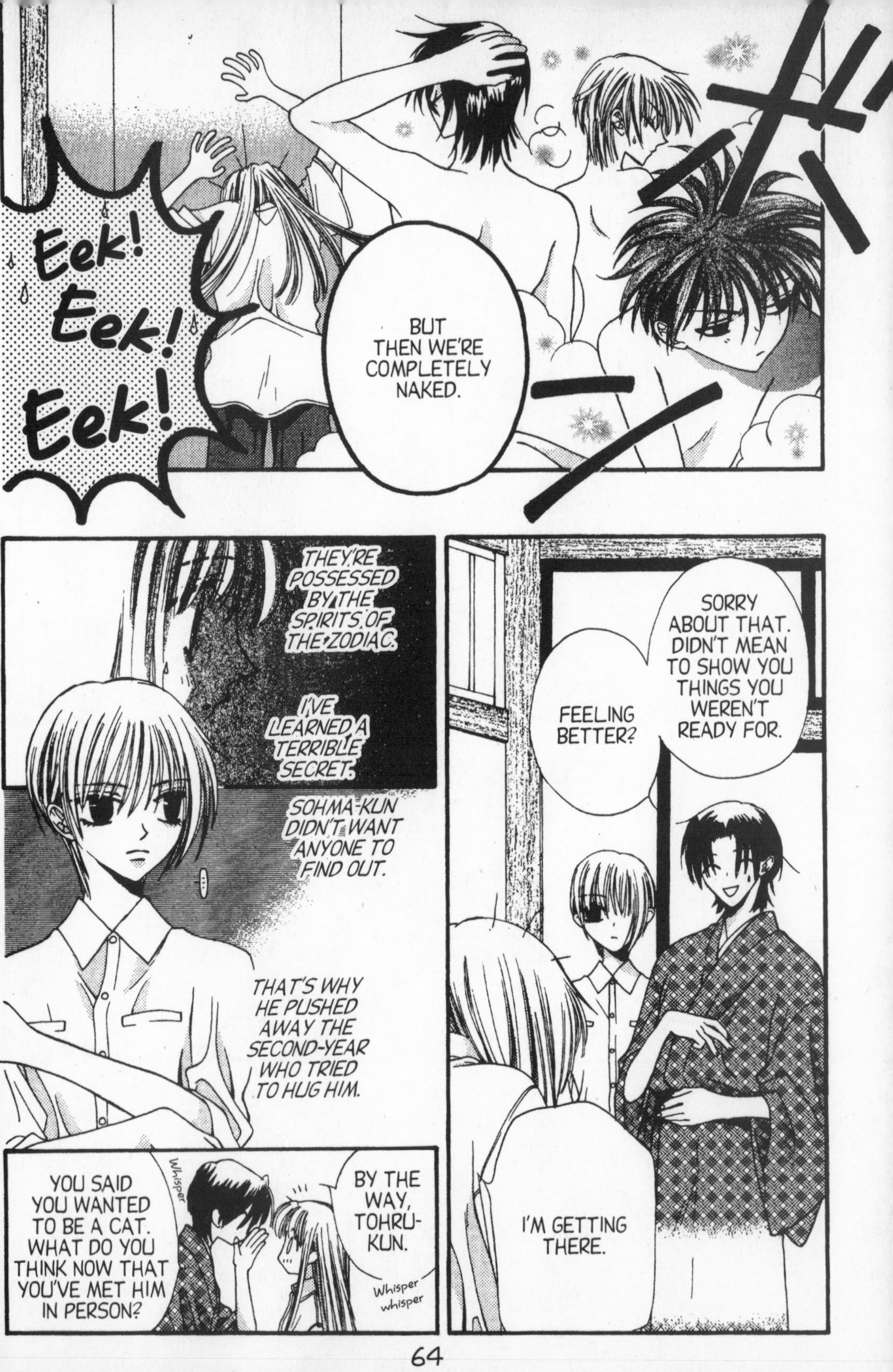
BUT THEN WE'RE COMPLETELY NAKED.
Eek! Eek! Eek!
SORRY ABOUT THAT. DIDN'T MEAN TO SHOW YOU THINGS YOU WEREN'T READY FOR.
FEELING BETTER?
I'M GETTING THERE.
THEY'RE POSSESSED BY THE SPIRITS OF THE ZODIAC.
I'VE LEARNED A TERRIBLE SECRET.
SOHMA-KUN DIDN'T WANT ANYONE TO FIND OUT.
THAT'S WHY HE PUSHED AWAY THE SECOND-YEAR WHO TRIED TO HUG HIM.
BY THE WAY, TOHRU-KUN.
Whisper
YOU SAID YOU WANTED TO BE A CAT. WHAT DO YOU THINK NOW THAT YOU'VE MET HIM IN PERSON?
Whisper whisper

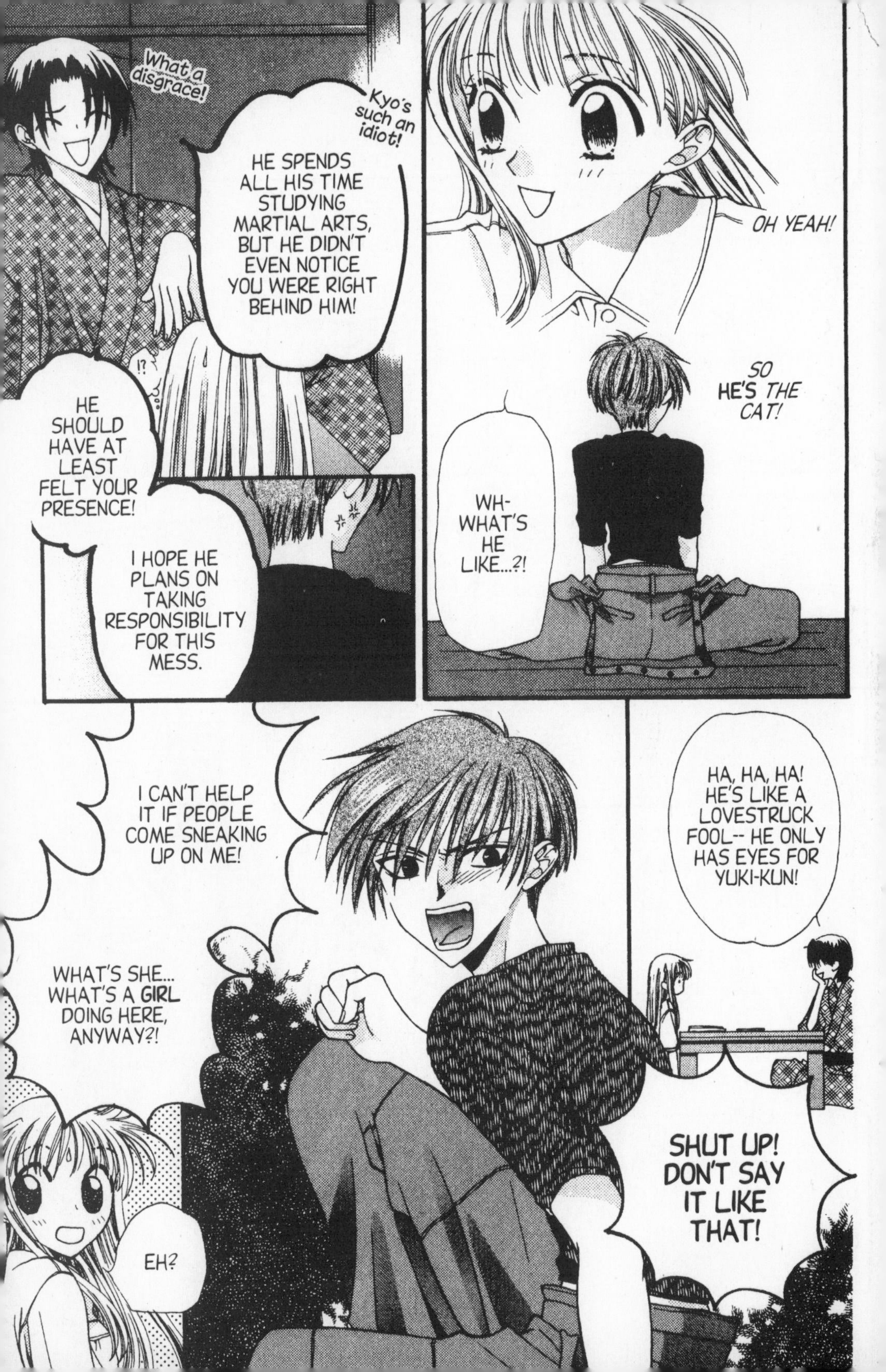
OH YEAH!
SO HE'S THE CAT!
WH-WHAT'S HE LIKE...?!
Kyo's such an idiot!
What a disgrace!
HE SPENDS ALL HIS TIME STUDYING MARTIAL ARTS, BUT HE DIDN'T EVEN NOTICE YOU WERE RIGHT BEHIND HIM!
!?
HE SHOULD HAVE AT LEAST FELT YOUR PRESENCE!
I HOPE HE PLANS ON TAKING RESPONSIBILITY FOR THIS MESS.
HA, HA, HA! HE'S LIKE A LOVESTRUCK FOOL-- HE ONLY HAS EYES FOR YUKI-KUN!
SHUT UP! DON'T SAY IT LIKE THAT!
I CAN'T HELP IT IF PEOPLE COME SNEAKING UP ON ME!
WHAT'S SHE... WHAT'S A GIRL DOING HERE, ANYWAY?!
EH?

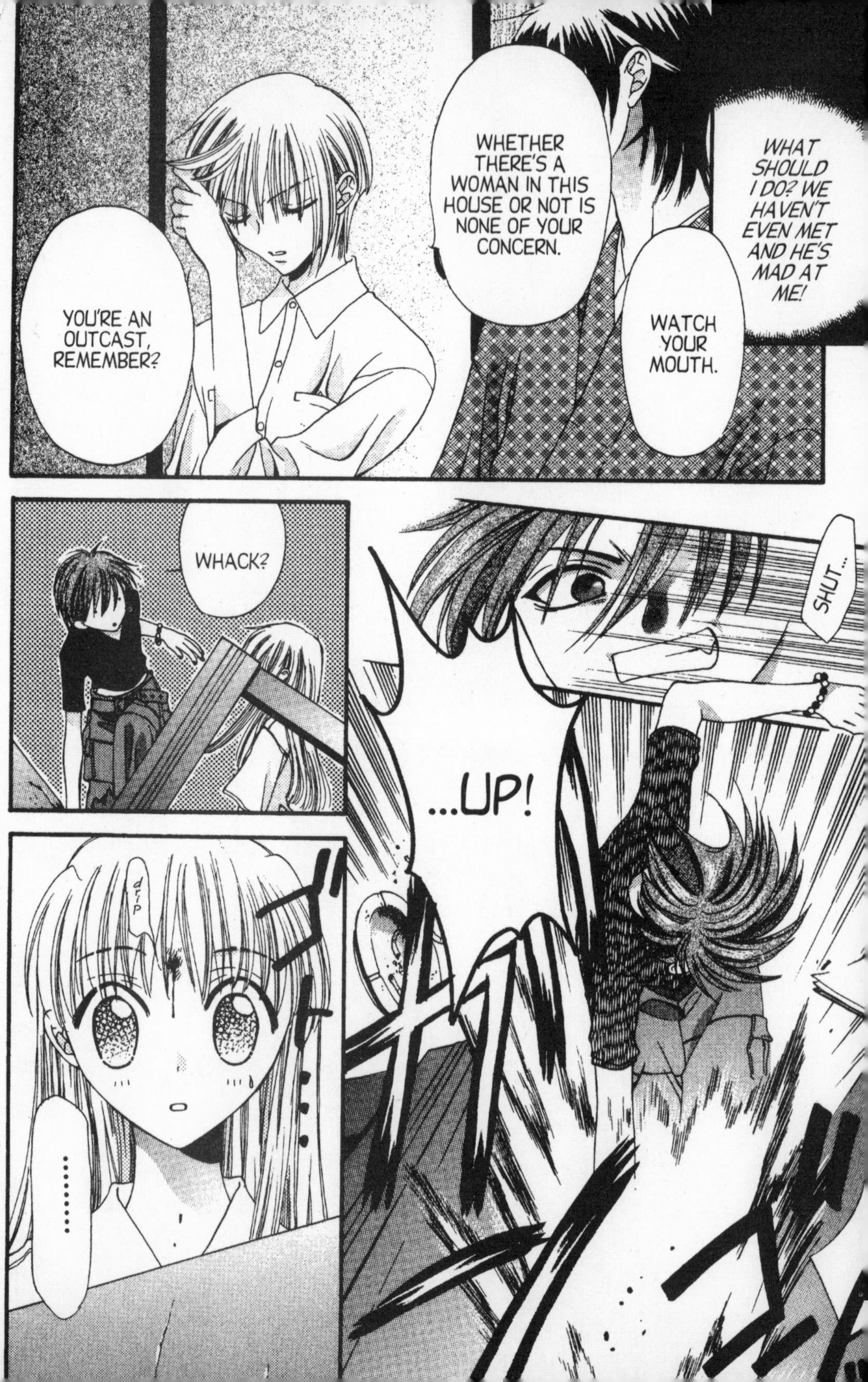
WHAT SHOULD I DO? WE HAVEN'T EVEN MET AND HE'S MAD AT ME!
WHETHER THERE'S A WOMAN IN THIS HOUSE OR NOT IS NONE OF YOUR CONCERN.
WATCH YOUR MOUTH.
YOU'RE AN OUTCAST, REMEMBER?
SHUT...
...UP!
WHACK?
drip
......

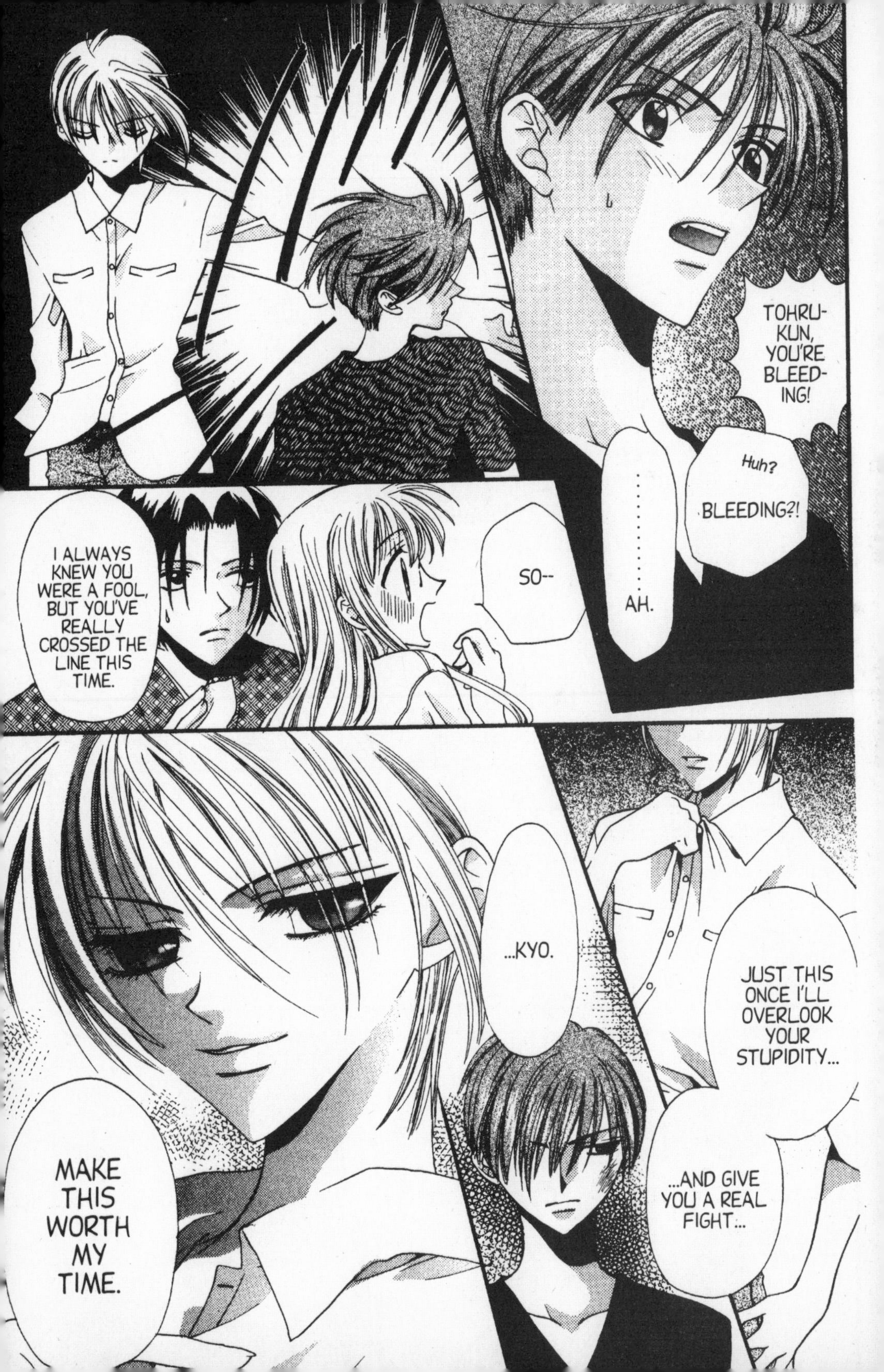
TOHRU-KUN, YOU'RE BLEEDING!
Huh? BLEEDING?!
......AH.
SO--
I ALWAYS KNEW YOU WERE A FOOL, BUT YOU'VE REALLY CROSSED THE LINE THIS TIME.
...KYO.
JUST THIS ONCE I'LL OVERLOOK YOUR STUPIDITY...
...AND GIVE YOU A REAL FIGHT...
MAKE THIS WORTH MY TIME.

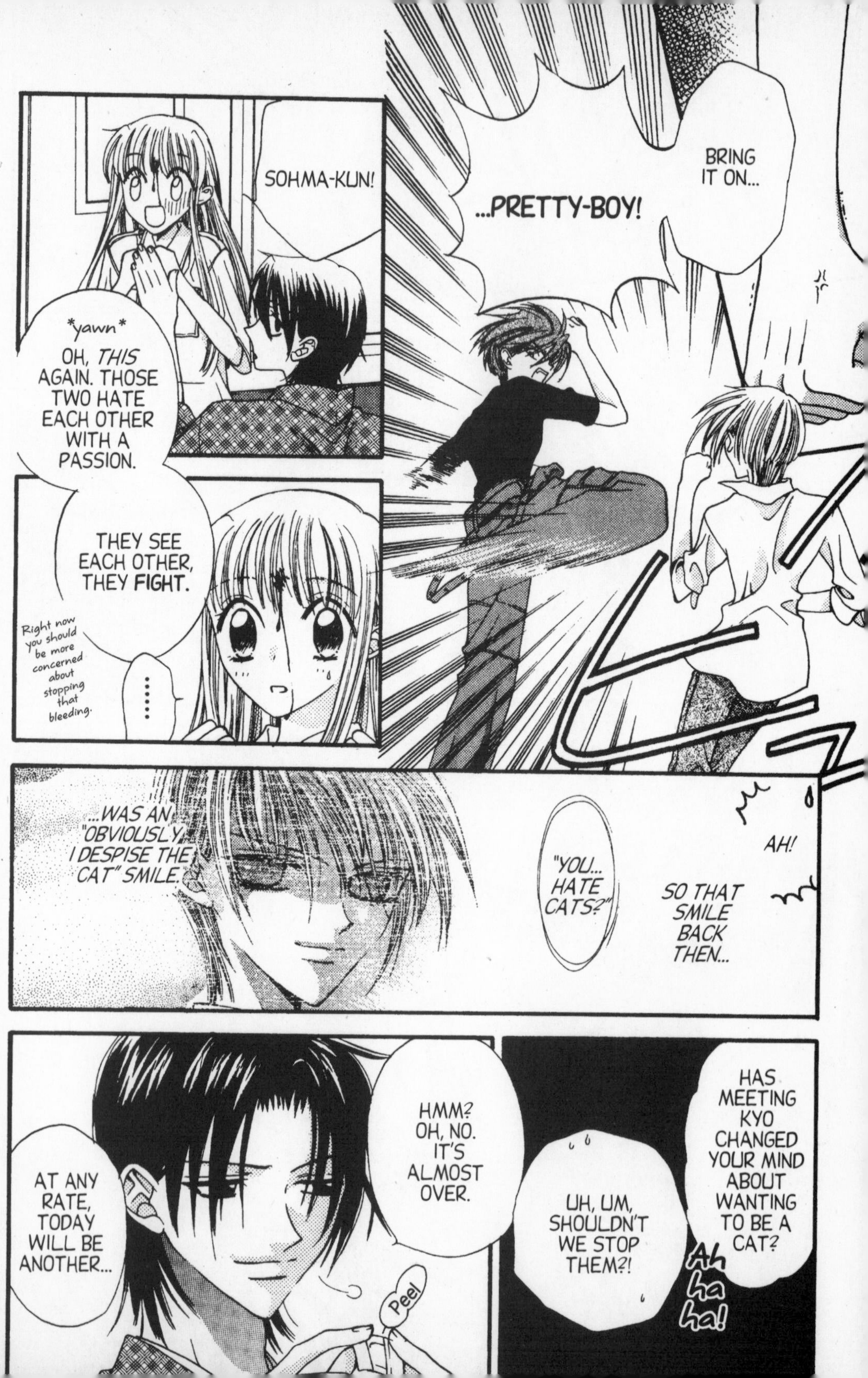
BRING IT ON...
...PRETTY-BOY!
SOHMA-KUN!
yawn OH, *THIS* AGAIN. THOSE TWO HATE EACH OTHER WITH A PASSION.
THEY SEE EACH OTHER, THEY **FIGHT**.
Right now you should be more concerned about stopping that bleeding.
......
AH!
SO THAT SMILE BACK THEN...
"YOU... HATE CATS?"
...WAS AN "OBVIOUSLY I DESPISE THE CAT" SMILE.
HAS MEETING KYO CHANGED YOUR MIND ABOUT WANTING TO BE A CAT?
Ah ha ha!
UH, UM, SHOULDN'T WE STOP THEM?!
HMM? OH, NO. IT'S ALMOST OVER.
Peel
AT ANY RATE, TODAY WILL BE ANOTHER...

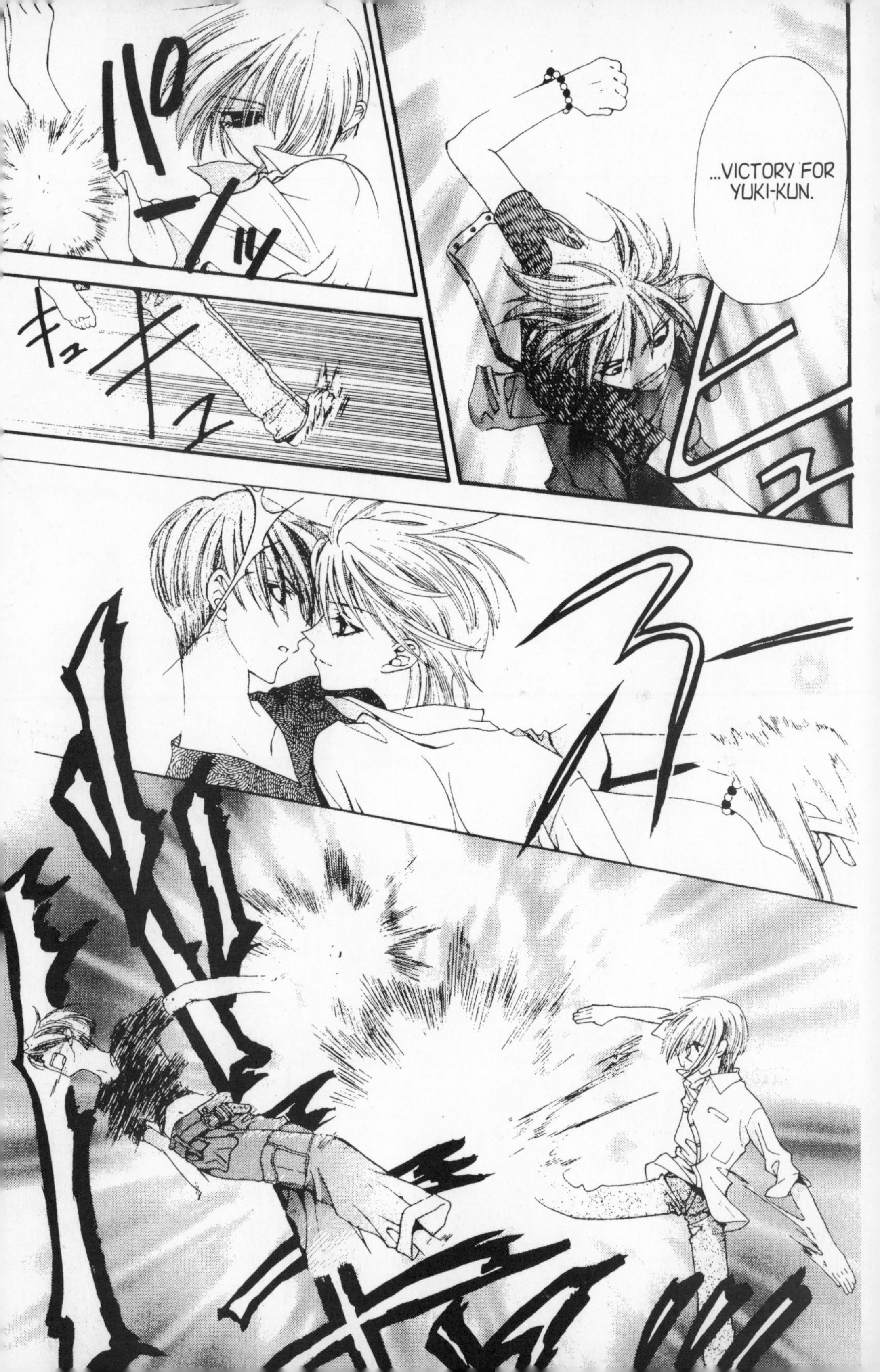
...VICTORY FOR YUKI-KUN.

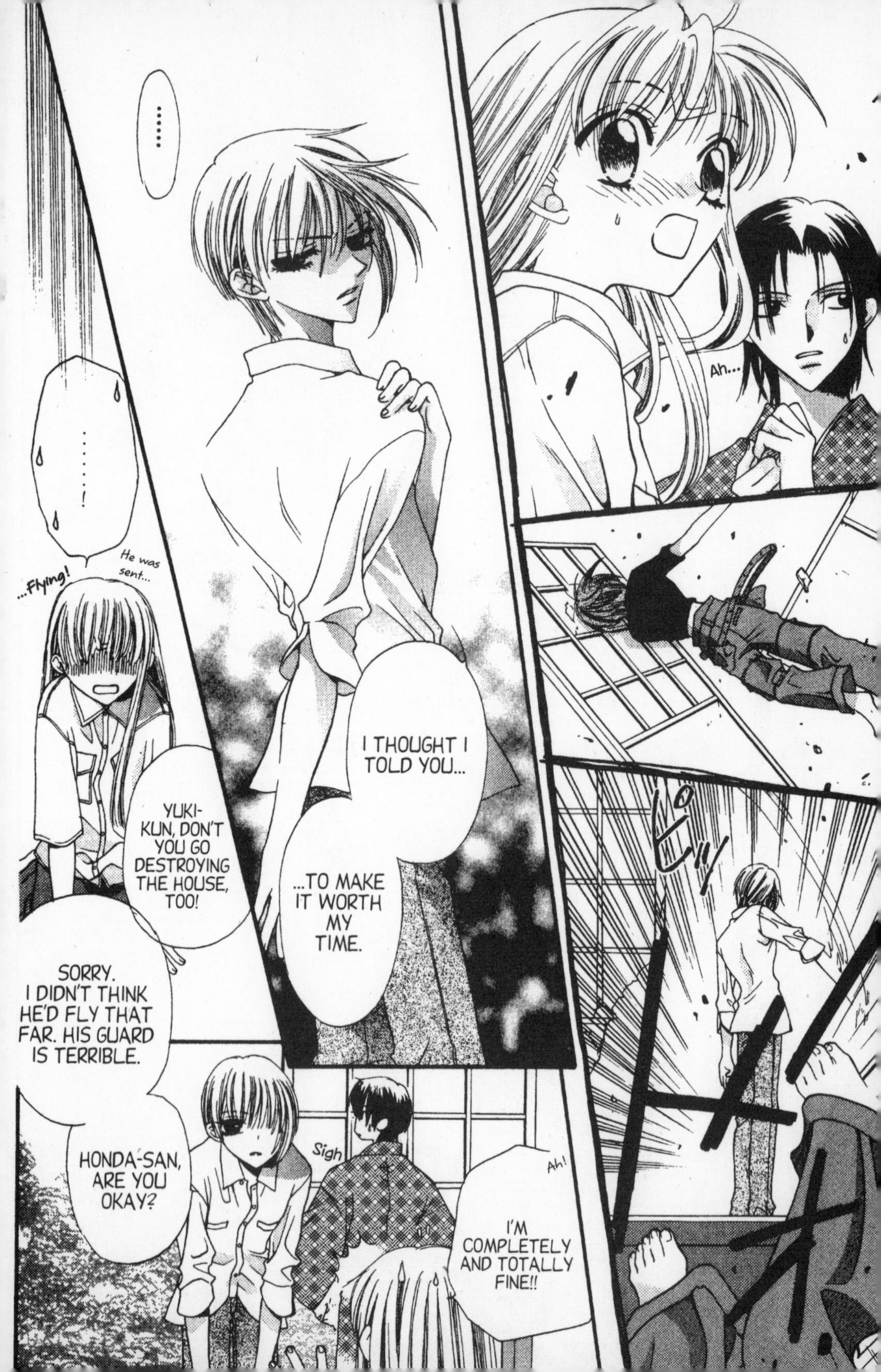
Ah...
I THOUGHT I TOLD YOU...
...TO MAKE IT WORTH MY TIME.
......
......!
He was sent...
...Flying!
YUKI-KUN, DON'T YOU GO DESTROYING THE HOUSE, TOO!
SORRY. I DIDN'T THINK HE'D FLY THAT FAR. HIS GUARD IS TERRIBLE.
Sigh
HONDA-SAN, ARE YOU OKAY?
Ah!
I'M COMPLETELY AND TOTALLY FINE!!

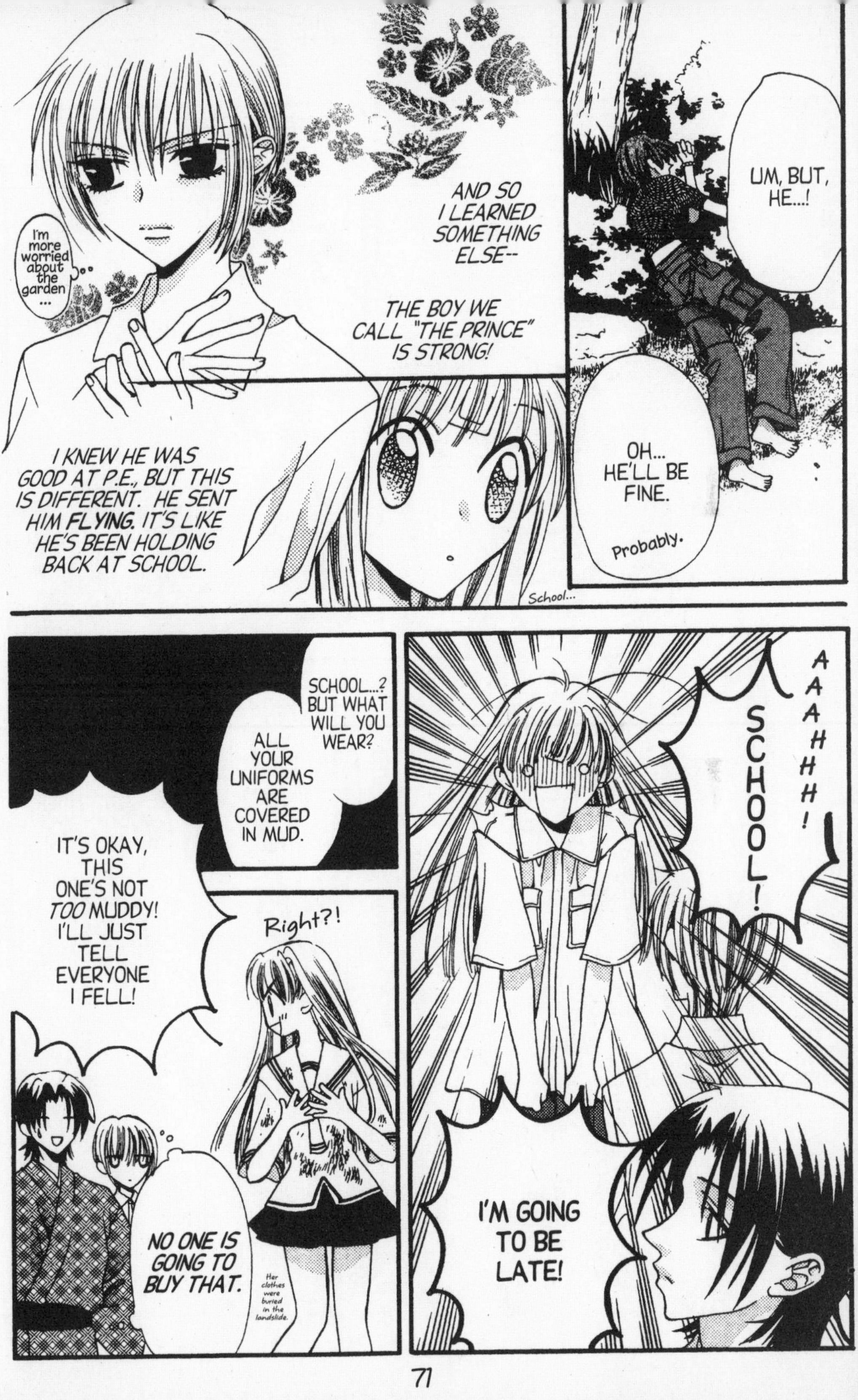
UM, BUT, HE...!
OH... HE'LL BE FINE.
Probably.
AND SO I LEARNED SOMETHING ELSE--
I'm more worried about the garden...
THE BOY WE CALL "THE PRINCE" IS STRONG!
I KNEW HE WAS GOOD AT P.E., BUT THIS IS DIFFERENT. HE SENT HIM FLYING. IT'S LIKE HE'S BEEN HOLDING BACK AT SCHOOL.
School...
AAAHHH! SCHOOL!
I'M GOING TO BE LATE!
SCHOOL...? BUT WHAT WILL YOU WEAR?
ALL YOUR UNIFORMS ARE COVERED IN MUD.
IT'S OKAY, THIS ONE'S NOT TOO MUDDY! I'LL JUST TELL EVERYONE I FELL!
Right?!
NO ONE IS GOING TO BUY THAT.
Her clothes were buried in the landslide.

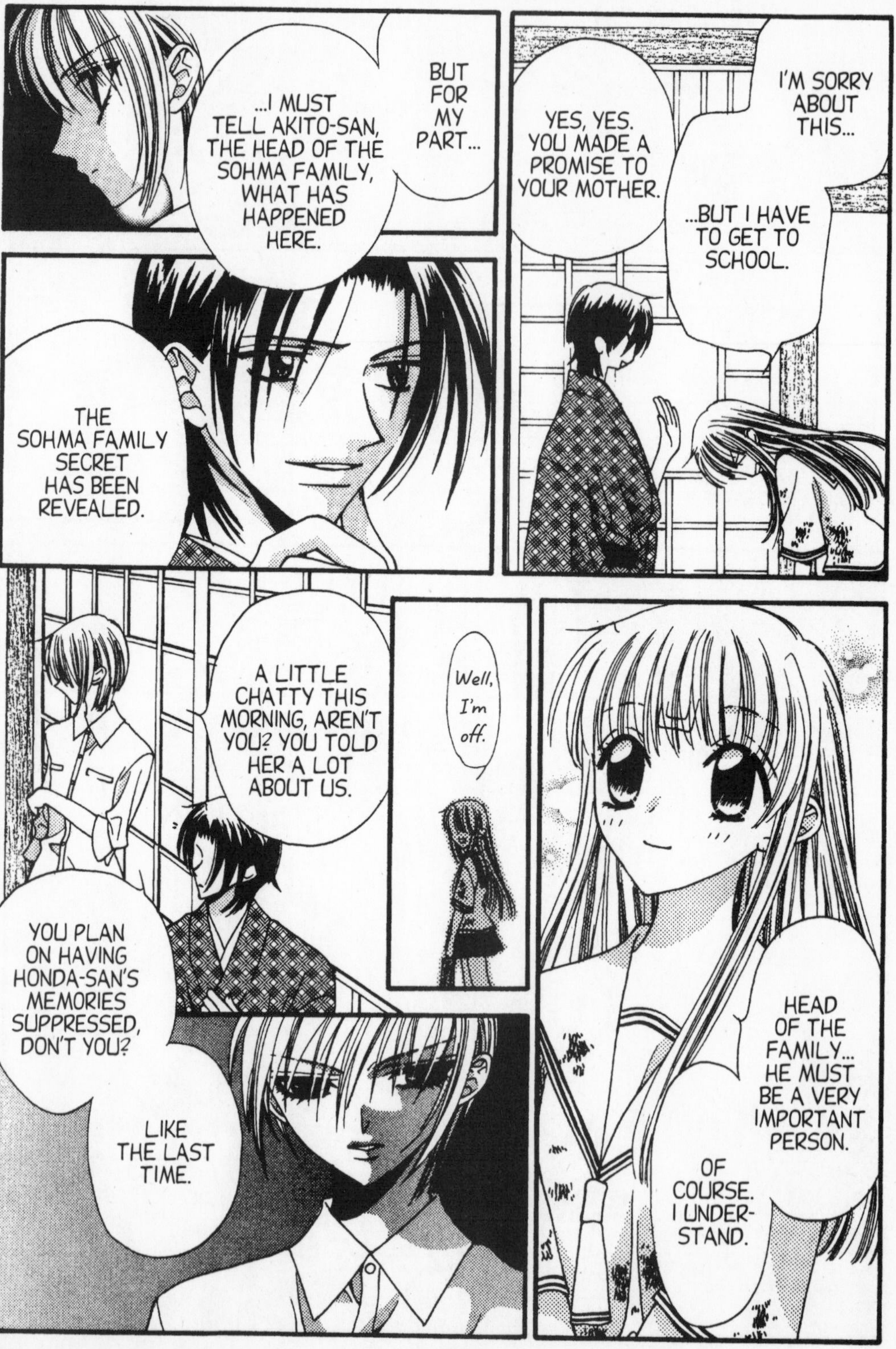

I'M SORRY ABOUT THIS...
...BUT I HAVE TO GET TO SCHOOL.
YES, YES. YOU MADE A PROMISE TO YOUR MOTHER.
BUT FOR MY PART...
...I MUST TELL AKITO-SAN, THE HEAD OF THE SOHMA FAMILY, WHAT HAS HAPPENED HERE.
THE SOHMA FAMILY SECRET HAS BEEN REVEALED.
HEAD OF THE FAMILY... HE MUST BE A VERY IMPORTANT PERSON.
OF COURSE. I UNDERSTAND.
Well, I'm off.
A LITTLE CHATTY THIS MORNING, AREN'T YOU? YOU TOLD HER A LOT ABOUT US.
YOU PLAN ON HAVING HONDA-SAN'S MEMORIES SUPPRESSED, DON'T YOU?
LIKE THE LAST TIME.

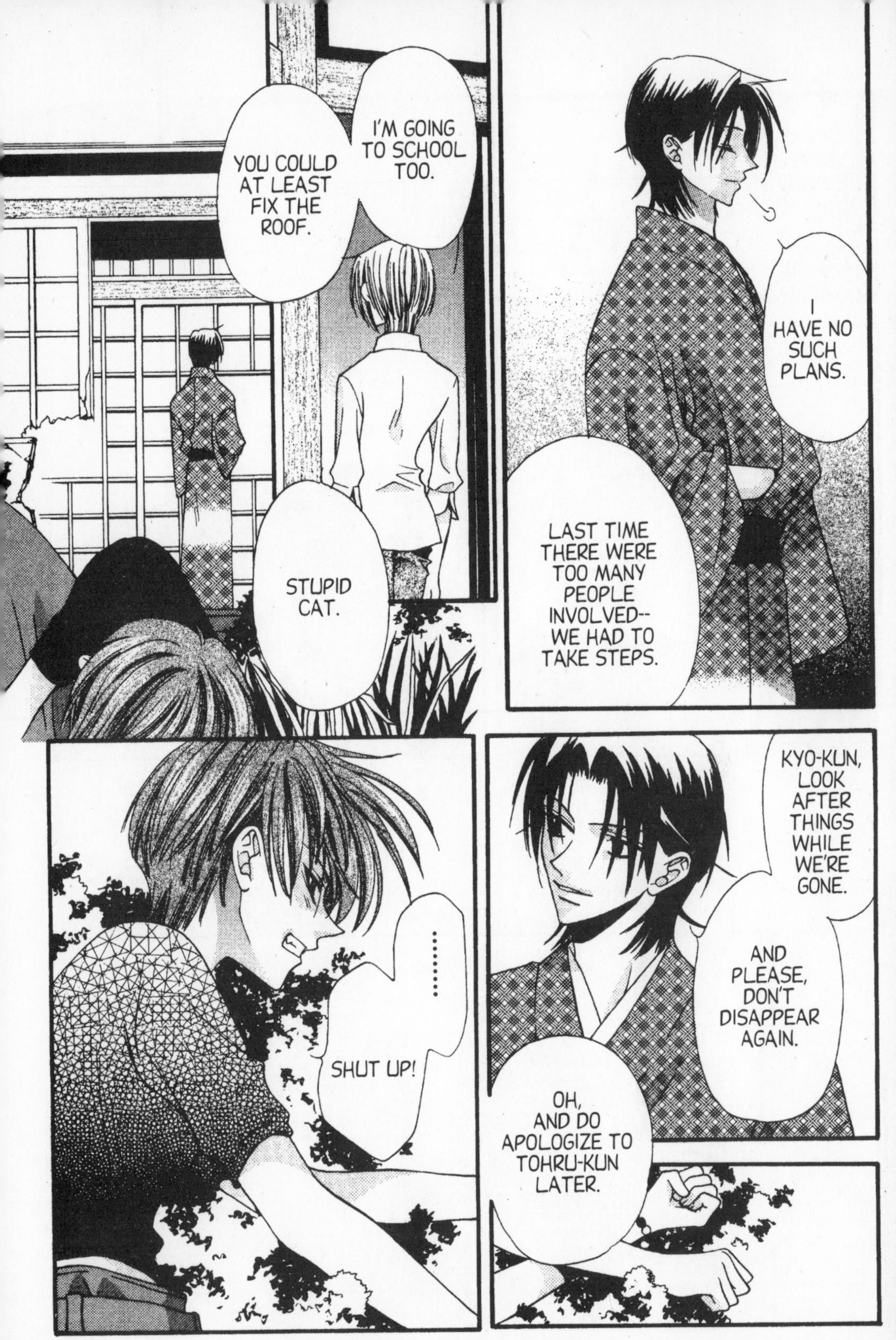
I HAVE NO SUCH PLANS.
LAST TIME THERE WERE TOO MANY PEOPLE INVOLVED-- WE HAD TO TAKE STEPS.
I'M GOING TO SCHOOL TOO.
YOU COULD AT LEAST FIX THE ROOF.
STUPID CAT.
KYO-KUN, LOOK AFTER THINGS WHILE WE'RE GONE.
AND PLEASE, DON'T DISAPPEAR AGAIN.
OH, AND DO APOLOGIZE TO TOHRU-KUN LATER.
......
SHUT UP!

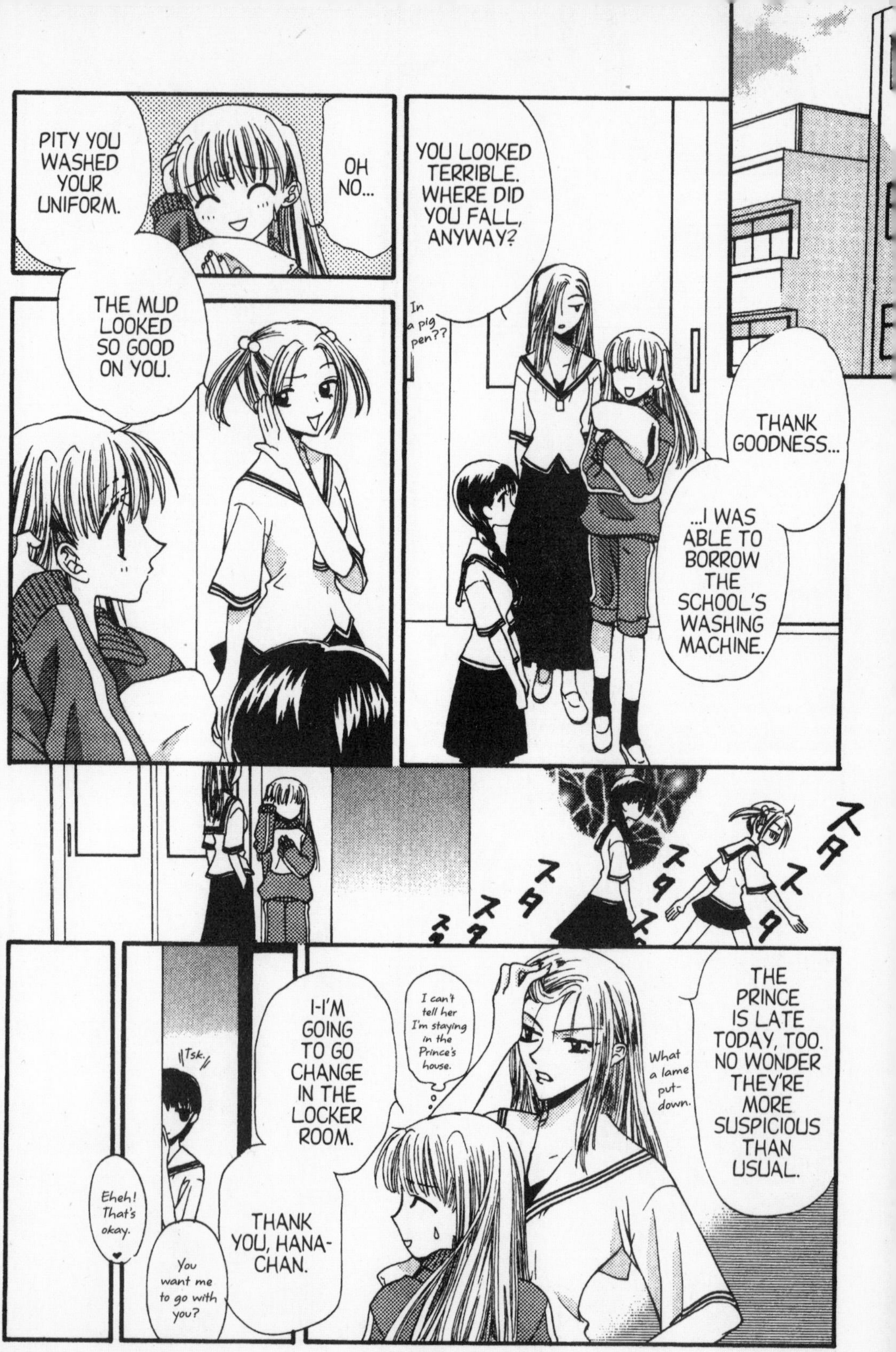
YOU LOOKED TERRIBLE. WHERE DID YOU FALL, ANYWAY?
In a pig pen??
THANK GOODNESS...
...I WAS ABLE TO BORROW THE SCHOOL'S WASHING MACHINE.
PITY YOU WASHED YOUR UNIFORM.
OH NO...
THE MUD LOOKED SO GOOD ON YOU.
スタスタスタ
スタスタスタ
THE PRINCE IS LATE TODAY, TOO. NO WONDER THEY'RE MORE SUSPICIOUS THAN USUAL.
What a lame put-down.
I can't tell her I'm staying in the Prince's house.
I-I'M GOING TO GO CHANGE IN THE LOCKER ROOM.
THANK YOU, HANA-CHAN.
You want me to go with you?
Eheh! That's okay.
Tsk.

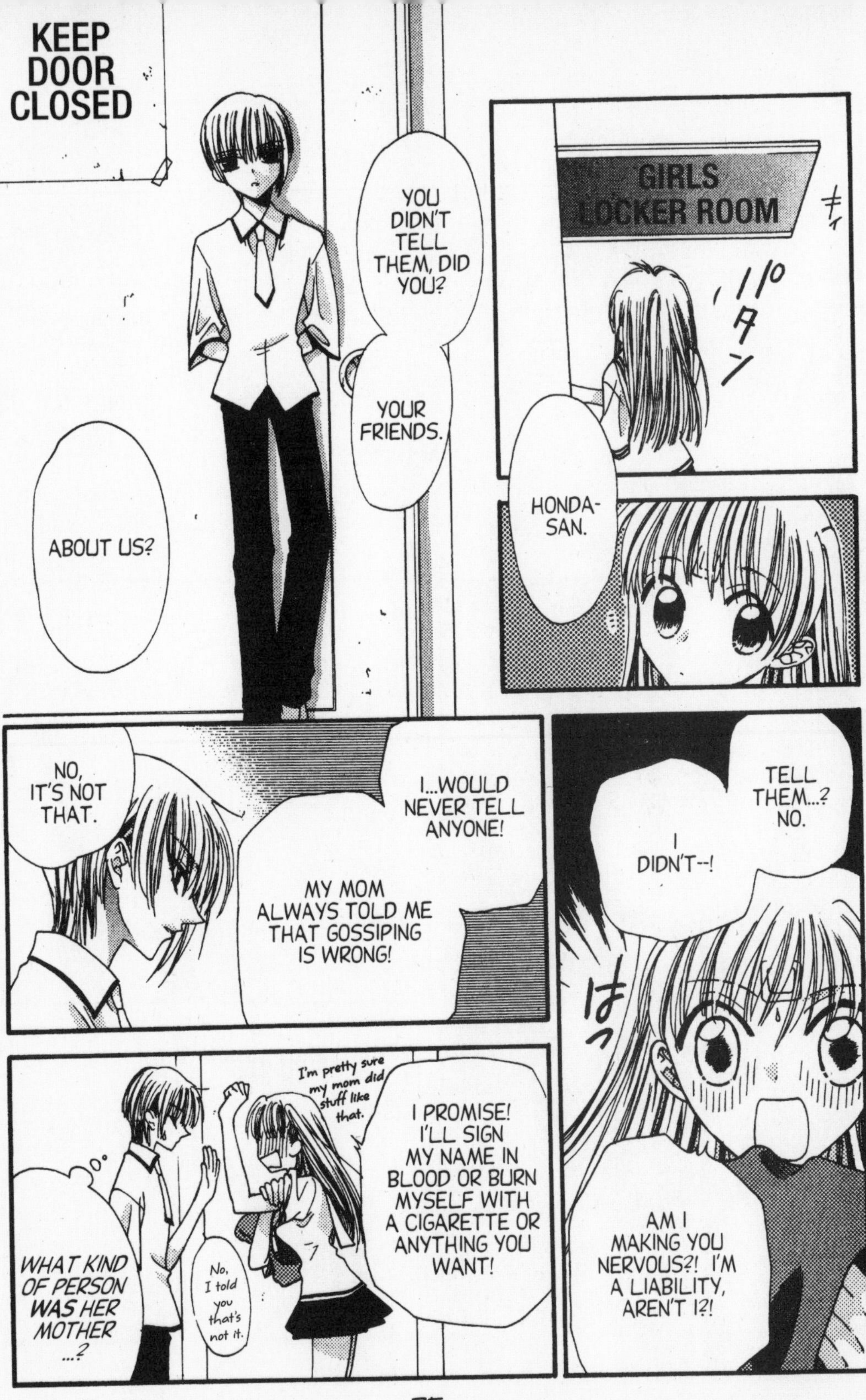
GIRLS LOCKER ROOM
キィ
パタン
HONDA-SAN.
YOU DIDN'T TELL THEM, DID YOU?
YOUR FRIENDS.
ABOUT US?
KEEP DOOR CLOSED
TELL THEM...? NO.
I DIDN'T--!
はっ
AM I MAKING YOU NERVOUS?! I'M A LIABILITY, AREN'T I?!
I...WOULD NEVER TELL ANYONE!
MY MOM ALWAYS TOLD ME THAT GOSSIPING IS WRONG!
NO, IT'S NOT THAT.
I PROMISE! I'LL SIGN MY NAME IN BLOOD OR BURN MYSELF WITH A CIGARETTE OR ANYTHING YOU WANT!
I'm pretty sure my mom did stuff like that.
No, I told you that's not it.
WHAT KIND OF PERSON WAS HER MOTHER ...?

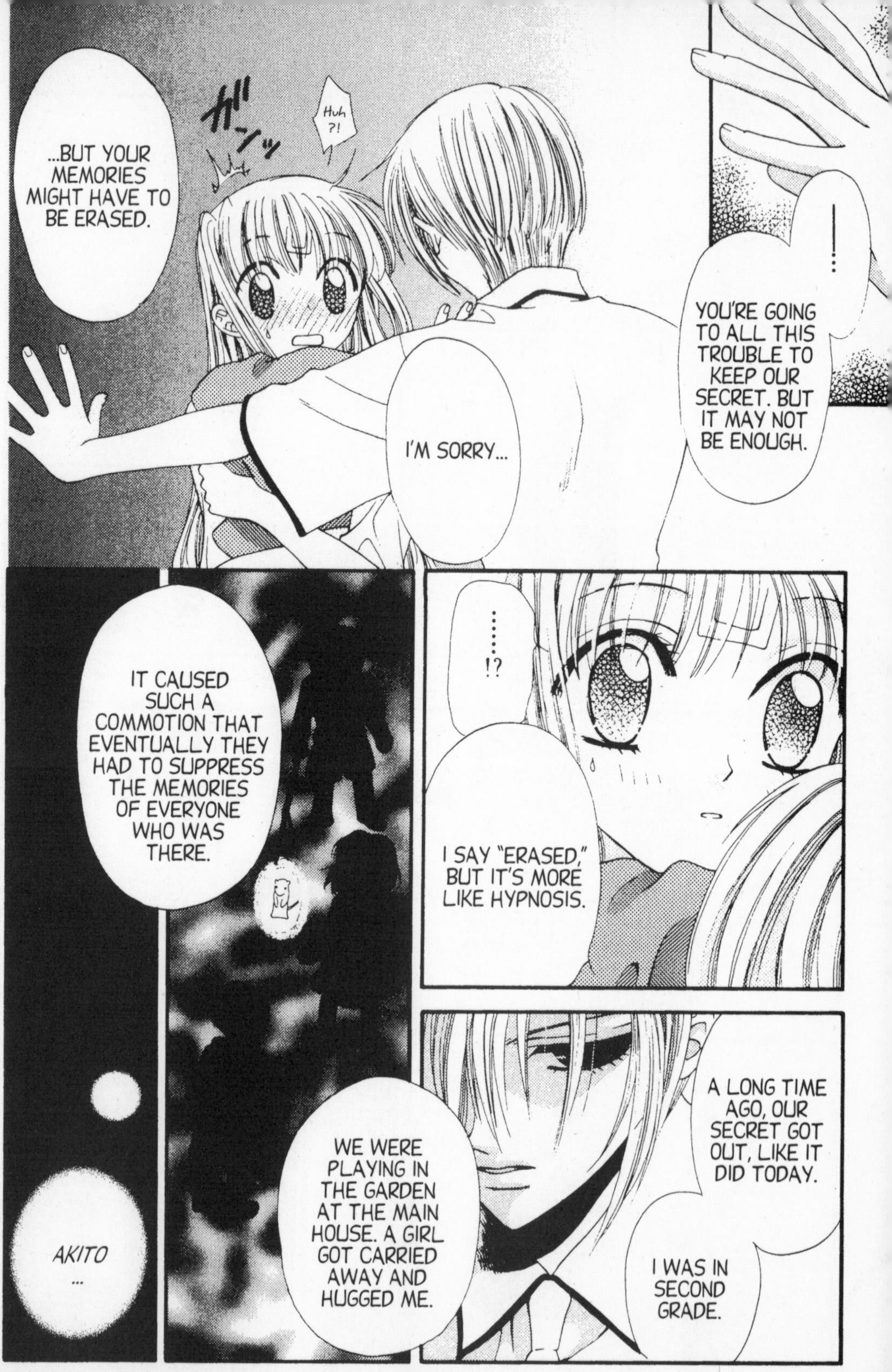
......!
YOU'RE GOING TO ALL THIS TROUBLE TO KEEP OUR SECRET. BUT IT MAY NOT BE ENOUGH.
I'M SORRY...
Huh ?!
...BUT YOUR MEMORIES MIGHT HAVE TO BE ERASED.
......!?
I SAY "ERASED," BUT IT'S MORE LIKE HYPNOSIS.
A LONG TIME AGO, OUR SECRET GOT OUT, LIKE IT DID TODAY.
I WAS IN SECOND GRADE.
WE WERE PLAYING IN THE GARDEN AT THE MAIN HOUSE. A GIRL GOT CARRIED AWAY AND HUGGED ME.
IT CAUSED SUCH A COMMOTION THAT EVENTUALLY THEY HAD TO SUPPRESS THE MEMORIES OF EVERYONE WHO WAS THERE.
AKITO ...

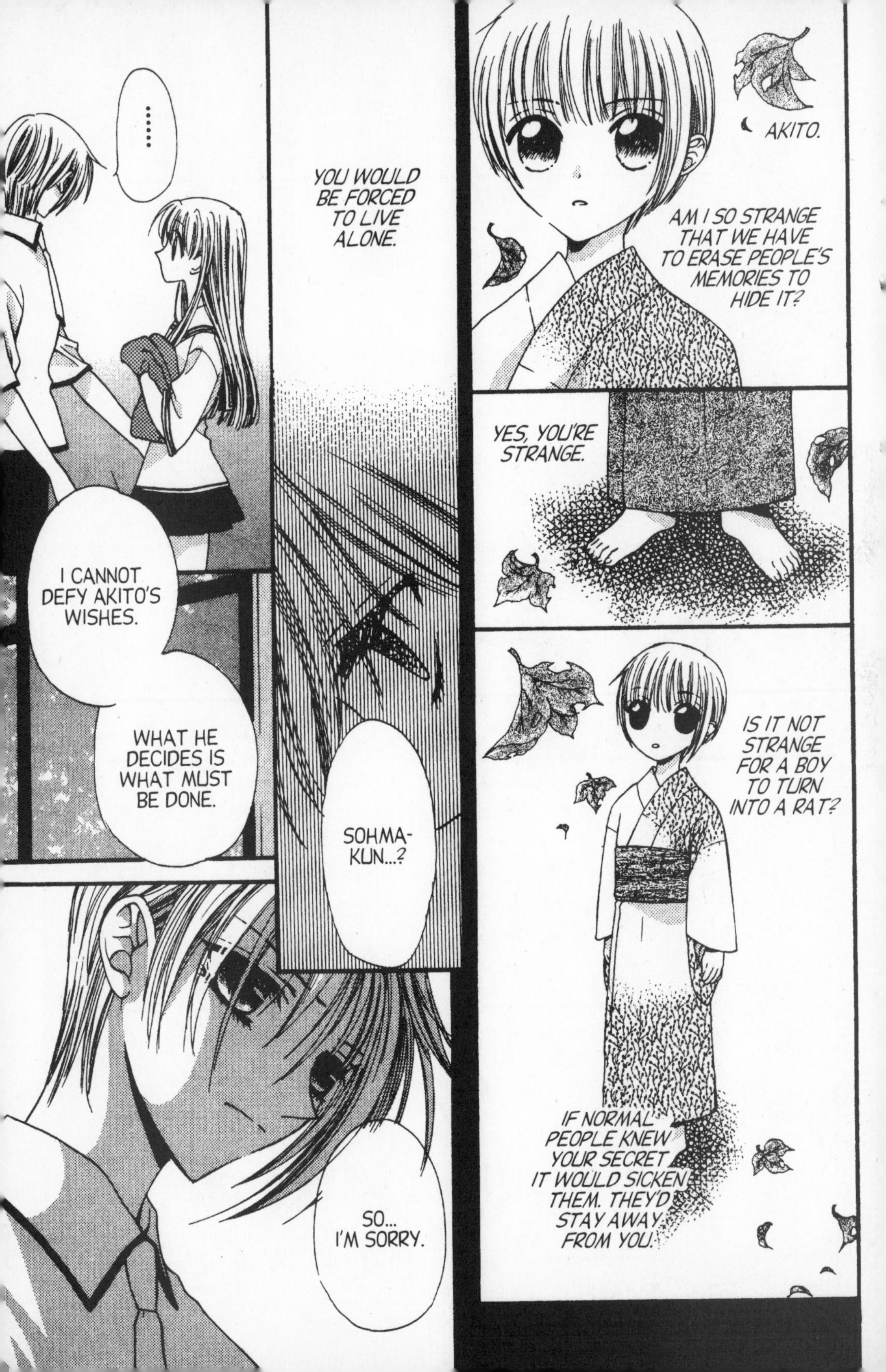
AKITO.
AM I SO STRANGE THAT WE HAVE TO ERASE PEOPLE'S MEMORIES TO HIDE IT?
YES, YOU'RE STRANGE.
IS IT NOT STRANGE FOR A BOY TO TURN INTO A RAT?
IF NORMAL PEOPLE KNEW YOUR SECRET IT WOULD SICKEN THEM. THEY'D STAY AWAY FROM YOU.
YOU WOULD BE FORCED TO LIVE ALONE.
......
I CANNOT DEFY AKITO'S WISHES.
WHAT HE DECIDES IS WHAT MUST BE DONE.
SOHMA-KUN...?
SO... I'M SORRY.

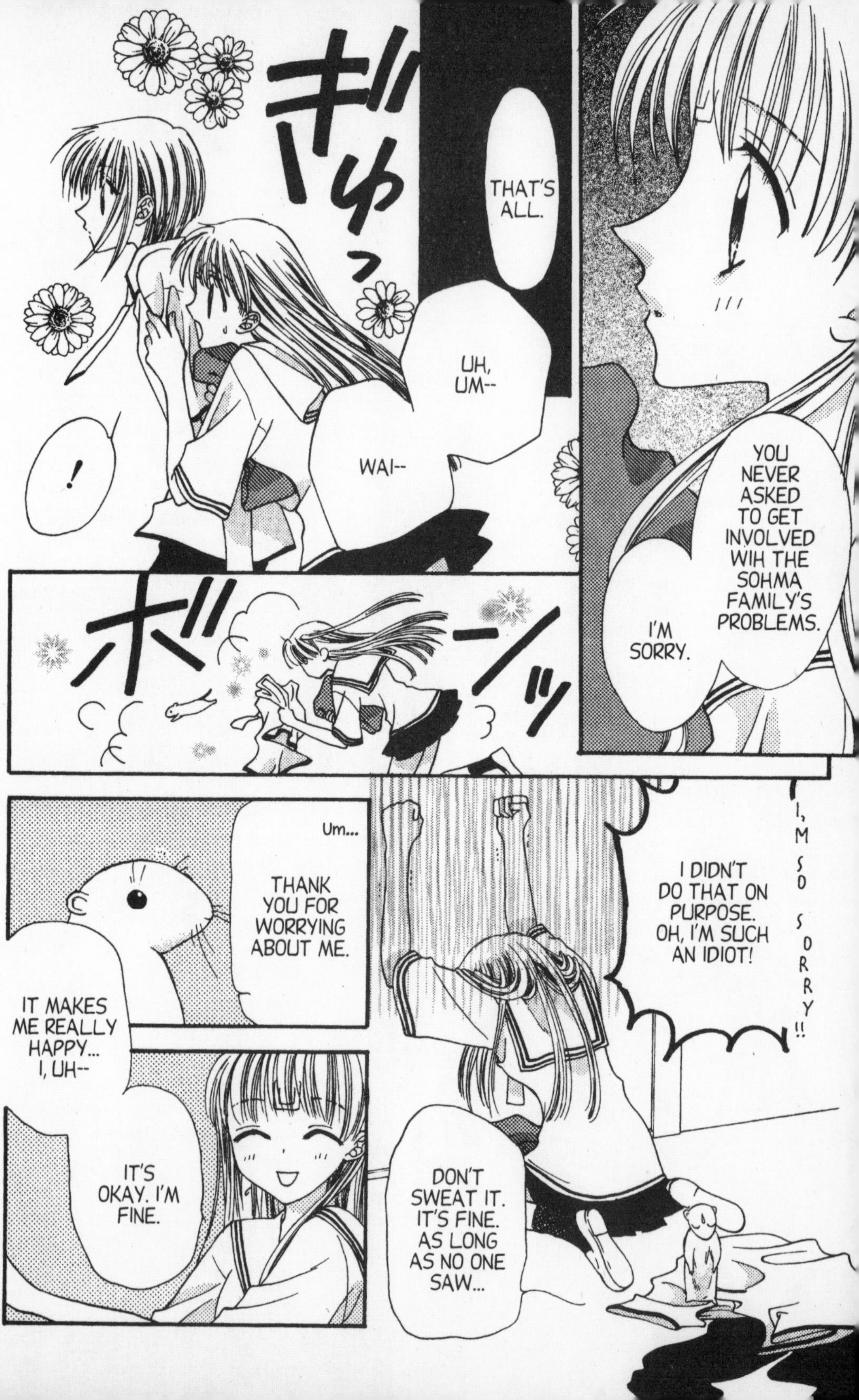
YOU NEVER ASKED TO GET INVOLVED WIH THE SOHMA FAMILY'S PROBLEMS.
I'M SORRY.
THAT'S ALL.
ぎゅっ
UH, UM--
WAI--
!
ボーンッ
I'M SO SORRY!!
I DIDN'T DO THAT ON PURPOSE. OH, I'M SUCH AN IDIOT!
DON'T SWEAT IT. IT'S FINE. AS LONG AS NO ONE SAW...
Um...
THANK YOU FOR WORRYING ABOUT ME.
IT MAKES ME REALLY HAPPY... I, UH--
IT'S OKAY. I'M FINE.

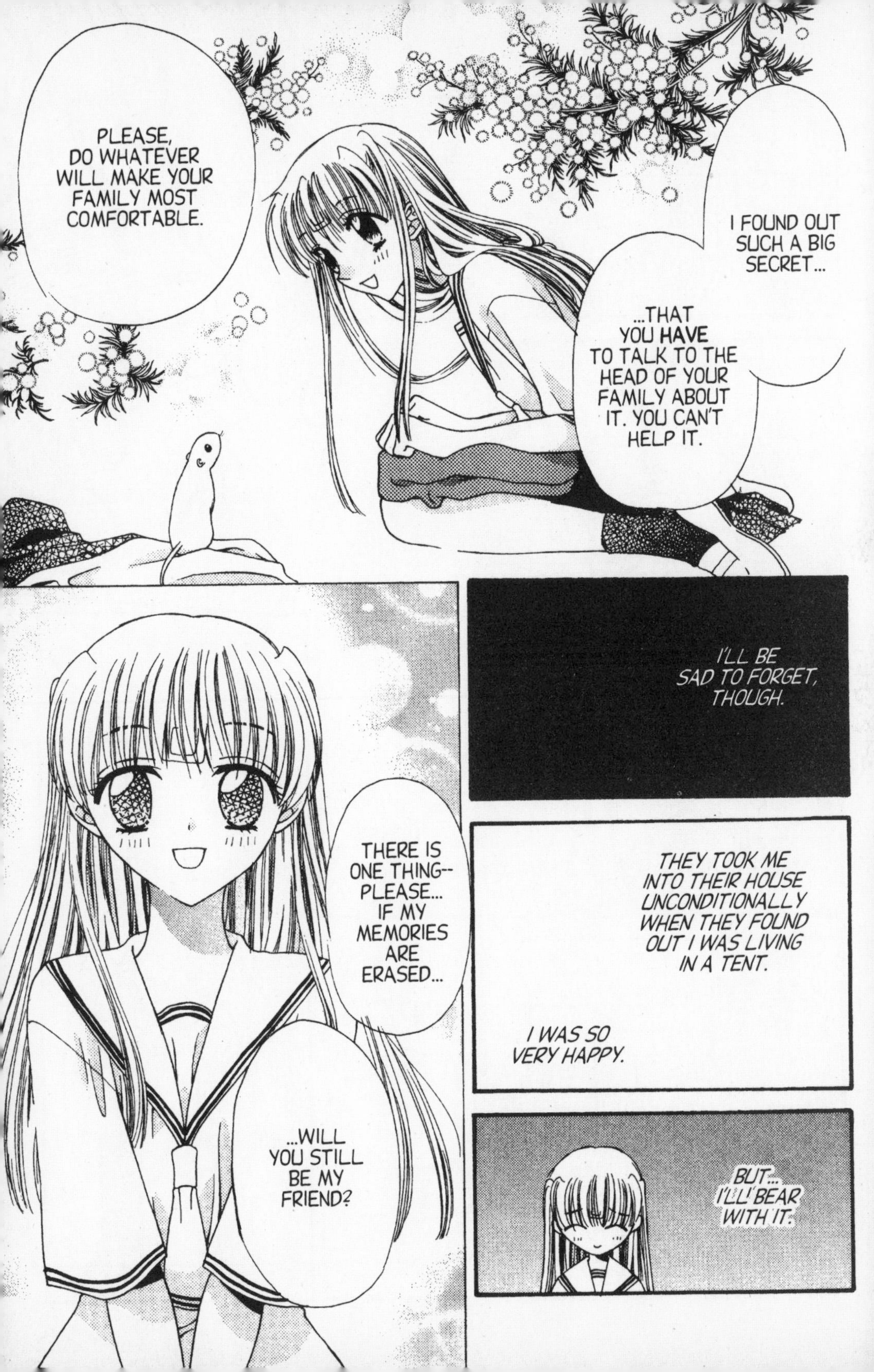
I FOUND OUT SUCH A BIG SECRET...
...THAT YOU **HAVE** TO TALK TO THE HEAD OF YOUR FAMILY ABOUT IT. YOU CAN'T HELP IT.
PLEASE, DO WHATEVER WILL MAKE YOUR FAMILY MOST COMFORTABLE.
I'LL BE SAD TO FORGET, THOUGH.
THEY TOOK ME INTO THEIR HOUSE UNCONDITIONALLY WHEN THEY FOUND OUT I WAS LIVING IN A TENT.
I WAS SO VERY HAPPY.
BUT... I'LL BEAR WITH IT.
THERE IS ONE THING-- PLEASE... IF MY MEMORIES ARE ERASED...
...WILL YOU STILL BE MY FRIEND?

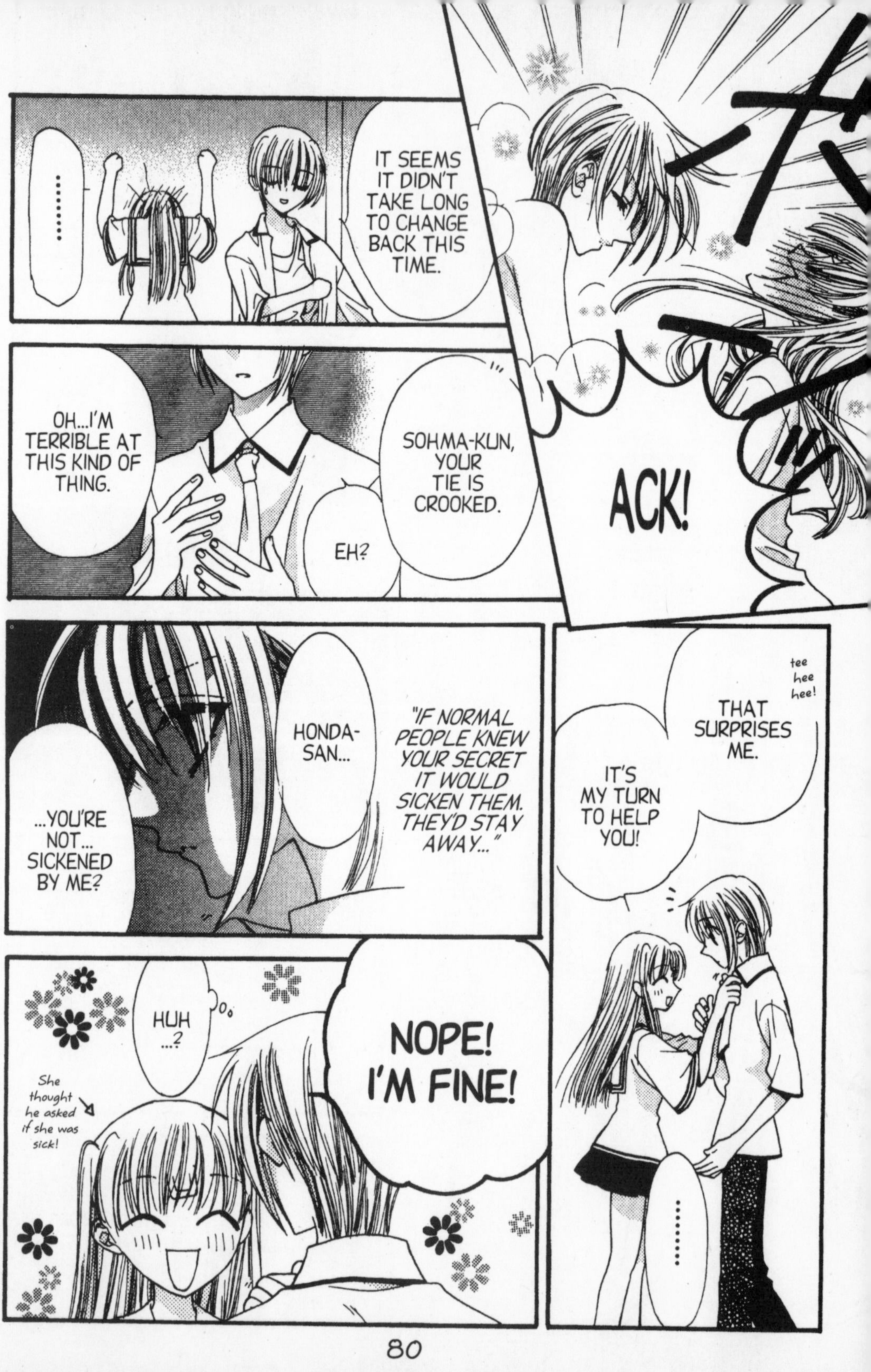
ACK!
IT SEEMS IT DIDN'T TAKE LONG TO CHANGE BACK THIS TIME.
......
SOHMA-KUN, YOUR TIE IS CROOKED.
EH?
OH...I'M TERRIBLE AT THIS KIND OF THING.
tee hee hee!
THAT SURPRISES ME.
IT'S MY TURN TO HELP YOU!
......
"IF NORMAL PEOPLE KNEW YOUR SECRET IT WOULD SICKEN THEM. THEY'D STAY AWAY..."
HONDA-SAN...
...YOU'RE NOT... SICKENED BY ME?
NOPE! I'M FINE!
HUH ...?
She thought he asked if she was sick!

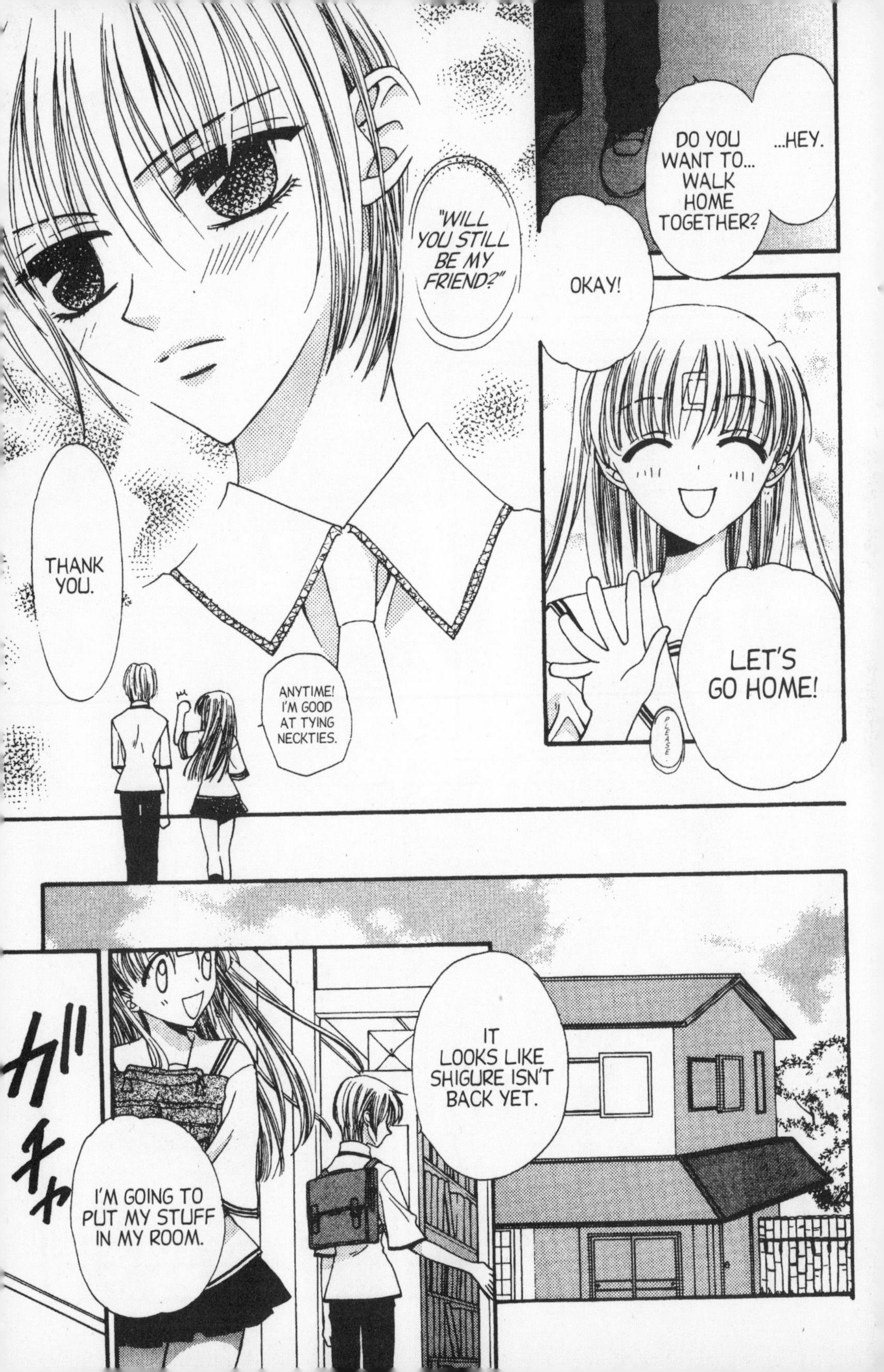
...HEY.
DO YOU WANT TO... WALK HOME TOGETHER?
OKAY!
LET'S GO HOME!
PLEASE.
"WILL YOU STILL BE MY FRIEND?"
THANK YOU.
ANYTIME! I'M GOOD AT TYING NECKTIES.
IT LOOKS LIKE SHIGURE ISN'T BACK YET.
ガチャ
I'M GOING TO PUT MY STUFF IN MY ROOM.

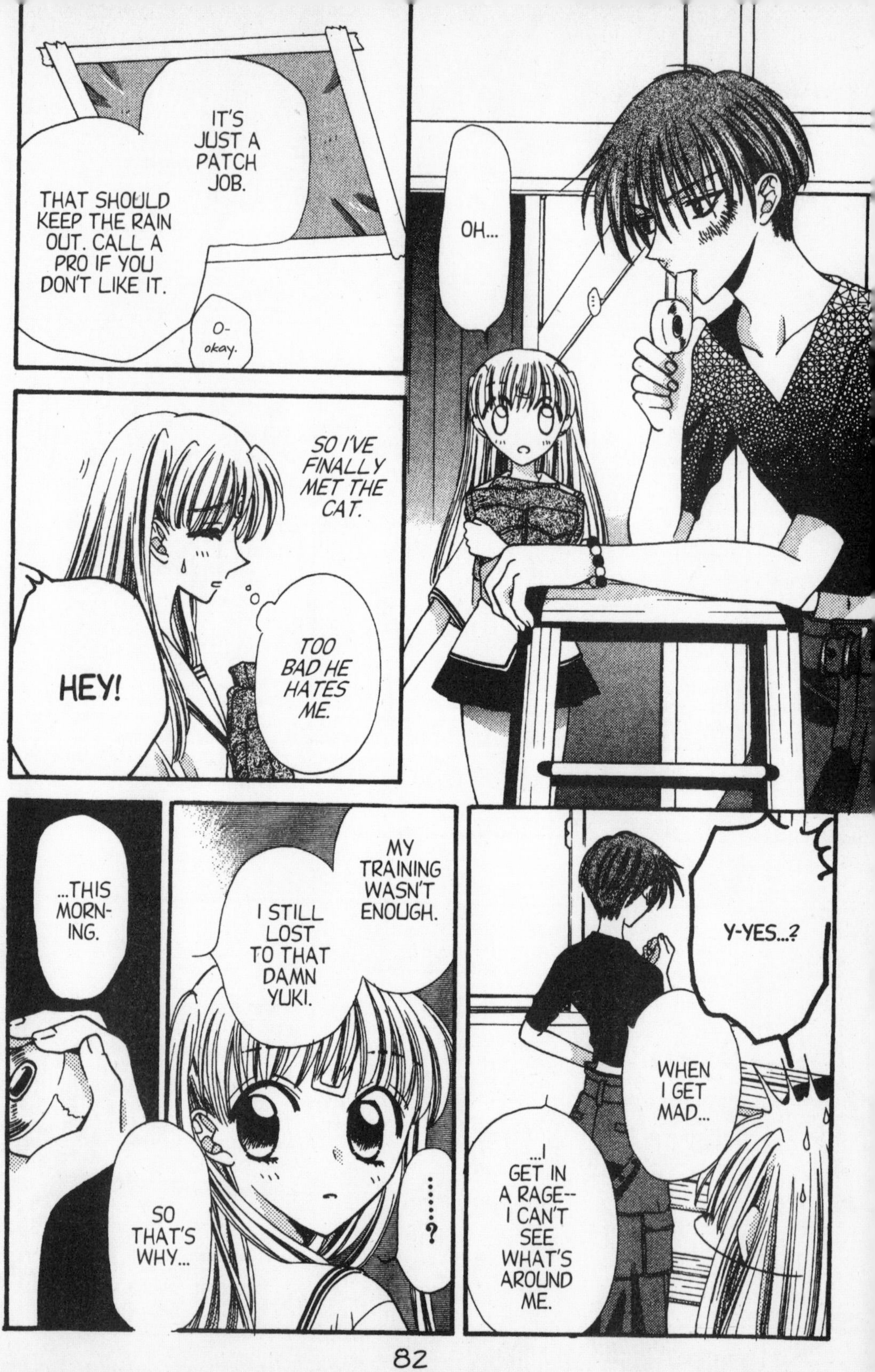
OH...
...
IT'S JUST A PATCH JOB.
THAT SHOULD KEEP THE RAIN OUT. CALL A PRO IF YOU DON'T LIKE IT.
O-okay.
SO I'VE FINALLY MET THE CAT.
TOO BAD HE HATES ME.
HEY!
Y-YES...?
WHEN I GET MAD...
...I GET IN A RAGE-- I CAN'T SEE WHAT'S AROUND ME.
MY TRAINING WASN'T ENOUGH.
I STILL LOST TO THAT DAMN YUKI.
......?
SO THAT'S WHY...
...THIS MORNING.

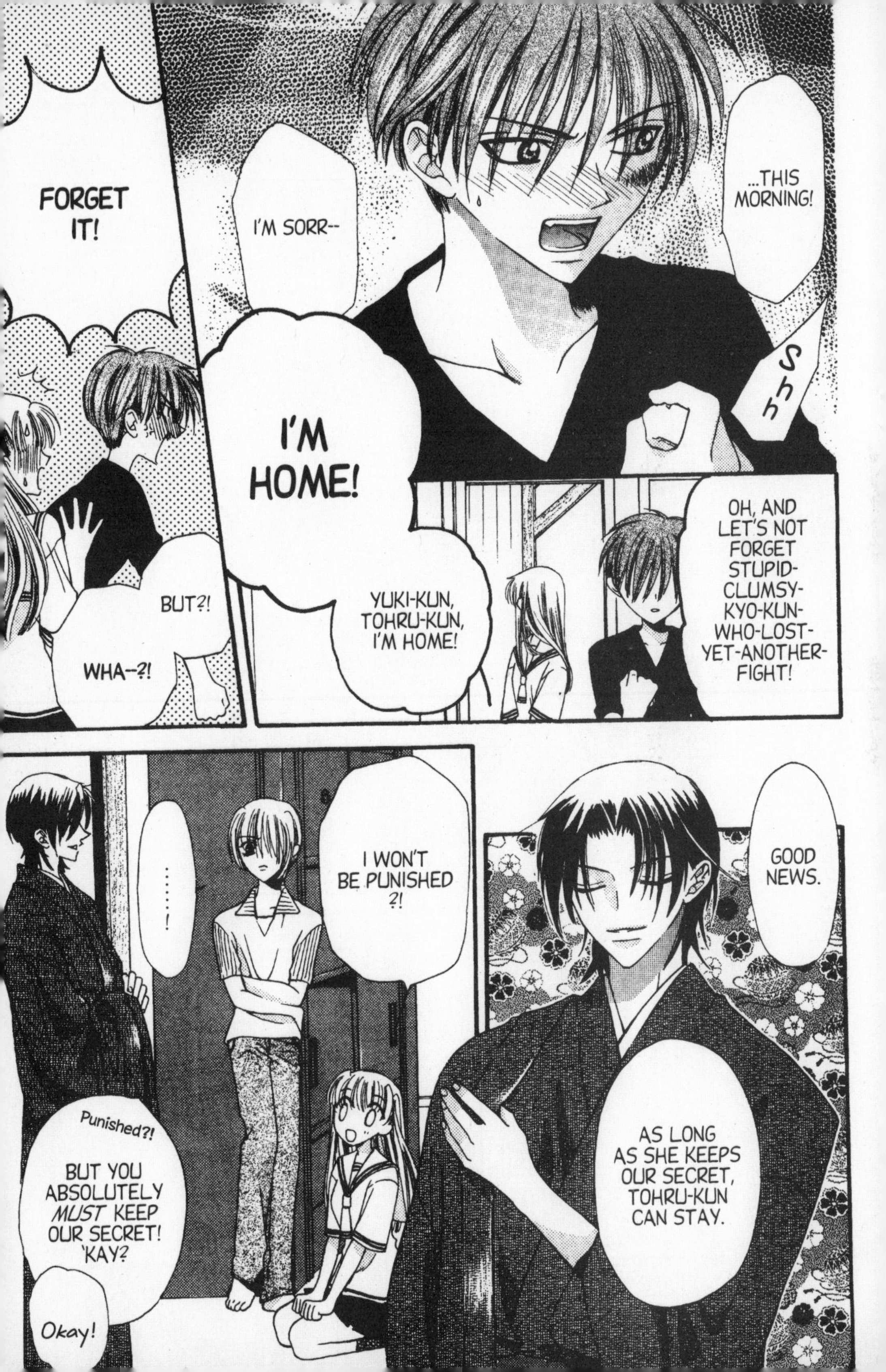
...THIS MORNING!
Shh
I'M SORR--
I'M HOME!
OH, AND LET'S NOT FORGET STUPID-CLUMSY-KYO-KUN-WHO-LOST-YET-ANOTHER-FIGHT!
YUKI-KUN, TOHRU-KUN, I'M HOME!
FORGET IT!
BUT?!
WHA--?!
GOOD NEWS.
AS LONG AS SHE KEEPS OUR SECRET, TOHRU-KUN CAN STAY.
I WON'T BE PUNISHED?!
......!
Punished?!
BUT YOU ABSOLUTELY *MUST* KEEP OUR SECRET! 'KAY?
Okay!

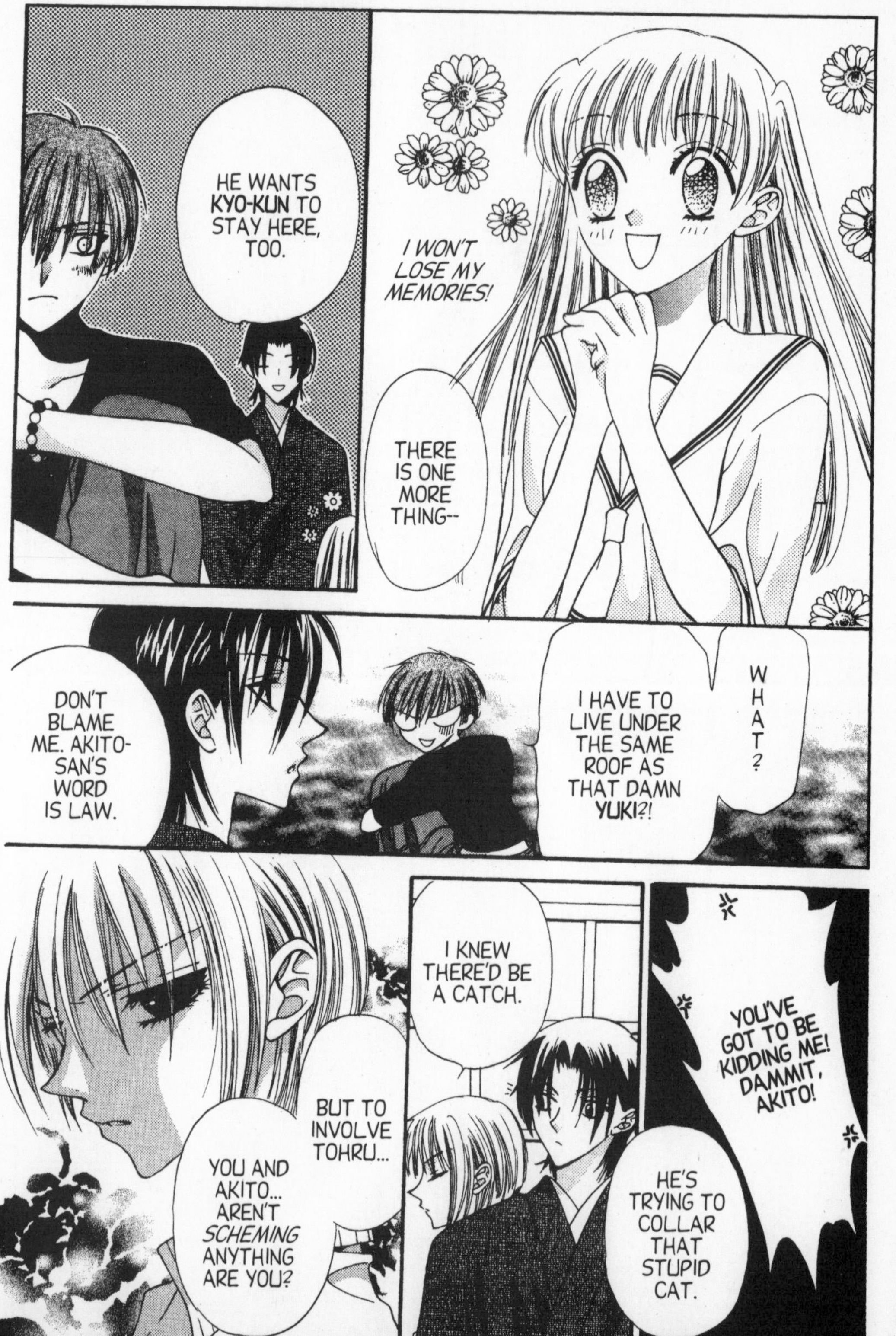
I WON'T LOSE MY MEMORIES!
THERE IS ONE MORE THING--
HE WANTS KYO-KUN TO STAY HERE, TOO.
WHAT?
I HAVE TO LIVE UNDER THE SAME ROOF AS THAT DAMN YUKI?!
DON'T BLAME ME. AKITO-SAN'S WORD IS LAW.
YOU'VE GOT TO BE KIDDING ME! DAMMIT, AKITO!
I KNEW THERE'D BE A CATCH.
HE'S TRYING TO COLLAR THAT STUPID CAT.
BUT TO INVOLVE TOHRU...
YOU AND AKITO... AREN'T *SCHEMING* ANYTHING ARE YOU?

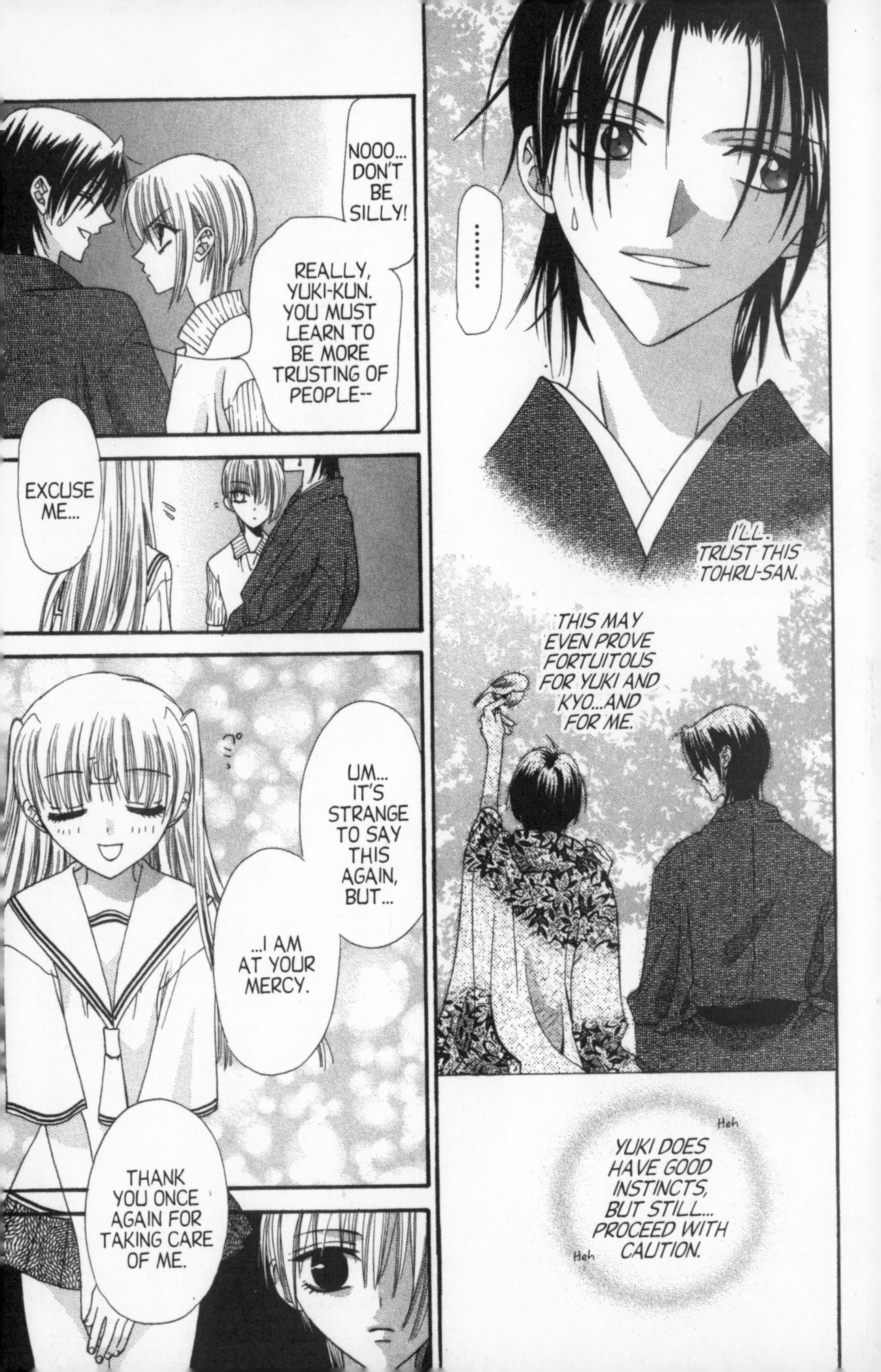
NOOO... DON'T BE SILLY!
REALLY, YUKI-KUN. YOU MUST LEARN TO BE MORE TRUSTING OF PEOPLE--
EXCUSE ME...
UM... IT'S STRANGE TO SAY THIS AGAIN, BUT...
...I AM AT YOUR MERCY.
THANK YOU ONCE AGAIN FOR TAKING CARE OF ME.
......
I'LL TRUST THIS TOHRU-SAN.
THIS MAY EVEN PROVE FORTUITOUS FOR YUKI AND KYO...AND FOR ME.
Heh
YUKI DOES HAVE GOOD INSTINCTS, BUT STILL... PROCEED WITH CAUTION.
Heh

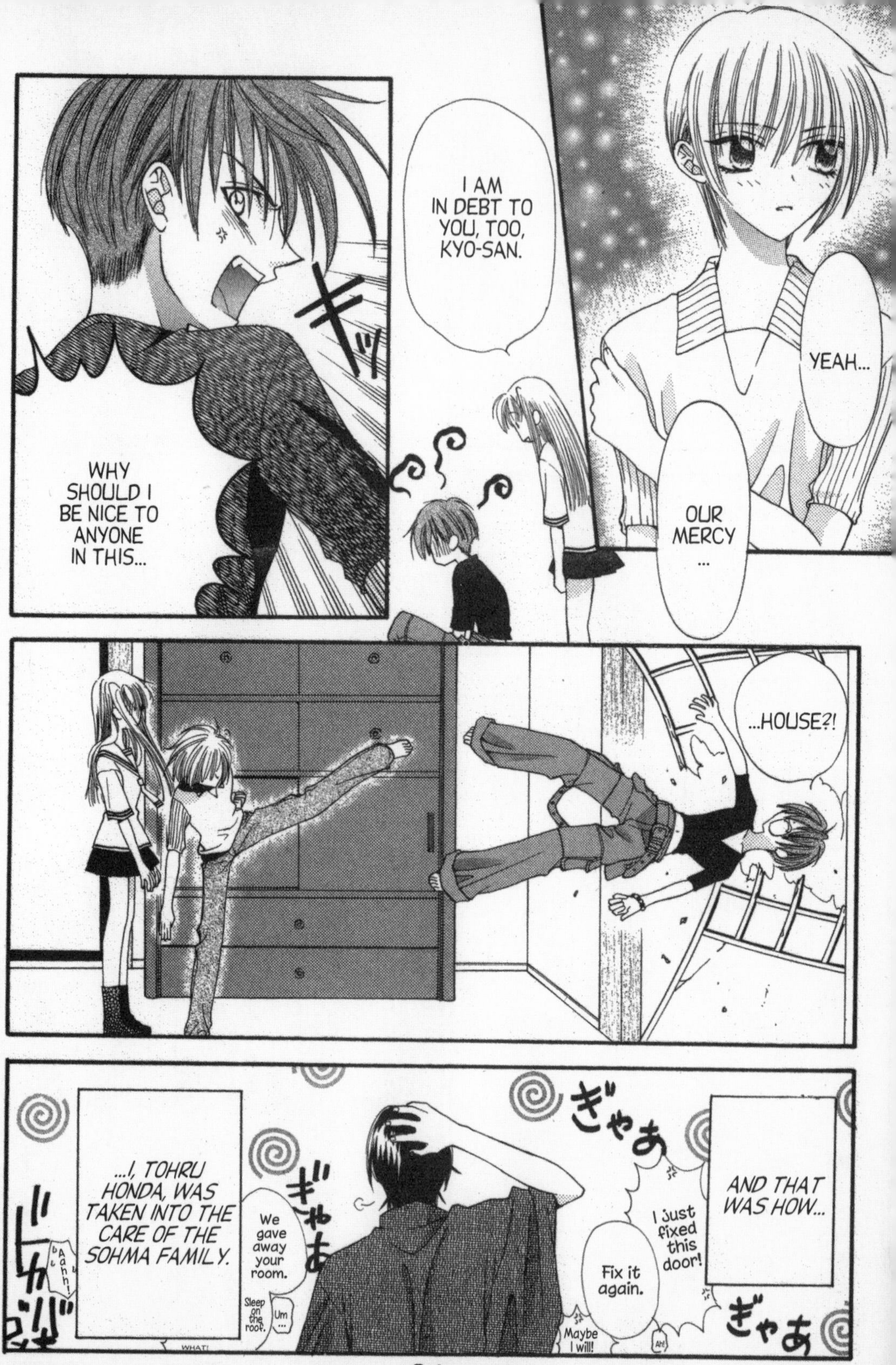
YEAH...
OUR MERCY ...
I AM IN DEBT TO YOU, TOO, KYO-SAN.
WHY SHOULD I BE NICE TO ANYONE IN THIS...
...HOUSE?!
AND THAT WAS HOW...
ぎゃあ
ぎゃあ
I just fixed this door!
Fix it again.
Maybe I will!
Ah!
ぎゃあ
We gave away your room.
Sleep on the roof.
Um ...
WHAT!
Aahh!
...I, TOHRU HONDA, WAS TAKEN INTO THE CARE OF THE SOHMA FAMILY.

Chapter 3

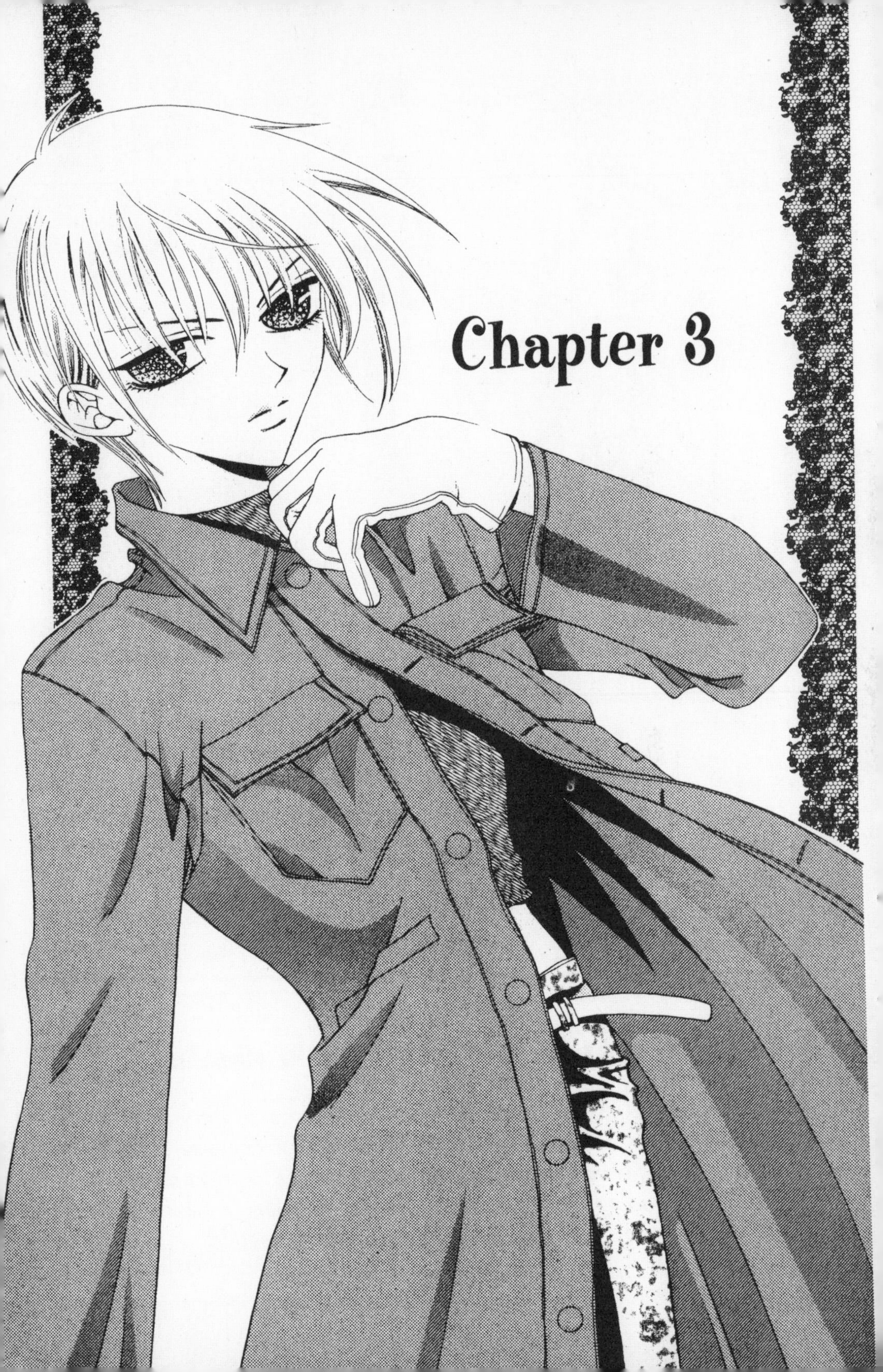

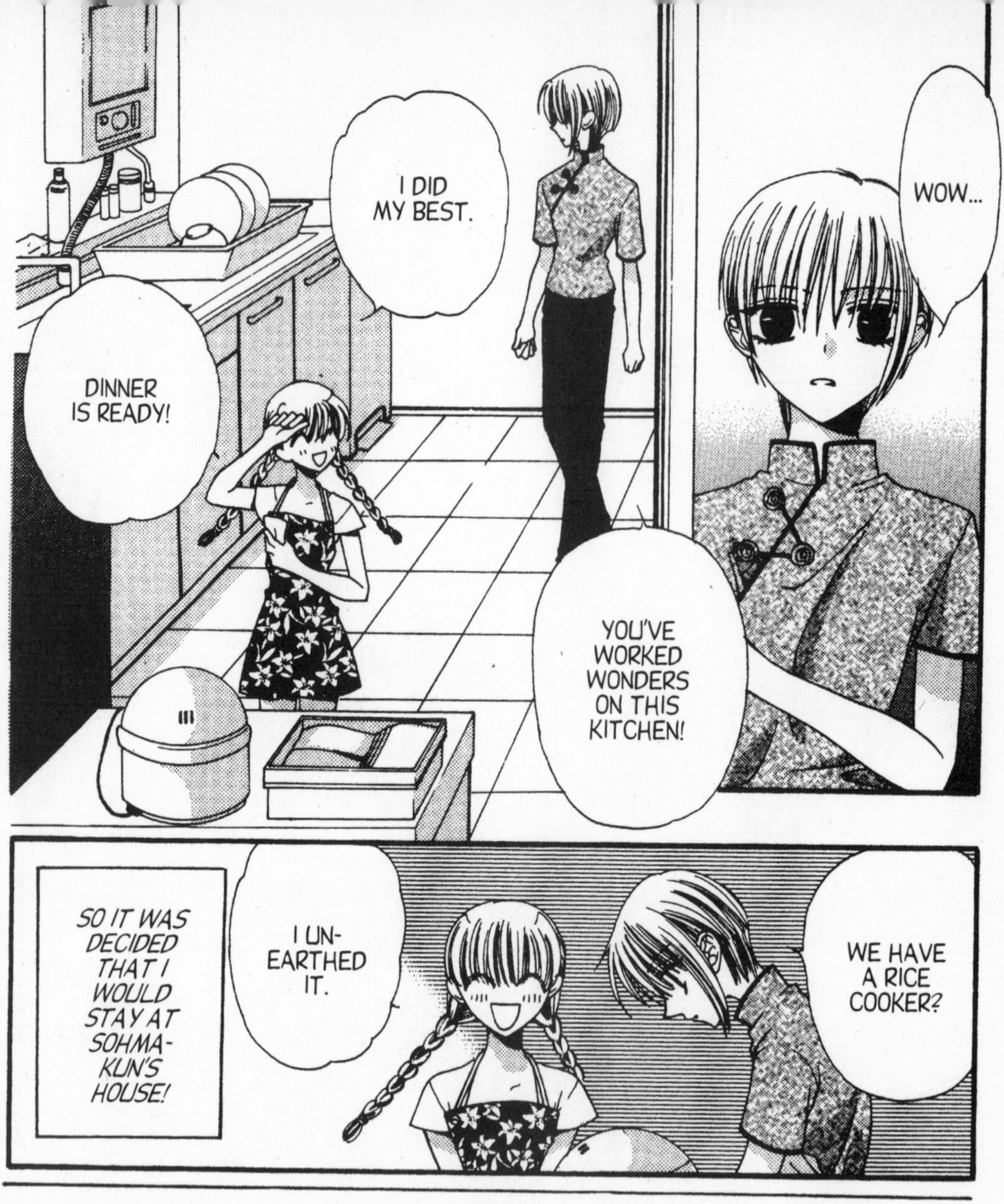
WOW...
YOU'VE WORKED WONDERS ON THIS KITCHEN!
I DID MY BEST.
DINNER IS READY!
WE HAVE A RICE COOKER?
I UN-EARTHED IT.
SO IT WAS DECIDED THAT I WOULD STAY AT SOHMA-KUN'S HOUSE!

ULTRA SPECIAL BLAH BLAH BLAH, NUMBER 2:

A martial artist has to have a firm body. They have to have muscles. But Yuki and Kyo are scrawny (ha ha). That's just because I don't like drawing muscles very much. I prefer a slender aesthetic for my men. Don't worry too much about it. Not that people had been pointing it out to me; I was just worried about it myself.

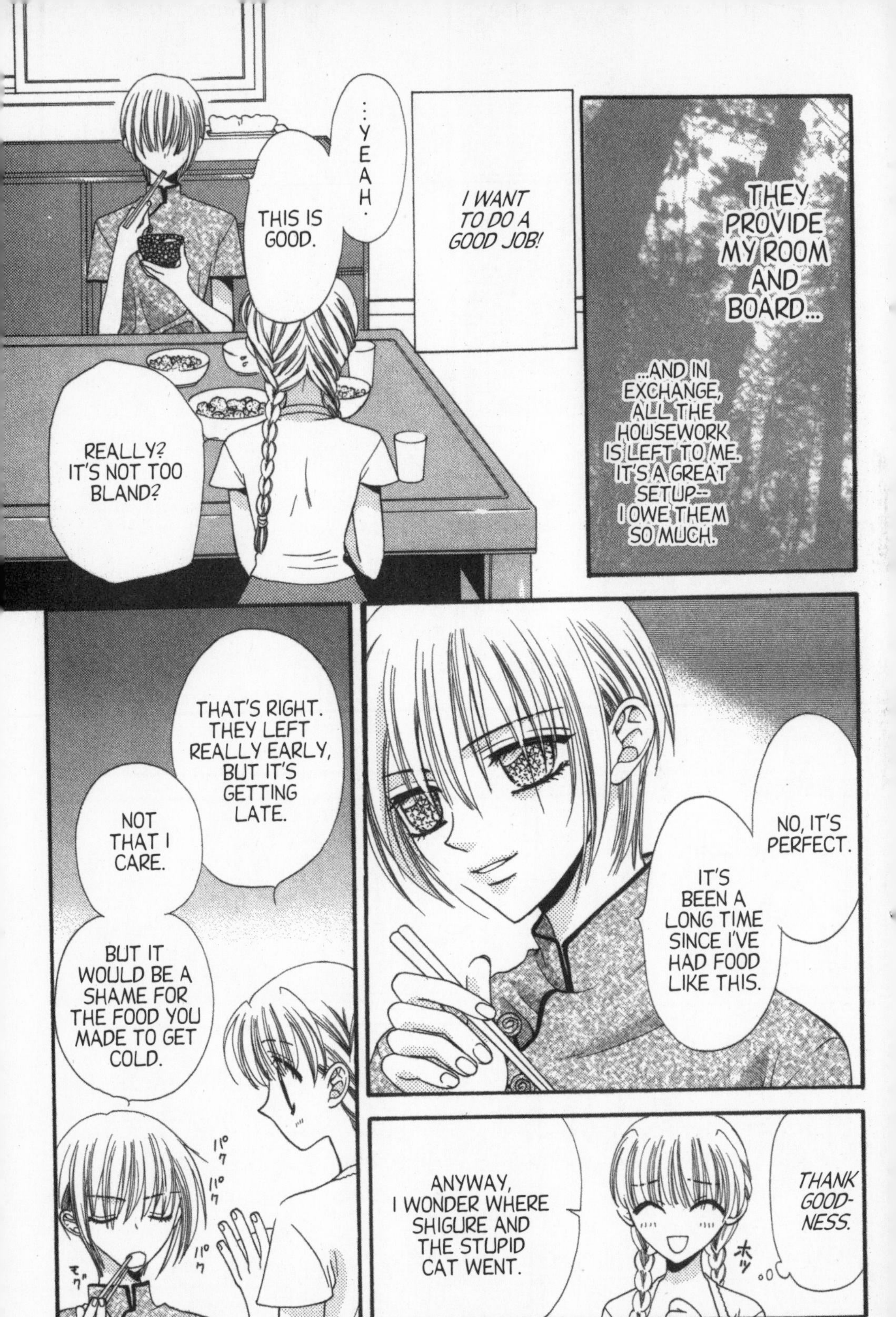
THEY PROVIDE MY ROOM AND BOARD...
...AND IN EXCHANGE, ALL THE HOUSEWORK IS LEFT TO ME. IT'S A GREAT SETUP-- I OWE THEM SO MUCH.
I WANT TO DO A GOOD JOB!
...YEAH.
THIS IS GOOD.
REALLY? IT'S NOT TOO BLAND?
NO, IT'S PERFECT.
IT'S BEEN A LONG TIME SINCE I'VE HAD FOOD LIKE THIS.
THANK GOODNESS.
ホッ
ANYWAY, I WONDER WHERE SHIGURE AND THE STUPID CAT WENT.
THAT'S RIGHT. THEY LEFT REALLY EARLY, BUT IT'S GETTING LATE.
NOT THAT I CARE.
BUT IT WOULD BE A SHAME FOR THE FOOD YOU MADE TO GET COLD.
パク
パク
パク
モグ

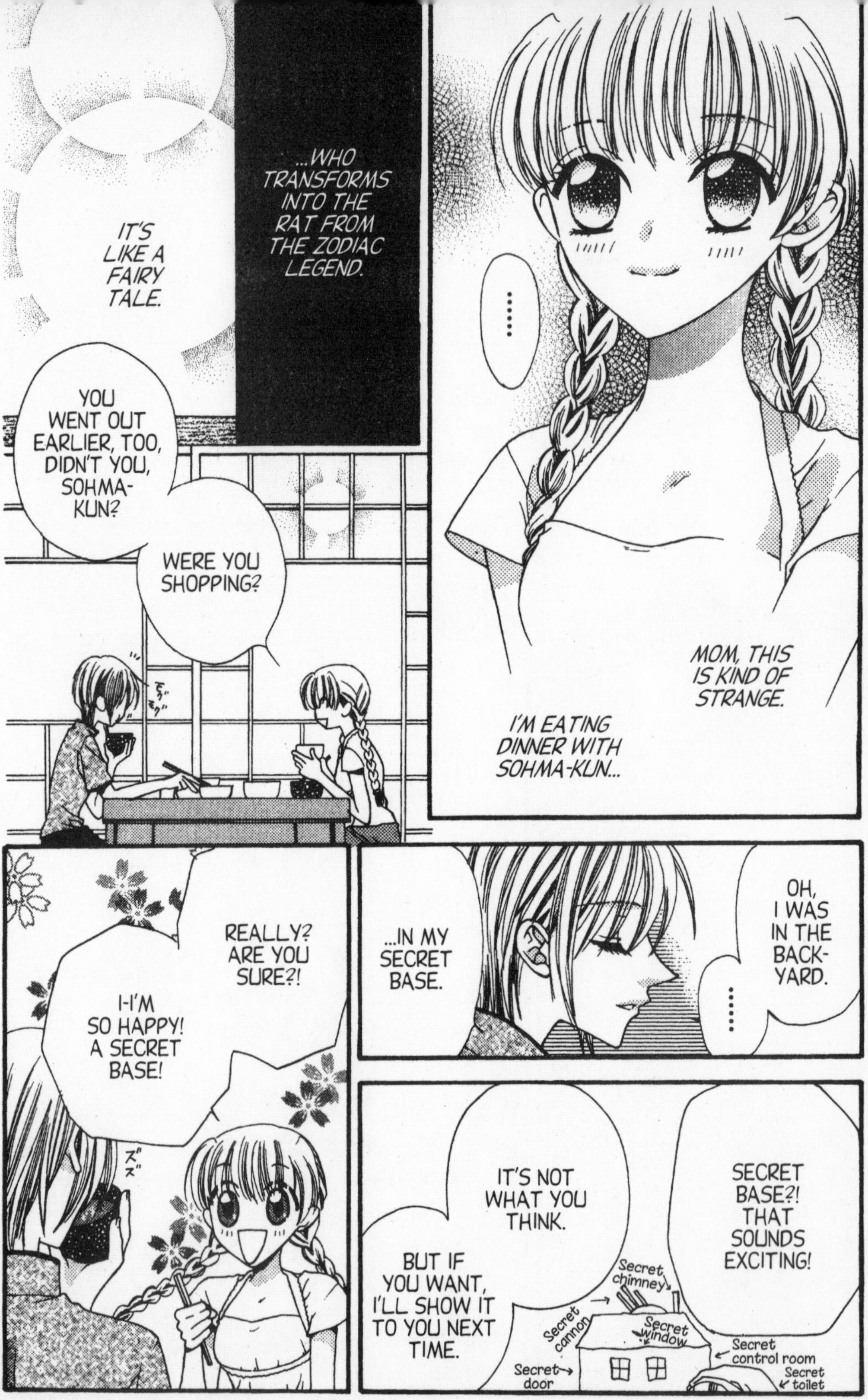
......
MOM, THIS IS KIND OF STRANGE.
I'M EATING DINNER WITH SOHMA-KUN...
...WHO TRANSFORMS INTO THE RAT FROM THE ZODIAC LEGEND.
IT'S LIKE A FAIRY TALE.
YOU WENT OUT EARLIER, TOO, DIDN'T YOU, SOHMA-KUN?
WERE YOU SHOPPING?
OH, I WAS IN THE BACK-YARD.
......
...IN MY SECRET BASE.
SECRET BASE?! THAT SOUNDS EXCITING!
IT'S NOT WHAT YOU THINK.
BUT IF YOU WANT, I'LL SHOW IT TO YOU NEXT TIME.
Secret chimney
Secret cannon
Secret window
Secret control room
Secret door
Secret toilet
REALLY? ARE YOU SURE?!
I-I'M SO HAPPY! A SECRET BASE!

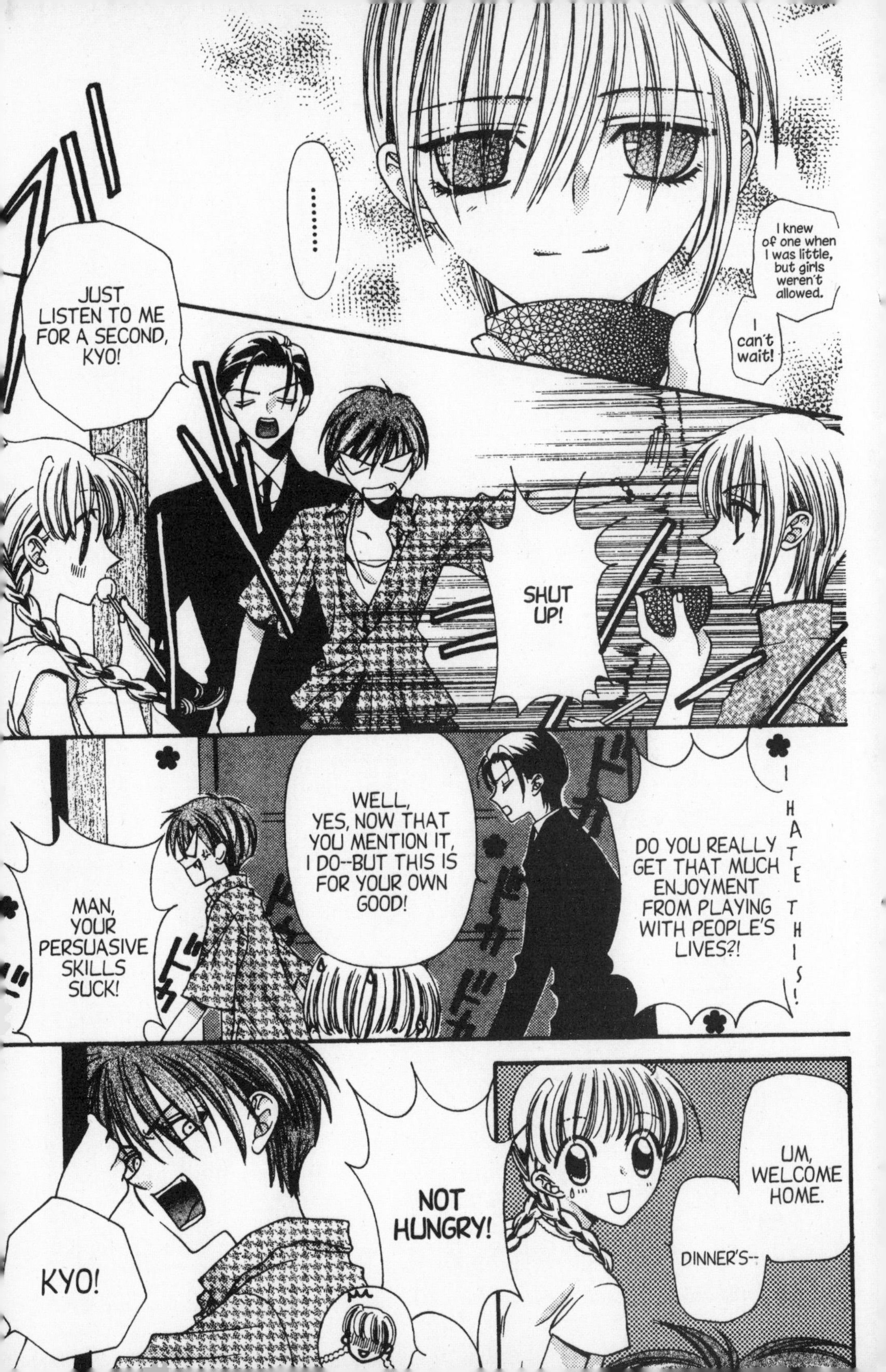
I knew of one when I was little, but girls weren't allowed.
I can't wait!
......
JUST LISTEN TO ME FOR A SECOND, KYO!
SHUT UP!
I HATE THIS!
DO YOU REALLY GET THAT MUCH ENJOYMENT FROM PLAYING WITH PEOPLE'S LIVES?!
WELL, YES, NOW THAT YOU MENTION IT, I DO--BUT THIS IS FOR YOUR OWN GOOD!
MAN, YOUR PERSUASIVE SKILLS SUCK!
UM, WELCOME HOME.
DINNER'S--
NOT HUNGRY!
KYO!

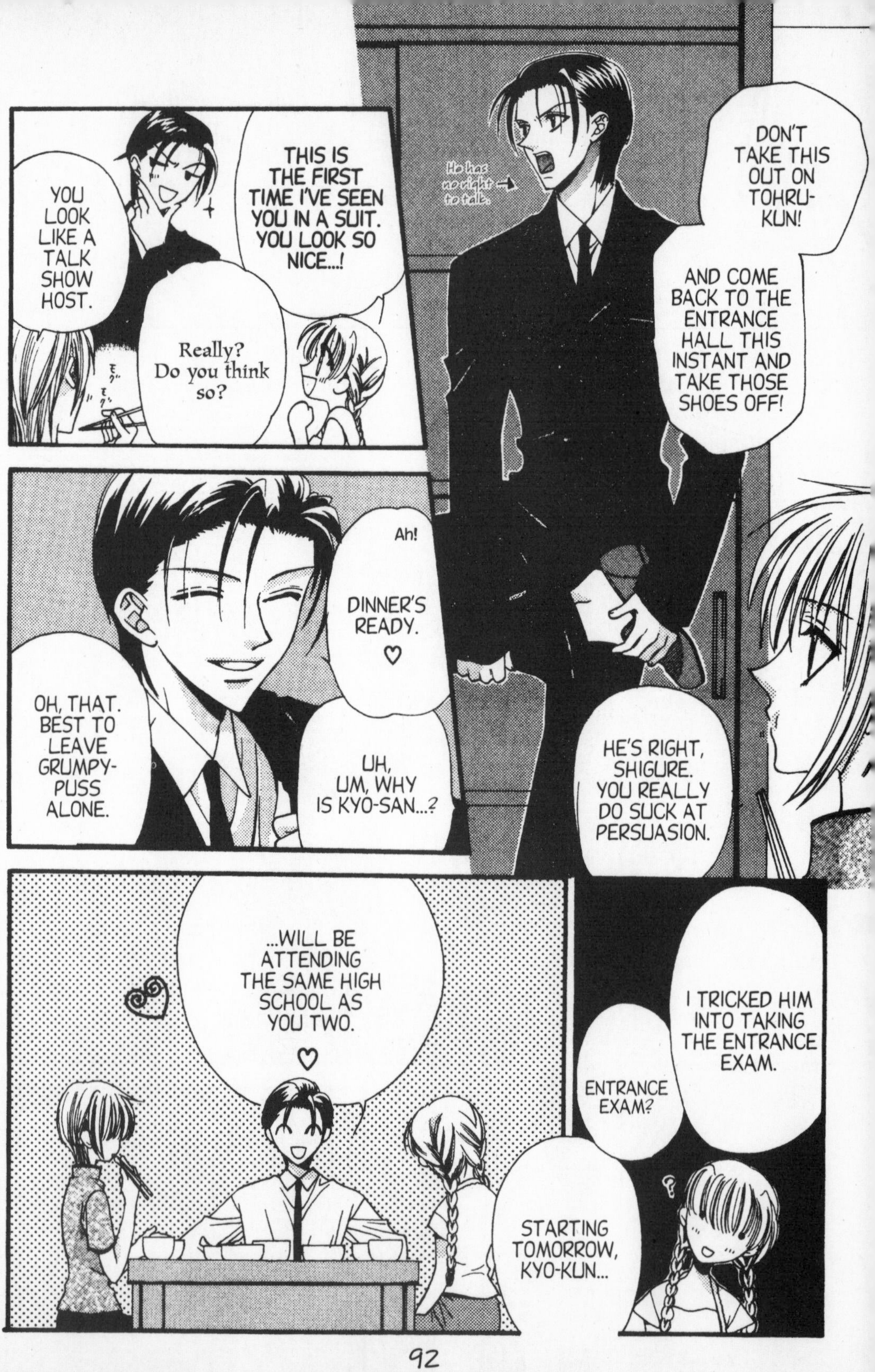
DON'T TAKE THIS OUT ON TOHRU-KUN!
He has no right to talk.
AND COME BACK TO THE ENTRANCE HALL THIS INSTANT AND TAKE THOSE SHOES OFF!
HE'S RIGHT, SHIGURE. YOU REALLY DO SUCK AT PERSUASION.
THIS IS THE FIRST TIME I'VE SEEN YOU IN A SUIT. YOU LOOK SO NICE...!
YOU LOOK LIKE A TALK SHOW HOST.
Really? Do you think so?
Ah!
DINNER'S READY. ♡
UH, UM, WHY IS KYO-SAN...?
OH, THAT. BEST TO LEAVE GRUMPY-PUSS ALONE.
I TRICKED HIM INTO TAKING THE ENTRANCE EXAM.
ENTRANCE EXAM?
STARTING TOMORROW, KYO-KUN...
...WILL BE ATTENDING THE SAME HIGH SCHOOL AS YOU TWO. ♡

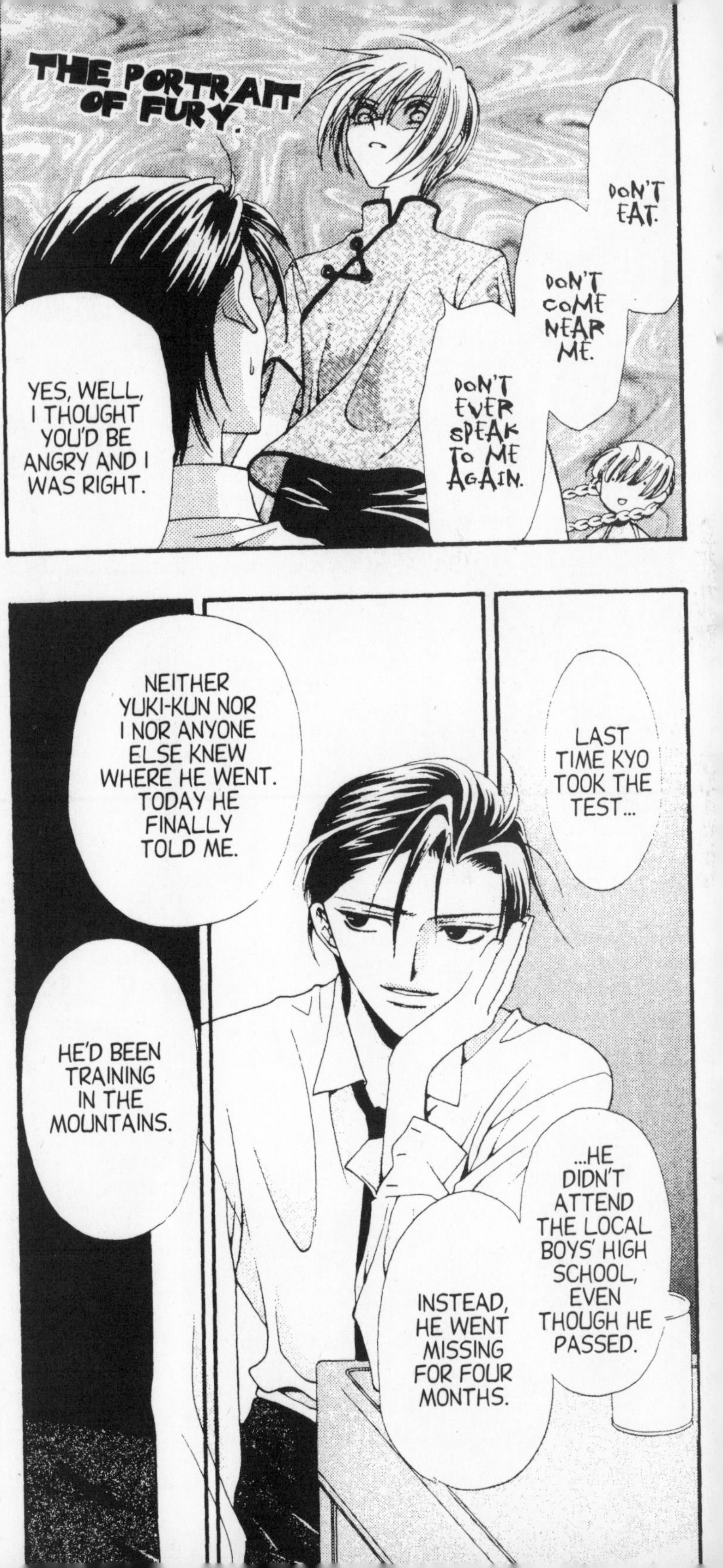
THE PORTRAIT OF FURY.
DON'T EAT.
DON'T COME NEAR ME.
DON'T EVER SPEAK TO ME AGAIN.
YES, WELL, I THOUGHT YOU'D BE ANGRY AND I WAS RIGHT.
LAST TIME KYO TOOK THE TEST...
...HE DIDN'T ATTEND THE LOCAL BOYS' HIGH SCHOOL, EVEN THOUGH HE PASSED.
INSTEAD, HE WENT MISSING FOR FOUR MONTHS.
NEITHER YUKI-KUN NOR I NOR ANYONE ELSE KNEW WHERE HE WENT. TODAY HE FINALLY TOLD ME.
HE'D BEEN TRAINING IN THE MOUNTAINS.

Number 4:

I finished "Romance of the Three Kingdoms," "Black Matrix" and "Pretty League." My characters were so strong that I won all the battles. I'm happy, but a little dramatic tension would've been nice, too (ha ha). I'll finish "Tokyo Friend" soon, too. It's a shame that all the main characters are guys, it would've been nice to play a girl! The one I'm waiting for now is "Teigaku Graph." (K-chan is looking forward to it more than I am.) I'm looking forward to "Knight R." And "Hey You, Pikachu!" Where will I ever find the time? I'll just sleep less! Then faint.

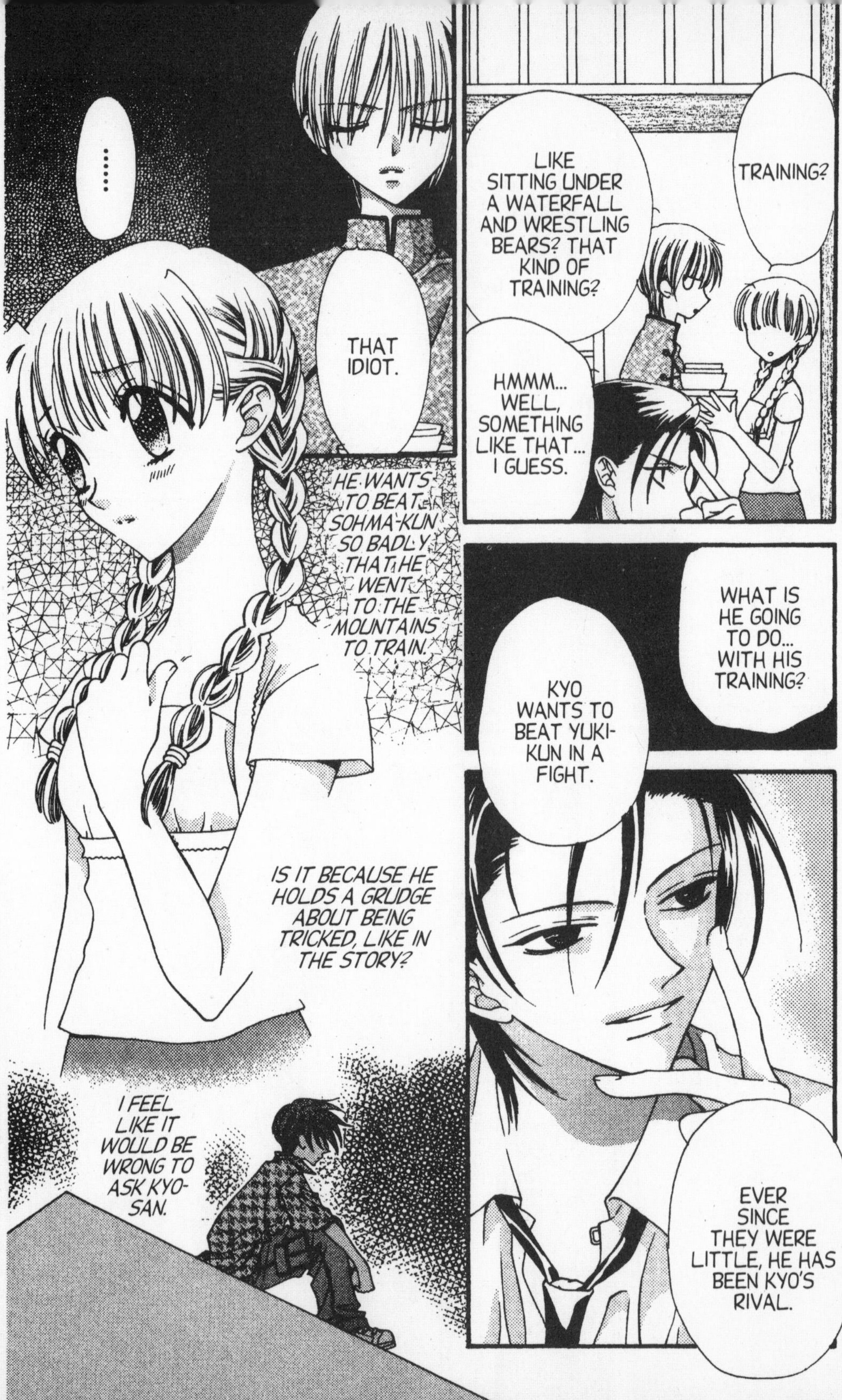
TRAINING?
LIKE SITTING UNDER A WATERFALL AND WRESTLING BEARS? THAT KIND OF TRAINING?
HMMM... WELL, SOMETHING LIKE THAT... I GUESS.
WHAT IS HE GOING TO DO... WITH HIS TRAINING?
KYO WANTS TO BEAT YUKI-KUN IN A FIGHT.
EVER SINCE THEY WERE LITTLE, HE HAS BEEN KYO'S RIVAL.
......
THAT IDIOT.
HE WANTS TO BEAT SOHMA-KUN SO BADLY THAT HE WENT TO THE MOUNTAINS TO TRAIN.
IS IT BECAUSE HE HOLDS A GRUDGE ABOUT BEING TRICKED, LIKE IN THE STORY?
I FEEL LIKE IT WOULD BE WRONG TO ASK KYO-SAN.

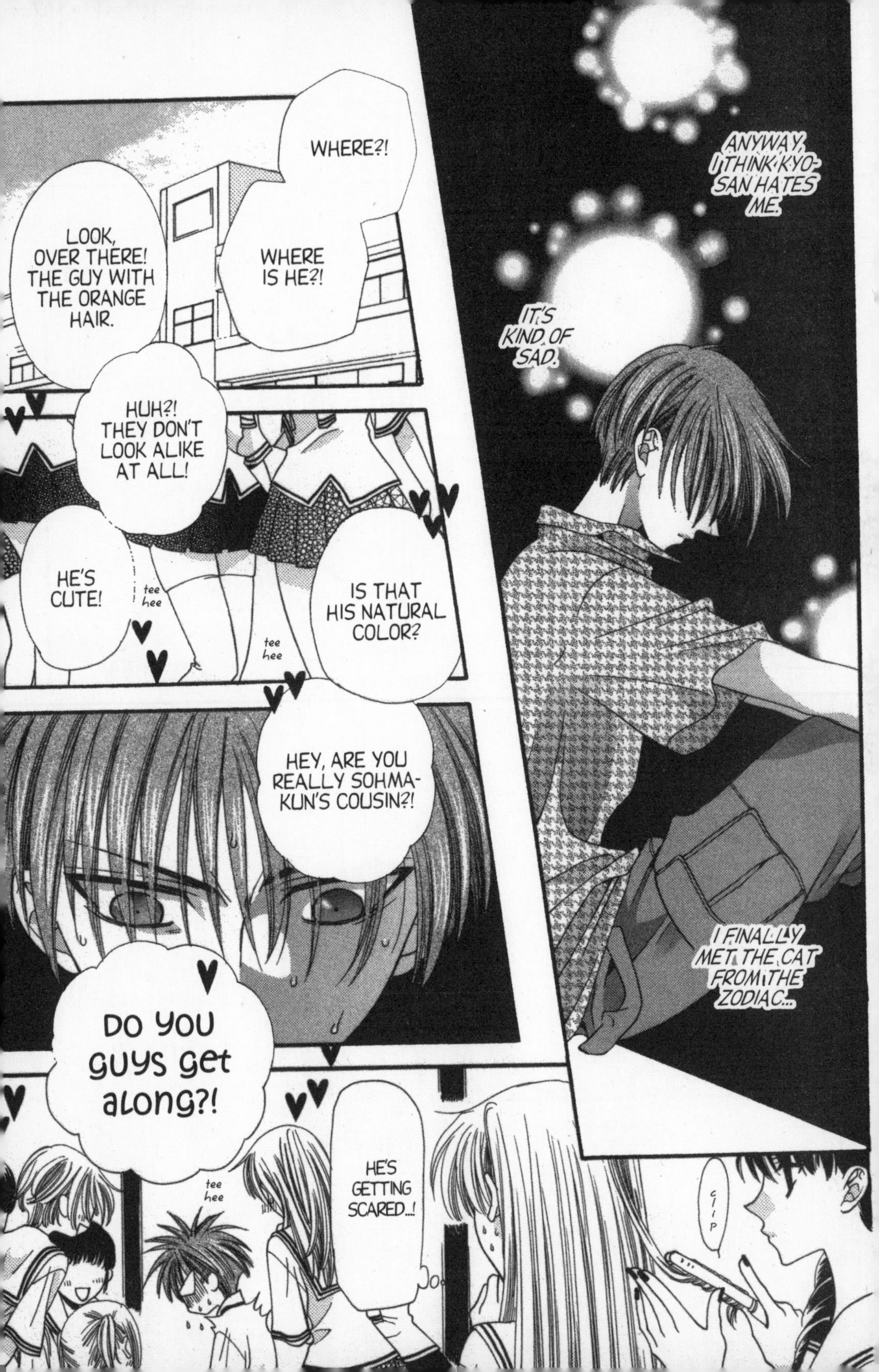
ANYWAY, I THINK KYO-SAN HATES ME.
IT'S KIND OF SAD.
I FINALLY MET THE CAT FROM THE ZODIAC...
WHERE?!
WHERE IS HE?!
LOOK, OVER THERE! THE GUY WITH THE ORANGE HAIR.
HUH?! THEY DON'T LOOK ALIKE AT ALL!
IS THAT HIS NATURAL COLOR?
tee hee
HE'S CUTE!
tee hee
HEY, ARE YOU REALLY SOHMA-KUN'S COUSIN?!
DO YOU GUYS GET ALONG?!
clip
HE'S GETTING SCARED...!
tee hee

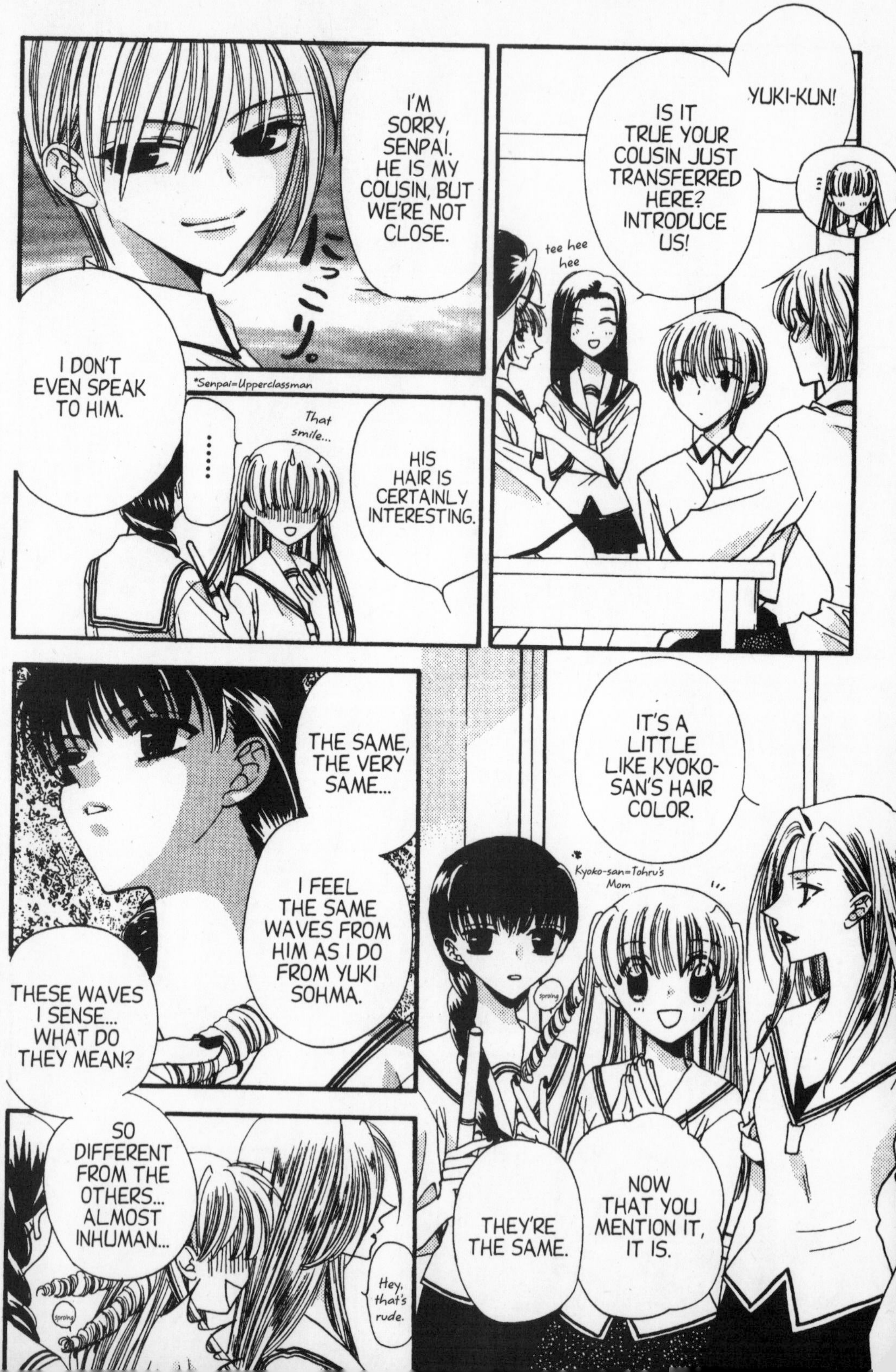
YUKI-KUN!
IS IT TRUE YOUR COUSIN JUST TRANSFERRED HERE? INTRODUCE US!
tee hee hee
I'M SORRY, SENPAI. HE IS MY COUSIN, BUT WE'RE NOT CLOSE.
I DON'T EVEN SPEAK TO HIM.
*Senpai=Upperclassman
HIS HAIR IS CERTAINLY INTERESTING.
That smile...
......
IT'S A LITTLE LIKE KYOKO-SAN'S HAIR COLOR.
Kyoko-san=Tohru's Mom
NOW THAT YOU MENTION IT, IT IS.
THEY'RE THE SAME.
THE SAME, THE VERY SAME...
I FEEL THE SAME WAVES FROM HIM AS I DO FROM YUKI SOHMA.
THESE WAVES I SENSE... WHAT DO THEY MEAN?
SO DIFFERENT FROM THE OTHERS... ALMOST INHUMAN...
Hey, that's rude.

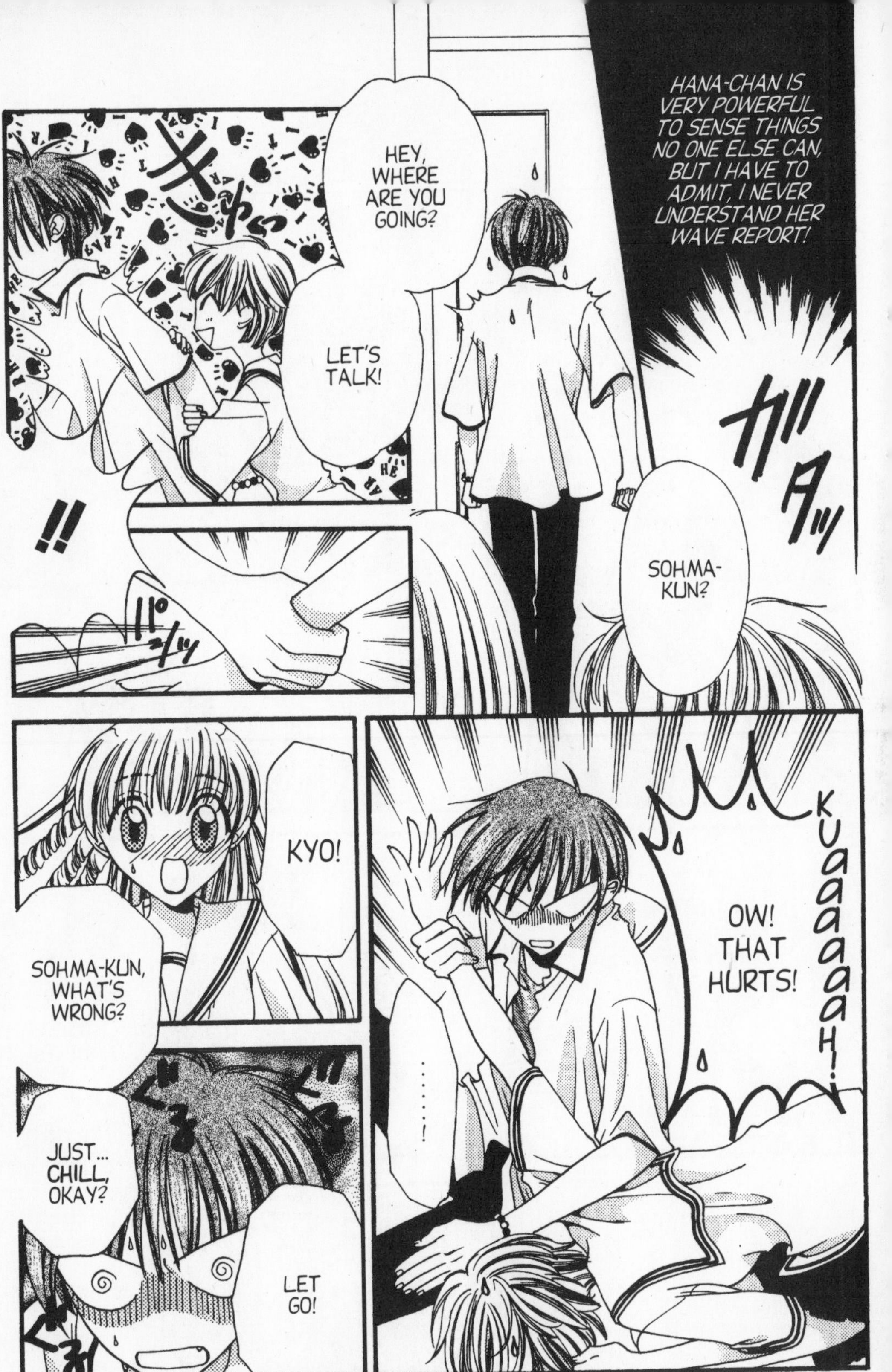

HANA-CHAN IS VERY POWERFUL TO SENSE THINGS NO ONE ELSE CAN, BUT I HAVE TO ADMIT, I NEVER UNDERSTAND HER WAVE REPORT!
SOHMA-KUN?
HEY, WHERE ARE YOU GOING?
LET'S TALK!
!!
KUAAAAAAAH!!
OW! THAT HURTS!
......!
KYO!
SOHMA-KUN, WHAT'S WRONG?
JUST... CHILL, OKAY?
LET GO!

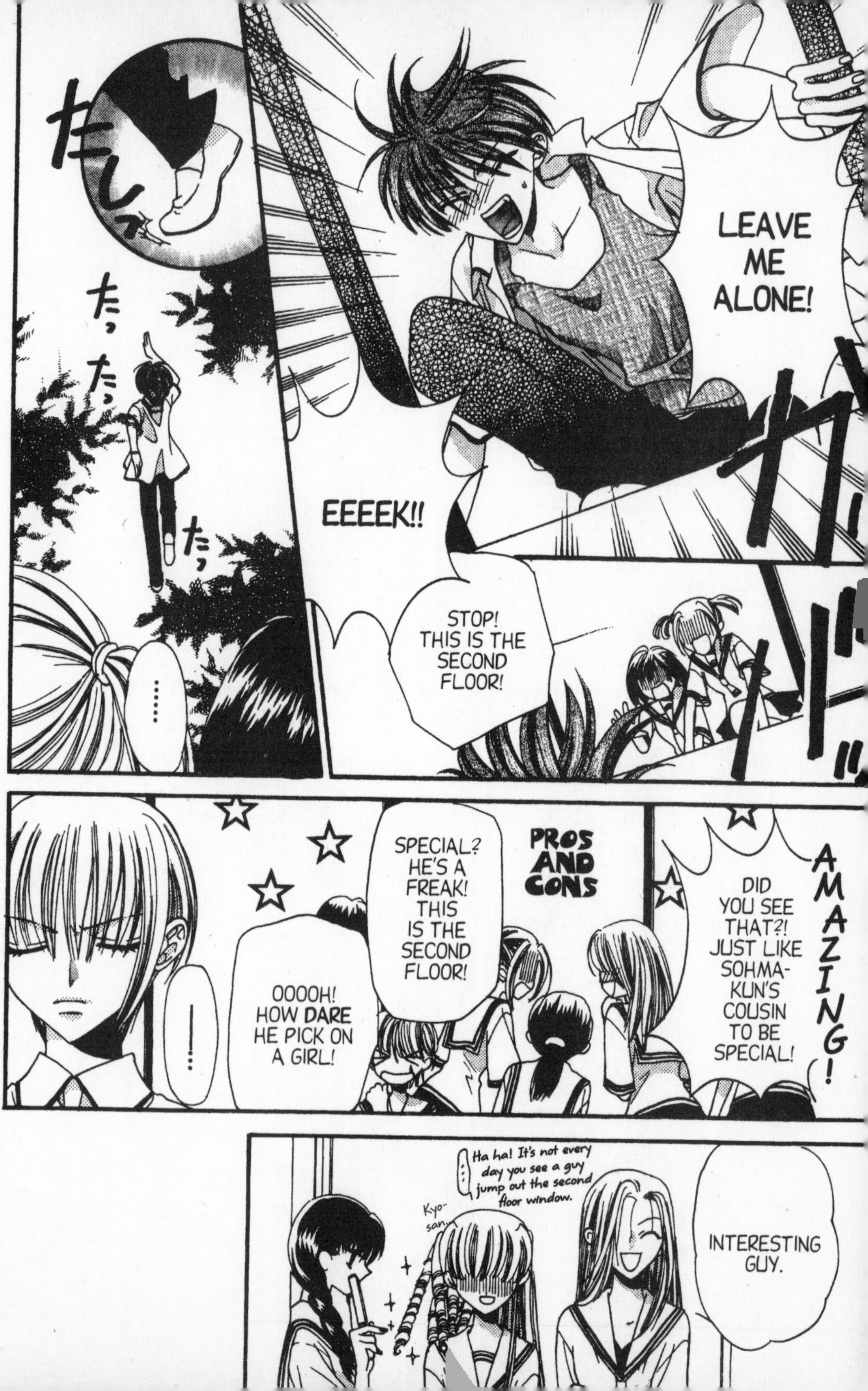
LEAVE ME ALONE!
EEEEK!!
STOP! THIS IS THE SECOND FLOOR!
たしっ
たっ たっ たっ
……
AMAZING!
DID YOU SEE THAT?! JUST LIKE SOHMA-KUN'S COUSIN TO BE SPECIAL!
PROS AND CONS
SPECIAL? HE'S A FREAK! THIS IS THE SECOND FLOOR!
OOOOH! HOW DARE HE PICK ON A GIRL!
……!
INTERESTING GUY.
Ha ha! It's not every day you see a guy jump out the second floor window.
…
Kyo-san…

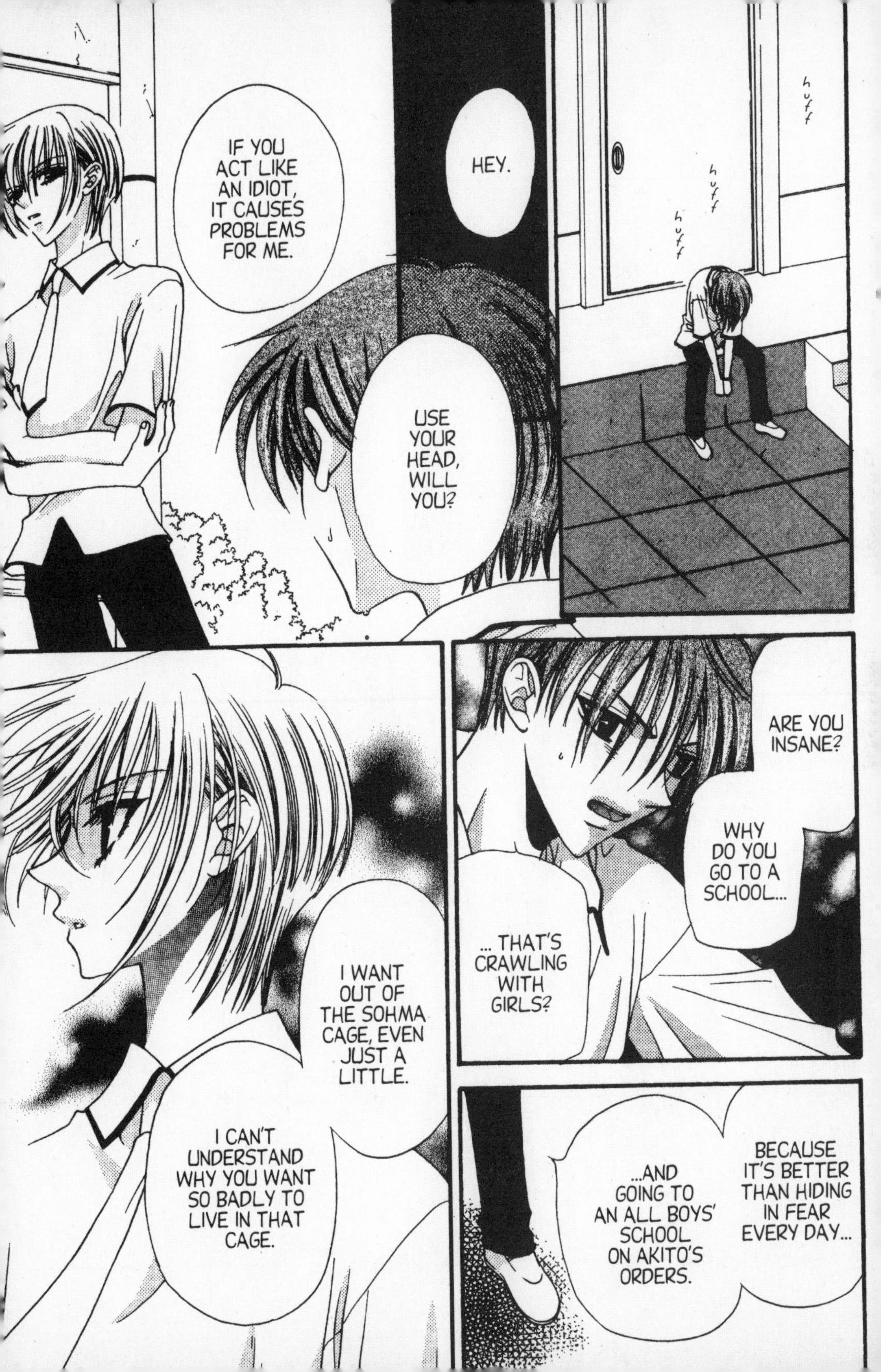
huff huff huff
HEY.
USE YOUR HEAD, WILL YOU?
IF YOU ACT LIKE AN IDIOT, IT CAUSES PROBLEMS FOR ME.
ARE YOU INSANE?
WHY DO YOU GO TO A SCHOOL...
... THAT'S CRAWLING WITH GIRLS?
BECAUSE IT'S BETTER THAN HIDING IN FEAR EVERY DAY...
...AND GOING TO AN ALL BOYS' SCHOOL ON AKITO'S ORDERS.
I WANT OUT OF THE SOHMA CAGE, EVEN JUST A LITTLE.
I CAN'T UNDERSTAND WHY YOU WANT SO BADLY TO LIVE IN THAT CAGE.

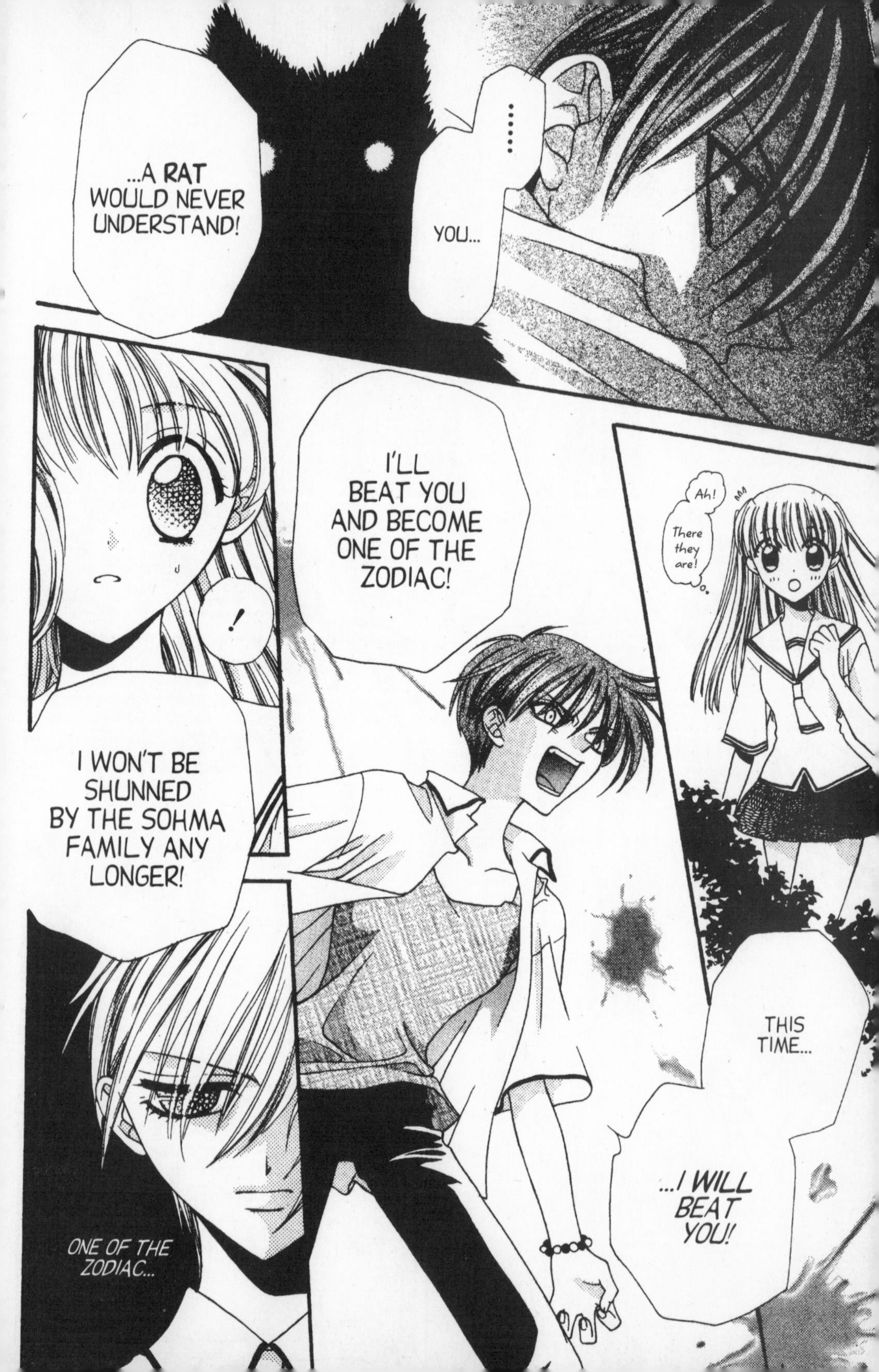
......
YOU...
...A RAT WOULD NEVER UNDERSTAND!
Ah!
There they are!
I'LL BEAT YOU AND BECOME ONE OF THE ZODIAC!
!
I WON'T BE SHUNNED BY THE SOHMA FAMILY ANY LONGER!
THIS TIME...
...I WILL BEAT YOU!
ONE OF THE ZODIAC...

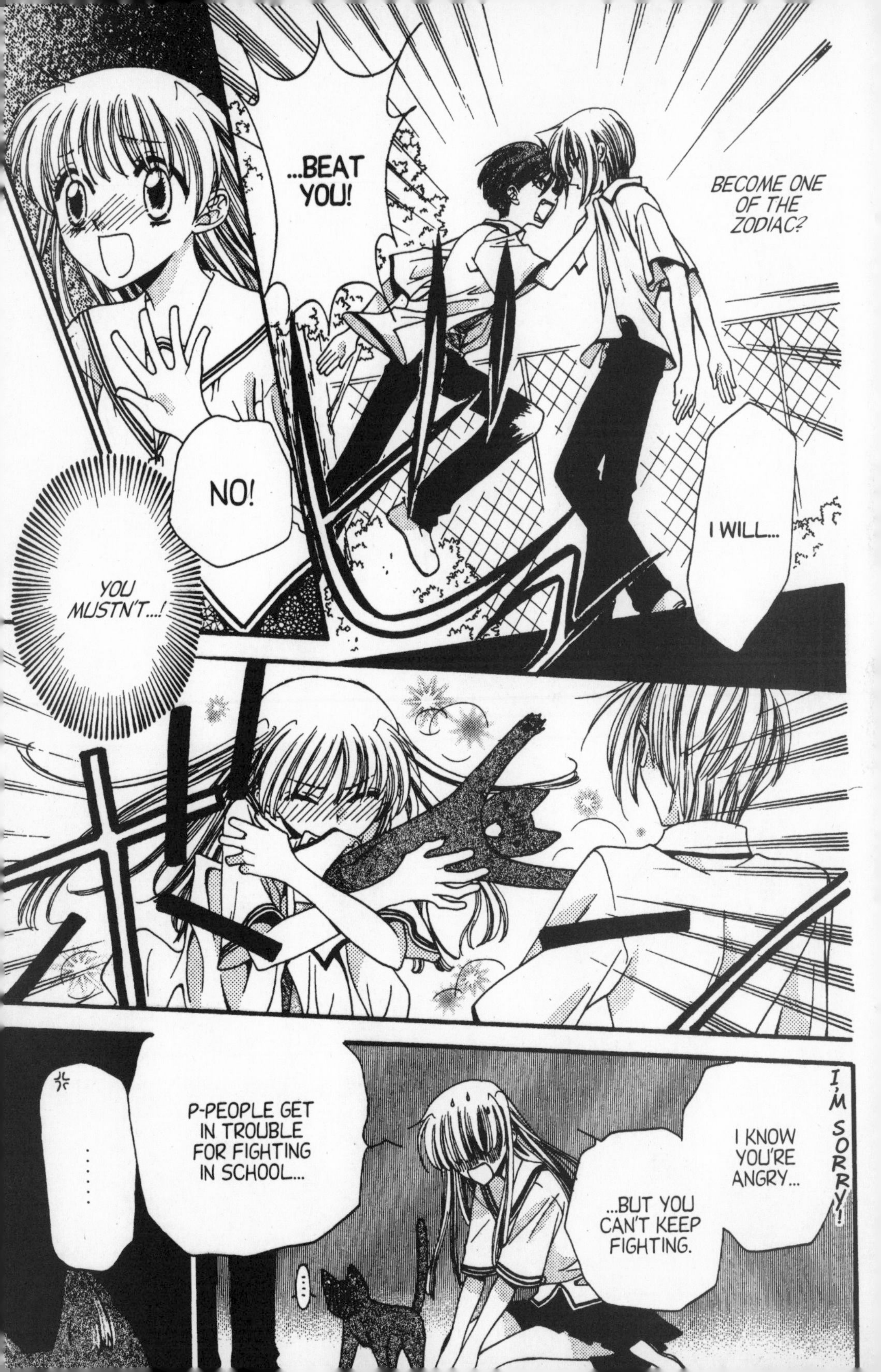
BECOME ONE OF THE ZODIAC?
I WILL...
...BEAT YOU!
NO!
YOU MUSTN'T...!
I'M SORRY!
I KNOW YOU'RE ANGRY...
...BUT YOU CAN'T KEEP FIGHTING.
P-PEOPLE GET IN TROUBLE FOR FIGHTING IN SCHOOL...
......
...

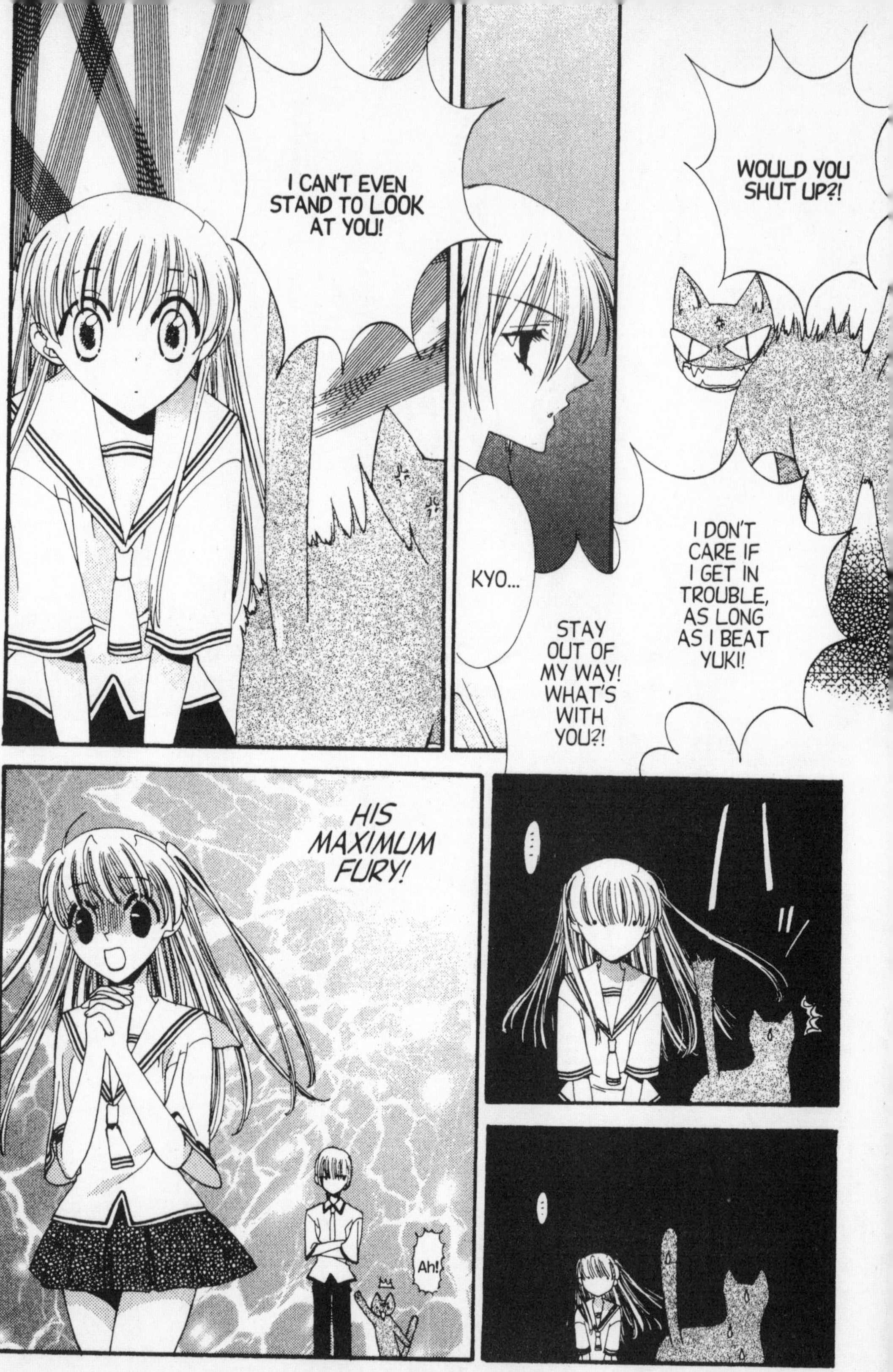
WOULD YOU SHUT UP?!
I DON'T CARE IF I GET IN TROUBLE, AS LONG AS I BEAT YUKI!
KYO...
STAY OUT OF MY WAY! WHAT'S WITH YOU?!
I CAN'T EVEN STAND TO LOOK AT YOU!
...
...
HIS MAXIMUM FURY!
Ah!

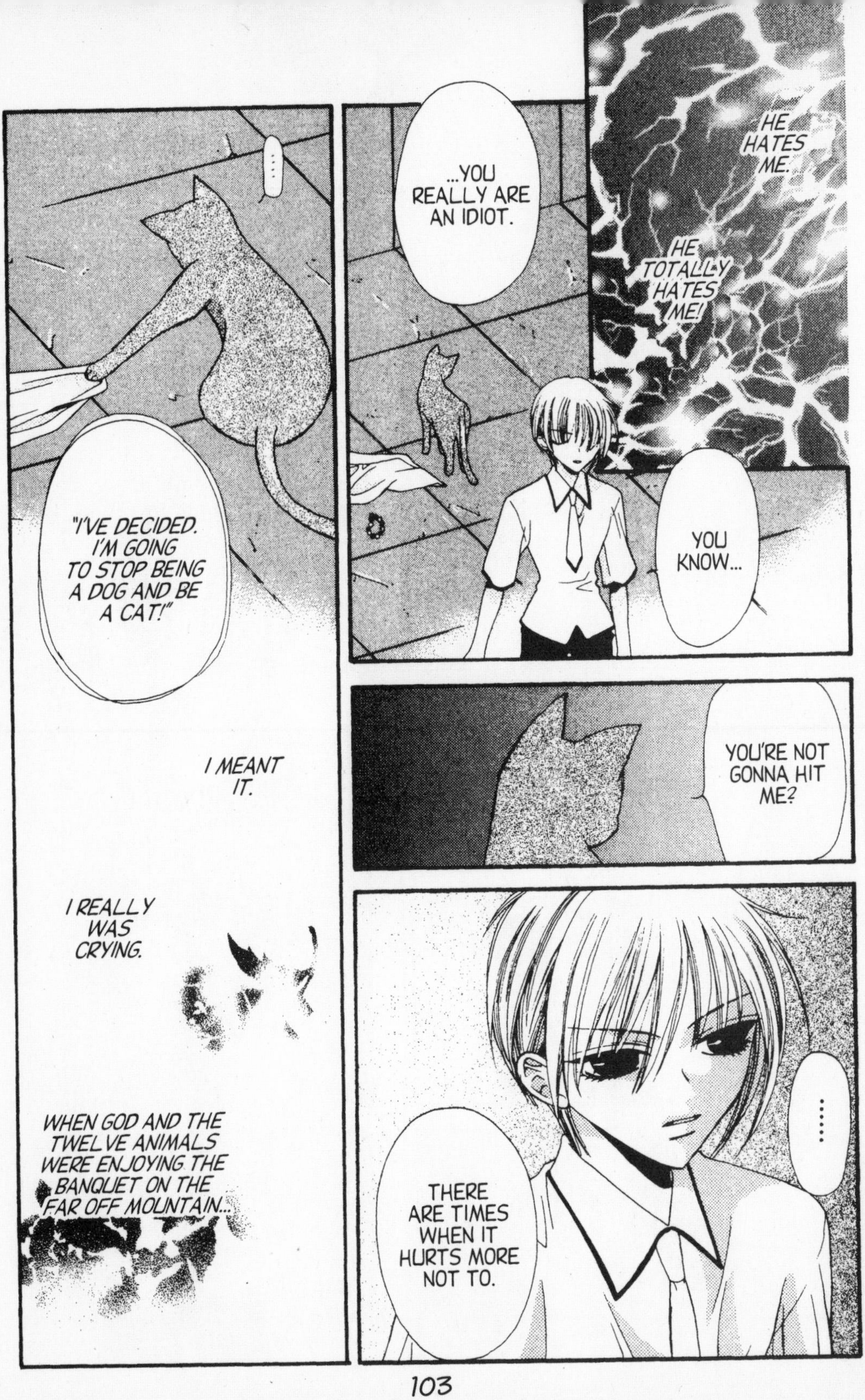
HE HATES ME.
HE TOTALLY HATES ME!
YOU KNOW...
...YOU REALLY ARE AN IDIOT.
YOU'RE NOT GONNA HIT ME?
......
THERE ARE TIMES WHEN IT HURTS MORE NOT TO.
....
"I'VE DECIDED. I'M GOING TO STOP BEING A DOG AND BE A CAT!"
I MEANT IT.
I REALLY WAS CRYING.
WHEN GOD AND THE TWELVE ANIMALS WERE ENJOYING THE BANQUET ON THE FAR OFF MOUNTAIN...

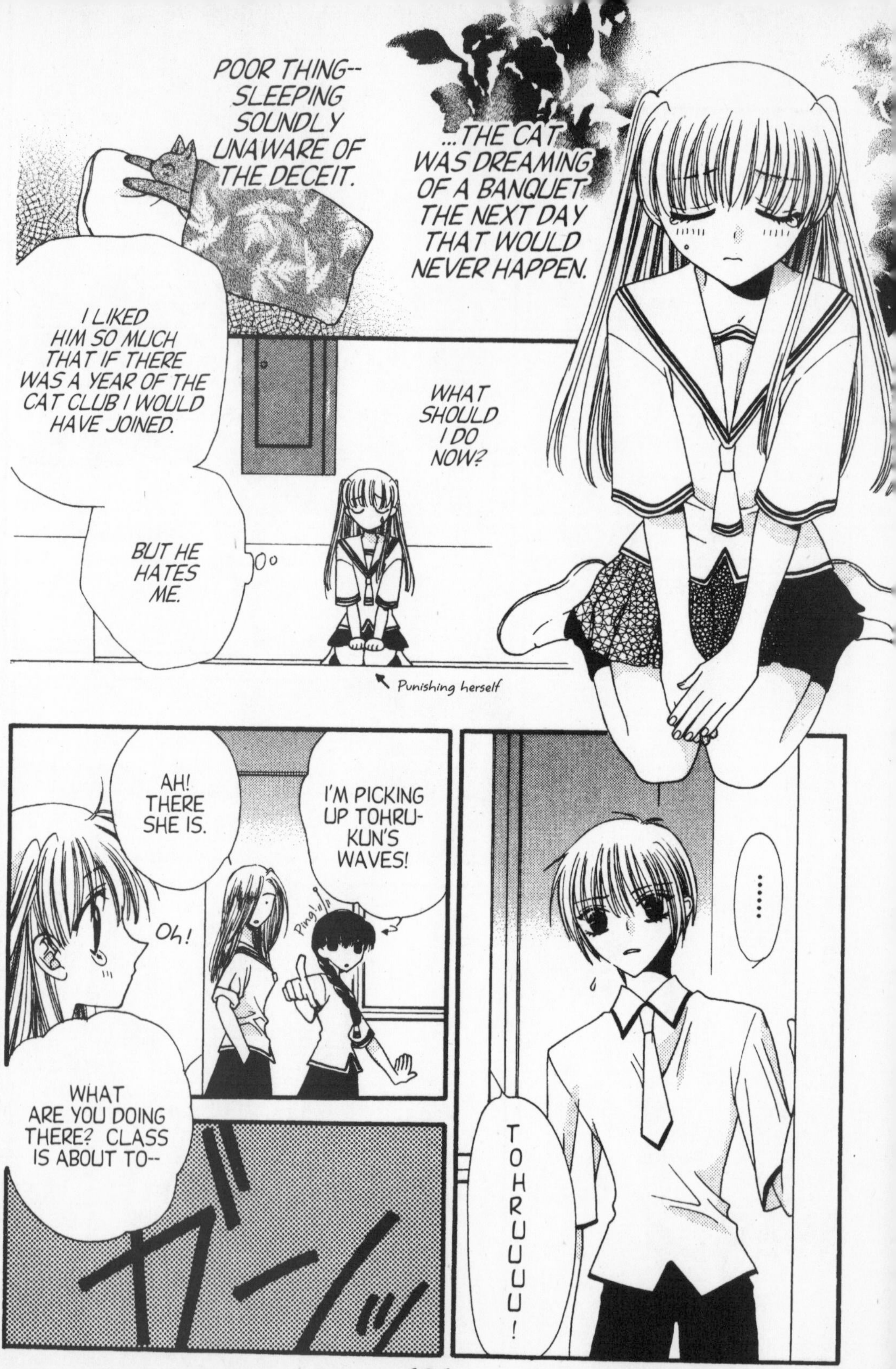
...THE CAT WAS DREAMING OF A BANQUET THE NEXT DAY THAT WOULD NEVER HAPPEN.
POOR THING-- SLEEPING SOUNDLY UNAWARE OF THE DECEIT.
WHAT SHOULD I DO NOW?
I LIKED HIM SO MUCH THAT IF THERE WAS A YEAR OF THE CAT CLUB I WOULD HAVE JOINED.
BUT HE HATES ME.
Punishing herself
......
TOHRUUUU!
I'M PICKING UP TOHRU-KUN'S WAVES!
Ping!
AH! THERE SHE IS.
Oh!
WHAT ARE YOU DOING THERE? CLASS IS ABOUT TO--

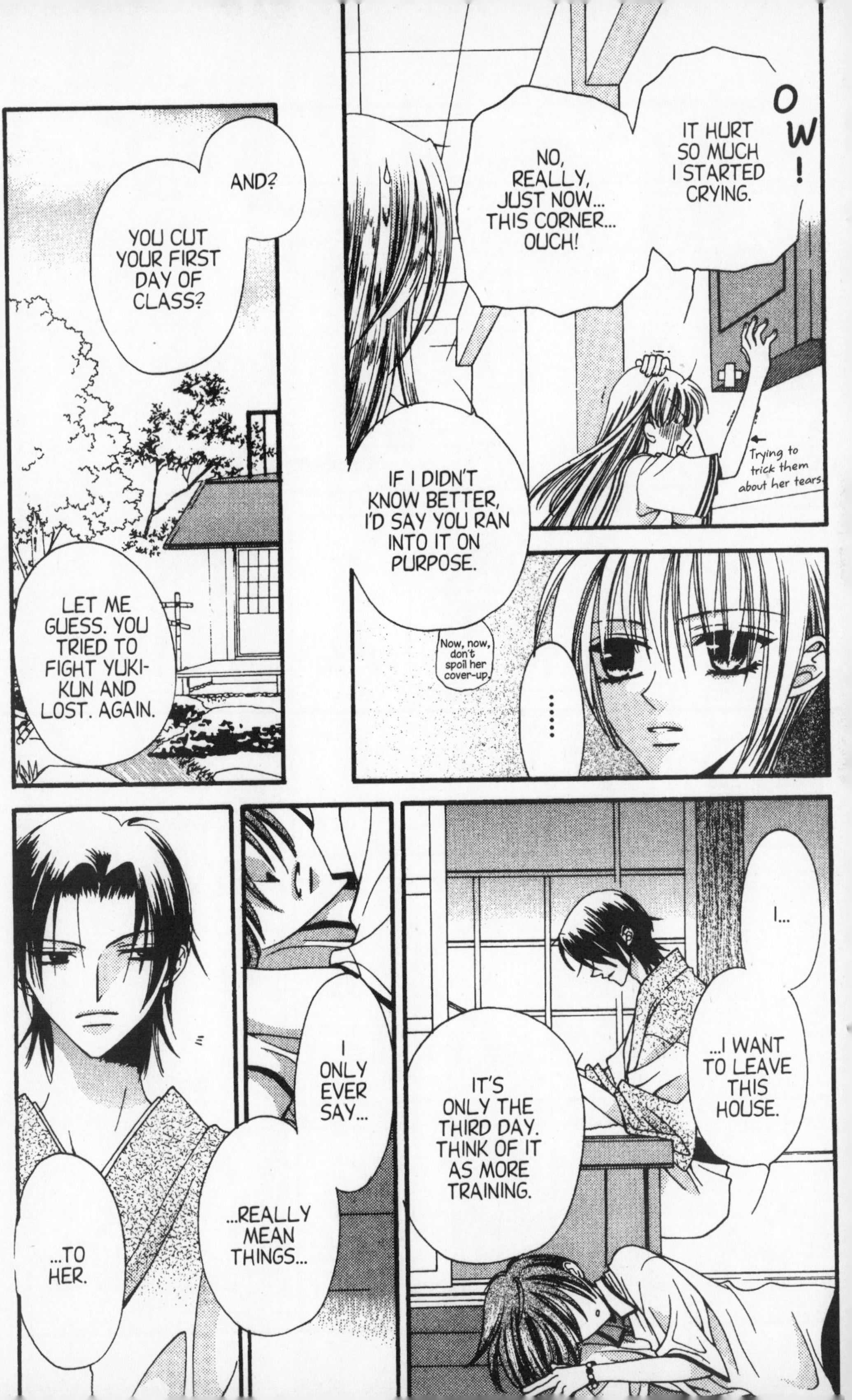
OW!
IT HURT SO MUCH I STARTED CRYING.
NO, REALLY, JUST NOW... THIS CORNER... OUCH!
Trying to trick them about her tears.
IF I DIDN'T KNOW BETTER, I'D SAY YOU RAN INTO IT ON PURPOSE.
......
Now, now, don't spoil her cover-up.
AND?
YOU CUT YOUR FIRST DAY OF CLASS?
LET ME GUESS. YOU TRIED TO FIGHT YUKI-KUN AND LOST. AGAIN.
I...
...I WANT TO LEAVE THIS HOUSE.
IT'S ONLY THE THIRD DAY. THINK OF IT AS MORE TRAINING.
I ONLY EVER SAY...
...REALLY MEAN THINGS...
...TO HER.

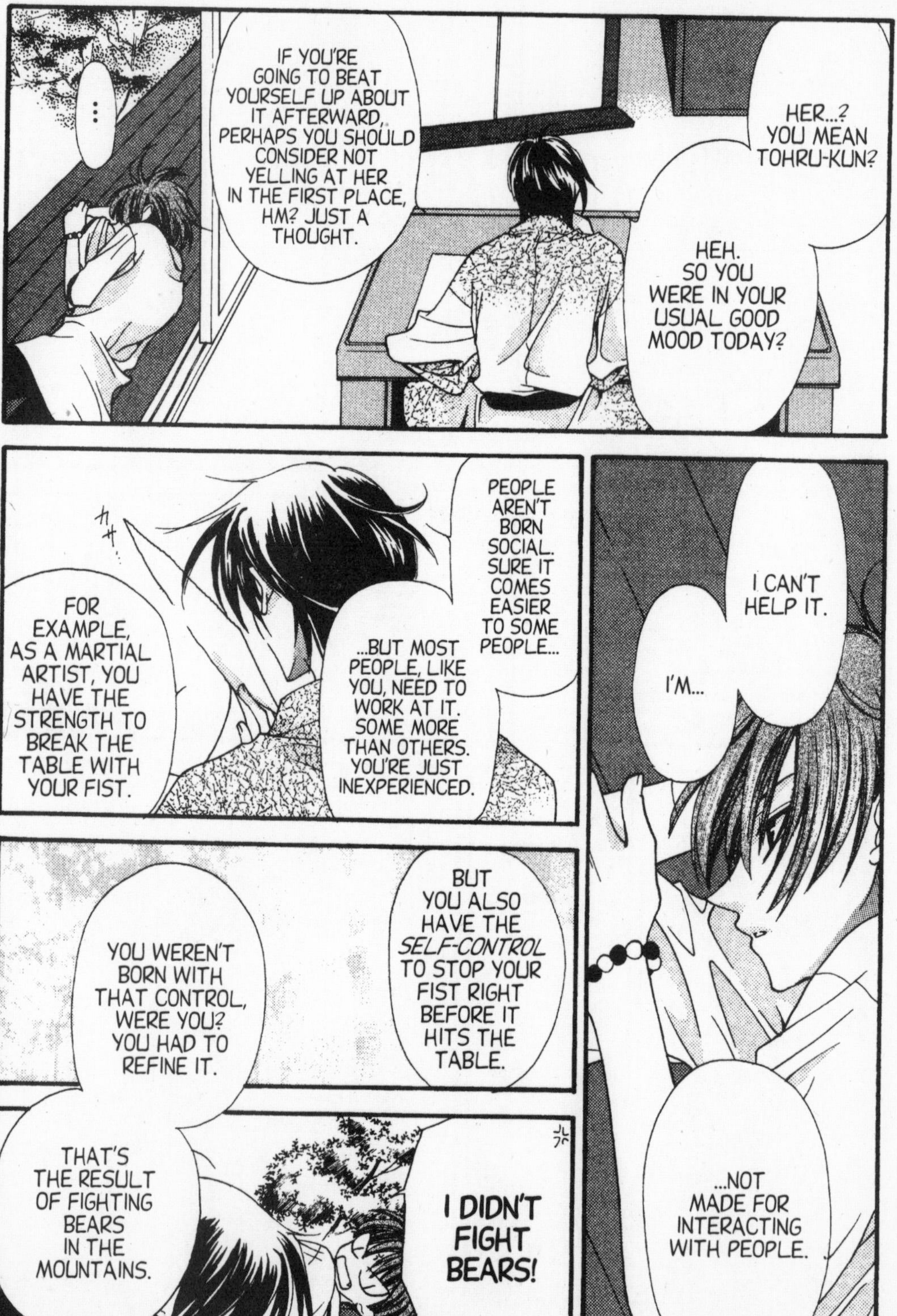

HER...? YOU MEAN TOHRU-KUN?
HEH. SO YOU WERE IN YOUR USUAL GOOD MOOD TODAY?
IF YOU'RE GOING TO BEAT YOURSELF UP ABOUT IT AFTERWARD, PERHAPS YOU SHOULD CONSIDER NOT YELLING AT HER IN THE FIRST PLACE, HM? JUST A THOUGHT.
...
I CAN'T HELP IT.
I'M...
...NOT MADE FOR INTERACTING WITH PEOPLE.
PEOPLE AREN'T BORN SOCIAL. SURE IT COMES EASIER TO SOME PEOPLE...
...BUT MOST PEOPLE, LIKE YOU, NEED TO WORK AT IT. SOME MORE THAN OTHERS. YOU'RE JUST INEXPERIENCED.
FOR EXAMPLE, AS A MARTIAL ARTIST, YOU HAVE THE STRENGTH TO BREAK THE TABLE WITH YOUR FIST.
BUT YOU ALSO HAVE THE *SELF-CONTROL* TO STOP YOUR FIST RIGHT BEFORE IT HITS THE TABLE.
YOU WEREN'T BORN WITH THAT CONTROL, WERE YOU? YOU HAD TO REFINE IT.
THAT'S THE RESULT OF FIGHTING BEARS IN THE MOUNTAINS.
I DIDN'T FIGHT BEARS!

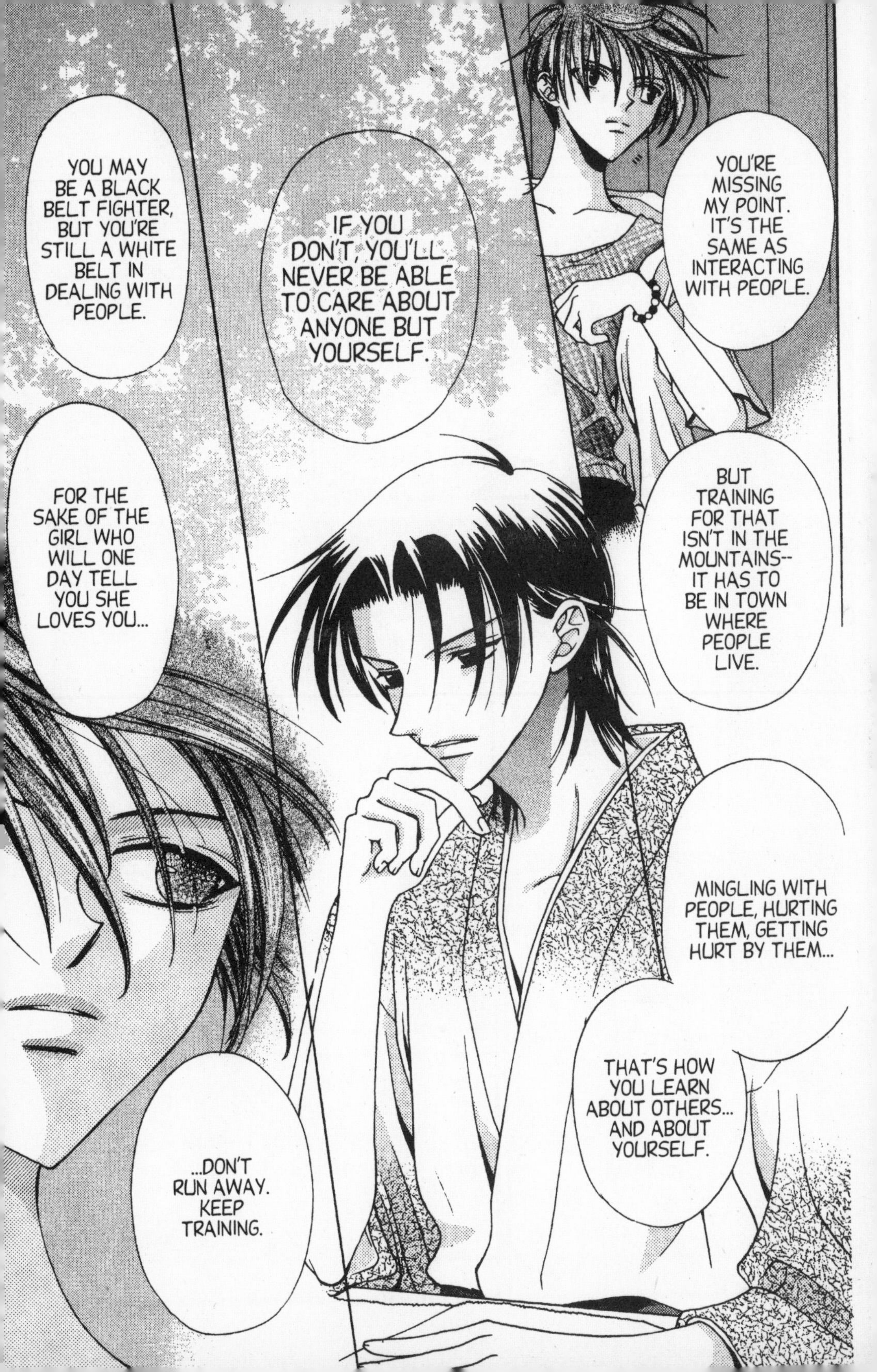

YOU'RE MISSING MY POINT. IT'S THE SAME AS INTERACTING WITH PEOPLE.
BUT TRAINING FOR THAT ISN'T IN THE MOUNTAINS-- IT HAS TO BE IN TOWN WHERE PEOPLE LIVE.
MINGLING WITH PEOPLE, HURTING THEM, GETTING HURT BY THEM...
THAT'S HOW YOU LEARN ABOUT OTHERS... AND ABOUT YOURSELF.
IF YOU DON'T, YOU'LL NEVER BE ABLE TO CARE ABOUT ANYONE BUT YOURSELF.
YOU MAY BE A BLACK BELT FIGHTER, BUT YOU'RE STILL A WHITE BELT IN DEALING WITH PEOPLE.
FOR THE SAKE OF THE GIRL WHO WILL ONE DAY TELL YOU SHE LOVES YOU...
...DON'T RUN AWAY. KEEP TRAINING.

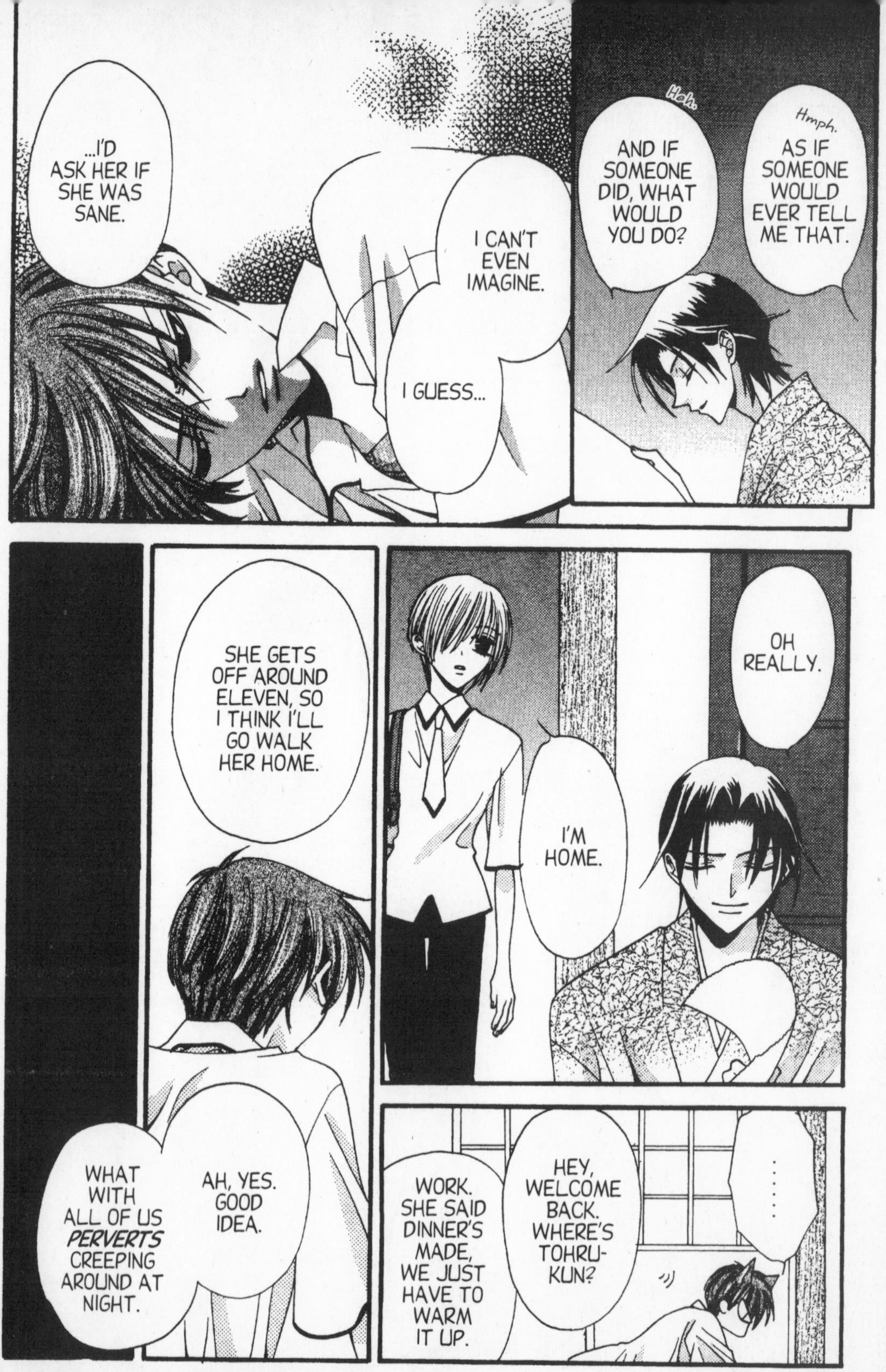
Hmph.
AS IF SOMEONE WOULD EVER TELL ME THAT.
Heh.
AND IF SOMEONE DID, WHAT WOULD YOU DO?
I CAN'T EVEN IMAGINE.
I GUESS...
...I'D ASK HER IF SHE WAS SANE.
OH REALLY.
I'M HOME.
.....
HEY, WELCOME BACK. WHERE'S TOHRU-KUN?
WORK. SHE SAID DINNER'S MADE, WE JUST HAVE TO WARM IT UP.
SHE GETS OFF AROUND ELEVEN, SO I THINK I'LL GO WALK HER HOME.
AH, YES. GOOD IDEA.
WHAT WITH ALL OF US *PERVERTS* CREEPING AROUND AT NIGHT.

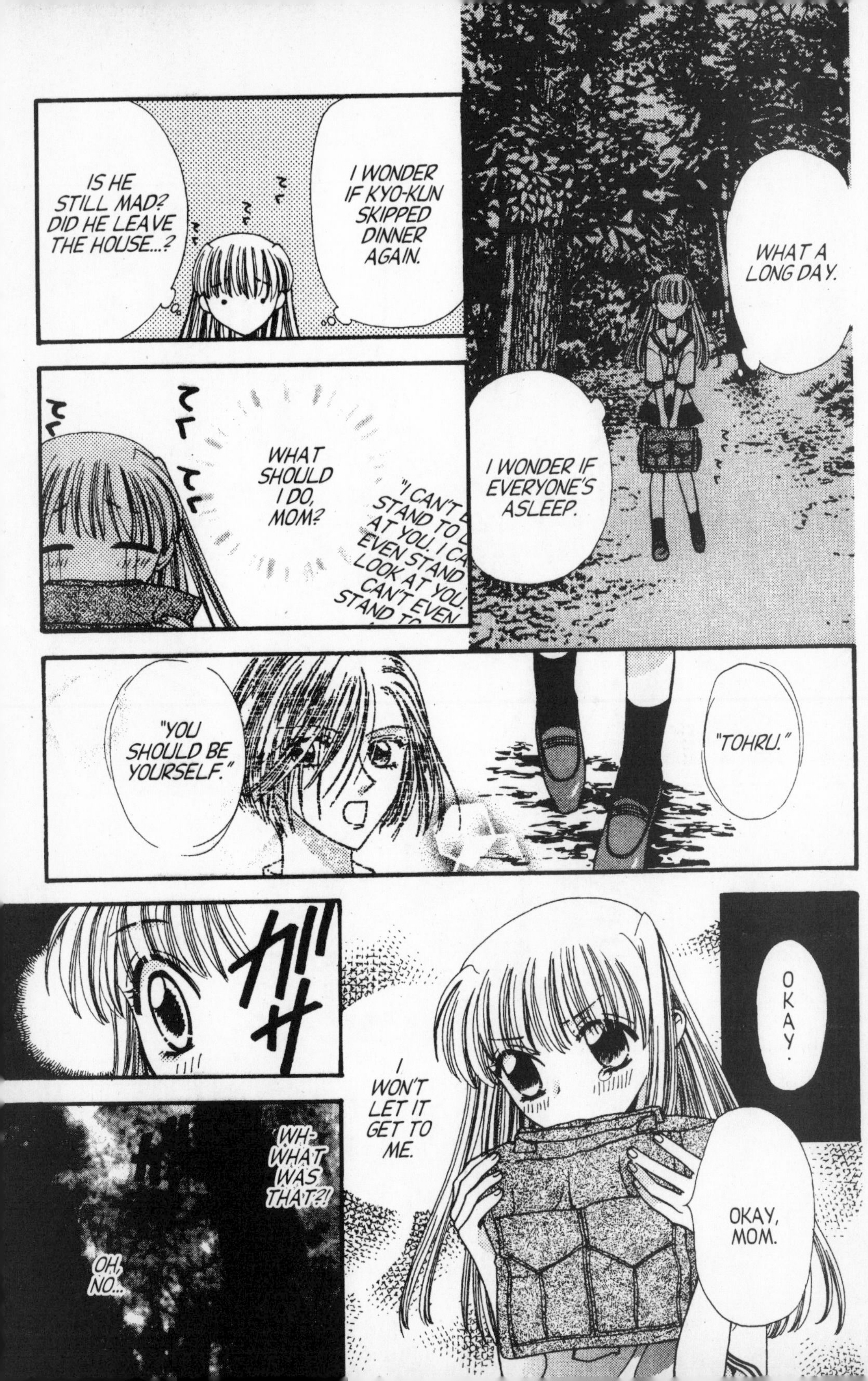
WHAT A LONG DAY.
I WONDER IF EVERYONE'S ASLEEP.
I WONDER IF KYO-KUN SKIPPED DINNER AGAIN.
IS HE STILL MAD? DID HE LEAVE THE HOUSE...?
WHAT SHOULD I DO, MOM?
"I CAN'T E STAND TO L AT YOU. I CA EVEN STAND LOOK AT YOU. CAN'T EVEN STAND TO
"TOHRU."
"YOU SHOULD BE YOURSELF."
OKAY.
I WON'T LET IT GET TO ME.
OKAY, MOM.
ガサ
WH-WHAT WAS THAT?!
OH, NO...

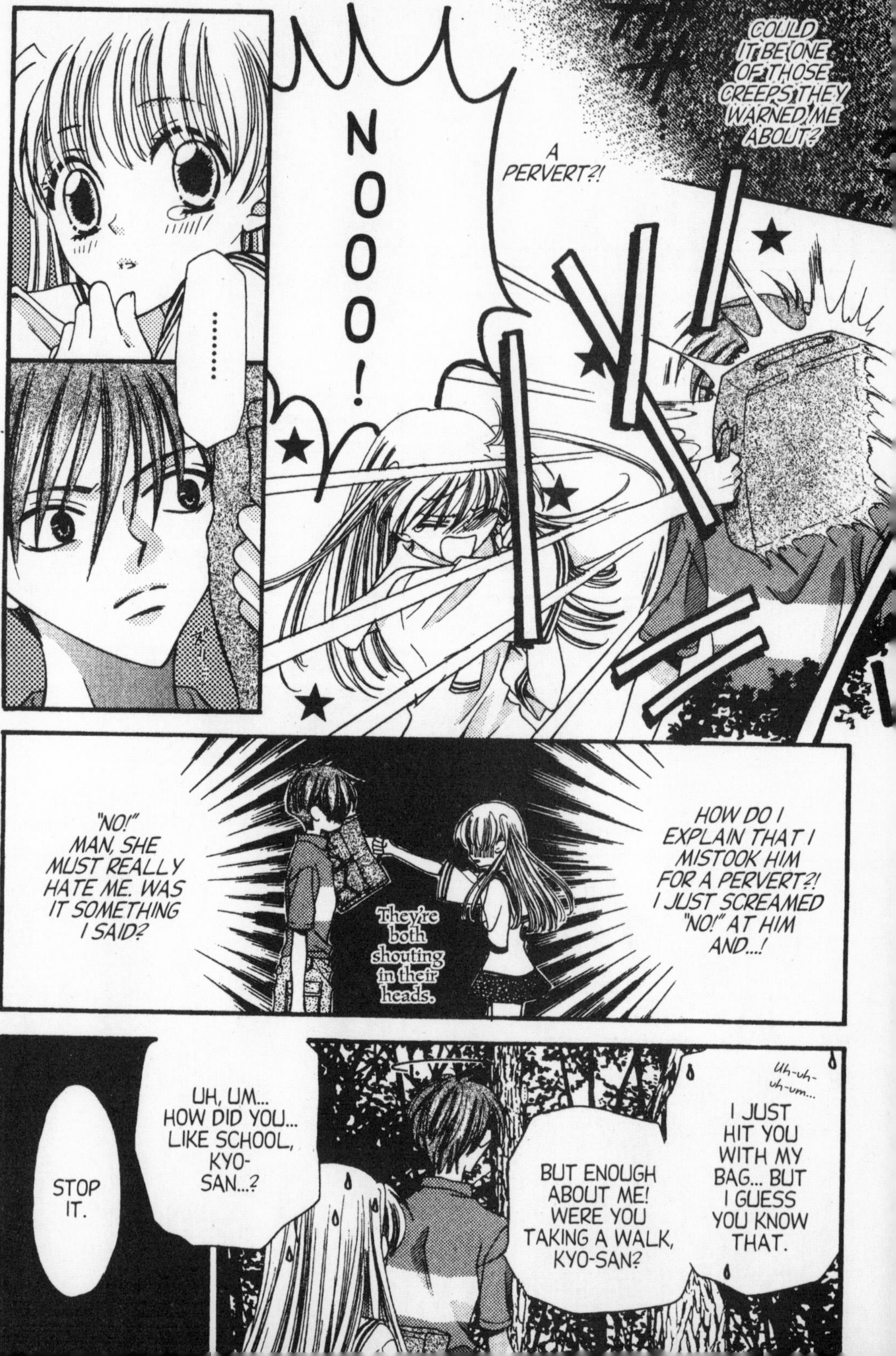
COULD IT BE ONE OF THOSE CREEPS THEY WARNED ME ABOUT?
A PERVERT?!
NOOOO!
......
HOW DO I EXPLAIN THAT I MISTOOK HIM FOR A PERVERT?! I JUST SCREAMED "NO!" AT HIM AND...!
"NO!" MAN, SHE MUST REALLY HATE ME. WAS IT SOMETHING I SAID?
They're both shouting in their heads.
uh-uh-uh-um...
I JUST HIT YOU WITH MY BAG... BUT I GUESS YOU KNOW THAT.
BUT ENOUGH ABOUT ME! WERE YOU TAKING A WALK, KYO-SAN?
UH, UM... HOW DID YOU... LIKE SCHOOL, KYO-SAN...?
STOP IT.

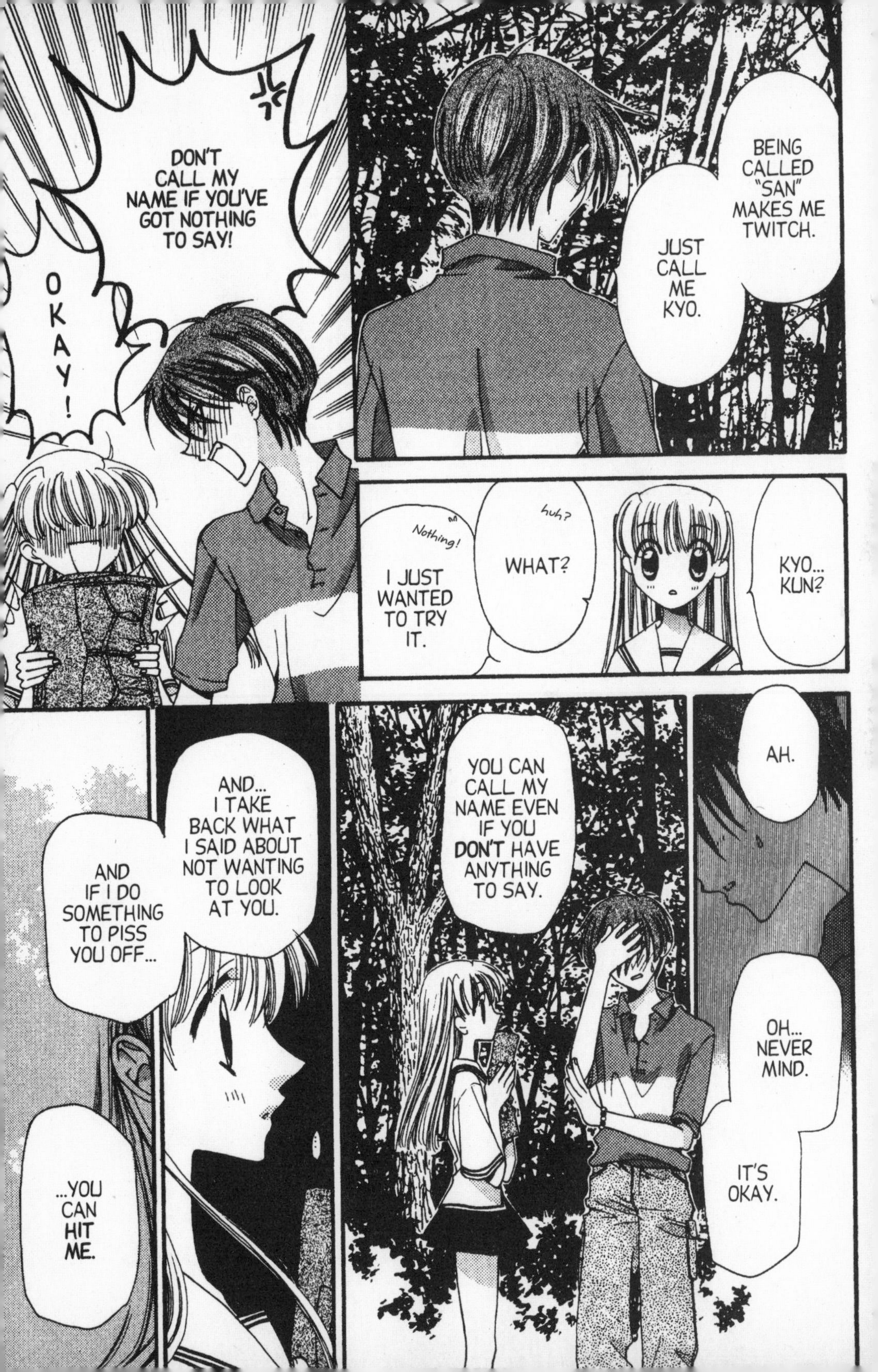
BEING CALLED "SAN" MAKES ME TWITCH.
JUST CALL ME KYO.
KYO... KUN?
huh?
WHAT?
Nothing!
I JUST WANTED TO TRY IT.
DON'T CALL MY NAME IF YOU'VE GOT NOTHING TO SAY!
OKAY!
AH.
OH... NEVER MIND.
IT'S OKAY.
YOU CAN CALL MY NAME EVEN IF YOU DON'T HAVE ANYTHING TO SAY.
AND... I TAKE BACK WHAT I SAID ABOUT NOT WANTING TO LOOK AT YOU.
AND IF I DO SOMETHING TO PISS YOU OFF...
...YOU CAN HIT ME.

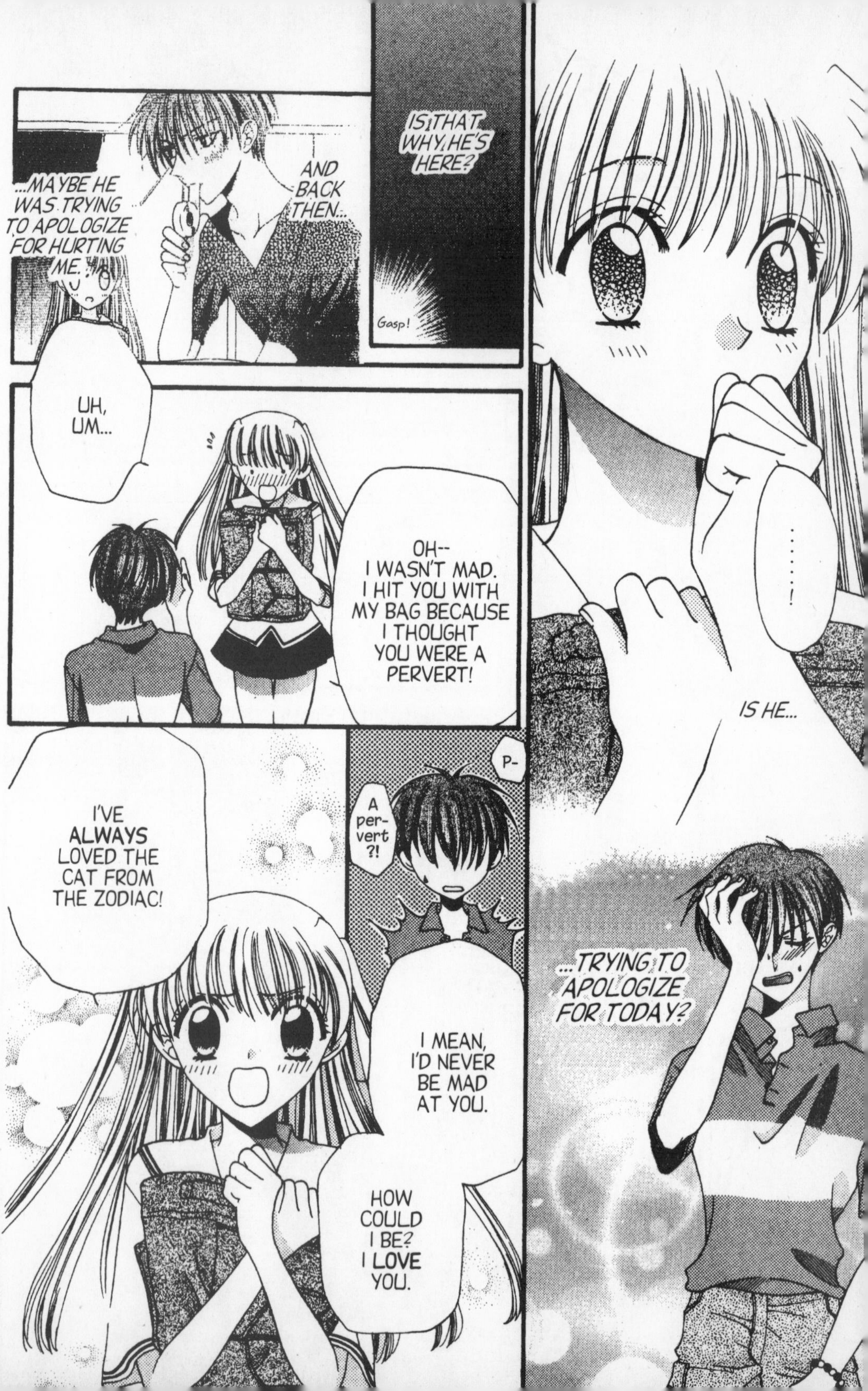
......!
IS HE...
...TRYING TO APOLOGIZE FOR TODAY?
IS THAT WHY HE'S HERE?
Gasp!
AND BACK THEN...
...MAYBE HE WAS TRYING TO APOLOGIZE FOR HURTING ME.
UH, UM...
OH-- I WASN'T MAD. I HIT YOU WITH MY BAG BECAUSE I THOUGHT YOU WERE A PERVERT!
P-
A per-vert?!
I MEAN, I'D NEVER BE MAD AT YOU.
HOW COULD I BE? I **LOVE** YOU.
I'VE **ALWAYS** LOVED THE CAT FROM THE ZODIAC!

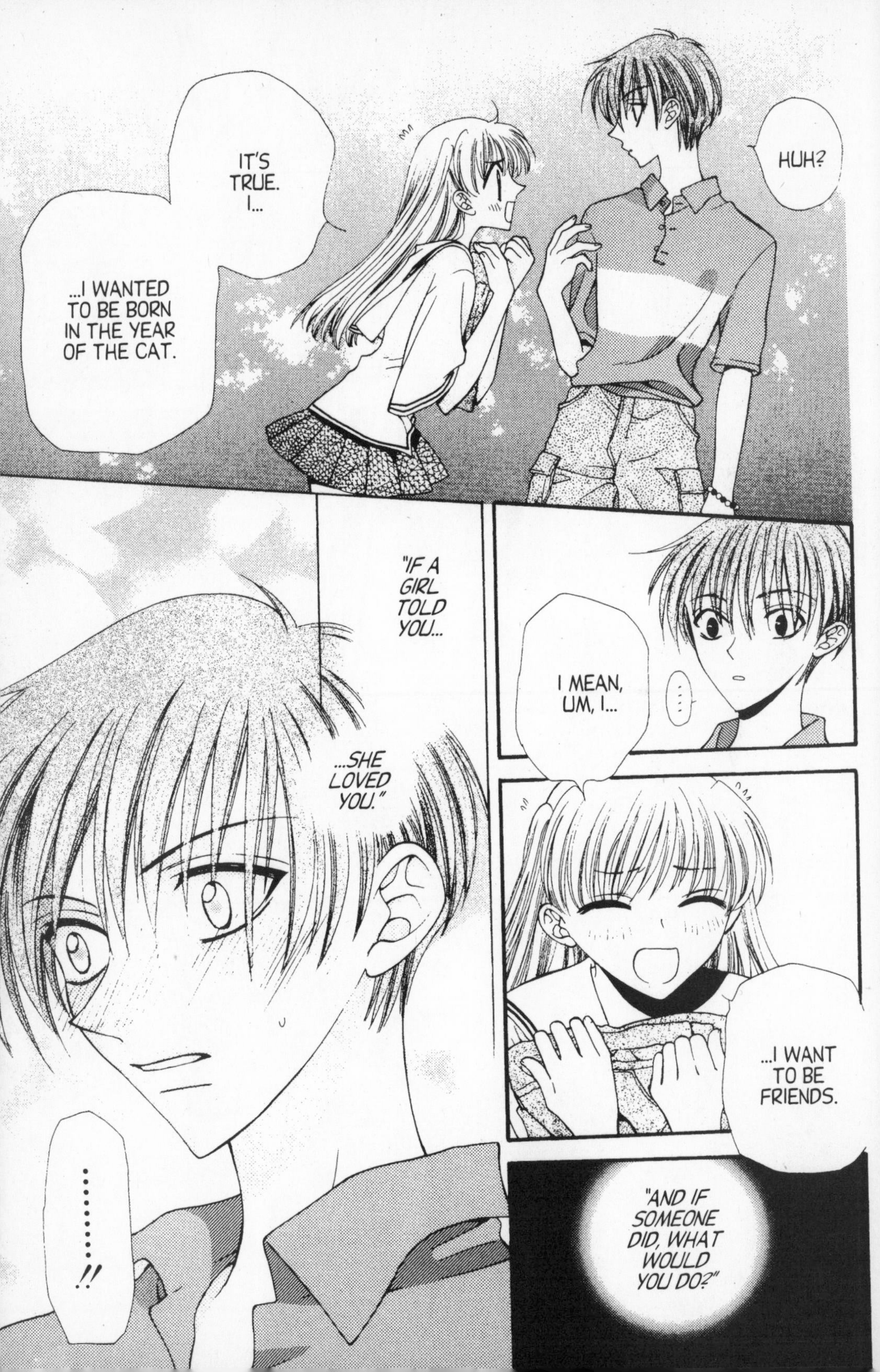
HUH?
IT'S TRUE. I...
...I WANTED TO BE BORN IN THE YEAR OF THE CAT.
...
I MEAN, UM, I...
...I WANT TO BE FRIENDS.
"AND IF SOMEONE DID, WHAT WOULD YOU DO?"
"IF A GIRL TOLD YOU...
...SHE LOVED YOU."
.......!!

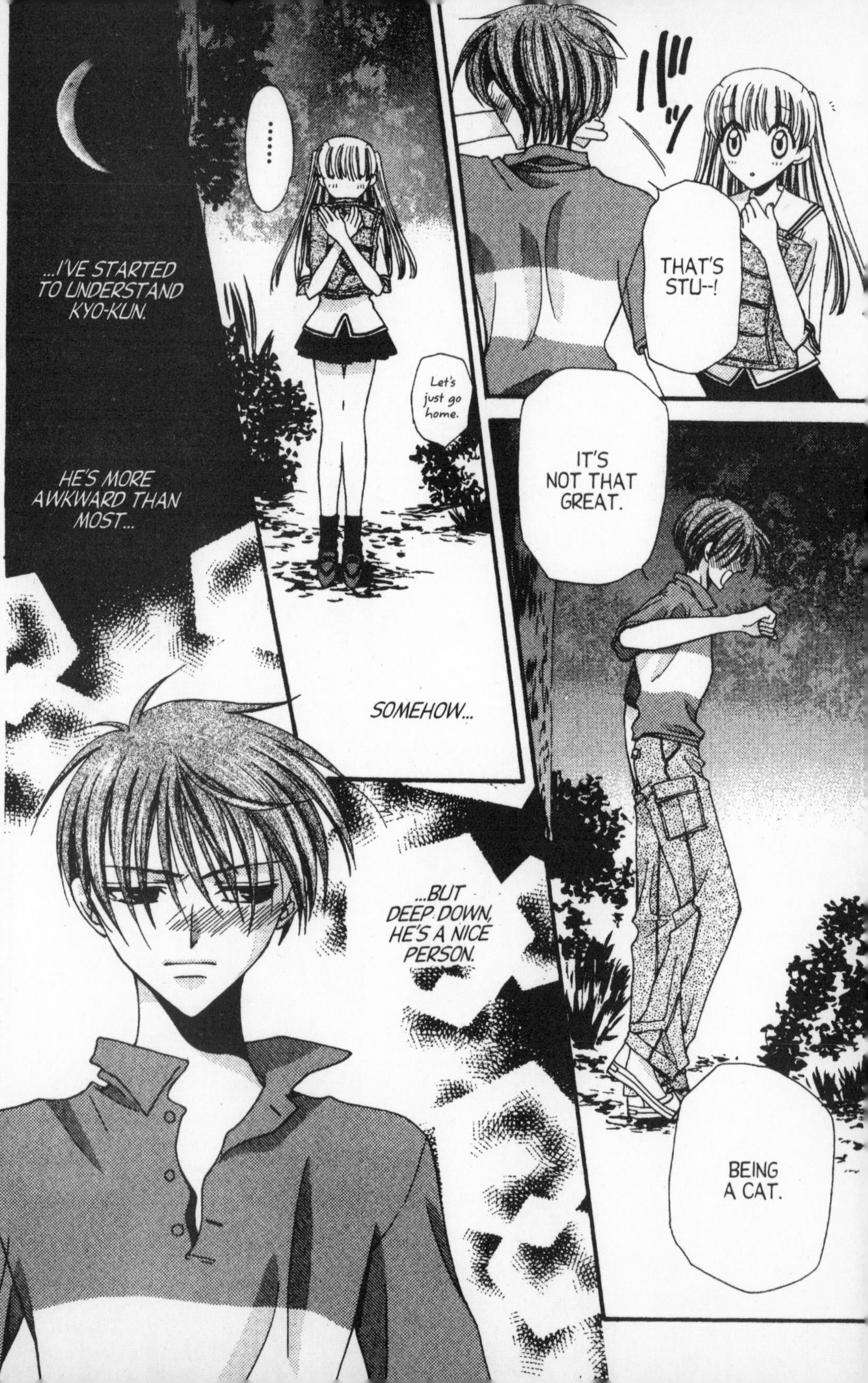
THAT'S STU--!
IT'S NOT THAT GREAT.
BEING A CAT.
......
Let's just go home.
SOMEHOW...
...I'VE STARTED TO UNDERSTAND KYO-KUN.
HE'S MORE AWKWARD THAN MOST...
...BUT DEEP DOWN, HE'S A NICE PERSON.

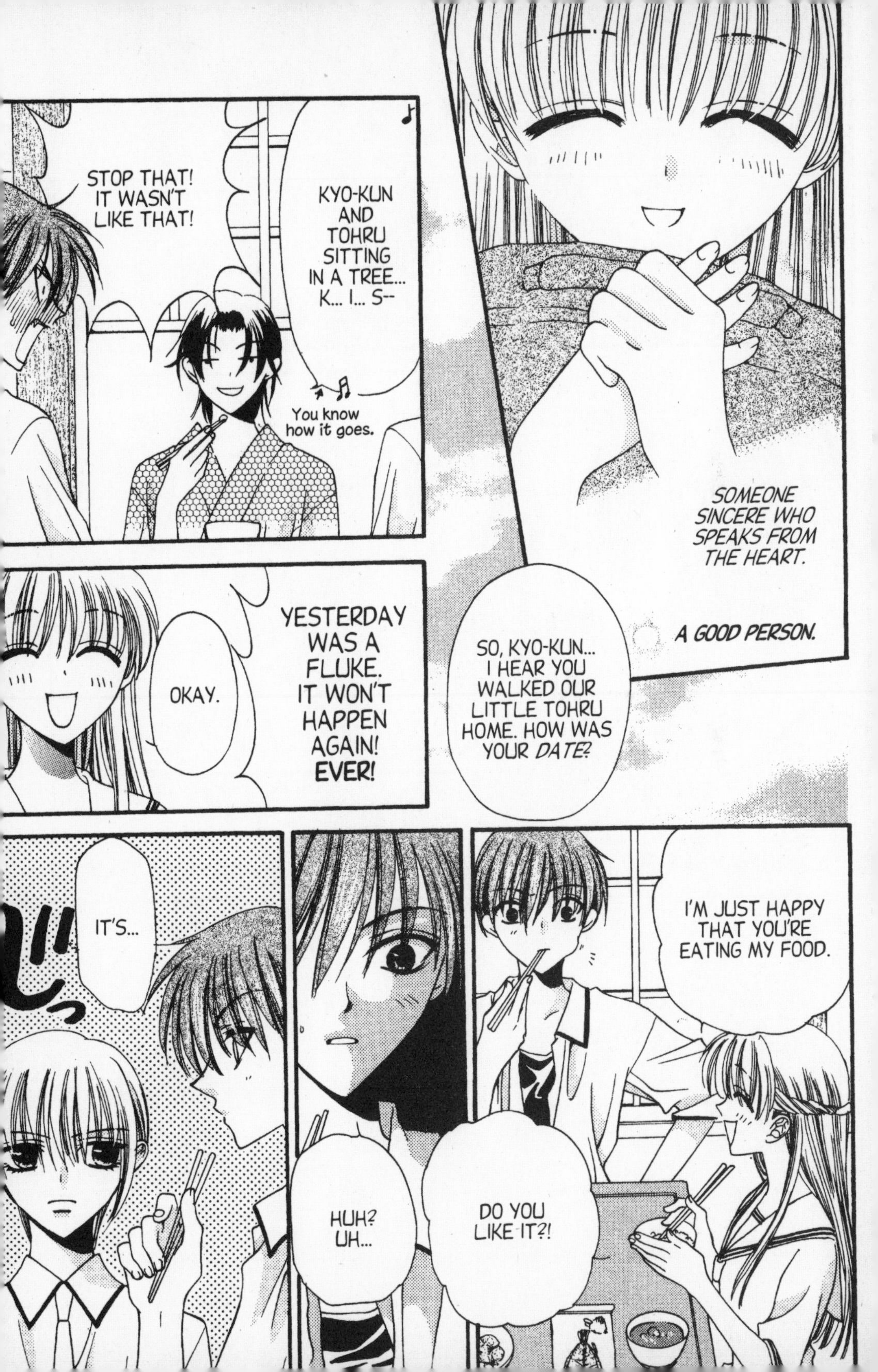
SOMEONE SINCERE WHO SPEAKS FROM THE HEART.
A GOOD PERSON.
SO, KYO-KUN... I HEAR YOU WALKED OUR LITTLE TOHRU HOME. HOW WAS YOUR *DATE*?
KYO-KUN AND TOHRU SITTING IN A TREE... K... I... S--
You know how it goes.
STOP THAT! IT WASN'T LIKE THAT!
YESTERDAY WAS A FLUKE. IT WON'T HAPPEN AGAIN! **EVER!**
OKAY.
I'M JUST HAPPY THAT YOU'RE EATING MY FOOD.
DO YOU LIKE IT?!
HUH? UH...
IT'S...

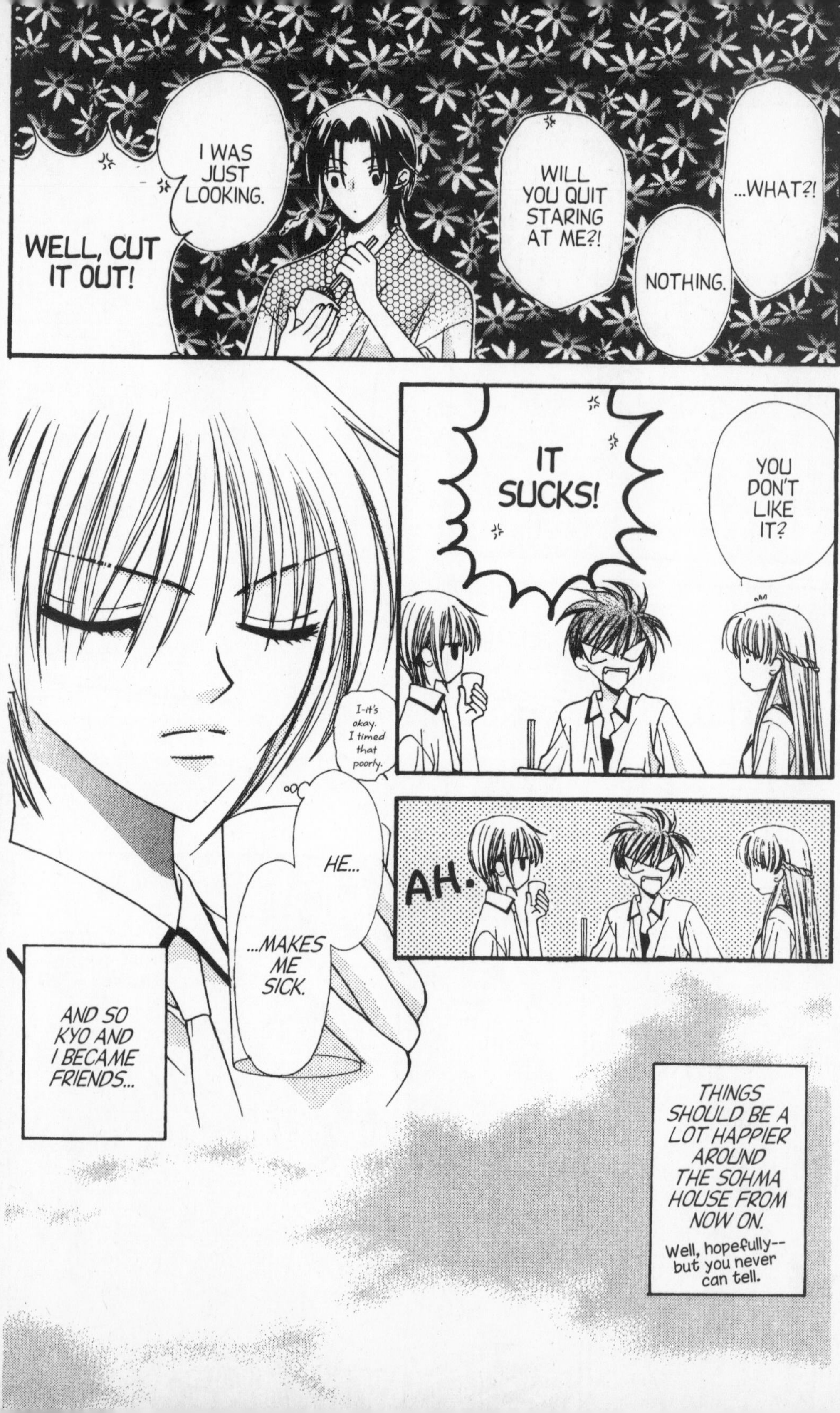
...WHAT?!
NOTHING.
WILL YOU QUIT STARING AT ME?!
I WAS JUST LOOKING.
WELL, CUT IT OUT!
YOU DON'T LIKE IT?
IT SUCKS!
I-it's okay. I timed that poorly.
AH.
HE...
...MAKES ME SICK.
AND SO KYO AND I BECAME FRIENDS...
THINGS SHOULD BE A LOT HAPPIER AROUND THE SOHMA HOUSE FROM NOW ON.
Well, hopefully--but you never can tell.

Chapter 4

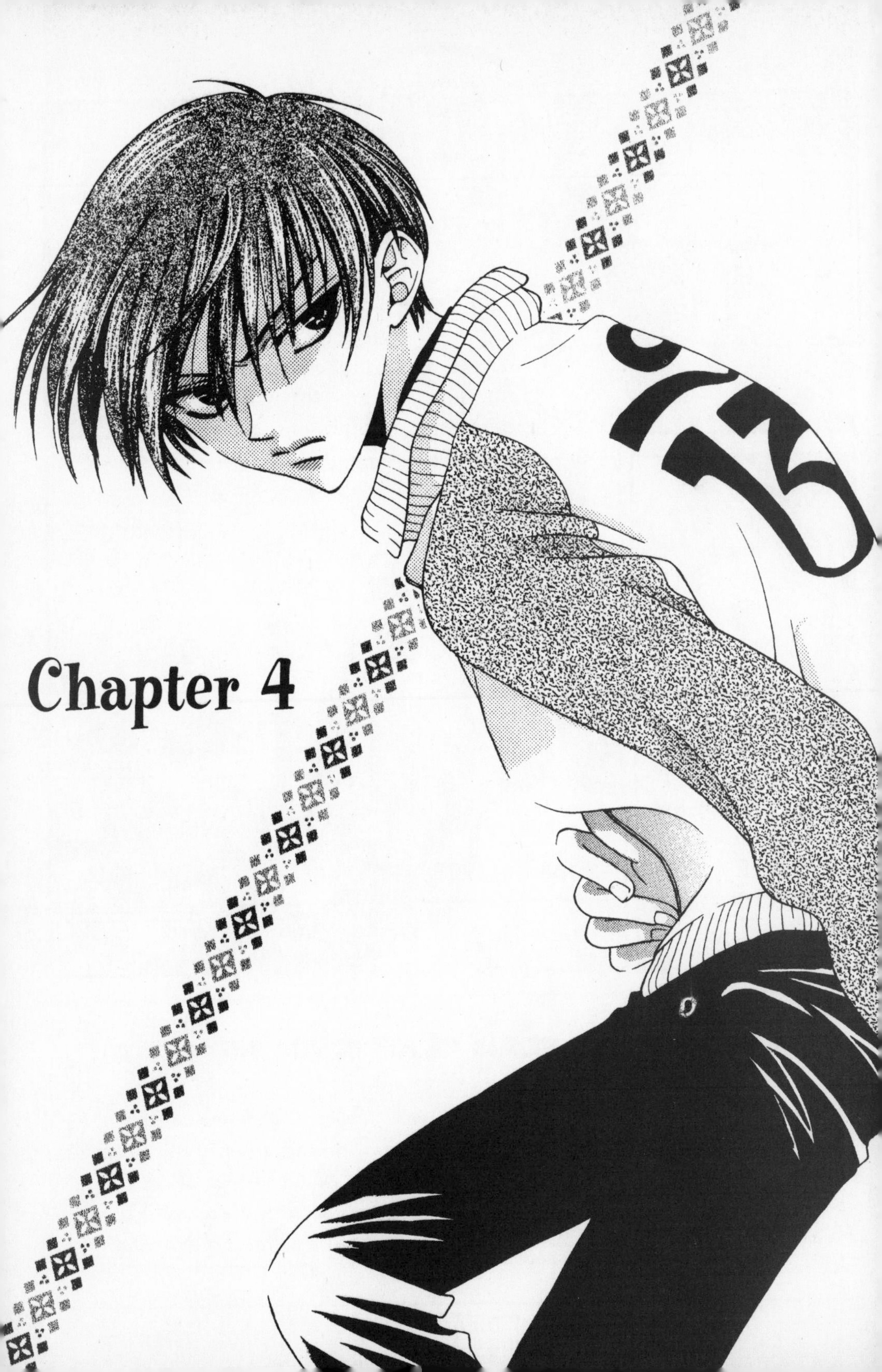

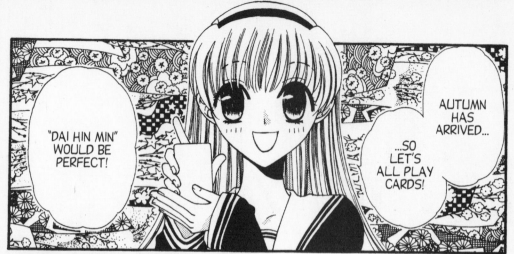

AUTUMN HAS ARRIVED...
...SO LET'S ALL PLAY CARDS!
"DAI HIN MIN" WOULD BE PERFECT!
ザワ
ザワ
ザワ
WHAT DOES DAI HIN MIN HAVE TO DO WITH AUTUMN?
IT'S REALLY POPULAR RIGHT NOW!
THEN IT HAS NOTHING TO DO WITH AUTUMN?
GO ASK THAT DAMN YUKI TO PLAY.
SOHMA-KUN'S NOT HERE.
Like I care.

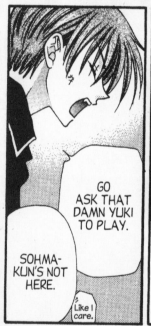

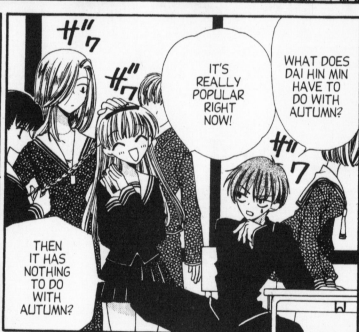

ULTRA SPECIAL BLAH BLAH BLAH, NUMBER 3:

When I drew Uo-chan, people asked me, "Sensei, did you used to be a Yankee?" Well, I wasn't a Yankee, but I wasn't exactly an honor student, either. Most people don't understand about Hana-chan's "poison waves," either. Apparently there's a video game called "Pange Reef" with poison waves, but I didn't play it until after I'd started the manga.

Number 5:

"How do you name your characters in video games?" I'm asked. Well, I usually put in my own name. I stopped for a while, but then I started doing it again. Of course, I say "my own name," but Natsuki Takaya is a pen name (laugh). If it was my real name, then, yeah, I might think it was a little embarrassing. I don't think it's bad though. Because it's my game to enjoy my own way. So now, when I become friends with people in the game "Tokyo Friend," they call me "Takayan."

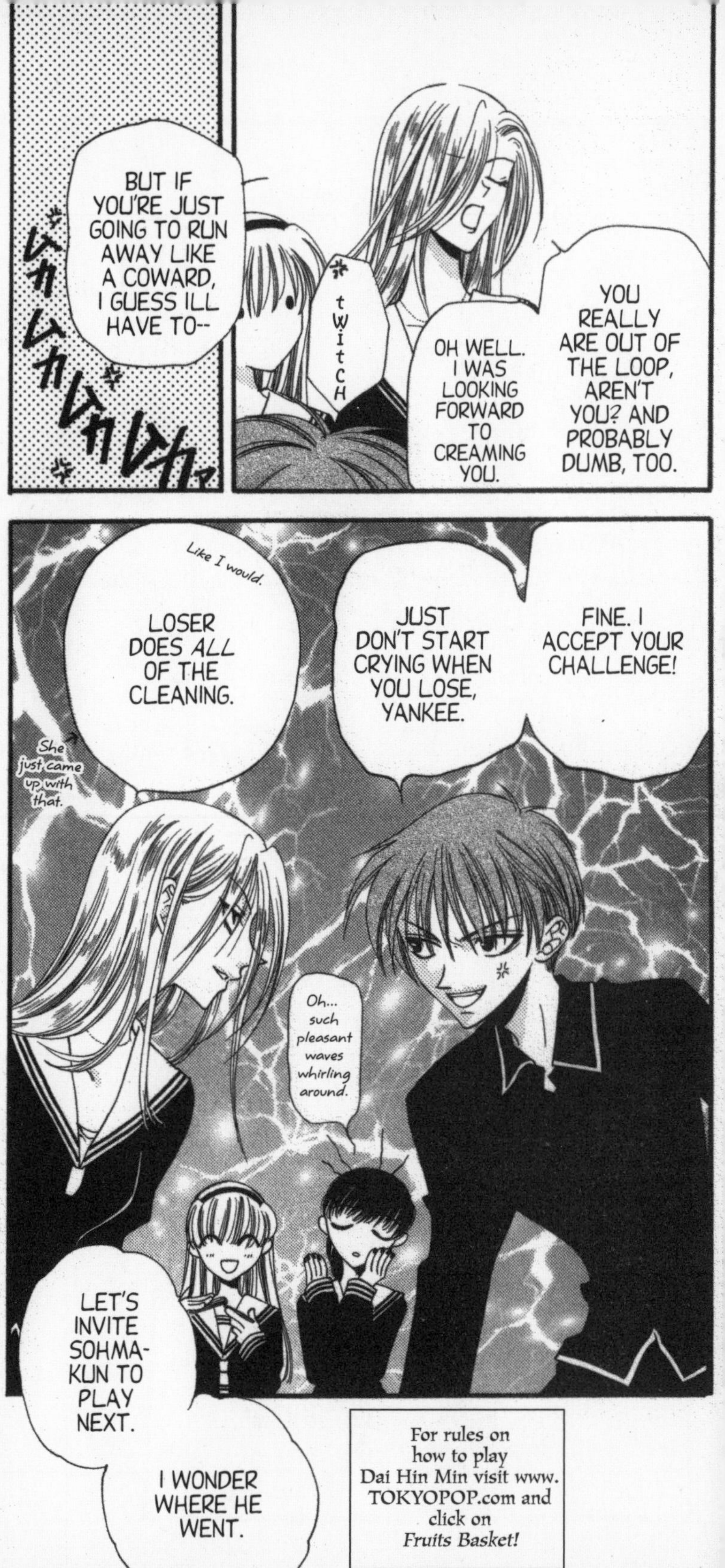
YOU REALLY ARE OUT OF THE LOOP, AREN'T YOU? AND PROBABLY DUMB, TOO.
OH WELL. I WAS LOOKING FORWARD TO CREAMING YOU.
tWITCH
BUT IF YOU'RE JUST GOING TO RUN AWAY LIKE A COWARD, I GUESS ILL HAVE TO--
FINE. I ACCEPT YOUR CHALLENGE!
JUST DON'T START CRYING WHEN YOU LOSE, YANKEE.
LOSER DOES *ALL* OF THE CLEANING.
Like I would.
She just came up with that.
Oh... such pleasant waves whirling around.
LET'S INVITE SOHMA-KUN TO PLAY NEXT.
I WONDER WHERE HE WENT.

For rules on how to play Dai Hin Min visit www.TOKYOPOP.com and click on *Fruits Basket!*

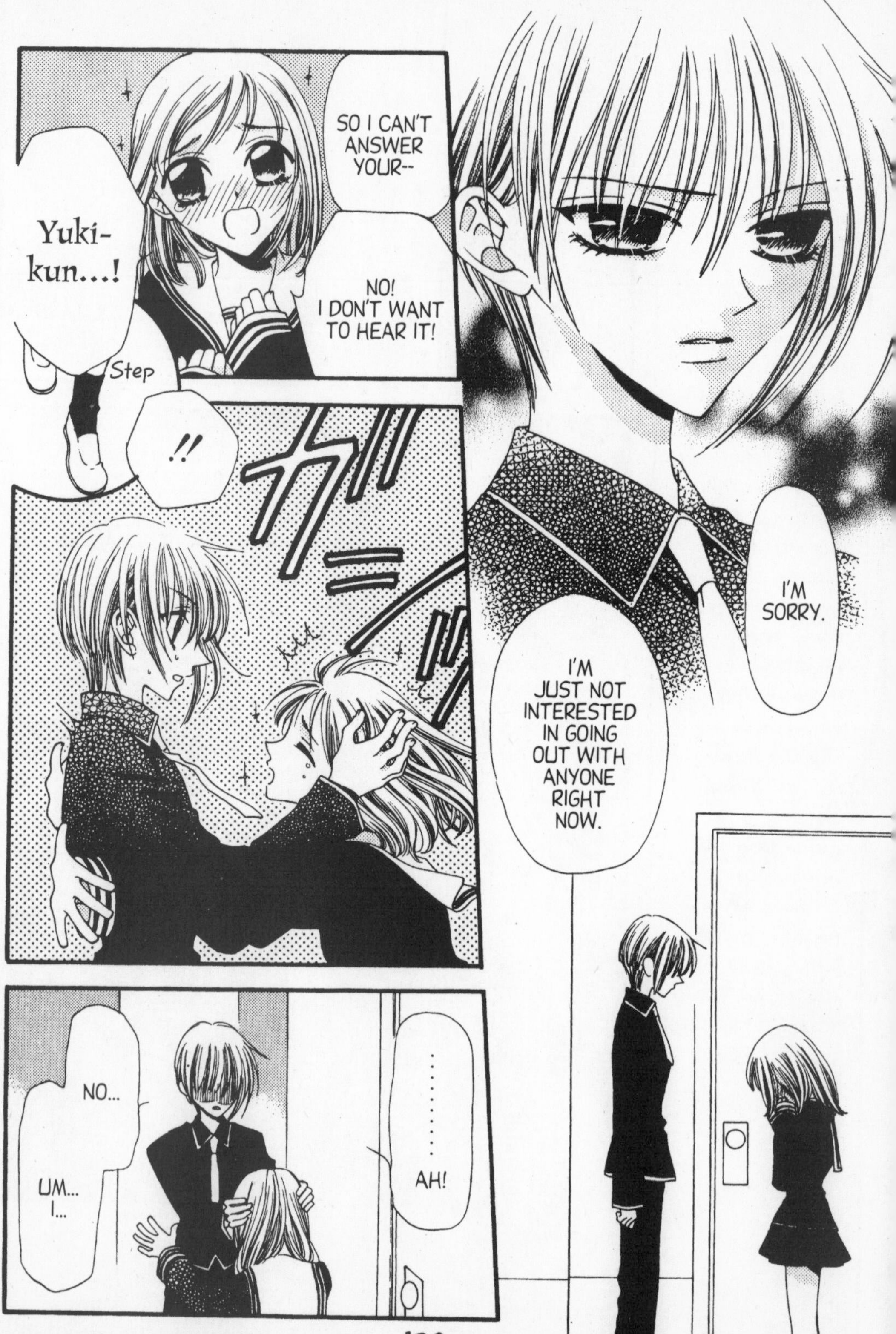
I'M SORRY.
I'M JUST NOT INTERESTED IN GOING OUT WITH ANYONE RIGHT NOW.
SO I CAN'T ANSWER YOUR--
NO! I DON'T WANT TO HEAR IT!
Yuki-kun...!
Step
!!
.........AH!
NO...
UM... I...

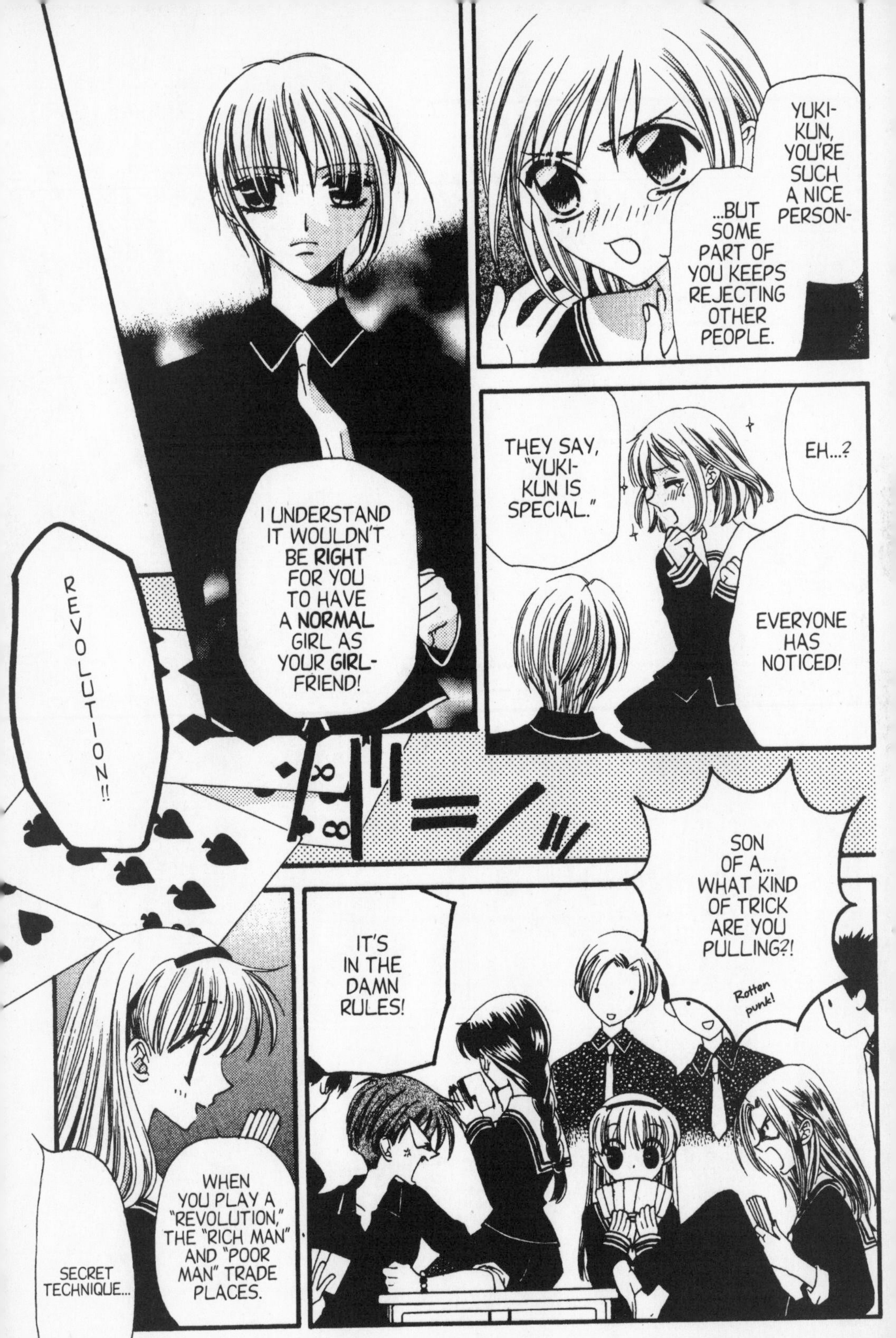
YUKI-KUN, YOU'RE SUCH A NICE PERSON-
...BUT SOME PART OF YOU KEEPS REJECTING OTHER PEOPLE.
EH...?
THEY SAY, "YUKI-KUN IS SPECIAL."
EVERYONE HAS NOTICED!
I UNDERSTAND IT WOULDN'T BE **RIGHT** FOR YOU TO HAVE A **NORMAL** GIRL AS YOUR **GIRL**-FRIEND!
REVOLUTION!!
SON OF A... WHAT KIND OF TRICK ARE YOU PULLING?!
Rotten punk!
IT'S IN THE DAMN RULES!
WHEN YOU PLAY A "REVOLUTION," THE "RICH MAN" AND "POOR MAN" TRADE PLACES.
SECRET TECHNIQUE...

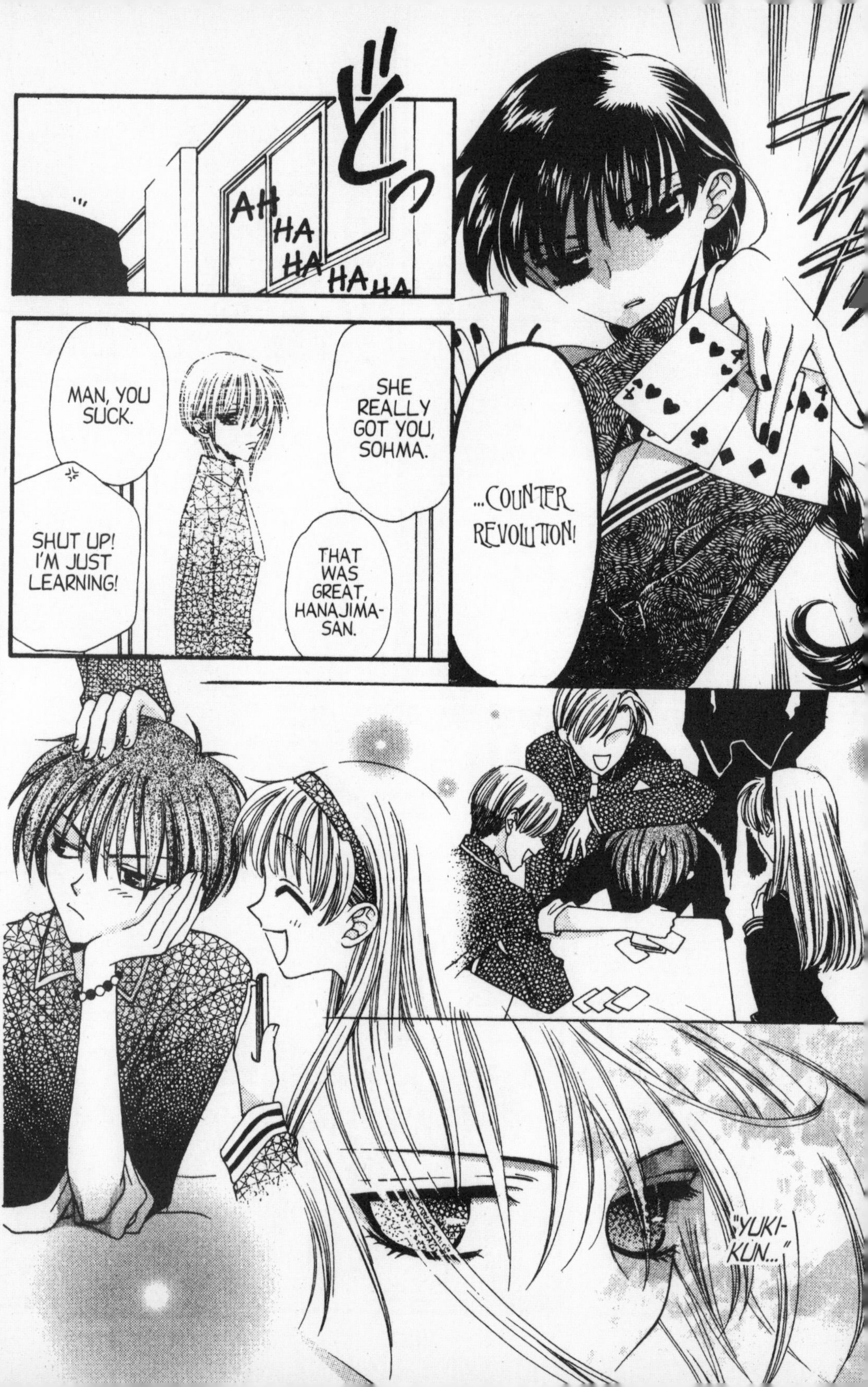
...COUNTER REVOLUTION!
どっ
AH HA HA HA HA
SHE REALLY GOT YOU, SOHMA.
MAN, YOU SUCK.
THAT WAS GREAT, HANAJIMA-SAN.
SHUT UP! I'M JUST LEARNING!
"YUKI-KUN..."

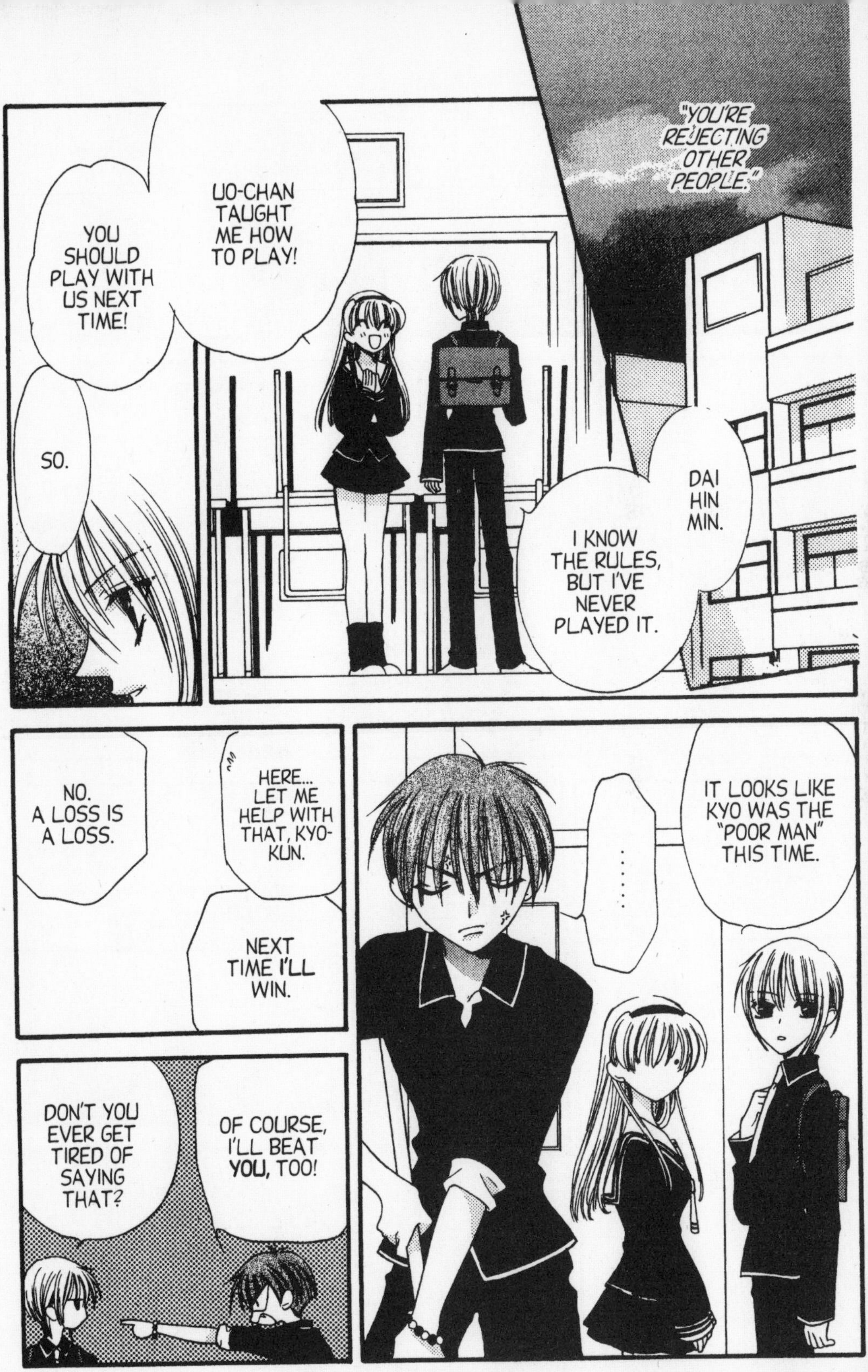
"YOU'RE REJECTING OTHER PEOPLE."
DAI HIN MIN.
I KNOW THE RULES, BUT I'VE NEVER PLAYED IT.
UO-CHAN TAUGHT ME HOW TO PLAY!
YOU SHOULD PLAY WITH US NEXT TIME!
SO.
IT LOOKS LIKE KYO WAS THE "POOR MAN" THIS TIME.
......
HERE... LET ME HELP WITH THAT, KYO-KUN.
NO. A LOSS IS A LOSS.
NEXT TIME I'LL WIN.
OF COURSE, I'LL BEAT YOU, TOO!
DON'T YOU EVER GET TIRED OF SAYING THAT?

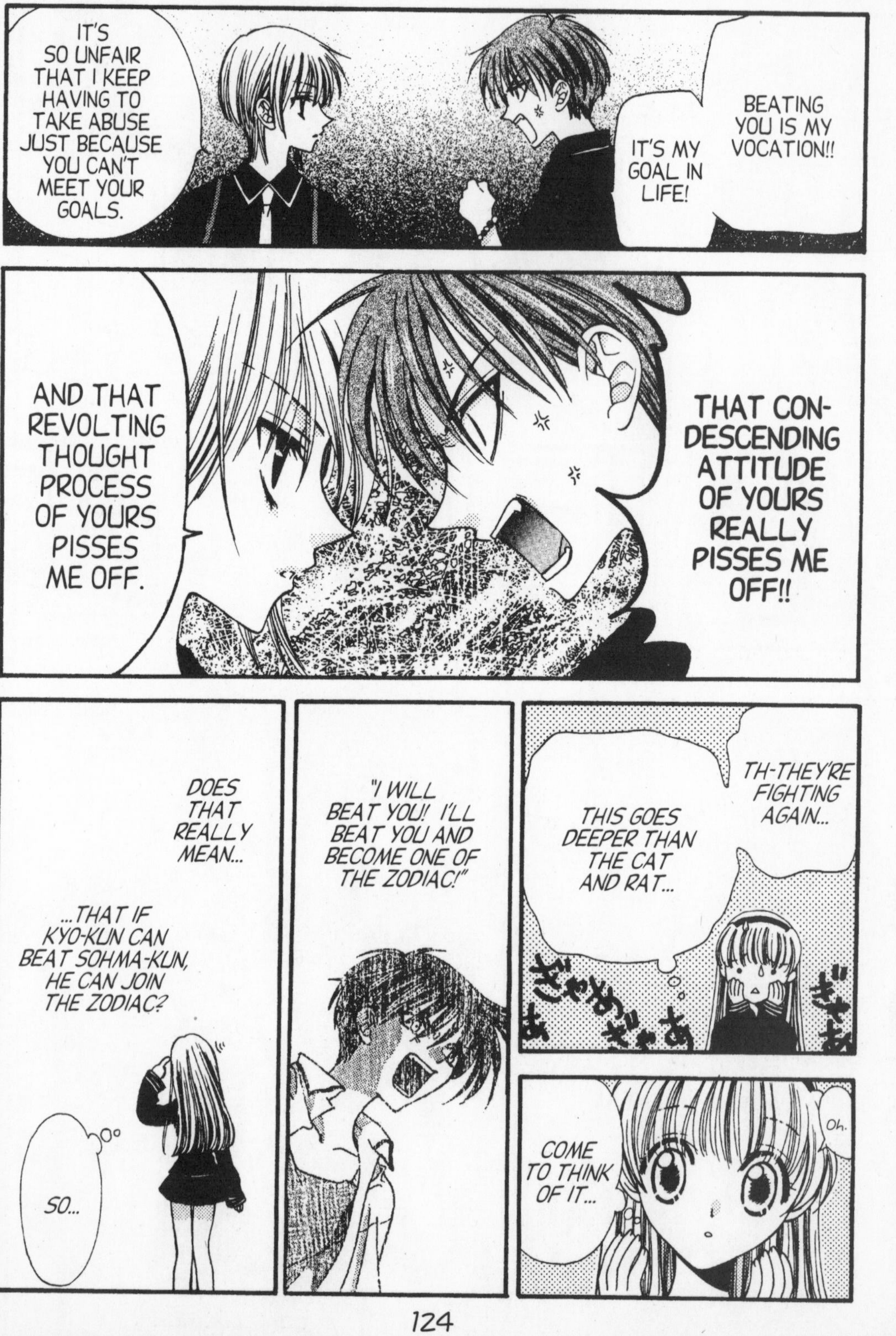
BEATING YOU IS MY VOCATION!!
IT'S MY GOAL IN LIFE!
IT'S SO UNFAIR THAT I KEEP HAVING TO TAKE ABUSE JUST BECAUSE YOU CAN'T MEET YOUR GOALS.
THAT CON-DESCENDING ATTITUDE OF YOURS REALLY PISSES ME OFF!!
AND THAT REVOLTING THOUGHT PROCESS OF YOURS PISSES ME OFF.
TH-THEY'RE FIGHTING AGAIN...
THIS GOES DEEPER THAN THE CAT AND RAT...
Oh.
COME TO THINK OF IT...
"I WILL BEAT YOU! I'LL BEAT YOU AND BECOME ONE OF THE ZODIAC!"
DOES THAT REALLY MEAN...
...THAT IF KYO-KUN CAN BEAT SOHMA-KUN, HE CAN JOIN THE ZODIAC?
SO...

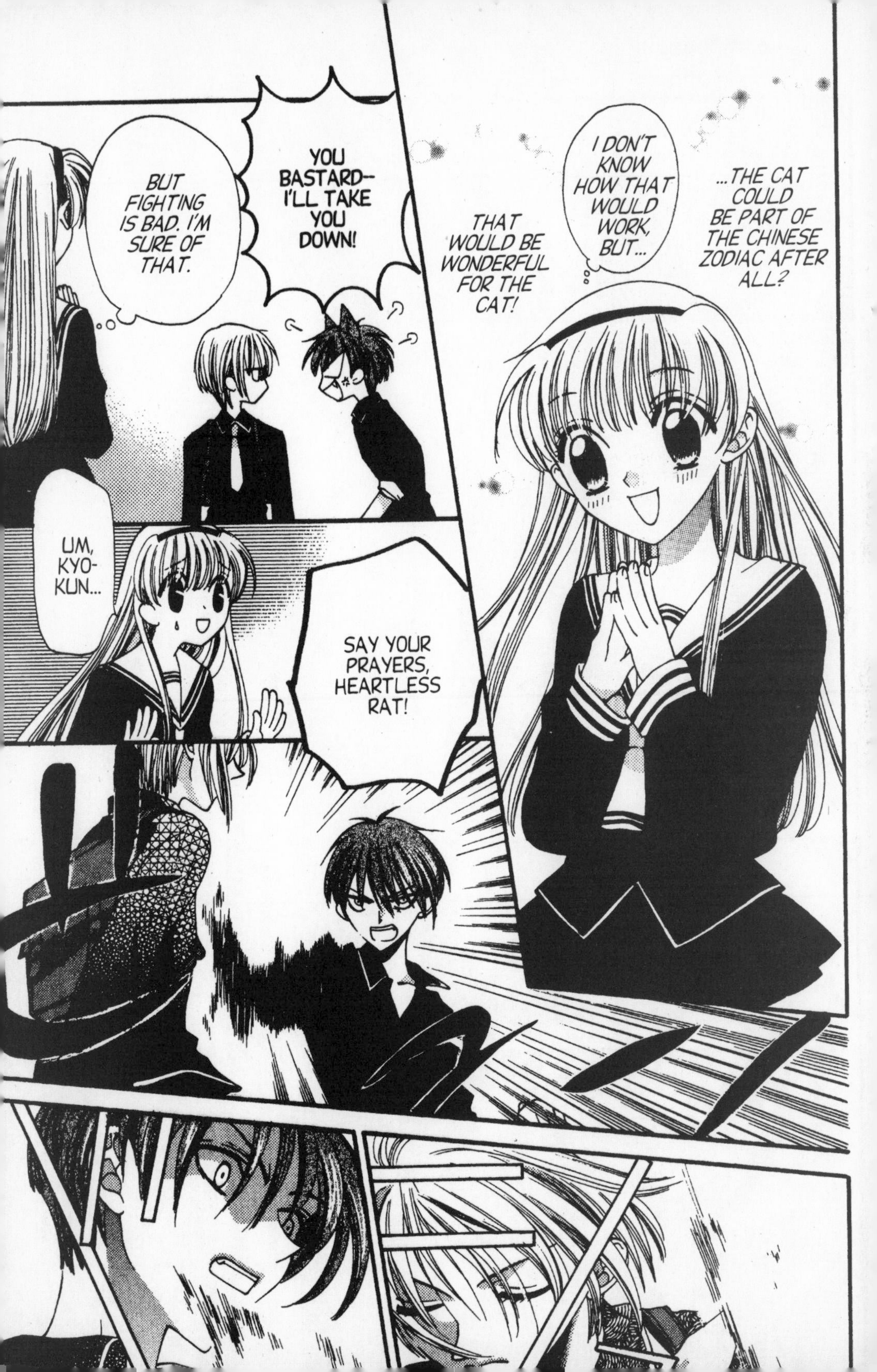
...THE CAT COULD BE PART OF THE CHINESE ZODIAC AFTER ALL?
I DON'T KNOW HOW THAT WOULD WORK, BUT...
THAT WOULD BE WONDERFUL FOR THE CAT!
YOU BASTARD-I'LL TAKE YOU DOWN!
BUT FIGHTING IS BAD. I'M SURE OF THAT.
SAY YOUR PRAYERS, HEARTLESS RAT!
UM, KYO-KUN...

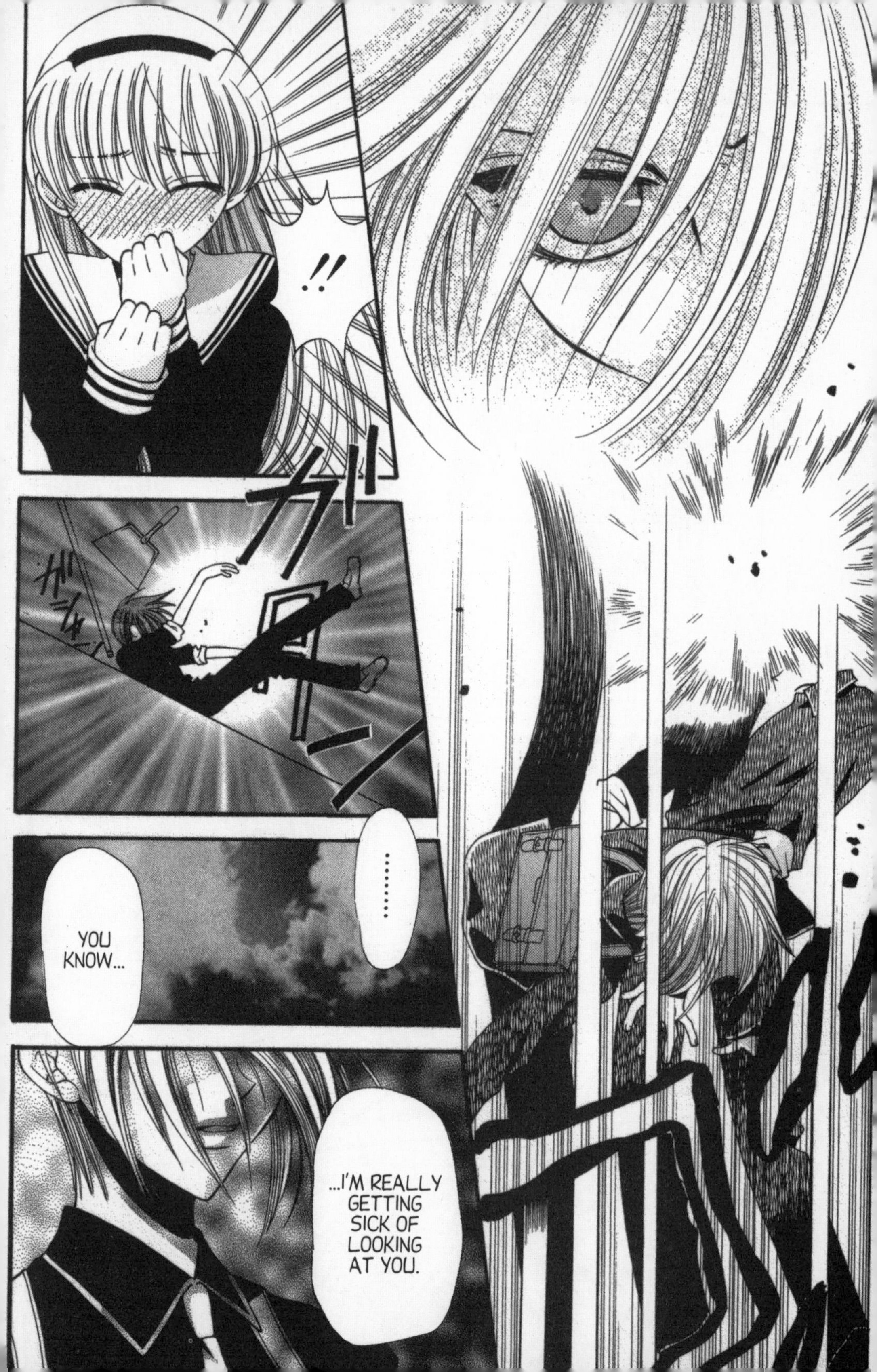
!!
....
YOU KNOW...
...I'M REALLY GETTING SICK OF LOOKING AT YOU.

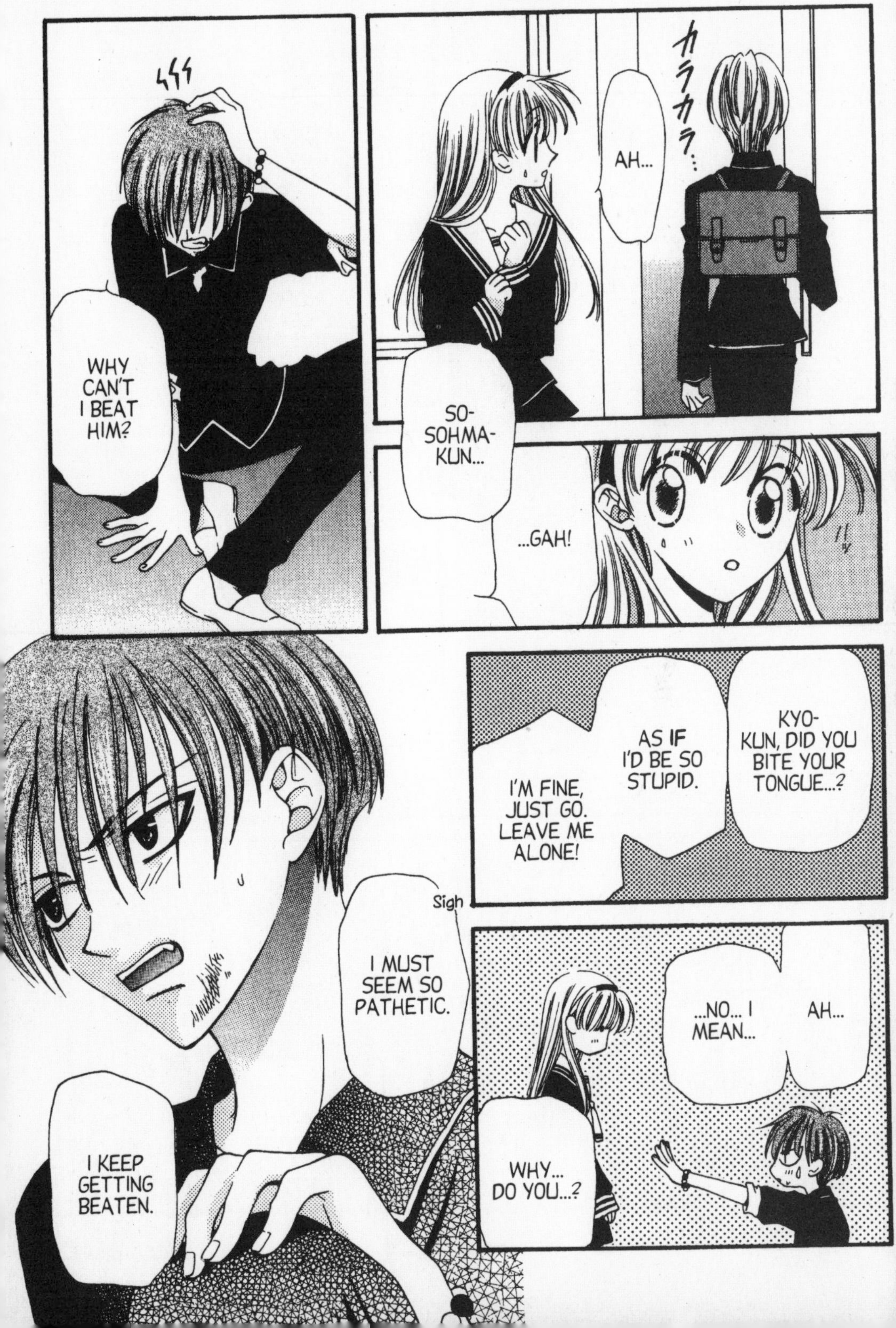
カラカラ…
AH...
SO-SOHMA-KUN...
...GAH!
WHY CAN'T I BEAT HIM?
KYO-KUN, DID YOU BITE YOUR TONGUE...?
AS IF I'D BE SO STUPID.
I'M FINE, JUST GO. LEAVE ME ALONE!
AH...
...NO... I MEAN...
WHY... DO YOU...?
Sigh
I MUST SEEM SO PATHETIC.
I KEEP GETTING BEATEN.

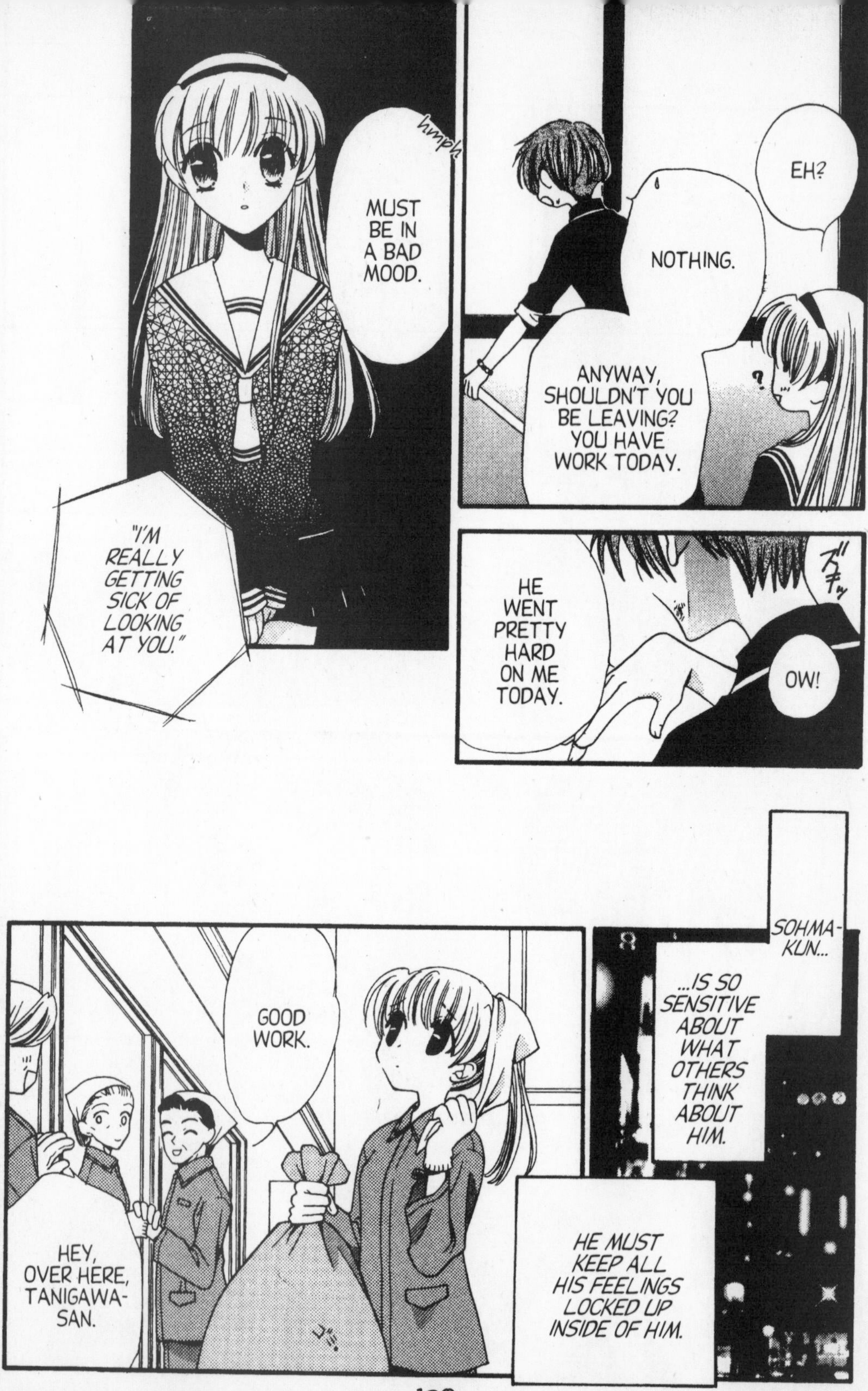
EH?
NOTHING.
ANYWAY, SHOULDN'T YOU BE LEAVING? YOU HAVE WORK TODAY.
ズキッ
OW!
HE WENT PRETTY HARD ON ME TODAY.
hmph
MUST BE IN A BAD MOOD.
"I'M REALLY GETTING SICK OF LOOKING AT YOU."
SOHMA-KUN...
...IS SO SENSITIVE ABOUT WHAT OTHERS THINK ABOUT HIM.
HE MUST KEEP ALL HIS FEELINGS LOCKED UP INSIDE OF HIM.
GOOD WORK.
HEY, OVER HERE, TANIGAWA-SAN.

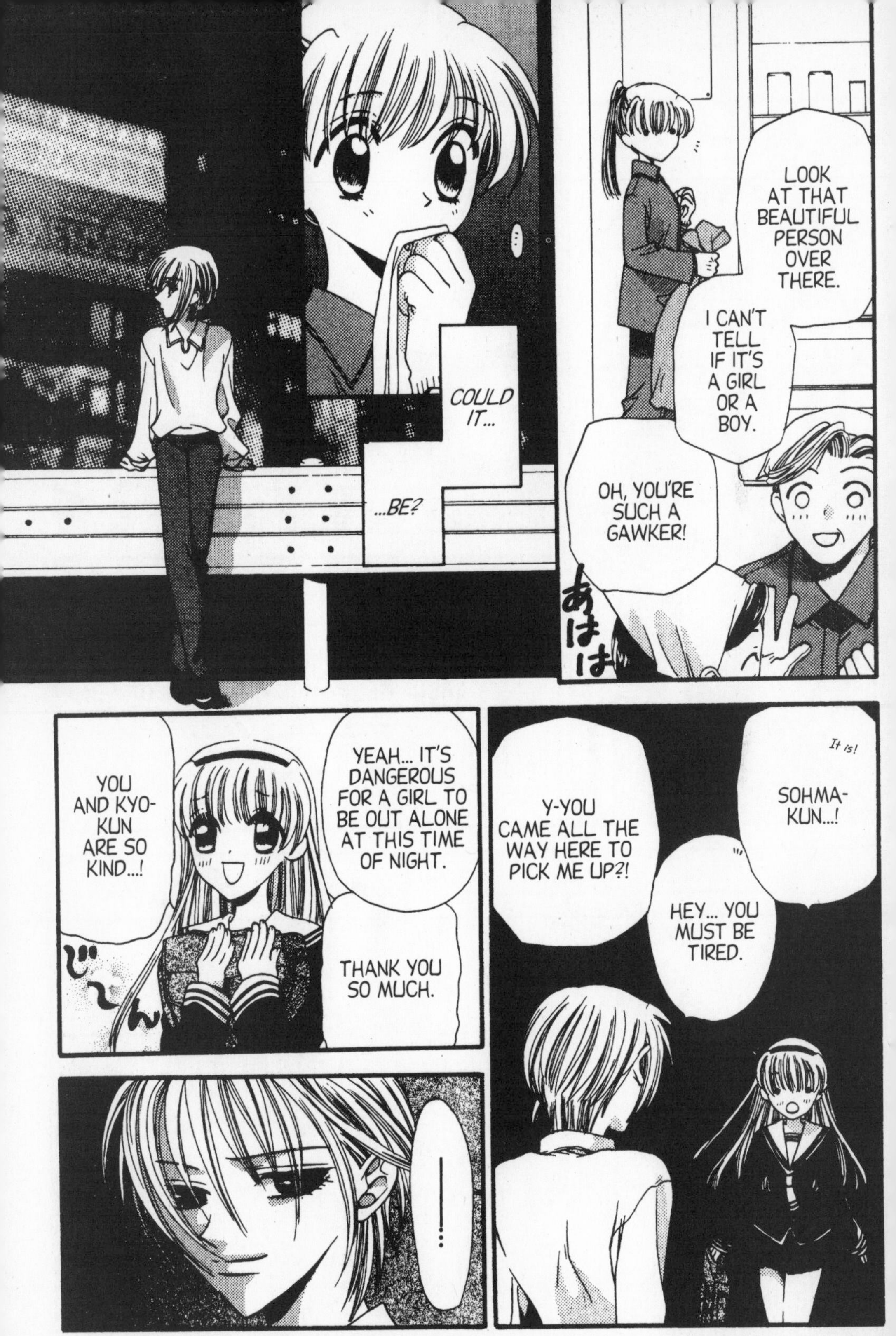
LOOK AT THAT BEAUTIFUL PERSON OVER THERE.
I CAN'T TELL IF IT'S A GIRL OR A BOY.
OH, YOU'RE SUCH A GAWKER!
あはは
...
COULD IT...
...BE?
It is!
SOHMA-KUN...!
Y-YOU CAME ALL THE WAY HERE TO PICK ME UP?!
HEY... YOU MUST BE TIRED.
YEAH... IT'S DANGEROUS FOR A GIRL TO BE OUT ALONE AT THIS TIME OF NIGHT.
THANK YOU SO MUCH.
YOU AND KYO-KUN ARE SO KIND...!
じ〜ん
...!

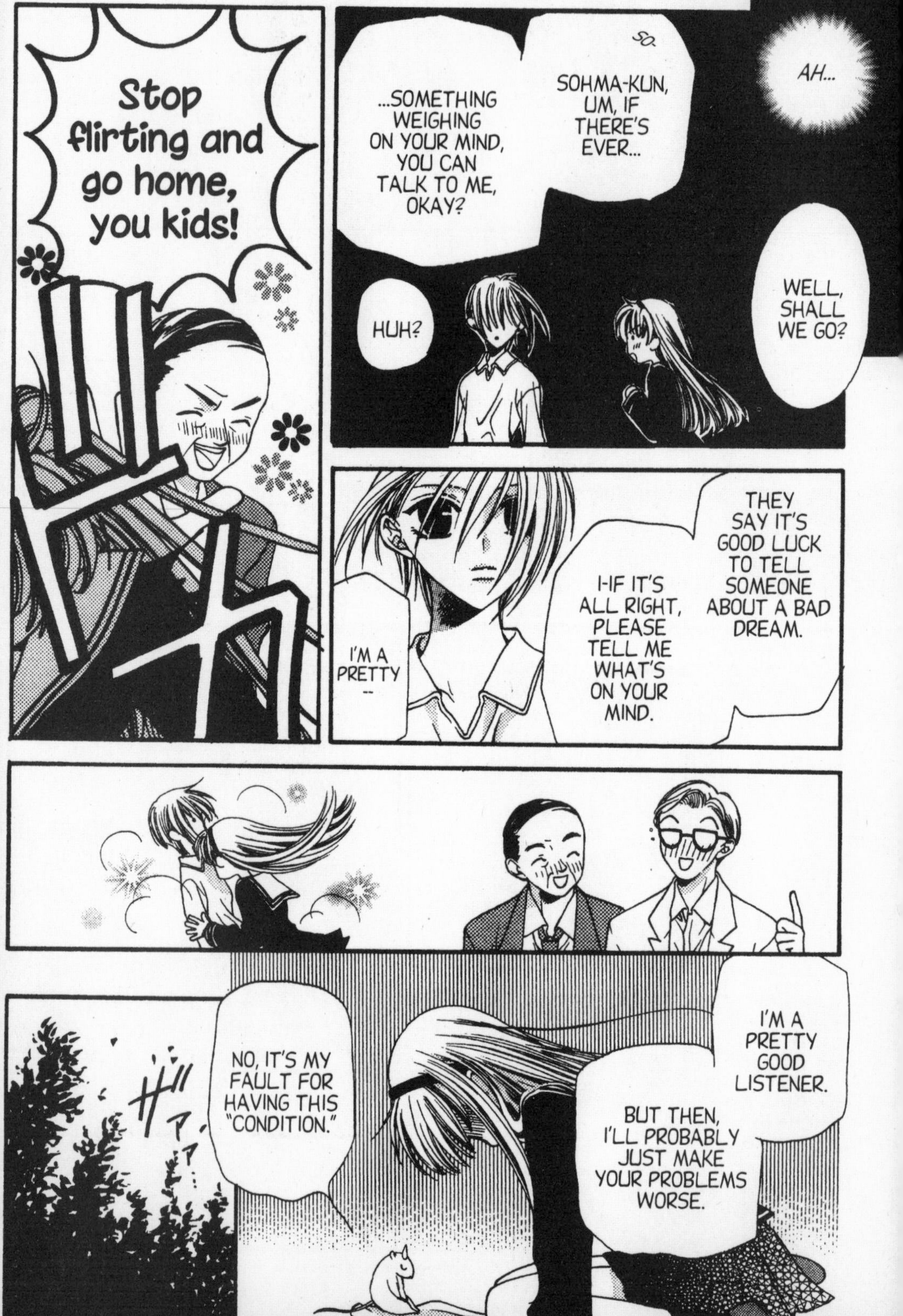
AH...
SO-
SOHMA-KUN, UM, IF THERE'S EVER...
...SOMETHING WEIGHING ON YOUR MIND, YOU CAN TALK TO ME, OKAY?
WELL, SHALL WE GO?
HUH?
THEY SAY IT'S GOOD LUCK TO TELL SOMEONE ABOUT A BAD DREAM.
I-IF IT'S ALL RIGHT, PLEASE TELL ME WHAT'S ON YOUR MIND.
I'M A PRETTY --
Stop flirting and go home, you kids!
I'M A PRETTY GOOD LISTENER.
BUT THEN, I'LL PROBABLY JUST MAKE YOUR PROBLEMS WORSE.
NO, IT'S MY FAULT FOR HAVING THIS "CONDITION."

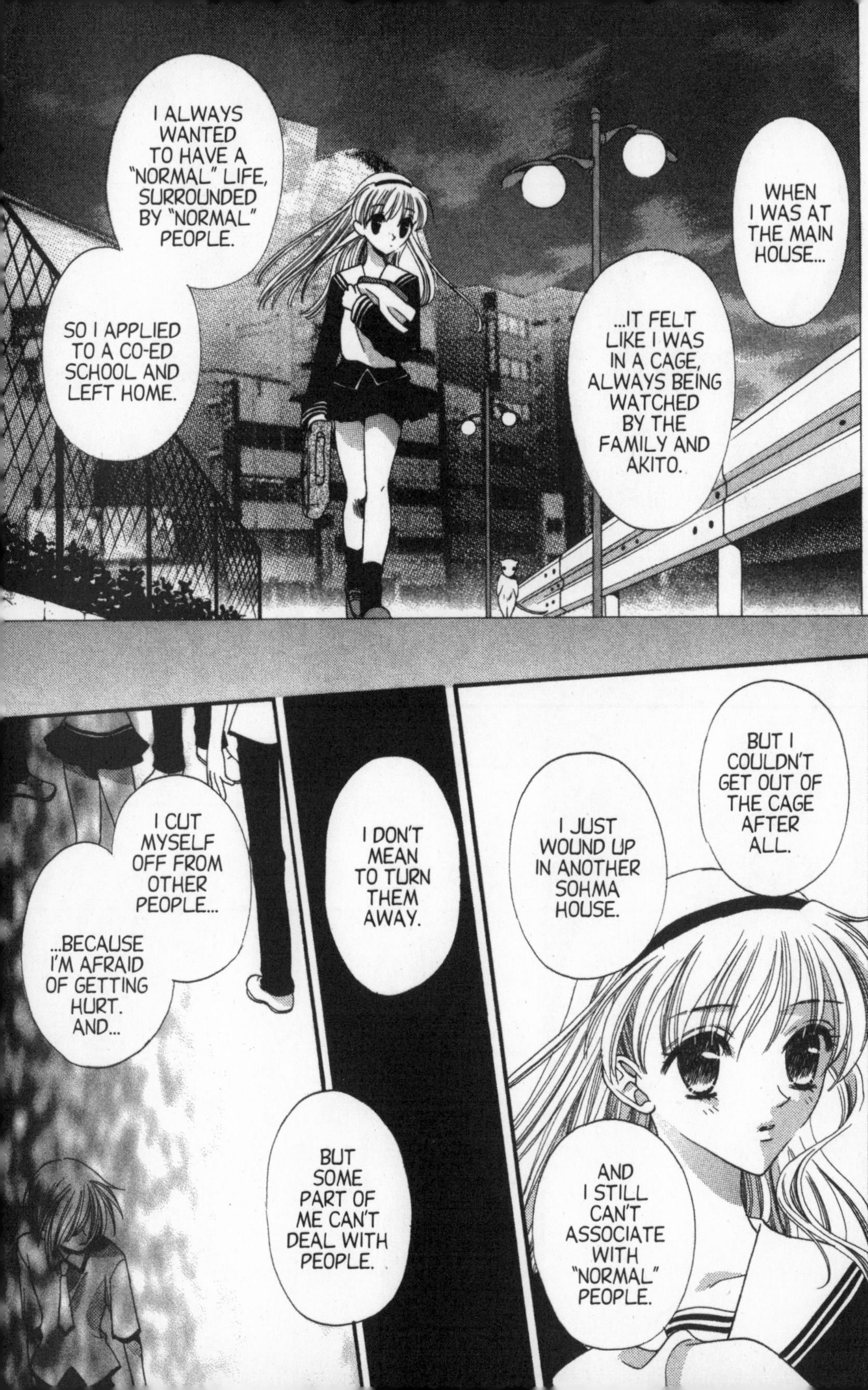
WHEN I WAS AT THE MAIN HOUSE...
...IT FELT LIKE I WAS IN A CAGE, ALWAYS BEING WATCHED BY THE FAMILY AND AKITO.
I ALWAYS WANTED TO HAVE A "NORMAL" LIFE, SURROUNDED BY "NORMAL" PEOPLE.
SO I APPLIED TO A CO-ED SCHOOL AND LEFT HOME.
BUT I COULDN'T GET OUT OF THE CAGE AFTER ALL.
I JUST WOUND UP IN ANOTHER SOHMA HOUSE.
AND I STILL CAN'T ASSOCIATE WITH "NORMAL" PEOPLE.
I DON'T MEAN TO TURN THEM AWAY.
BUT SOME PART OF ME CAN'T DEAL WITH PEOPLE.
I CUT MYSELF OFF FROM OTHER PEOPLE...
...BECAUSE I'M AFRAID OF GETTING HURT. AND...

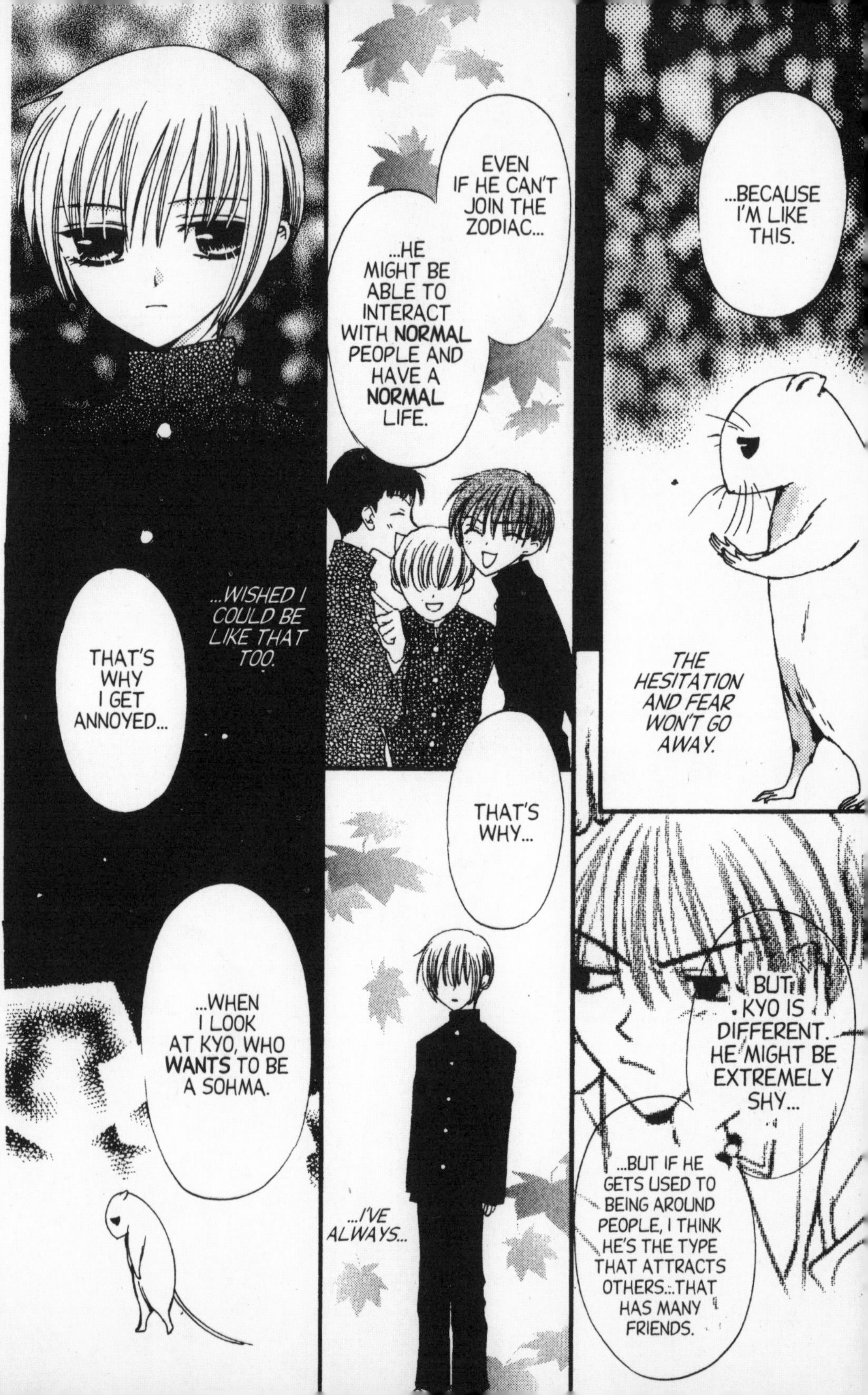
...BECAUSE I'M LIKE THIS.
THE HESITATION AND FEAR WON'T GO AWAY.
BUT KYO IS DIFFERENT. HE MIGHT BE EXTREMELY SHY...
...BUT IF HE GETS USED TO BEING AROUND PEOPLE, I THINK HE'S THE TYPE THAT ATTRACTS OTHERS...THAT HAS MANY FRIENDS.
EVEN IF HE CAN'T JOIN THE ZODIAC...
...HE MIGHT BE ABLE TO INTERACT WITH NORMAL PEOPLE AND HAVE A NORMAL LIFE.
THAT'S WHY...
...I'VE ALWAYS...
...WISHED I COULD BE LIKE THAT TOO.
THAT'S WHY I GET ANNOYED...
...WHEN I LOOK AT KYO, WHO WANTS TO BE A SOHMA.

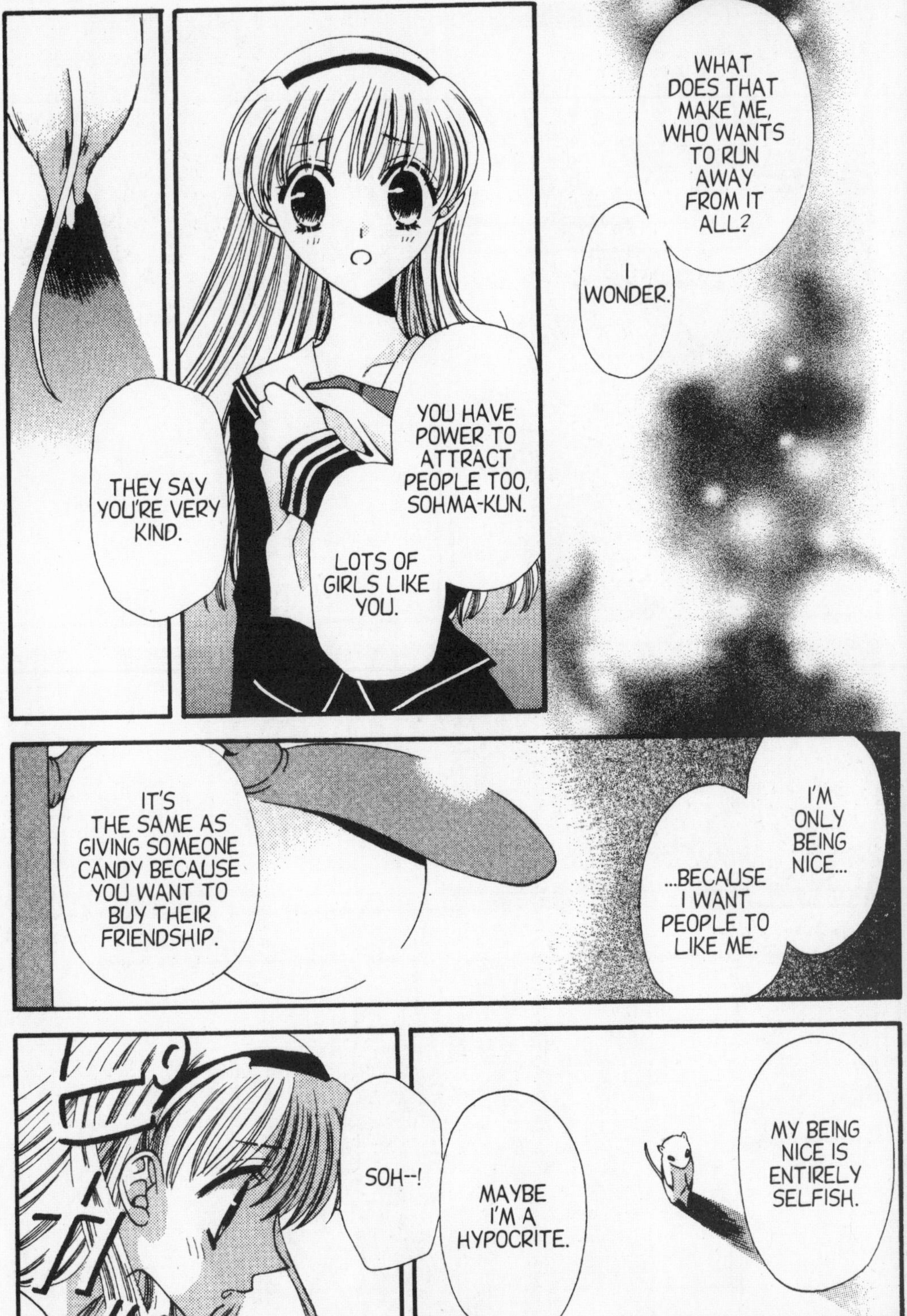
WHAT DOES THAT MAKE ME, WHO WANTS TO RUN AWAY FROM IT ALL?
I WONDER.
YOU HAVE POWER TO ATTRACT PEOPLE TOO, SOHMA-KUN.
LOTS OF GIRLS LIKE YOU.
THEY SAY YOU'RE VERY KIND.
I'M ONLY BEING NICE...
...BECAUSE I WANT PEOPLE TO LIKE ME.
IT'S THE SAME AS GIVING SOMEONE CANDY BECAUSE YOU WANT TO BUY THEIR FRIENDSHIP.
MY BEING NICE IS ENTIRELY SELFISH.
MAYBE I'M A HYPOCRITE.
SOH--!

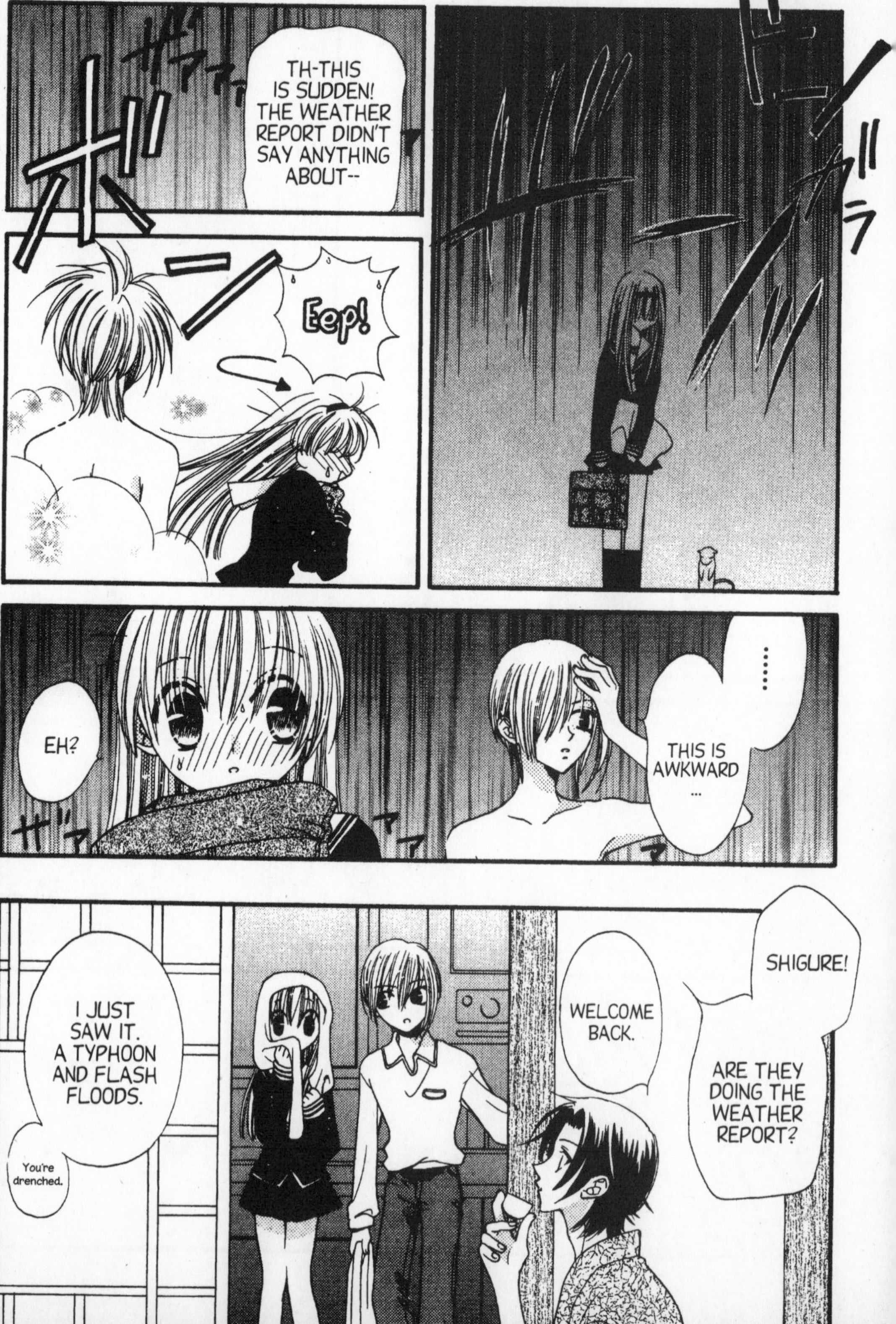
TH-THIS IS SUDDEN! THE WEATHER REPORT DIDN'T SAY ANYTHING ABOUT--
Eep!
......
THIS IS AWKWARD ...
EH?
SHIGURE!
WELCOME BACK.
ARE THEY DOING THE WEATHER REPORT?
I JUST SAW IT. A TYPHOON AND FLASH FLOODS.
You're drenched.

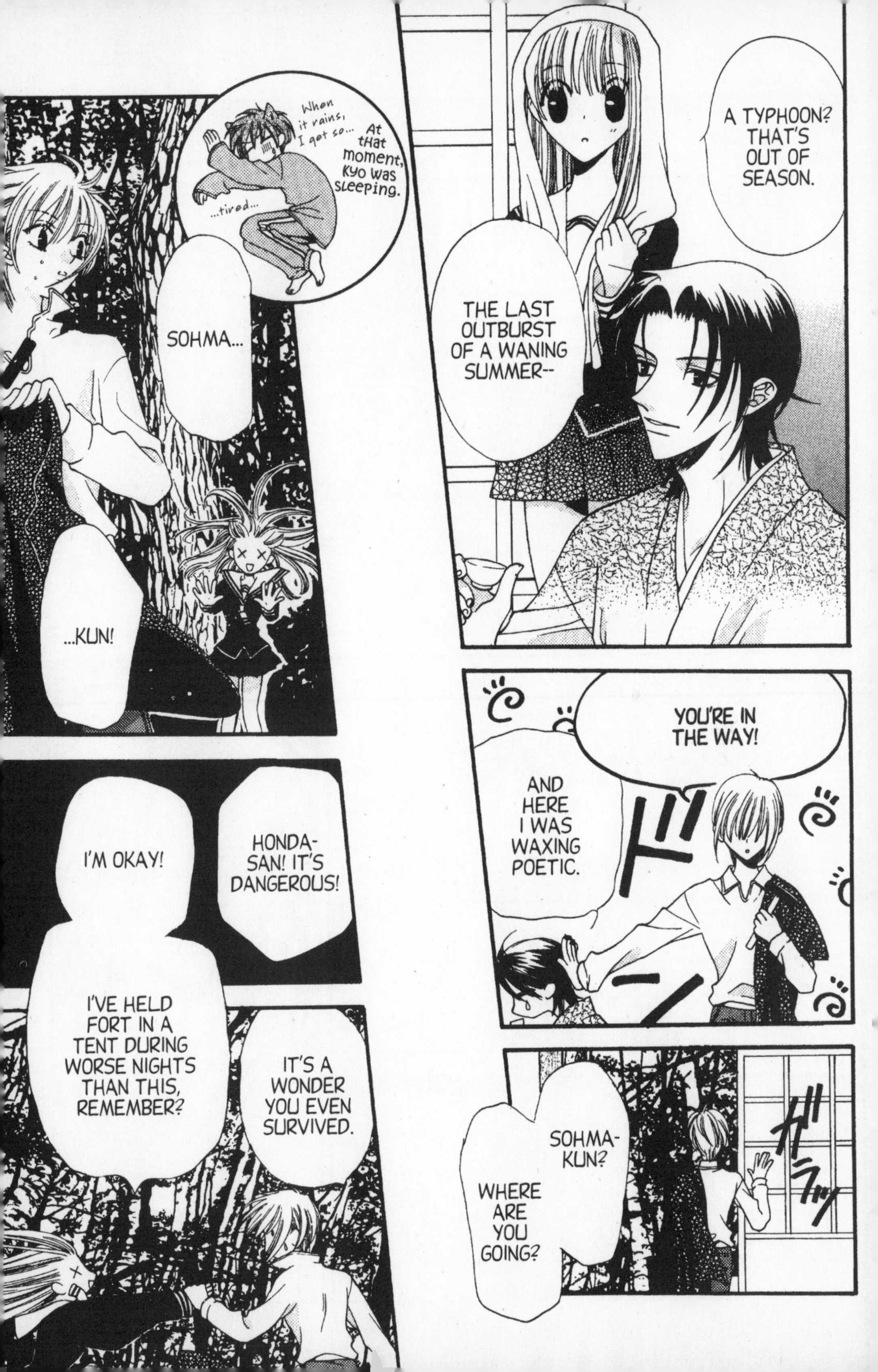
A TYPHOON? THAT'S OUT OF SEASON.
THE LAST OUTBURST OF A WANING SUMMER--
YOU'RE IN THE WAY!
AND HERE I WAS WAXING POETIC.
SOHMA-KUN?
WHERE ARE YOU GOING?
When it rains, I get so...
...tired...
At that moment, Kyo was sleeping.
SOHMA...
...KUN!
HONDA-SAN! IT'S DANGEROUS!
I'M OKAY!
I'VE HELD FORT IN A TENT DURING WORSE NIGHTS THAN THIS, REMEMBER?
IT'S A WONDER YOU EVEN SURVIVED.

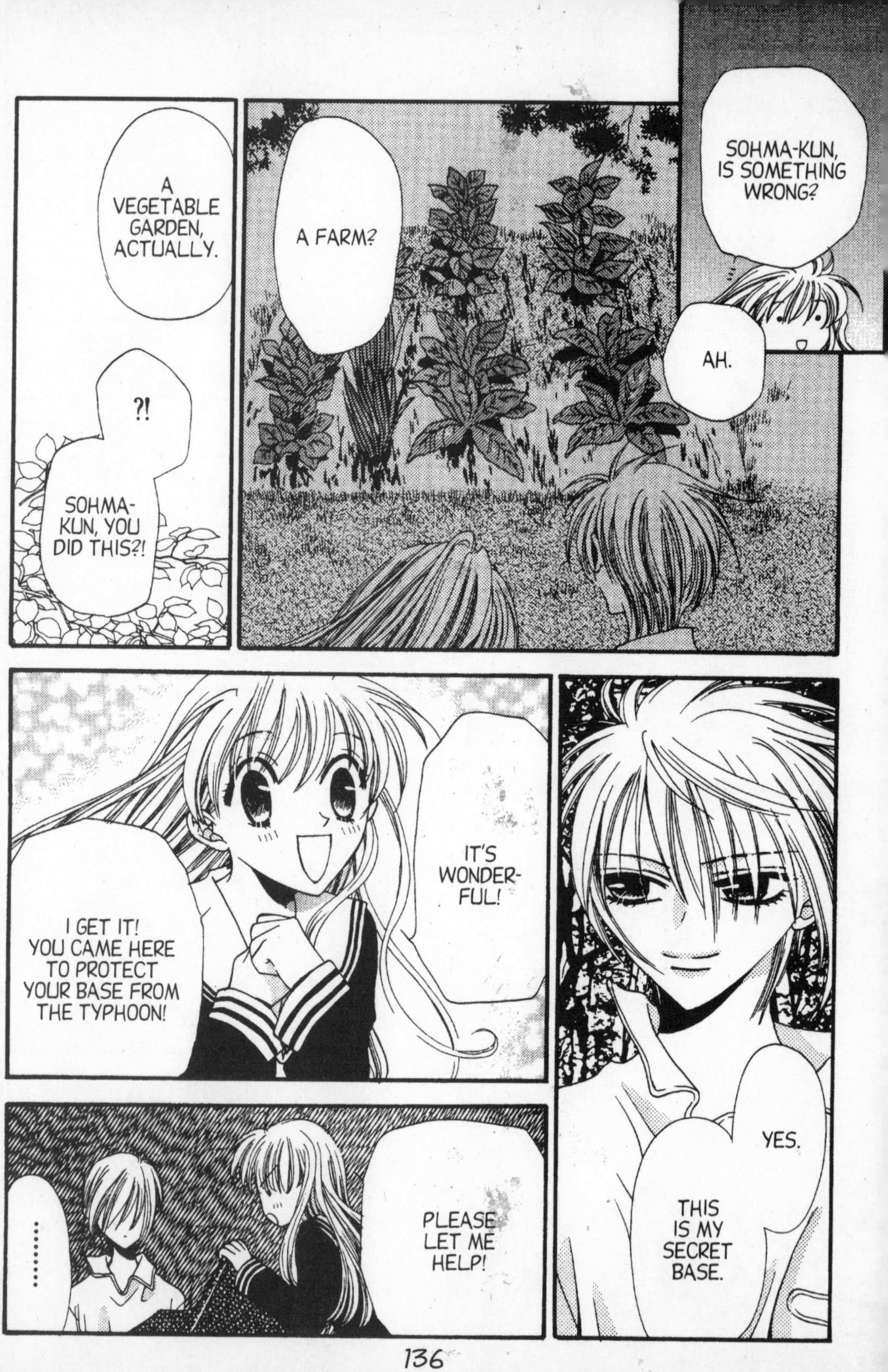
SOHMA-KUN, IS SOMETHING WRONG?
AH.
A FARM?
A VEGETABLE GARDEN, ACTUALLY.
?!
SOHMA-KUN, YOU DID THIS?!
YES.
THIS IS MY SECRET BASE.
IT'S WONDERFUL!
I GET IT! YOU CAME HERE TO PROTECT YOUR BASE FROM THE TYPHOON!
PLEASE LET ME HELP!
....

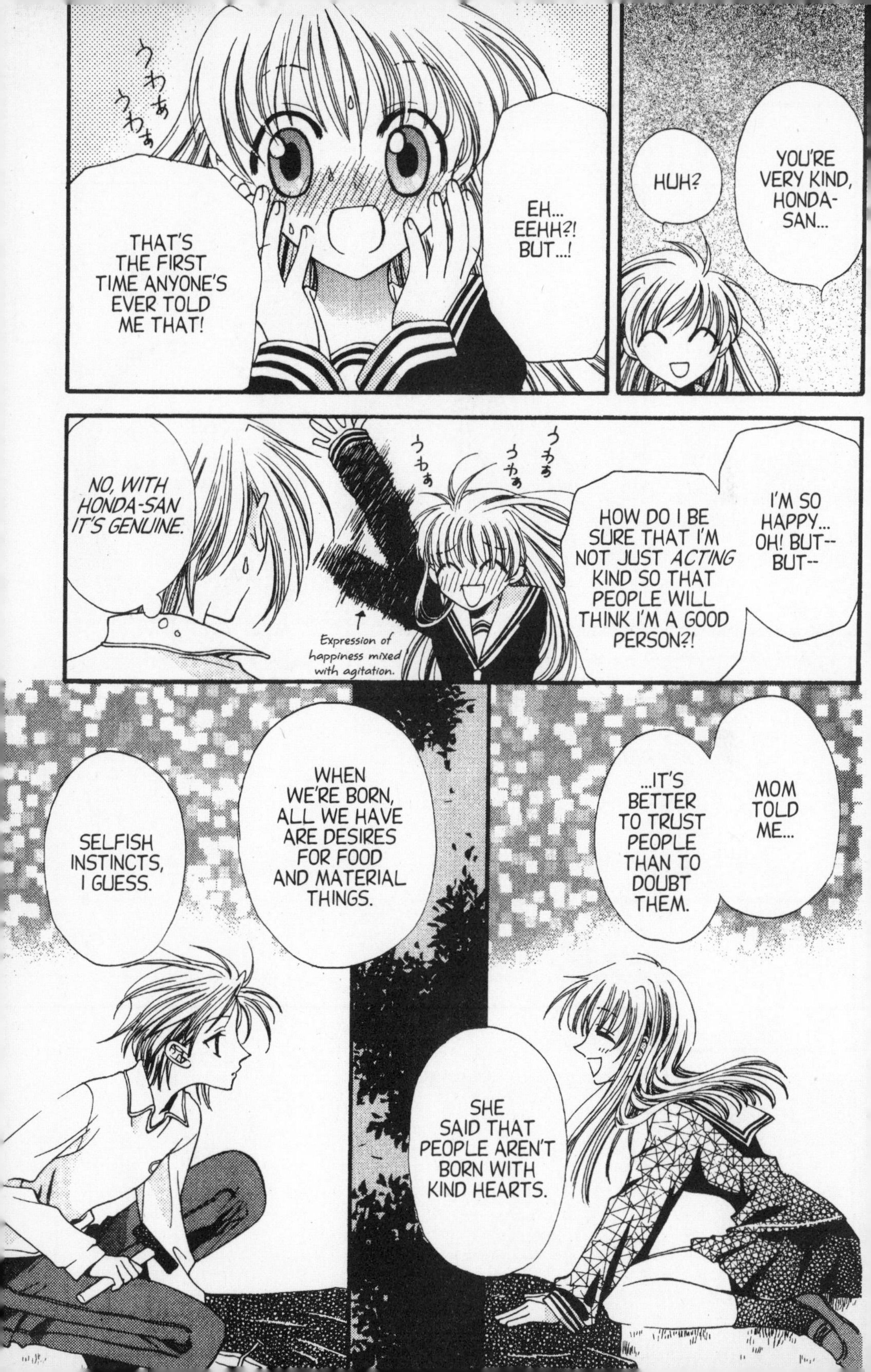
YOU'RE VERY KIND, HONDA-SAN...
HUH?
うわぁ うわぁ
EH... EEHH?! BUT...!
THAT'S THE FIRST TIME ANYONE'S EVER TOLD ME THAT!
I'M SO HAPPY... OH! BUT-- BUT--
HOW DO I BE SURE THAT I'M NOT JUST *ACTING* KIND SO THAT PEOPLE WILL THINK I'M A GOOD PERSON?!
うわぁ うわぁ
Expression of happiness mixed with agitation.
NO, WITH HONDA-SAN IT'S GENUINE.
MOM TOLD ME...
...IT'S BETTER TO TRUST PEOPLE THAN TO DOUBT THEM.
SHE SAID THAT PEOPLE AREN'T BORN WITH KIND HEARTS.
WHEN WE'RE BORN, ALL WE HAVE ARE DESIRES FOR FOOD AND MATERIAL THINGS.
SELFISH INSTINCTS, I GUESS.

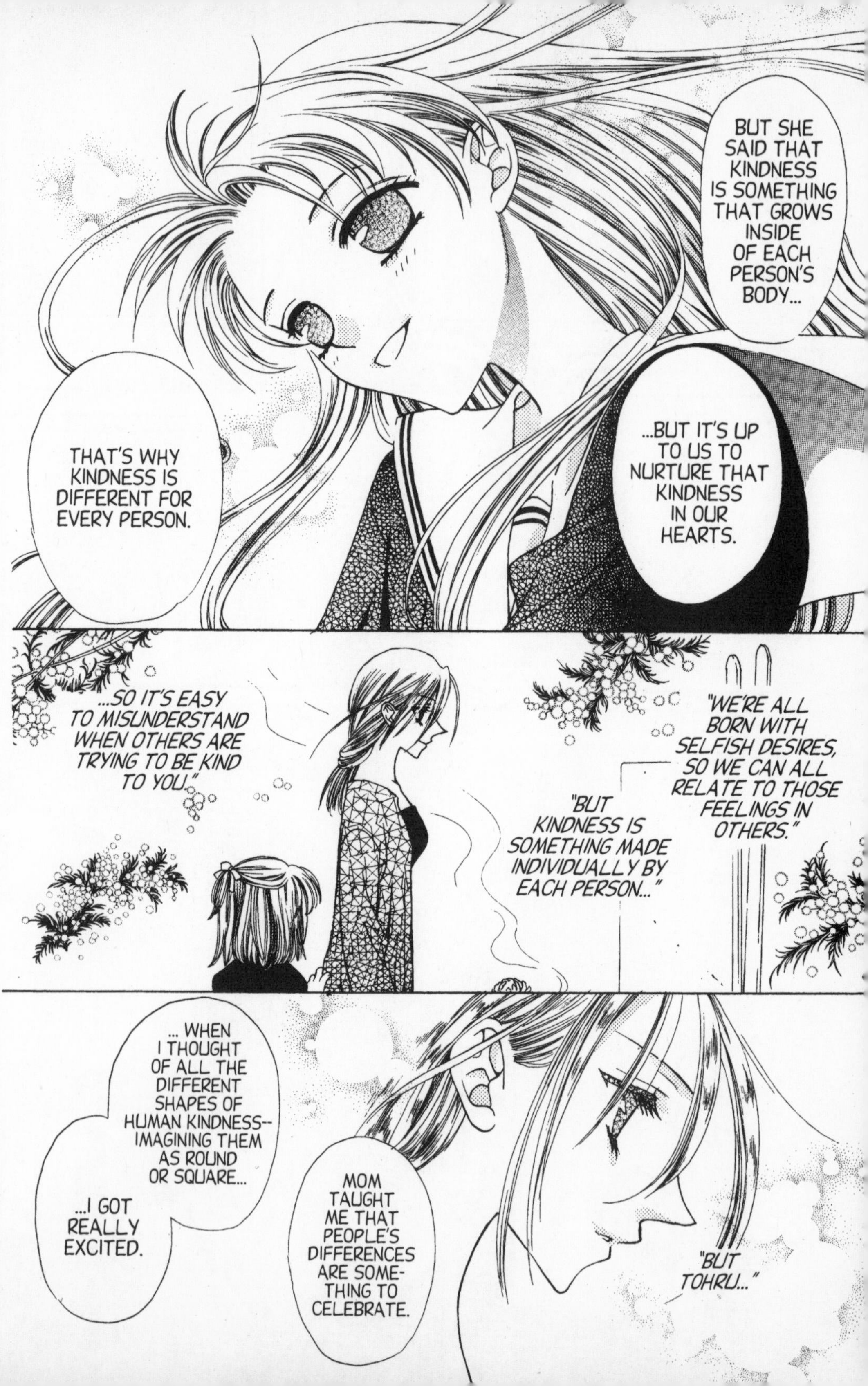
BUT SHE SAID THAT KINDNESS IS SOMETHING THAT GROWS INSIDE OF EACH PERSON'S BODY...
...BUT IT'S UP TO US TO NURTURE THAT KINDNESS IN OUR HEARTS.
THAT'S WHY KINDNESS IS DIFFERENT FOR EVERY PERSON.
"WE'RE ALL BORN WITH SELFISH DESIRES, SO WE CAN ALL RELATE TO THOSE FEELINGS IN OTHERS."
"BUT KINDNESS IS SOMETHING MADE INDIVIDUALLY BY EACH PERSON..."
...SO IT'S EASY TO MISUNDERSTAND WHEN OTHERS ARE TRYING TO BE KIND TO YOU."
"BUT TOHRU..."
MOM TAUGHT ME THAT PEOPLE'S DIFFERENCES ARE SOME-THING TO CELEBRATE.
... WHEN I THOUGHT OF ALL THE DIFFERENT SHAPES OF HUMAN KINDNESS--IMAGINING THEM AS ROUND OR SQUARE...
...I GOT REALLY EXCITED.

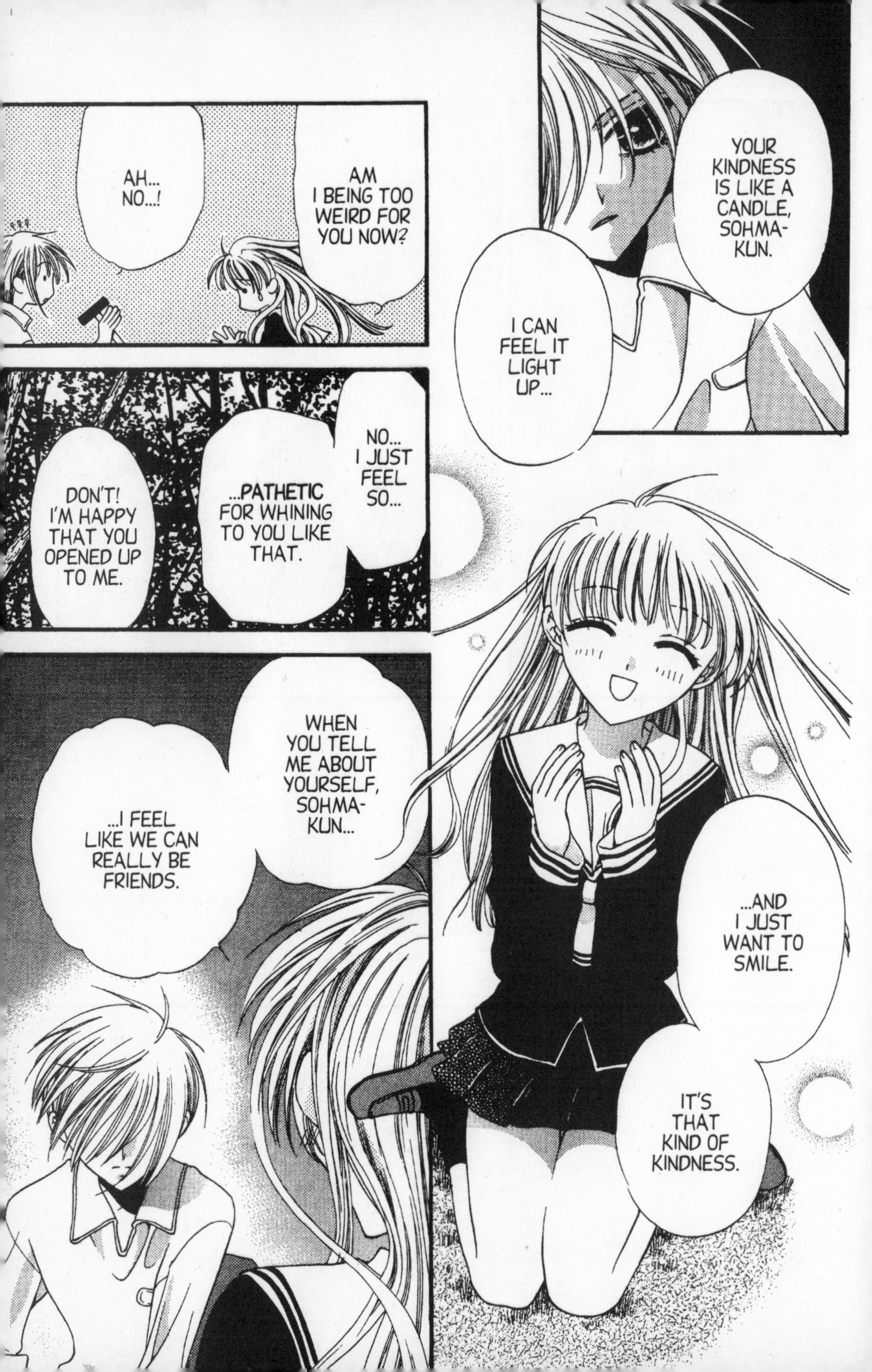
YOUR KINDNESS IS LIKE A CANDLE, SOHMA-KUN.
I CAN FEEL IT LIGHT UP...
...AND I JUST WANT TO SMILE.
IT'S THAT KIND OF KINDNESS.
AM I BEING TOO WEIRD FOR YOU NOW?
AH... NO...!
NO... I JUST FEEL SO...
...PATHETIC FOR WHINING TO YOU LIKE THAT.
DON'T! I'M HAPPY THAT YOU OPENED UP TO ME.
WHEN YOU TELL ME ABOUT YOURSELF, SOHMA-KUN...
...I FEEL LIKE WE CAN REALLY BE FRIENDS.

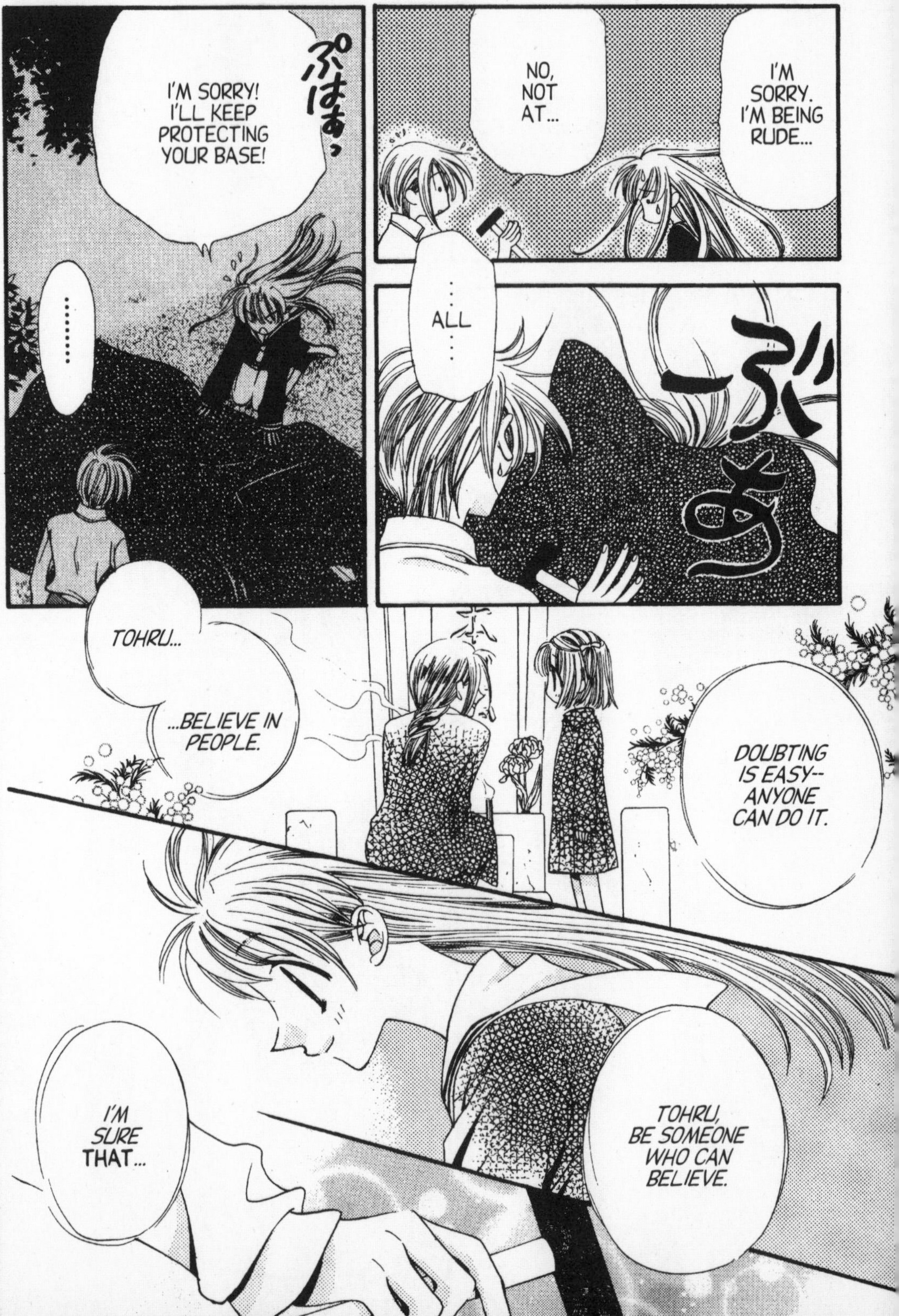
I'M SORRY. I'M BEING RUDE...
NO, NOT AT...
...ALL...
ぷはぁっ
I'M SORRY! I'LL KEEP PROTECTING YOUR BASE!
....
DOUBTING IS EASY-- ANYONE CAN DO IT.
TOHRU...
...BELIEVE IN PEOPLE.
TOHRU, BE SOMEONE WHO CAN BELIEVE.
I'M SURE THAT...

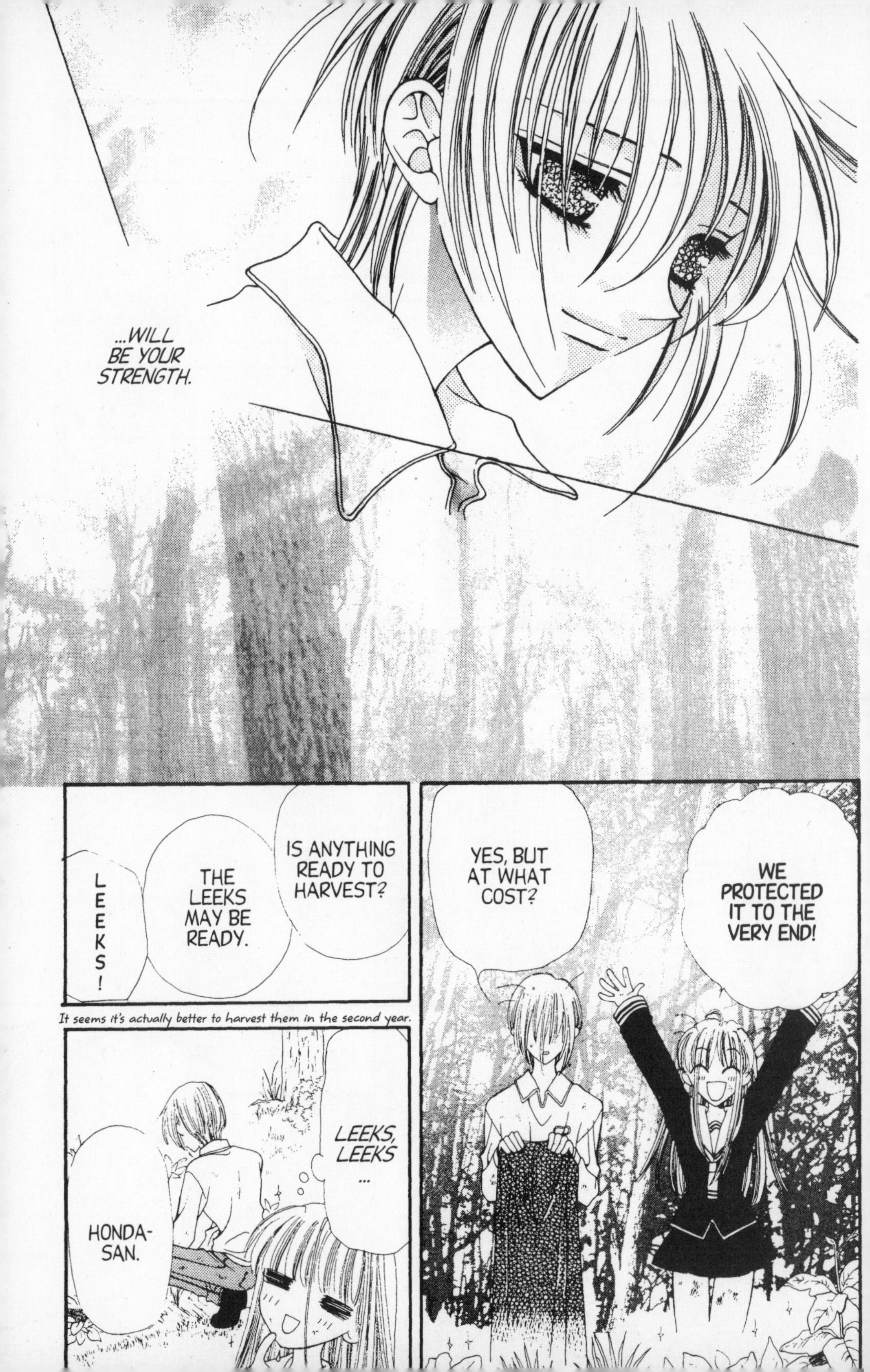
...WILL BE YOUR STRENGTH.
WE PROTECTED IT TO THE VERY END!
YES, BUT AT WHAT COST?
IS ANYTHING READY TO HARVEST?
THE LEEKS MAY BE READY.
LEEKS!
It seems it's actually better to harvest them in the second year.
LEEKS, LEEKS ...
HONDA-SAN.

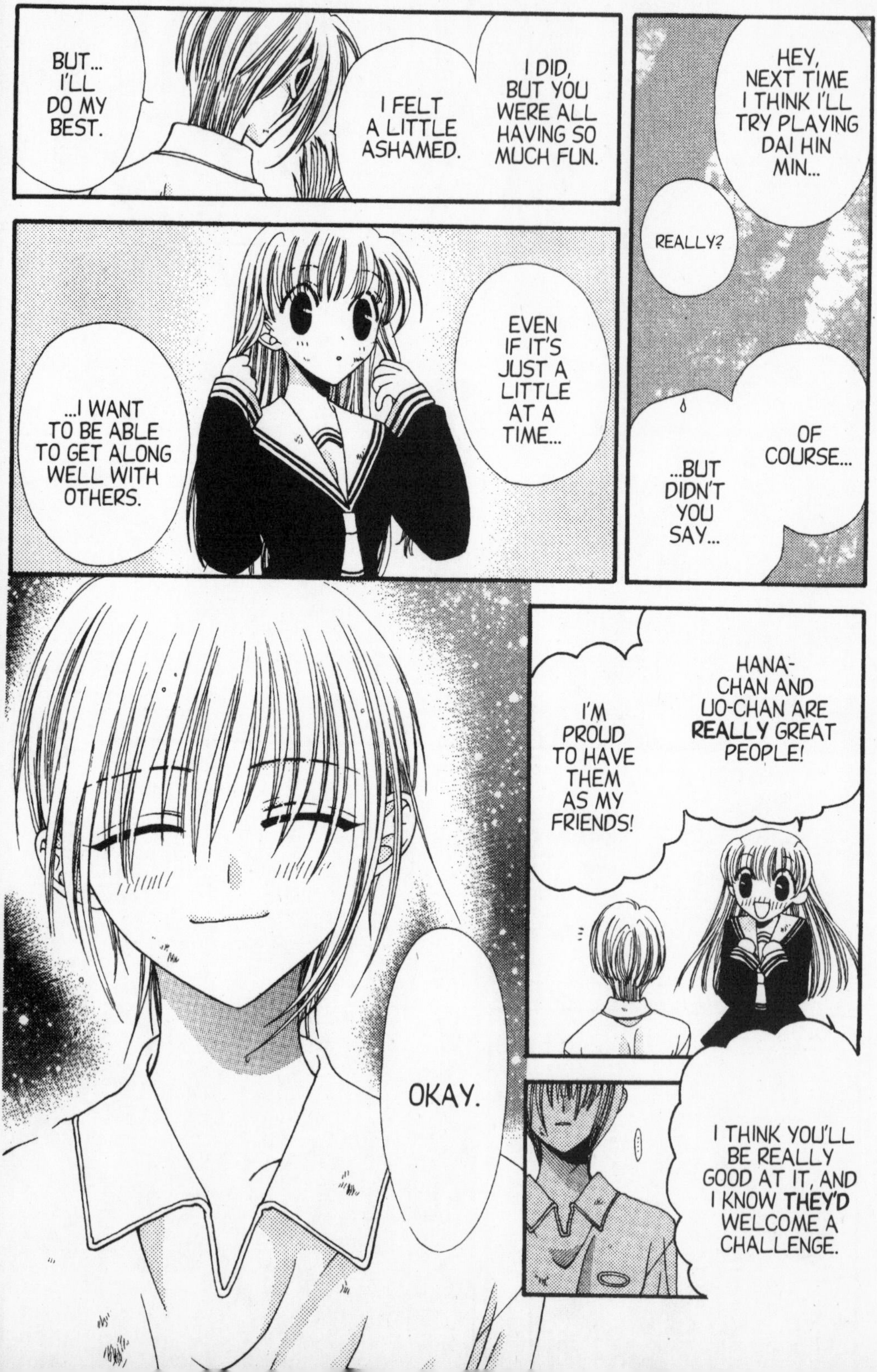
HEY, NEXT TIME I THINK I'LL TRY PLAYING DAI HIN MIN...
REALLY?
OF COURSE...
...BUT DIDN'T YOU SAY...
I DID, BUT YOU WERE ALL HAVING SO MUCH FUN.
I FELT A LITTLE ASHAMED.
BUT... I'LL DO MY BEST.
EVEN IF IT'S JUST A LITTLE AT A TIME...
...I WANT TO BE ABLE TO GET ALONG WELL WITH OTHERS.
HANA-CHAN AND UO-CHAN ARE **REALLY** GREAT PEOPLE!
I'M PROUD TO HAVE THEM AS MY FRIENDS!
I THINK YOU'LL BE REALLY GOOD AT IT, AND I KNOW **THEY'D** WELCOME A CHALLENGE.
......
OKAY.

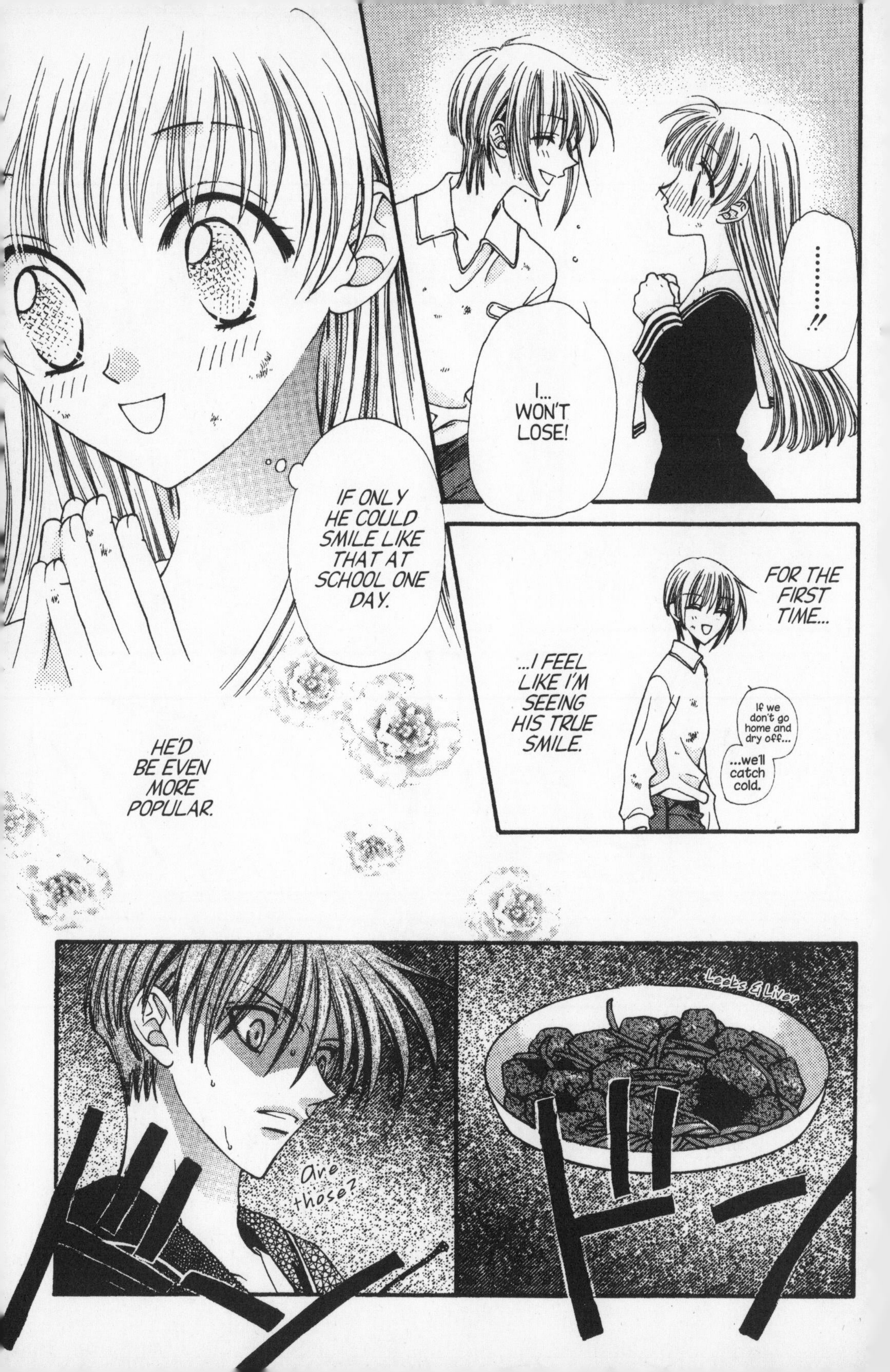

......!!
I... WON'T LOSE!
FOR THE FIRST TIME...
...I FEEL LIKE I'M SEEING HIS TRUE SMILE.
If we don't go home and dry off...
...we'll catch cold.
IF ONLY HE COULD SMILE LIKE THAT AT SCHOOL ONE DAY.
HE'D BE EVEN MORE POPULAR.
Leeks & Liver
Are those?

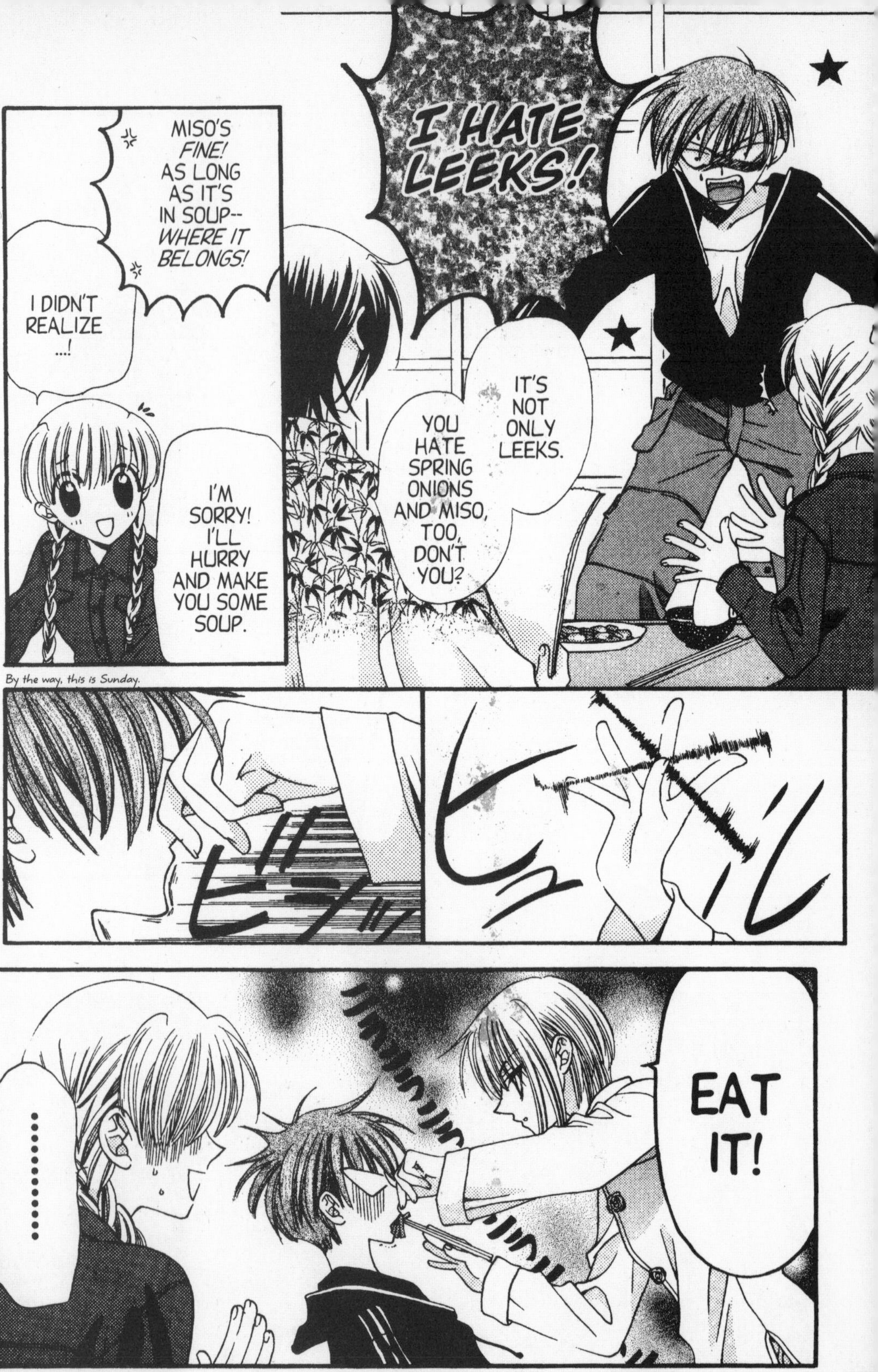
I HATE LEEKS!
IT'S NOT ONLY LEEKS.
YOU HATE SPRING ONIONS AND MISO, TOO, DON'T YOU?
MISO'S *FINE!* AS LONG AS IT'S IN SOUP-- *WHERE IT BELONGS!*
I DIDN'T REALIZE ...!
I'M SORRY! I'LL HURRY AND MAKE YOU SOME SOUP.
By the way, this is Sunday.
EAT IT!
....

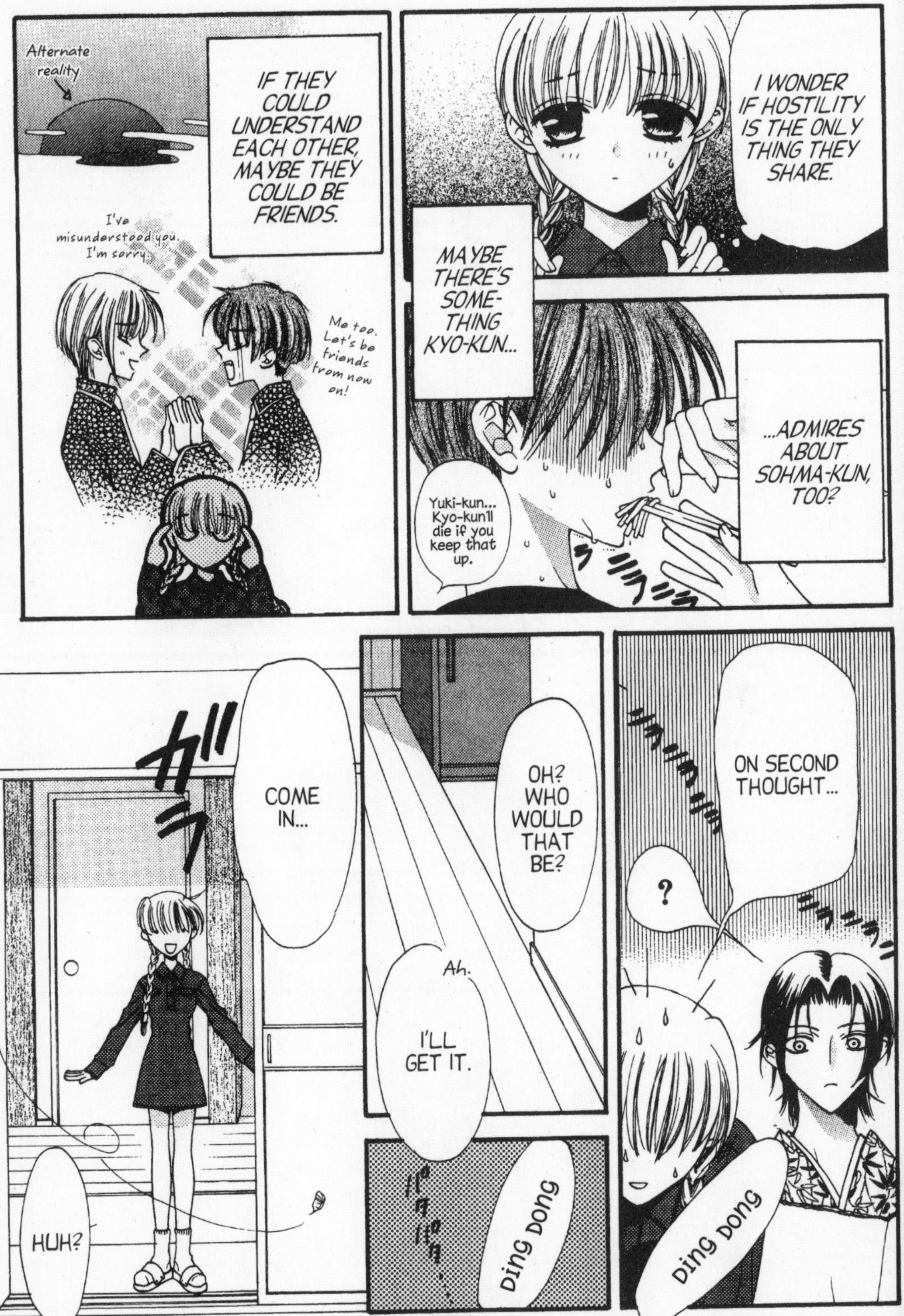
I WONDER IF HOSTILITY IS THE ONLY THING THEY SHARE.
MAYBE THERE'S SOME-THING KYO-KUN...
...ADMIRES ABOUT SOHMA-KUN, TOO?
Yuki-kun... Kyo-kun'll die if you keep that up.
IF THEY COULD UNDERSTAND EACH OTHER, MAYBE THEY COULD BE FRIENDS.
Alternate reality
I've misunderstood you. I'm sorry.
Me too. Let's be friends from now on!
ON SECOND THOUGHT...
?
DING DONG
OH? WHO WOULD THAT BE?
Ah.
I'LL GET IT.
DING DONG
COME IN...
HUH?

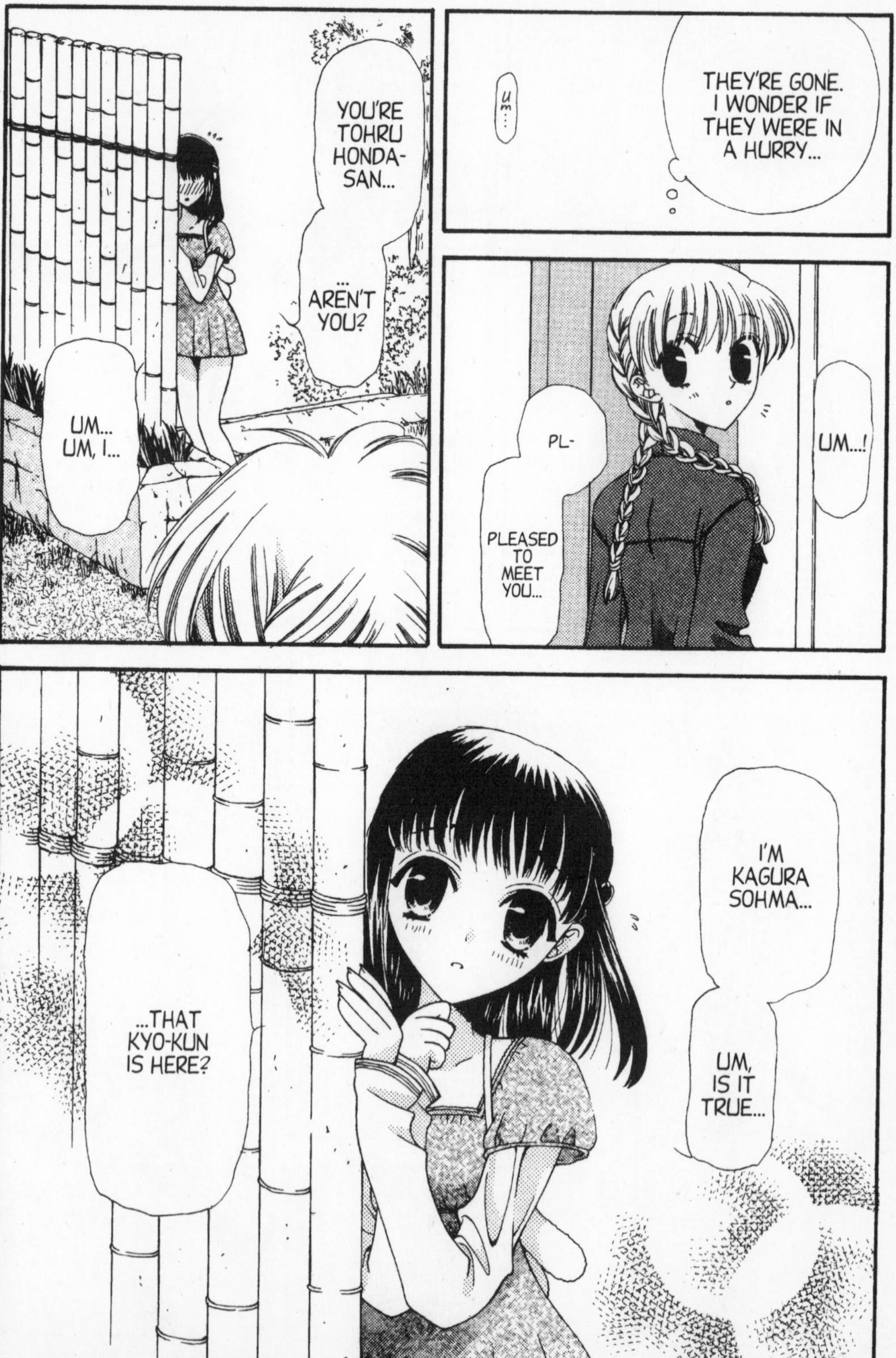
THEY'RE GONE. I WONDER IF THEY WERE IN A HURRY...
um...
UM...!
PL-
PLEASED TO MEET YOU...
YOU'RE TOHRU HONDA-SAN...
...AREN'T YOU?
UM... UM, I...
I'M KAGURA SOHMA...
UM, IS IT TRUE...
...THAT KYO-KUN IS HERE?

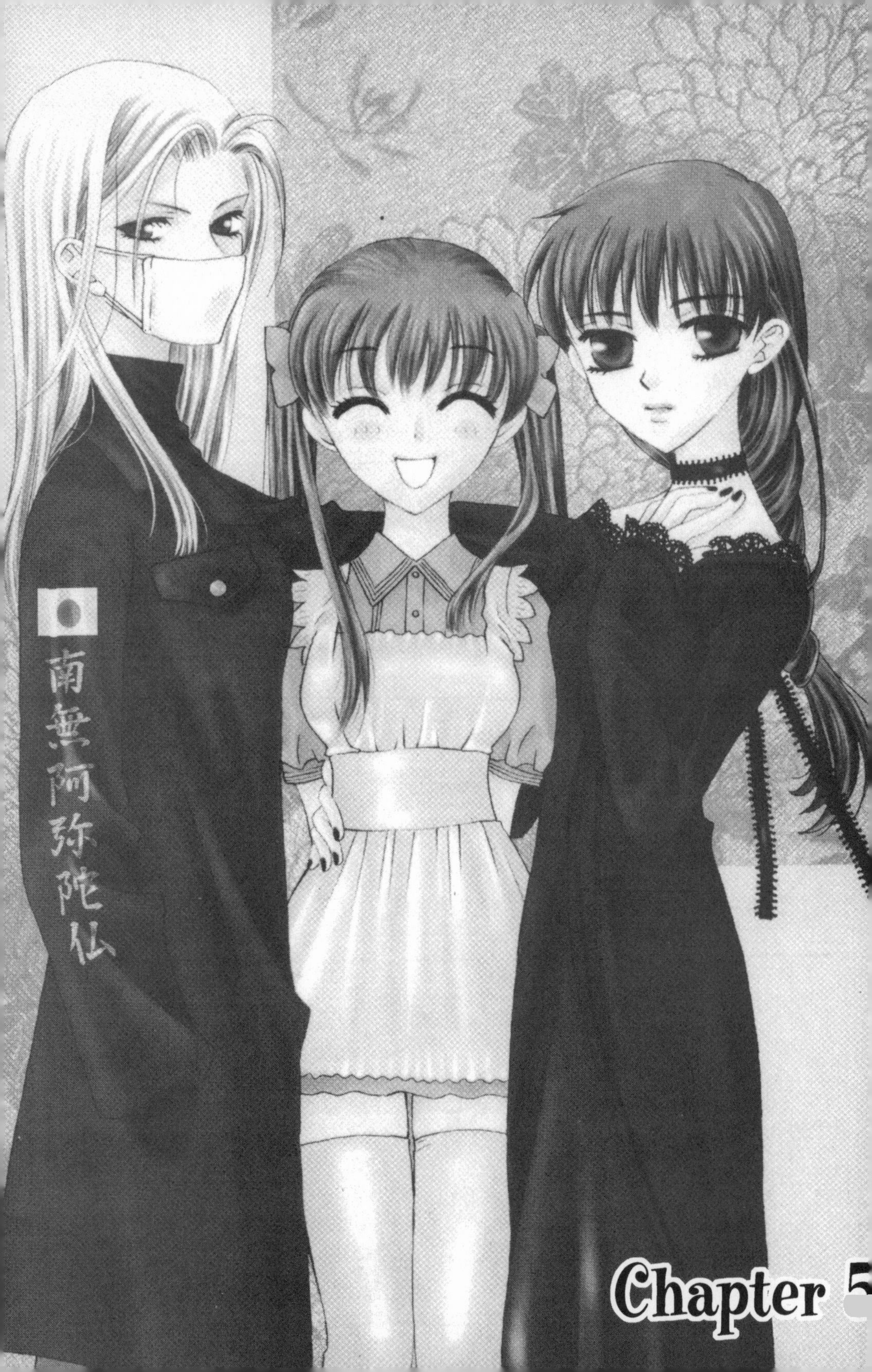
南無阿弥陀仏
Chapter 5

Omake Theater 3: Are you kidding or are you serious?

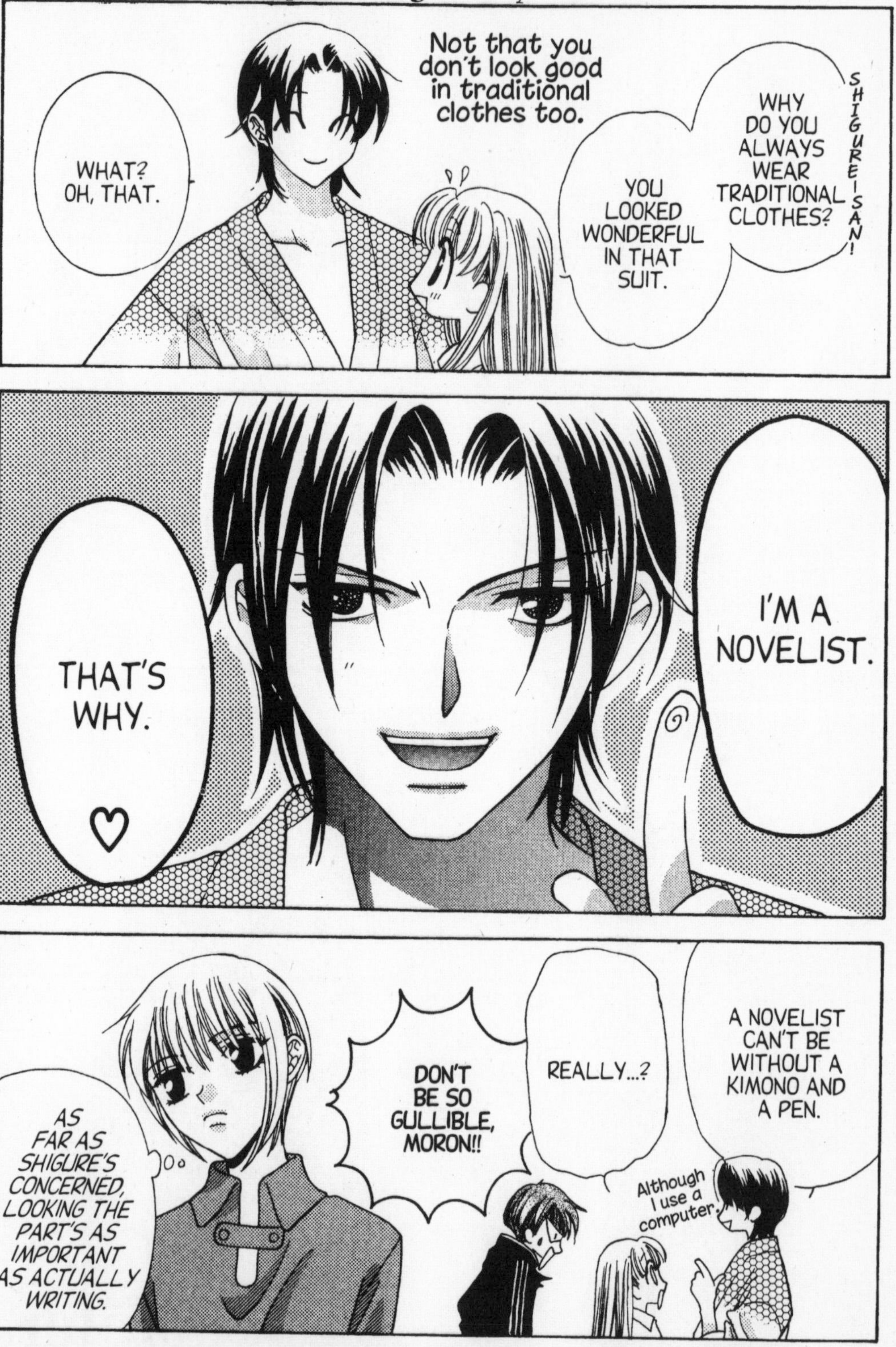
SHIGURE-SAN!
WHY DO YOU ALWAYS WEAR TRADITIONAL CLOTHES?
YOU LOOKED WONDERFUL IN THAT SUIT.
Not that you don't look good in traditional clothes too.
WHAT? OH, THAT.
I'M A NOVELIST.
THAT'S WHY. ♡
A NOVELIST CAN'T BE WITHOUT A KIMONO AND A PEN.
Although I use a computer.
REALLY...?
DON'T BE SO GULLIBLE, MORON!!
AS FAR AS SHIGURE'S CONCERNED, LOOKING THE PART'S AS IMPORTANT AS ACTUALLY WRITING.

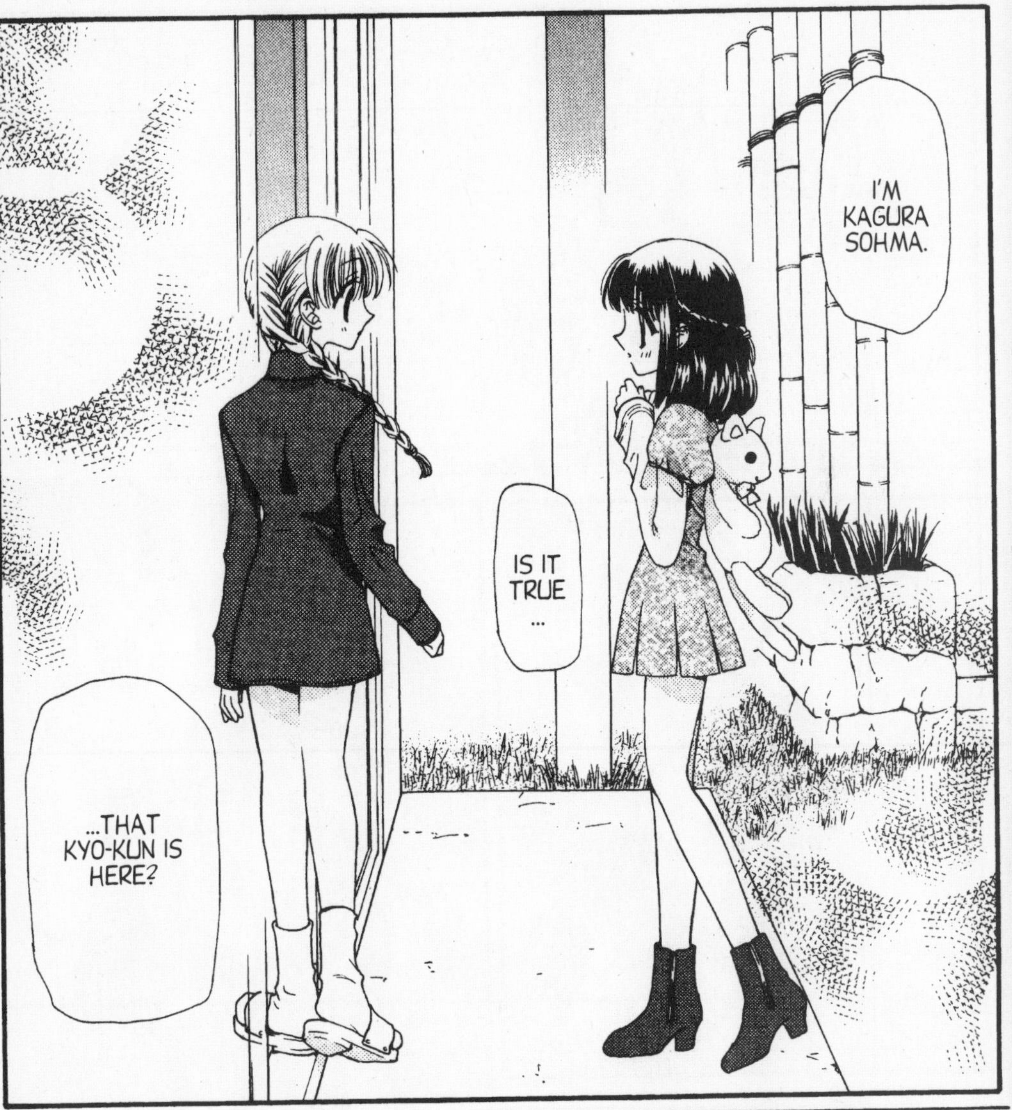
I'M KAGURA SOHMA.
IS IT TRUE ...
...THAT KYO-KUN IS HERE?

ULTRA SPECIAL BLAH BLAH BLAH, NUMBER 4:

I couldn't help wanting to draw a girl like Kagura. So I'm pleased (ha ha). I thought the opinions on her would be divided between, "She's hilarious!" and "Why does she hit him? That's so mean!" and I was right. She hits him because she loves him. It's the ultimate expression of love (ha ha).

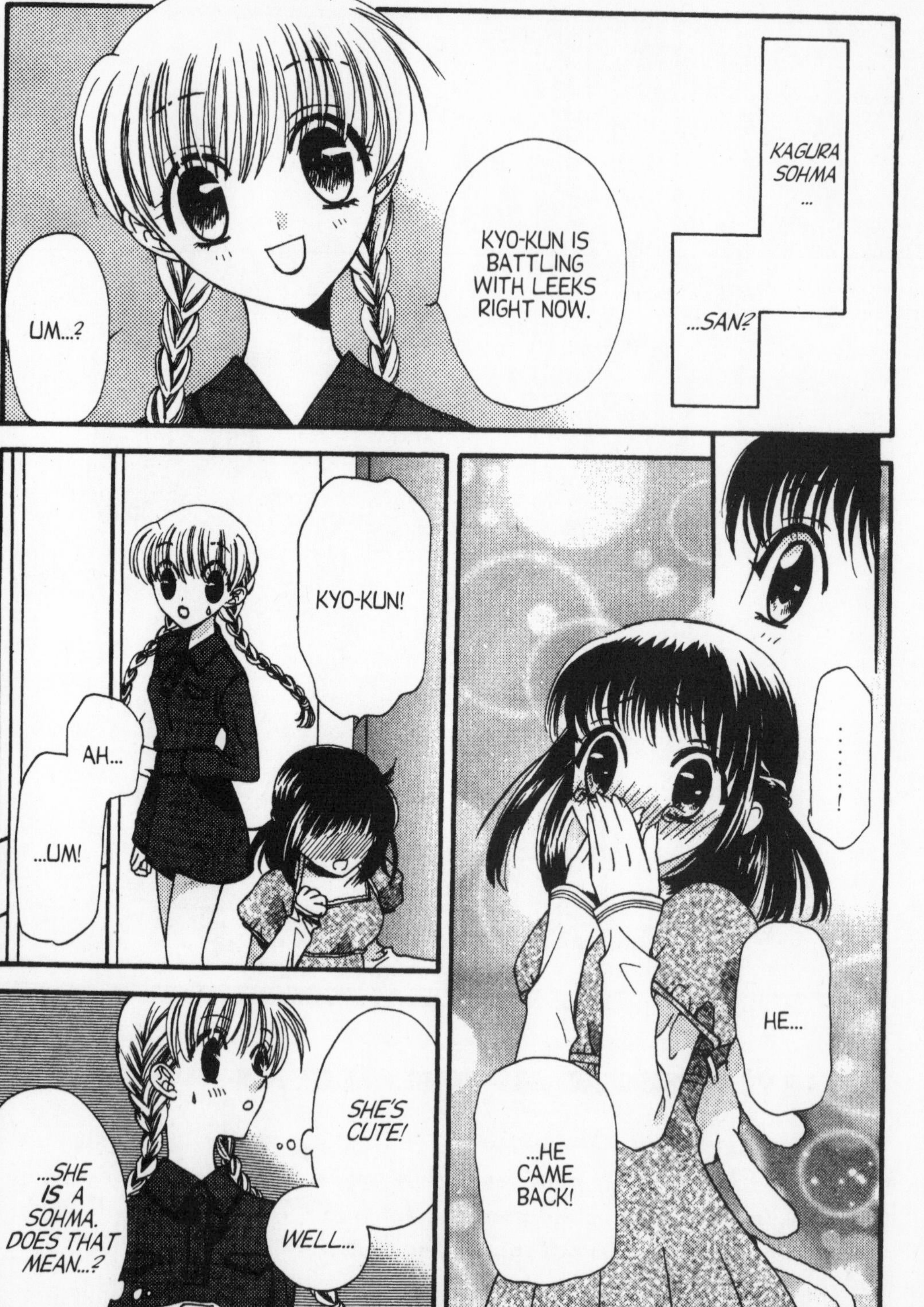
KAGURA SOHMA ...
...SAN?
KYO-KUN IS BATTLING WITH LEEKS RIGHT NOW.
UM...?
......!
HE...
...HE CAME BACK!
KYO-KUN!
AH...
...UM!
SHE'S CUTE!
WELL...
...SHE IS A SOHMA. DOES THAT MEAN...?

Number 6:

I have the Internet now. I feel weird about the Internet. I think it's a world that's there but not, and fake but real; I don't know what to call it (ha ha). It reminds me of "Soul Hackers." Yeah! I'm about half way through that game right now. Oh, no... I'm bubbling again- stay on target! I'm really getting into surfing around and checking out people's home pages. Home pages, huh...? I think I'd like to make one of my own, but I don't know how. If someone started one for me...? (ha ha) My home page would probably just talk about video games all the time!

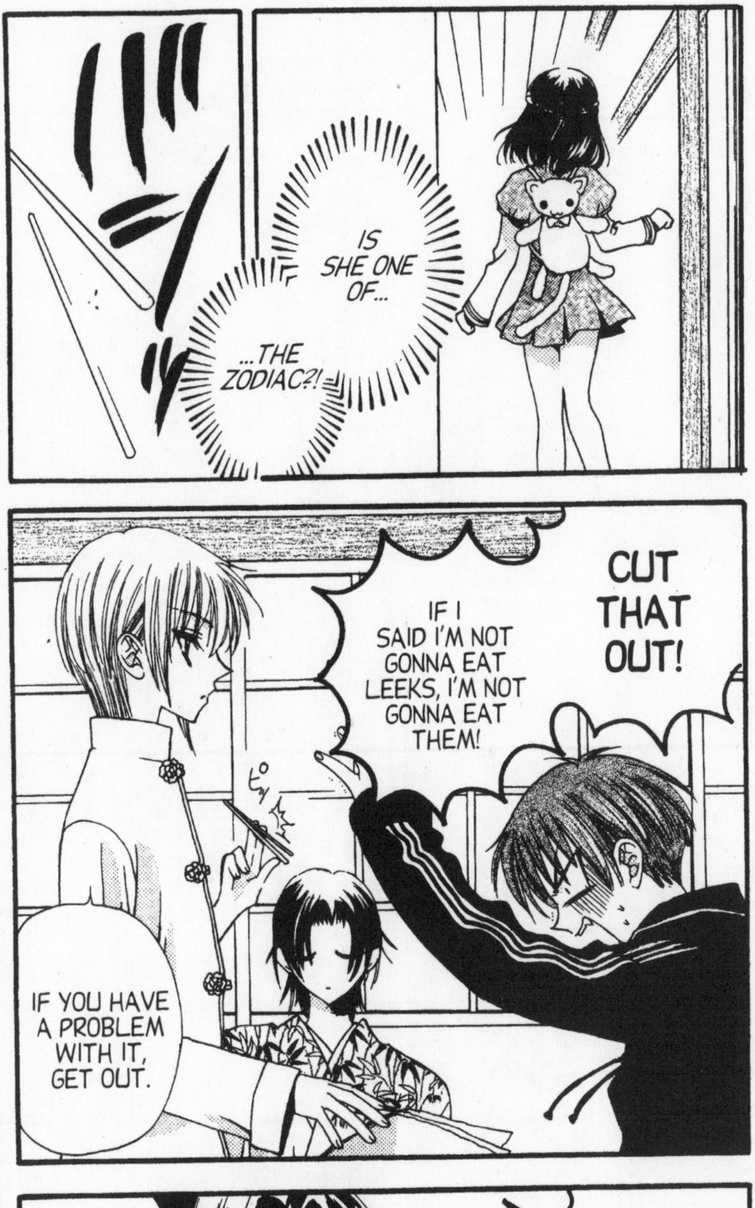
IS SHE ONE OF...
...THE ZODIAC?!
CUT THAT OUT!
IF I SAID I'M NOT GONNA EAT LEEKS, I'M NOT GONNA EAT THEM!
IF YOU HAVE A PROBLEM WITH IT, GET OUT.
YOU DON'T HAVE TO CONVINCE ME TO GET OUT OF THIS HOUSE!
THEY FIGHT LIKE A MARRIED COUPLE.
NOW, NOW... YUKI-KUN, KYO-KUN...

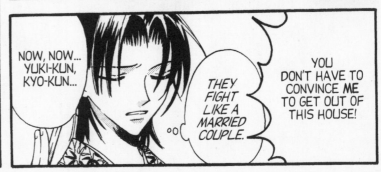

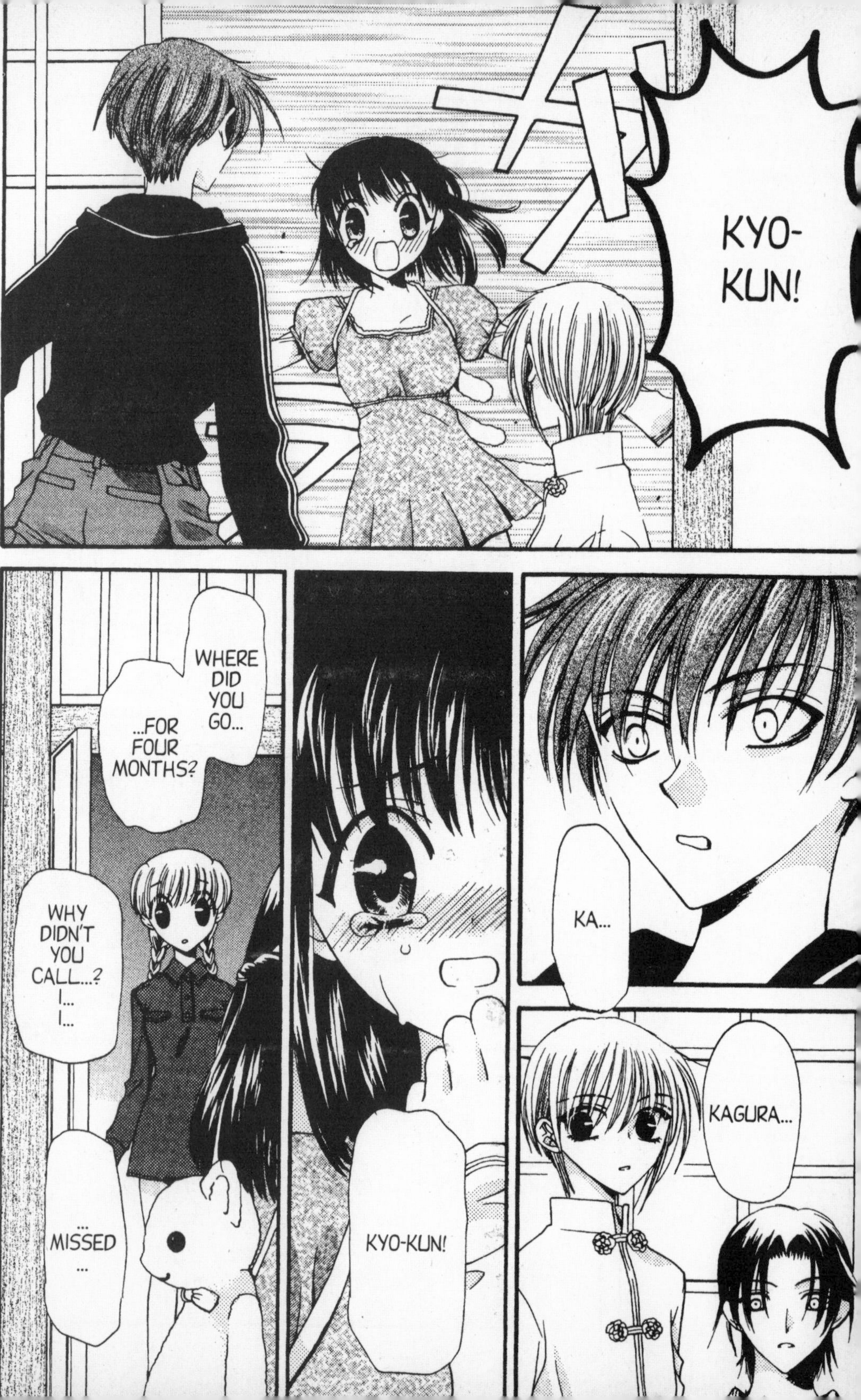
KYO-KUN!
KA...
KAGURA...
KYO-KUN!
WHERE DID YOU GO...
...FOR FOUR MONTHS?
WHY DIDN'T YOU CALL...? I... I...
...MISSED...

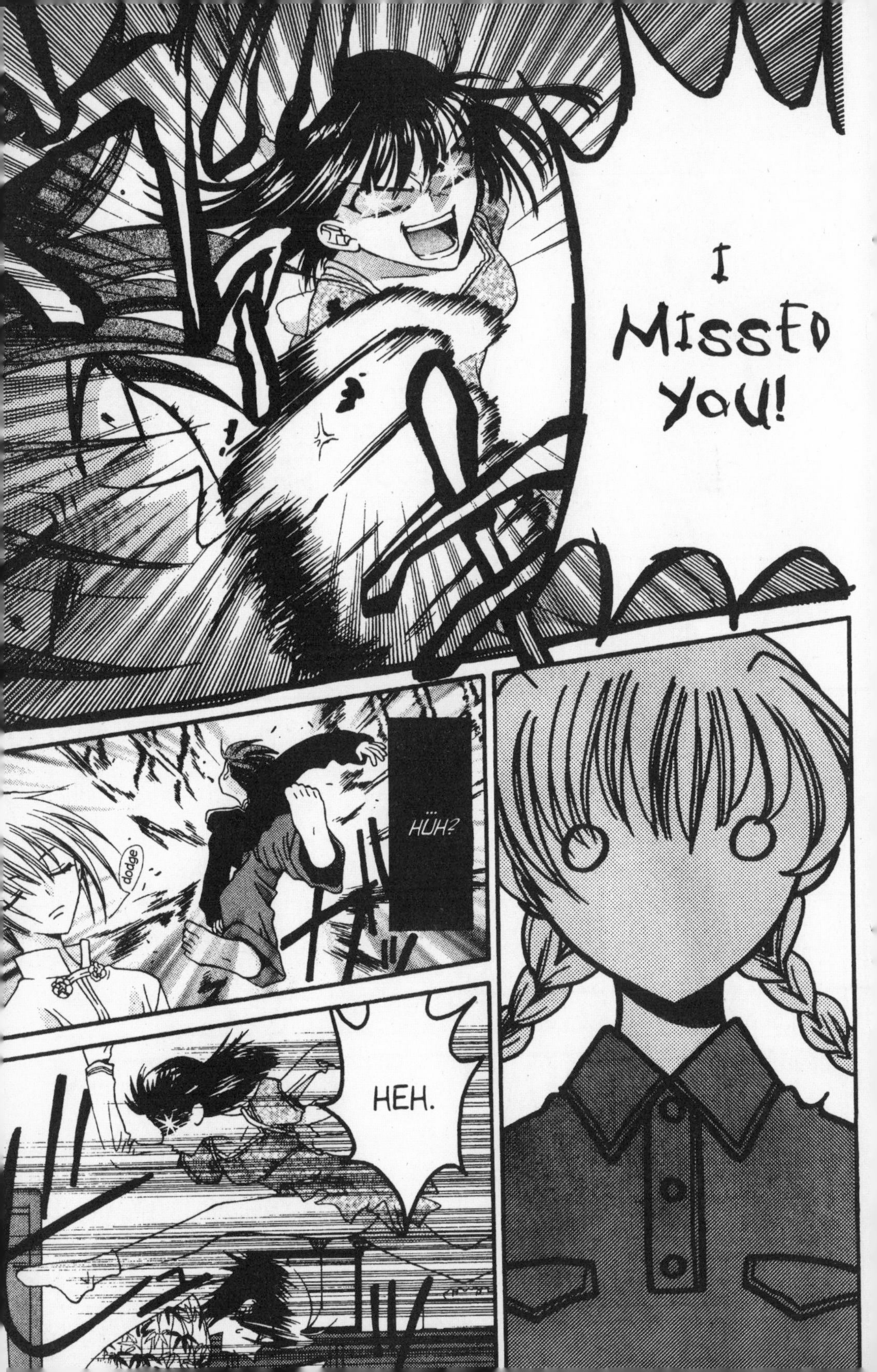
I MISSED YOU!
...HUH?
dodge
HEH.

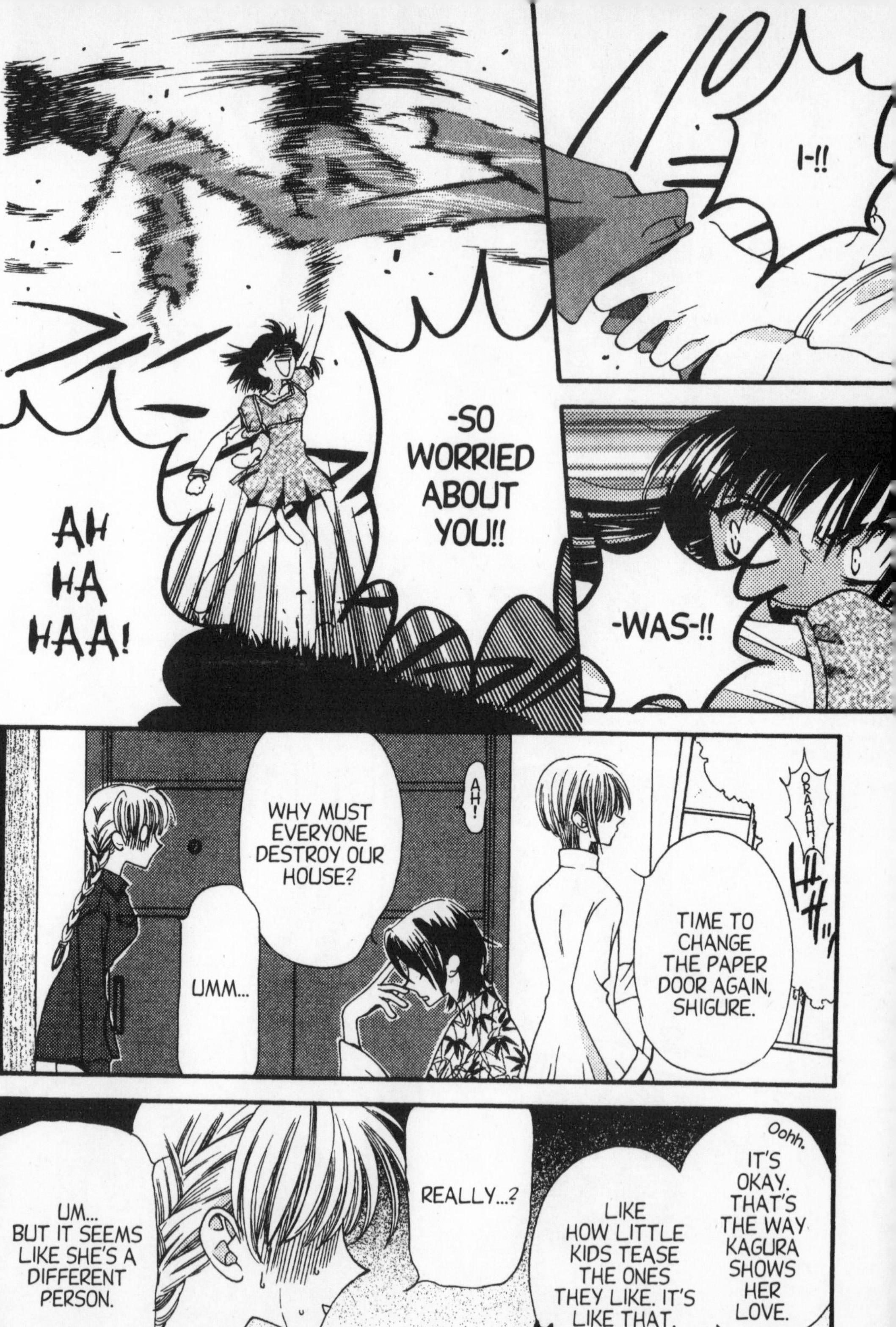
I-!!
-WAS-!!
-SO WORRIED ABOUT YOU!!
AH HA HAA!
ORAAH!!
TIME TO CHANGE THE PAPER DOOR AGAIN, SHIGURE.
AH!
WHY MUST EVERYONE DESTROY OUR HOUSE?
UMM...
Oohh.
IT'S OKAY. THAT'S THE WAY KAGURA SHOWS HER LOVE.
LIKE HOW LITTLE KIDS TEASE THE ONES THEY LIKE. IT'S LIKE THAT.
REALLY...?
UM... BUT IT SEEMS LIKE SHE'S A DIFFERENT PERSON.

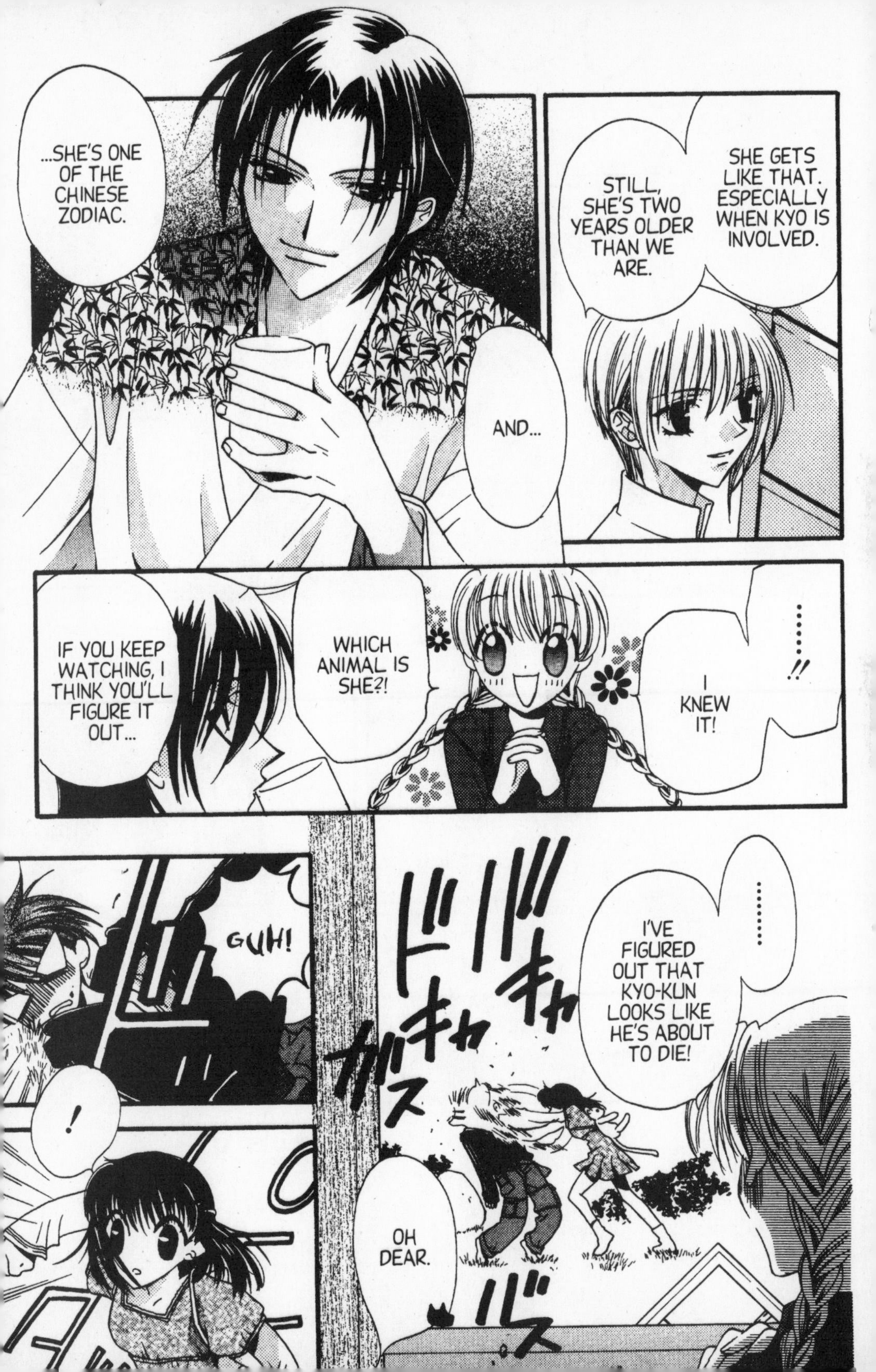
SHE GETS LIKE THAT. ESPECIALLY WHEN KYO IS INVOLVED.
STILL, SHE'S TWO YEARS OLDER THAN WE ARE.
AND...
...SHE'S ONE OF THE CHINESE ZODIAC.
......!!
I KNEW IT!
WHICH ANIMAL IS SHE?!
IF YOU KEEP WATCHING, I THINK YOU'LL FIGURE IT OUT...
......
I'VE FIGURED OUT THAT KYO-KUN LOOKS LIKE HE'S ABOUT TO DIE!
OH DEAR.
GUH!
!

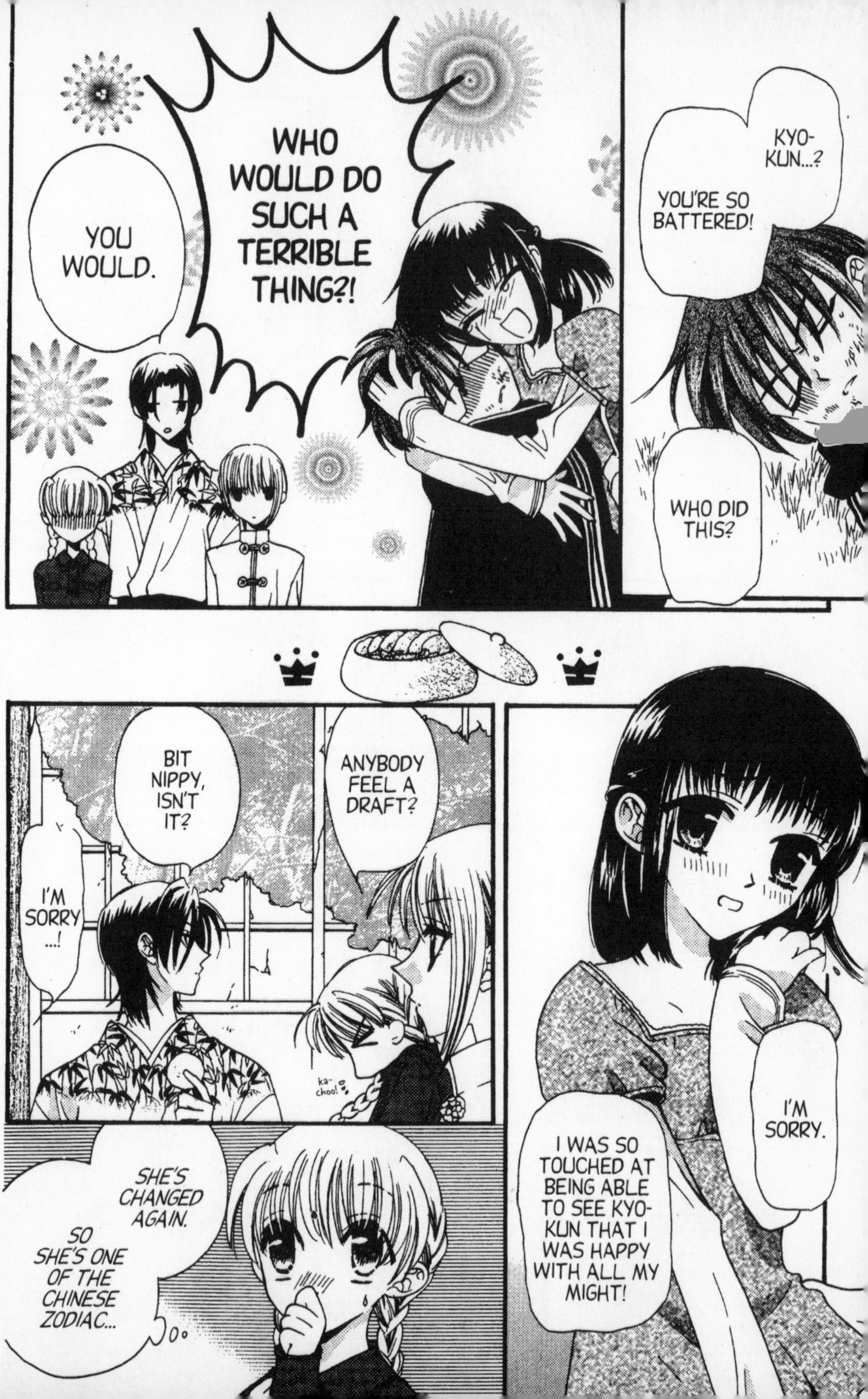
KYO-KUN...?
YOU'RE SO BATTERED!
WHO DID THIS?
WHO WOULD DO SUCH A TERRIBLE THING?!
YOU WOULD.
I'M SORRY.
I WAS SO TOUCHED AT BEING ABLE TO SEE KYO-KUN THAT I WAS HAPPY WITH ALL MY MIGHT!
ANYBODY FEEL A DRAFT?
BIT NIPPY, ISN'T IT?
I'M SORRY ...!
ka-choo!
SHE'S CHANGED AGAIN.
SO SHE'S ONE OF THE CHINESE ZODIAC...

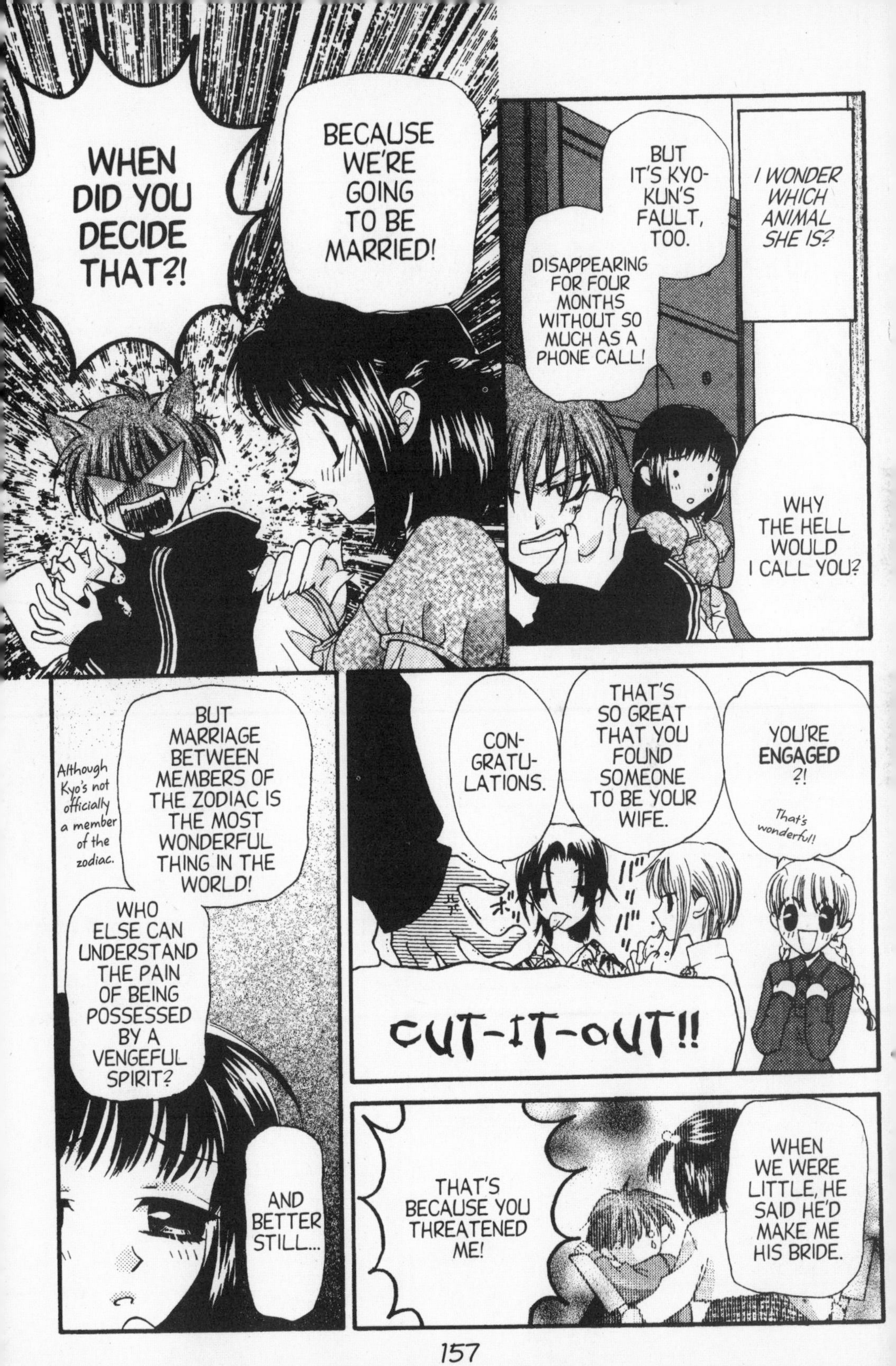
I WONDER WHICH ANIMAL SHE IS?
BUT IT'S KYO-KUN'S FAULT, TOO.
DISAPPEARING FOR FOUR MONTHS WITHOUT SO MUCH AS A PHONE CALL!
WHY THE HELL WOULD I CALL YOU?
BECAUSE WE'RE GOING TO BE MARRIED!
WHEN DID YOU DECIDE THAT?!
YOU'RE **ENGAGED**?!
That's wonderful!
THAT'S SO GREAT THAT YOU FOUND SOMEONE TO BE YOUR WIFE.
CON-GRATU-LATIONS.
CUT-IT-OUT!!
WHEN WE WERE LITTLE, HE SAID HE'D MAKE ME HIS BRIDE.
THAT'S BECAUSE YOU THREATENED ME!
BUT MARRIAGE BETWEEN MEMBERS OF THE ZODIAC IS THE MOST WONDERFUL THING IN THE WORLD!
Although Kyo's not officially a member of the zodiac.
WHO ELSE CAN UNDERSTAND THE PAIN OF BEING POSSESSED BY A VENGEFUL SPIRIT?
AND BETTER STILL...

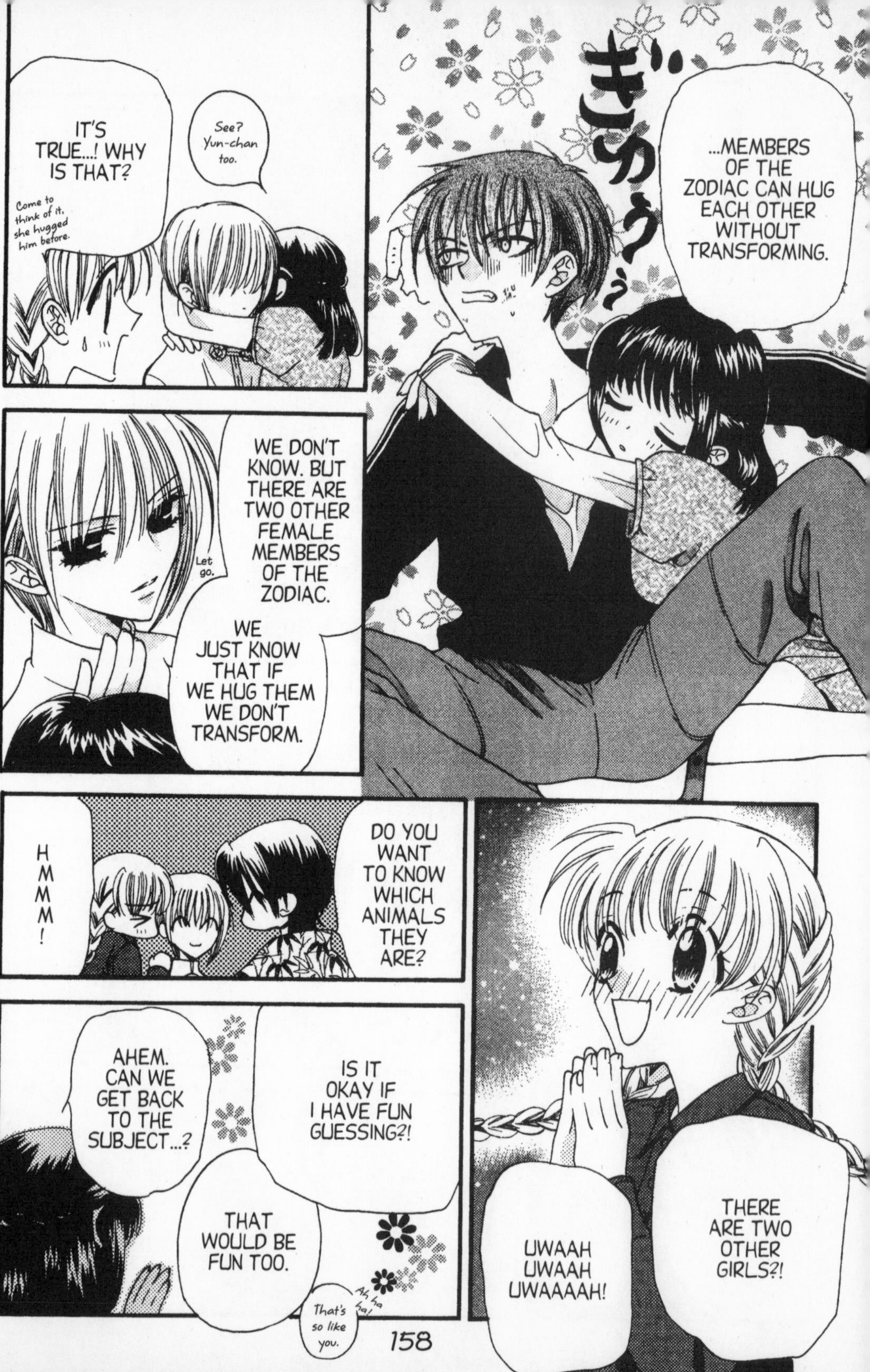
ぎゅう～
...MEMBERS OF THE ZODIAC CAN HUG EACH OTHER WITHOUT TRANSFORMING.
See? Yun-chan too.
IT'S TRUE...! WHY IS THAT?
Come to think of it, she hugged him before.
WE DON'T KNOW. BUT THERE ARE TWO OTHER FEMALE MEMBERS OF THE ZODIAC.
Let go.
WE JUST KNOW THAT IF WE HUG THEM WE DON'T TRANSFORM.
THERE ARE TWO OTHER GIRLS?!
UWAAH UWAAH UWAAAAH!
DO YOU WANT TO KNOW WHICH ANIMALS THEY ARE?
HMMM!
IS IT OKAY IF I HAVE FUN GUESSING?!
AHEM. CAN WE GET BACK TO THE SUBJECT...?
THAT WOULD BE FUN TOO.
Ah ha ha!
That's so like you.

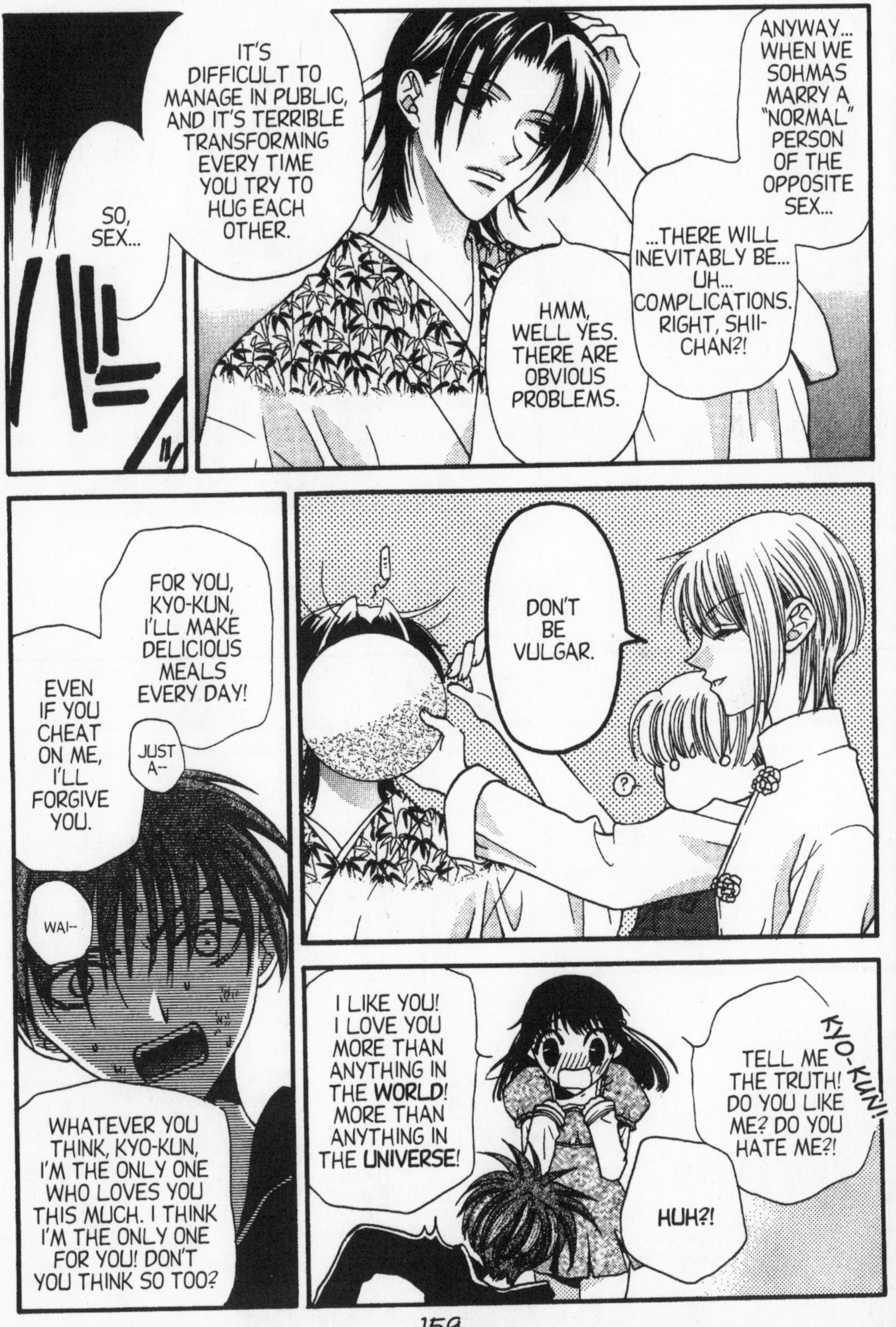
ANYWAY... WHEN WE SOHMAS MARRY A "NORMAL" PERSON OF THE OPPOSITE SEX...
...THERE WILL INEVITABLY BE... UH... COMPLICATIONS. RIGHT, SHII-CHAN?!
HMM, WELL YES. THERE ARE OBVIOUS PROBLEMS.
IT'S DIFFICULT TO MANAGE IN PUBLIC, AND IT'S TERRIBLE TRANSFORMING EVERY TIME YOU TRY TO HUG EACH OTHER.
SO, SEX...
DON'T BE VULGAR.
KYO-KUN!
TELL ME THE TRUTH! DO YOU LIKE ME? DO YOU HATE ME?!
HUH?!
I LIKE YOU! I LOVE YOU MORE THAN ANYTHING IN THE **WORLD**! MORE THAN ANYTHING IN THE **UNIVERSE**!
FOR YOU, KYO-KUN, I'LL MAKE DELICIOUS MEALS EVERY DAY!
JUST A--
EVEN IF YOU CHEAT ON ME, I'LL FORGIVE YOU.
WAI--
WHATEVER YOU THINK, KYO-KUN, I'M THE ONLY ONE WHO LOVES YOU THIS MUCH. I THINK I'M THE ONLY ONE FOR YOU! DON'T YOU THINK SO TOO?

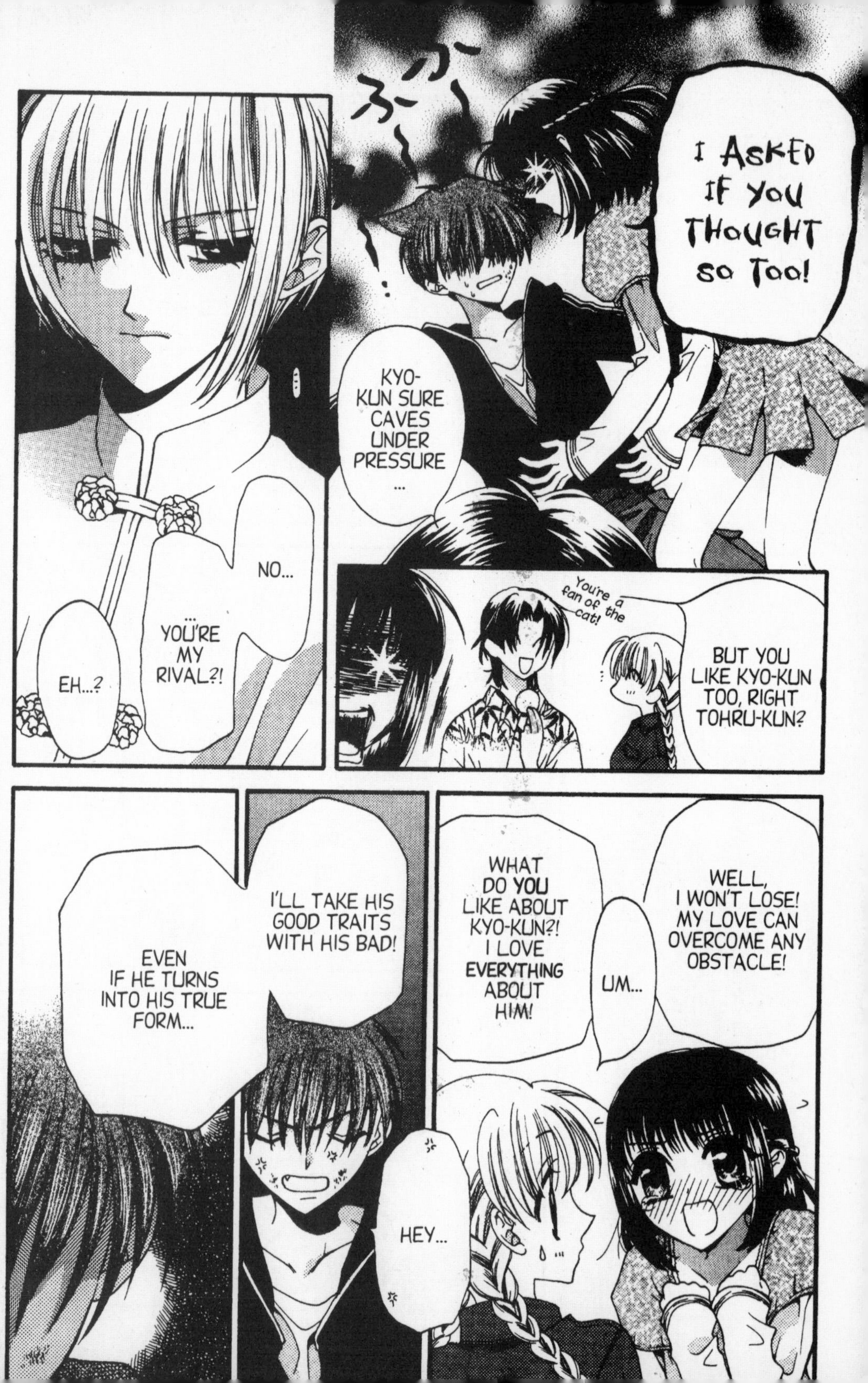
ぷ〜ぷ〜
I ASKED IF YOU THOUGHT SO TOO!
KYO-KUN SURE CAVES UNDER PRESSURE ...
BUT YOU LIKE KYO-KUN TOO, RIGHT TOHRU-KUN?
You're a fan of the cat!
NO...
... YOU'RE MY RIVAL?!
EH...?
WELL, I WON'T LOSE! MY LOVE CAN OVERCOME ANY OBSTACLE!
UM...
WHAT DO YOU LIKE ABOUT KYO-KUN?! I LOVE EVERYTHING ABOUT HIM!
HEY...
I'LL TAKE HIS GOOD TRAITS WITH HIS BAD!
EVEN IF HE TURNS INTO HIS TRUE FORM...

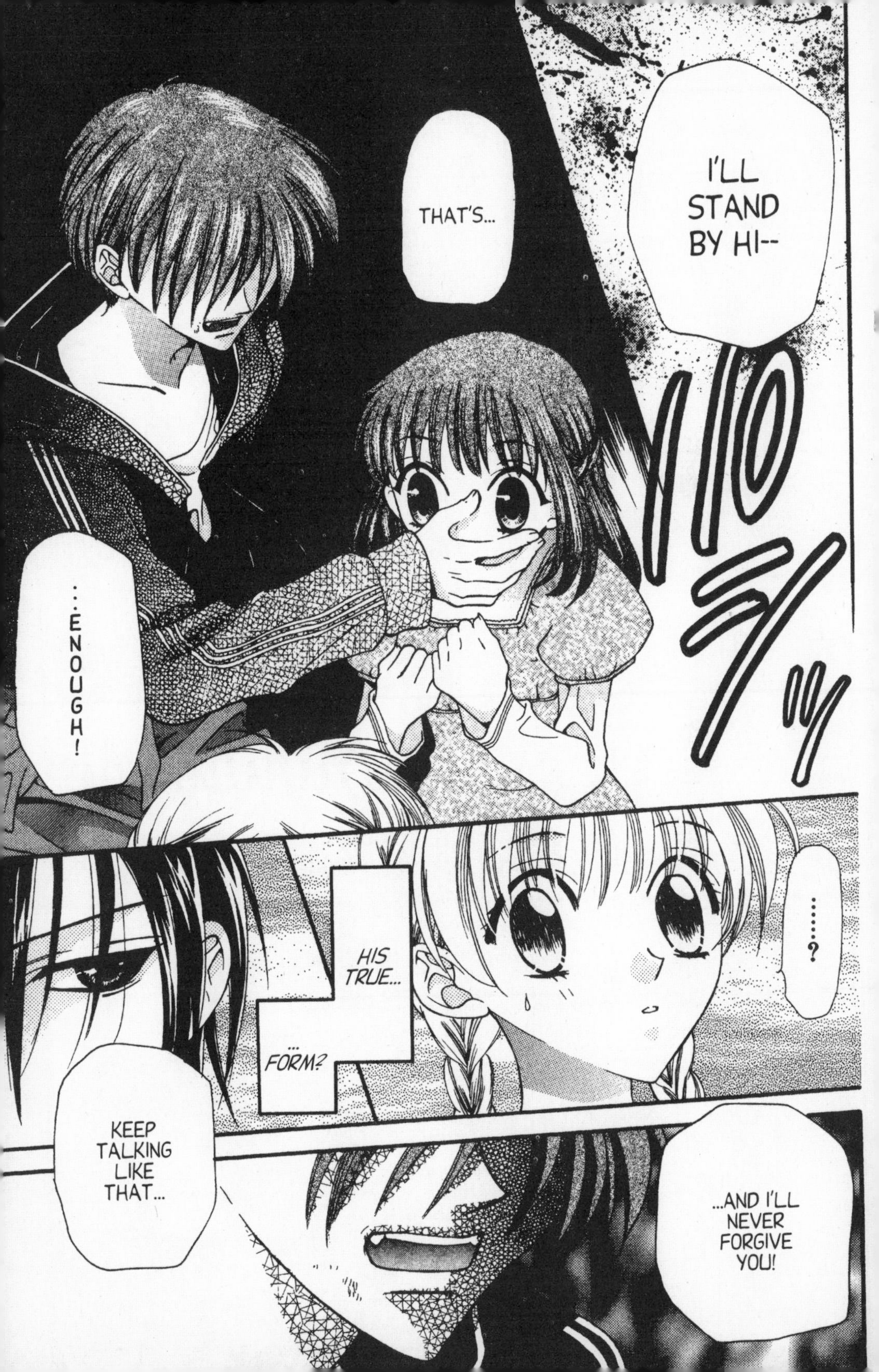
I'LL STAND BY HI--
THAT'S...
...ENOUGH!
......?
HIS TRUE...
...FORM?
KEEP TALKING LIKE THAT...
...AND I'LL NEVER FORGIVE YOU!

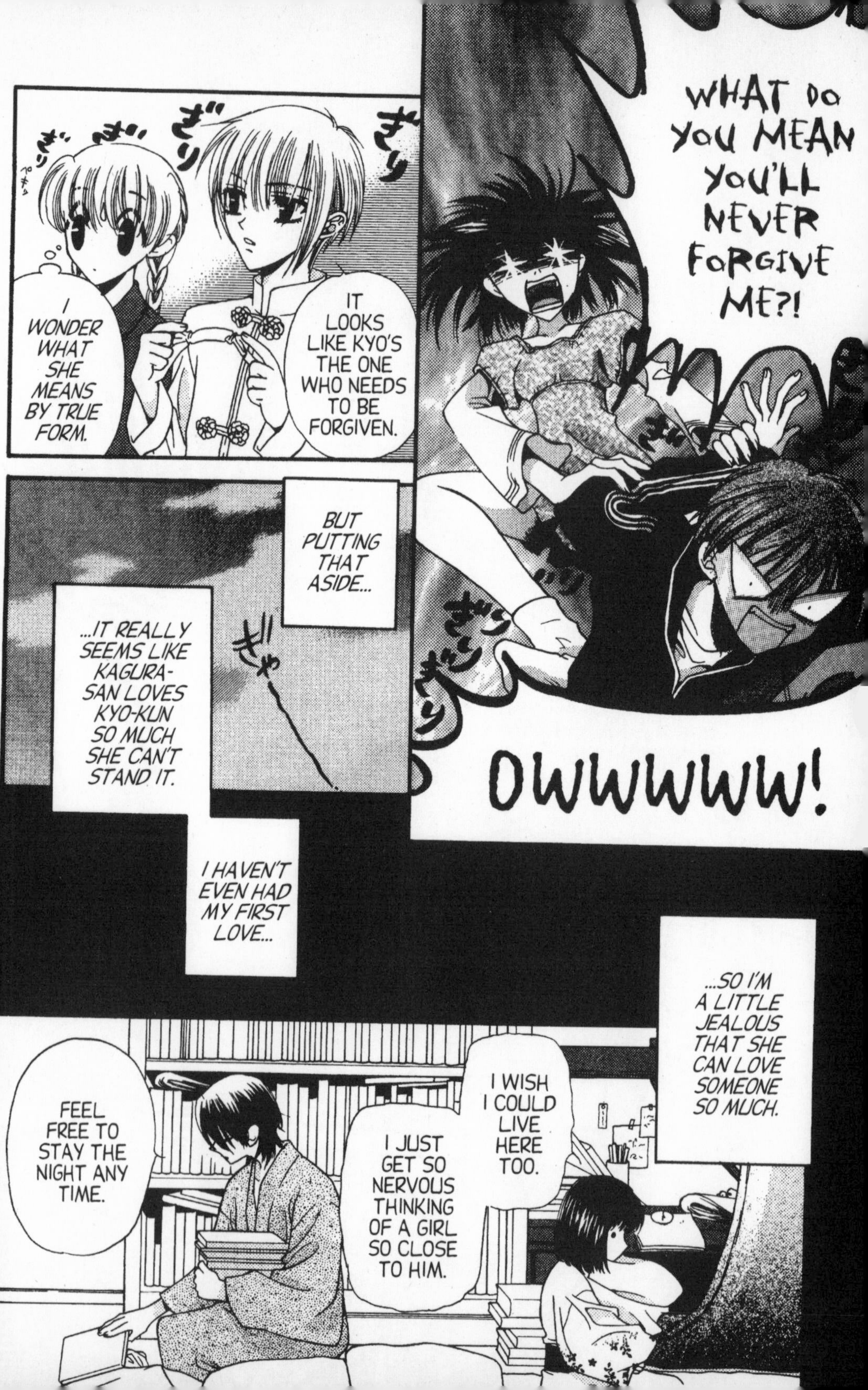
WHAT DO YOU MEAN YOU'LL NEVER FORGIVE ME?!
OWWWWW!
ぎり
IT LOOKS LIKE KYO'S THE ONE WHO NEEDS TO BE FORGIVEN.
I WONDER WHAT SHE MEANS BY TRUE FORM.
BUT PUTTING THAT ASIDE...
...IT REALLY SEEMS LIKE KAGURA-SAN LOVES KYO-KUN SO MUCH SHE CAN'T STAND IT.
ぎゃ
I HAVEN'T EVEN HAD MY FIRST LOVE...
...SO I'M A LITTLE JEALOUS THAT SHE CAN LOVE SOMEONE SO MUCH.
I WISH I COULD LIVE HERE TOO.
I JUST GET SO NERVOUS THINKING OF A GIRL SO CLOSE TO HIM.
FEEL FREE TO STAY THE NIGHT ANY TIME.

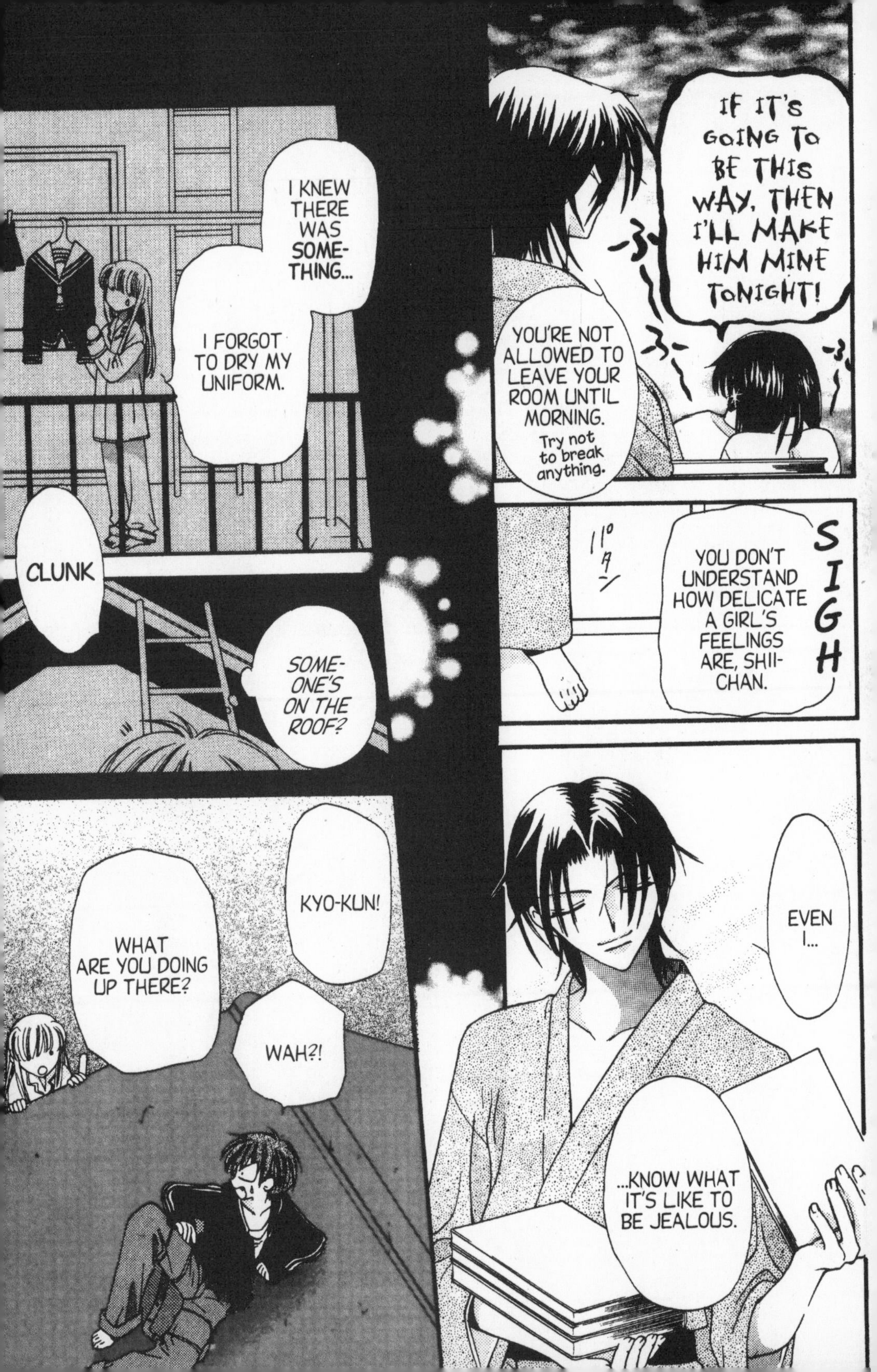
IF IT'S GOING TO BE THIS WAY, THEN I'LL MAKE HIM MINE TONIGHT!
YOU'RE NOT ALLOWED TO LEAVE YOUR ROOM UNTIL MORNING.
Try not to break anything.
SIGH
YOU DON'T UNDERSTAND HOW DELICATE A GIRL'S FEELINGS ARE, SHII-CHAN.
EVEN I...
...KNOW WHAT IT'S LIKE TO BE JEALOUS.
I KNEW THERE WAS SOME-THING...
I FORGOT TO DRY MY UNIFORM.
CLUNK
SOME-ONE'S ON THE ROOF?
KYO-KUN!
WHAT ARE YOU DOING UP THERE?
WAH?!

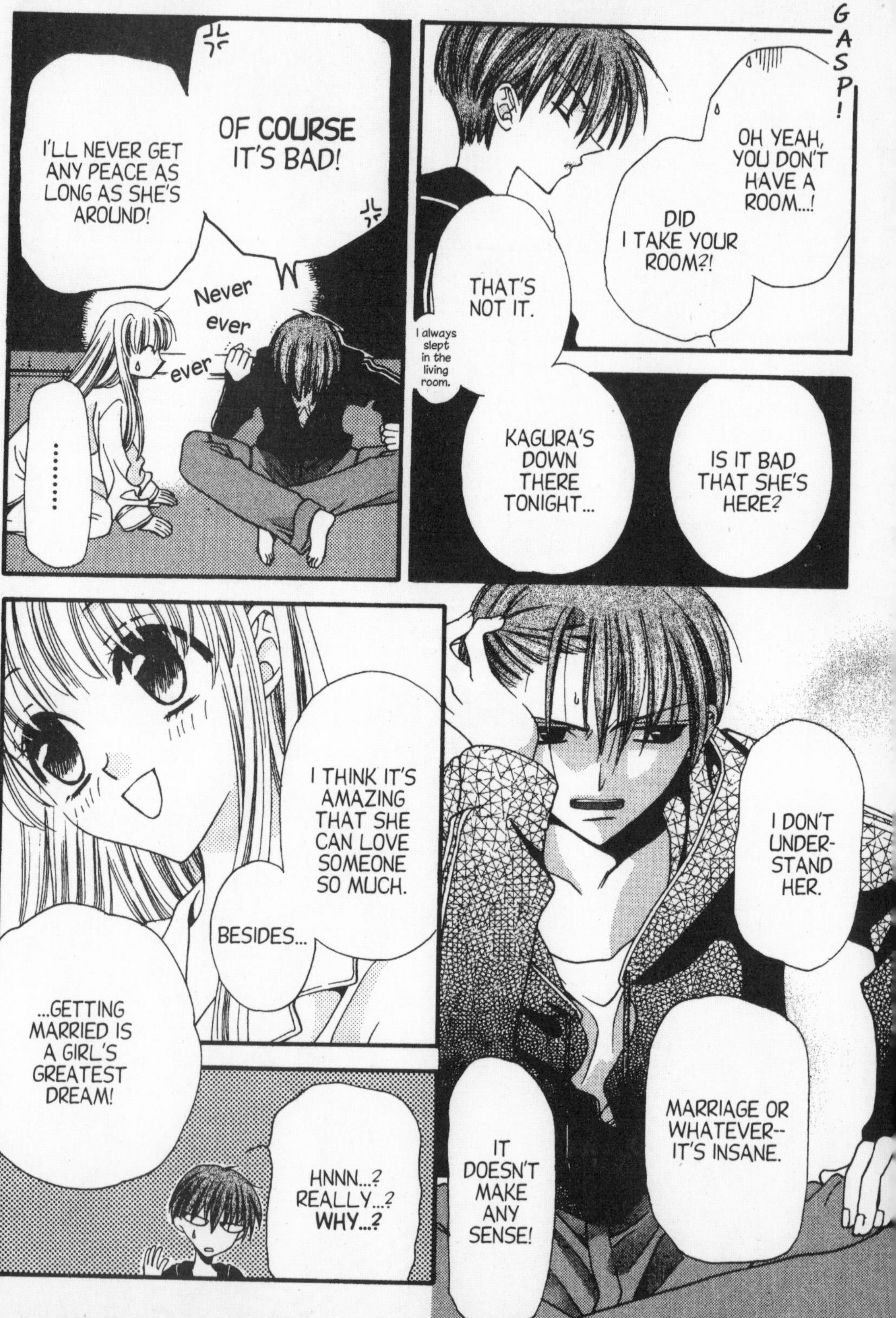
GASP!
OH YEAH, YOU DON'T HAVE A ROOM...!
DID I TAKE YOUR ROOM?!
THAT'S NOT IT.
I always slept in the living room.
IS IT BAD THAT SHE'S HERE?
KAGURA'S DOWN THERE TONIGHT...
OF COURSE IT'S BAD!
I'LL NEVER GET ANY PEACE AS LONG AS SHE'S AROUND!
Never ever ever
....
I DON'T UNDER-STAND HER.
MARRIAGE OR WHATEVER-- IT'S INSANE.
IT DOESN'T MAKE ANY SENSE!
I THINK IT'S AMAZING THAT SHE CAN LOVE SOMEONE SO MUCH.
BESIDES...
...GETTING MARRIED IS A GIRL'S GREATEST DREAM!
HNNN...? REALLY...? WHY...?

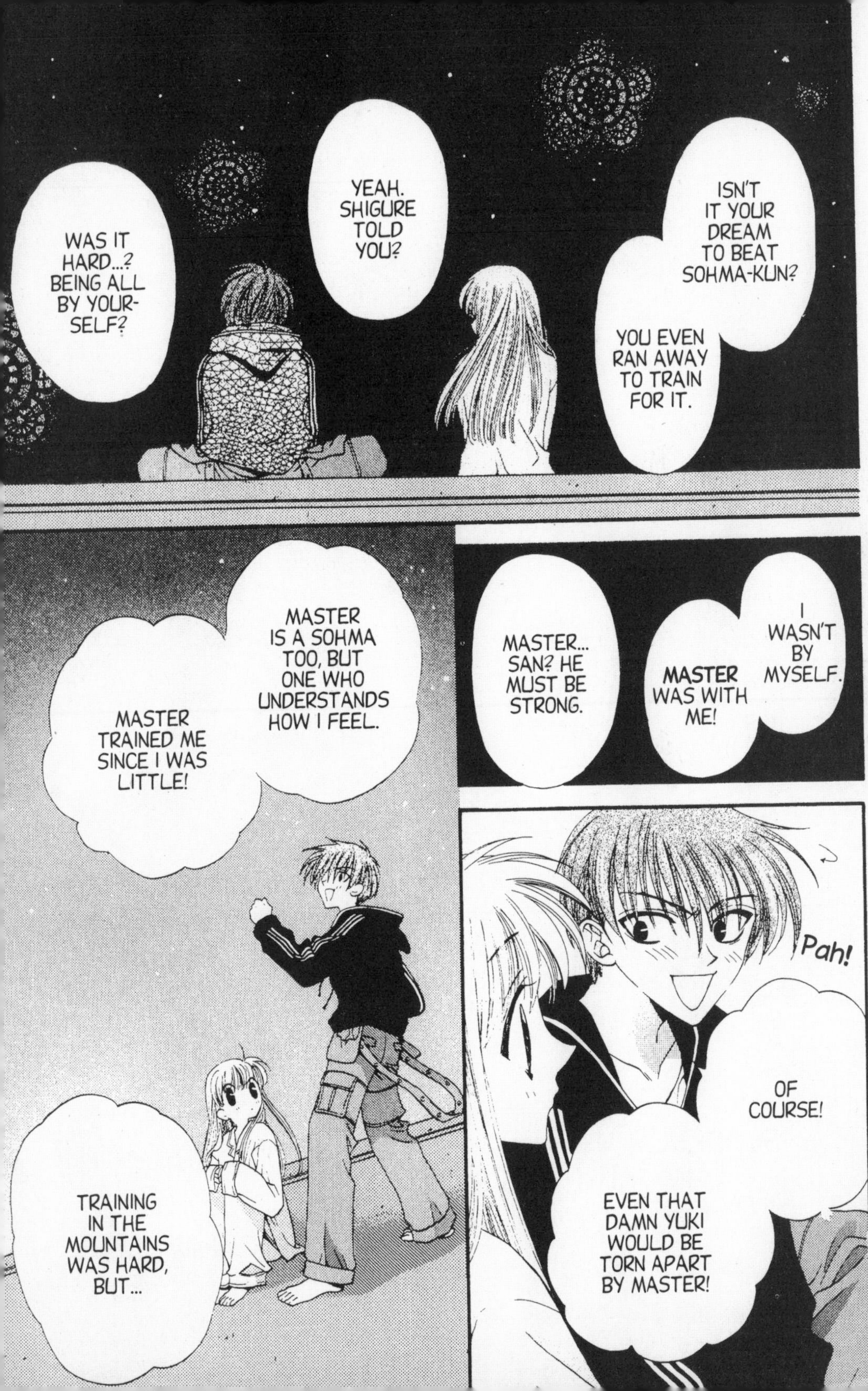
ISN'T IT YOUR DREAM TO BEAT SOHMA-KUN?
YOU EVEN RAN AWAY TO TRAIN FOR IT.
YEAH. SHIGURE TOLD YOU?
WAS IT HARD...? BEING ALL BY YOUR-SELF?
I WASN'T BY MYSELF.
MASTER WAS WITH ME!
MASTER... SAN? HE MUST BE STRONG.
Pah!
OF COURSE!
EVEN THAT DAMN YUKI WOULD BE TORN APART BY MASTER!
MASTER IS A SOHMA TOO, BUT ONE WHO UNDERSTANDS HOW I FEEL.
MASTER TRAINED ME SINCE I WAS LITTLE!
TRAINING IN THE MOUNTAINS WAS HARD, BUT...

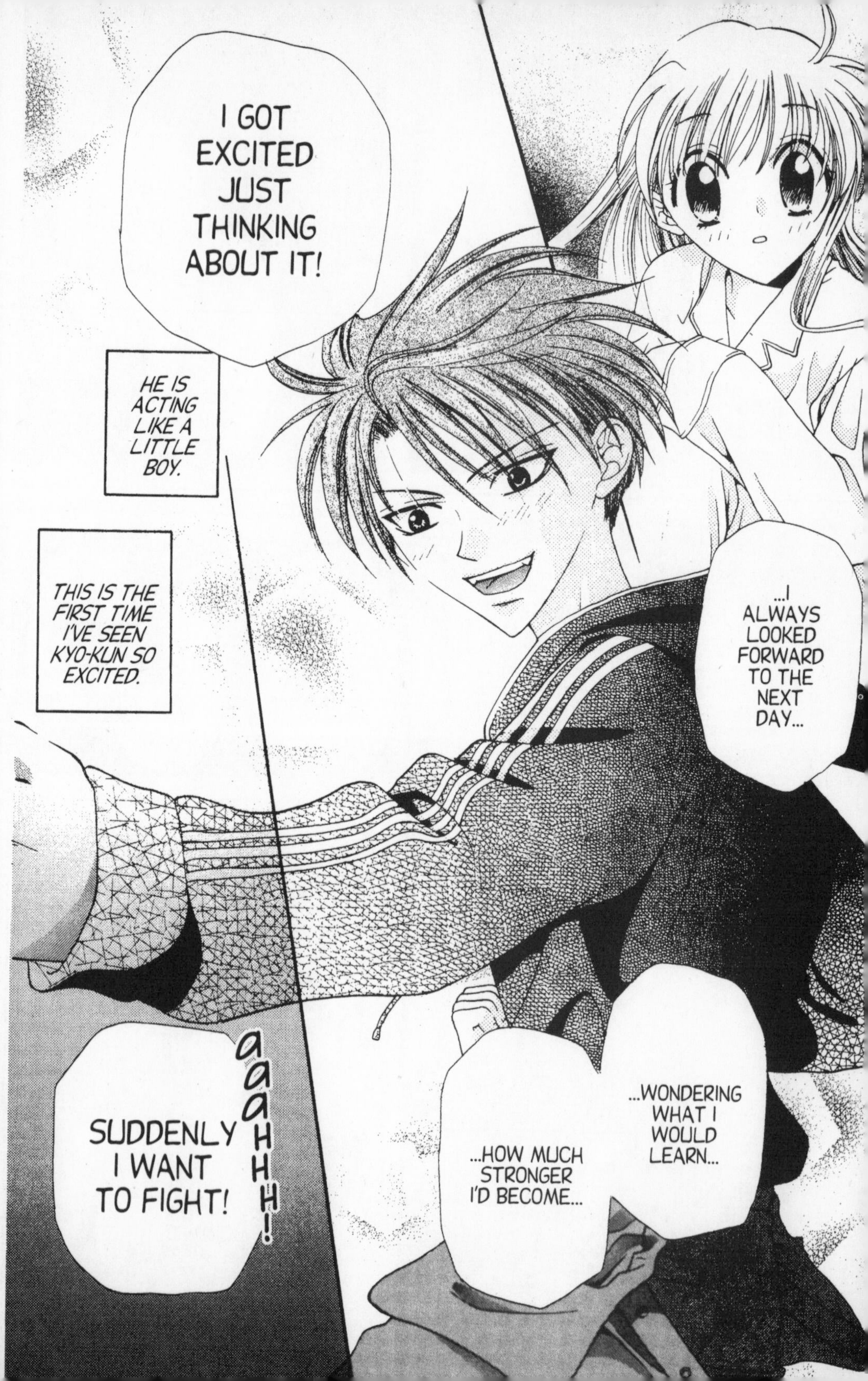
...I ALWAYS LOOKED FORWARD TO THE NEXT DAY...
...WONDERING WHAT I WOULD LEARN...
...HOW MUCH STRONGER I'D BECOME...
I GOT EXCITED JUST THINKING ABOUT IT!
HE IS ACTING LIKE A LITTLE BOY.
THIS IS THE FIRST TIME I'VE SEEN KYO-KUN SO EXCITED.
SUDDENLY I WANT TO FIGHT!
aaaHHHH!

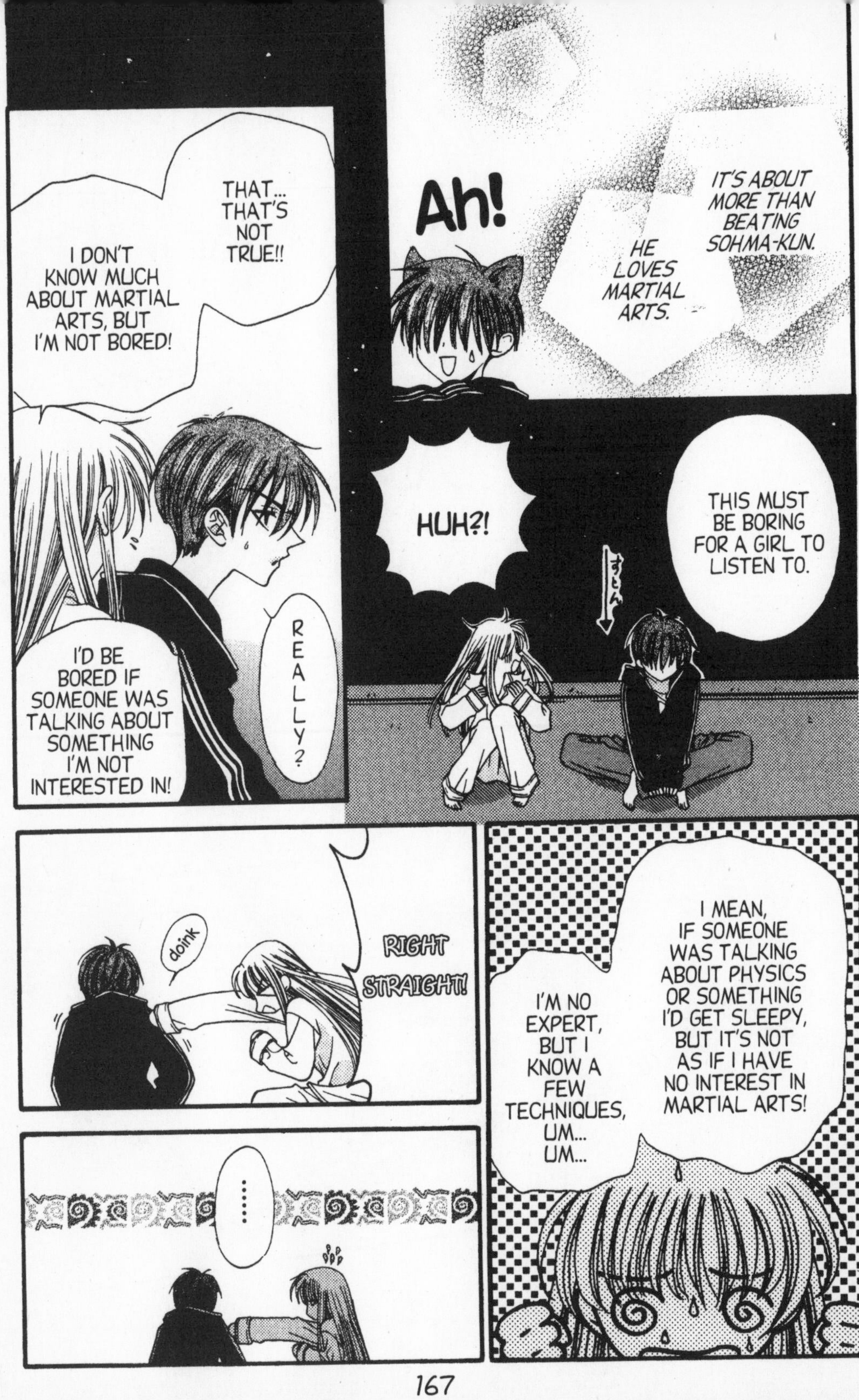

IT'S ABOUT MORE THAN BEATING SOHMA-KUN.
HE LOVES MARTIAL ARTS.
Ah!
THIS MUST BE BORING FOR A GIRL TO LISTEN TO.
HUH?!
THAT... THAT'S NOT TRUE!!
I DON'T KNOW MUCH ABOUT MARTIAL ARTS, BUT I'M NOT BORED!
REALLY?
I'D BE BORED IF SOMEONE WAS TALKING ABOUT SOMETHING I'M NOT INTERESTED IN!
I MEAN, IF SOMEONE WAS TALKING ABOUT PHYSICS OR SOMETHING I'D GET SLEEPY, BUT IT'S NOT AS IF I HAVE NO INTEREST IN MARTIAL ARTS!
I'M NO EXPERT, BUT I KNOW A FEW TECHNIQUES, UM... UM...
RIGHT STRAIGHT!
doink
......

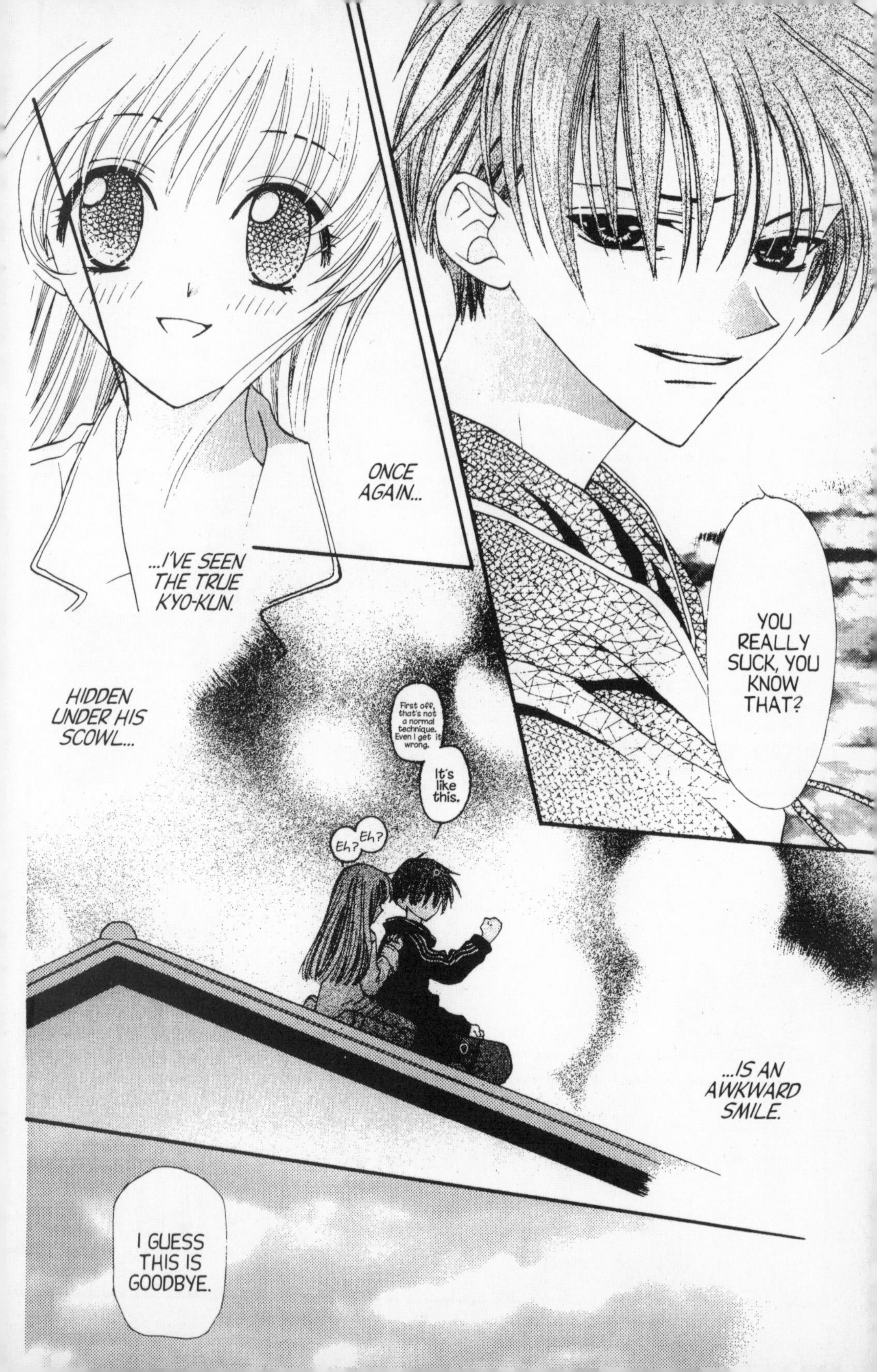

YOU REALLY SUCK, YOU KNOW THAT?
ONCE AGAIN...
...I'VE SEEN THE TRUE KYO-KUN.
HIDDEN UNDER HIS SCOWL...
First off, that's not a normal technique. Even I get it wrong.
It's like this.
Eh? Eh?
...IS AN AWKWARD SMILE.
I GUESS THIS IS GOODBYE.

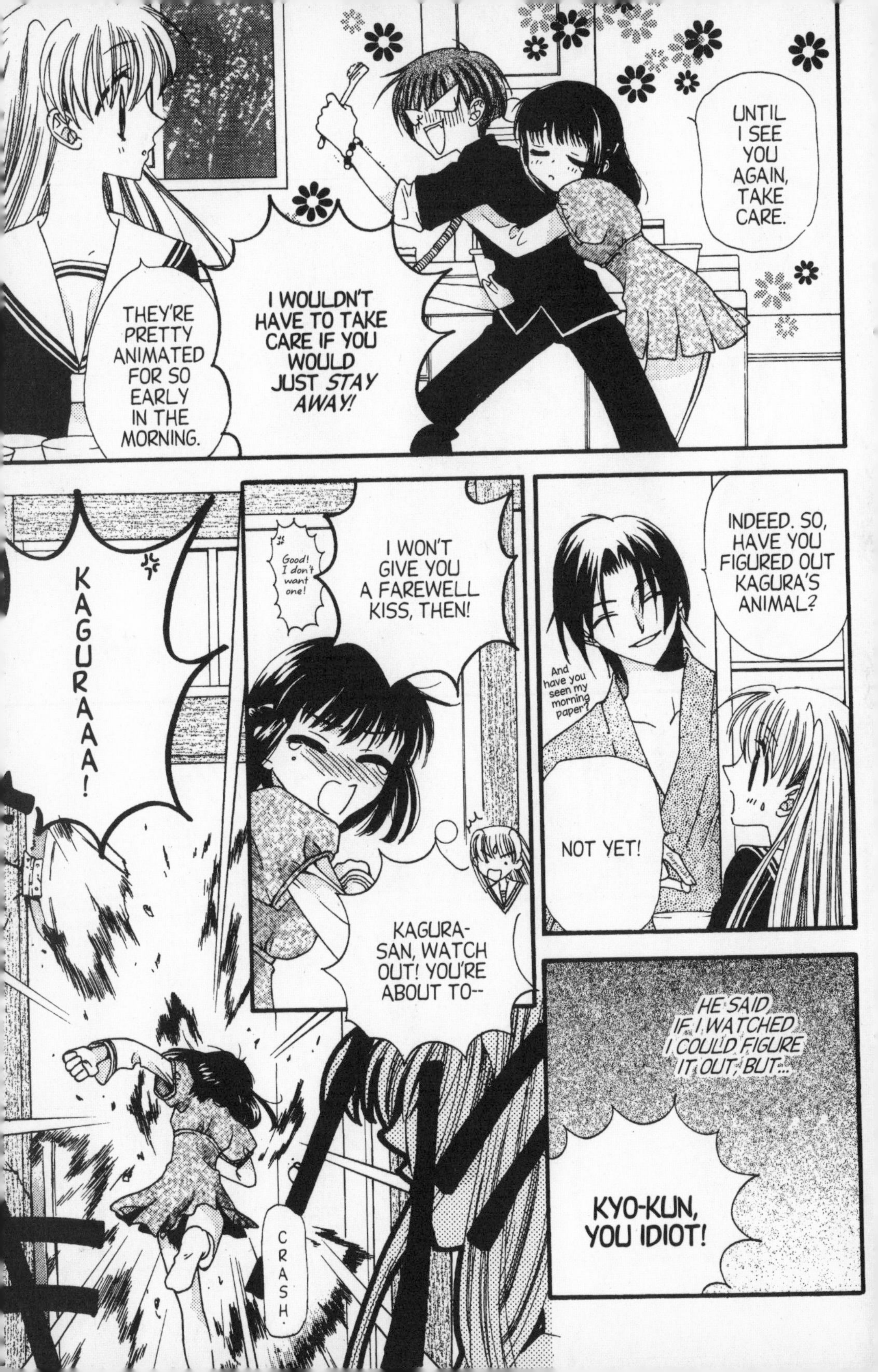
UNTIL I SEE YOU AGAIN, TAKE CARE.
I WOULDN'T HAVE TO TAKE CARE IF YOU WOULD JUST *STAY AWAY!*
THEY'RE PRETTY ANIMATED FOR SO EARLY IN THE MORNING.
INDEED. SO, HAVE YOU FIGURED OUT KAGURA'S ANIMAL?
And have you seen my morning paper?
NOT YET!
I WON'T GIVE YOU A FAREWELL KISS, THEN!
Good! I don't want one!
KAGURA-SAN, WATCH OUT! YOU'RE ABOUT TO--
KAGURAAAA!
CRASH.
HE SAID IF I WATCHED I COULD FIGURE IT OUT, BUT...
KYO-KUN, YOU IDIOT!

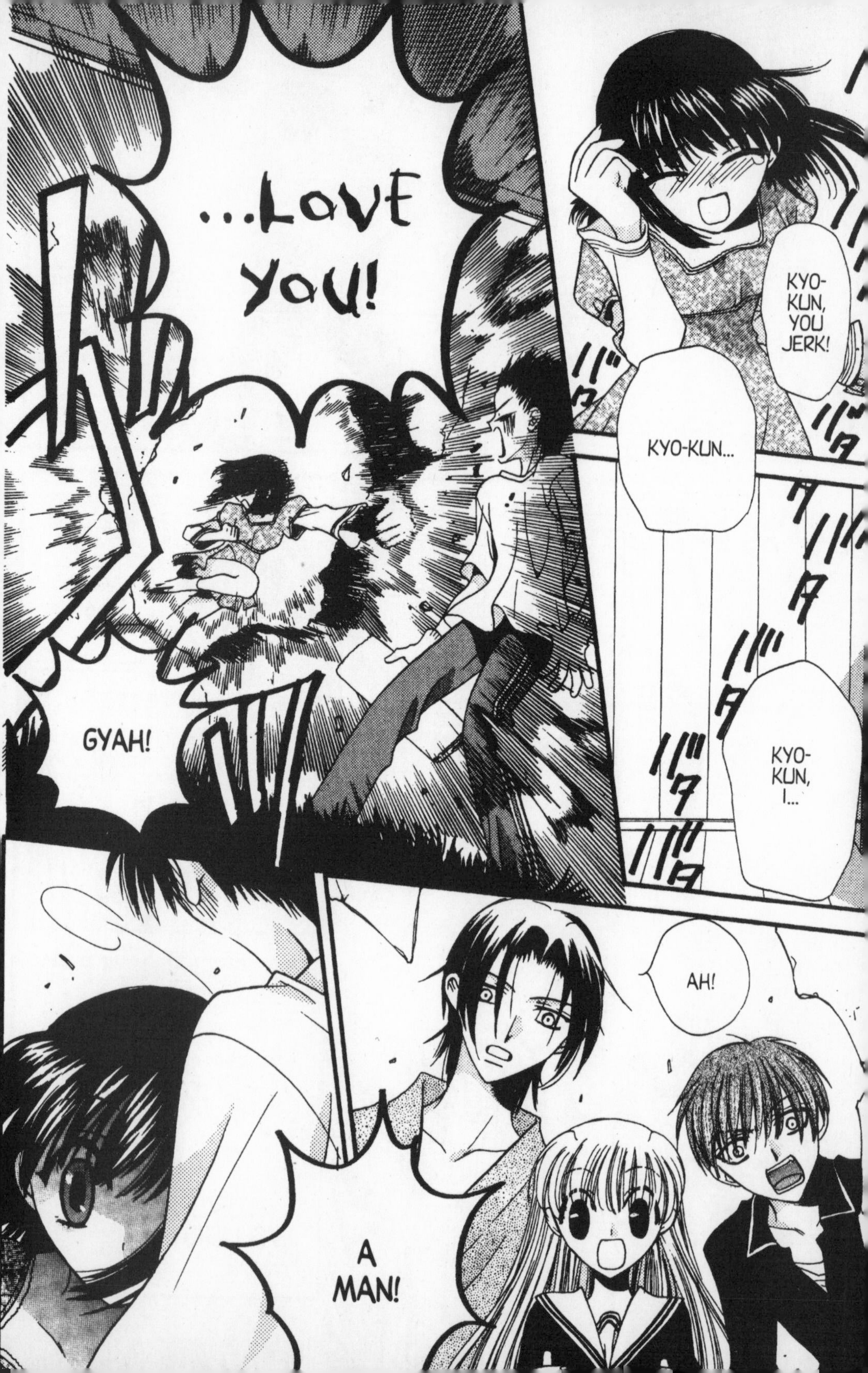

KYO-KUN, YOU JERK!
KYO-KUN...
KYO-KUN, I...
...LOVE YOU!
GYAH!
AH!
A MAN!

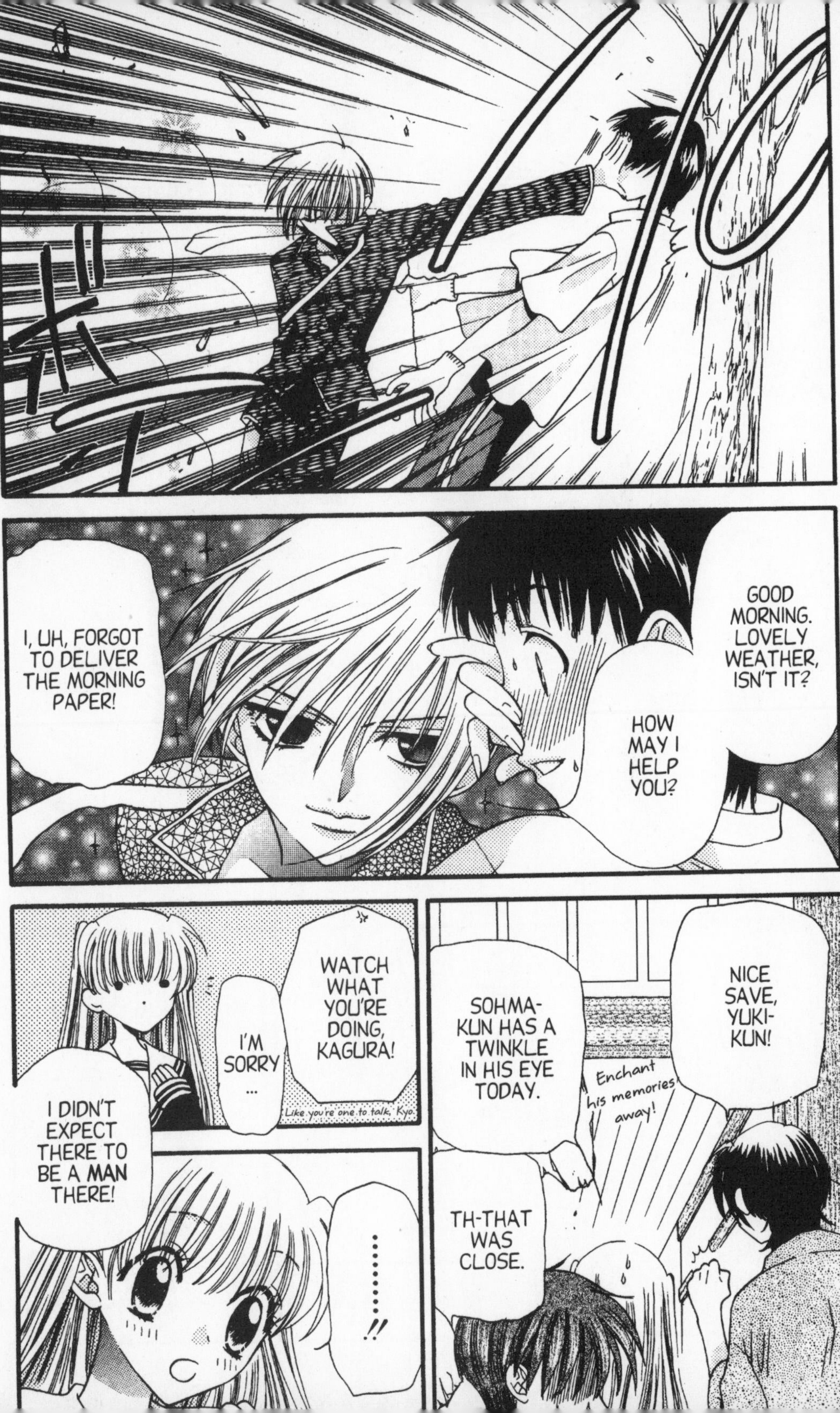
GOOD MORNING. LOVELY WEATHER, ISN'T IT?
HOW MAY I HELP YOU?
I, UH, FORGOT TO DELIVER THE MORNING PAPER!
NICE SAVE, YUKI-KUN!
SOHMA-KUN HAS A TWINKLE IN HIS EYE TODAY.
Enchant his memories away!
TH-THAT WAS CLOSE.
WATCH WHAT YOU'RE DOING, KAGURA!
I'M SORRY...
Like you're one to talk, Kyo.
......!!
I DIDN'T EXPECT THERE TO BE A MAN THERE!

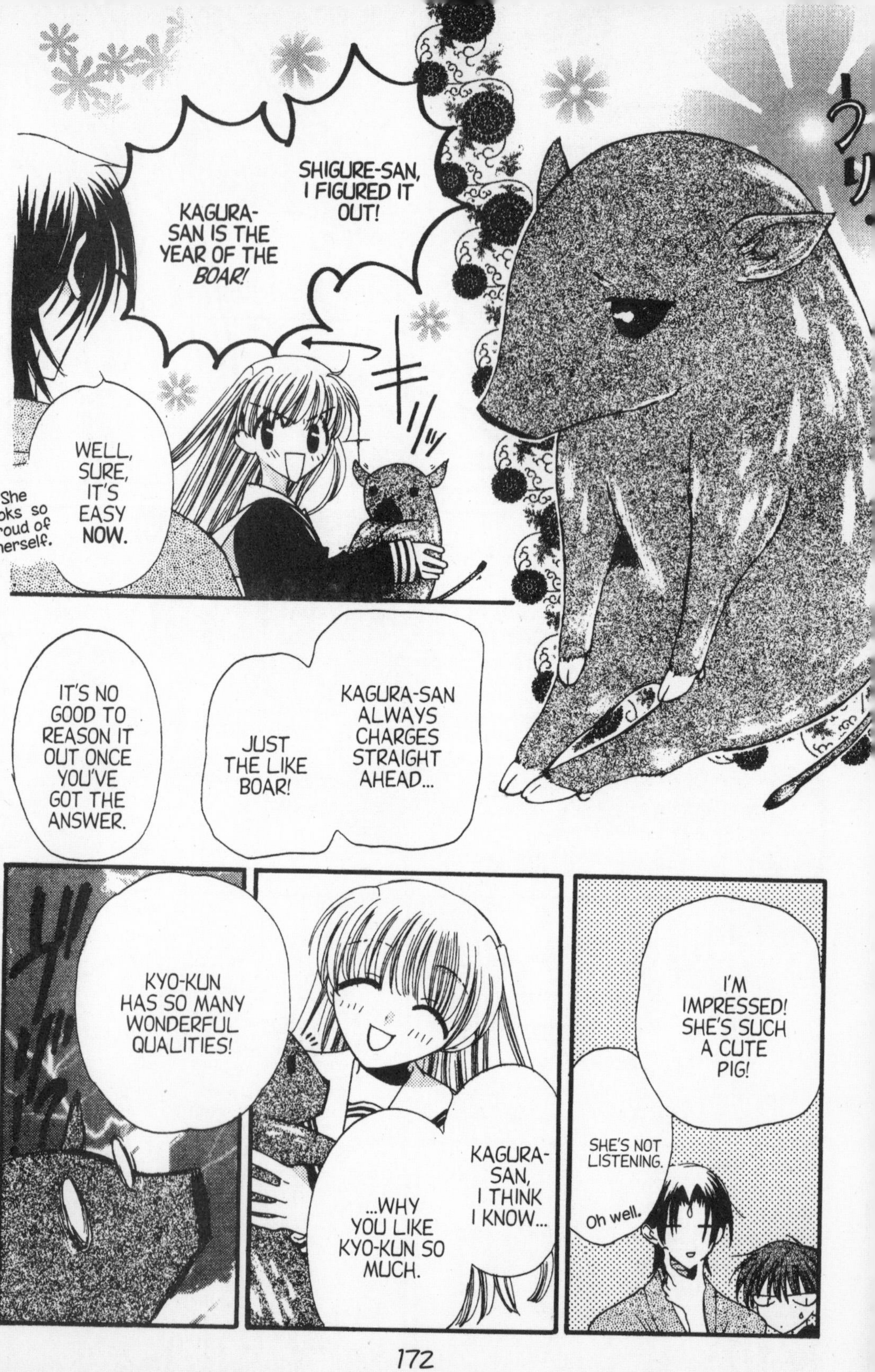
うり・
SHIGURE-SAN, I FIGURED IT OUT!
KAGURA-SAN IS THE YEAR OF THE *BOAR!*
WELL, SURE, IT'S EASY NOW.
She looks so proud of herself.
KAGURA-SAN ALWAYS CHARGES STRAIGHT AHEAD...
JUST THE LIKE BOAR!
IT'S NO GOOD TO REASON IT OUT ONCE YOU'VE GOT THE ANSWER.
I'M IMPRESSED! SHE'S SUCH A CUTE PIG!
SHE'S NOT LISTENING.
Oh well.
KAGURA-SAN, I THINK I KNOW...
...WHY YOU LIKE KYO-KUN SO MUCH.
KYO-KUN HAS SO MANY WONDERFUL QUALITIES!

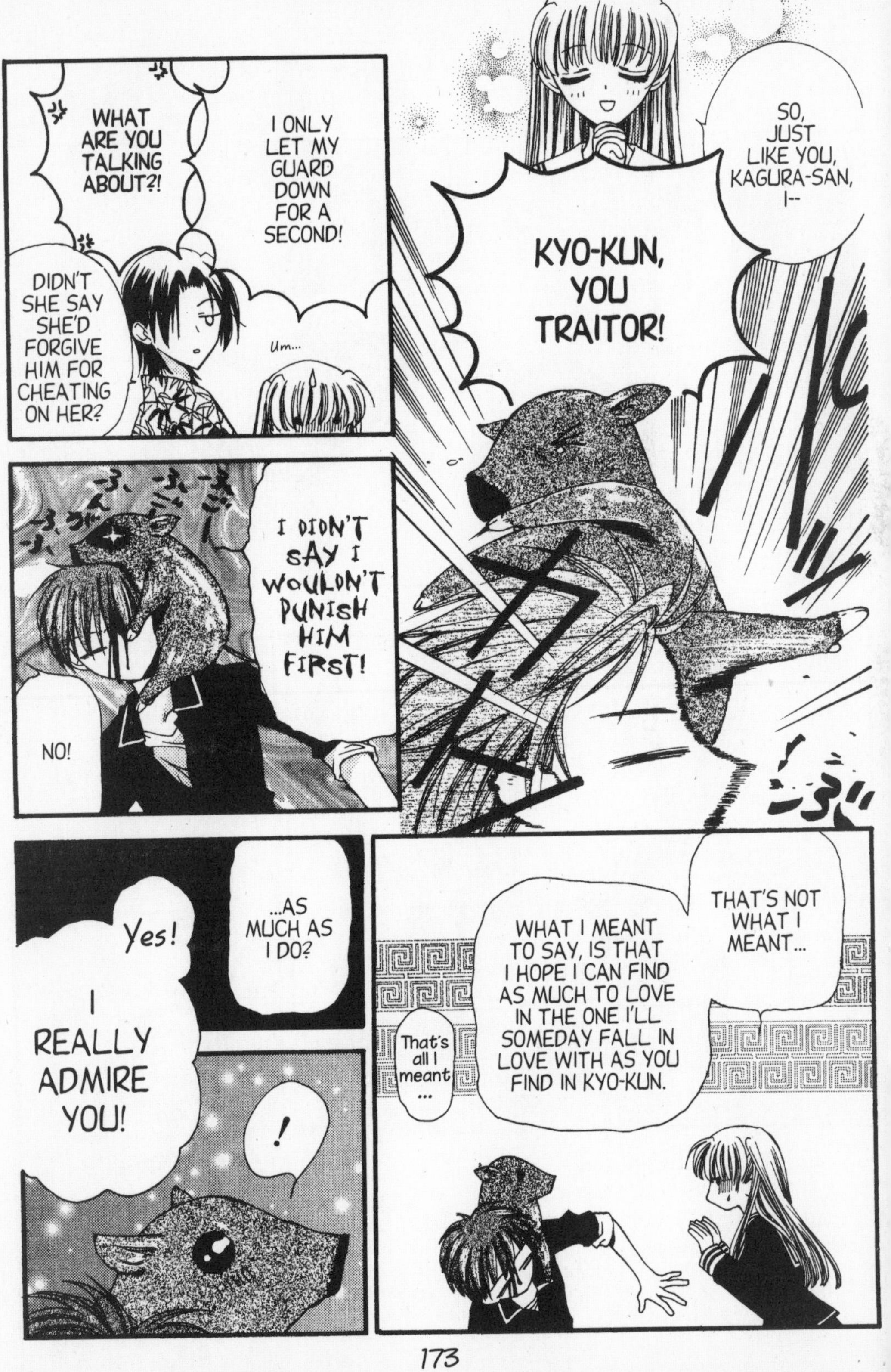
SO, JUST LIKE YOU, KAGURA-SAN, I--
KYO-KUN, YOU TRAITOR!
I ONLY LET MY GUARD DOWN FOR A SECOND!
WHAT ARE YOU TALKING ABOUT?!
DIDN'T SHE SAY SHE'D FORGIVE HIM FOR CHEATING ON HER?
Um...
I DIDN'T SAY I WOULDN'T PUNISH HIM FIRST!
NO!
THAT'S NOT WHAT I MEANT...
WHAT I MEANT TO SAY, IS THAT I HOPE I CAN FIND AS MUCH TO LOVE IN THE ONE I'LL SOMEDAY FALL IN LOVE WITH AS YOU FIND IN KYO-KUN.
That's all I meant ...
...AS MUCH AS I DO?
Yes!
I REALLY ADMIRE YOU!
!

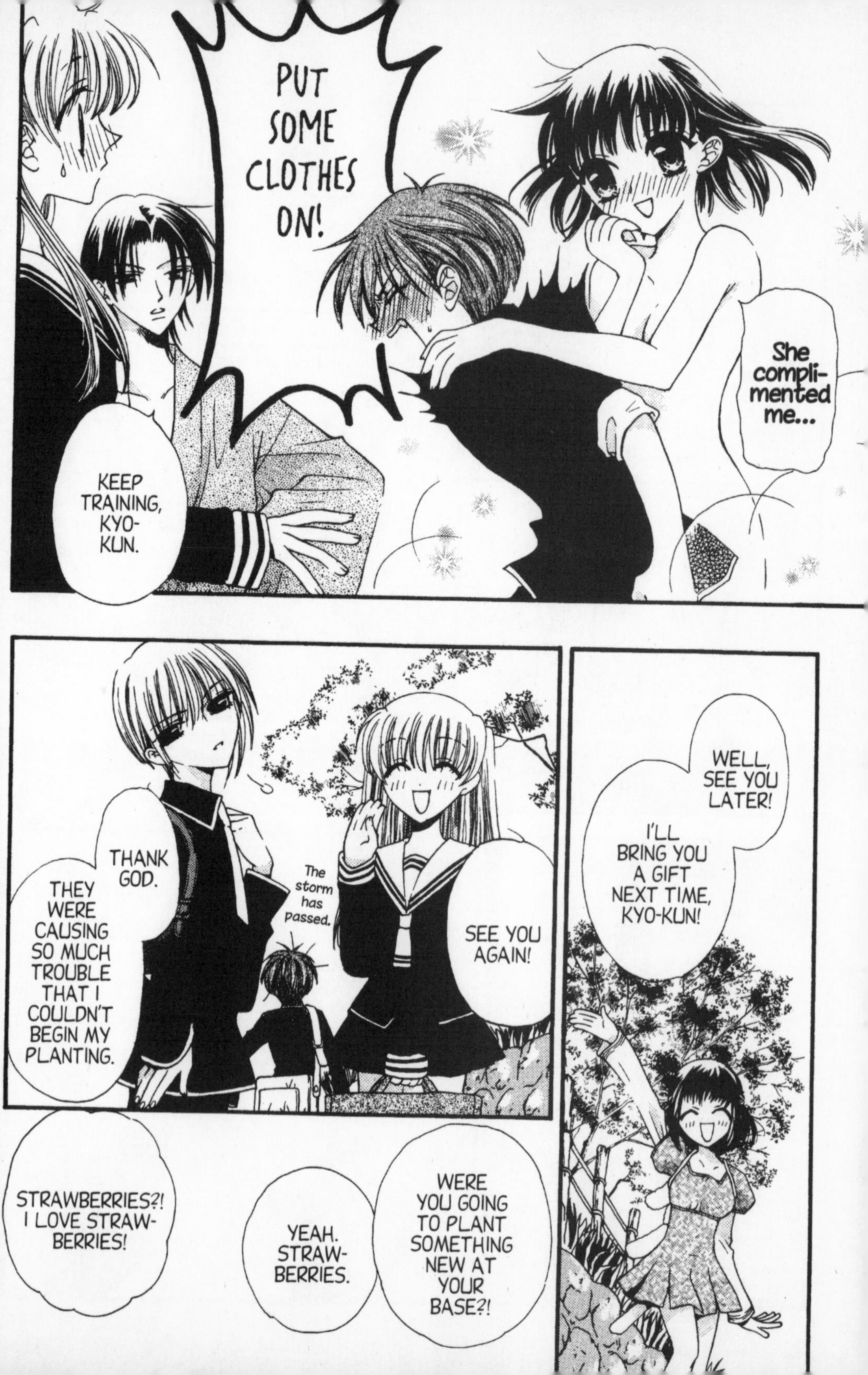
She compli- mented me...
PUT SOME CLOTHES ON!
KEEP TRAINING, KYO-KUN.
WELL, SEE YOU LATER!
I'LL BRING YOU A GIFT NEXT TIME, KYO-KUN!
SEE YOU AGAIN!
The storm has passed.
THANK GOD.
THEY WERE CAUSING SO MUCH TROUBLE THAT I COULDN'T BEGIN MY PLANTING.
WERE YOU GOING TO PLANT SOMETHING NEW AT YOUR BASE?!
YEAH. STRAW- BERRIES.
STRAWBERRIES?! I LOVE STRAW- BERRIES!

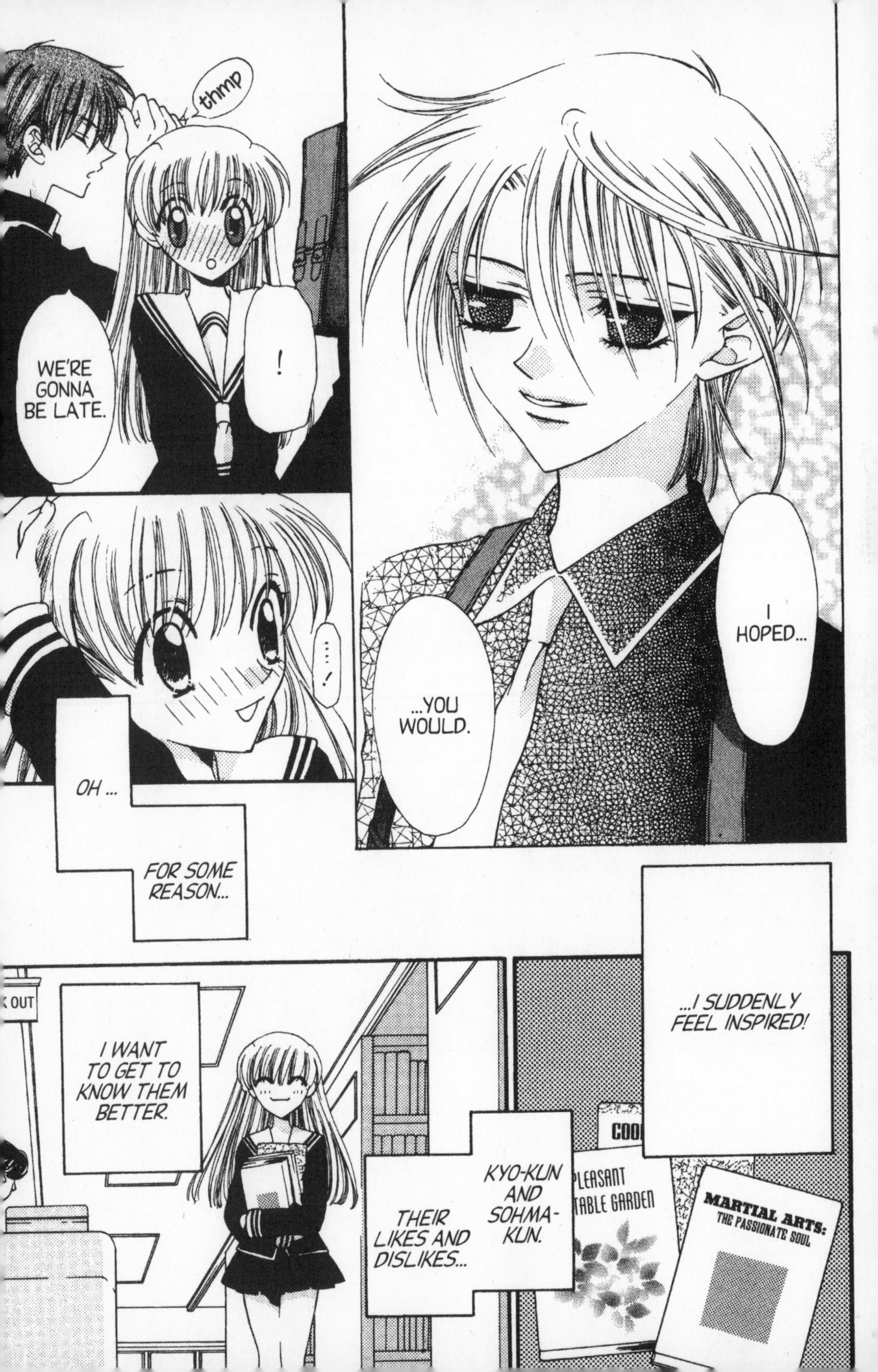
I HOPED...
...YOU WOULD.
thmp
WE'RE GONNA BE LATE.
!
...!
OH ...
FOR SOME REASON...
...I SUDDENLY FEEL INSPIRED!
MARTIAL ARTS: THE PASSIONATE SOUL
PLEASANT
TABLE GARDEN
KYO-KUN AND SOHMA-KUN.
THEIR LIKES AND DISLIKES...
I WANT TO GET TO KNOW THEM BETTER.
K OUT

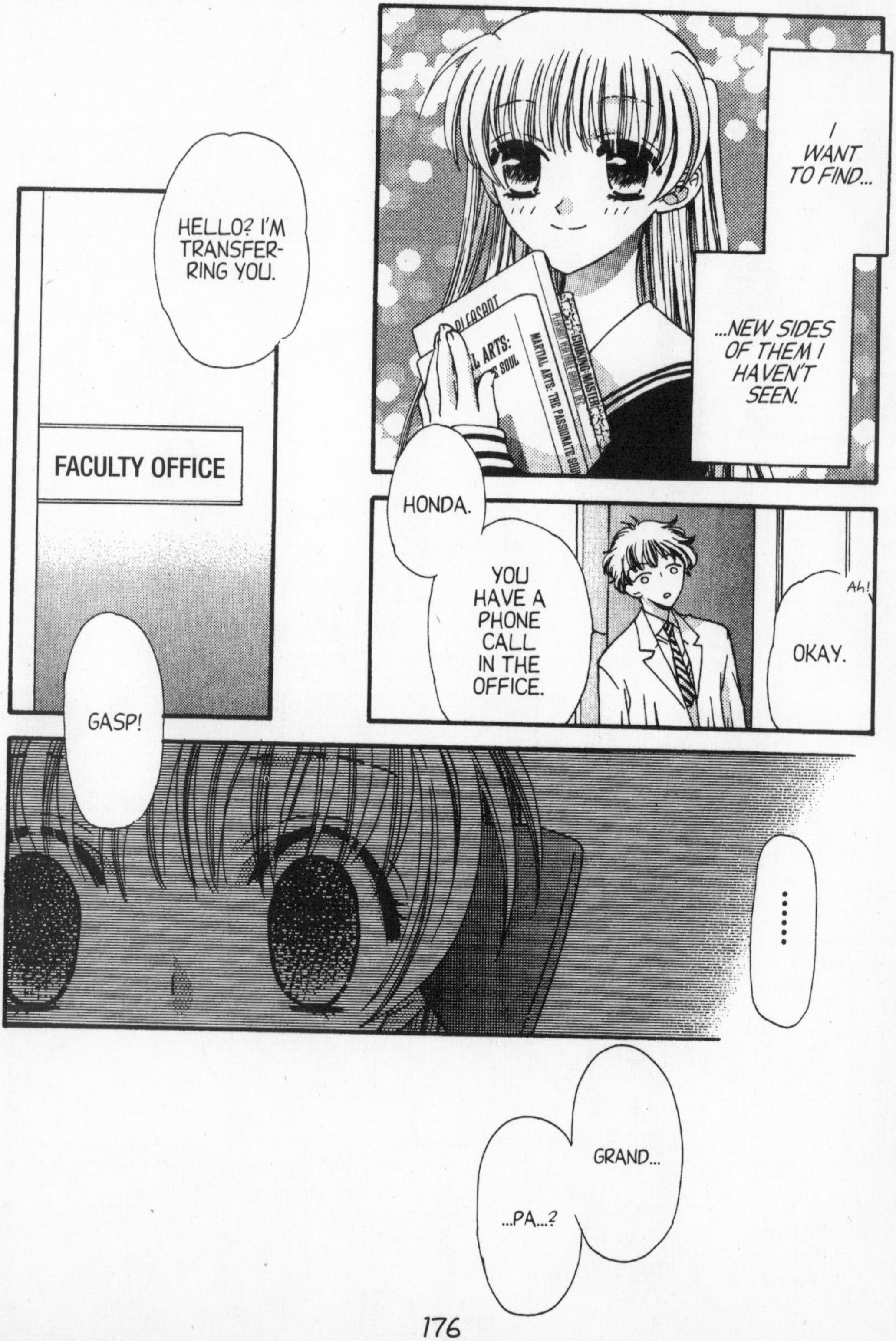
I WANT TO FIND...
...NEW SIDES OF THEM I HAVEN'T SEEN.
COOKING MASTER
MARTIAL ARTS: THE PASSIONATE SOUL
HONDA.
YOU HAVE A PHONE CALL IN THE OFFICE.
Ah!
OKAY.
HELLO? I'M TRANSFERRING YOU.
FACULTY OFFICE
GASP!
......
GRAND...
...PA...?

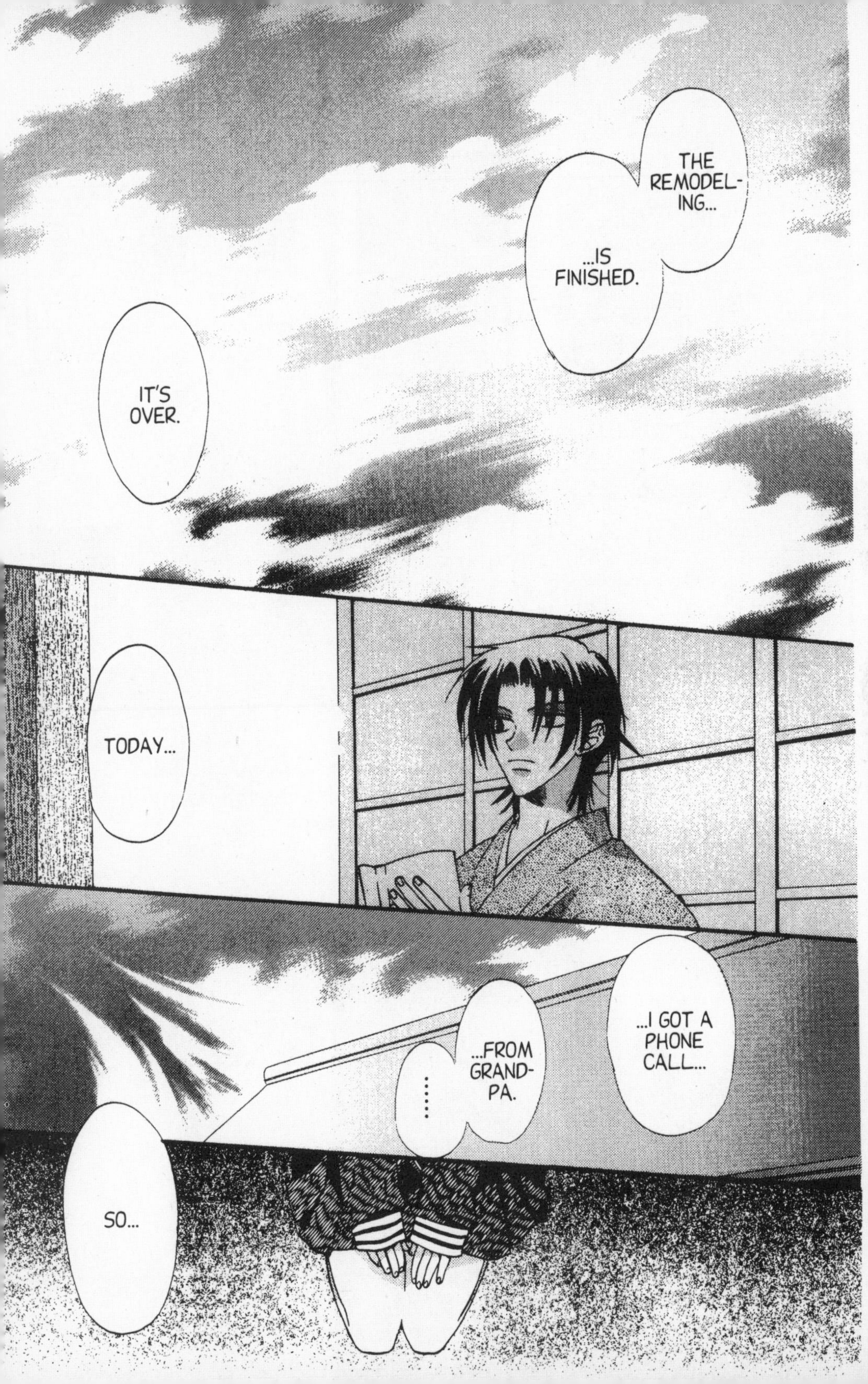
THE REMODEL-ING...
...IS FINISHED.
IT'S OVER.
TODAY...
...I GOT A PHONE CALL...
...FROM GRAND-PA.
......
SO...

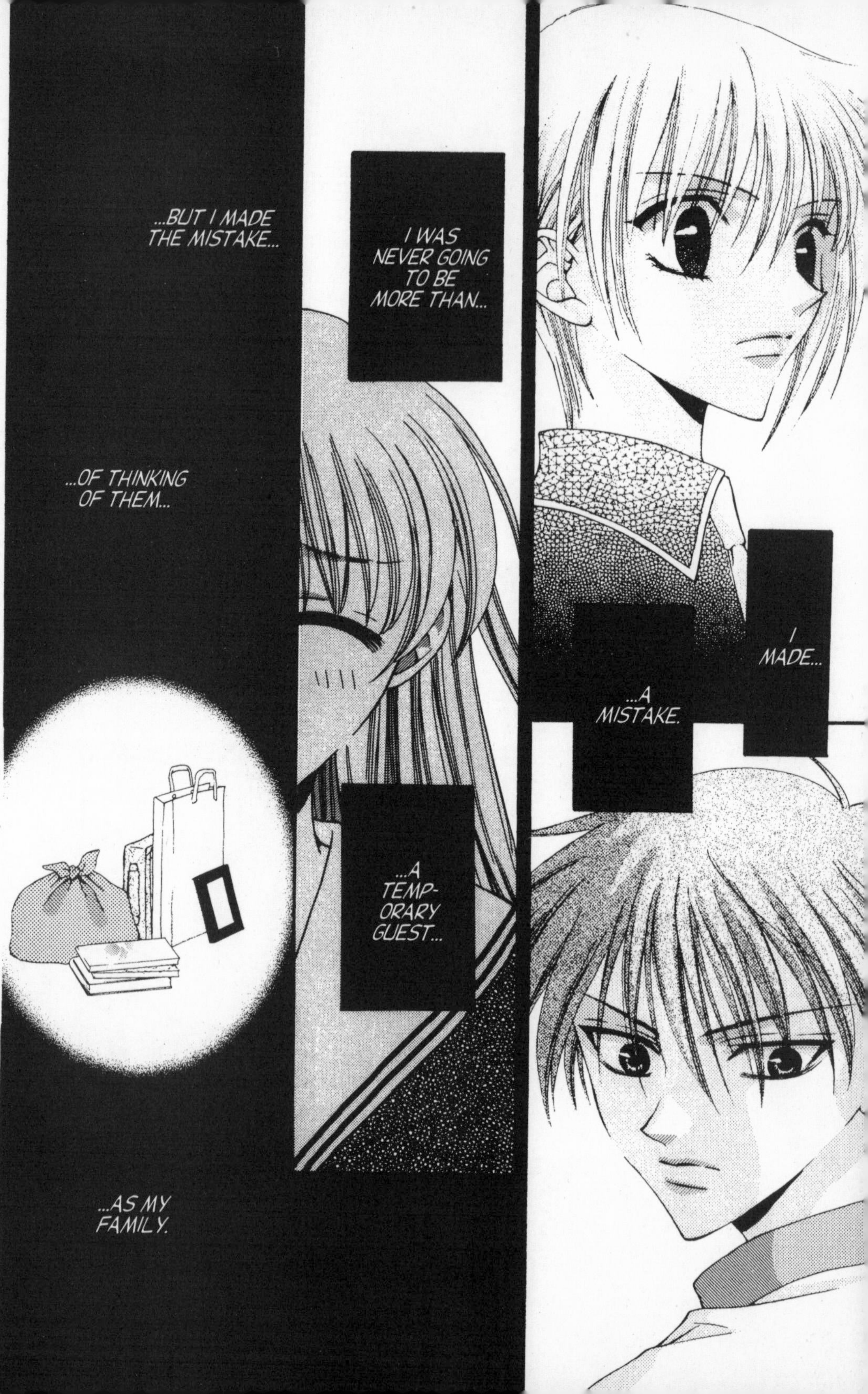
I MADE...
...A MISTAKE.
I WAS NEVER GOING TO BE MORE THAN...
...A TEMPORARY GUEST...
...BUT I MADE THE MISTAKE...
...OF THINKING OF THEM...
...AS MY FAMILY.

Chapter 6

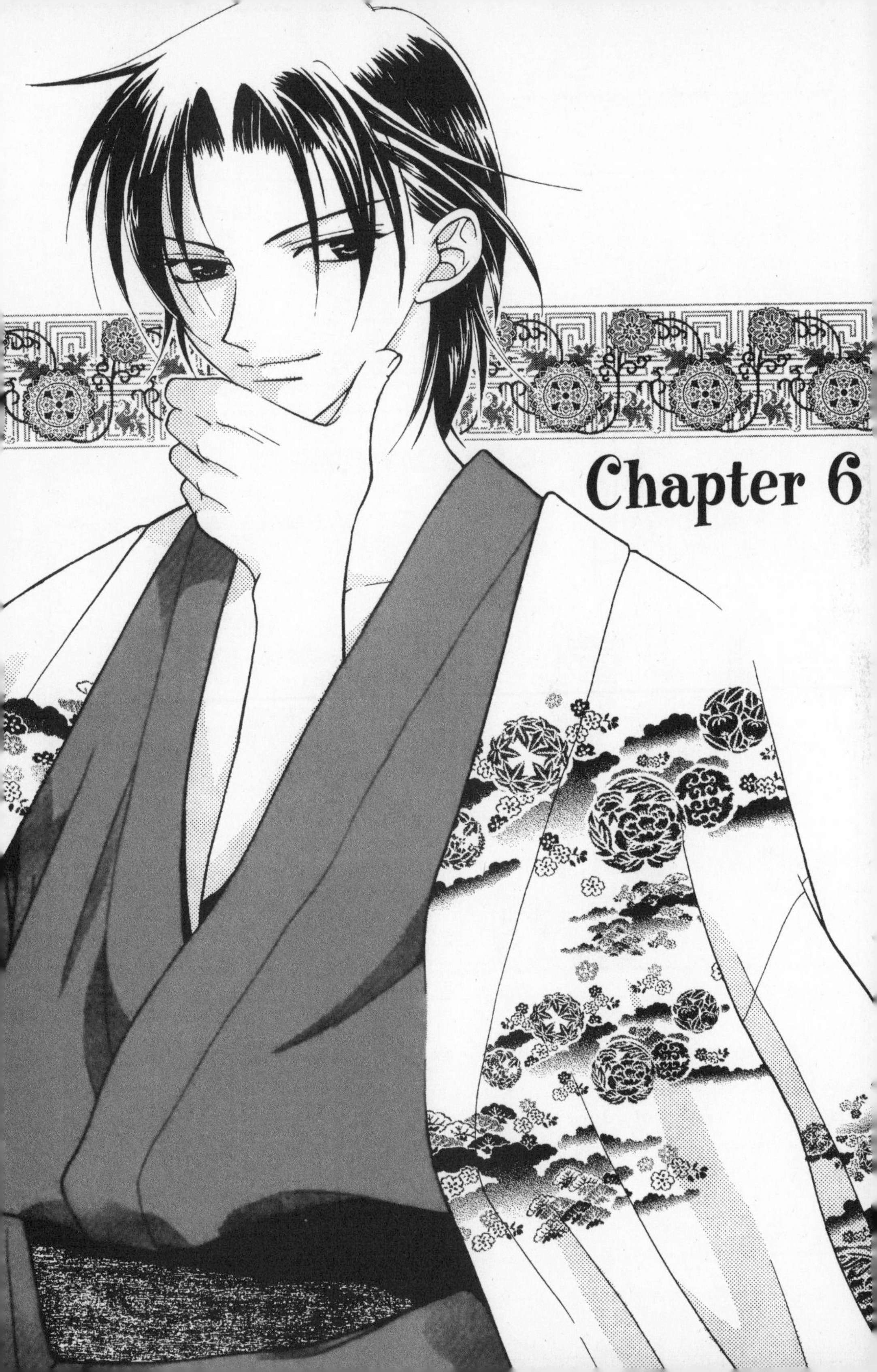

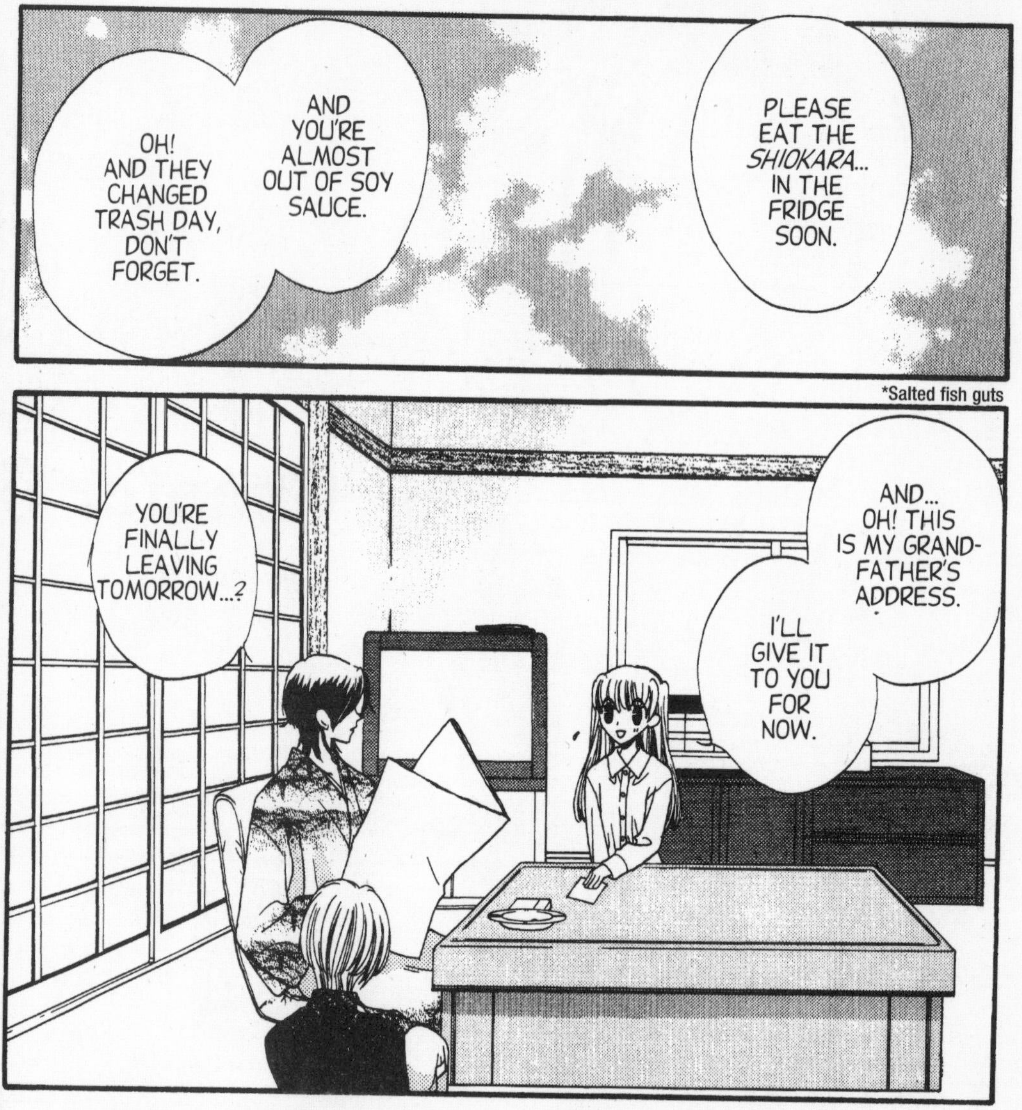
PLEASE EAT THE *SHIOKARA*... IN THE FRIDGE SOON.
AND YOU'RE ALMOST OUT OF SOY SAUCE.
OH! AND THEY CHANGED TRASH DAY, DON'T FORGET.
AND... OH! THIS IS MY GRANDFATHER'S ADDRESS.
I'LL GIVE IT TO YOU FOR NOW.
YOU'RE FINALLY LEAVING TOMORROW...?
*Salted fish guts

ULTRA SPECIAL BLAH BLAH BLAH, NUMBER 5:

This series is kind of turning into a sitcom, but I don't really think of it as a comedy when I draw it. I mean -- it is funny (Of course I don't mind if people call it a comedy. I love comedies. Especially dry humor). I just kind of feel like, "Oh. Is it?" I have no idea what I'm trying to say.

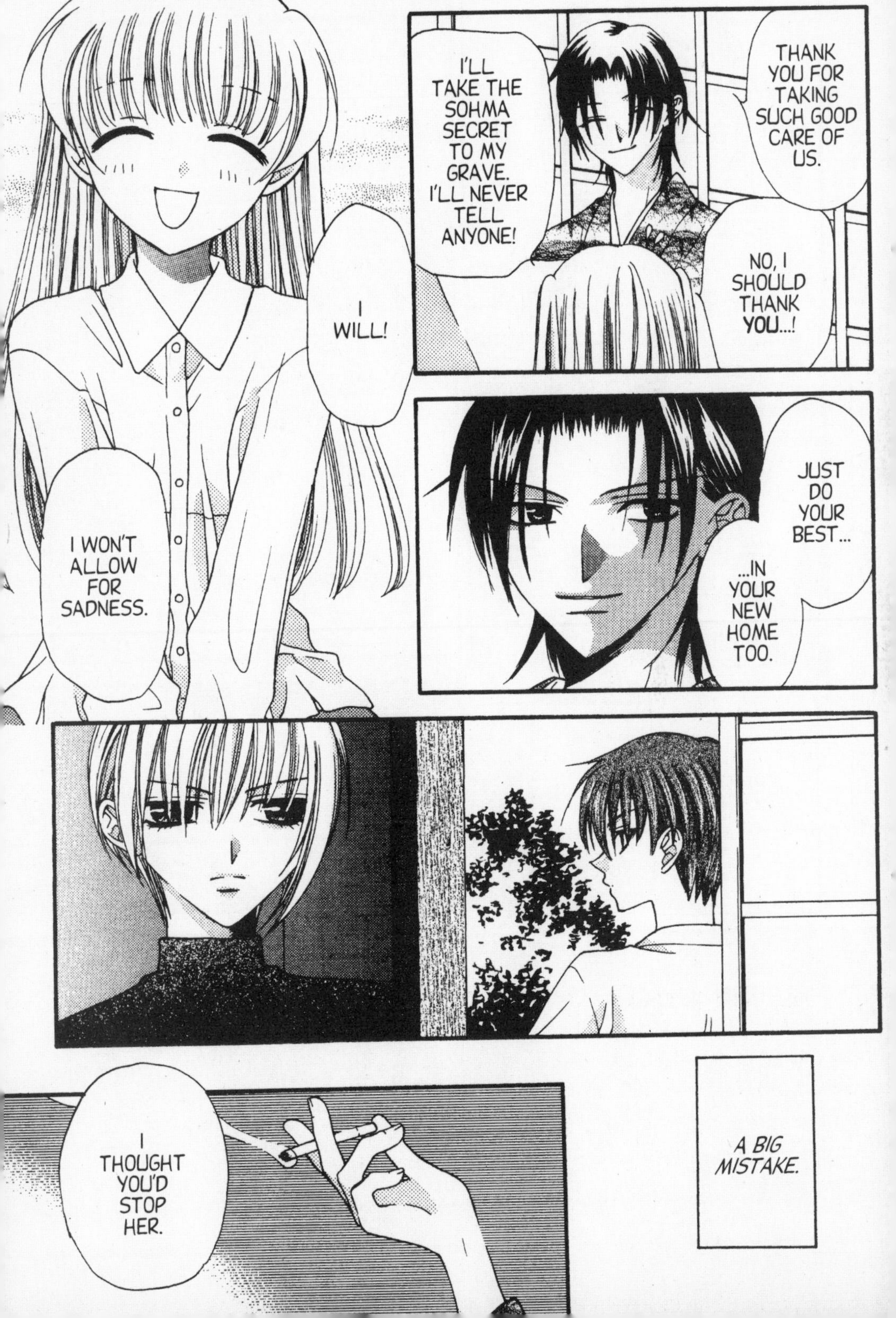
THANK YOU FOR TAKING SUCH GOOD CARE OF US.
NO, I SHOULD THANK **YOU**...!
I'LL TAKE THE SOHMA SECRET TO MY GRAVE. I'LL NEVER TELL ANYONE!
JUST DO YOUR BEST...
...IN YOUR NEW HOME TOO.
I WILL!
I WON'T ALLOW FOR SADNESS.
A BIG MISTAKE.
I THOUGHT YOU'D STOP HER.

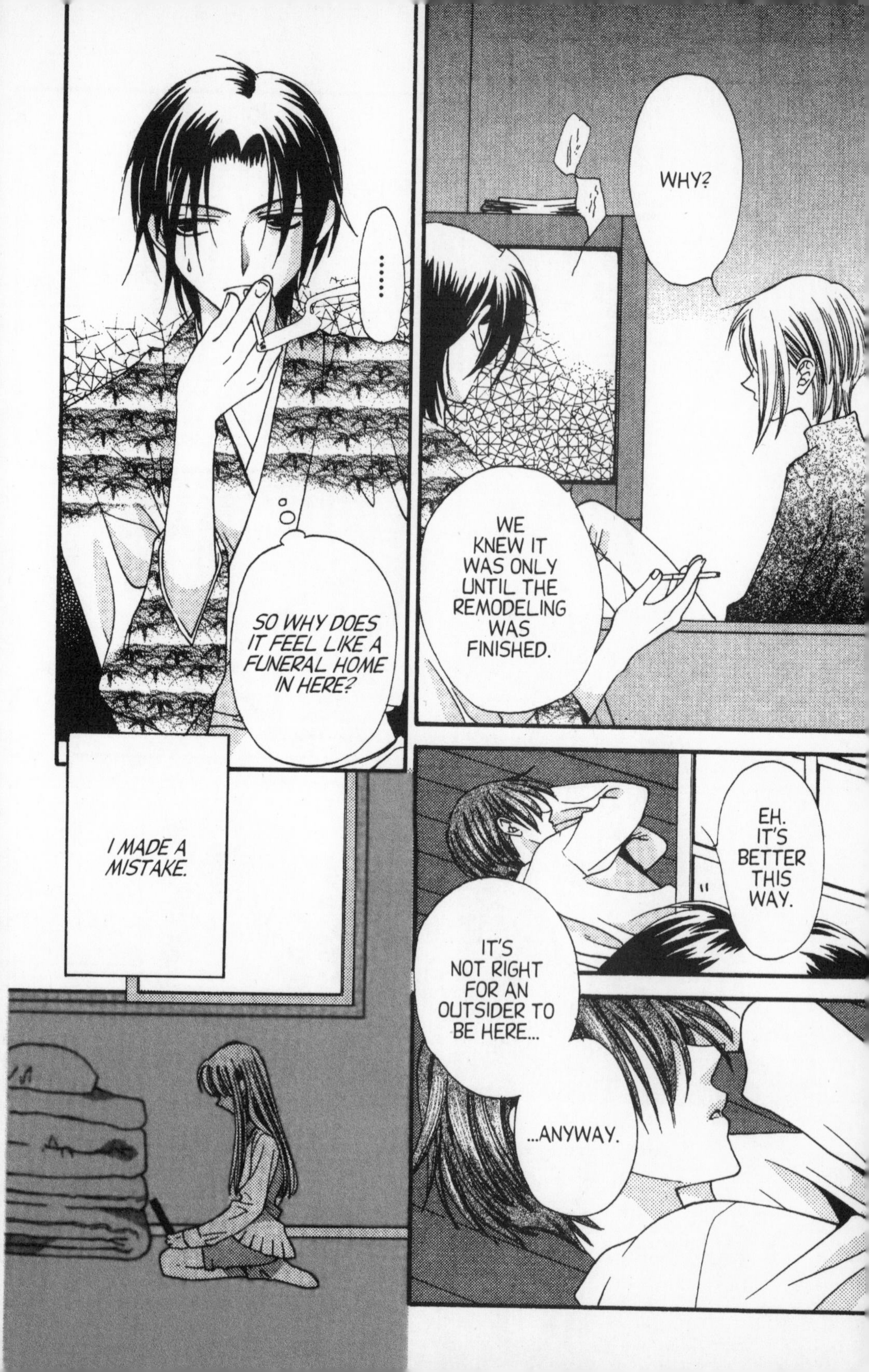
WHY?
WE KNEW IT WAS ONLY UNTIL THE REMODELING WAS FINISHED.
......
SO WHY DOES IT FEEL LIKE A FUNERAL HOME IN HERE?
EH. IT'S BETTER THIS WAY.
IT'S NOT RIGHT FOR AN OUTSIDER TO BE HERE...
...ANYWAY.
I MADE A MISTAKE.

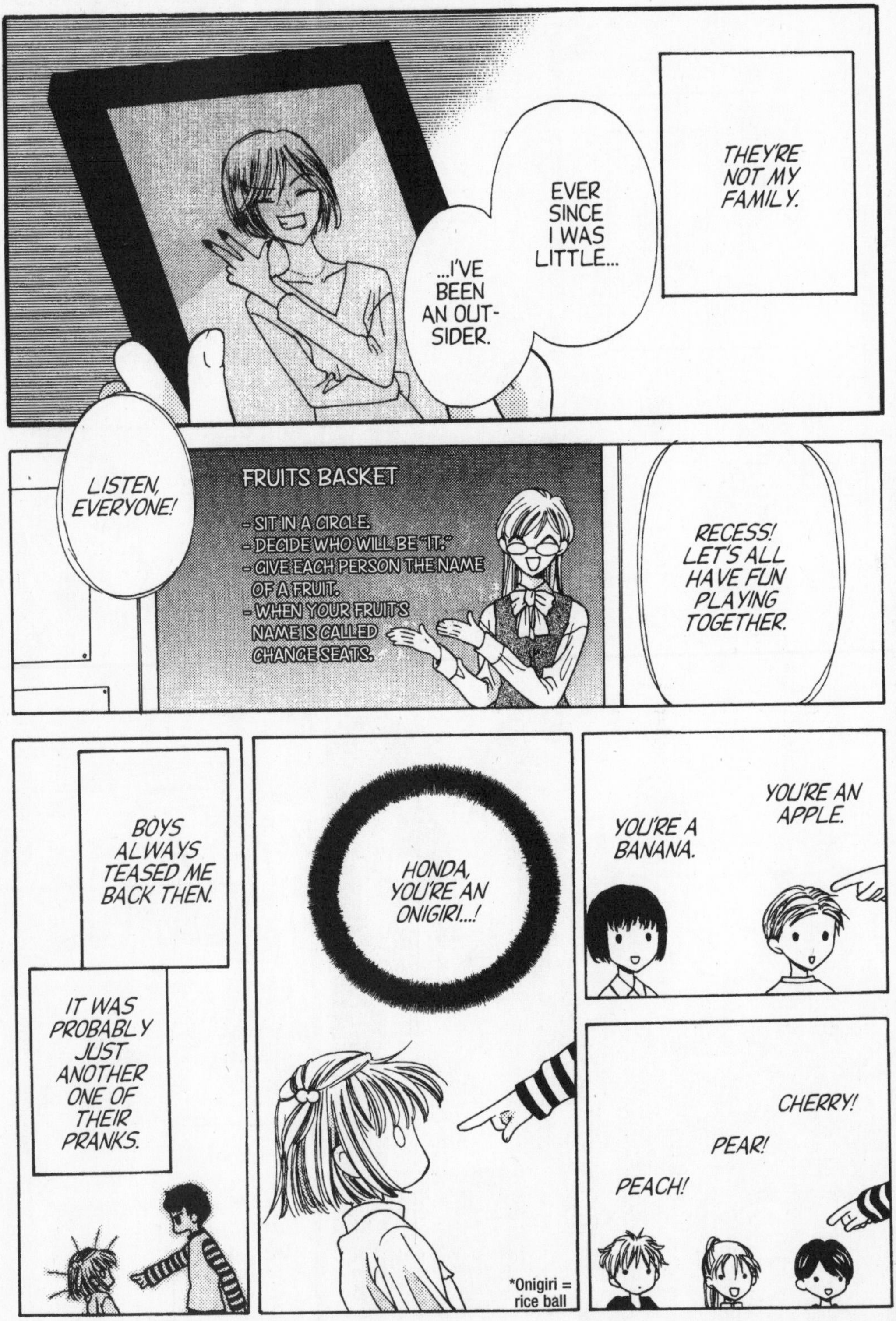
THEY'RE NOT MY FAMILY.
EVER SINCE I WAS LITTLE...
...I'VE BEEN AN OUT-SIDER.
RECESS! LET'S ALL HAVE FUN PLAYING TOGETHER.
FRUITS BASKET
- SIT IN A CIRCLE.
- DECIDE WHO WILL BE "IT."
- GIVE EACH PERSON THE NAME OF A FRUIT.
- WHEN YOUR FRUITS NAME IS CALLED CHANGE SEATS.
LISTEN, EVERYONE!
YOU'RE AN APPLE.
YOU'RE A BANANA.
CHERRY!
PEAR!
PEACH!
HONDA, YOU'RE AN ONIGIRI...!
*Onigiri = rice ball
BOYS ALWAYS TEASED ME BACK THEN.
IT WAS PROBABLY JUST ANOTHER ONE OF THEIR PRANKS.

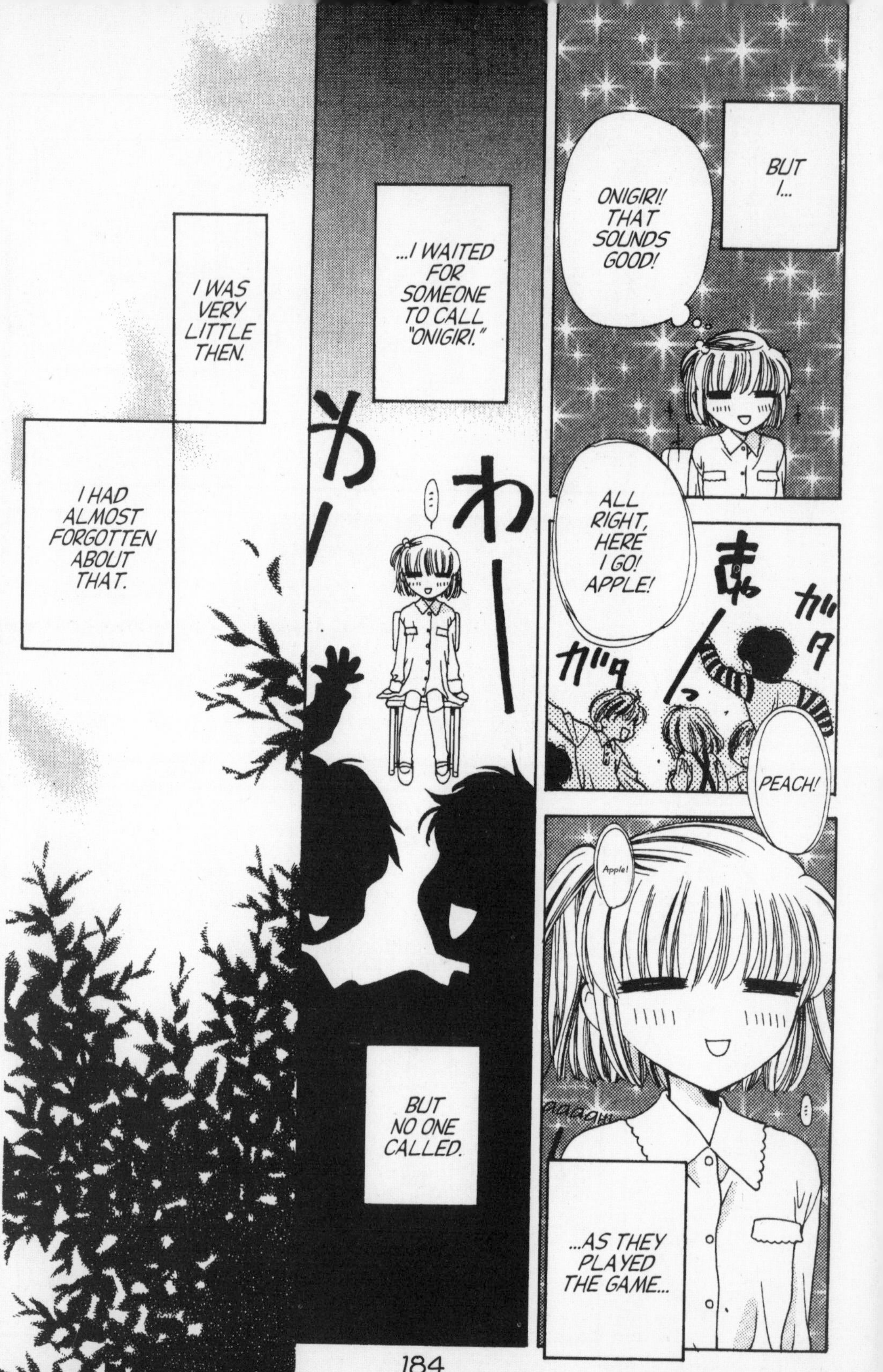
BUT I...
ONIGIRI! THAT SOUNDS GOOD!
ALL RIGHT, HERE I GO! APPLE!
ガタ
ガタ
PEACH!
Apple!
...AS THEY PLAYED THE GAME...
...I WAITED FOR SOMEONE TO CALL "ONIGIRI."
わー
BUT NO ONE CALLED.
I WAS VERY LITTLE THEN.
I HAD ALMOST FORGOTTEN ABOUT THAT.

Number 7:
When "Furuba" started in "Hana to Yume Magazine," there was a popularity contest.
Here are the results:
First place... Yuki.
Second place... Tohru.
Third place... Kyo.
Fourth place... Shigure.
Fifth place... Hana.
Sixth place... Uo.
Seventh place... Mama.
If we do it now, we might have different results. Like, Kyo had only been around for one chapter. No one had a chance to fall in love with him yet!
Oh, and remember when Shigure teases Kyo with a song? The original words were "kyo-o-kun no su-ke-be." (Kyo-kun is a pervert). Can you guess the tune? Don't worry about it. I don't think anyone would really know it anyway. It'll just be my secret!

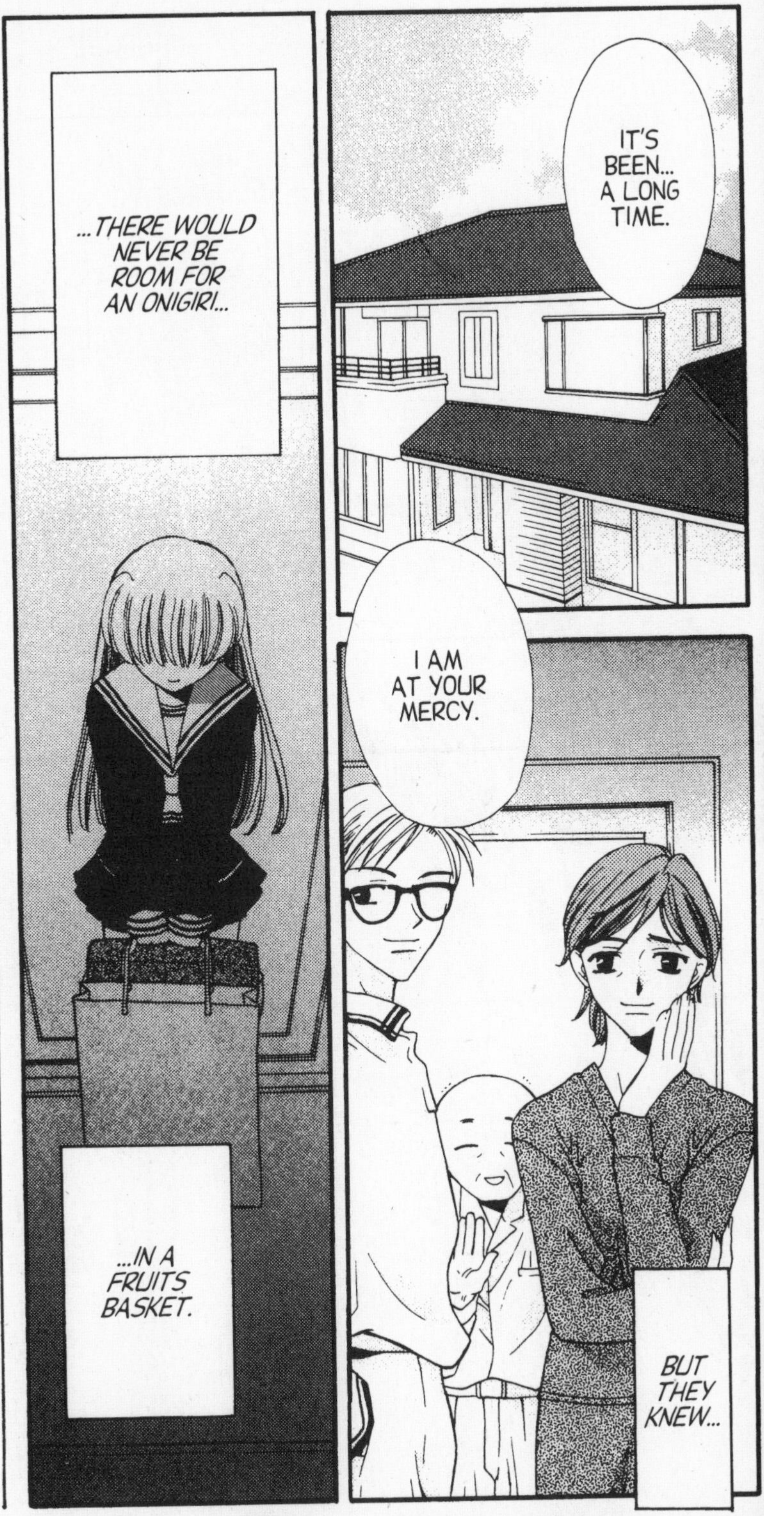

IT'S BEEN... A LONG TIME.
I AM AT YOUR MERCY.
BUT THEY KNEW...
...THERE WOULD NEVER BE ROOM FOR AN ONIGIRI...
...IN A FRUITS BASKET.

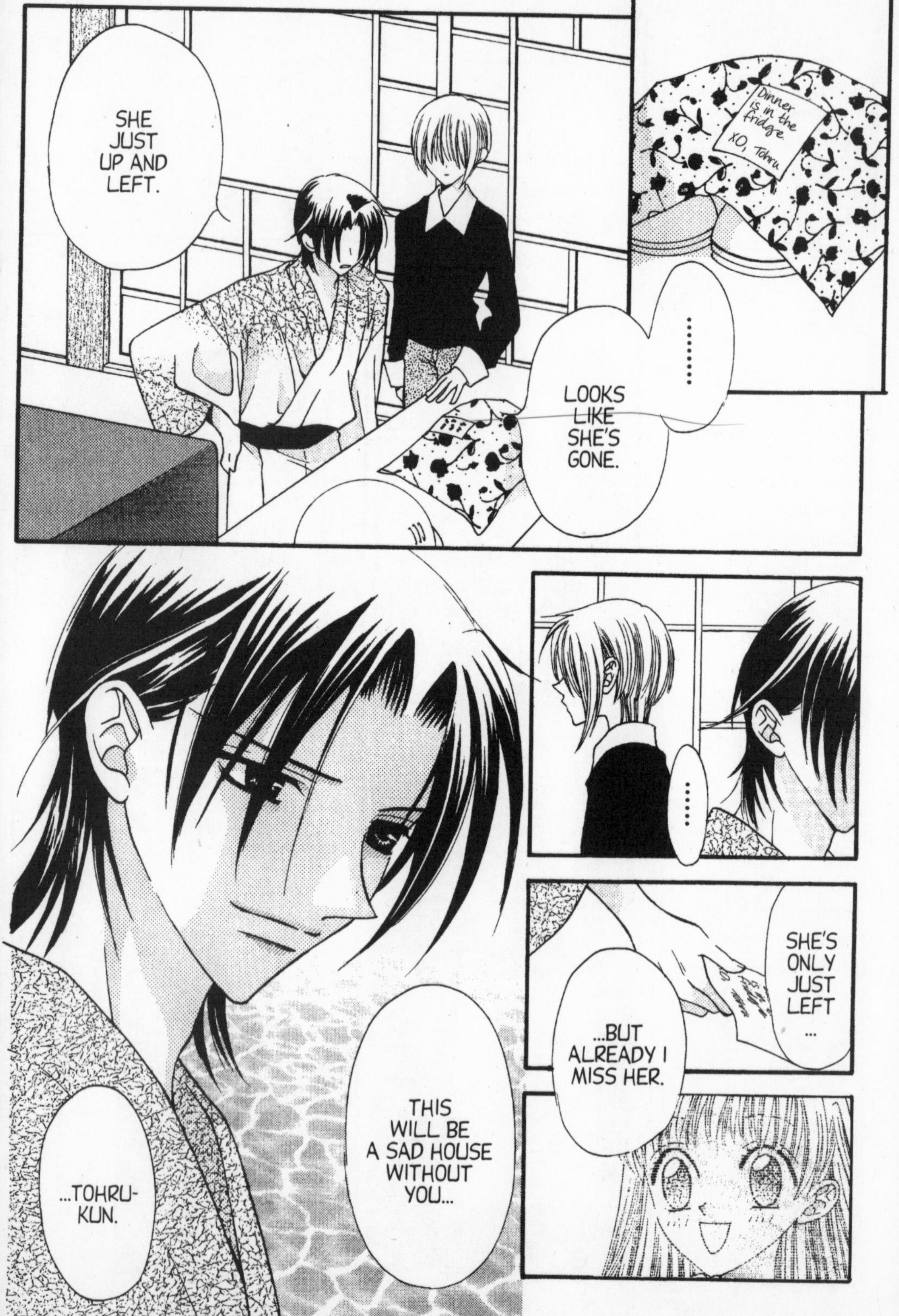
Dinner is in the fridge
XO, Tohru
......
LOOKS LIKE SHE'S GONE.
SHE JUST UP AND LEFT.
......
SHE'S ONLY JUST LEFT...
...BUT ALREADY I MISS HER.
THIS WILL BE A SAD HOUSE WITHOUT YOU...
...TOHRU-KUN.

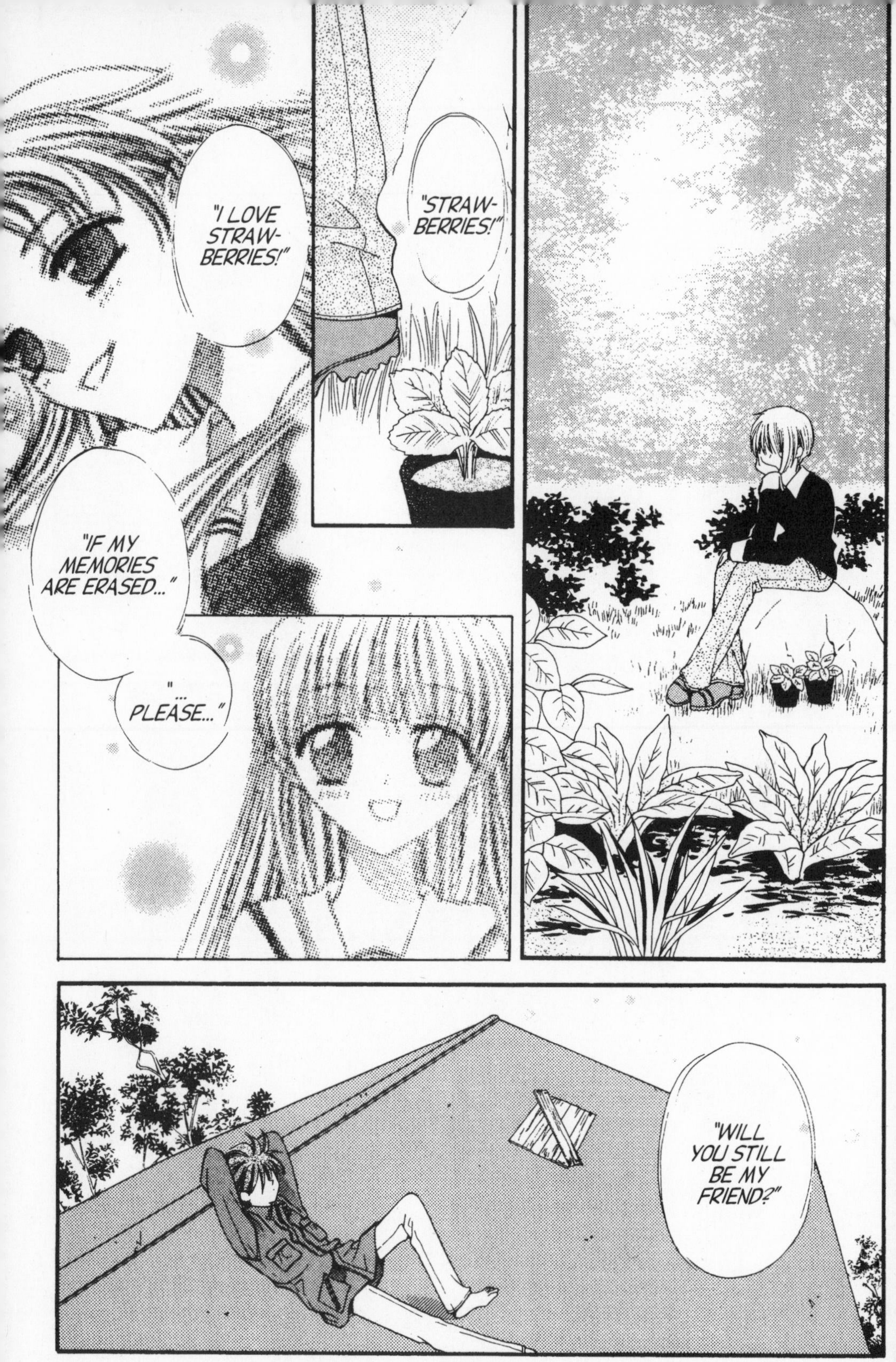
"STRAW-BERRIES!"
"I LOVE STRAW-BERRIES!"
"IF MY MEMORIES ARE ERASED..."
"... PLEASE..."
"WILL YOU STILL BE MY FRIEND?"

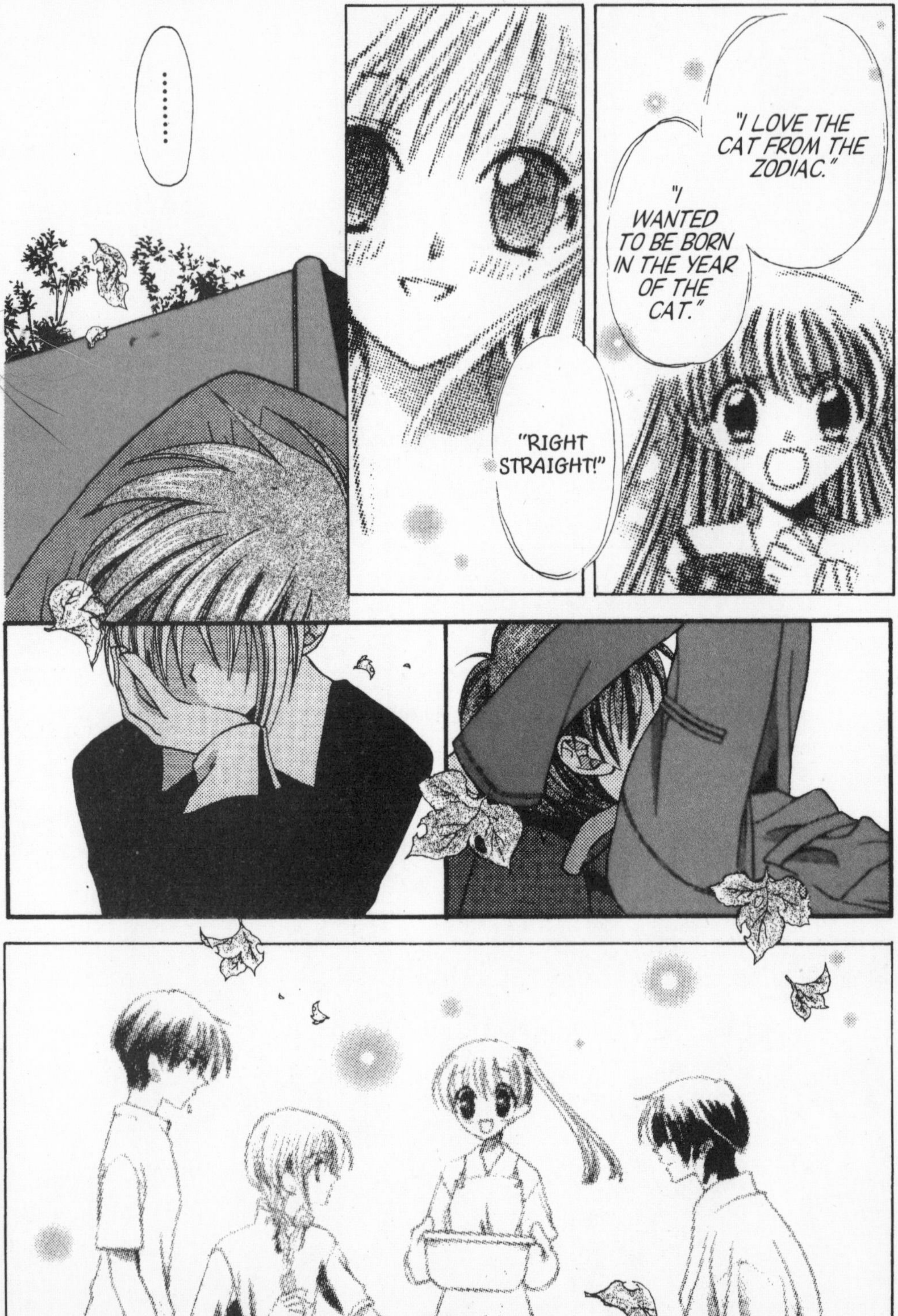
"I LOVE THE CAT FROM THE ZODIAC."
"I WANTED TO BE BORN IN THE YEAR OF THE CAT."
"RIGHT STRAIGHT!"
......

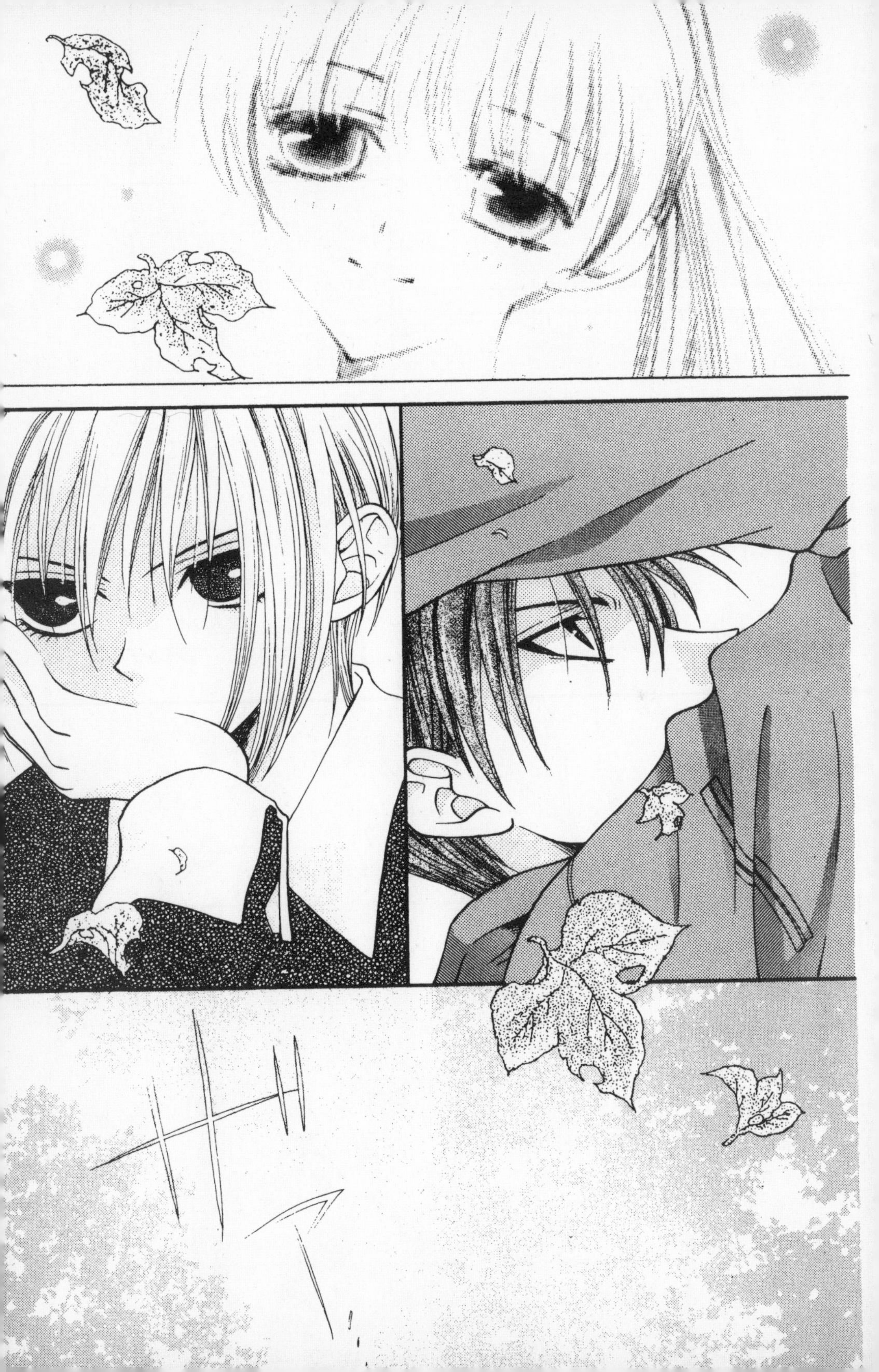

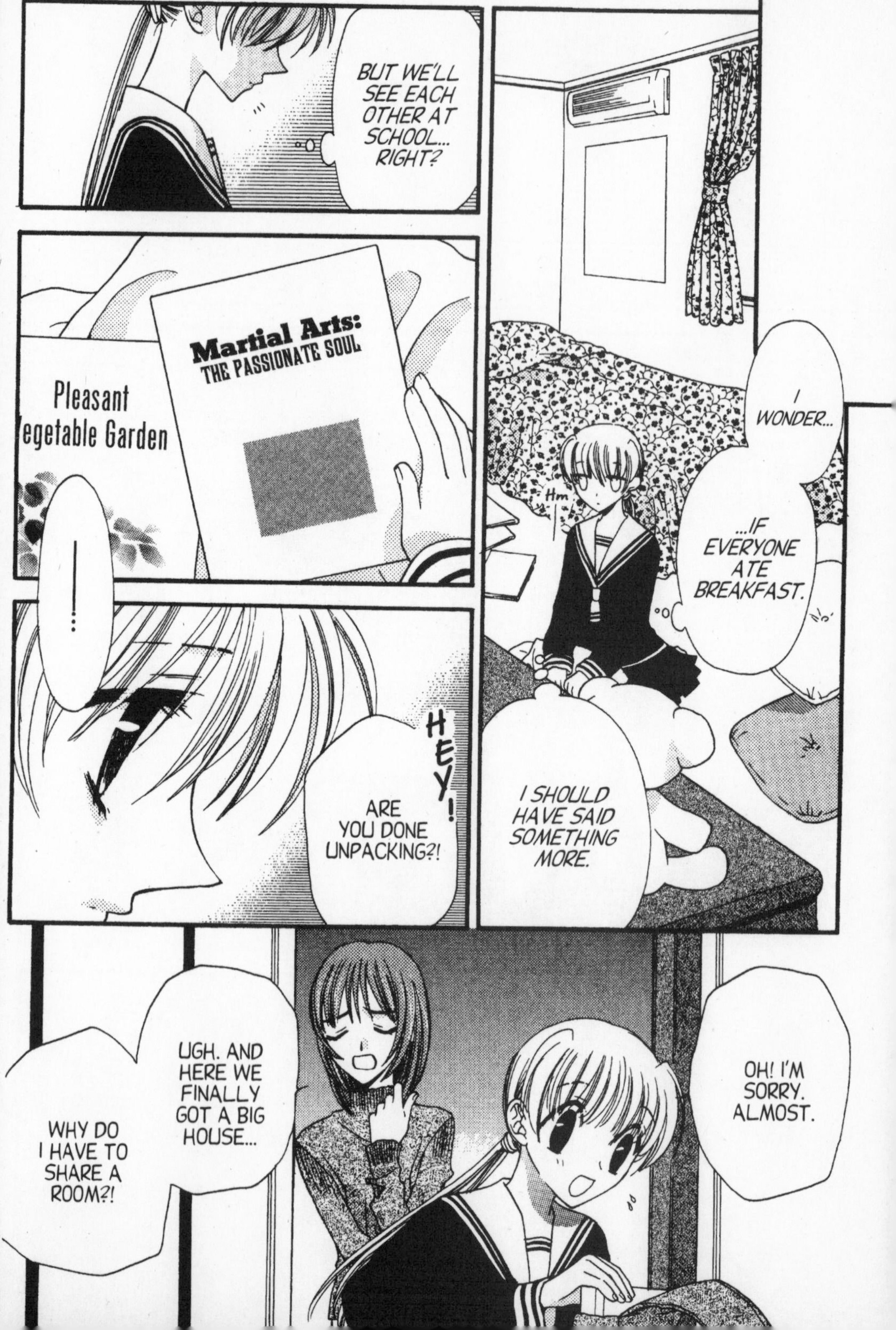
I WONDER...
...IF EVERYONE ATE BREAKFAST.
Hm
I SHOULD HAVE SAID SOMETHING MORE.
BUT WE'LL SEE EACH OTHER AT SCHOOL... RIGHT?
Martial Arts: THE PASSIONATE SOUL
Pleasant
egetable Garden
...
HEY!
ARE YOU DONE UNPACKING?!
OH! I'M SORRY. ALMOST.
UGH. AND HERE WE FINALLY GOT A BIG HOUSE...
WHY DO I HAVE TO SHARE A ROOM?!

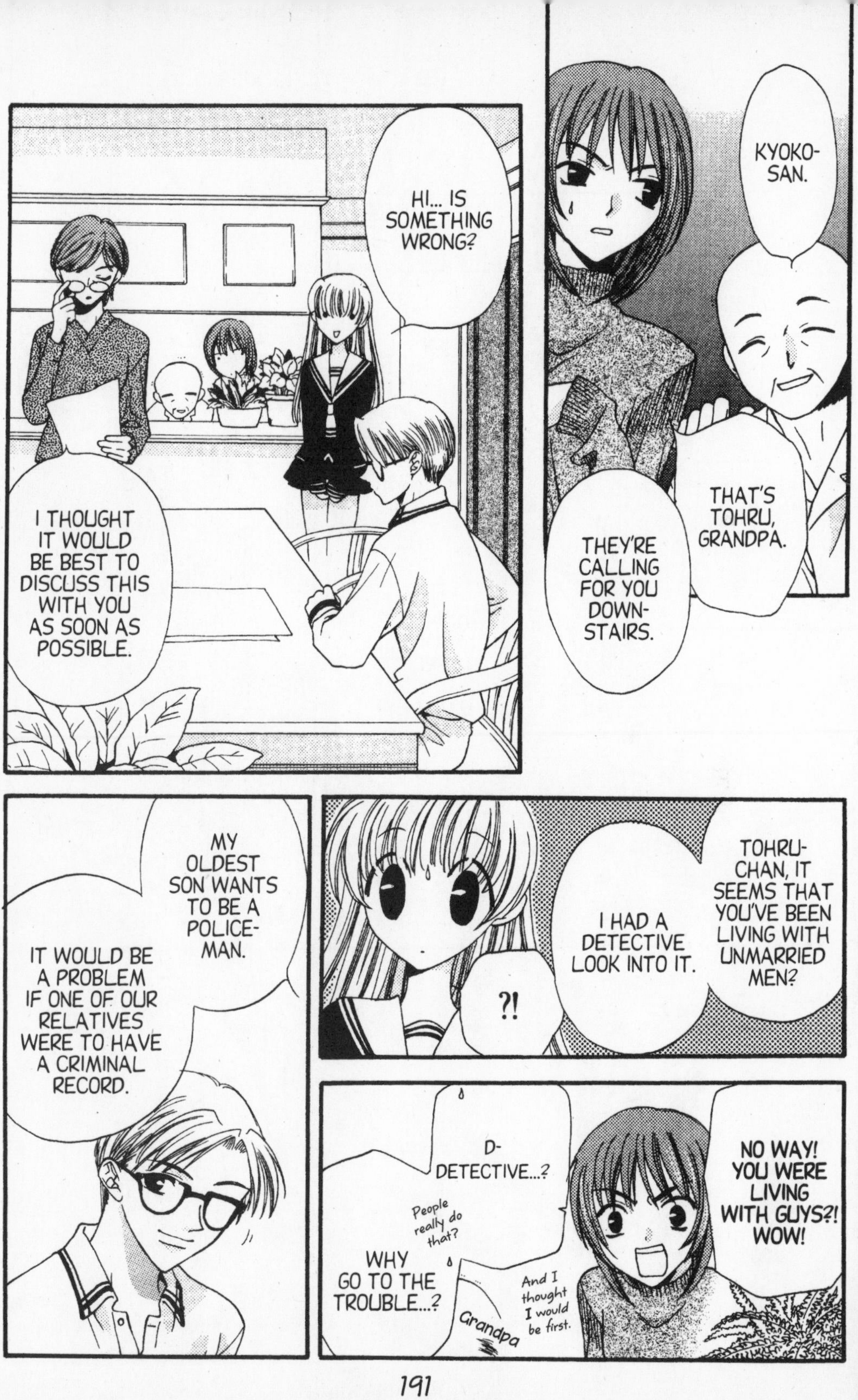
KYOKO-SAN.
THAT'S TOHRU, GRANDPA.
THEY'RE CALLING FOR YOU DOWN-STAIRS.
HI... IS SOMETHING WRONG?
I THOUGHT IT WOULD BE BEST TO DISCUSS THIS WITH YOU AS SOON AS POSSIBLE.
TOHRU-CHAN, IT SEEMS THAT YOU'VE BEEN LIVING WITH UNMARRIED MEN?
I HAD A DETECTIVE LOOK INTO IT.
?!
NO WAY! YOU WERE LIVING WITH GUYS?! WOW!
And I thought I would be first.
D-DETECTIVE...?
People really do that?
WHY GO TO THE TROUBLE...?
Grandpa
MY OLDEST SON WANTS TO BE A POLICE-MAN.
IT WOULD BE A PROBLEM IF ONE OF OUR RELATIVES WERE TO HAVE A CRIMINAL RECORD.

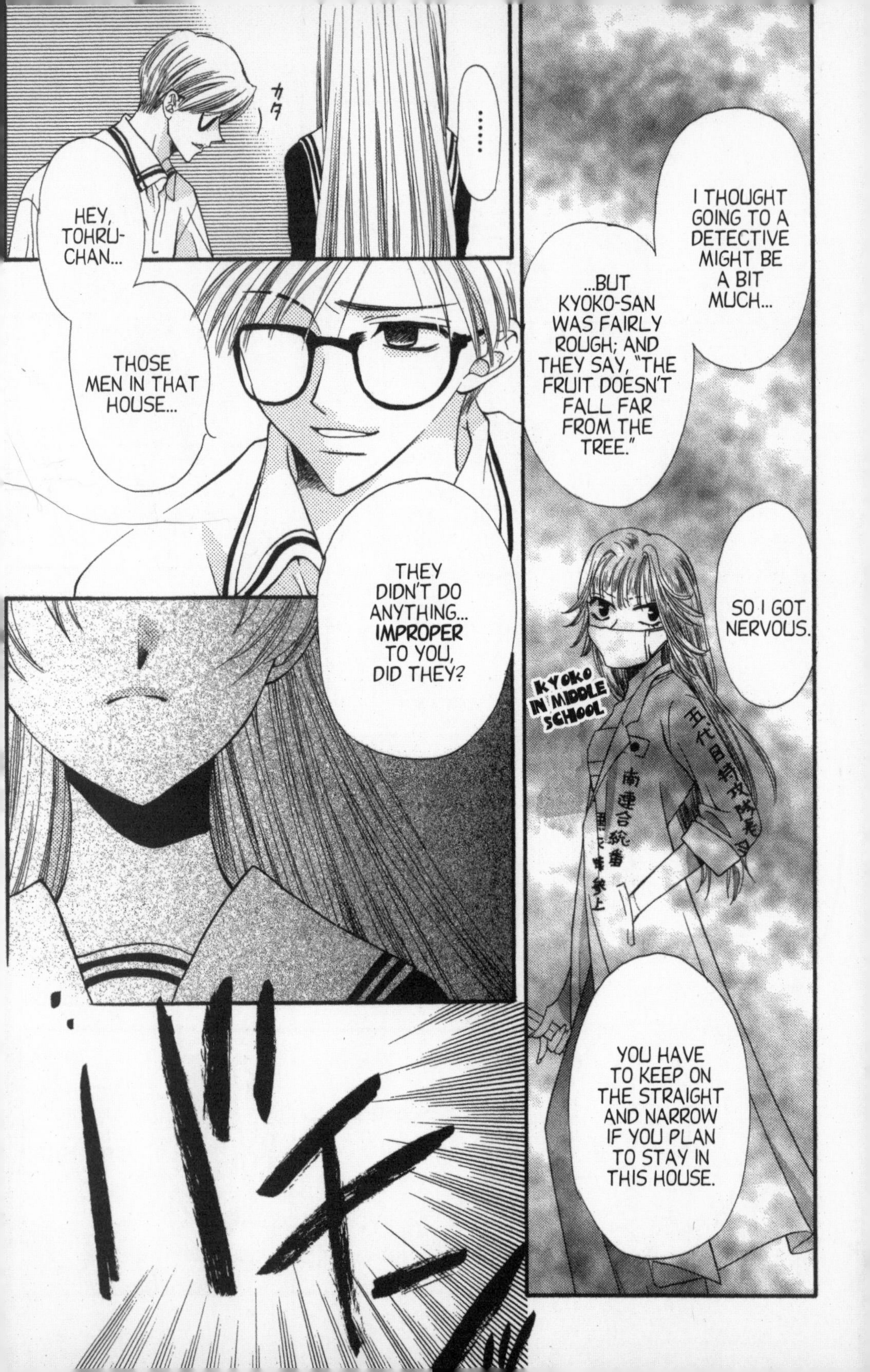
I THOUGHT GOING TO A DETECTIVE MIGHT BE A BIT MUCH...
...BUT KYOKO-SAN WAS FAIRLY ROUGH; AND THEY SAY, "THE FRUIT DOESN'T FALL FAR FROM THE TREE."
SO I GOT NERVOUS.
KYOKO IN MIDDLE SCHOOL
YOU HAVE TO KEEP ON THE STRAIGHT AND NARROW IF YOU PLAN TO STAY IN THIS HOUSE.
......
カタ
HEY, TOHRU-CHAN...
THOSE MEN IN THAT HOUSE...
THEY DIDN'T DO ANYTHING... **IMPROPER** TO YOU, DID THEY?

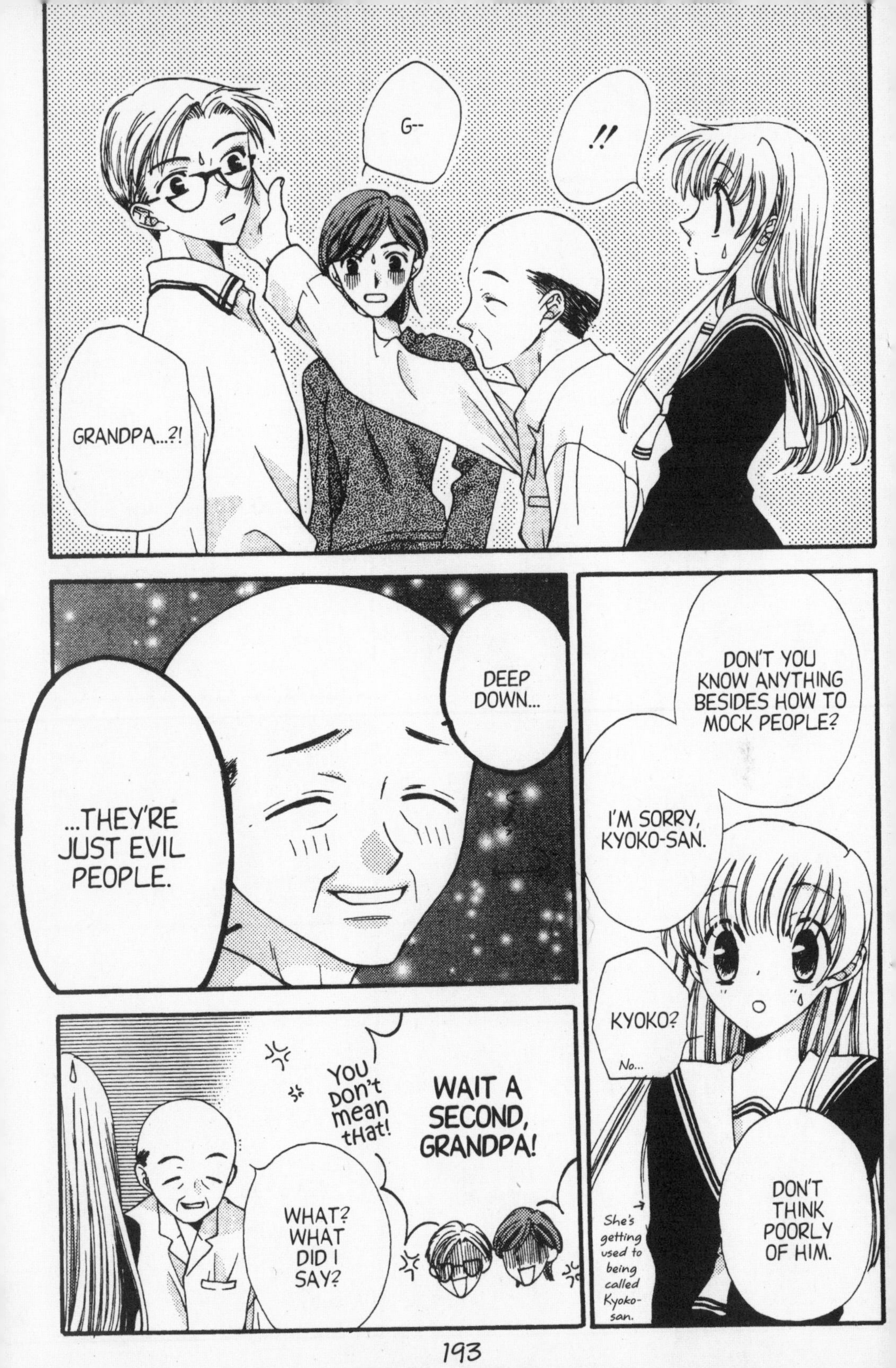
!!
G--
GRANDPA...?!
DON'T YOU KNOW ANYTHING BESIDES HOW TO MOCK PEOPLE?
I'M SORRY, KYOKO-SAN.
KYOKO?
No...
DON'T THINK POORLY OF HIM.
She's getting used to being called Kyoko-san.
DEEP DOWN...
...THEY'RE JUST EVIL PEOPLE.
WAIT A SECOND, GRANDPA!
YOU DON'T MEAN THAT!
WHAT? WHAT DID I SAY?

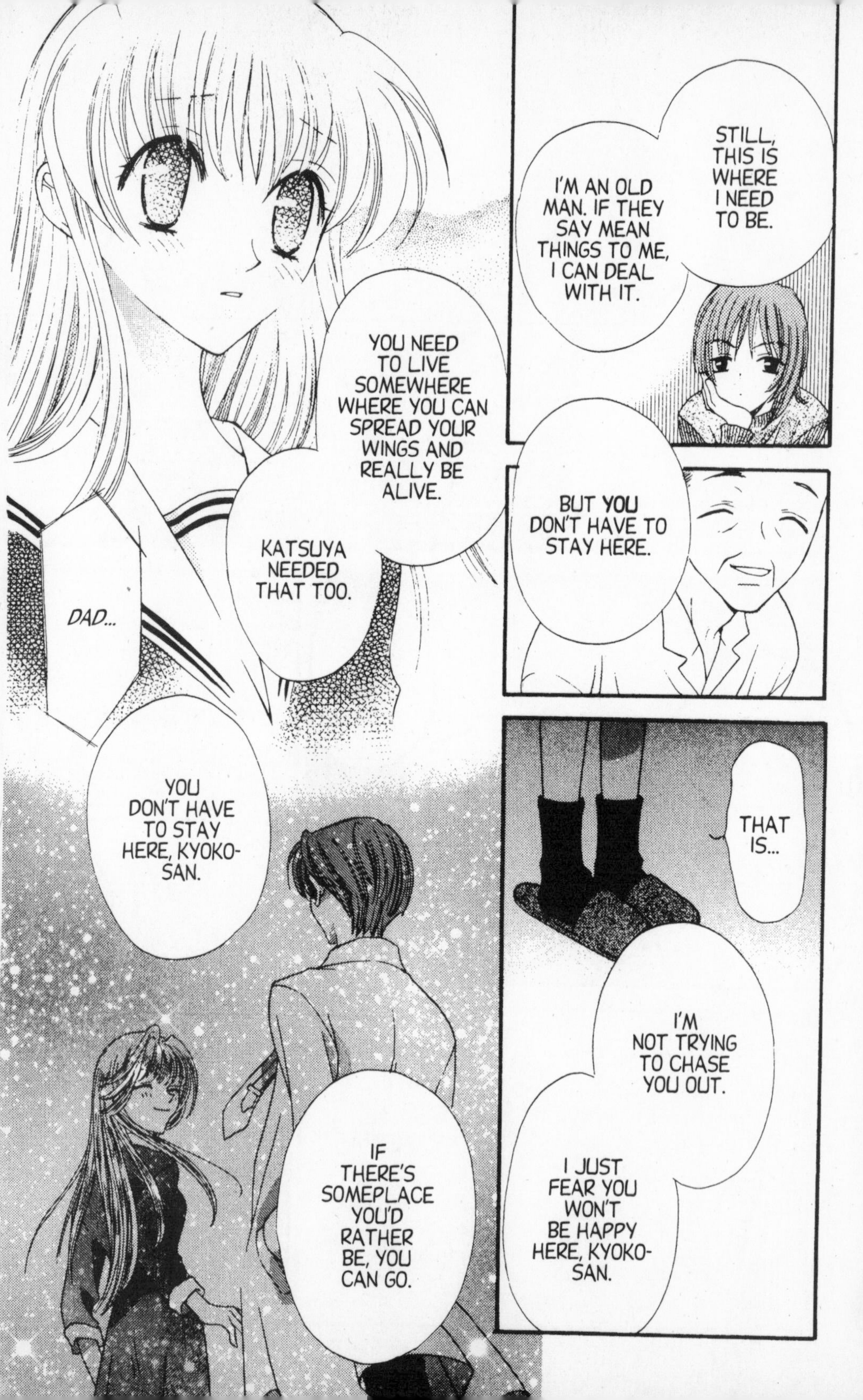
STILL, THIS IS WHERE I NEED TO BE.
I'M AN OLD MAN. IF THEY SAY MEAN THINGS TO ME, I CAN DEAL WITH IT.
BUT YOU DON'T HAVE TO STAY HERE.
THAT IS...
I'M NOT TRYING TO CHASE YOU OUT.
I JUST FEAR YOU WON'T BE HAPPY HERE, KYOKO-SAN.
YOU NEED TO LIVE SOMEWHERE WHERE YOU CAN SPREAD YOUR WINGS AND REALLY BE ALIVE.
KATSUYA NEEDED THAT TOO.
DAD...
YOU DON'T HAVE TO STAY HERE, KYOKO-SAN.
IF THERE'S SOMEPLACE YOU'D RATHER BE, YOU CAN GO.

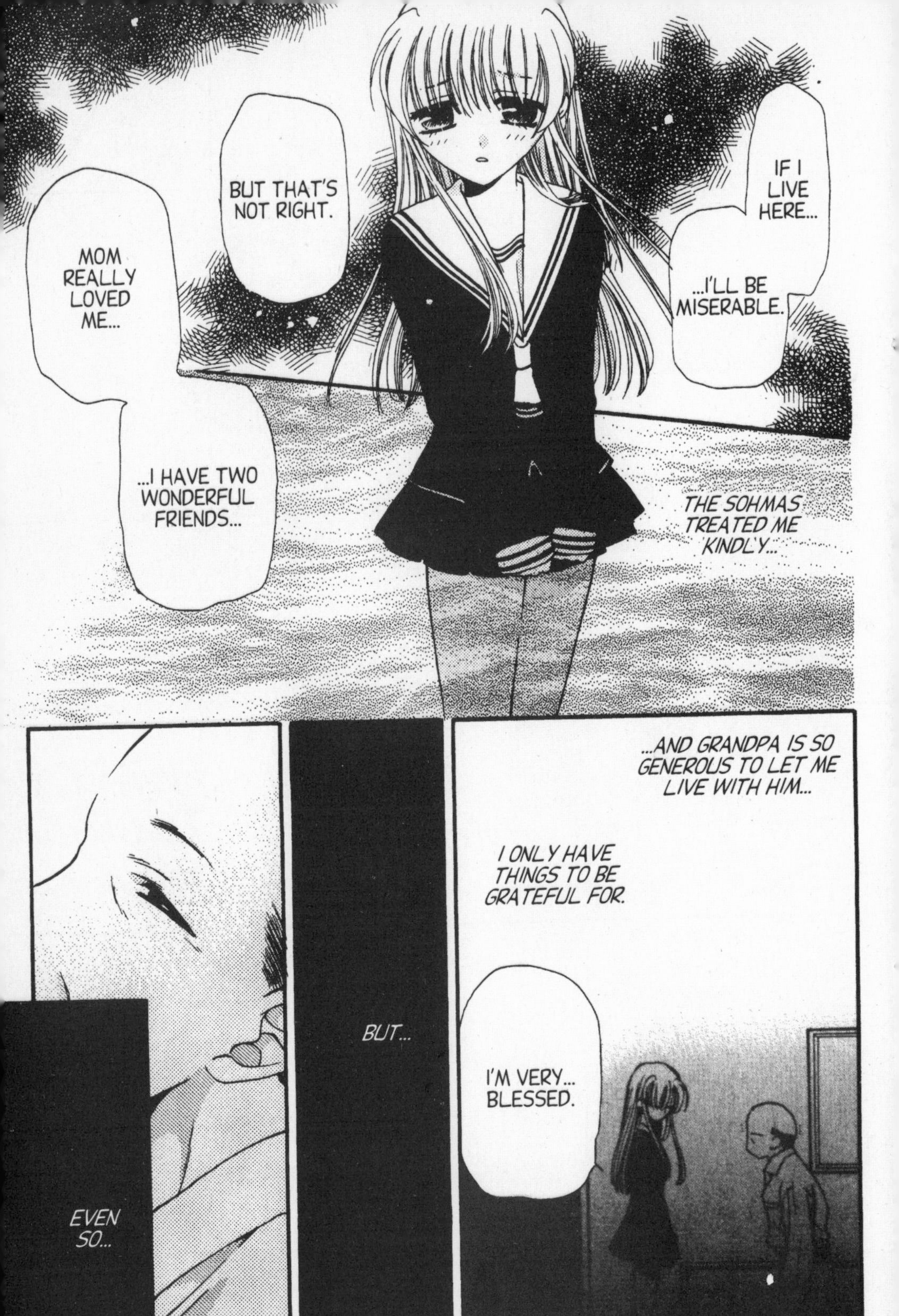
IF I LIVE HERE...
...I'LL BE MISERABLE.
BUT THAT'S NOT RIGHT.
MOM REALLY LOVED ME...
...I HAVE TWO WONDERFUL FRIENDS...
THE SOHMAS TREATED ME KINDLY...
...AND GRANDPA IS SO GENEROUS TO LET ME LIVE WITH HIM...
I ONLY HAVE THINGS TO BE GRATEFUL FOR.
I'M VERY... BLESSED.
BUT...
EVEN SO...

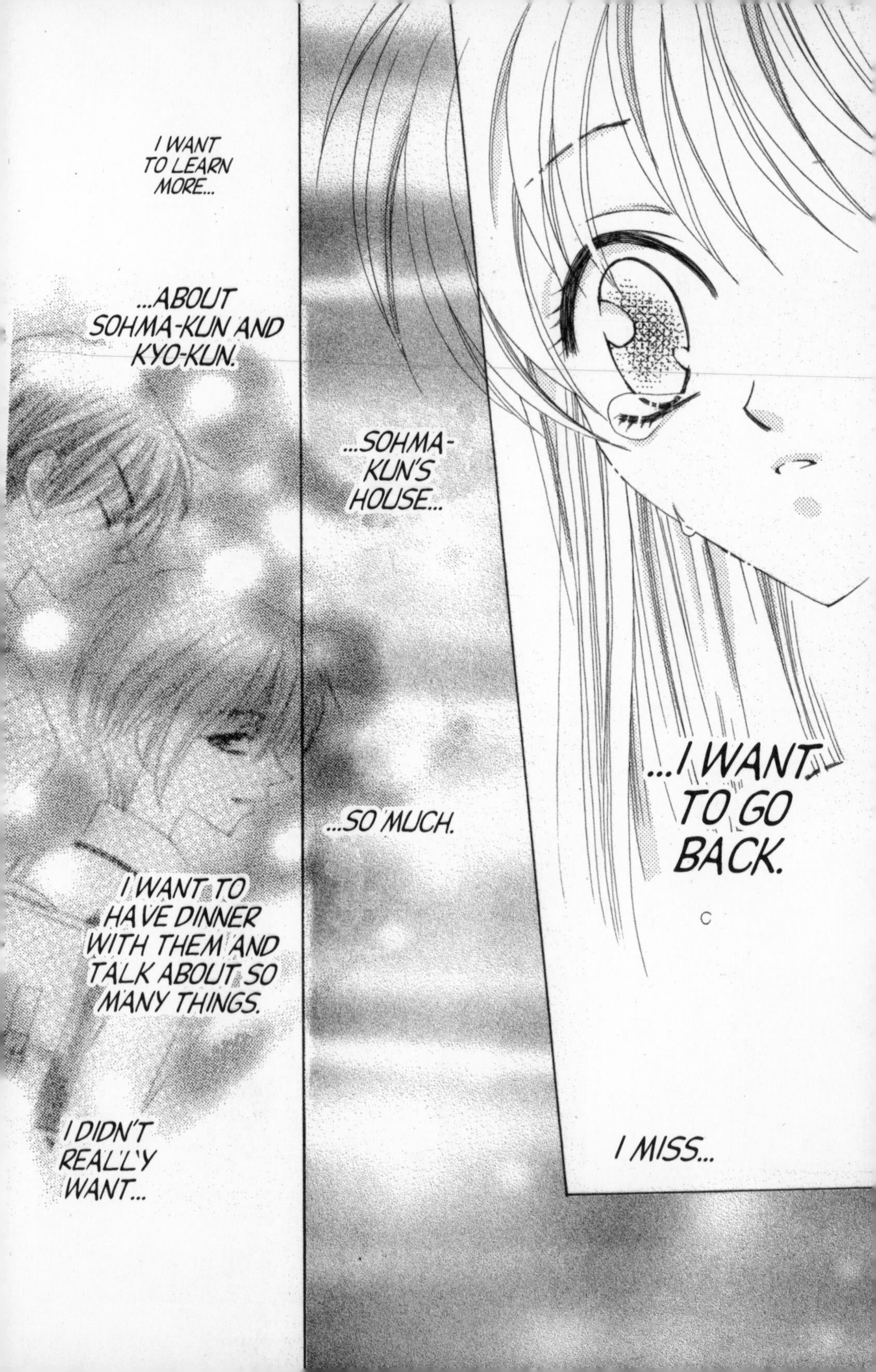
...I WANT TO GO BACK.
I MISS...
...SOHMA-KUN'S HOUSE...
...SO MUCH.
I WANT TO LEARN MORE...
...ABOUT SOHMA-KUN AND KYO-KUN.
I WANT TO HAVE DINNER WITH THEM AND TALK ABOUT SO MANY THINGS.
I DIDN'T REALLY WANT...

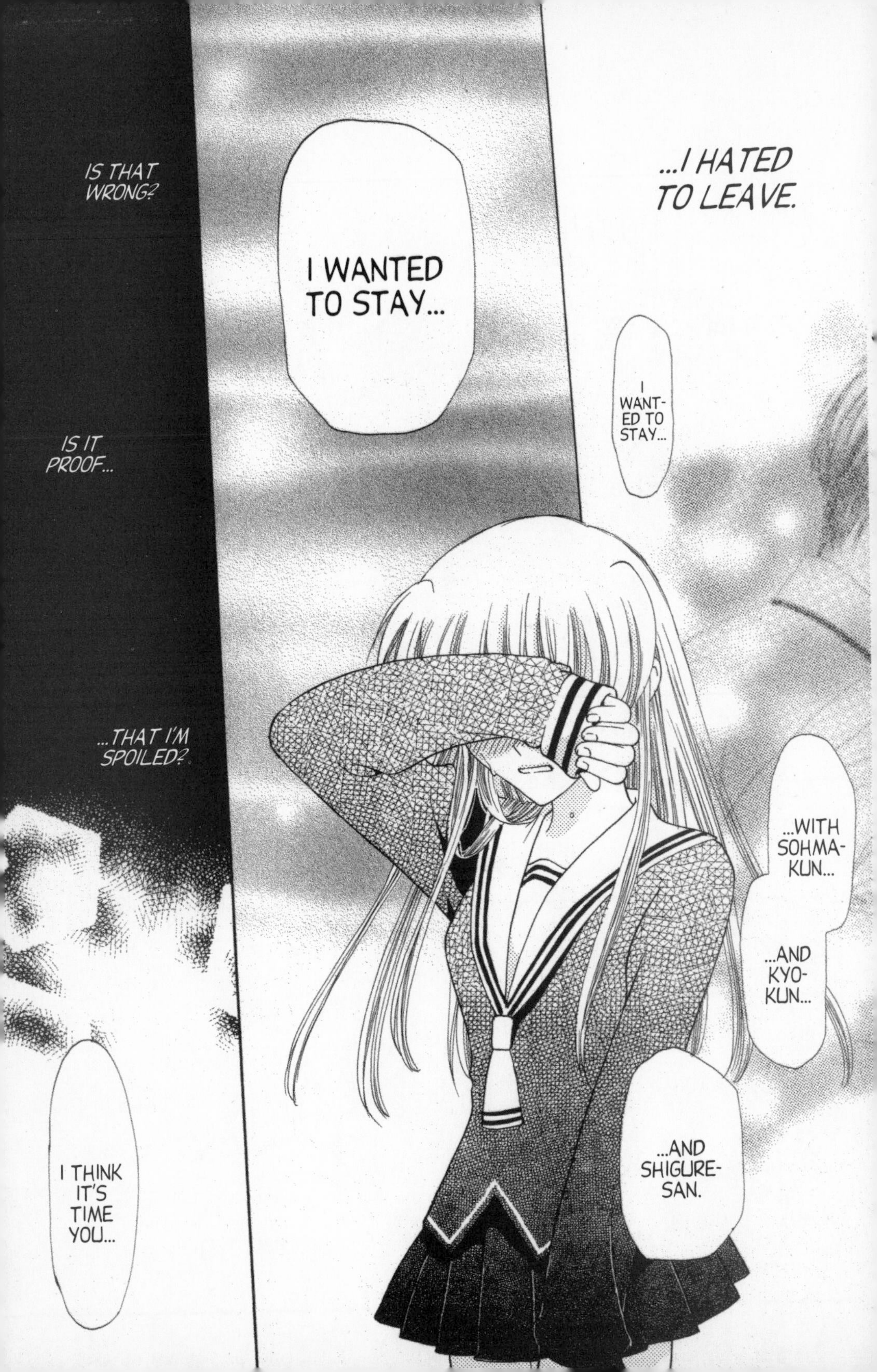
...I HATED TO LEAVE.
I WANTED TO STAY...
...WITH SOHMA-KUN...
...AND KYO-KUN...
...AND SHIGURE-SAN.
I WANTED TO STAY...
IS THAT WRONG?
IS IT PROOF...
...THAT I'M SPOILED?
I THINK IT'S TIME YOU...

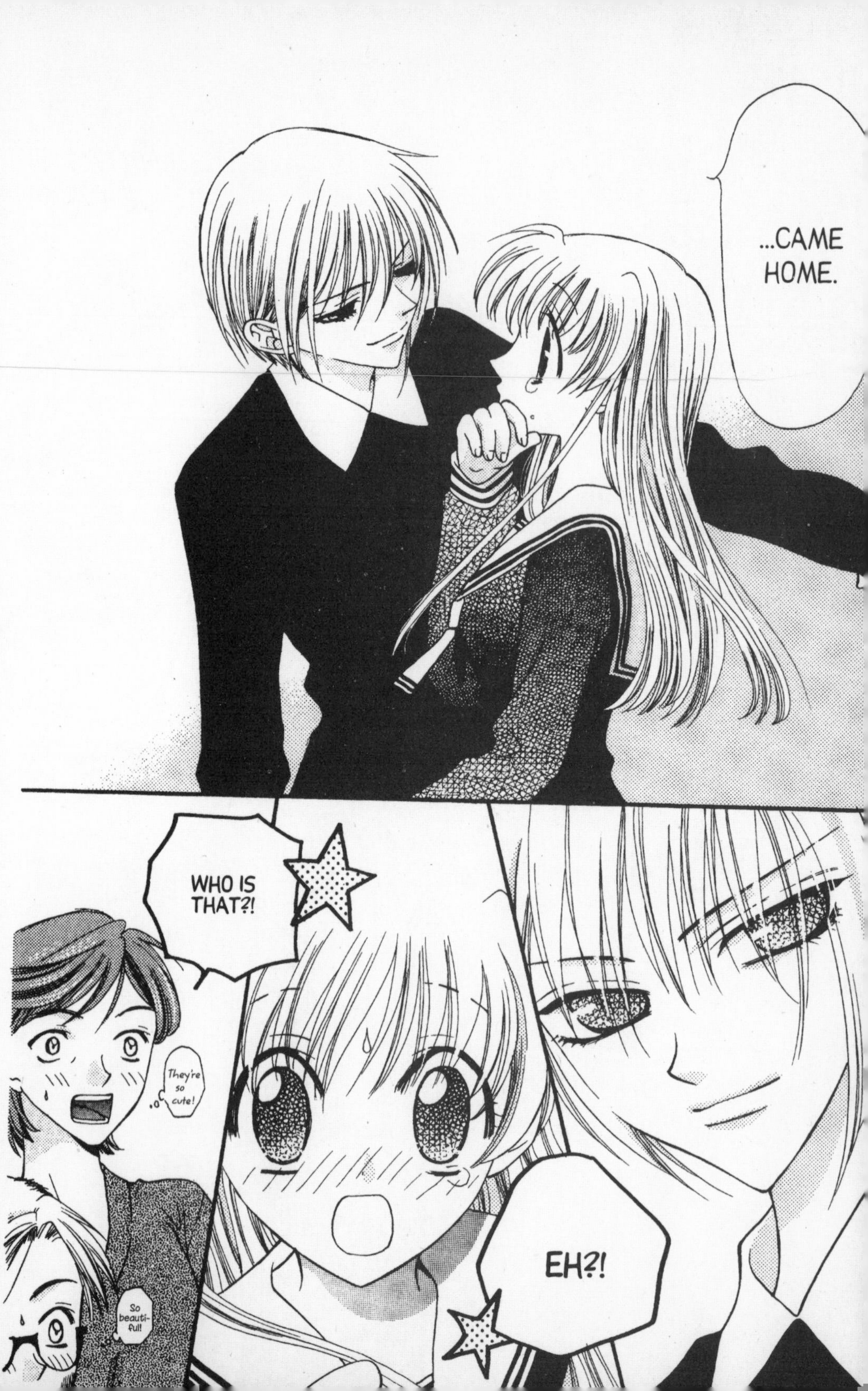
...CAME HOME.
EH?!
WHO IS THAT?!
They're so cute!
So beauti-ful!

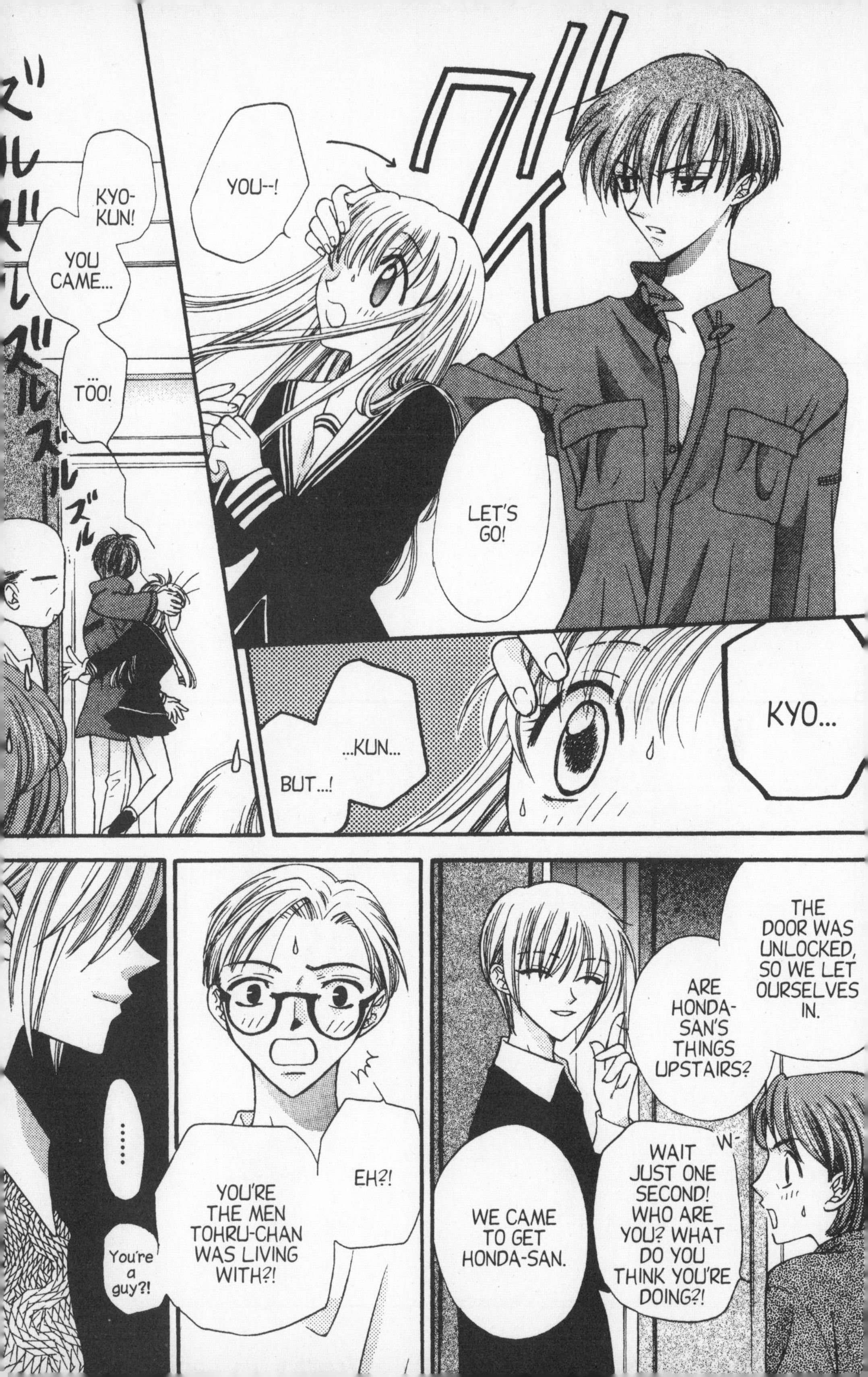
YOU--!
LET'S GO!
KYO-KUN! YOU CAME... ...TOO!
KYO...
...KUN... BUT...!
THE DOOR WAS UNLOCKED, SO WE LET OURSELVES IN.
ARE HONDA-SAN'S THINGS UPSTAIRS?
W-
WAIT JUST ONE SECOND! WHO ARE YOU? WHAT DO YOU THINK YOU'RE DOING?!
WE CAME TO GET HONDA-SAN.
EH?!
YOU'RE THE MEN TOHRU-CHAN WAS LIVING WITH?!
......
You're a guy?!

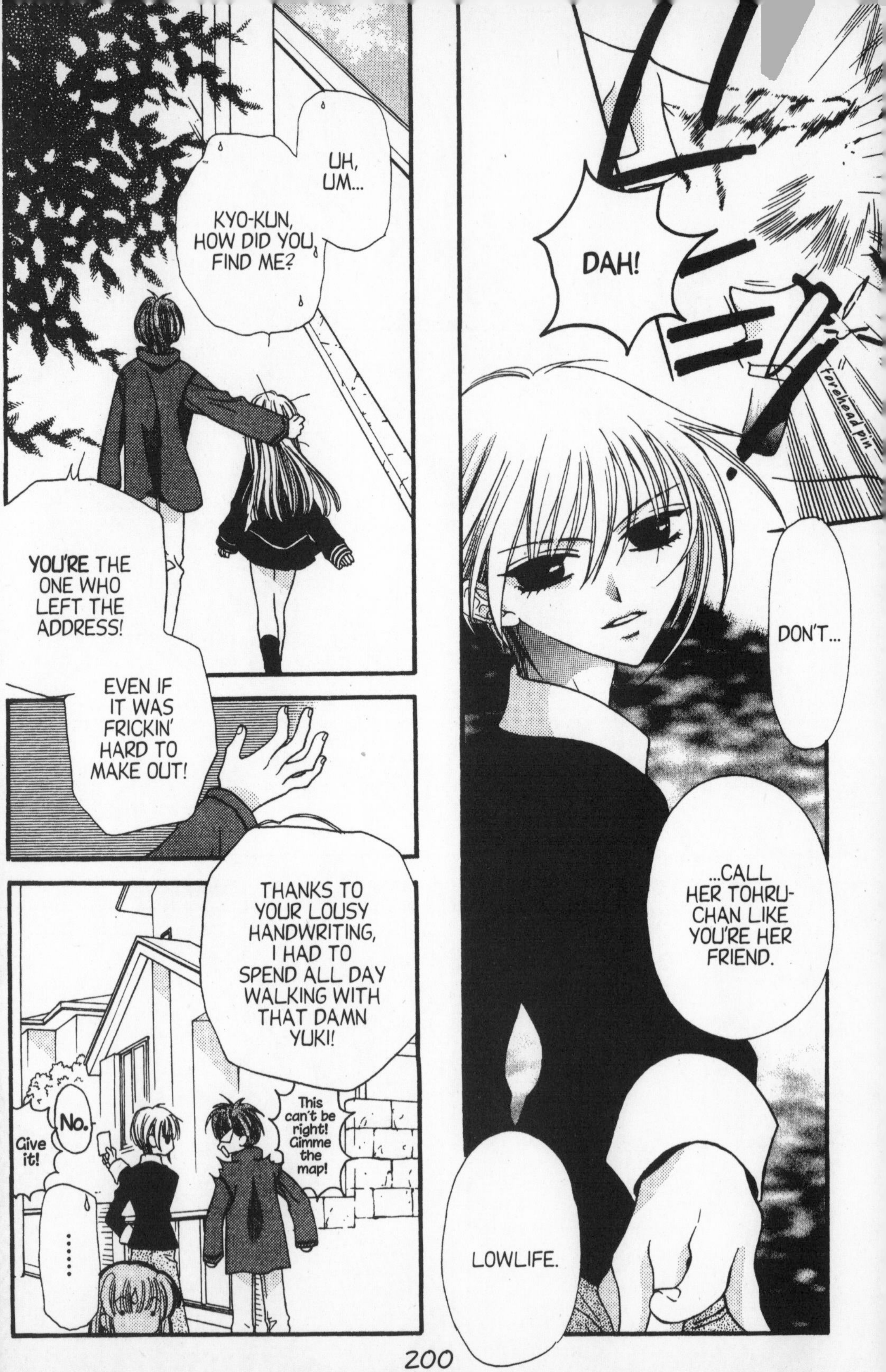
DAH!
forehead pin
DON'T...
...CALL HER TOHRU-CHAN LIKE YOU'RE HER FRIEND.
LOWLIFE.
UH, UM...
KYO-KUN, HOW DID YOU FIND ME?
YOU'RE THE ONE WHO LEFT THE ADDRESS!
EVEN IF IT WAS FRICKIN' HARD TO MAKE OUT!
THANKS TO YOUR LOUSY HANDWRITING, I HAD TO SPEND ALL DAY WALKING WITH THAT DAMN YUKI!
This can't be right! Gimme the map!
No.
Give it!
......

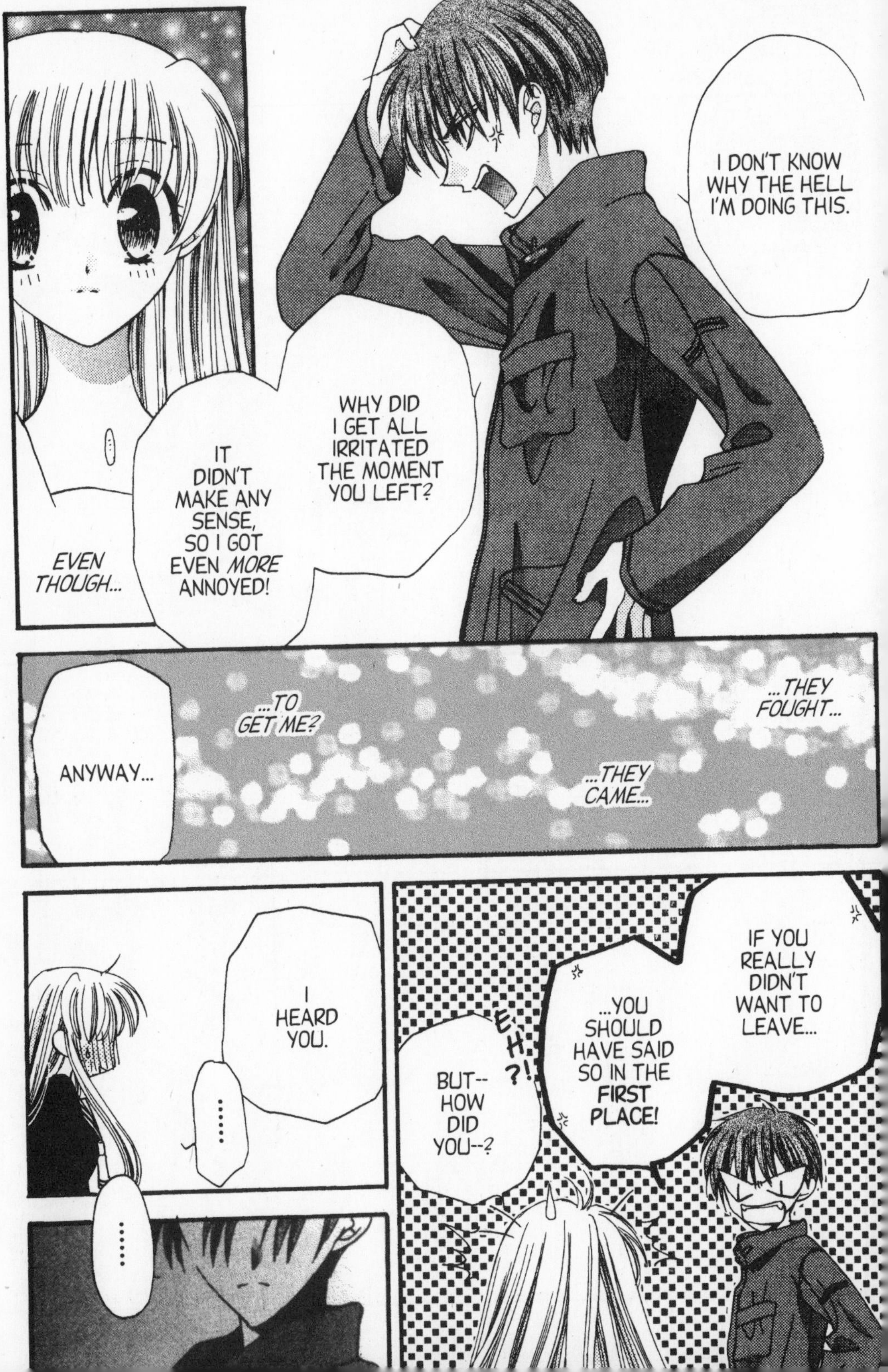

I DON'T KNOW WHY THE HELL I'M DOING THIS.
WHY DID I GET ALL IRRITATED THE MOMENT YOU LEFT?
IT DIDN'T MAKE ANY SENSE, SO I GOT EVEN *MORE* ANNOYED!
...
EVEN THOUGH...
...THEY FOUGHT...
...THEY CAME...
...TO GET ME?
ANYWAY...
IF YOU REALLY DIDN'T WANT TO LEAVE...
...YOU SHOULD HAVE SAID SO IN THE **FIRST PLACE!**
EH?!
BUT-- HOW DID YOU--?
I HEARD YOU.
......
......

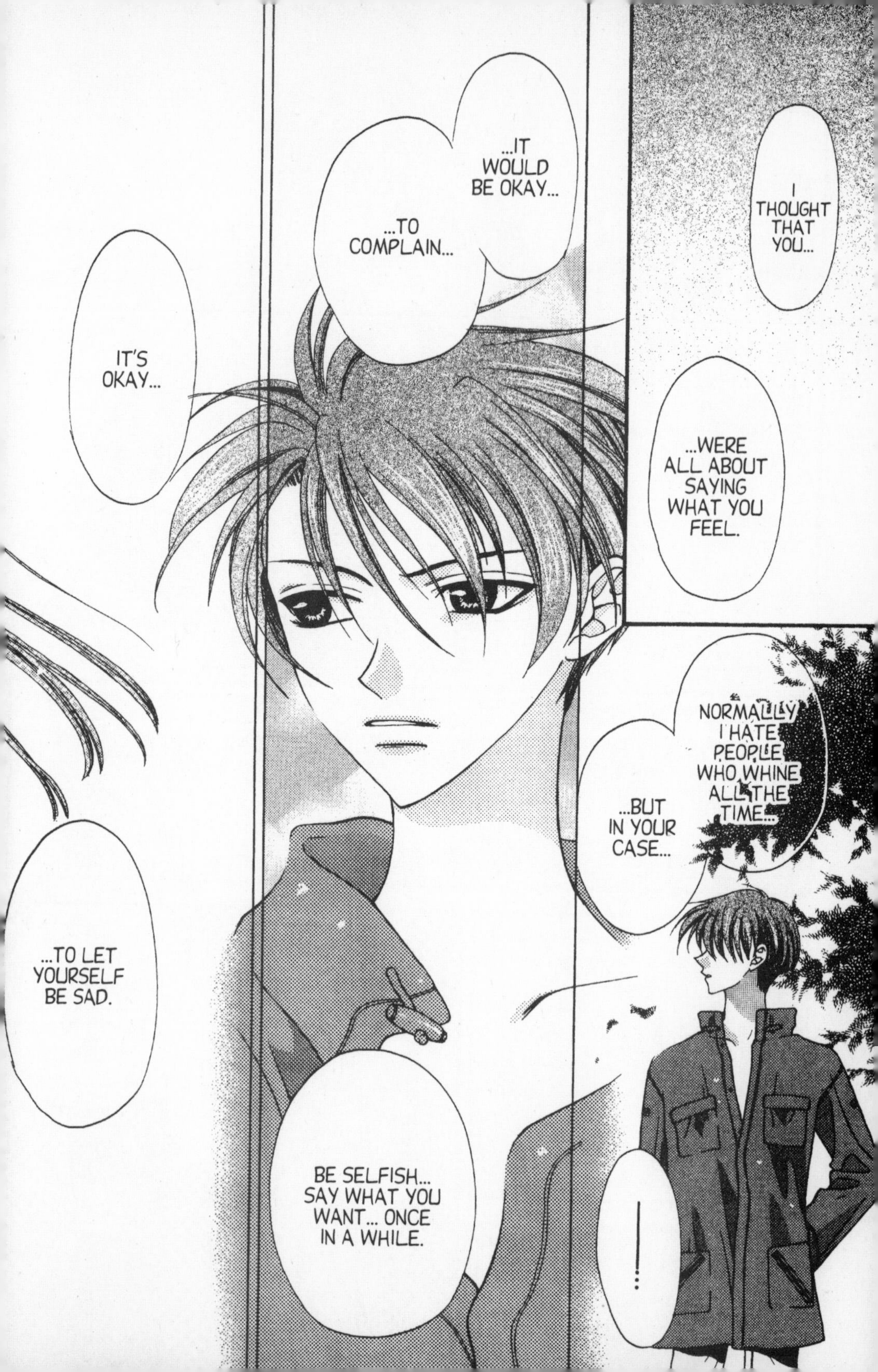
I THOUGHT THAT YOU...
...WERE ALL ABOUT SAYING WHAT YOU FEEL.
NORMALLY I HATE PEOPLE WHO WHINE ALL THE TIME...
...BUT IN YOUR CASE...
...IT WOULD BE OKAY...
...TO COMPLAIN...
BE SELFISH... SAY WHAT YOU WANT... ONCE IN A WHILE.
IT'S OKAY...
...TO LET YOURSELF BE SAD.

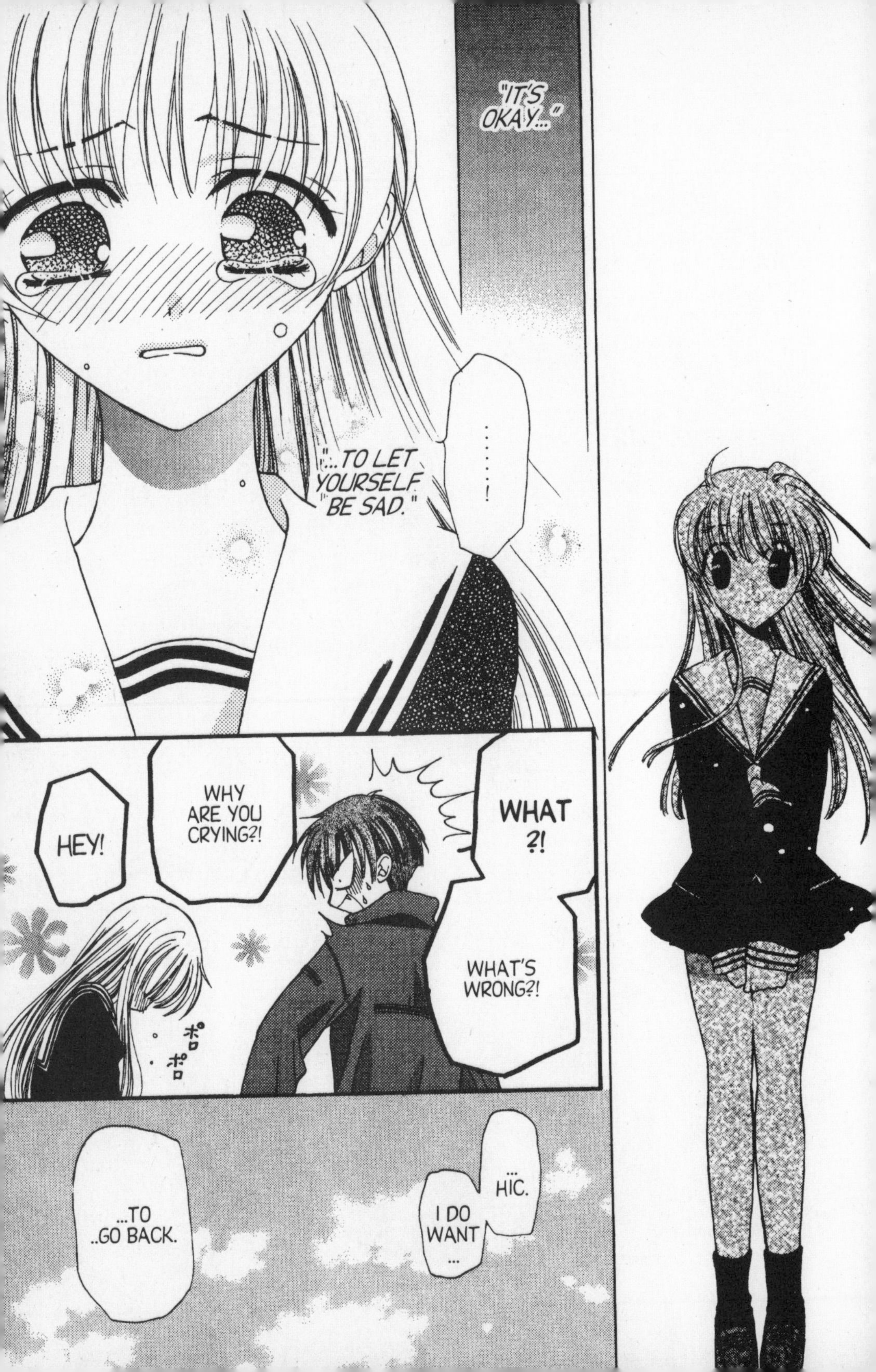

"IT'S OKAY..."
......!
"...TO LET YOURSELF BE SAD."
WHAT?!
WHAT'S WRONG?!
WHY ARE YOU CRYING?!
HEY!
ポロ ポロ
... HIC.
I DO WANT ...
...TO ..GO BACK.

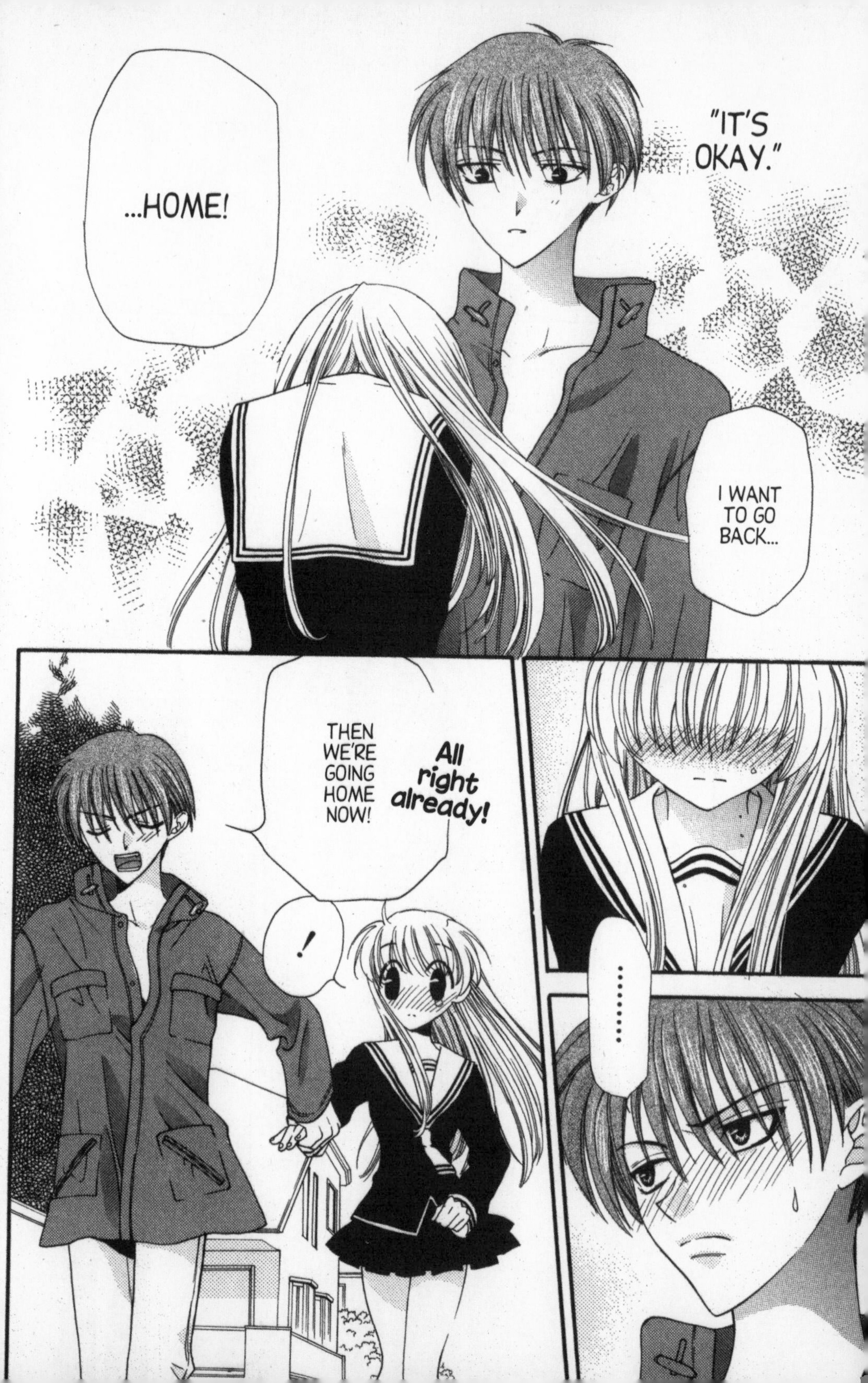
"IT'S OKAY."
I WANT TO GO BACK...
...HOME!
......
All right already!
THEN WE'RE GOING HOME NOW!
!

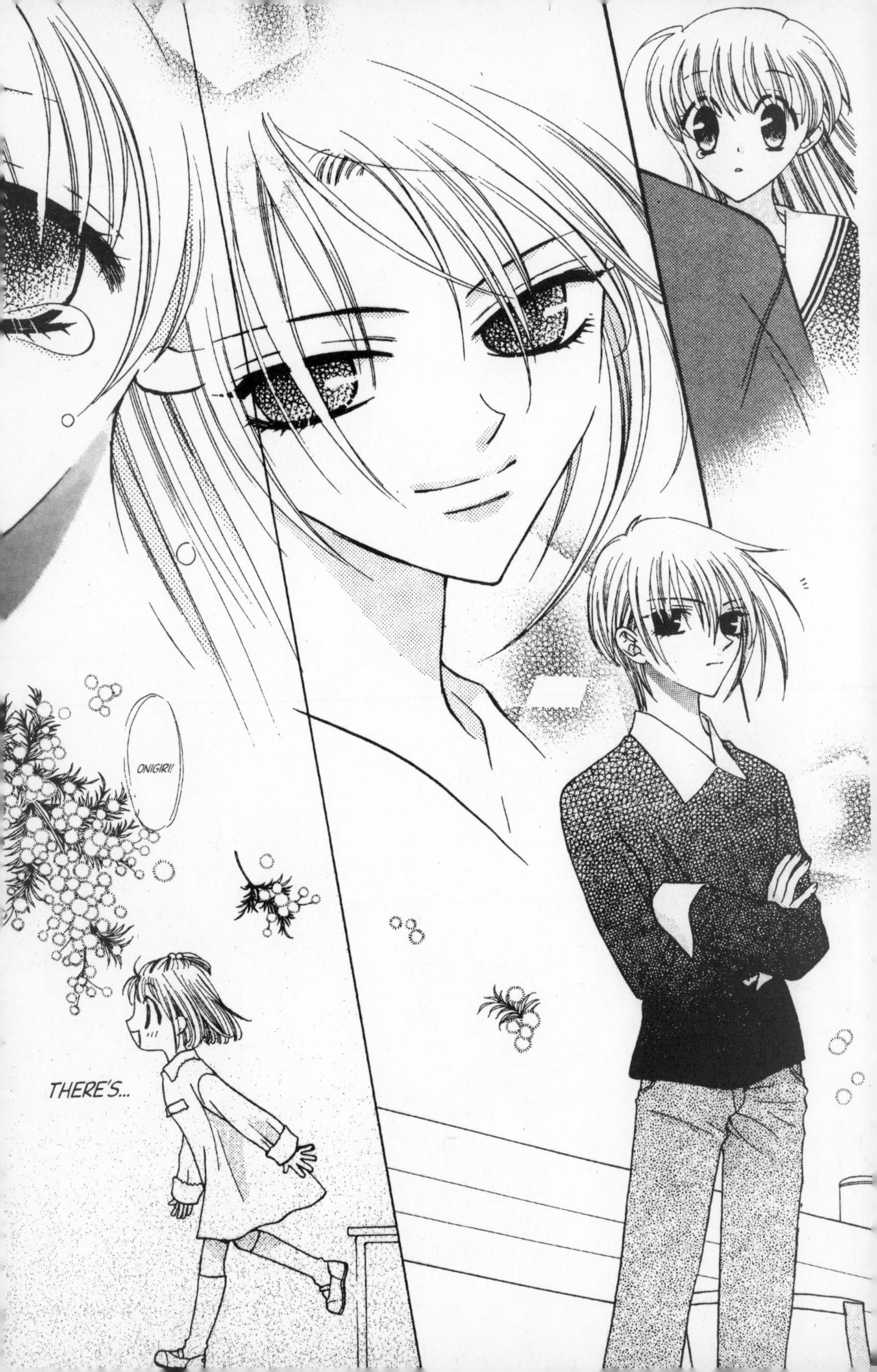
ONIGIRI!
THERE'S...

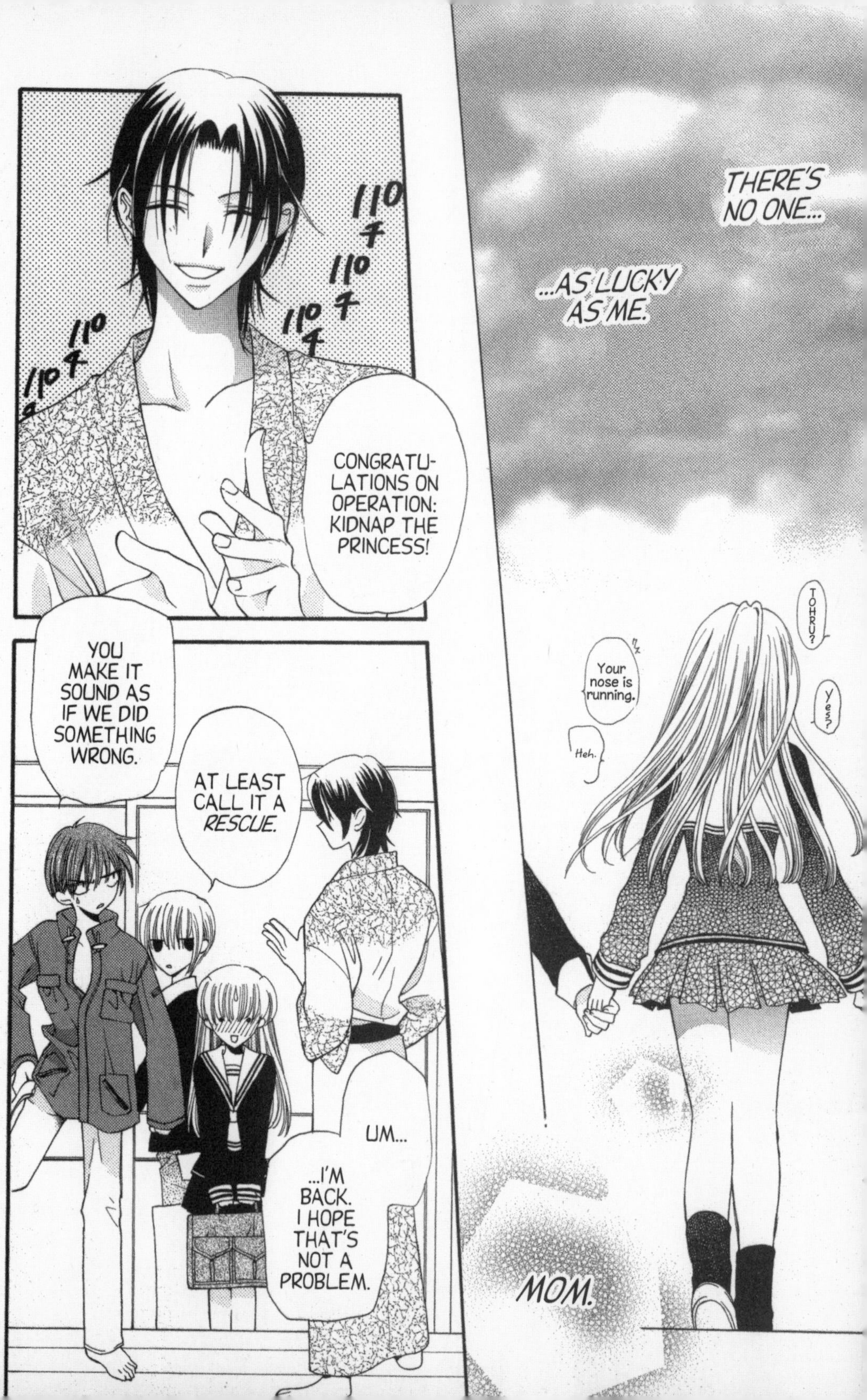
THERE'S NO ONE...
...AS LUCKY AS ME.
TOHRU?
Yes?
Your nose is running.
Heh.
MOM.
CONGRATULATIONS ON OPERATION: KIDNAP THE PRINCESS!
YOU MAKE IT SOUND AS IF WE DID SOMETHING WRONG.
AT LEAST CALL IT A RESCUE.
UM...
...I'M BACK. I HOPE THAT'S NOT A PROBLEM.

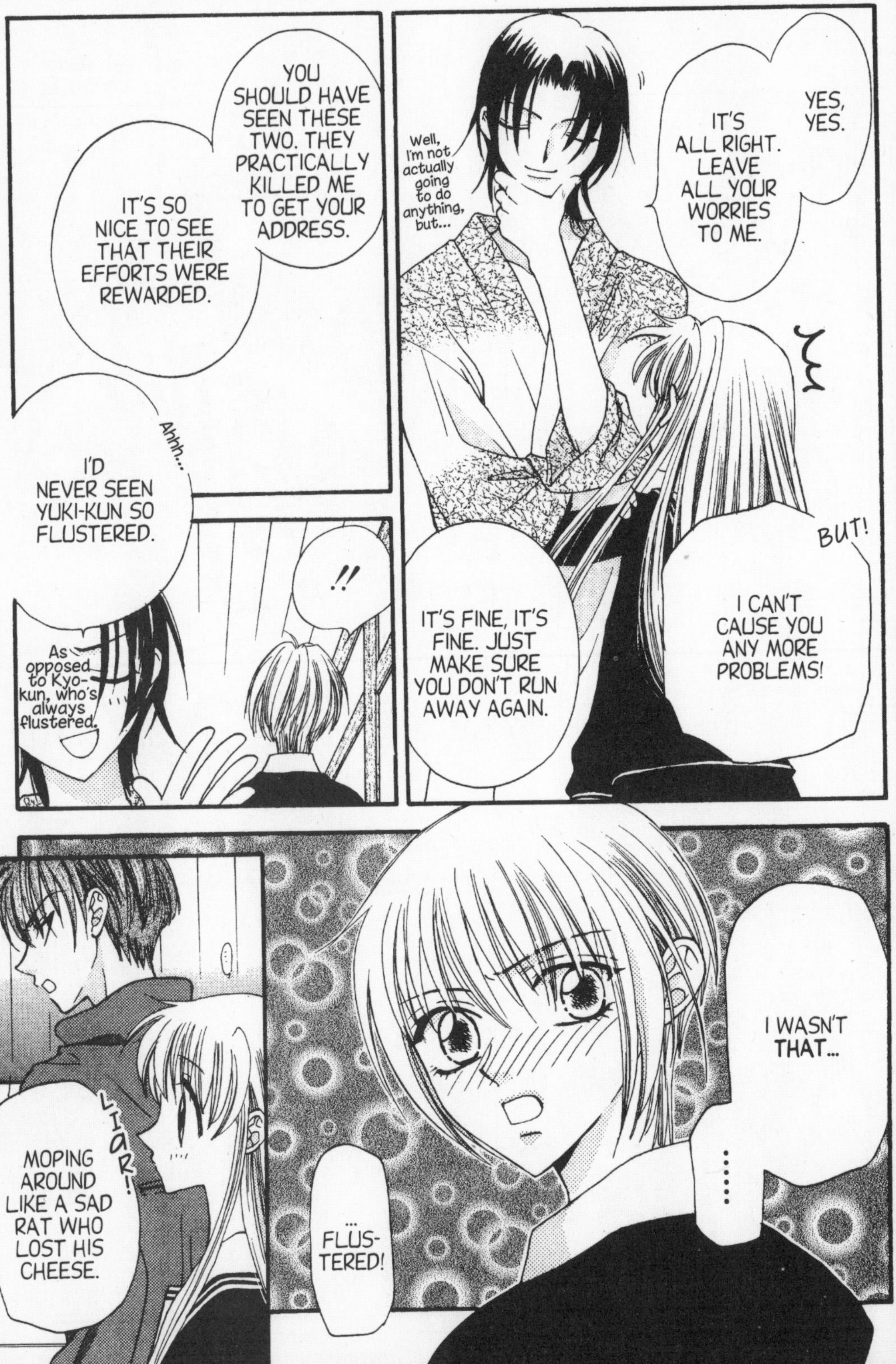
YES, YES.
IT'S ALL RIGHT. LEAVE ALL YOUR WORRIES TO ME.
Well, I'm not actually going to do anything, but...
BUT!
I CAN'T CAUSE YOU ANY MORE PROBLEMS!
IT'S FINE, IT'S FINE. JUST MAKE SURE YOU DON'T RUN AWAY AGAIN.
YOU SHOULD HAVE SEEN THESE TWO. THEY PRACTICALLY KILLED ME TO GET YOUR ADDRESS.
IT'S SO NICE TO SEE THAT THEIR EFFORTS WERE REWARDED.
Ahhh...
I'D NEVER SEEN YUKI-KUN SO FLUSTERED.
!!
As opposed to Kyo-kun, who's always flustered.
I WASN'T THAT...
......
...FLUS-TERED!
LIAR!
MOPING AROUND LIKE A SAD RAT WHO LOST HIS CHEESE.

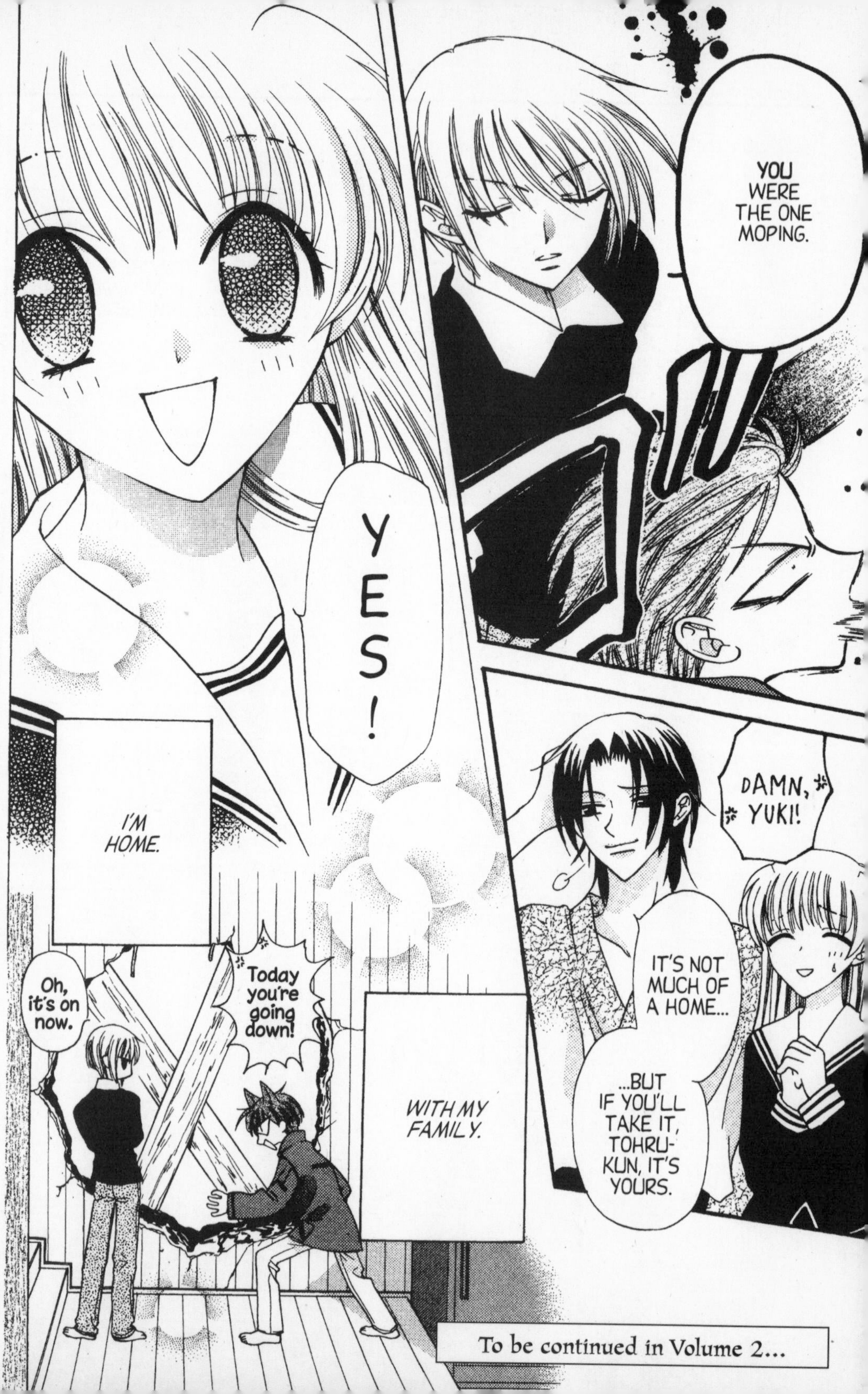
YOU WERE THE ONE MOPING.
DAMN, YUKI!
IT'S NOT MUCH OF A HOME...
...BUT IF YOU'LL TAKE IT, TOHRU-KUN, IT'S YOURS.
YES!
I'M HOME.
WITH MY FAMILY.
Today you're going down!
Oh, it's on now.

To be continued in Volume 2...

Omake Theater 4: This question isn't on the S.A.T....

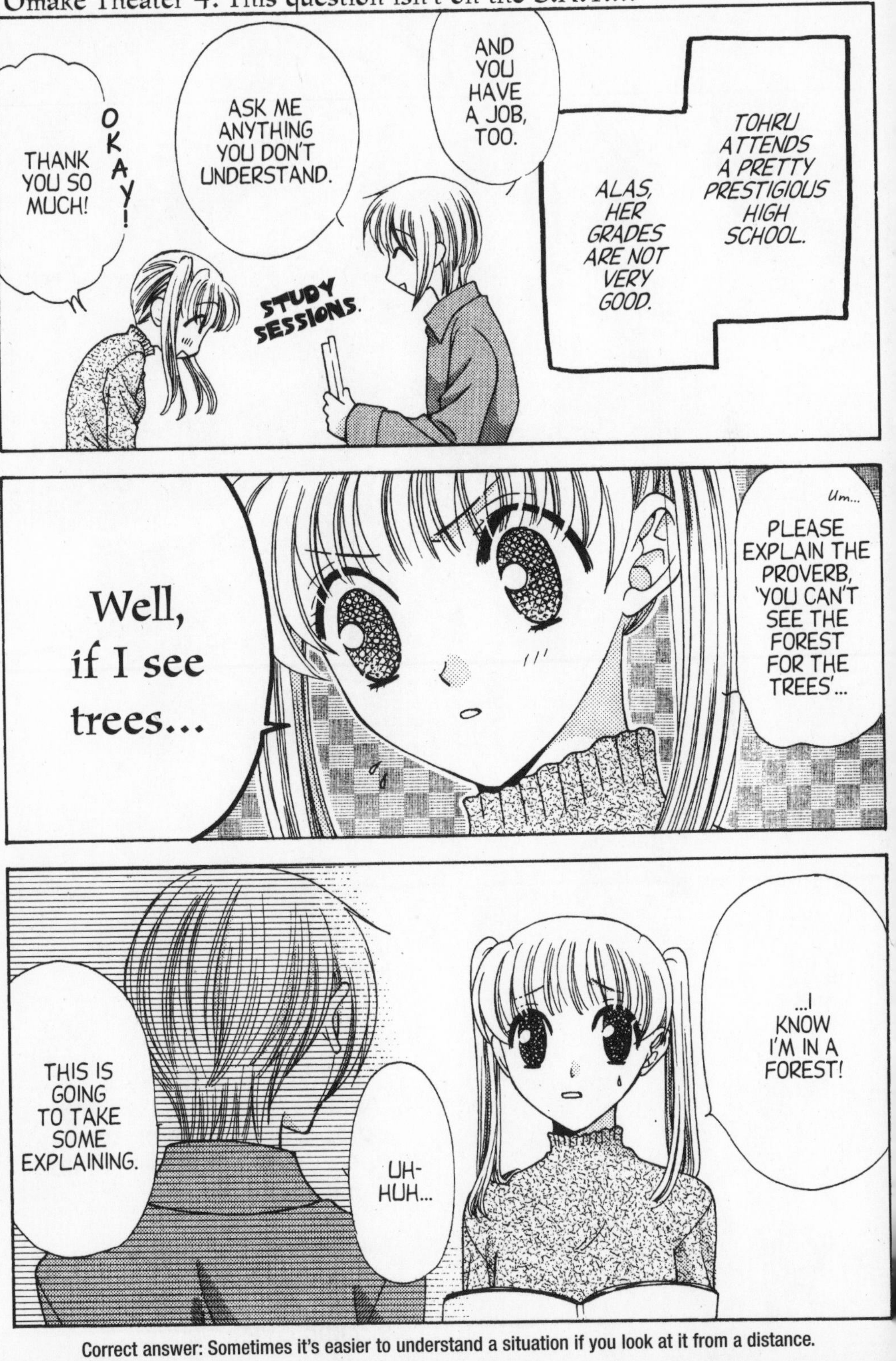
TOHRU ATTENDS A PRETTY PRESTIGIOUS HIGH SCHOOL.
ALAS, HER GRADES ARE NOT VERY GOOD.
AND YOU HAVE A JOB, TOO.
ASK ME ANYTHING YOU DON'T UNDERSTAND.
STUDY SESSIONS.
OKAY!
THANK YOU SO MUCH!
Um...
PLEASE EXPLAIN THE PROVERB, 'YOU CAN'T SEE THE FOREST FOR THE TREES'...
Well, if I see trees...
...I KNOW I'M IN A FOREST!
UH-HUH...
THIS IS GOING TO TAKE SOME EXPLAINING.

Correct answer: Sometimes it's easier to understand a situation if you look at it from a distance.

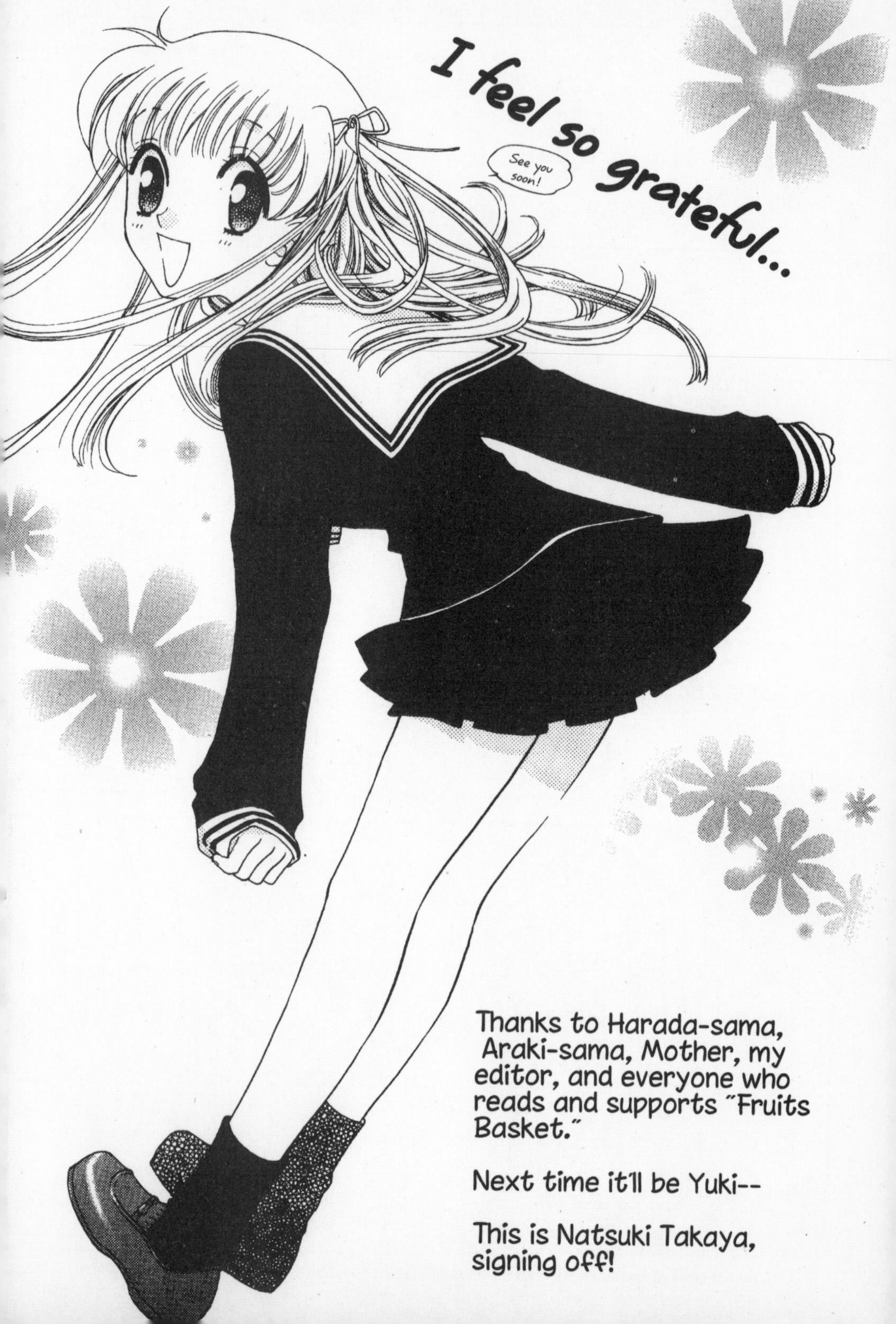
I feel so grateful...
See you soon!

Thanks to Harada-sama, Araki-sama, Mother, my editor, and everyone who reads and supports "Fruits Basket."

Next time it'll be Yuki--

This is Natsuki Takaya, signing off!

Next time in...

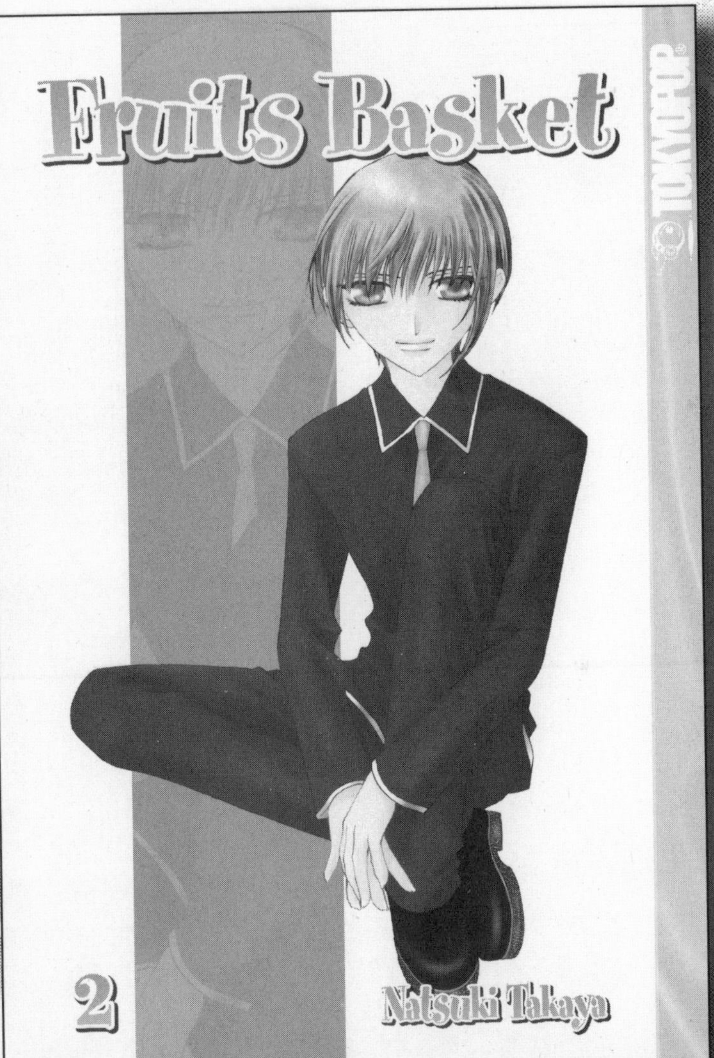
Fruits Basket
TOKYOPOP
2
Natsuki Takaya

Old Friends and New Family

The Sohma family is just starting to get used to life with Tohru, but can they survive a sleepover visit by her two best friends without their secret being exposed? Things aren't any easier at school where crowd-shy Kyo must deal with sudden popularity—and a surprise visit by two other members of the Sohma clan!

Boar

Years: 1971, 1983, 1995, 2007
Positive: reliable, sincere, tolerant
Negative: shy, short tempered

Dog

Years: 1970, 1982, 1994, 2006
Positive: honest, generous, faithful
Negative: quiet, cynical

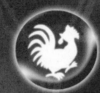

Rooster

Years: 1969, 1981, 1993, 2005
Positive: courageous, hardworking, skilled
Negative: arrogant, selfish

Monkey

Years: 1968, 1980, 1992, 2004
Positive: inventive, entertaining, magnetic personality
Negative: distrusting, untrusting

Dragon

Years: 1964, 1976, 1988, 2000
Positive: intelligent, enthusiastic, softhearted
Negative: bossy, loud

Sheep

Years: 1967, 1979, 1991, 2003
Positive: creative, honest, passionate
Negative: disorganized, timid

Snake

Years: 1965, 1977, 1989, 2001
Positive: romantic, clever, beautiful
Negative: vain, procrastinators

Horse

Years: 1966, 1978, 1990, 2002
Positive: cunning, adventurous, cheerful
Negative: impatient, selfish

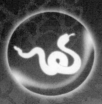

Fruits Basket's

The Chinese Zodiac – Part 1: History Lesson

Fables, myths, and legends abound in every culture of the world. Some of the most ancient of them stem from a basic need to place some type of meaning on those events that are out of our control. The exact origins of the Chinese Zodiac remain a mystery, but their influence is still being felt even today.

The Chinese once viewed time as a cyclical journey consisting of highs and lows that would eventually come full circle. This concept of time would become the basis for the Chinese Lunar Calendar, a 12-year calendar built around 60-year cycles that were delegated by the longitude of the sun and the phases of the moon.

The calendar itself dates back to around 2637 B.C. and consists of 10 Heavenly Steams (elements with yin and yang characteristics) and 12 Earthly Branches (animals of the zodiac) that are clumped together to become the name of the year. When the steams and branches, also known as "Jikkan Junishi," are combined in sequential order, they do not repeat until 60 years have passed. So in essence no one person will ever see any given year more than twice in their own lifetime.

Unfortunately, much of the population was illiterate and unable to fully grasp the complexity of the calendar so the 12 Earthly Branches came to be represented by animals so that everyone could remember them better. The version of the calendar that has been passed down also incorporates the five Chinese elements (Metal, Water, Wood, Fire, and Earth) into its design. The elements themselves each have a yin and yang variation, but the zodiac animals are always either yin or yang. For example, an odd year is yin and an even year is yang.

Japan was introduced to the Chinese calendar in approximately 604 A.D. during the reign of the Empress Suiko-Tenno, when she made an active attempt to spread the many wonders of Buddhism throughout the island nation. By this time though, the calendar was all ready being used for a number of things including telling the time of day through two-hour intervals and even pointing out cardinal directions.

As time went on, the animals became the core basis of Asian astrology, which dictates that one's personality can be divined from the year in which they were born. When combined with the elemental aspects of the calendar, Chinese astrology can even point out which partner will be more dominant in a relationship. Needless to say, the vast majority of the population does not take this seriously anymore.

Still, the Chinese Zodiac does have its uses in modern society. Instead of being rude and asking someone how old they are, one would instead ask what their animal where they born under. With a little math—just add or subtract 12—you'll have your answer. And let us not forget the Chinese New Year, which is celebrated every year in either late January or early February.

Cow

Years: 1961, 1973, 1985, 1997
Positive: inspiring, conservative, natural born leaders
Negative: stubborn, unyielding personality

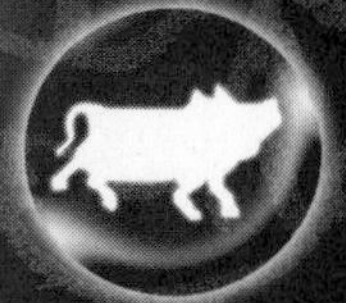

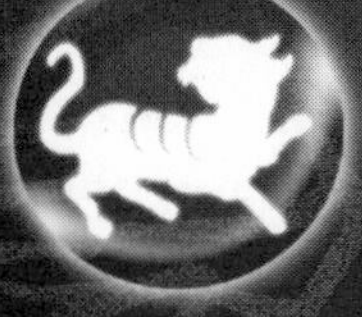

Tiger

Years: 1962, 1974, 1986, 1998
Positive: courageous, unpredictable, loving
Negative: overly aggressive, highly emotional

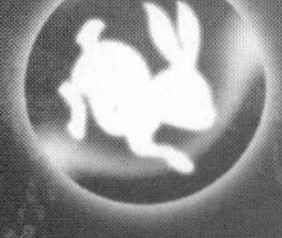

Rabbit

Years: 1963, 1975, 1987, 1999
Positive: affectionate, pleasant, talented
Negative: too sentimental, avoids conflict

Rat

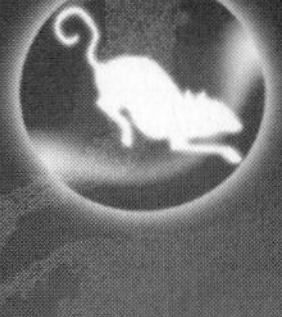

Years: 1960, 1972, 1984, 1996
Positive: imaginative, ambitious, generous to loved ones
Negative: hot-tempered,

A conversation with Laura Bailey.
the English voice of Tohru Honda

You genuinely care about every storyline.

TP: How did you prepare for the role of Tohru Honda? How was this character different from other anime characters that you've played?

LB: In preparing for the part, I researched the series on the Internet and watched the Japanese version. Tohru was the first innocent character I'd played. The more I researched, the more I fell in love with that innocence.

TP: How does the original Japanese performance influence your own interpretation of a character?

LB: Well, it helped me form a basis for Tohru's mannerisms and inflections. I think when the original is so wonderful, you don't want to stray from that. Why mess with a good thing, y'know?

TP: Many of Tohru's humble behaviors and speech patterns must have been very difficult to translate to English. What did you find most challenging about capturing her character in your performance?

LB: Actually, I was asked a similar question by Mr. Daichi (Japanese director) himself, during a panel discussion. He wanted to make sure that her sweetness and formal nature didn't get lost in the translation. I think that, while we in America don't have that same speech formality, the humble nature can still be communicated through inflections and tone. I guess the challenging part was just making sure to always use those softer inflections.

TP: What about Tohru's character do you most relate to? What do you find difficult to relate to?

LB: Her desire to turn any situation into a positive one—that's what I most connected with. Not to say that I always succeed ... but I certainly try to remain optimistic. I think it was her formal nature that I found most difficult. Luckily, John Burgmeier did a wonderful job with the dialogue, which made things easier.

TOKYOPOP: Could you briefly explain the process of voice acting for Fruits Basket?

Laura Bailey: I, as an actress, become involved after the translated script has been completed and the director has an idea of what he wants from the episode. Justin Cook, my voice director on Fruits Basket, usually has pretty specific ideas and is great about filling me in on what's happening throughout the show. He'll give me the background of other characters and help me decide where Tohru is coming from during her interaction with others. That's especially helpful when I'm the first actor to record on an episode. All actors record separately due to the difficulty of ADR; but I always prefer to be the last to record so that I can have Justin play the other actors in my headphones when I go in. It's easier to be believable when you know what you're reacting to. One of the great things about Tohru was, though she had a lot of dialogue, most of it was spoken off screen. That helped to speed up recording because I didn't have to match mouth flaps and could use the timing that I wanted to. Often, on the narration, I could get through it in one take.

TP: When you first became involved with Fruits Basket, were you aware of the huge international following that the series has? What is it about Fruits Basket, do you think, that makes it such a fan favorite series with many viewers and readers outside of the usual shojo market?

LB: I had no idea Fruits Basket had the following it did, but I could tell from the first episode I watched that it wasn't an average series. I think what makes Fruits Basket so special is the depth of all the characters.

Laura Bailey

TP: How is acting for anime different from other acting jobs you do?

LB: Well I can look like sin for one thing. I love that. And anime is the only thing I do in which I act after the fact. Dubbing is a craft unto itself; it takes a completely different approach. You don't always get to decide how you want to say a line, because your way doesn't work with the timing. Anime means taking something very specific, and making it work for you.

TP: Do you have a favorite anime or manga series?

LB: I feel like a cheese for saying so, but Fruits Basket is my favorite. When I found out you guys were releasing the manga in English, I was ecstatic.

TP: What's your zodiac animal? Are you happy being that animal or would you rather be something else?

LB: I'm a cock. I wouldn't change that either; just 'cause it's fun to say, "I'm a cock."

TP: Okay, I have to ask... If you were in Tohru's shoes and you had to pick one guy, who would you choose Kyo or Yuki?

LB: I don't know ... I've tried to make that choice about a thousand times. At first I thought Kyo because, c'mon, he's awesome. He's got the whole bad boy thing working for him; but then I think about Yuki, and how much he truly cares about Tohru and how wonderful a person he is ... and I'm back at square one. It's an endless circle.

TP: Tohru is a very emotional character who is often moved to tears of joy or sadness. Was it difficult to bring out her emotions out in your performance?

LB: It wasn't so much difficult as it was draining. In the last few episodes especially, Tohru goes though a lot of extreme emotions. Those days of recording were the hardest. The emotion you feel as the character attaches itself to you, so I left the booth very depressed and frustrated.

TP: What was it like working with the other members of the Fruits Basket cast? What was your involvement with the other actors?

LB: Justin did a great job of casting the show. When listening to the final product, I kept wishing that I had been able to be involved with their recording sessions as well. Luckily, I'm friends with a lot of the cast, so I could still tell them how much I enjoyed what they did.

TP: How did you feel when the series was over?

LB: I was so upset. I loved working on Fruits Basket; there's no doubt that I would jump at the chance to continue it.

TP: What was your first voice acting role for anime?

LB: The first thing I did was kid Dende on Dragonball Z. I was filling in for the woman who originally did that voice, as she wasn't available. It turns out, though, she came back to the studio after me, and rerecorded everything I'd done. Which really sucked, let me tell you. Soon after, though, I was cast as kid Trunks. So I guess it was all for the best in the end.

TP: Is there a favorite anime role that you've performed?

LB: Tohru. I just loved everything about her.

TP: What was the most challenging role you've ever played?

LB: That's a tough question. Either Tohru or Marlene in Blue Gender. Both had some intense moments throughout their series.

Fruits Basket™

Volume 2

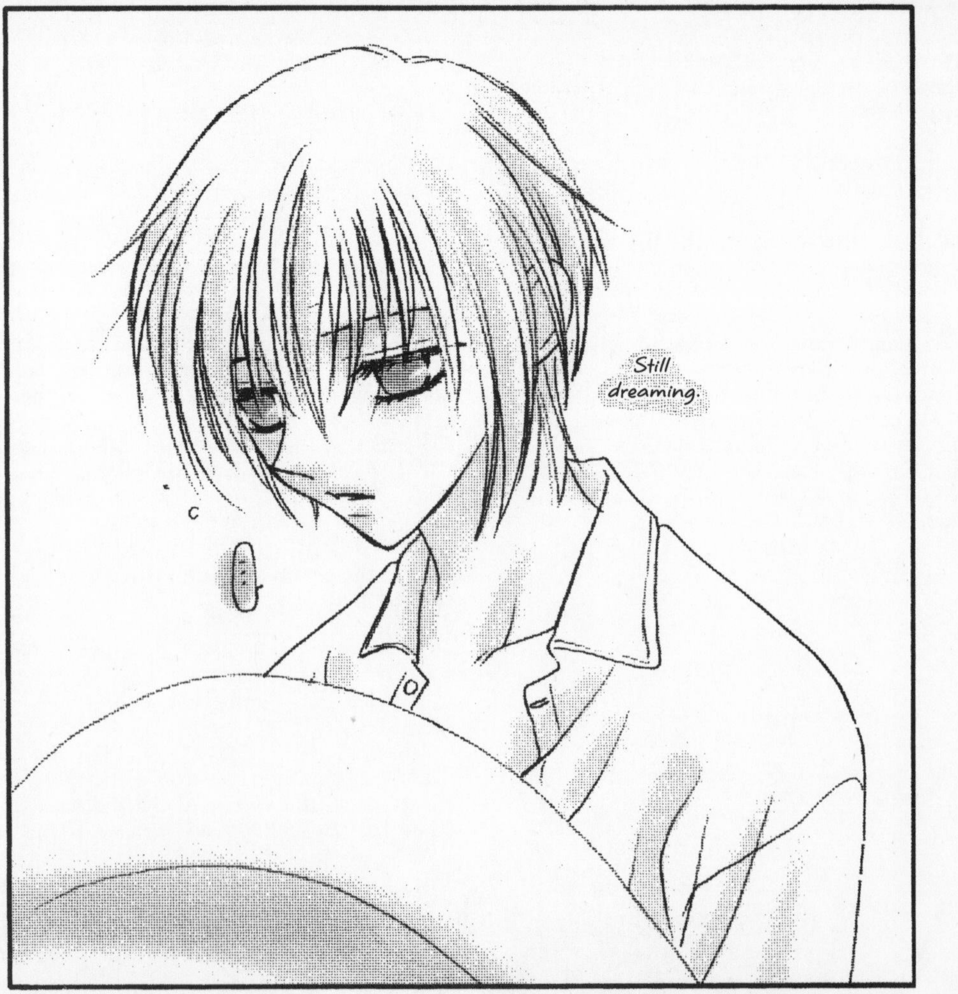
Still dreaming.

Natsuki Takaya

Fruits Basket

Volume 2

Table of Contents

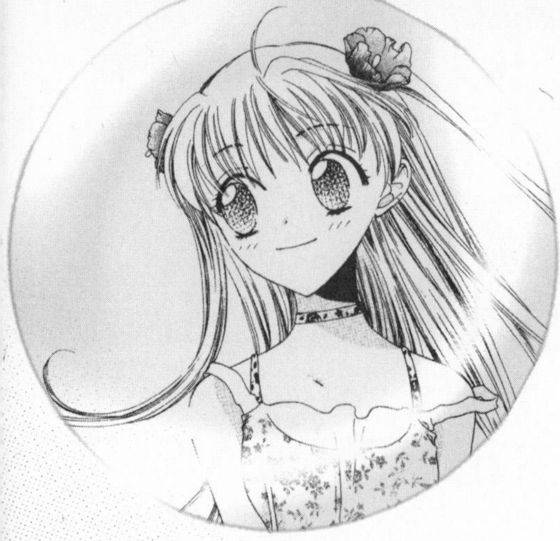

Tohru Honda

The ever-optimistic hero of our story. Recently orphaned, Tohru has taken up residence in Shigure Sohma's house, along with Yuki and Kyo. She's the only person outside of the Sohma family who knows about their Zodiac curse.

Yuki Sohma

At school he's known as Prince Charming. Polite and soft-spoken, he's the polar opposite of Kyo. Yuki is possessed by the spirit of the Rat.

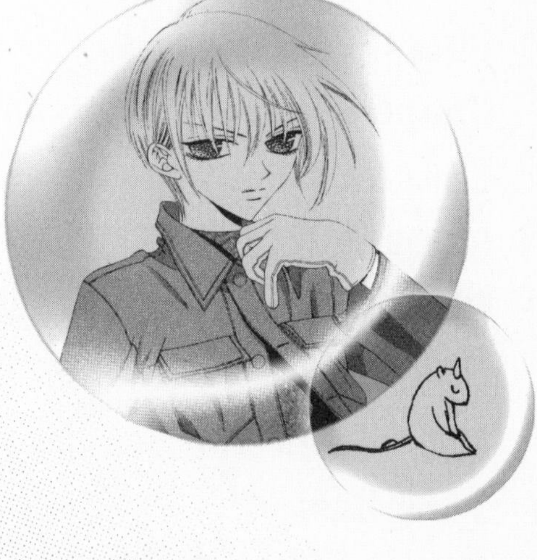

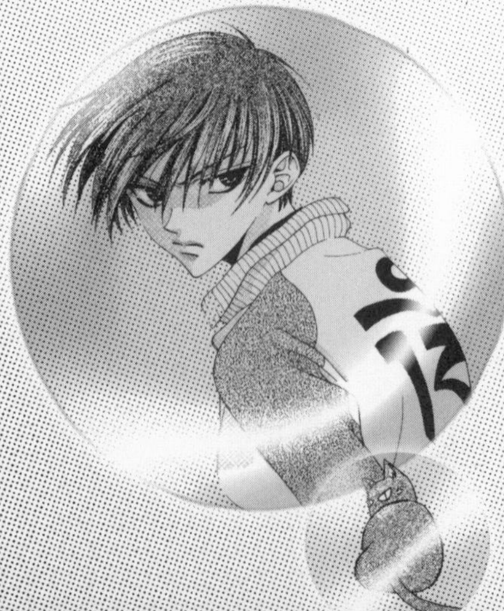

Kyo Sohma

Just as the Cat of legend (whose spirit possesses him) was left out of the Zodiac, Kyo is ostracized by the Sohma family. His greatest wish in life is to defeat Yuki in battle and win his rightful place in the zodiac.

Fruits Basket Characters

Shigure Sohma

The enigmatic Shigure keeps a house outside of the Sohma estate where he lives with Yuki, Kyo and Tohru. He may act perverted at times, but he has a good heart. His Zodiac spirit is the Dog.

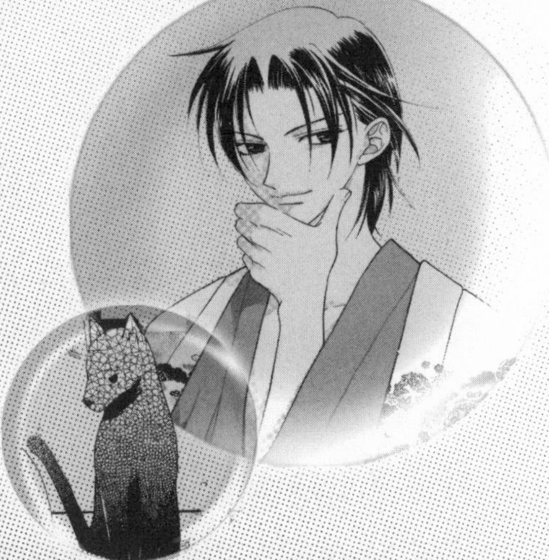

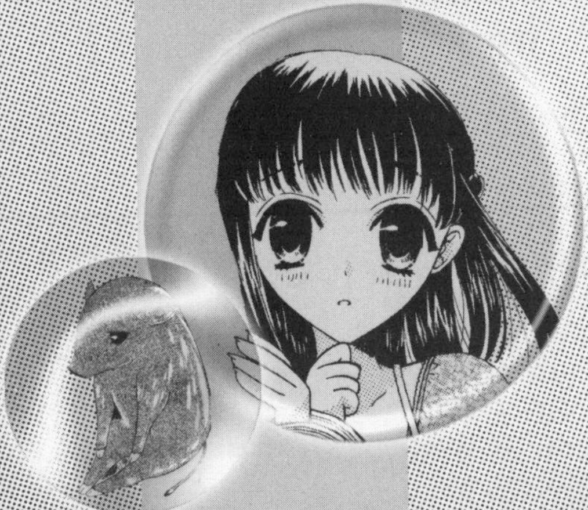

Kagura Sohma

Stubborn and jealous as her zodiac symbol, the boar, Kagura is determined to marry Kyo…even if she kills him in the process.

Hanajima & Arisa

The two best friends a girl could hope for. They always look out for Tohru, but they don't know about her new living arrangements…yet.

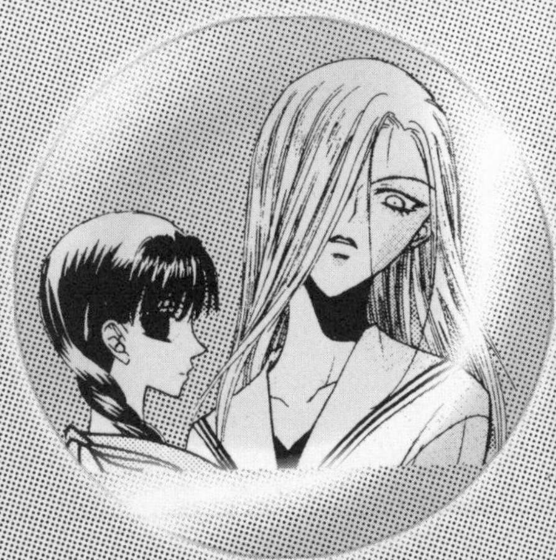

STORY SO FAR...

Hello, I'm Tohru Honda and I have come to know a terrible secret. After the death of my mother, I was living by myself in a tent, when the Sohma family took me in. I soon learned that the Sohma family lives with a curse! Each family member is possessed by the vengeful spirit of an animal from the Chinese Zodiac. Whenever one of them becomes weak or is hugged by a member of the opposite sex, they change into their Zodiac animal!

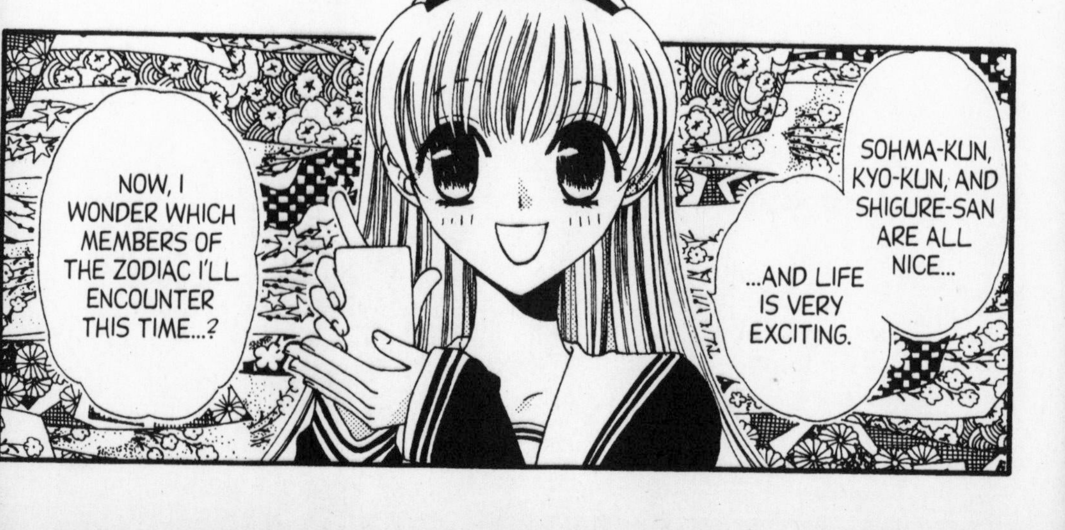
SOHMA-KUN, KYO-KUN, AND SHIGURE-SAN ARE ALL NICE...
...AND LIFE IS VERY EXCITING.
NOW, I WONDER WHICH MEMBERS OF THE ZODIAC I'LL ENCOUNTER THIS TIME...?

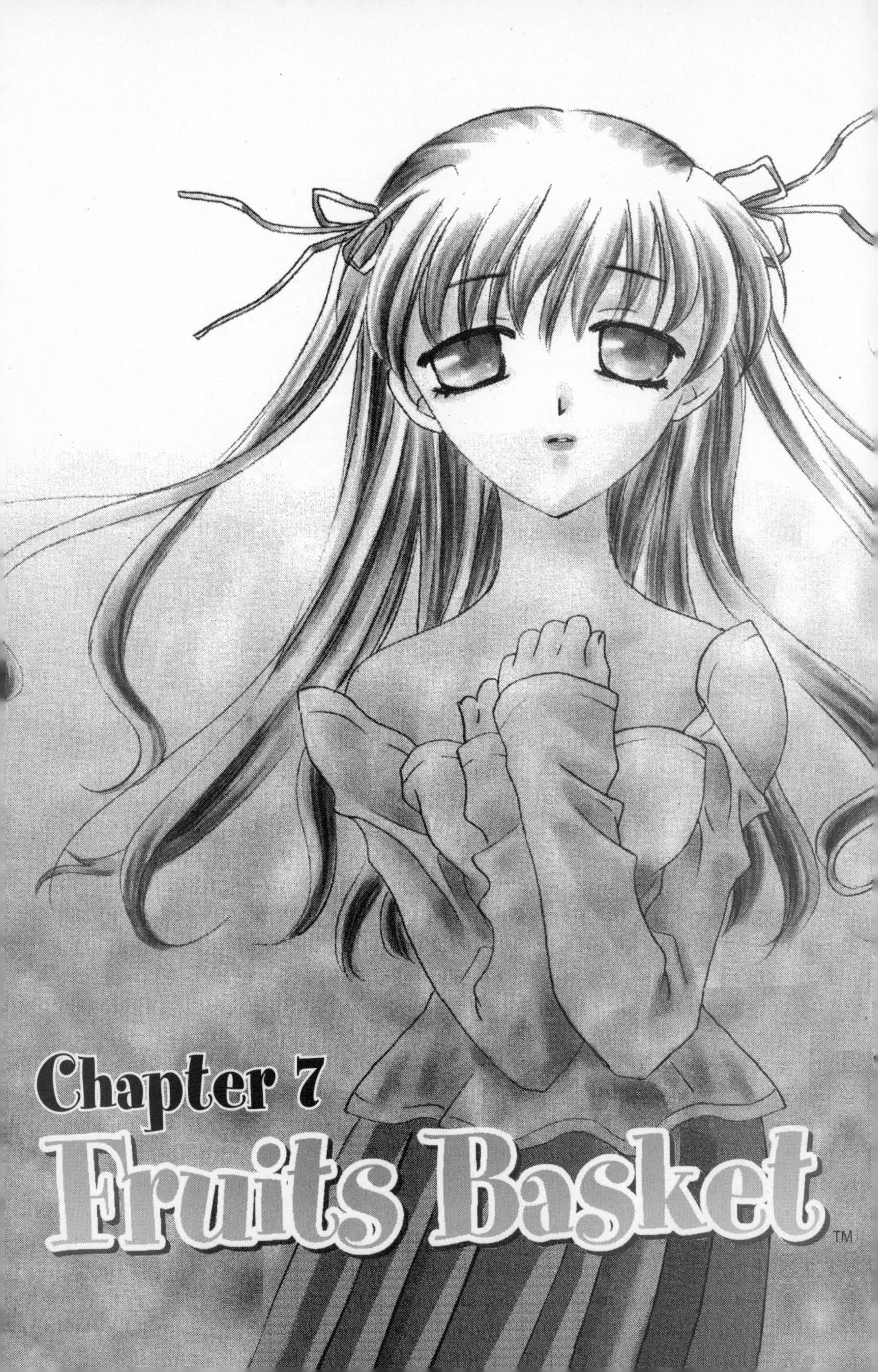
Chapter 7
Fruits Basket™

Omake Theater: That's right. Hana-chan is an older sister.

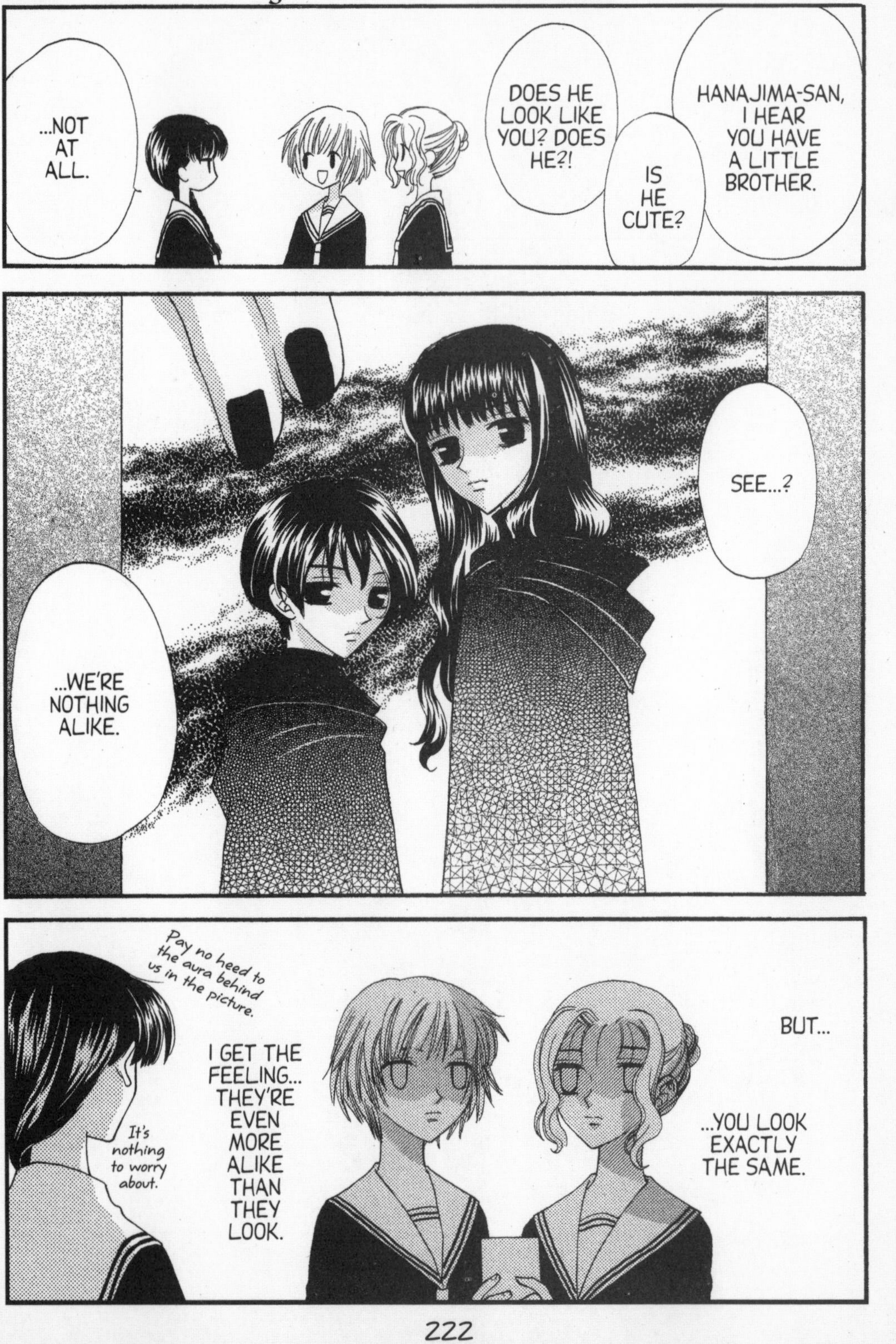

HANAJIMA-SAN, I HEAR YOU HAVE A LITTLE BROTHER.
IS HE CUTE?
DOES HE LOOK LIKE YOU? DOES HE?!
...NOT AT ALL.
SEE...?
...WE'RE NOTHING ALIKE.
BUT...
...YOU LOOK EXACTLY THE SAME.
I GET THE FEELING... THEY'RE EVEN MORE ALIKE THAN THEY LOOK.
Pay no heed to the aura behind us in the picture.
It's nothing to worry about.

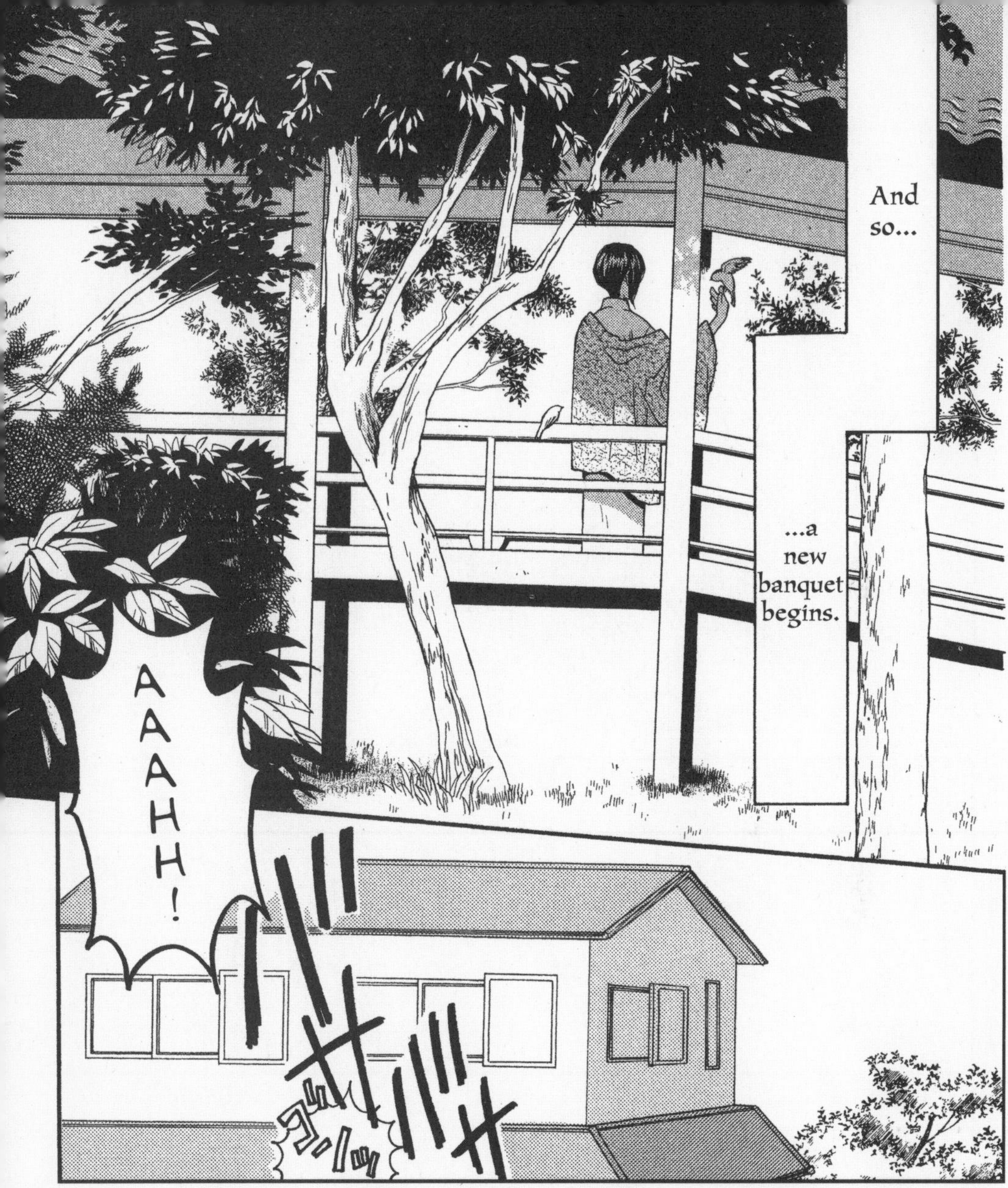
And so...
...a new banquet begins.
AAAHH!

ULTRA SPECIAL BLAH BLAH BLAH 1

I get a lot of letters from people asking me to teach them how to play Dai Hinmin. The way I learned was by playing the video game Sakura Wars 2! (ha ha) But the rules I learned were Sakura rules, so I don't think they're the actual rules. Maybe they're regional rules, or something like that. Like how in Final Fantasy VIII, the card game rules change in each city you visit.

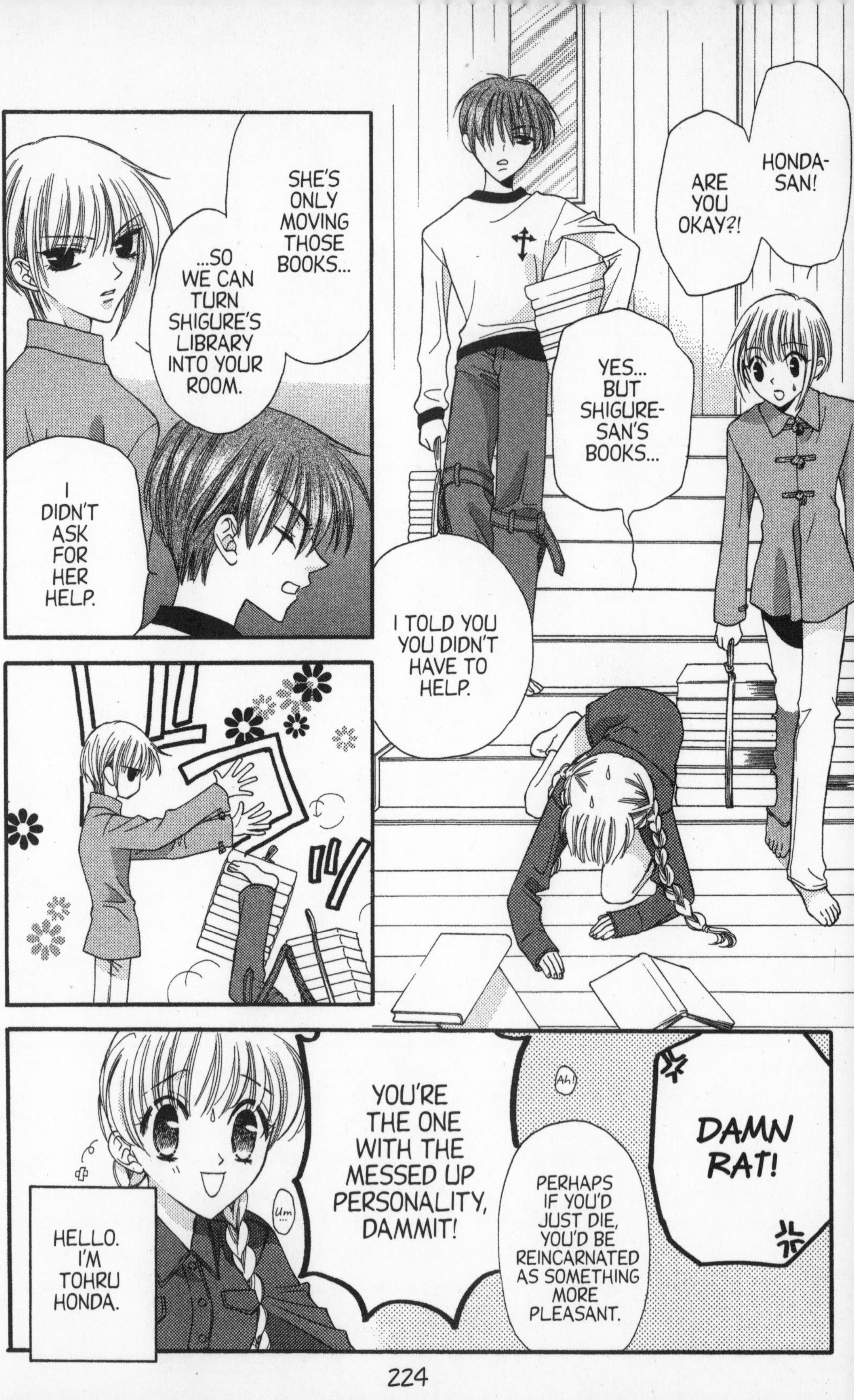
HONDA-SAN!
ARE YOU OKAY?!
YES... BUT SHIGURE-SAN'S BOOKS...
I TOLD YOU YOU DIDN'T HAVE TO HELP.
SHE'S ONLY MOVING THOSE BOOKS...
...SO WE CAN TURN SHIGURE'S LIBRARY INTO YOUR ROOM.
I DIDN'T ASK FOR HER HELP.
DAMN RAT!
Ah!
PERHAPS IF YOU'D JUST DIE, YOU'D BE REINCARNATED AS SOMETHING MORE PLEASANT.
YOU'RE THE ONE WITH THE MESSED UP PERSONALITY, DAMMIT!
Um...
HELLO. I'M TOHRU HONDA.

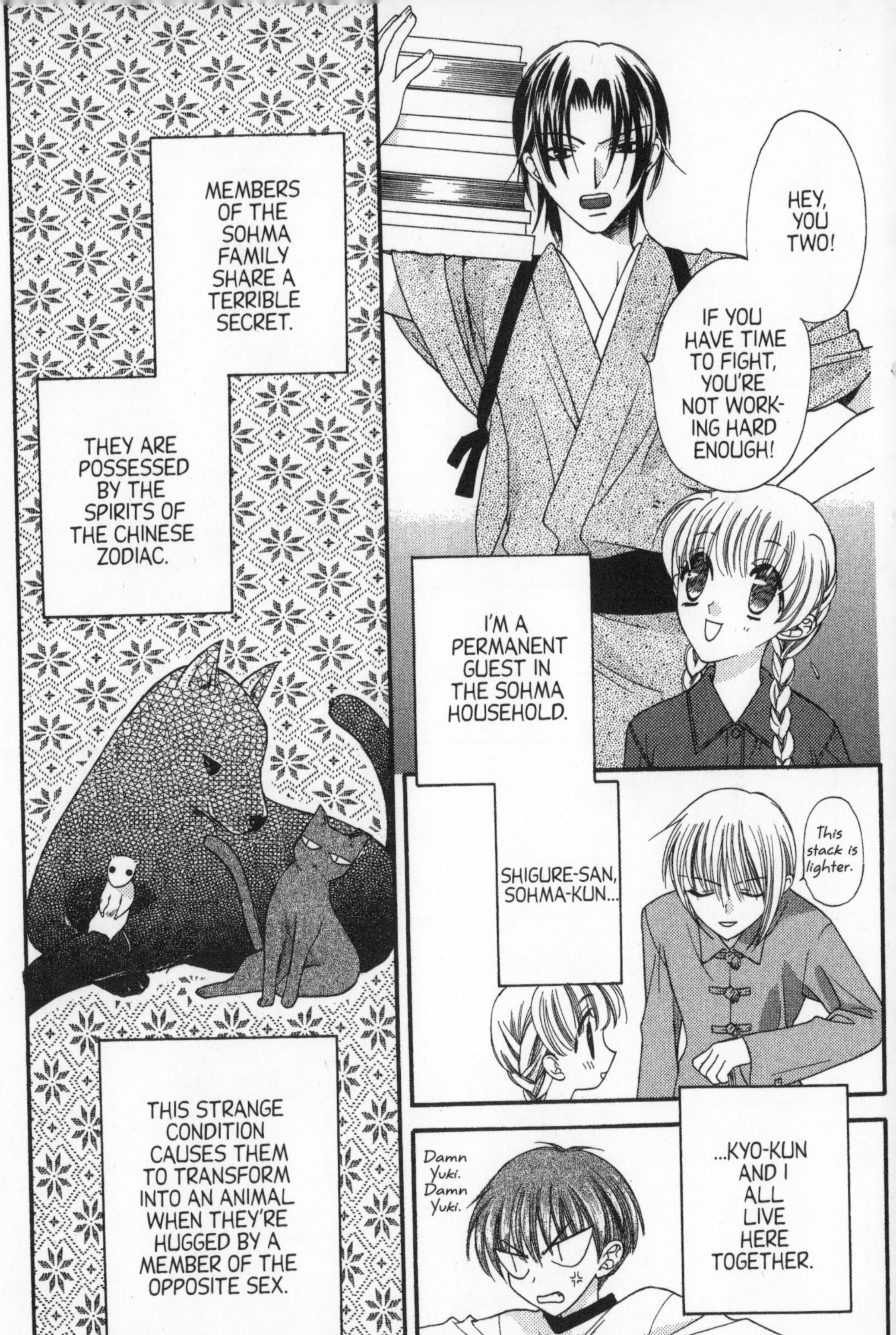
HEY, YOU TWO!
IF YOU HAVE TIME TO FIGHT, YOU'RE NOT WORKING HARD ENOUGH!
I'M A PERMANENT GUEST IN THE SOHMA HOUSEHOLD.
SHIGURE-SAN, SOHMA-KUN...
This stack is lighter.
...KYO-KUN AND I ALL LIVE HERE TOGETHER.
Damn Yuki. Damn Yuki.
MEMBERS OF THE SOHMA FAMILY SHARE A TERRIBLE SECRET.
THEY ARE POSSESSED BY THE SPIRITS OF THE CHINESE ZODIAC.
THIS STRANGE CONDITION CAUSES THEM TO TRANSFORM INTO AN ANIMAL WHEN THEY'RE HUGGED BY A MEMBER OF THE OPPOSITE SEX.

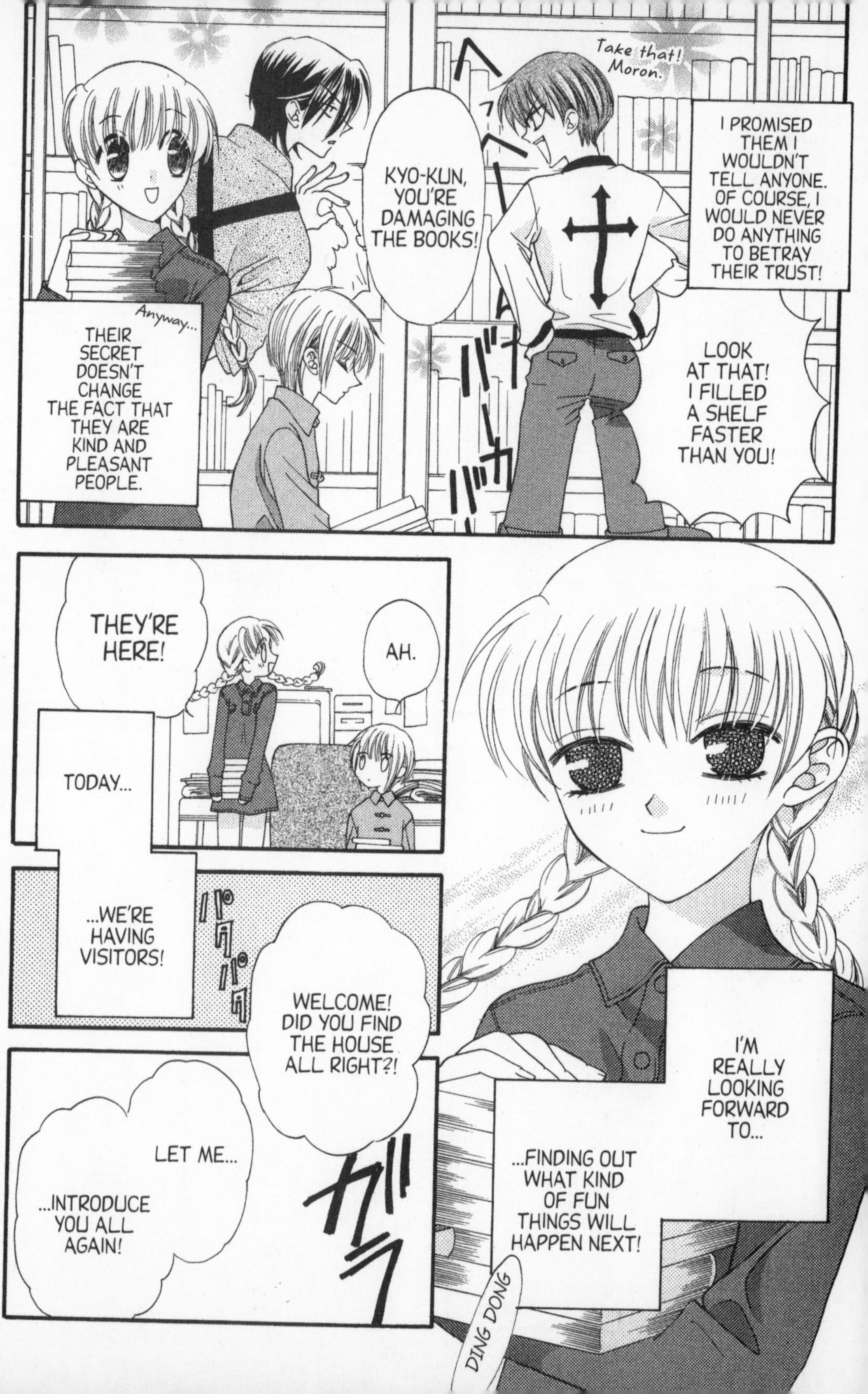
Take that! Moron.
I PROMISED THEM I WOULDN'T TELL ANYONE. OF COURSE, I WOULD NEVER DO ANYTHING TO BETRAY THEIR TRUST!
KYO-KUN, YOU'RE DAMAGING THE BOOKS!
LOOK AT THAT! I FILLED A SHELF FASTER THAN YOU!
Anyway...
THEIR SECRET DOESN'T CHANGE THE FACT THAT THEY ARE KIND AND PLEASANT PEOPLE.
I'M REALLY LOOKING FORWARD TO...
...FINDING OUT WHAT KIND OF FUN THINGS WILL HAPPEN NEXT!
DING DONG
THEY'RE HERE!
AH.
TODAY...
...WE'RE HAVING VISITORS!
WELCOME! DID YOU FIND THE HOUSE ALL RIGHT?!
LET ME...
...INTRODUCE YOU ALL AGAIN!

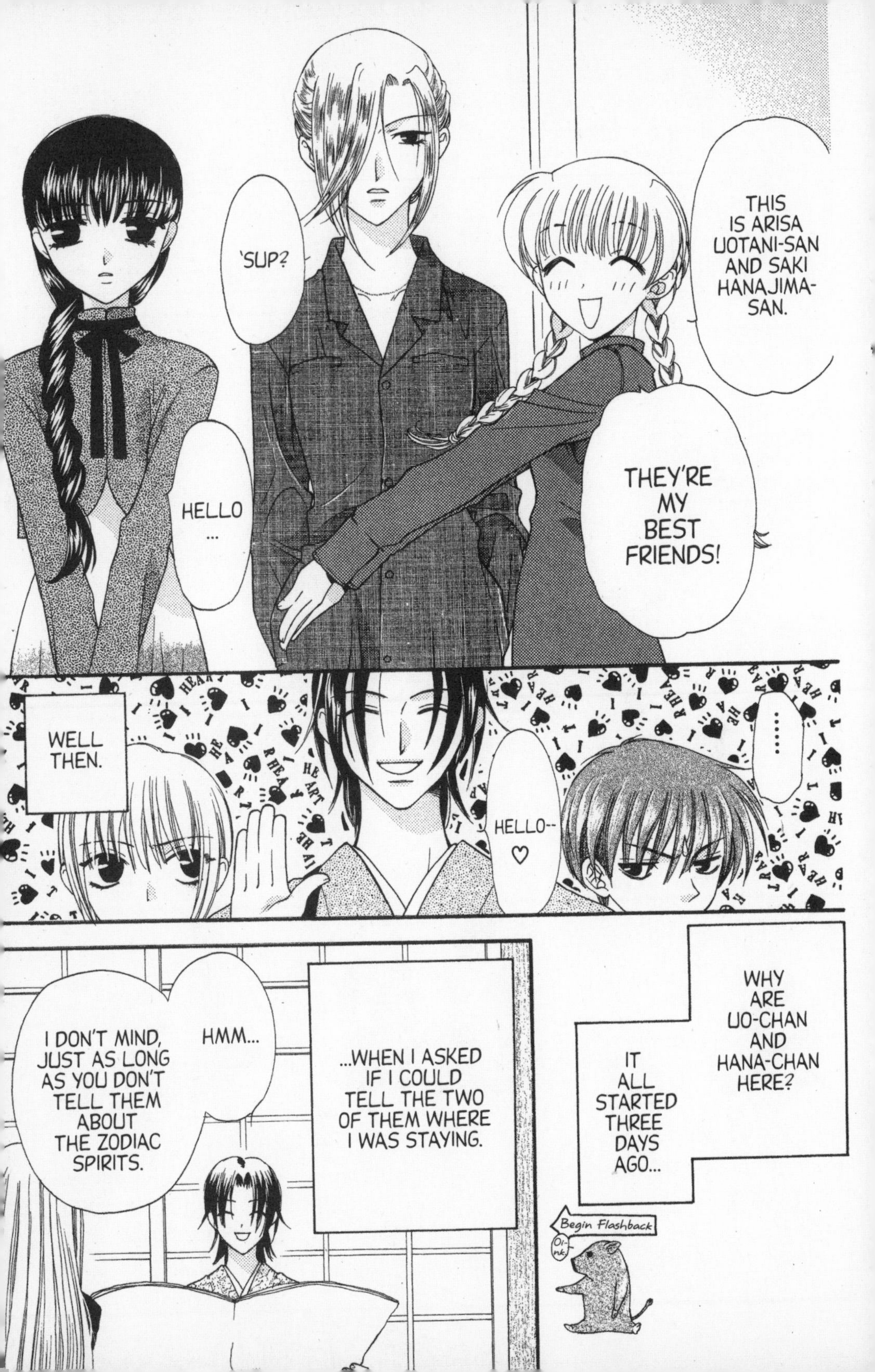
THIS IS ARISA UOTANI-SAN AND SAKI HANAJIMA-SAN.
THEY'RE MY BEST FRIENDS!
'SUP?
HELLO ...
......
HELLO-- ♡
WELL THEN.
WHY ARE UO-CHAN AND HANA-CHAN HERE?
IT ALL STARTED THREE DAYS AGO...
...WHEN I ASKED IF I COULD TELL THE TWO OF THEM WHERE I WAS STAYING.
HMM...
I DON'T MIND, JUST AS LONG AS YOU DON'T TELL THEM ABOUT THE ZODIAC SPIRITS.
Begin Flashback
Oi-nk

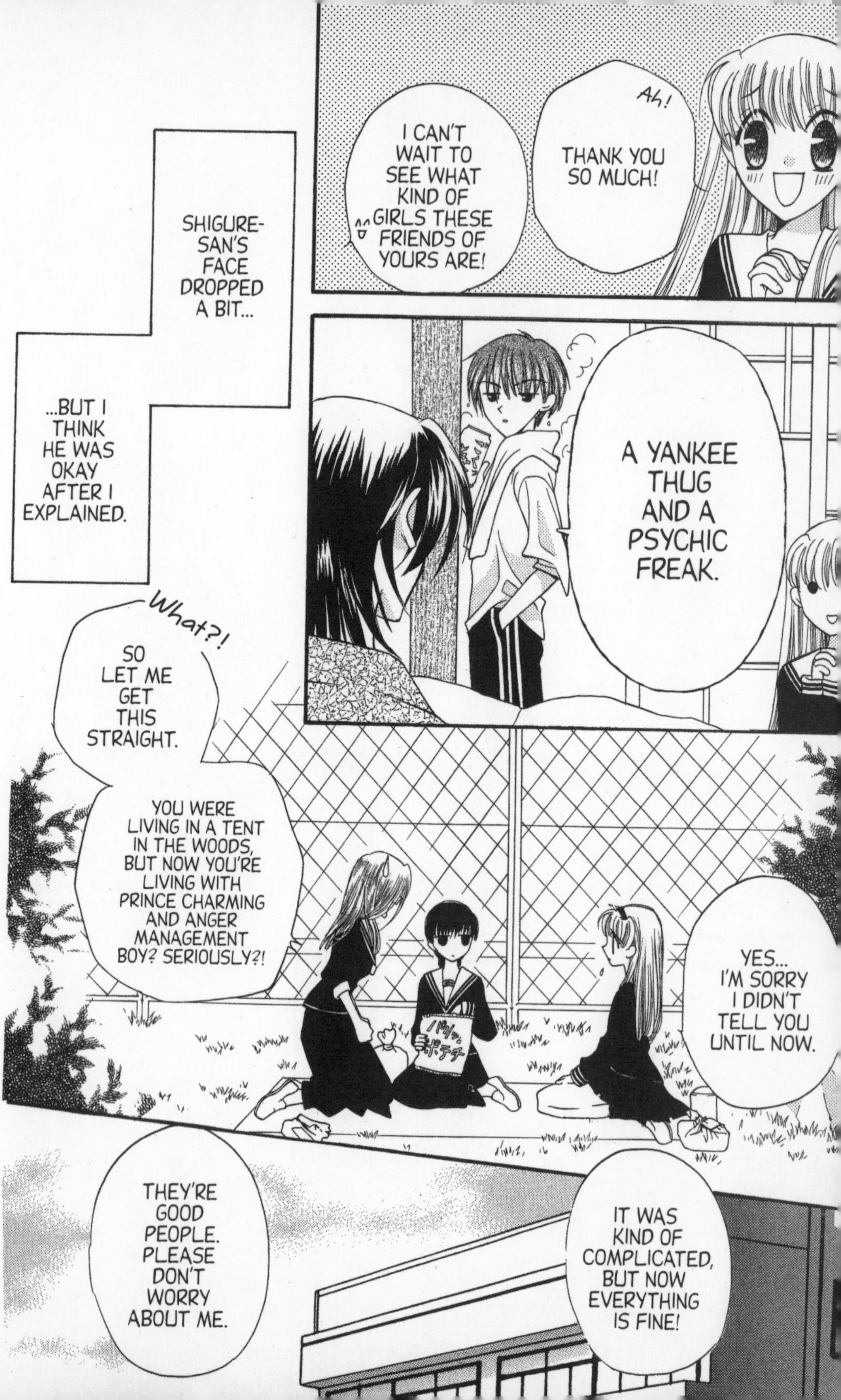
Ah!
THANK YOU SO MUCH!
I CAN'T WAIT TO SEE WHAT KIND OF GIRLS THESE FRIENDS OF YOURS ARE!
A YANKEE THUG AND A PSYCHIC FREAK.
SHIGURE-SAN'S FACE DROPPED A BIT...
...BUT I THINK HE WAS OKAY AFTER I EXPLAINED.
What?!
SO LET ME GET THIS STRAIGHT.
YOU WERE LIVING IN A TENT IN THE WOODS, BUT NOW YOU'RE LIVING WITH PRINCE CHARMING AND ANGER MANAGEMENT BOY? SERIOUSLY?!
YES... I'M SORRY I DIDN'T TELL YOU UNTIL NOW.
IT WAS KIND OF COMPLICATED, BUT NOW EVERYTHING IS FINE!
THEY'RE GOOD PEOPLE. PLEASE DON'T WORRY ABOUT ME.

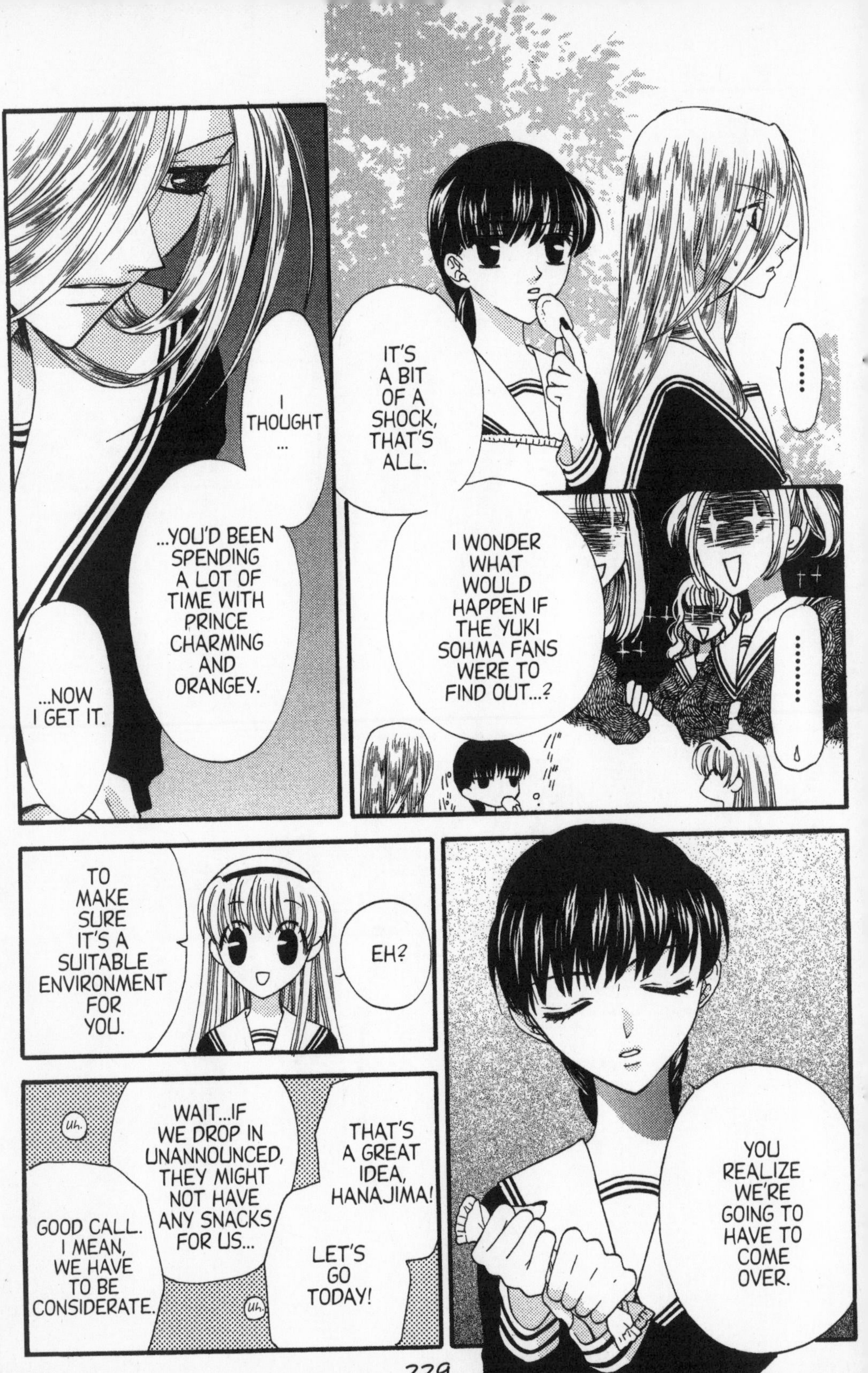
......
IT'S A BIT OF A SHOCK, THAT'S ALL.
......
I WONDER WHAT WOULD HAPPEN IF THE YUKI SOHMA FANS WERE TO FIND OUT...?
I THOUGHT...
...YOU'D BEEN SPENDING A LOT OF TIME WITH PRINCE CHARMING AND ORANGEY.
...NOW I GET IT.
YOU REALIZE WE'RE GOING TO HAVE TO COME OVER.
EH?
TO MAKE SURE IT'S A SUITABLE ENVIRONMENT FOR YOU.
THAT'S A GREAT IDEA, HANAJIMA!
LET'S GO TODAY!
WAIT...IF WE DROP IN UNANNOUNCED, THEY MIGHT NOT HAVE ANY SNACKS FOR US...
Uh.
GOOD CALL. I MEAN, WE HAVE TO BE CONSIDERATE.
Uh.

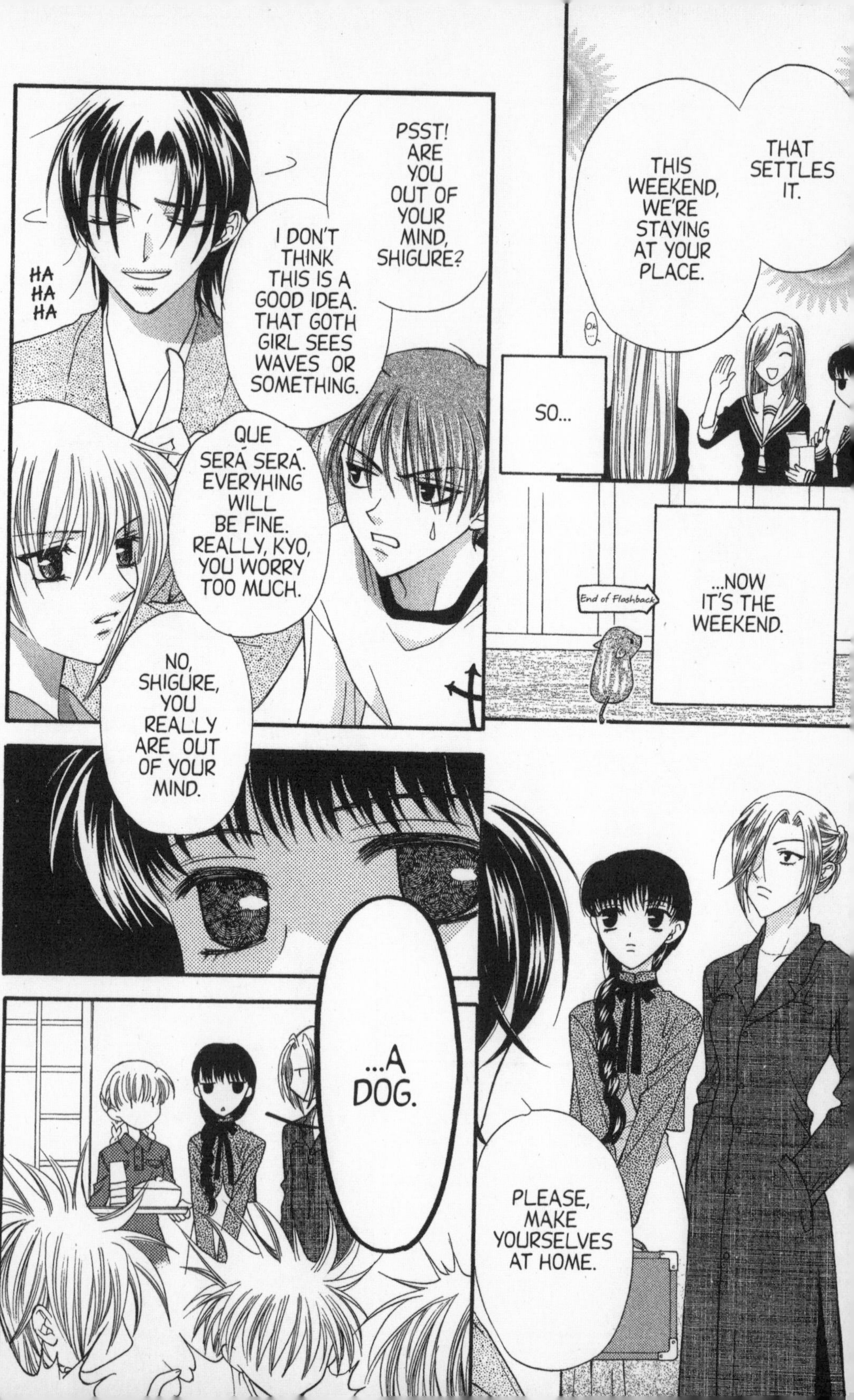
THAT SETTLES IT.
THIS WEEKEND, WE'RE STAYING AT YOUR PLACE.
SO...
End of Flashback
...NOW IT'S THE WEEKEND.
PSST! ARE YOU OUT OF YOUR MIND, SHIGURE?
I DON'T THINK THIS IS A GOOD IDEA. THAT GOTH GIRL SEES WAVES OR SOMETHING.
HA HA HA
QUE SERÁ SERÁ. EVERYHING WILL BE FINE. REALLY, KYO, YOU WORRY TOO MUCH.
NO, SHIGURE, YOU REALLY ARE OUT OF YOUR MIND.
PLEASE, MAKE YOURSELVES AT HOME.
...A DOG.

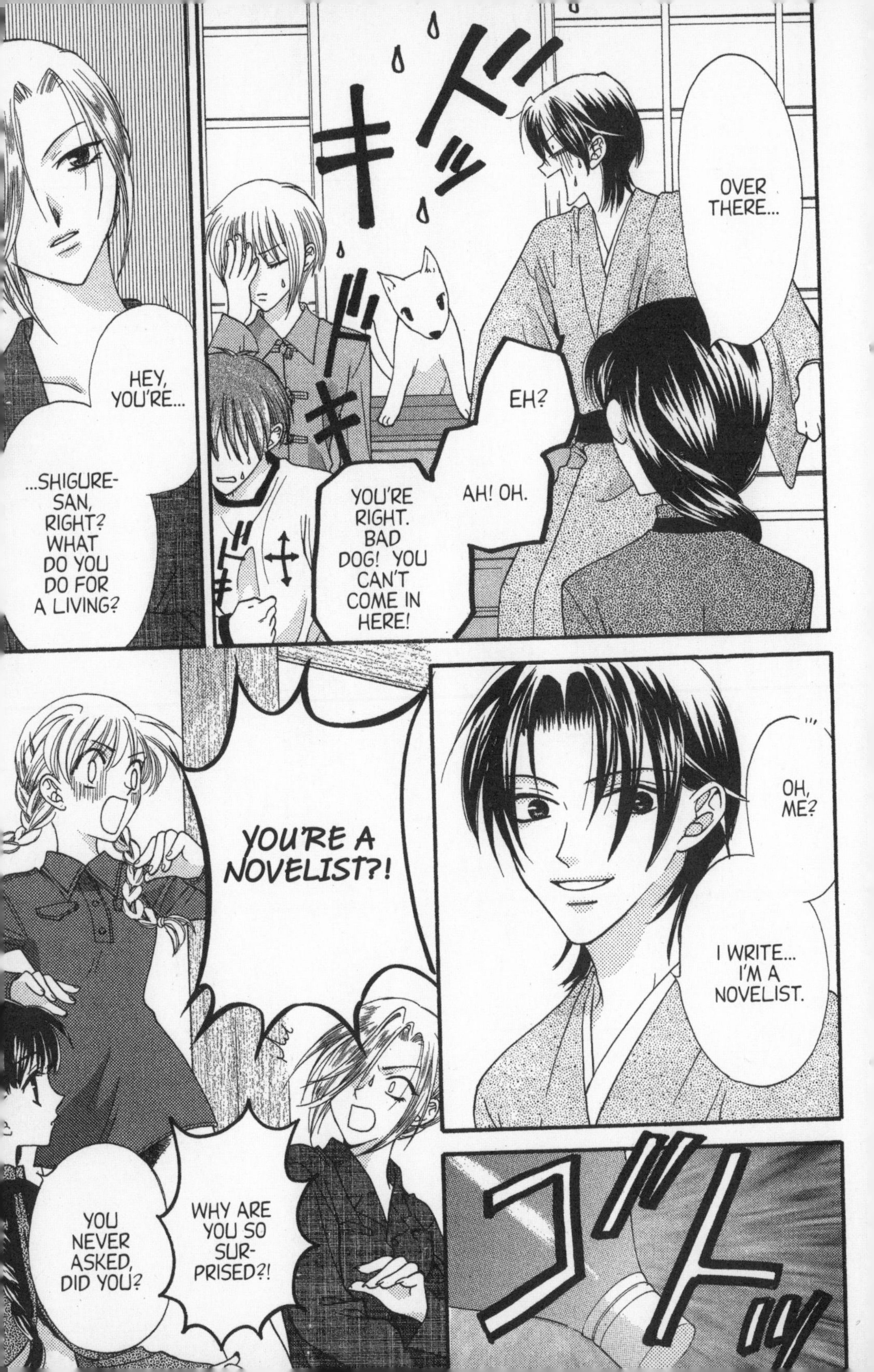
OVER THERE...
EH?
AH! OH.
YOU'RE RIGHT. BAD DOG! YOU CAN'T COME IN HERE!
HEY, YOU'RE...
...SHIGURE-SAN, RIGHT? WHAT DO YOU DO FOR A LIVING?
OH, ME?
I WRITE... I'M A NOVELIST.
YOU'RE A NOVELIST?!
WHY ARE YOU SO SUR-PRISED?!
YOU NEVER ASKED, DID YOU?

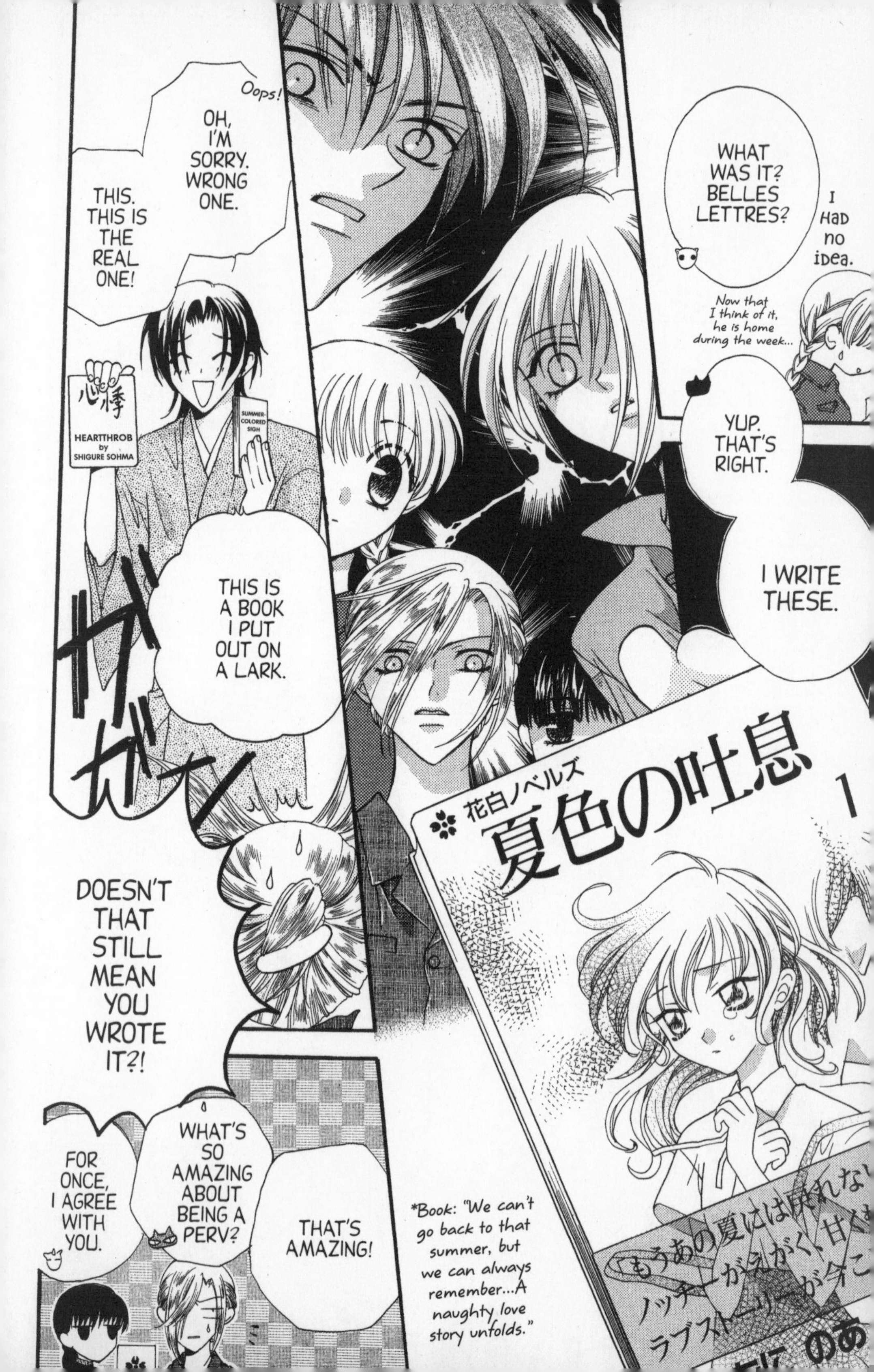
WHAT WAS IT? BELLES LETTRES?
I HAD no idea.
Now that I think of it, he is home during the week...
YUP. THAT'S RIGHT.
I WRITE THESE.
Oops!
OH, I'M SORRY. WRONG ONE.
THIS. THIS IS THE REAL ONE!
心悸
HEARTTHROB by SHIGURE SOHMA
SUMMER-COLORED SIGH
THIS IS A BOOK I PUT OUT ON A LARK.
花白ノベルズ
夏色の吐息
1
DOESN'T THAT STILL MEAN YOU WROTE IT?!
*Book: "We can't go back to that summer, but we can always remember...A naughty love story unfolds."
THAT'S AMAZING!
WHAT'S SO AMAZING ABOUT BEING A PERV?
FOR ONCE, I AGREE WITH YOU.

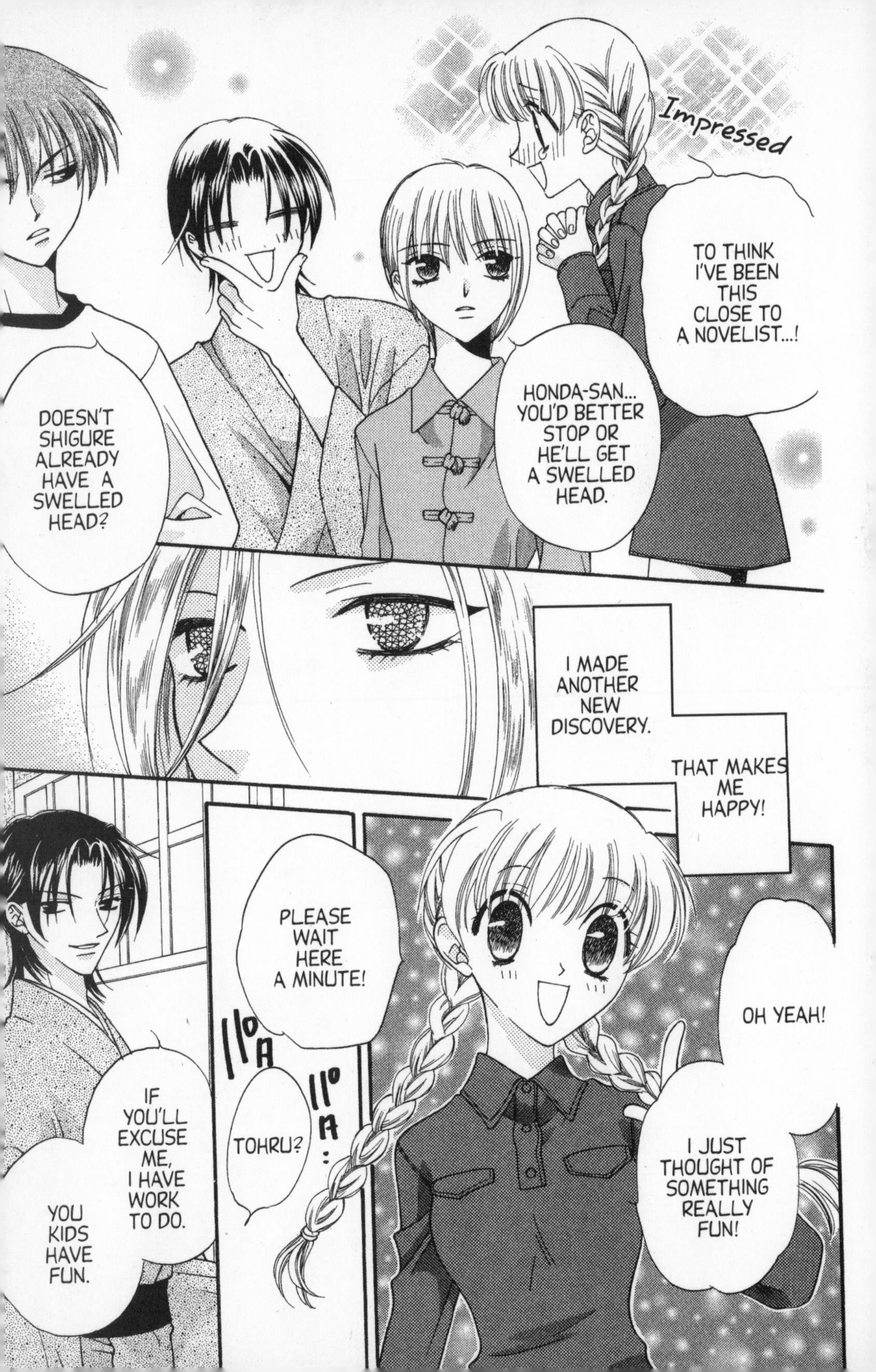
Impressed
TO THINK I'VE BEEN THIS CLOSE TO A NOVELIST...!
HONDA-SAN... YOU'D BETTER STOP OR HE'LL GET A SWELLED HEAD.
DOESN'T SHIGURE ALREADY HAVE A SWELLED HEAD?
I MADE ANOTHER NEW DISCOVERY.
THAT MAKES ME HAPPY!
OH YEAH!
I JUST THOUGHT OF SOMETHING REALLY FUN!
PLEASE WAIT HERE A MINUTE!
TOHRU?
IF YOU'LL EXCUSE ME, I HAVE WORK TO DO.
YOU KIDS HAVE FUN.

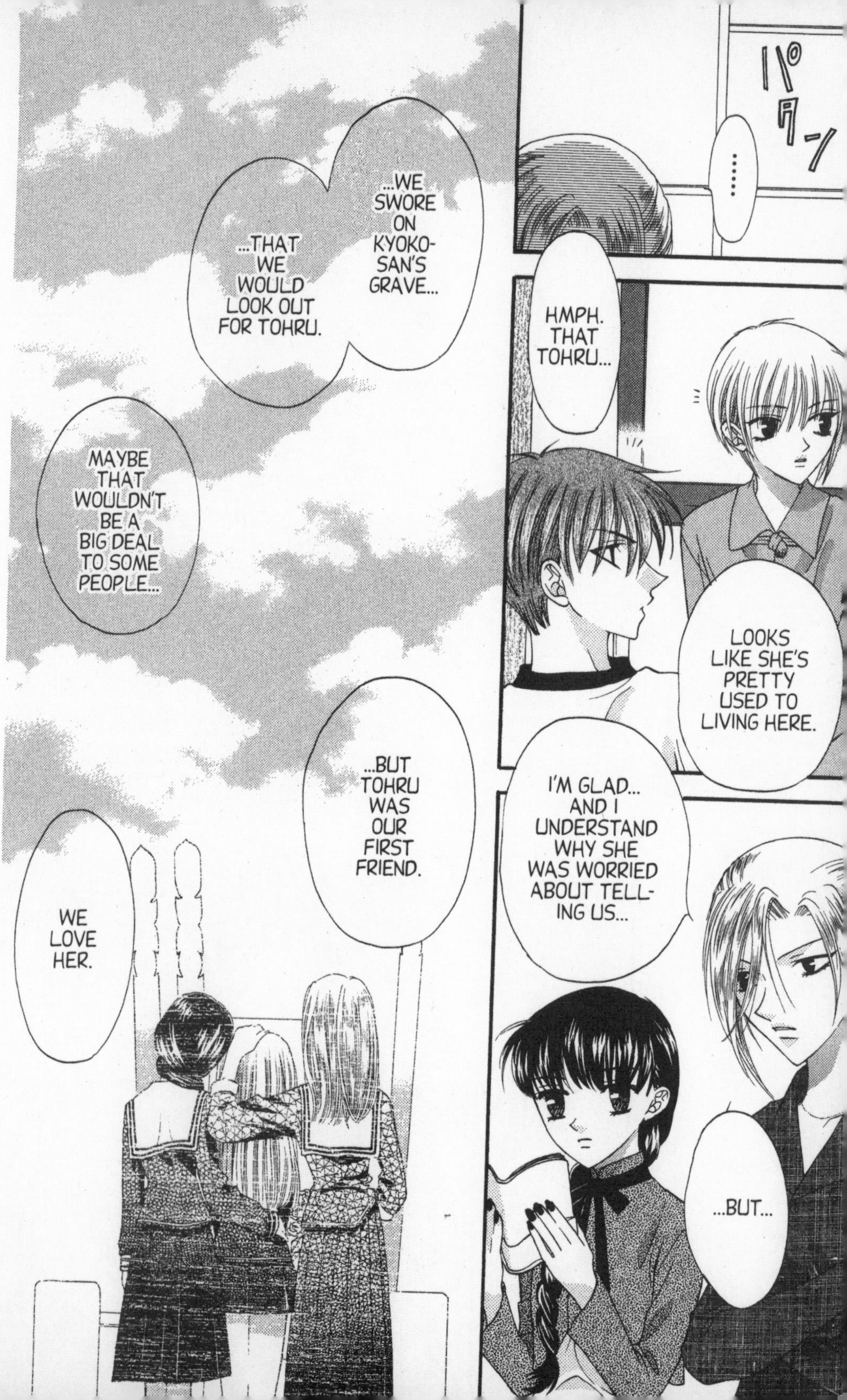
パタン
......
HMPH. THAT TOHRU...
LOOKS LIKE SHE'S PRETTY USED TO LIVING HERE.
I'M GLAD... AND I UNDERSTAND WHY SHE WAS WORRIED ABOUT TELLING US...
...BUT...
...WE SWORE ON KYOKO-SAN'S GRAVE...
...THAT WE WOULD LOOK OUT FOR TOHRU.
MAYBE THAT WOULDN'T BE A BIG DEAL TO SOME PEOPLE...
...BUT TOHRU WAS OUR FIRST FRIEND.
WE LOVE HER.

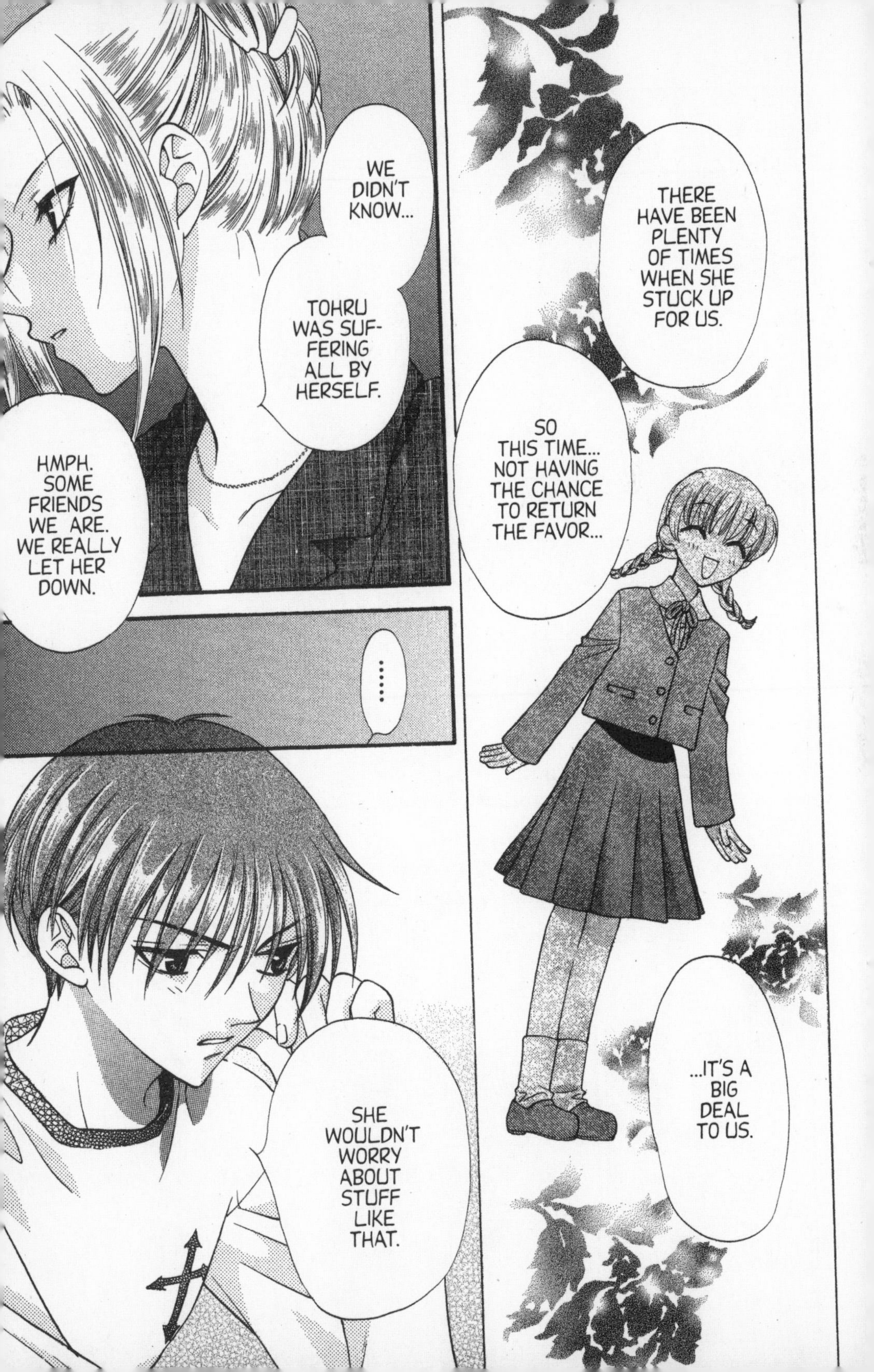
THERE HAVE BEEN PLENTY OF TIMES WHEN SHE STUCK UP FOR US.
SO THIS TIME... NOT HAVING THE CHANCE TO RETURN THE FAVOR...
...IT'S A BIG DEAL TO US.
WE DIDN'T KNOW...
TOHRU WAS SUF-FERING ALL BY HERSELF.
HMPH. SOME FRIENDS WE ARE. WE REALLY LET HER DOWN.
......
SHE WOULDN'T WORRY ABOUT STUFF LIKE THAT.

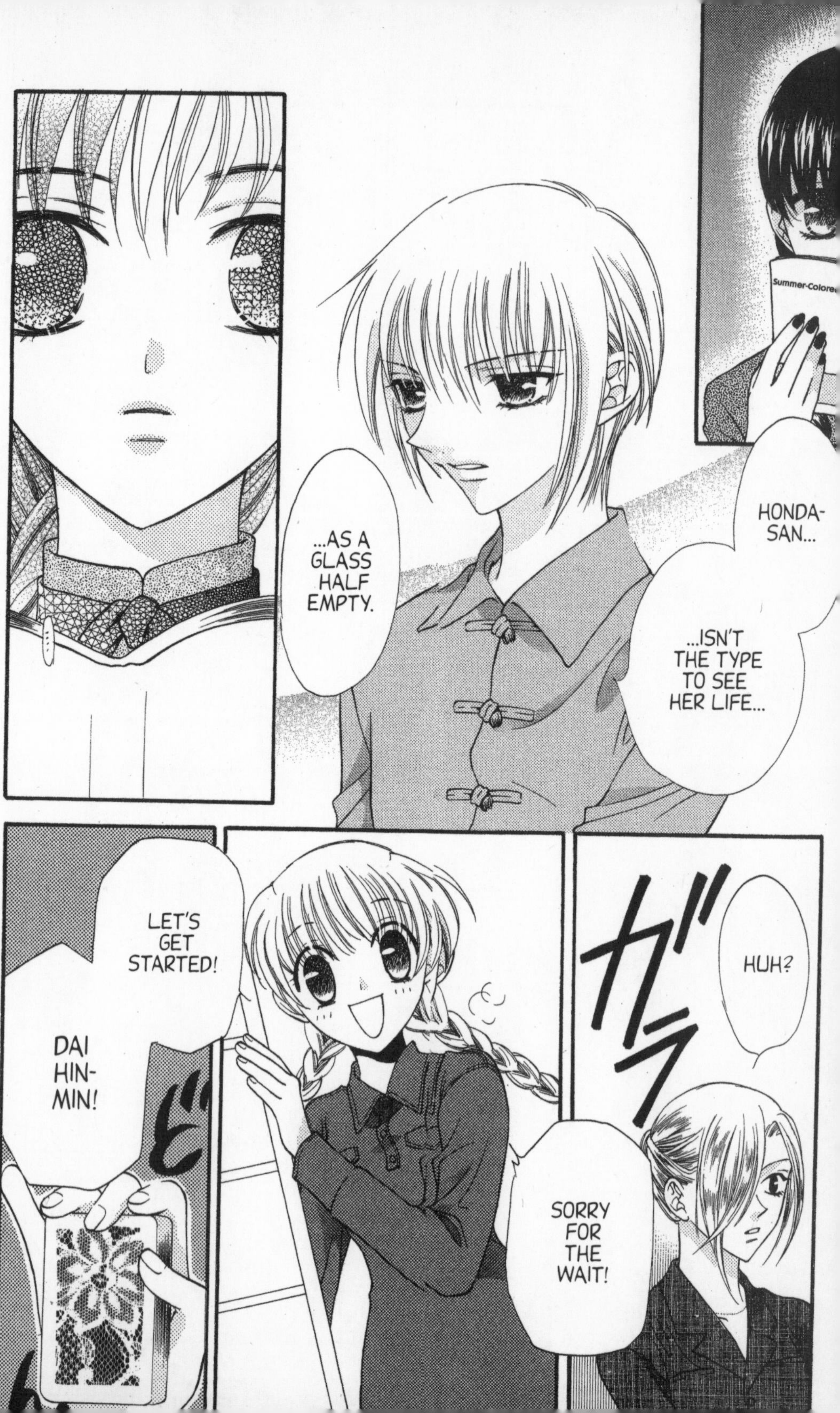
HONDA-SAN...
...ISN'T THE TYPE TO SEE HER LIFE...
...AS A GLASS HALF EMPTY.
ガラ
HUH?
SORRY FOR THE WAIT!
LET'S GET STARTED!
DAI HIN-MIN!
ど

Fruits Basket 2 Part 1:

Nice to meet you and hello. This is Takaya. This is volume 2 of Fruits Basket. It's Prince Charming this time (ha!). This is a bit sudden, but how does everyone shorten the title? Furuba? Furubasu? FB? ...I like "FB"; it's kind of like FF (Final Fantasy!) And Furuba makes me think "Furuba=furui basho," which means "old town" and Furubasu makes me think "Furubasu=furui basu,"which means "old bus" (ha!)! Let's agree to shorten it as Furuba. Now, please enjoy volume 2 of Furuba (ha ha)!

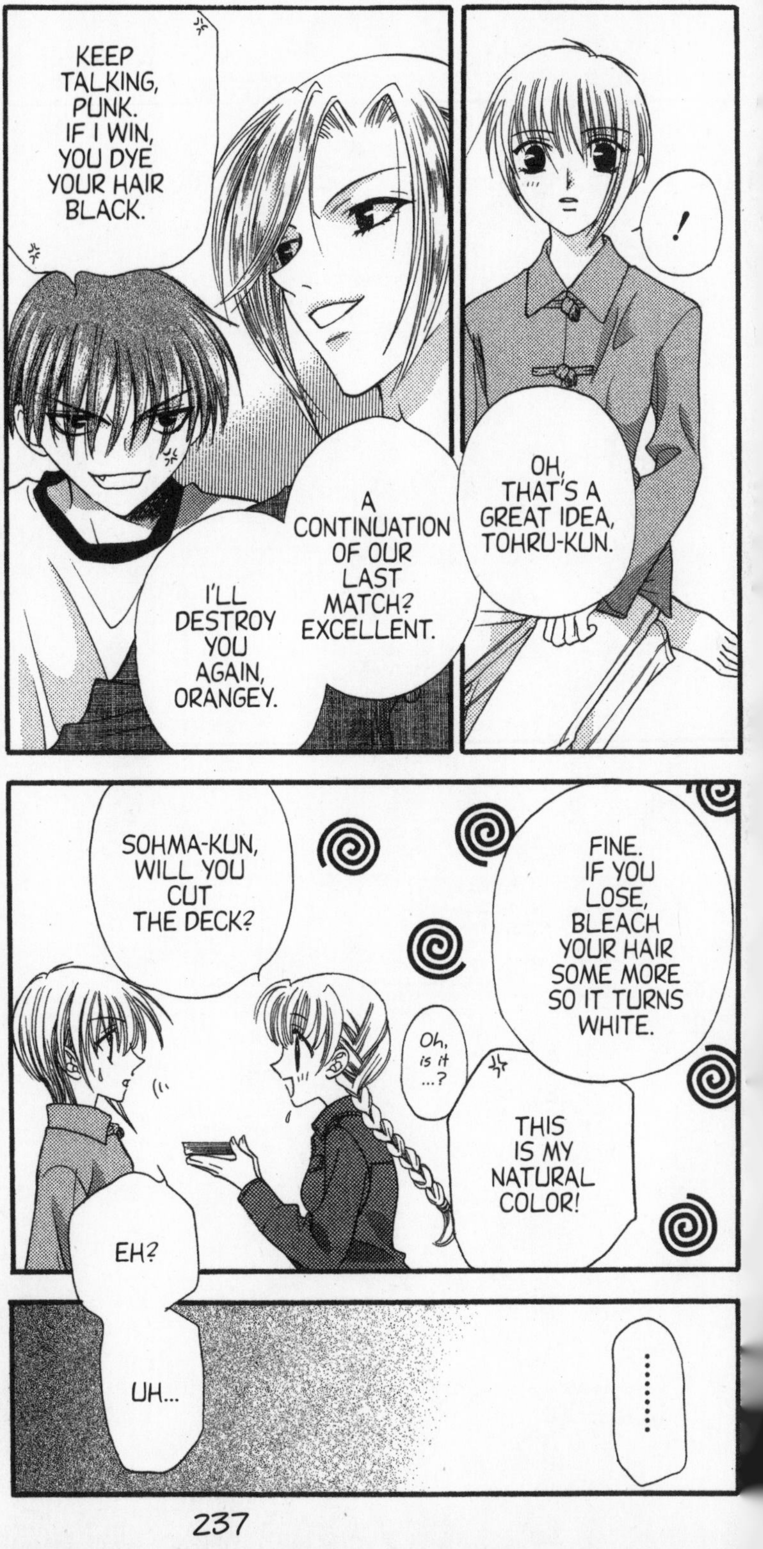
!
OH, THAT'S A GREAT IDEA, TOHRU-KUN.
A CONTINUATION OF OUR LAST MATCH? EXCELLENT.
I'LL DESTROY YOU AGAIN, ORANGEY.
KEEP TALKING, PUNK. IF I WIN, YOU DYE YOUR HAIR BLACK.
FINE. IF YOU LOSE, BLEACH YOUR HAIR SOME MORE SO IT TURNS WHITE.
SOHMA-KUN, WILL YOU CUT THE DECK?
Oh, is it ...?
THIS IS MY NATURAL COLOR!
EH?
....
UH...

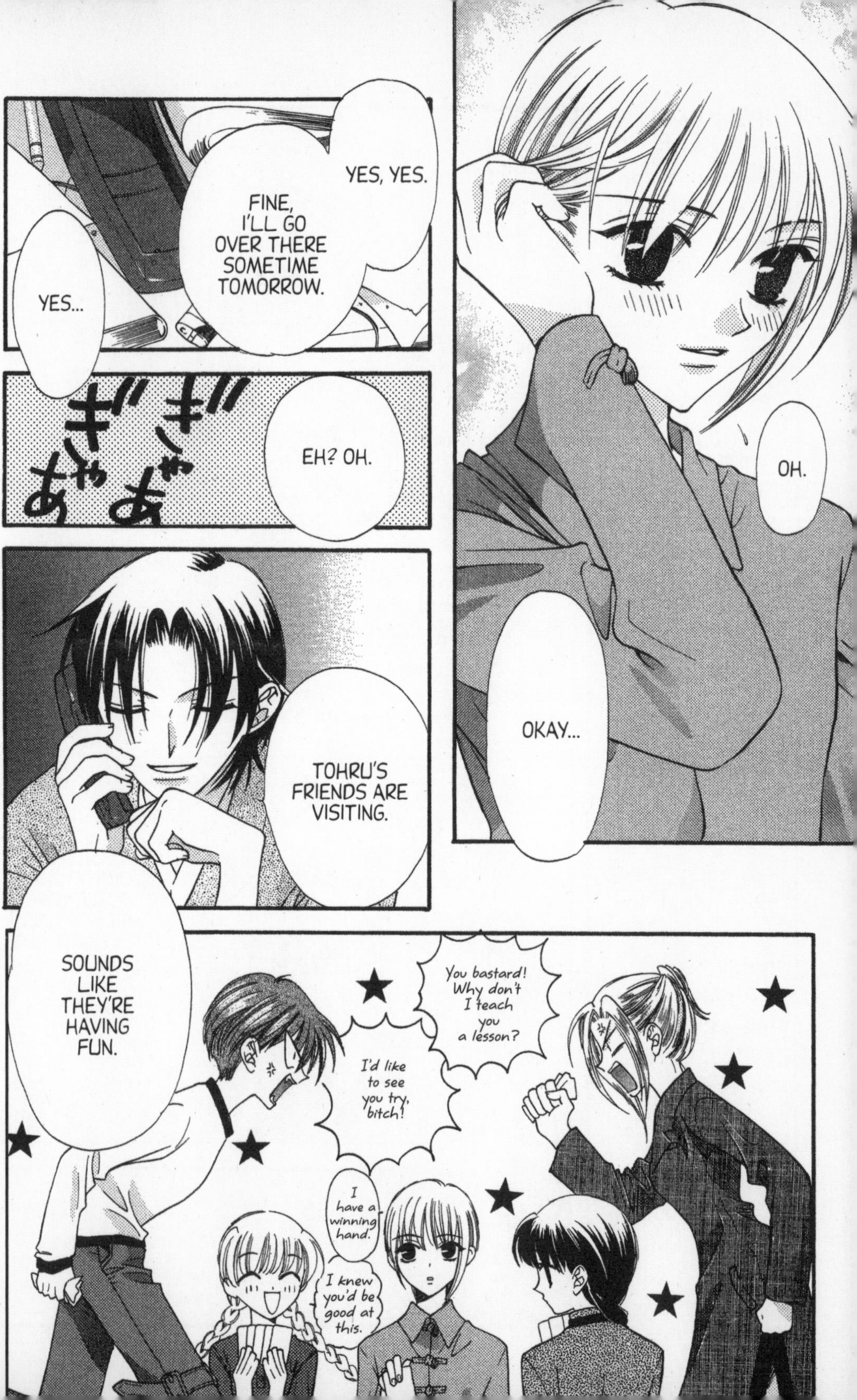
OH.
OKAY...
YES, YES.
FINE, I'LL GO OVER THERE SOMETIME TOMORROW.
YES...
EH? OH.
ぎゃあ ぎゃあ
TOHRU'S FRIENDS ARE VISITING.
SOUNDS LIKE THEY'RE HAVING FUN.
You bastard! Why don't I teach you a lesson?
I'd like to see you try, bitch!
I have a winning hand.
I knew you'd be good at this.

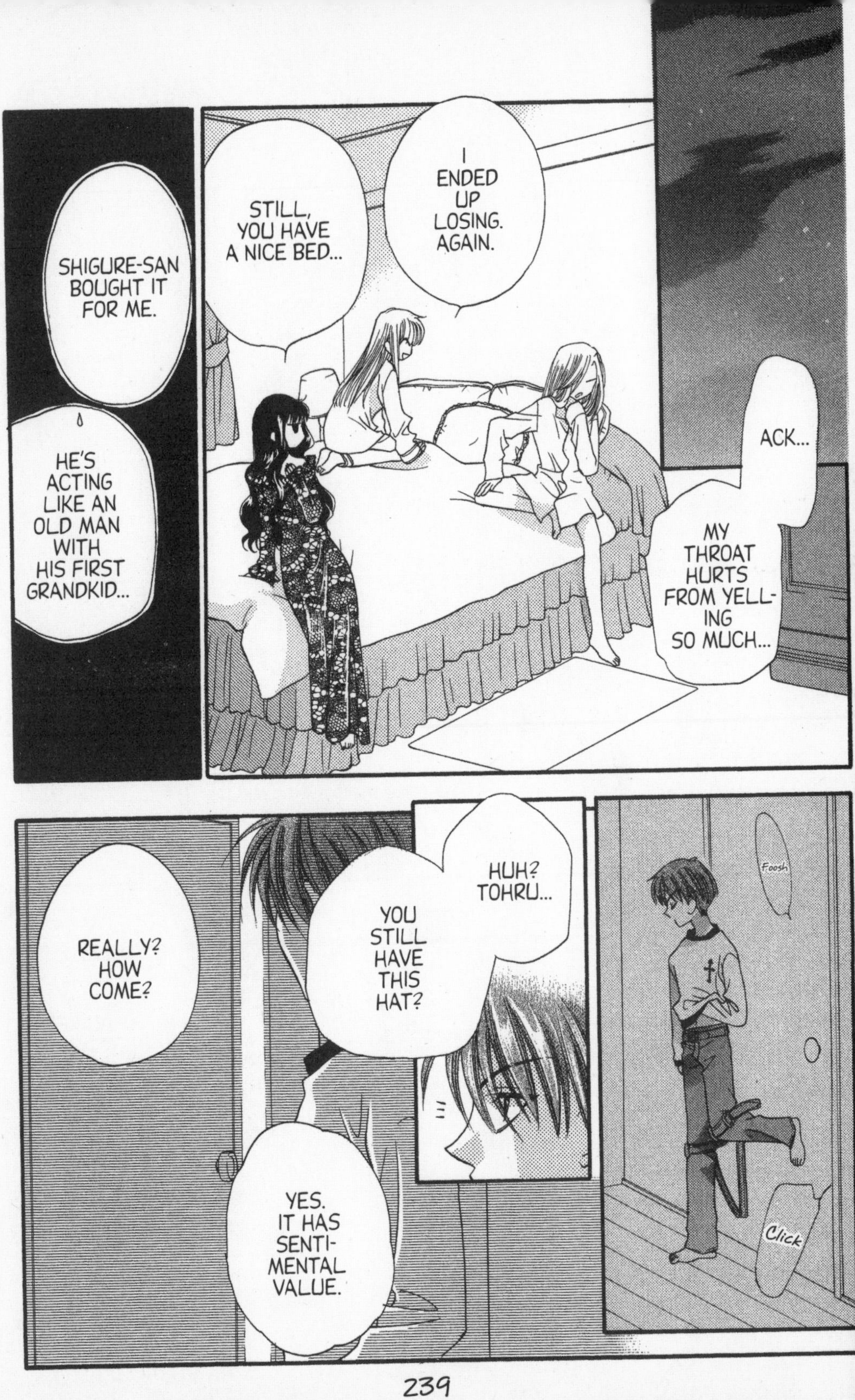
I ENDED UP LOSING. AGAIN.
ACK...
MY THROAT HURTS FROM YELL-ING SO MUCH...
STILL, YOU HAVE A NICE BED...
SHIGURE-SAN BOUGHT IT FOR ME.
HE'S ACTING LIKE AN OLD MAN WITH HIS FIRST GRANDKID...
Foosh
Click
HUH? TOHRU...
YOU STILL HAVE THIS HAT?
YES. IT HAS SENTI-MENTAL VALUE.
REALLY? HOW COME?

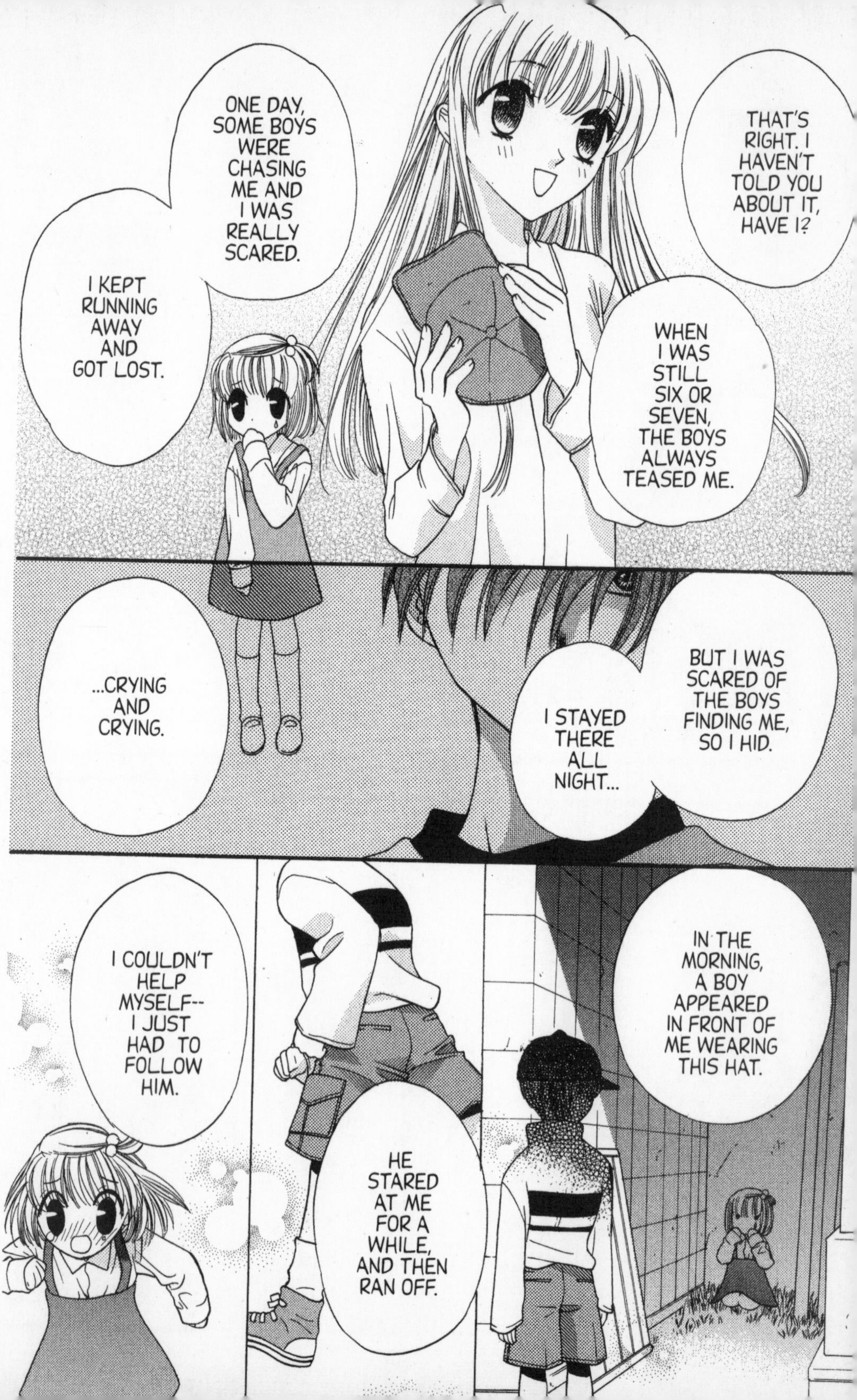
THAT'S RIGHT. I HAVEN'T TOLD YOU ABOUT IT, HAVE I?
WHEN I WAS STILL SIX OR SEVEN, THE BOYS ALWAYS TEASED ME.
ONE DAY, SOME BOYS WERE CHASING ME AND I WAS REALLY SCARED.
I KEPT RUNNING AWAY AND GOT LOST.
BUT I WAS SCARED OF THE BOYS FINDING ME, SO I HID.
I STAYED THERE ALL NIGHT...
...CRYING AND CRYING.
IN THE MORNING, A BOY APPEARED IN FRONT OF ME WEARING THIS HAT.
HE STARED AT ME FOR A WHILE, AND THEN RAN OFF.
I COULDN'T HELP MYSELF-- I JUST HAD TO FOLLOW HIM.

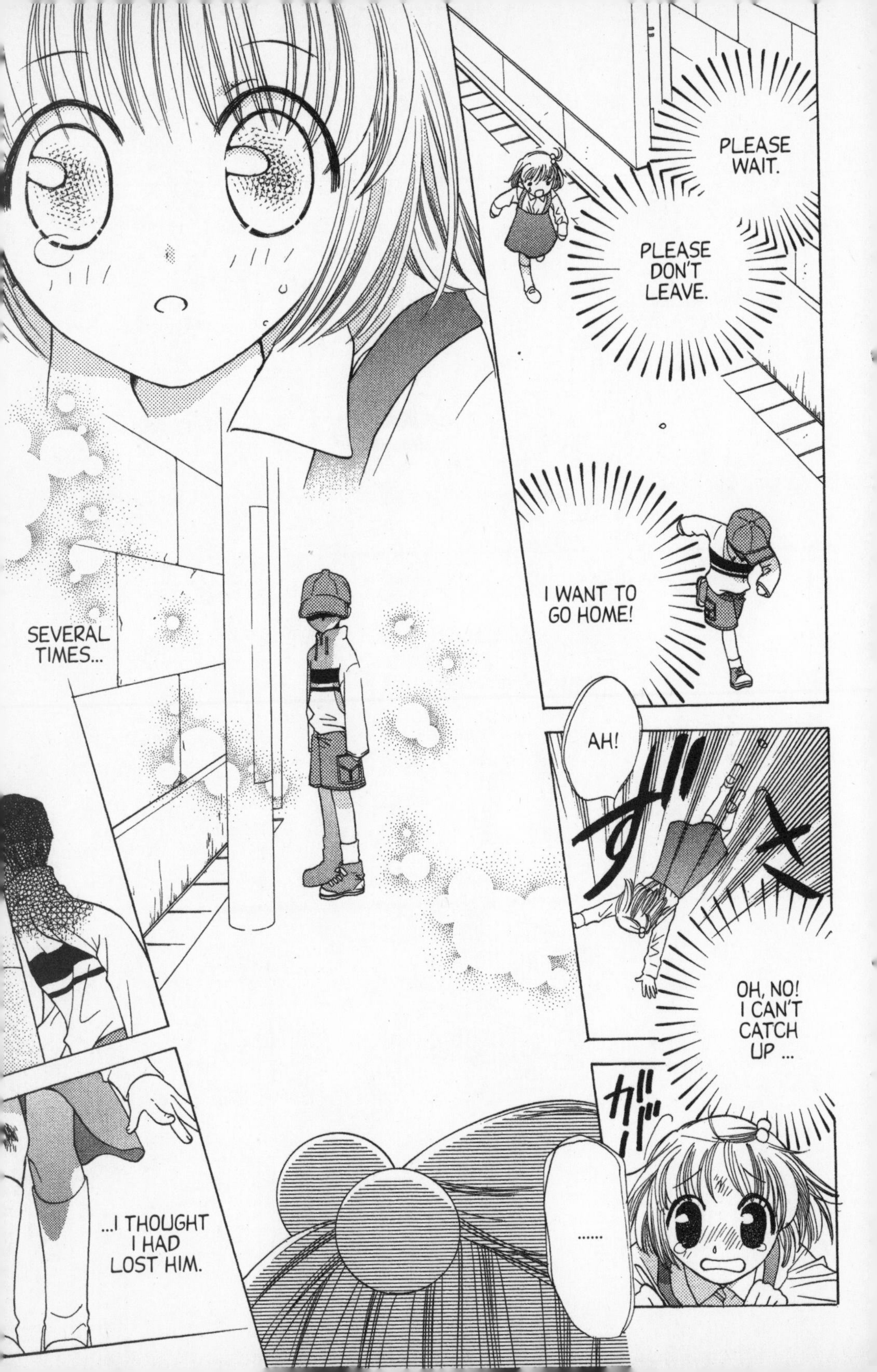
PLEASE WAIT.
PLEASE DON'T LEAVE.
I WANT TO GO HOME!
AH!
OH, NO! I CAN'T CATCH UP ...
......
SEVERAL TIMES...
...I THOUGHT I HAD LOST HIM.

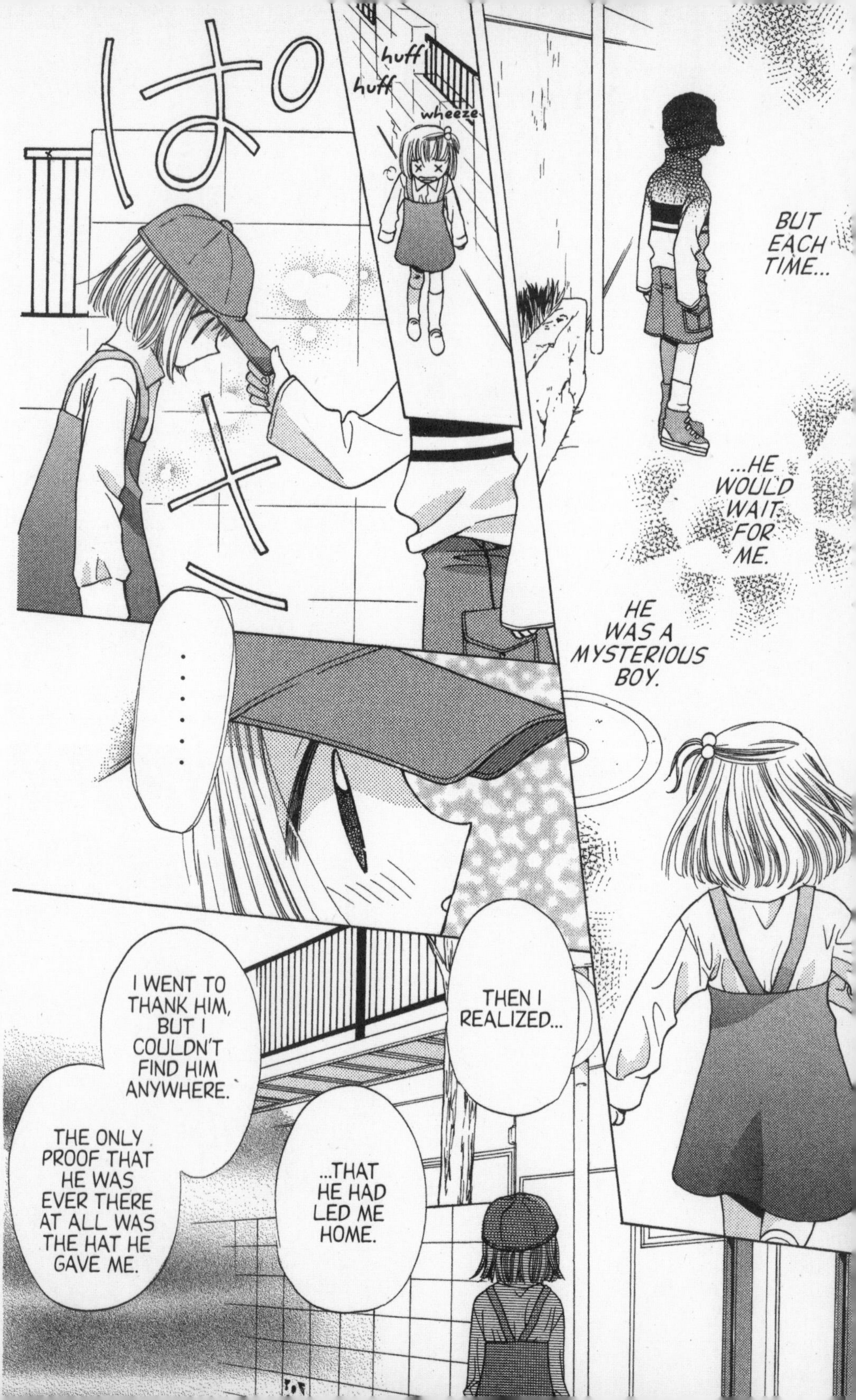
BUT EACH TIME...
...HE WOULD WAIT FOR ME.
huff
huff
wheeze
HE WAS A MYSTERIOUS BOY.
......
THEN I REALIZED...
...THAT HE HAD LED ME HOME.
I WENT TO THANK HIM, BUT I COULDN'T FIND HIM ANYWHERE.
THE ONLY PROOF THAT HE WAS EVER THERE AT ALL WAS THE HAT HE GAVE ME.

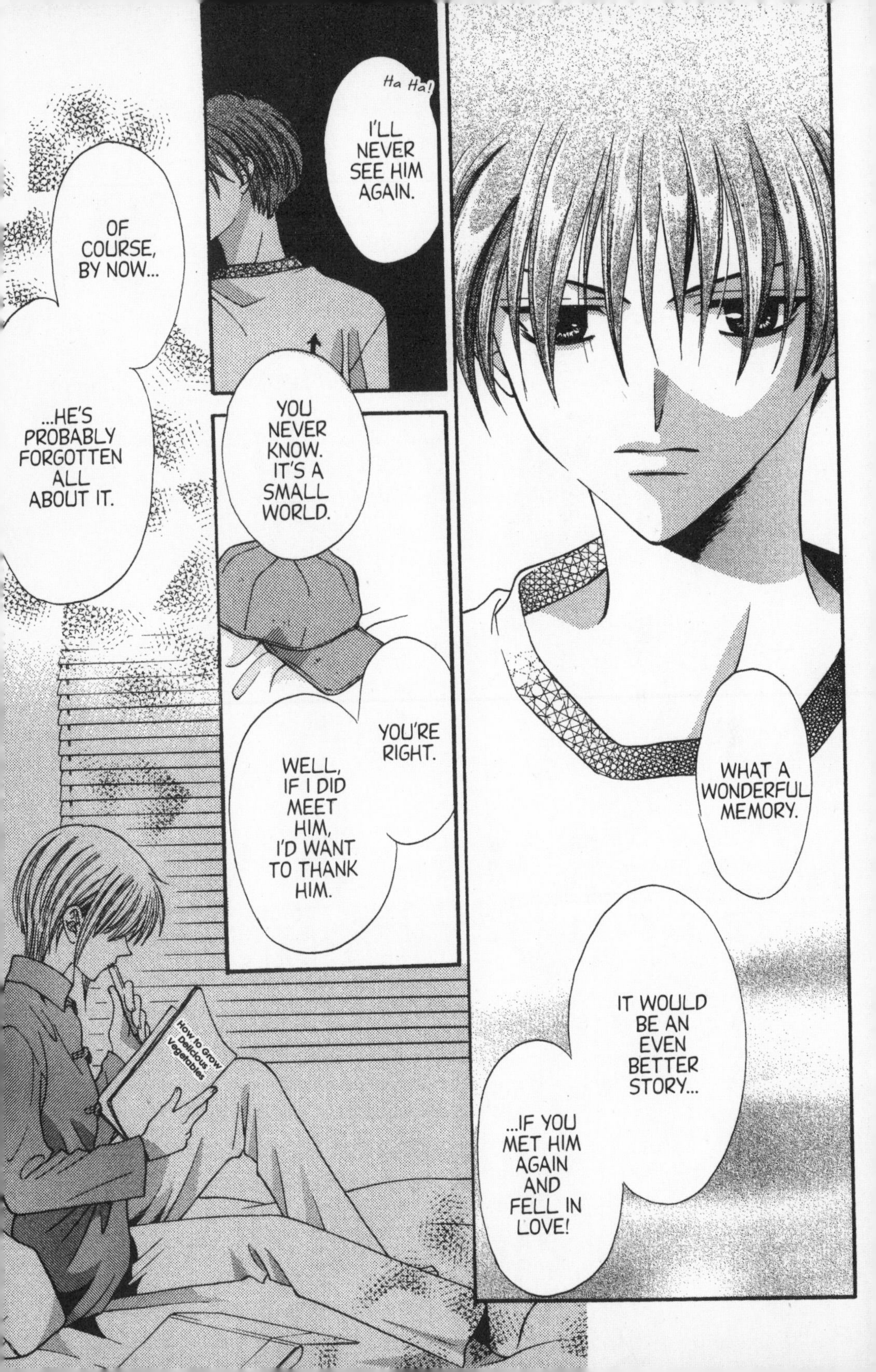
WHAT A WONDERFUL MEMORY.
IT WOULD BE AN EVEN BETTER STORY...
...IF YOU MET HIM AGAIN AND FELL IN LOVE!
Ha Ha!
I'LL NEVER SEE HIM AGAIN.
OF COURSE, BY NOW...
...HE'S PROBABLY FORGOTTEN ALL ABOUT IT.
YOU NEVER KNOW. IT'S A SMALL WORLD.
YOU'RE RIGHT.
WELL, IF I DID MEET HIM, I'D WANT TO THANK HIM.
How to Grow Delicious Vegetables

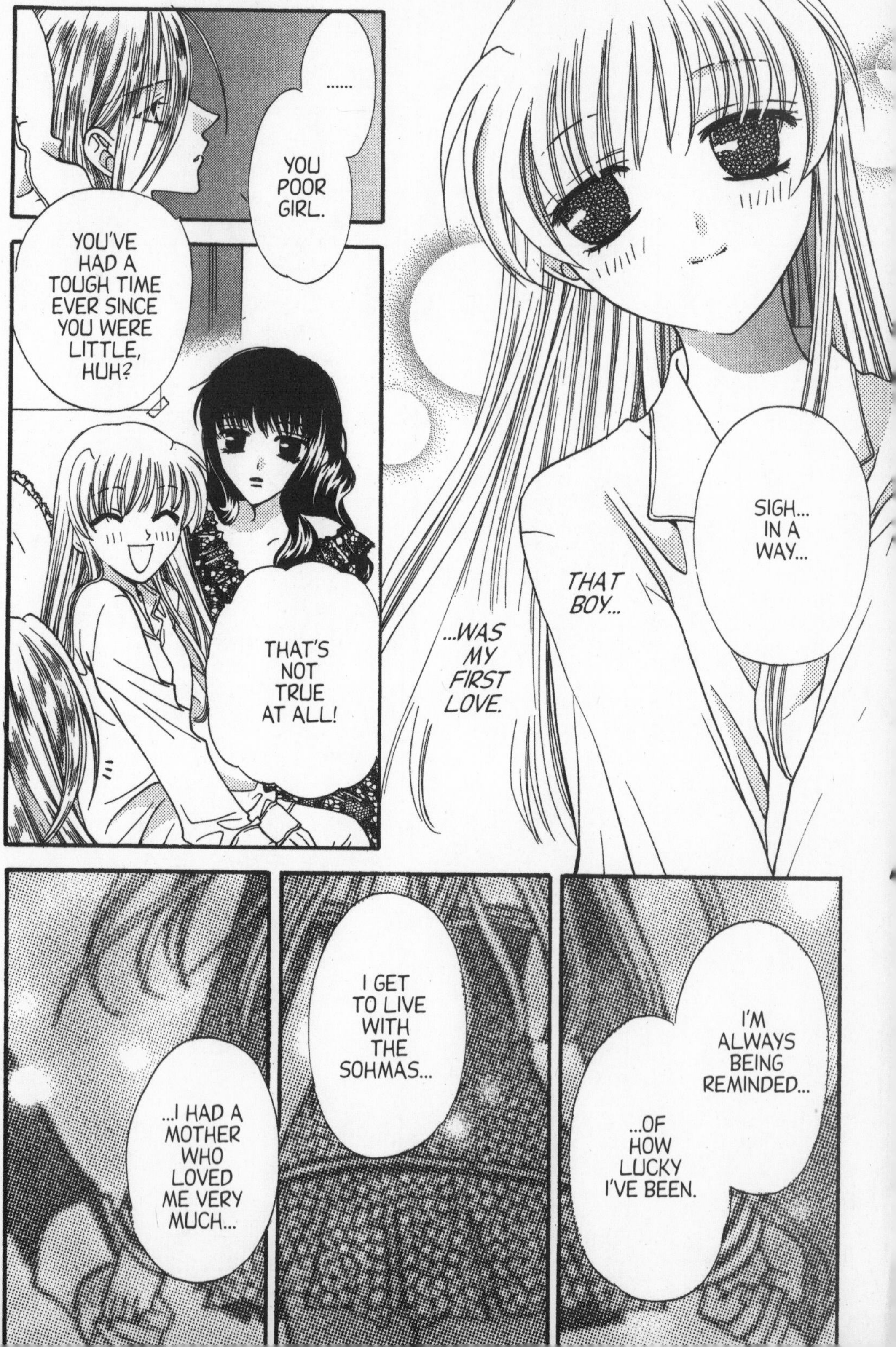
SIGH... IN A WAY...
THAT BOY...
...WAS MY FIRST LOVE.
......
YOU POOR GIRL.
YOU'VE HAD A TOUGH TIME EVER SINCE YOU WERE LITTLE, HUH?
THAT'S NOT TRUE AT ALL!
I'M ALWAYS BEING REMINDED...
...OF HOW LUCKY I'VE BEEN.
I GET TO LIVE WITH THE SOHMAS...
...I HAD A MOTHER WHO LOVED ME VERY MUCH...

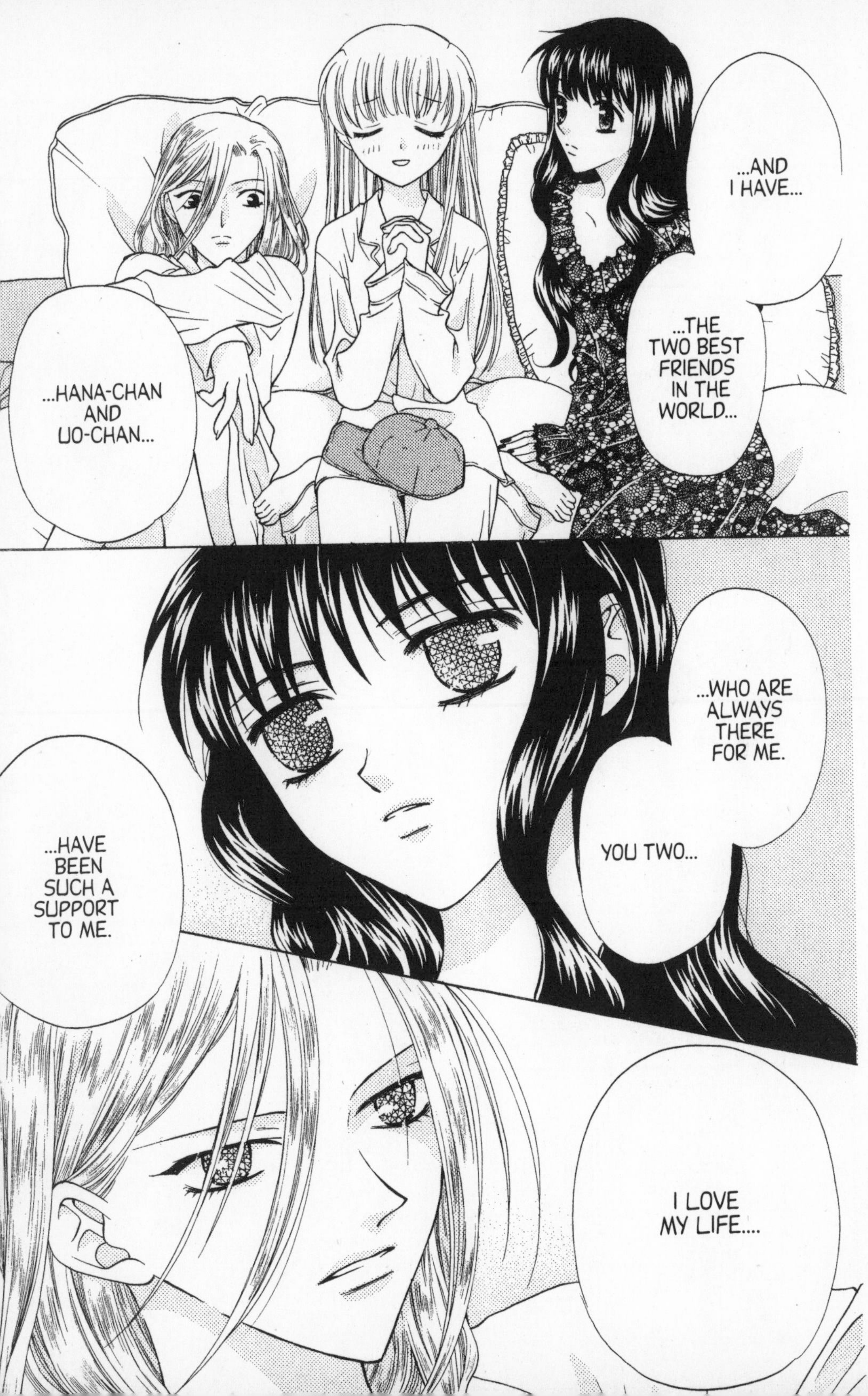
...AND I HAVE...
...THE TWO BEST FRIENDS IN THE WORLD...
...HANA-CHAN AND UO-CHAN...
...WHO ARE ALWAYS THERE FOR ME.
YOU TWO...
...HAVE BEEN SUCH A SUPPORT TO ME.
I LOVE MY LIFE....

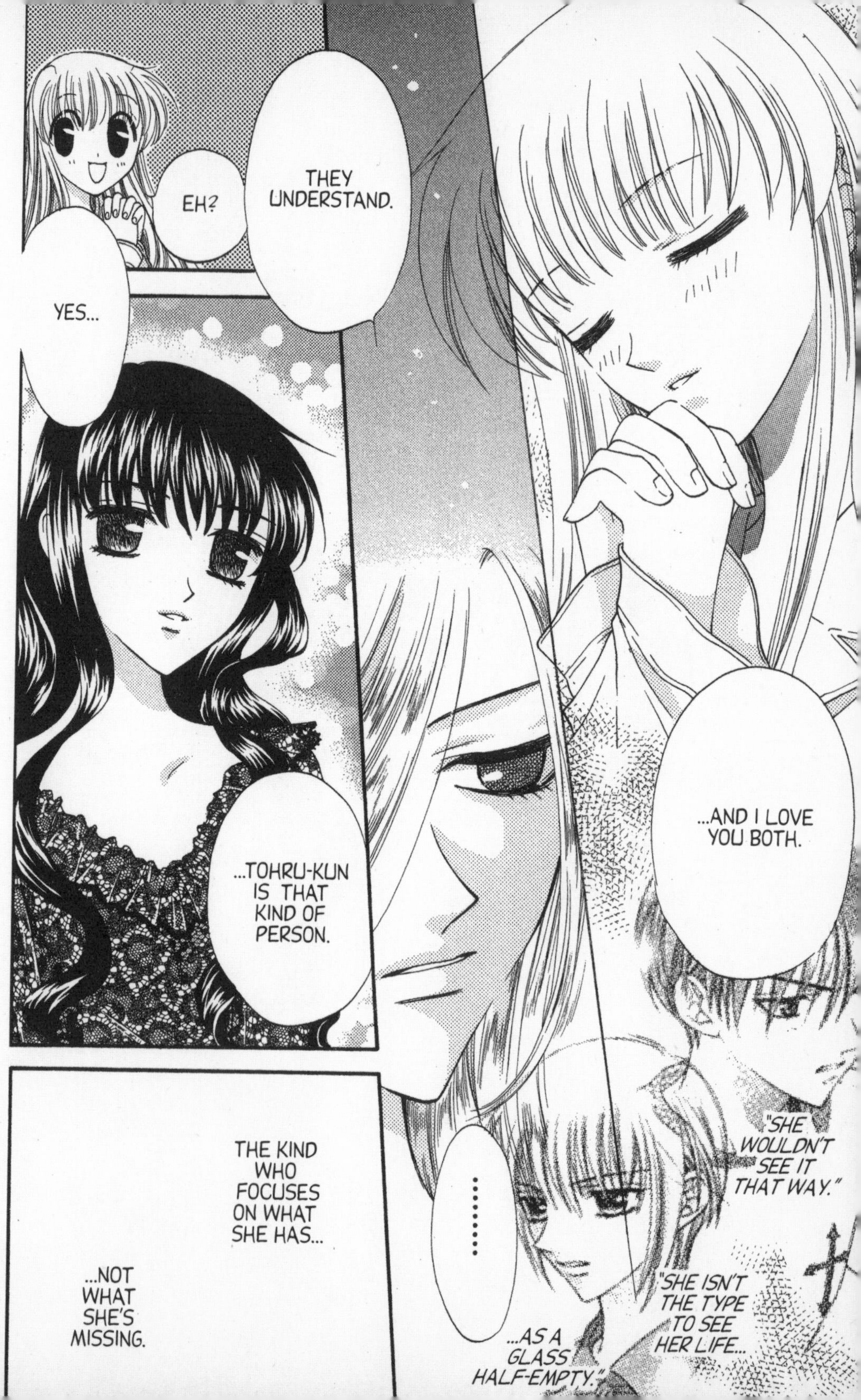
...AND I LOVE YOU BOTH.
THEY UNDERSTAND.
EH?
YES...
...TOHRU-KUN IS THAT KIND OF PERSON.
"SHE WOULDN'T SEE IT THAT WAY."
"SHE ISN'T THE TYPE TO SEE HER LIFE...
...AS A GLASS HALF-EMPTY."
......
THE KIND WHO FOCUSES ON WHAT SHE HAS...
...NOT WHAT SHE'S MISSING.

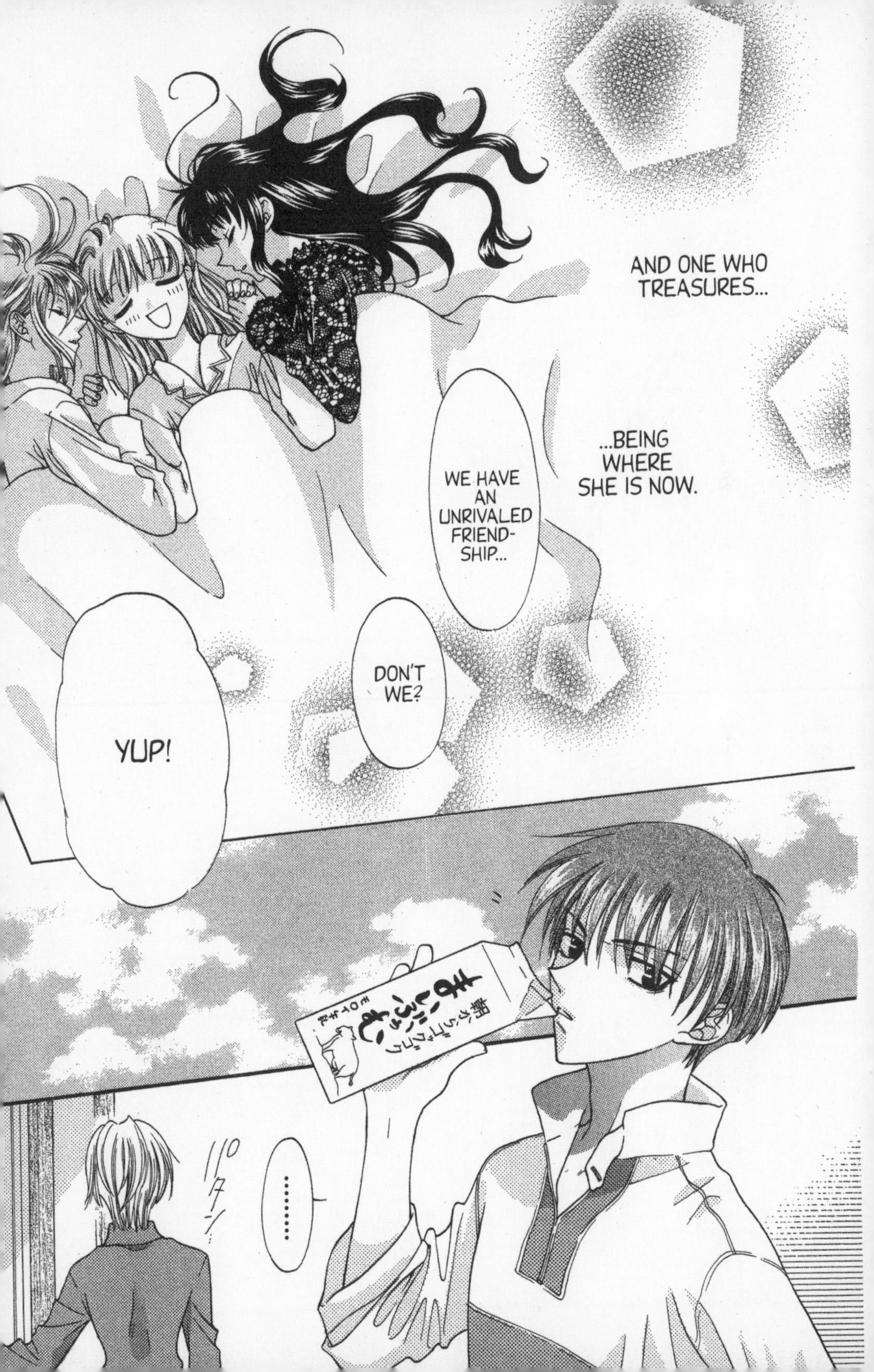
AND ONE WHO TREASURES...
...BEING WHERE SHE IS NOW.
WE HAVE AN UNRIVALED FRIEND-SHIP...
DON'T WE?
YUP!
....

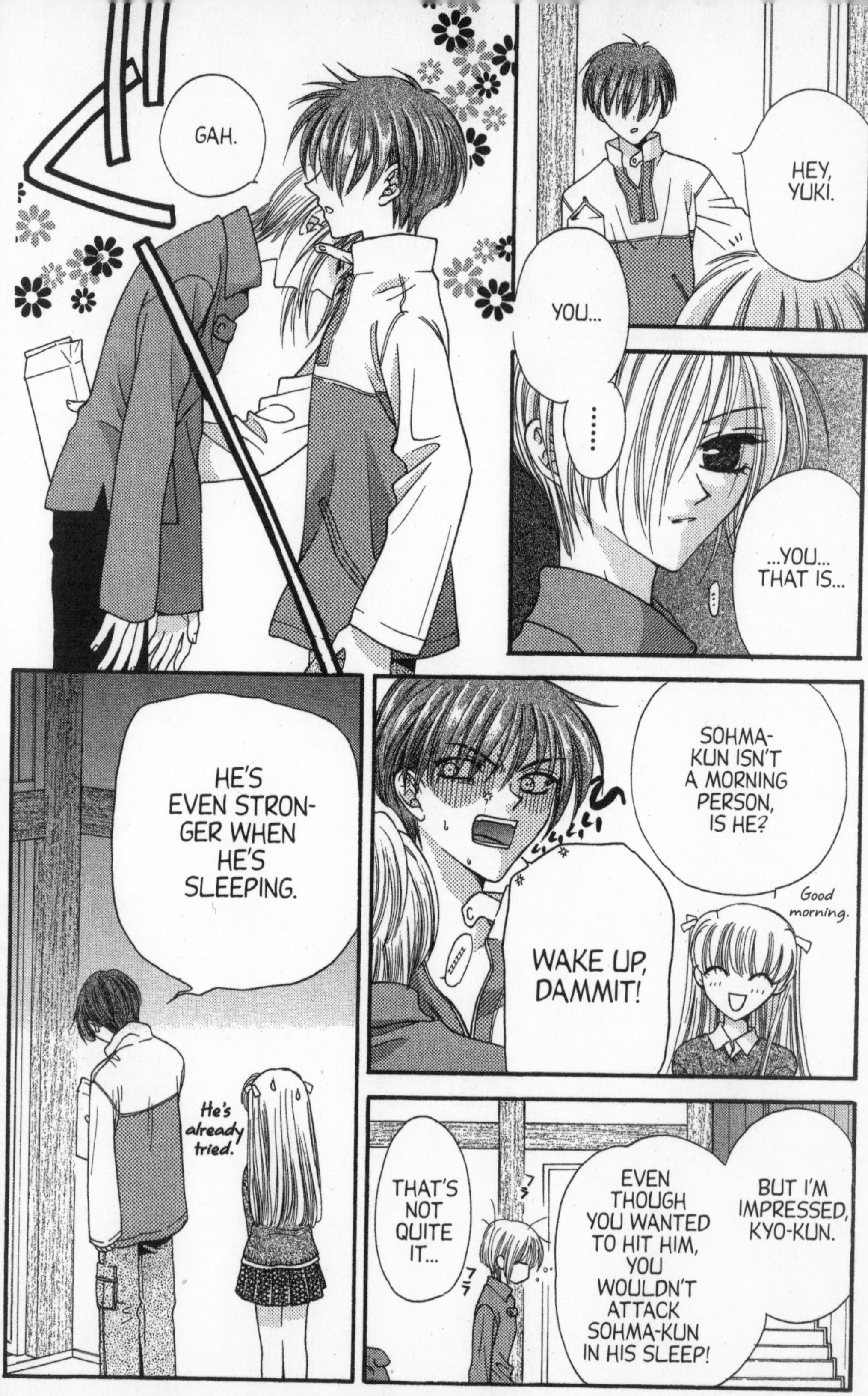
HEY, YUKI.
YOU...
......
...YOU... THAT IS...
GAH.
Good morning.
SOHMA-KUN ISN'T A MORNING PERSON, IS HE?
WAKE UP, DAMMIT!
BUT I'M IMPRESSED, KYO-KUN.
EVEN THOUGH YOU WANTED TO HIT HIM, YOU WOULDN'T ATTACK SOHMA-KUN IN HIS SLEEP!
THAT'S NOT QUITE IT...
HE'S EVEN STRONGER WHEN HE'S SLEEPING.
He's already tried.

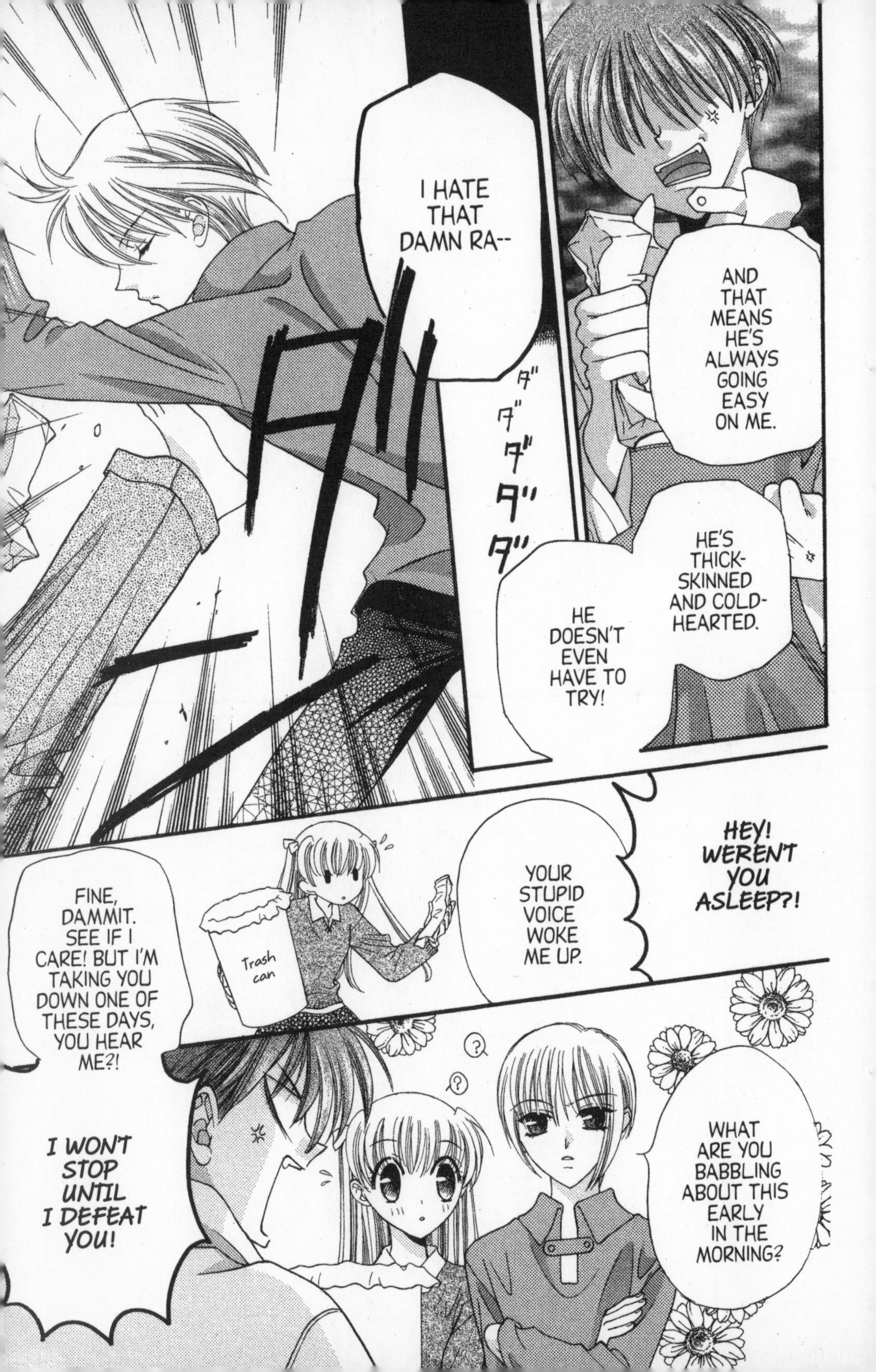
AND THAT MEANS HE'S ALWAYS GOING EASY ON ME.
HE'S THICK-SKINNED AND COLD-HEARTED.
HE DOESN'T EVEN HAVE TO TRY!
I HATE THAT DAMN RA--
ダダダダダ
HEY! WEREN'T YOU ASLEEP?!
YOUR STUPID VOICE WOKE ME UP.
Trash can
FINE, DAMMIT. SEE IF I CARE! BUT I'M TAKING YOU DOWN ONE OF THESE DAYS, YOU HEAR ME?!
WHAT ARE YOU BABBLING ABOUT THIS EARLY IN THE MORNING?
I WON'T STOP UNTIL I DEFEAT YOU!

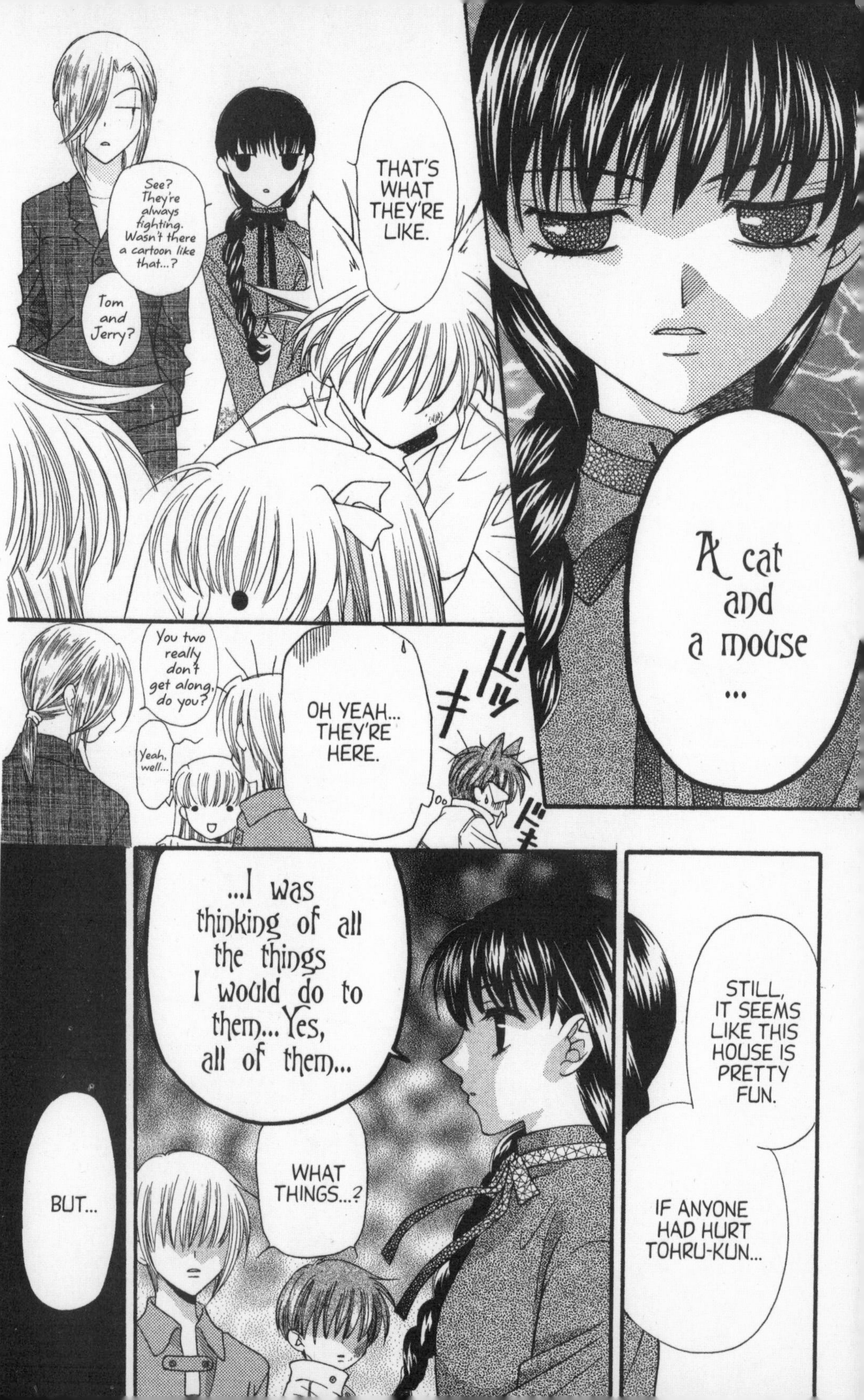
A cat and a mouse ...
THAT'S WHAT THEY'RE LIKE.
See? They're always fighting. Wasn't there a cartoon like that...?
Tom and Jerry?
OH YEAH... THEY'RE HERE.
You two really don't get along, do you?
Yeah, well...
STILL, IT SEEMS LIKE THIS HOUSE IS PRETTY FUN.
IF ANYONE HAD HURT TOHRU-KUN...
...I was thinking of all the things I would do to them... Yes, all of them...
WHAT THINGS...?
BUT...

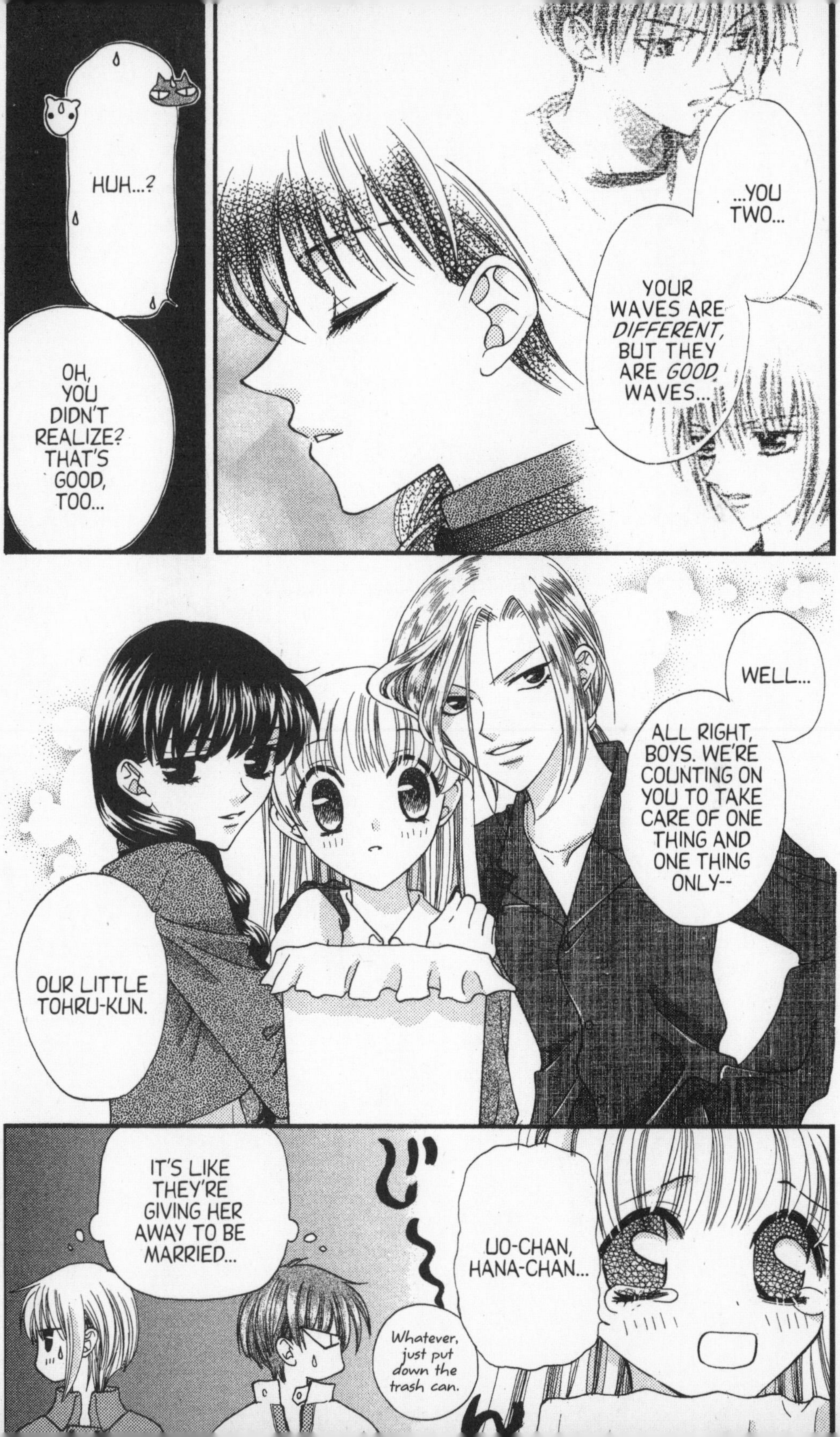
...YOU TWO...
YOUR WAVES ARE *DIFFERENT*, BUT THEY ARE *GOOD* WAVES...
HUH...?
OH, YOU DIDN'T REALIZE? THAT'S GOOD, TOO...
WELL...
ALL RIGHT, BOYS. WE'RE COUNTING ON YOU TO TAKE CARE OF ONE THING AND ONE THING ONLY--
OUR LITTLE TOHRU-KUN.
UO-CHAN, HANA-CHAN...
じ~
IT'S LIKE THEY'RE GIVING HER AWAY TO BE MARRIED...
Whatever, just put down the trash can.

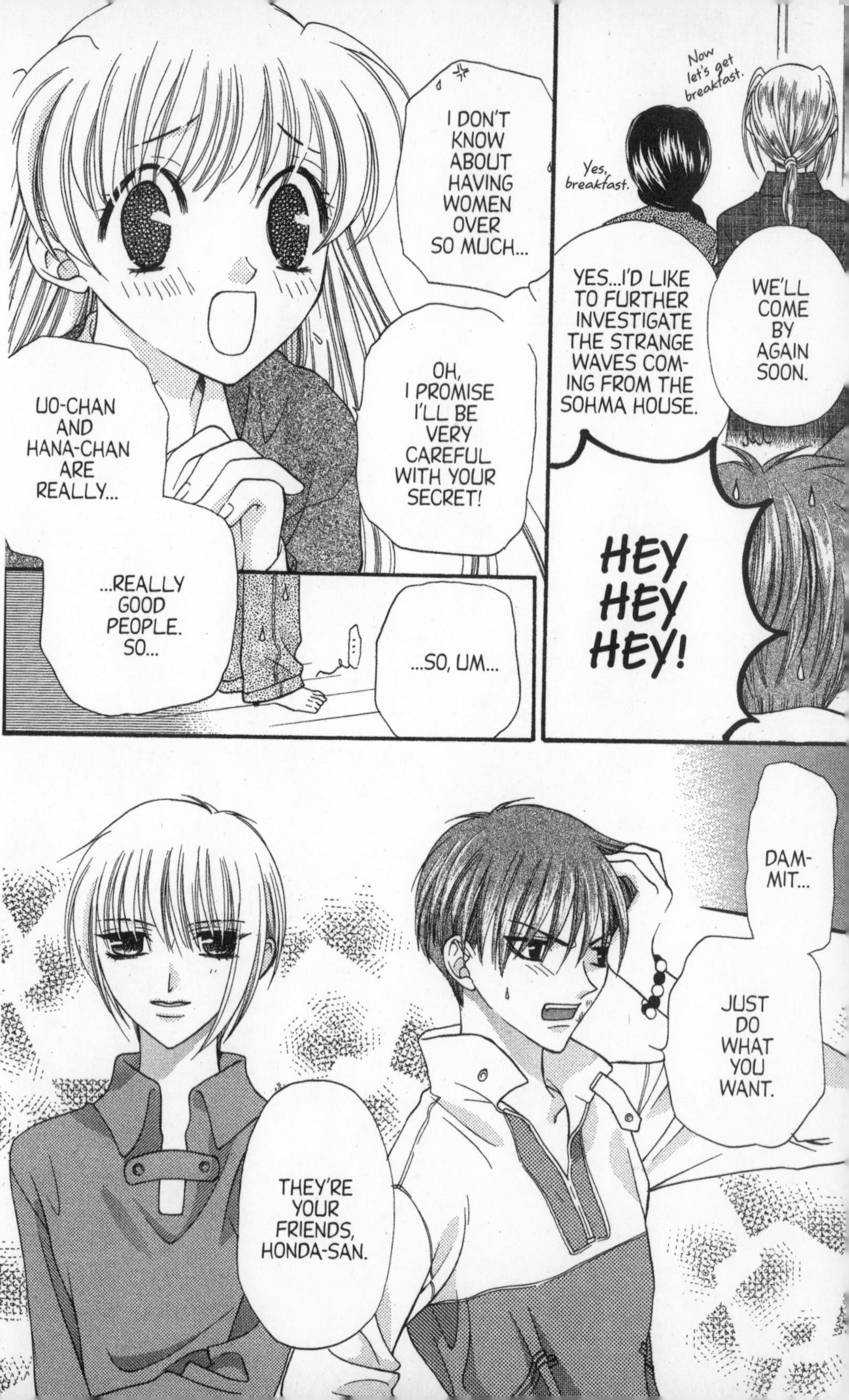
Now let's get breakfast.
Yes, breakfast.
WE'LL COME BY AGAIN SOON.
YES...I'D LIKE TO FURTHER INVESTIGATE THE STRANGE WAVES COMING FROM THE SOHMA HOUSE.
HEY HEY HEY!
I DON'T KNOW ABOUT HAVING WOMEN OVER SO MUCH...
OH, I PROMISE I'LL BE VERY CAREFUL WITH YOUR SECRET!
UO-CHAN AND HANA-CHAN ARE REALLY...
...REALLY GOOD PEOPLE. SO...
...
...SO, UM...
DAM-MIT...
JUST DO WHAT YOU WANT.
THEY'RE YOUR FRIENDS, HONDA-SAN.

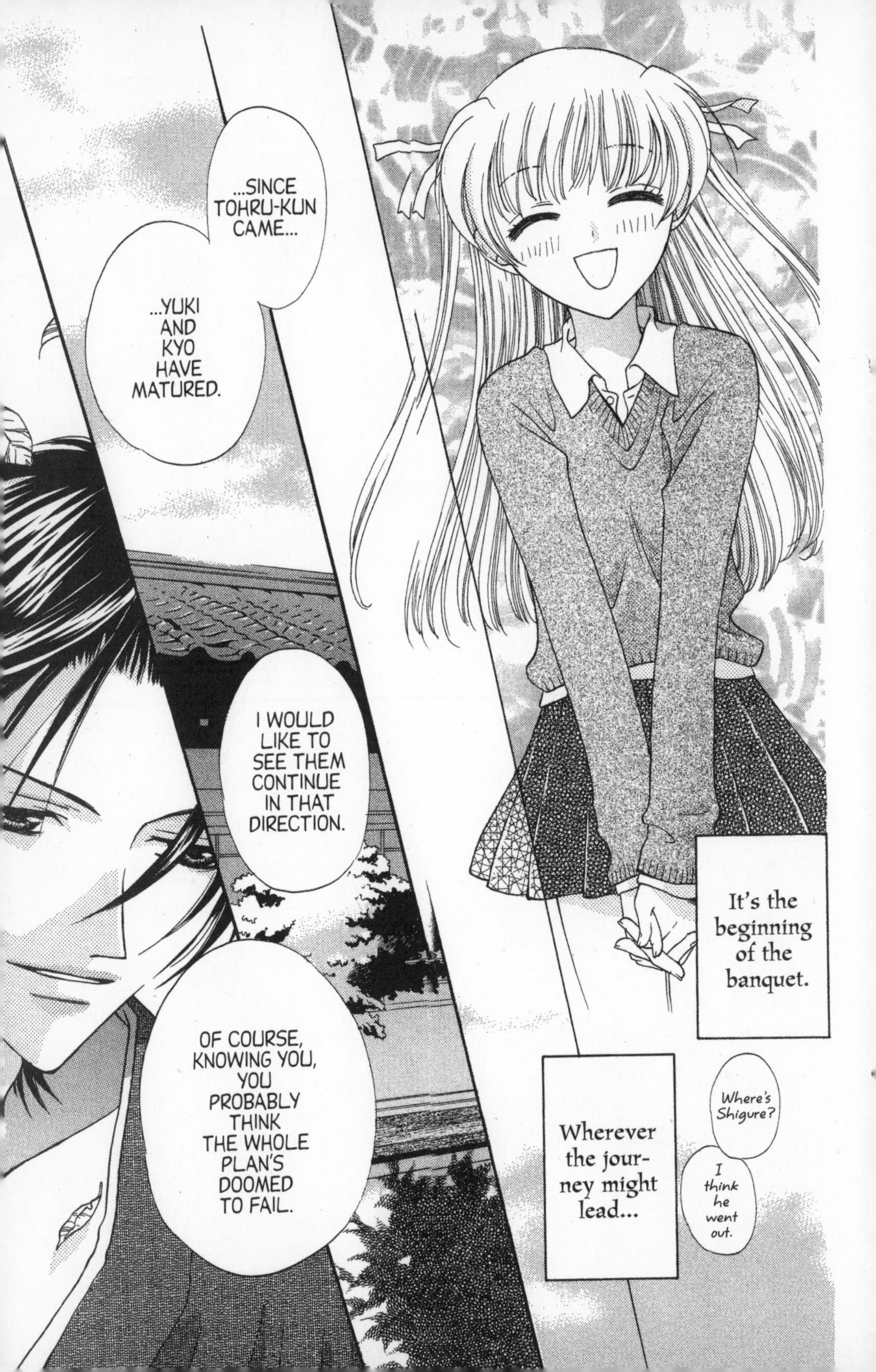
It's the beginning of the banquet.
Wherever the journey might lead...
Where's Shigure?
I think he went out.
...SINCE TOHRU-KUN CAME...
...YUKI AND KYO HAVE MATURED.
I WOULD LIKE TO SEE THEM CONTINUE IN THAT DIRECTION.
OF COURSE, KNOWING YOU, YOU PROBABLY THINK THE WHOLE PLAN'S DOOMED TO FAIL.

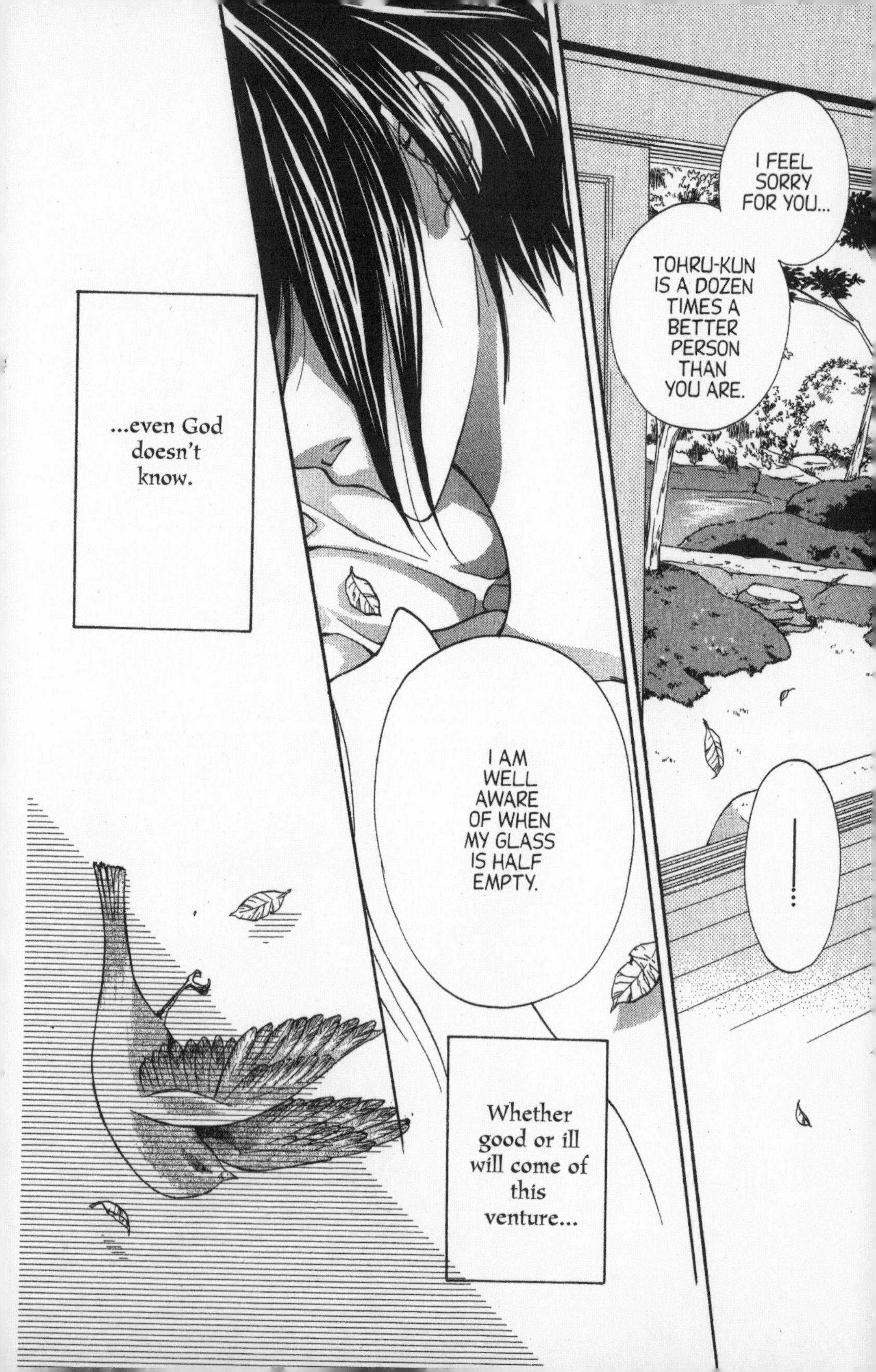
I FEEL SORRY FOR YOU...
TOHRU-KUN IS A DOZEN TIMES A BETTER PERSON THAN YOU ARE.
......
I AM WELL AWARE OF WHEN MY GLASS IS HALF EMPTY.
Whether good or ill will come of this venture...
...even God doesn't know.

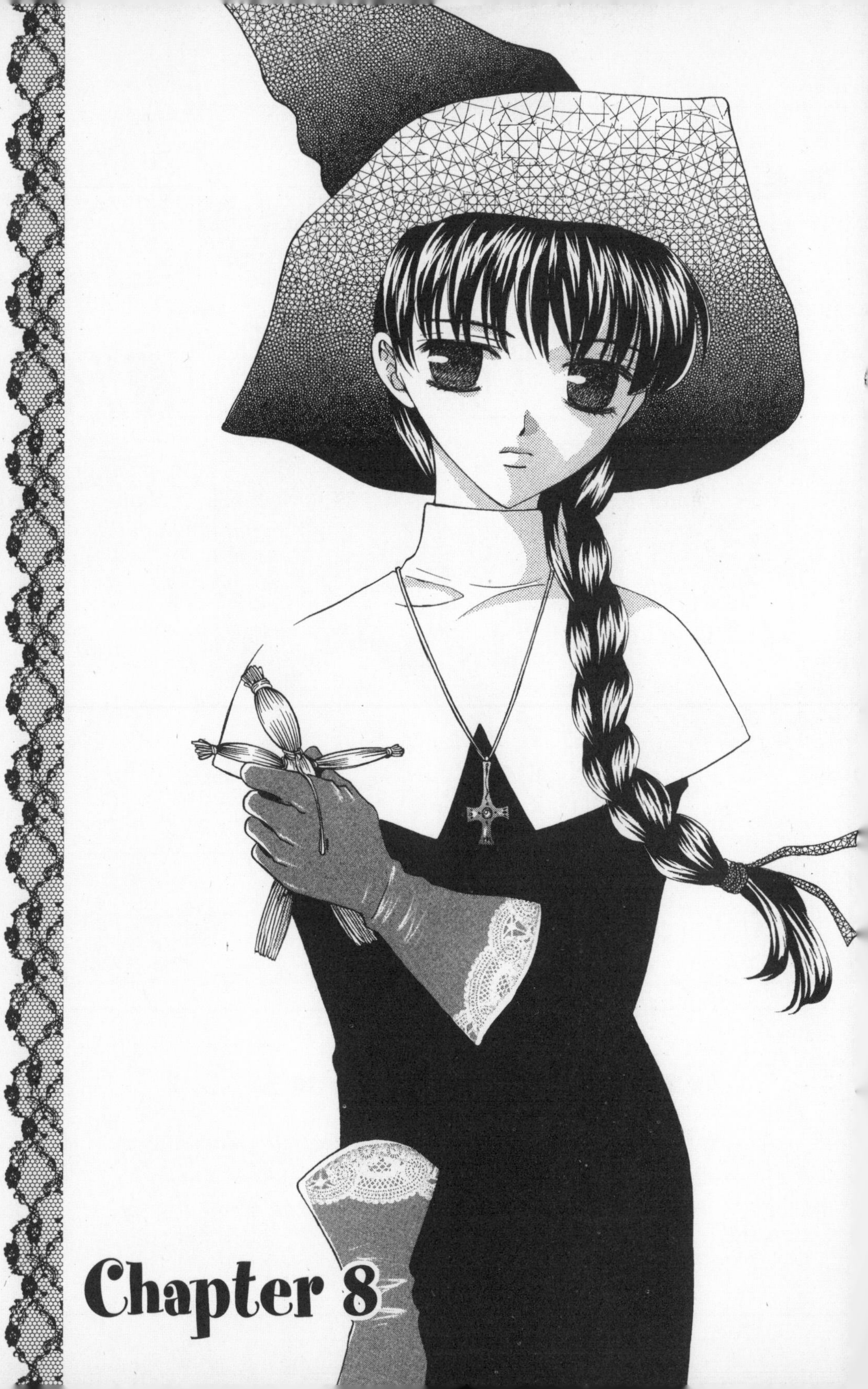

Chapter 8

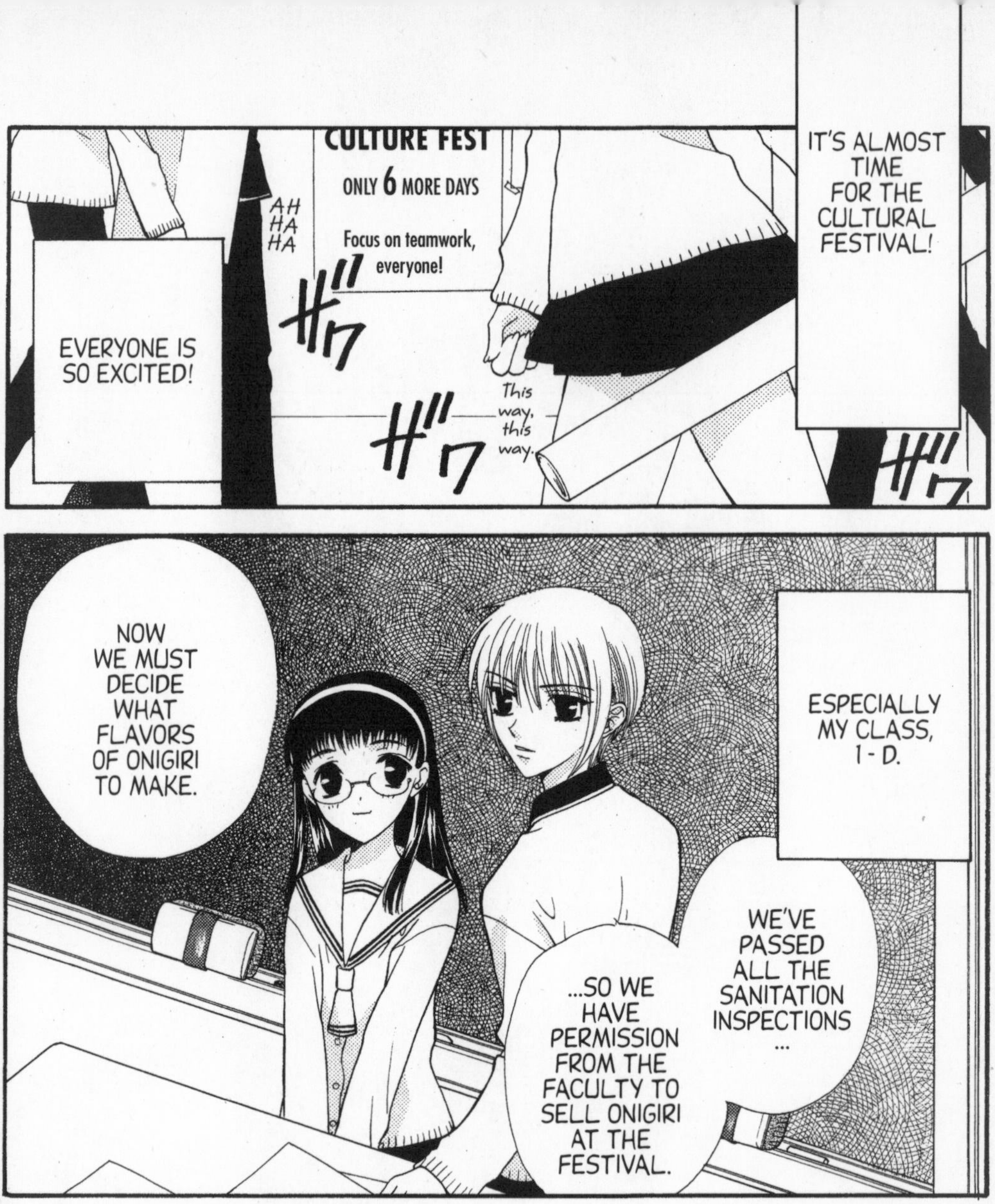
IT'S ALMOST TIME FOR THE CULTURAL FESTIVAL!
ザワ
This way, this way.
ザワ
CULTURE FEST
ONLY 6 MORE DAYS
Focus on teamwork, everyone!
ザワ
AH HA HA
EVERYONE IS SO EXCITED!
ESPECIALLY MY CLASS, 1 - D.
WE'VE PASSED ALL THE SANITATION INSPECTIONS ...
...SO WE HAVE PERMISSION FROM THE FACULTY TO SELL ONIGIRI AT THE FESTIVAL.
NOW WE MUST DECIDE WHAT FLAVORS OF ONIGIRI TO MAKE.

ULTRA SPECIAL BLAH BLAH BLAH 2

If you'd like to know what Momiji is saying in German, he says, "What a surprise! How lucky!" "Nice to meet you," "I'm so happy to meet you," and "You're so cute!". This will all make sense shortly! (Ha ha!)

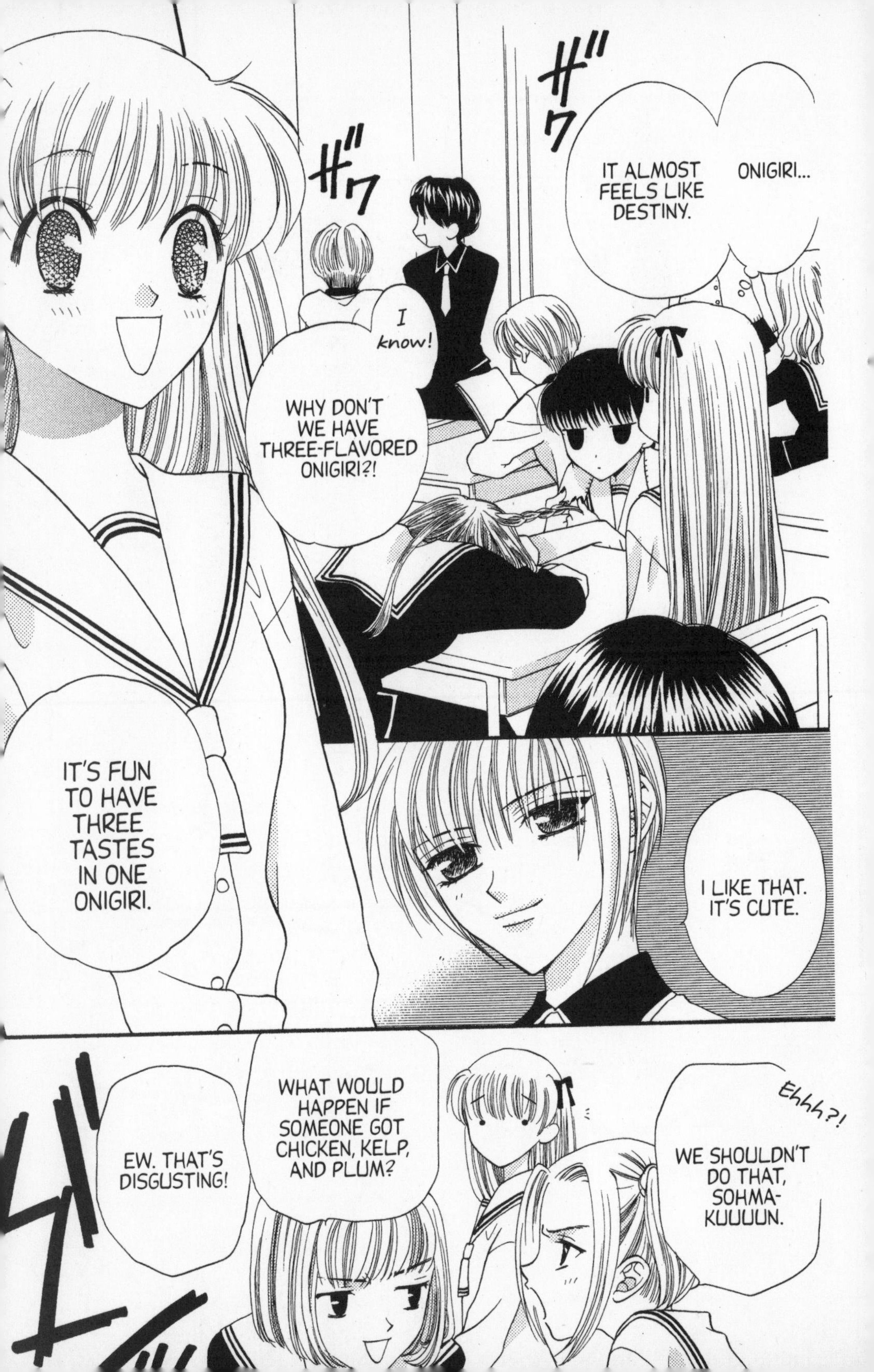
ザワ
ONIGIRI...
IT ALMOST FEELS LIKE DESTINY.
ザワ
I know!
WHY DON'T WE HAVE THREE-FLAVORED ONIGIRI?!
I LIKE THAT. IT'S CUTE.
IT'S FUN TO HAVE THREE TASTES IN ONE ONIGIRI.
Ehhh?!
WE SHOULDN'T DO THAT, SOHMA-KUUUUN.
WHAT WOULD HAPPEN IF SOMEONE GOT CHICKEN, KELP, AND PLUM?
EW. THAT'S DISGUSTING!

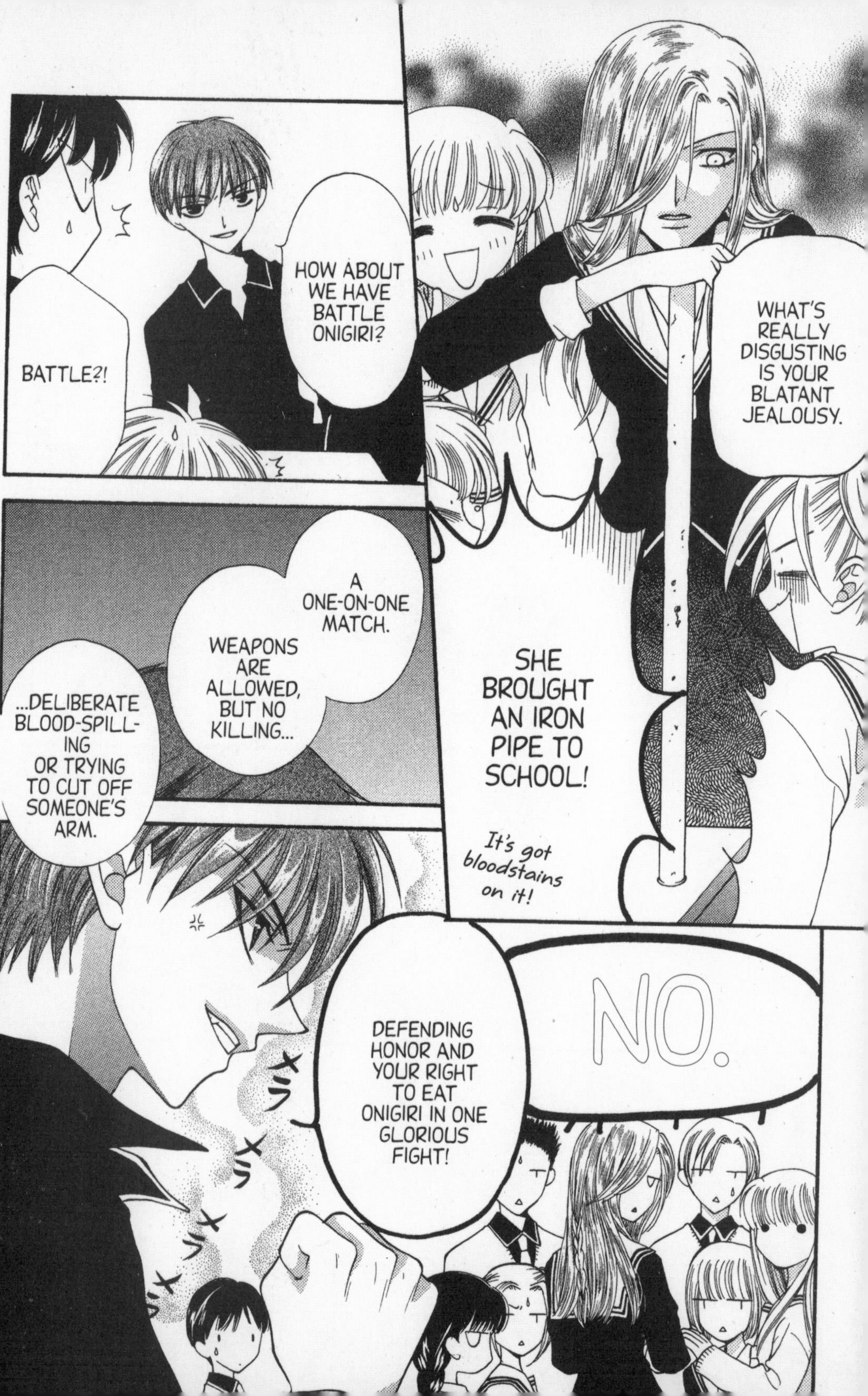
WHAT'S REALLY DISGUSTING IS YOUR BLATANT JEALOUSY.
SHE BROUGHT AN IRON PIPE TO SCHOOL!
It's got bloodstains on it!
HOW ABOUT WE HAVE BATTLE ONIGIRI?
BATTLE?!
A ONE-ON-ONE MATCH.
WEAPONS ARE ALLOWED, BUT NO KILLING...
...DELIBERATE BLOOD-SPILLING OR TRYING TO CUT OFF SOMEONE'S ARM.
NO.
DEFENDING HONOR AND YOUR RIGHT TO EAT ONIGIRI IN ONE GLORIOUS FIGHT!

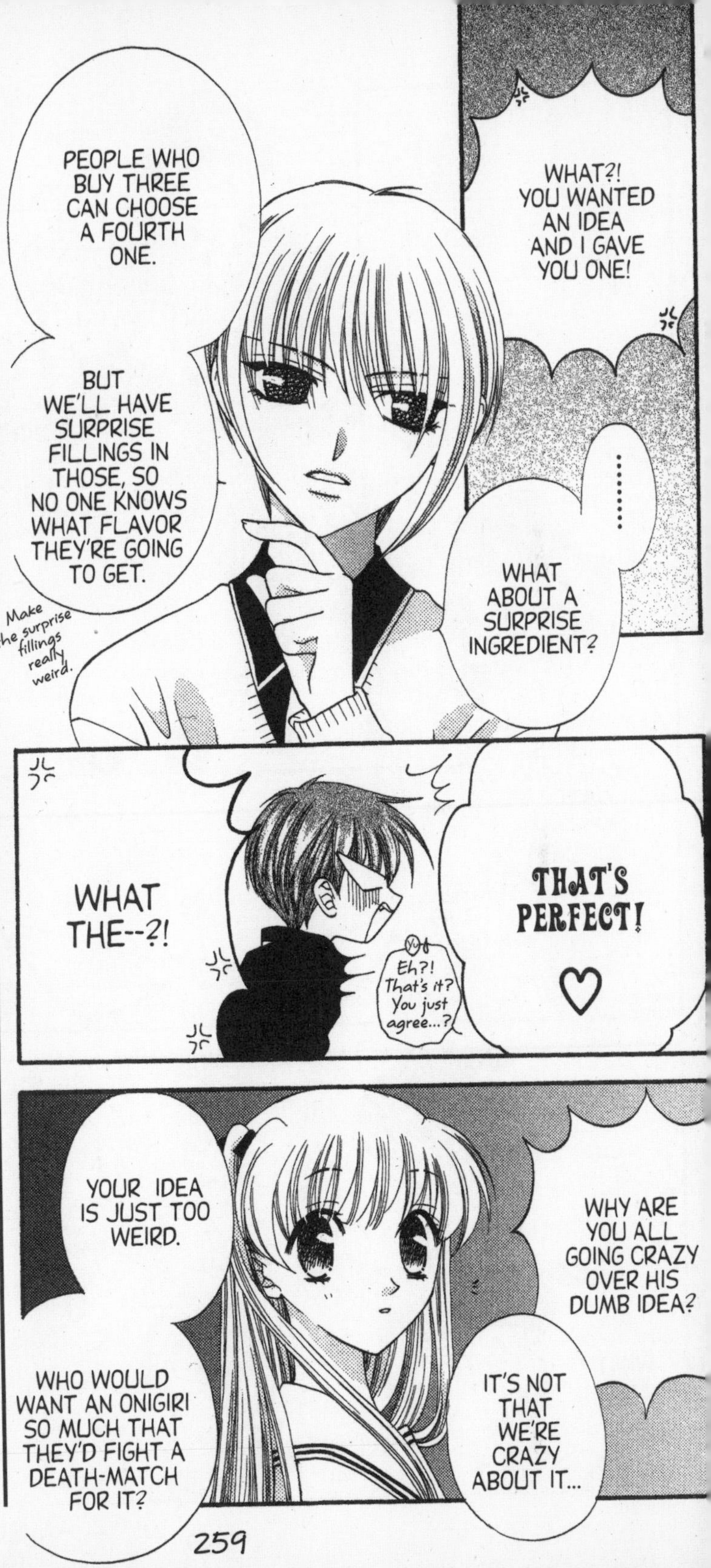
WHAT?! YOU WANTED AN IDEA AND I GAVE YOU ONE!
......
WHAT ABOUT A SURPRISE INGREDIENT?
PEOPLE WHO BUY THREE CAN CHOOSE A FOURTH ONE.
BUT WE'LL HAVE SURPRISE FILLINGS IN THOSE, SO NO ONE KNOWS WHAT FLAVOR THEY'RE GOING TO GET.
Make the surprise fillings really weird.
THAT'S PERFECT! ♡
Eh?! That's it? You just agree...?
WHAT THE--?!
WHY ARE YOU ALL GOING CRAZY OVER HIS DUMB IDEA?
IT'S NOT THAT WE'RE CRAZY ABOUT IT...
YOUR IDEA IS JUST TOO WEIRD.
WHO WOULD WANT AN ONIGIRI SO MUCH THAT THEY'D FIGHT A DEATH-MATCH FOR IT?

Fruits Basket 2 Part 2:

I'll start from the beginning. This is the story of a video game. That's right, Final Fantasy 8. This has spoilers in it, so if you are in the middle the game or plan on playing it, I recommend that you not read this. Okay? Here I go. Let's go back one game first. I played FF7, and beat it normally. (Oy.) I think, somehow, it was special. I've been playing FF since number 4, but the first time I broke down crying was 7. I had never cried about a game before. It still makes me cry. Whenever I hear Aeris's theme, I cry. And of course I think it's stupid to keep crying, but still. Such sadness and pain and helplessness—why couldn't I have done more? To be continued...

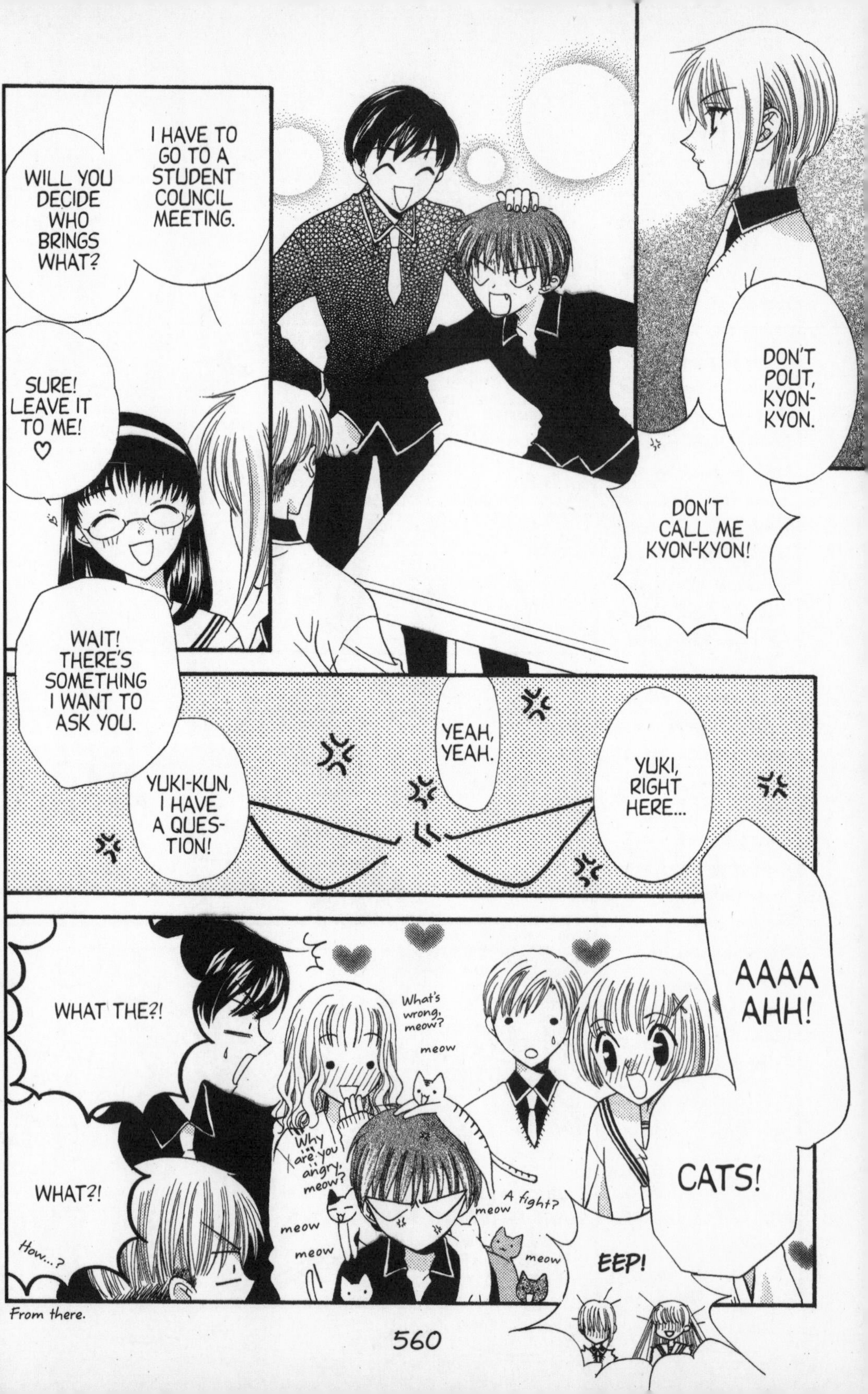
DON'T POUT, KYON-KYON.
DON'T CALL ME KYON-KYON!
I HAVE TO GO TO A STUDENT COUNCIL MEETING.
WILL YOU DECIDE WHO BRINGS WHAT?
SURE! LEAVE IT TO ME! ♡
WAIT! THERE'S SOMETHING I WANT TO ASK YOU.
YUKI, RIGHT HERE...
YEAH, YEAH.
YUKI-KUN, I HAVE A QUESTION!
AAAA AHH!
CATS!
EEP!
What's wrong, meow?
meow
A fight?
meow
meow
Why are you angry, meow?
meow
meow
WHAT THE?!
WHAT?!
How...?
From there.

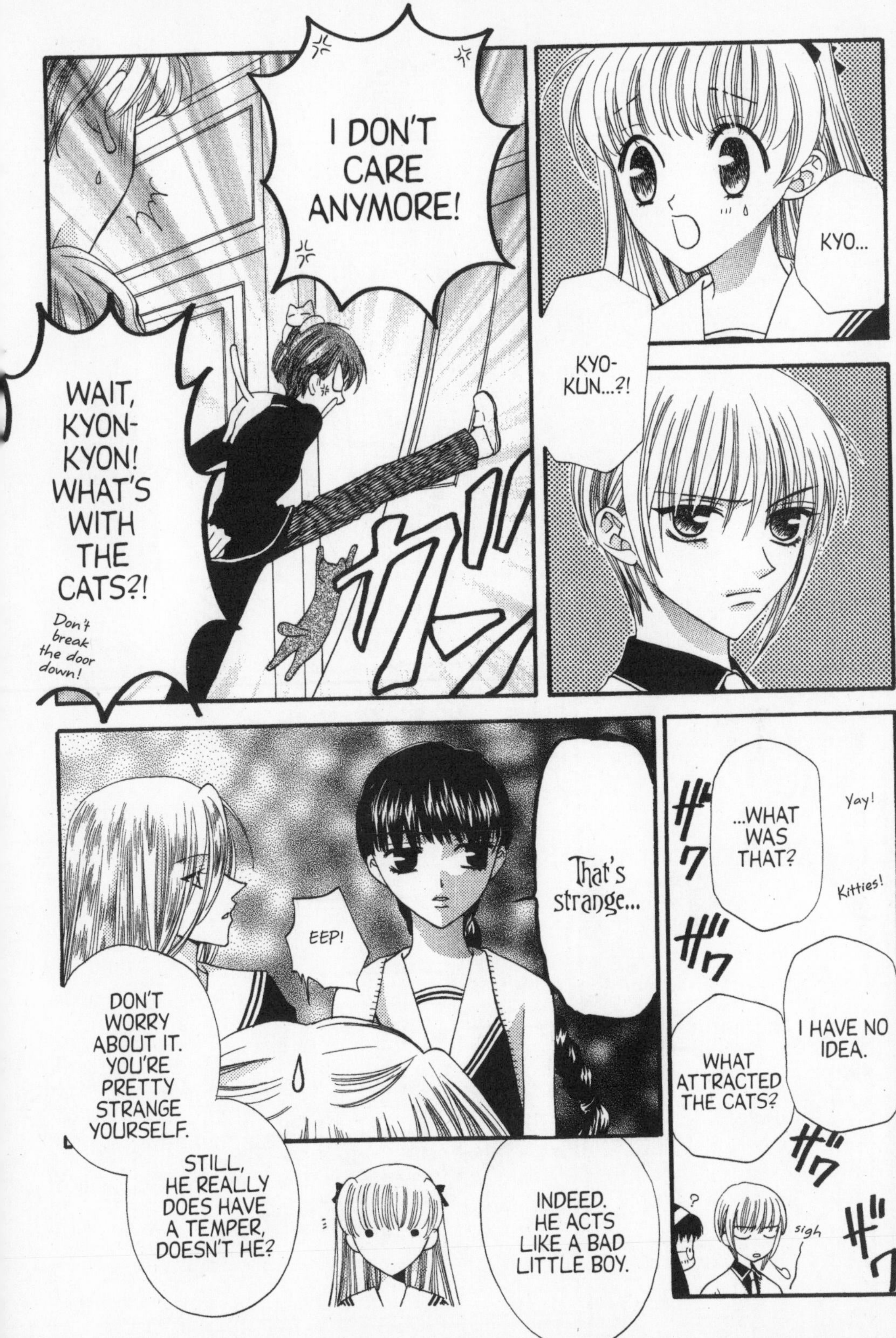
KYO...
KYO-KUN...?!
I DON'T CARE ANYMORE!
WAIT, KYON-KYON! WHAT'S WITH THE CATS?!
Don't break the door down!
ガン
...WHAT WAS THAT?
Yay!
Kitties!
ザワ
ザワ
I HAVE NO IDEA.
WHAT ATTRACTED THE CATS?
ザワ
ザワ
sigh
That's strange...
EEP!
DON'T WORRY ABOUT IT. YOU'RE PRETTY STRANGE YOURSELF.
STILL, HE REALLY DOES HAVE A TEMPER, DOESN'T HE?
INDEED. HE ACTS LIKE A BAD LITTLE BOY.

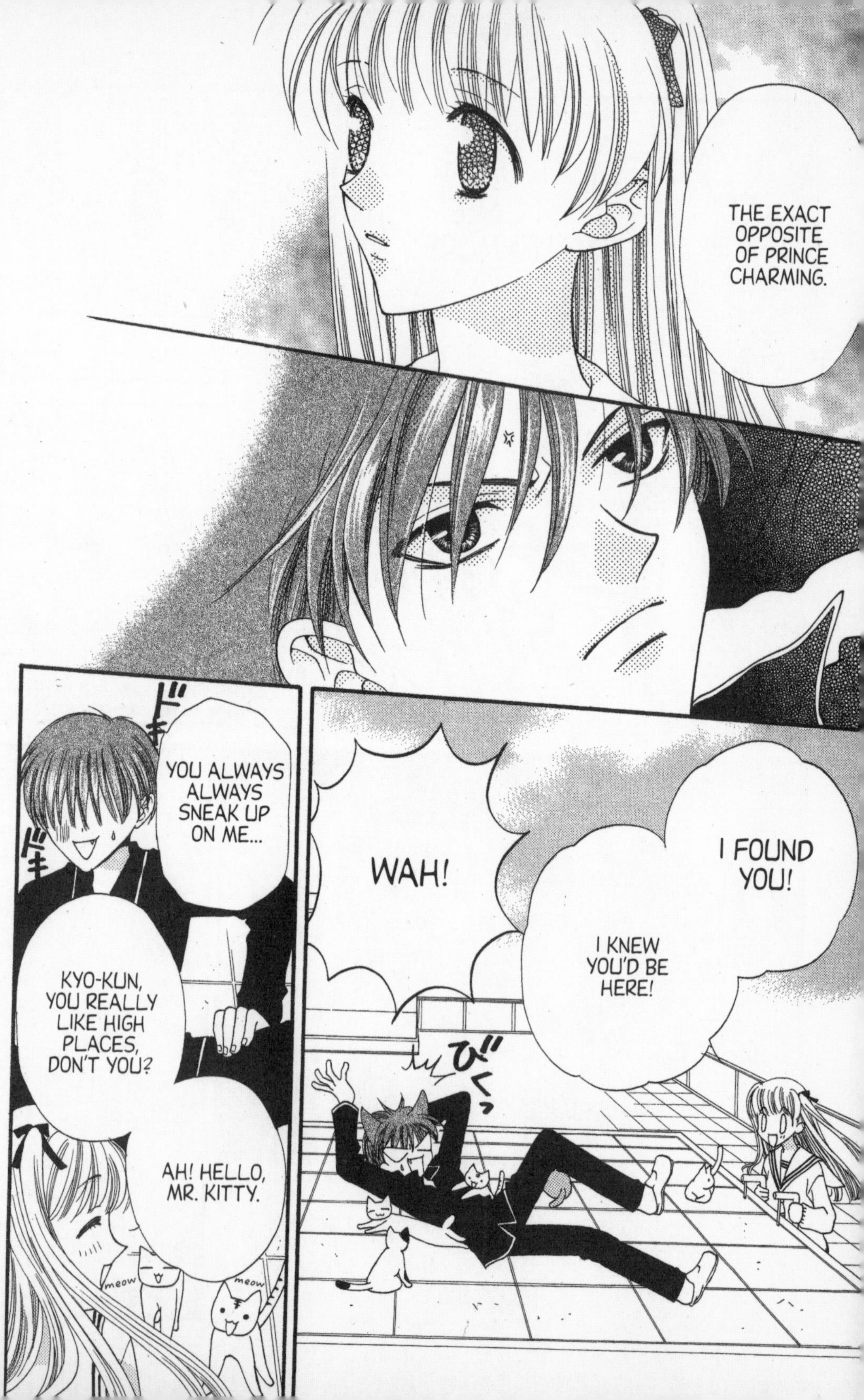
THE EXACT OPPOSITE OF PRINCE CHARMING.
I FOUND YOU!
I KNEW YOU'D BE HERE!
WAH!
YOU ALWAYS ALWAYS SNEAK UP ON ME...
KYO-KUN, YOU REALLY LIKE HIGH PLACES, DON'T YOU?
AH! HELLO, MR. KITTY.
meow
meow

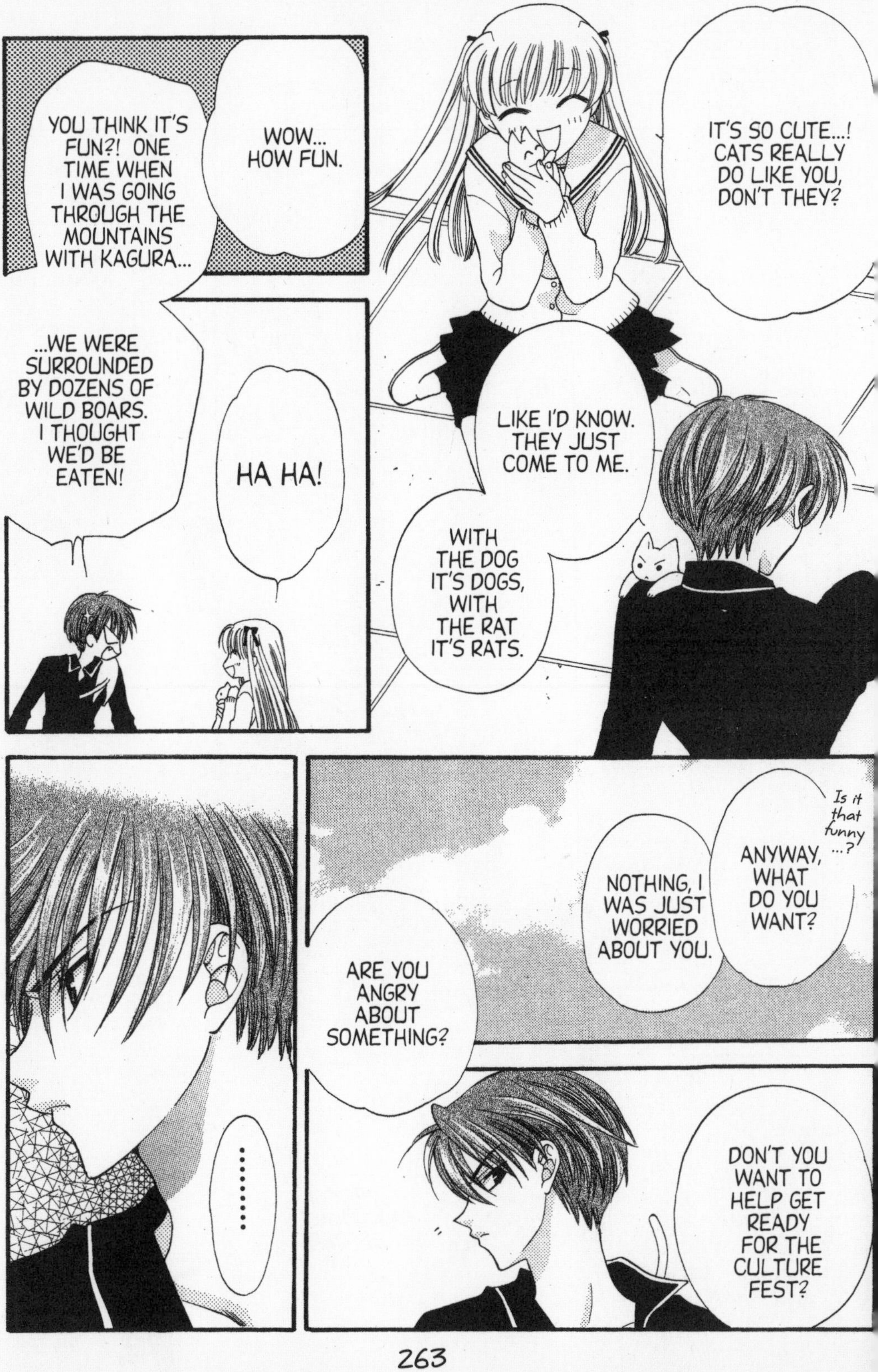
IT'S SO CUTE...! CATS REALLY DO LIKE YOU, DON'T THEY?
LIKE I'D KNOW. THEY JUST COME TO ME.
WITH THE DOG IT'S DOGS, WITH THE RAT IT'S RATS.
WOW... HOW FUN.
YOU THINK IT'S FUN?! ONE TIME WHEN I WAS GOING THROUGH THE MOUNTAINS WITH KAGURA...
...WE WERE SURROUNDED BY DOZENS OF WILD BOARS. I THOUGHT WE'D BE EATEN!
HA HA!
Is it that funny ...?
ANYWAY, WHAT DO YOU WANT?
NOTHING, I WAS JUST WORRIED ABOUT YOU.
ARE YOU ANGRY ABOUT SOMETHING?
DON'T YOU WANT TO HELP GET READY FOR THE CULTURE FEST?
....

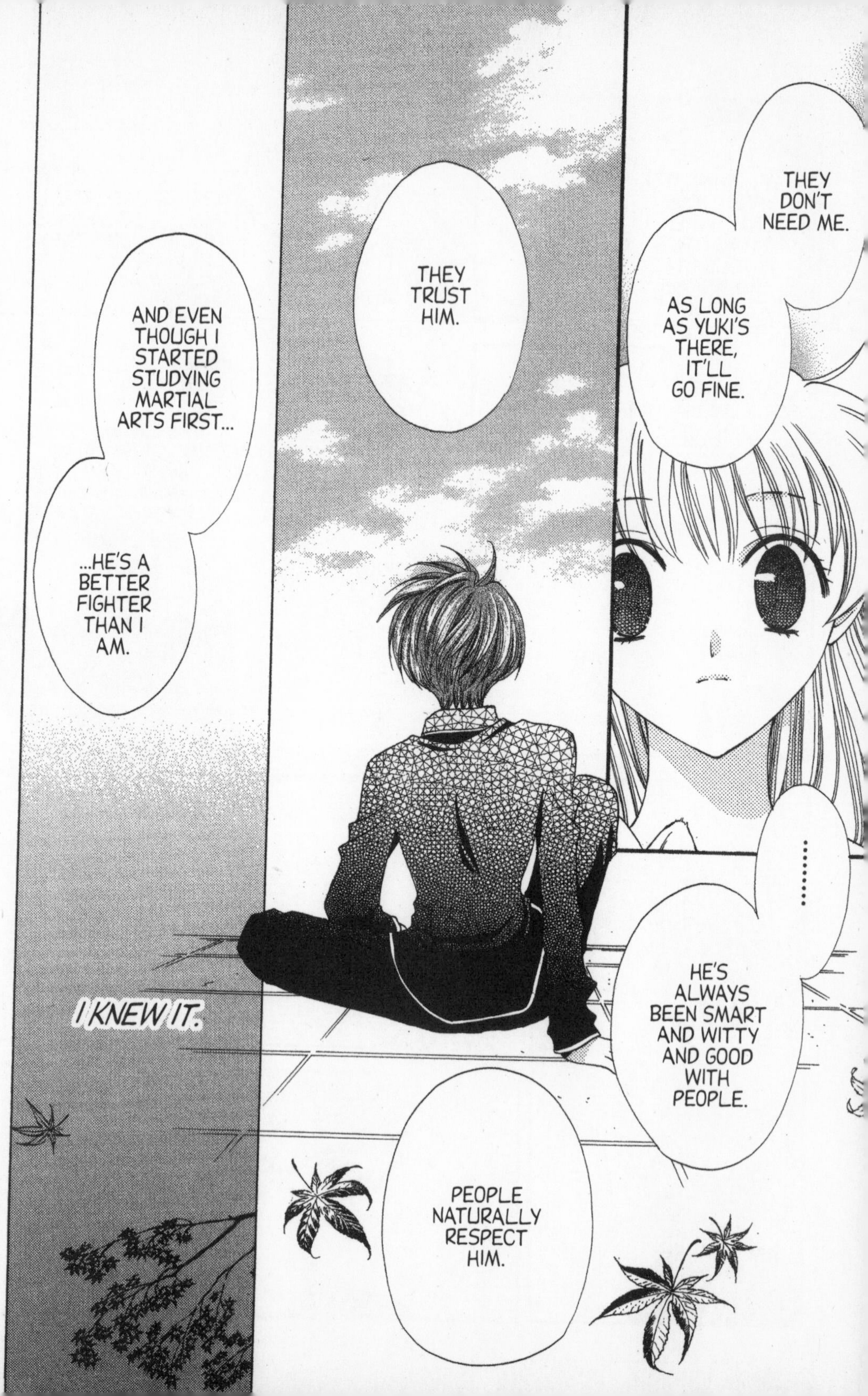
THEY DON'T NEED ME.
AS LONG AS YUKI'S THERE, IT'LL GO FINE.
......
HE'S ALWAYS BEEN SMART AND WITTY AND GOOD WITH PEOPLE.
PEOPLE NATURALLY RESPECT HIM.
THEY TRUST HIM.
AND EVEN THOUGH I STARTED STUDYING MARTIAL ARTS FIRST...
...HE'S A BETTER FIGHTER THAN I AM.
I KNEW IT.

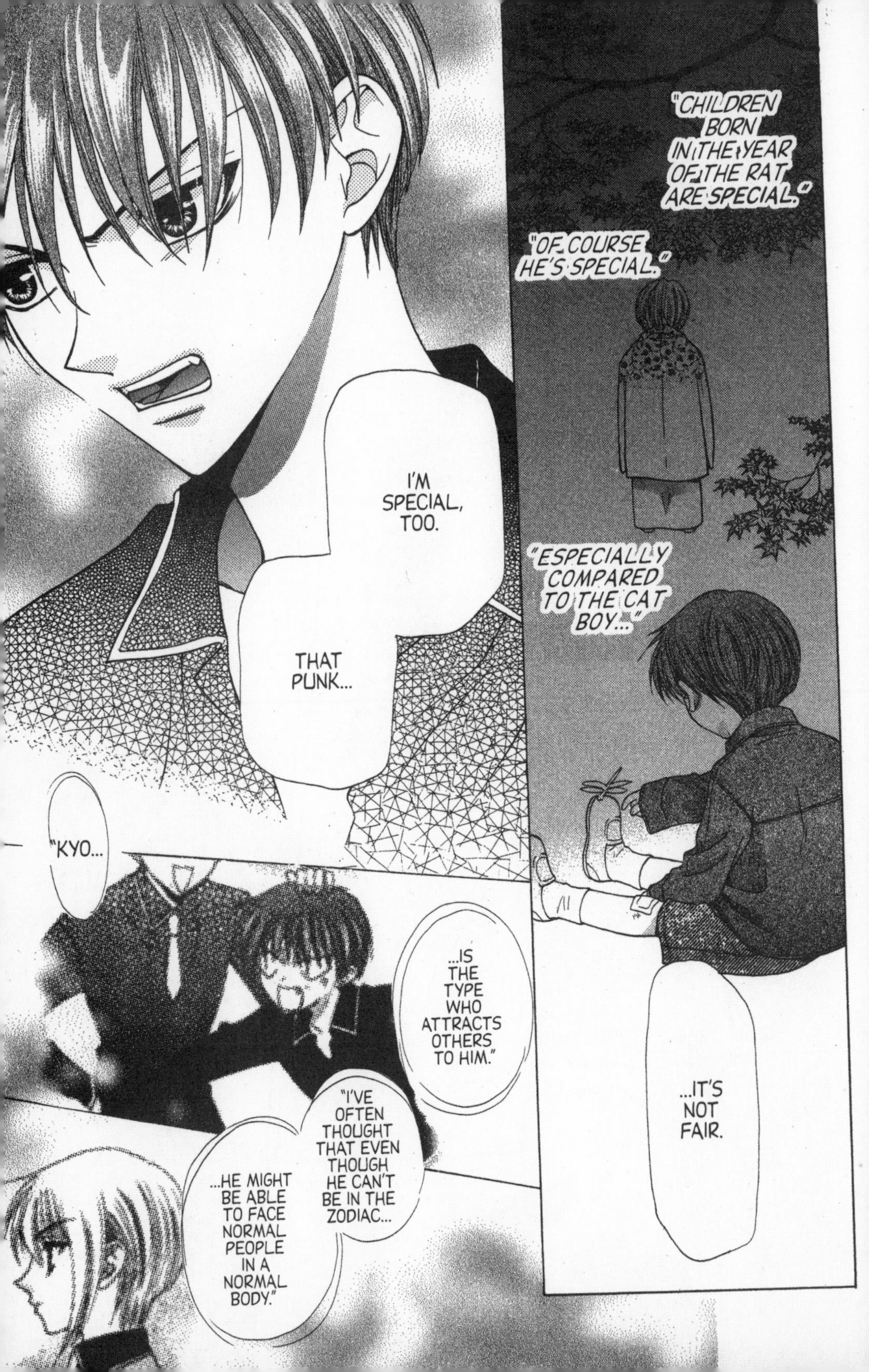
"CHILDREN BORN IN THE YEAR OF THE RAT ARE SPECIAL."
"OF COURSE HE'S SPECIAL."
"ESPECIALLY COMPARED TO THE CAT BOY..."
...IT'S NOT FAIR.
I'M SPECIAL, TOO.
THAT PUNK...
"KYO...
...IS THE TYPE WHO ATTRACTS OTHERS TO HIM."
"I'VE OFTEN THOUGHT THAT EVEN THOUGH HE CAN'T BE IN THE ZODIAC...
...HE MIGHT BE ABLE TO FACE NORMAL PEOPLE IN A NORMAL BODY."

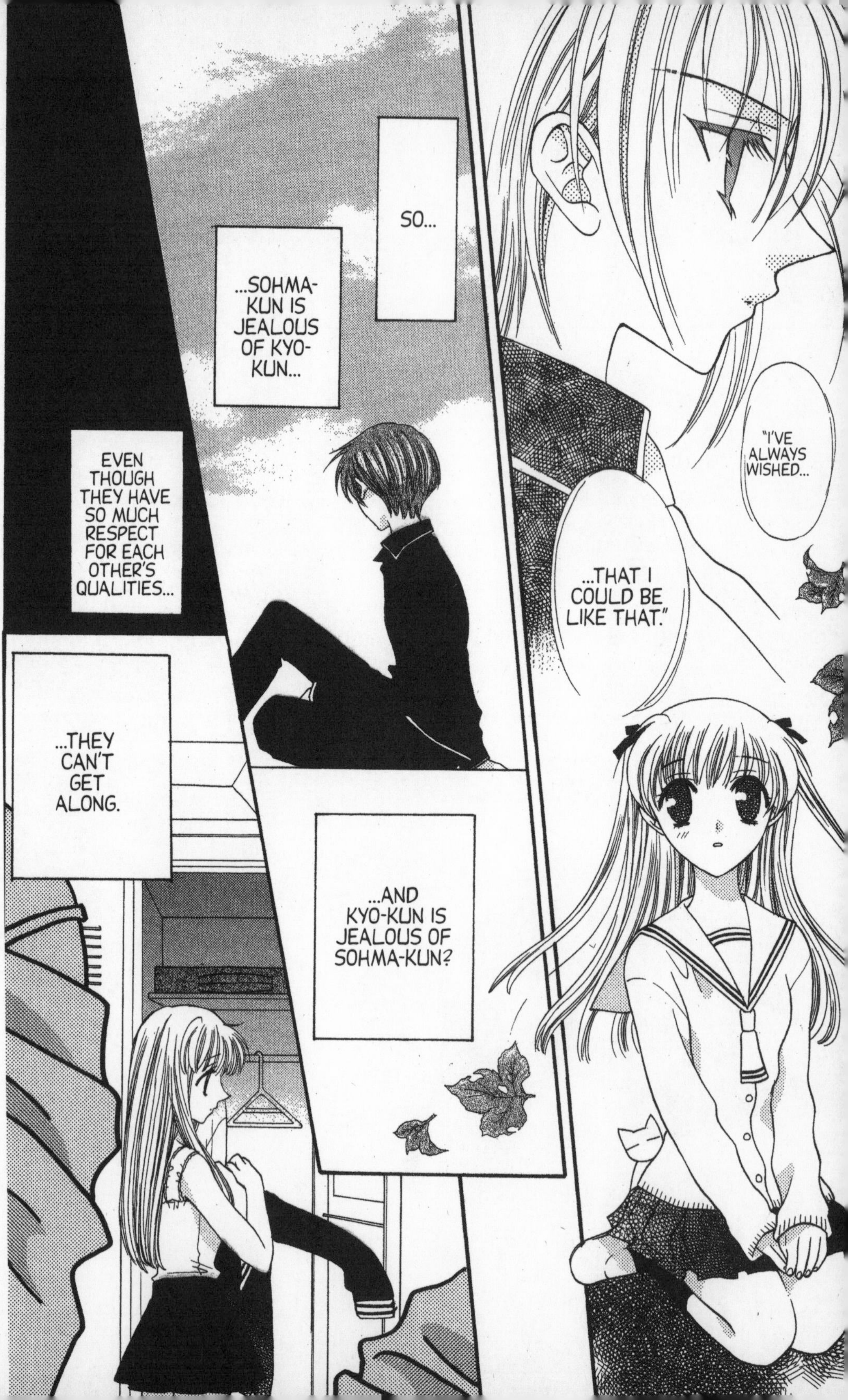
"I'VE ALWAYS WISHED...
...THAT I COULD BE LIKE THAT."
SO...
...SOHMA-KUN IS JEALOUS OF KYO-KUN...
...AND KYO-KUN IS JEALOUS OF SOHMA-KUN?
EVEN THOUGH THEY HAVE SO MUCH RESPECT FOR EACH OTHER'S QUALITIES...
...THEY CAN'T GET ALONG.

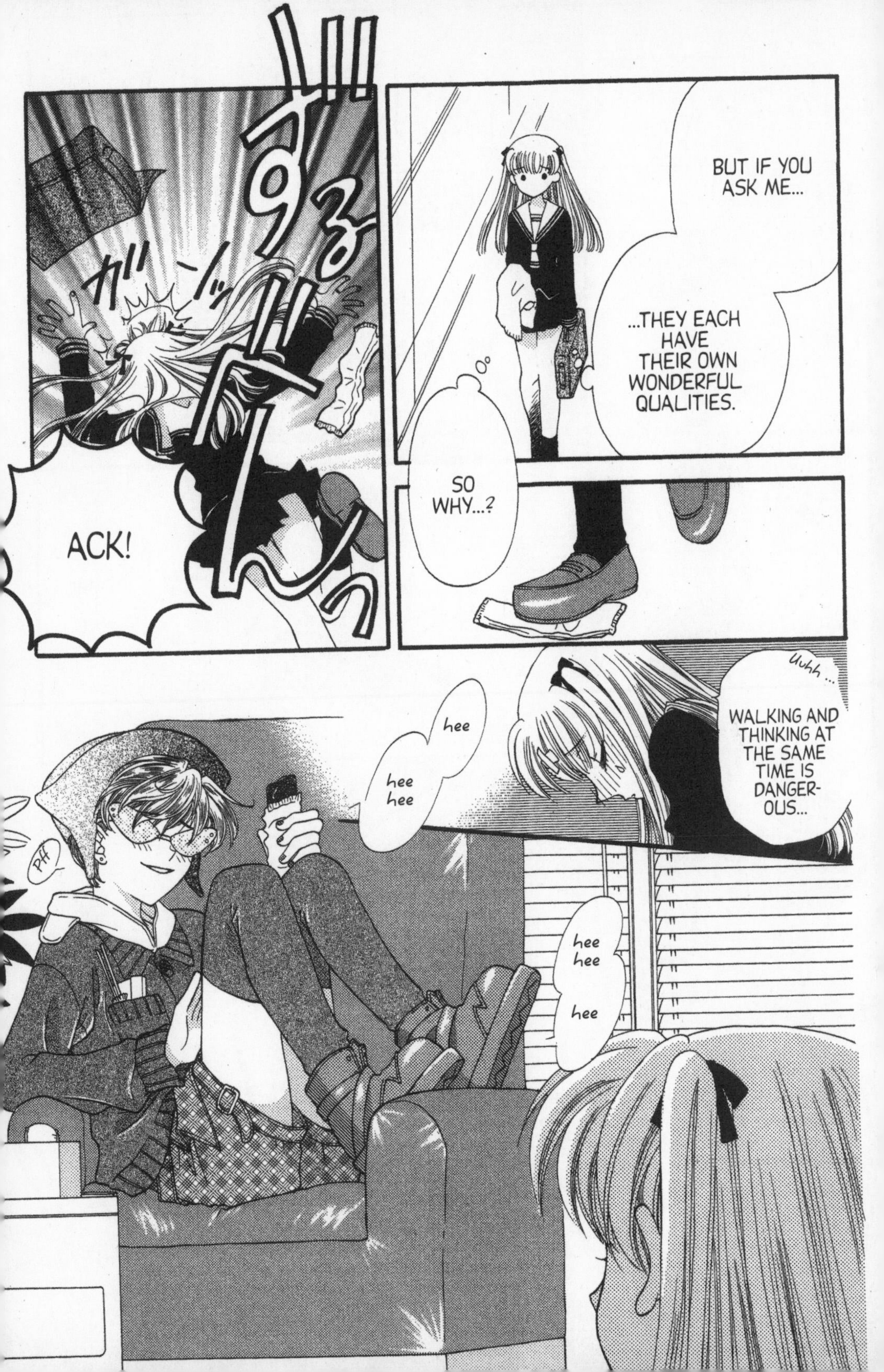
BUT IF YOU ASK ME...
...THEY EACH HAVE THEIR OWN WONDERFUL QUALITIES.
SO WHY...?
ACK!
Uuhh...
WALKING AND THINKING AT THE SAME TIME IS DANGER-OUS...
hee
hee hee
hee hee
hee

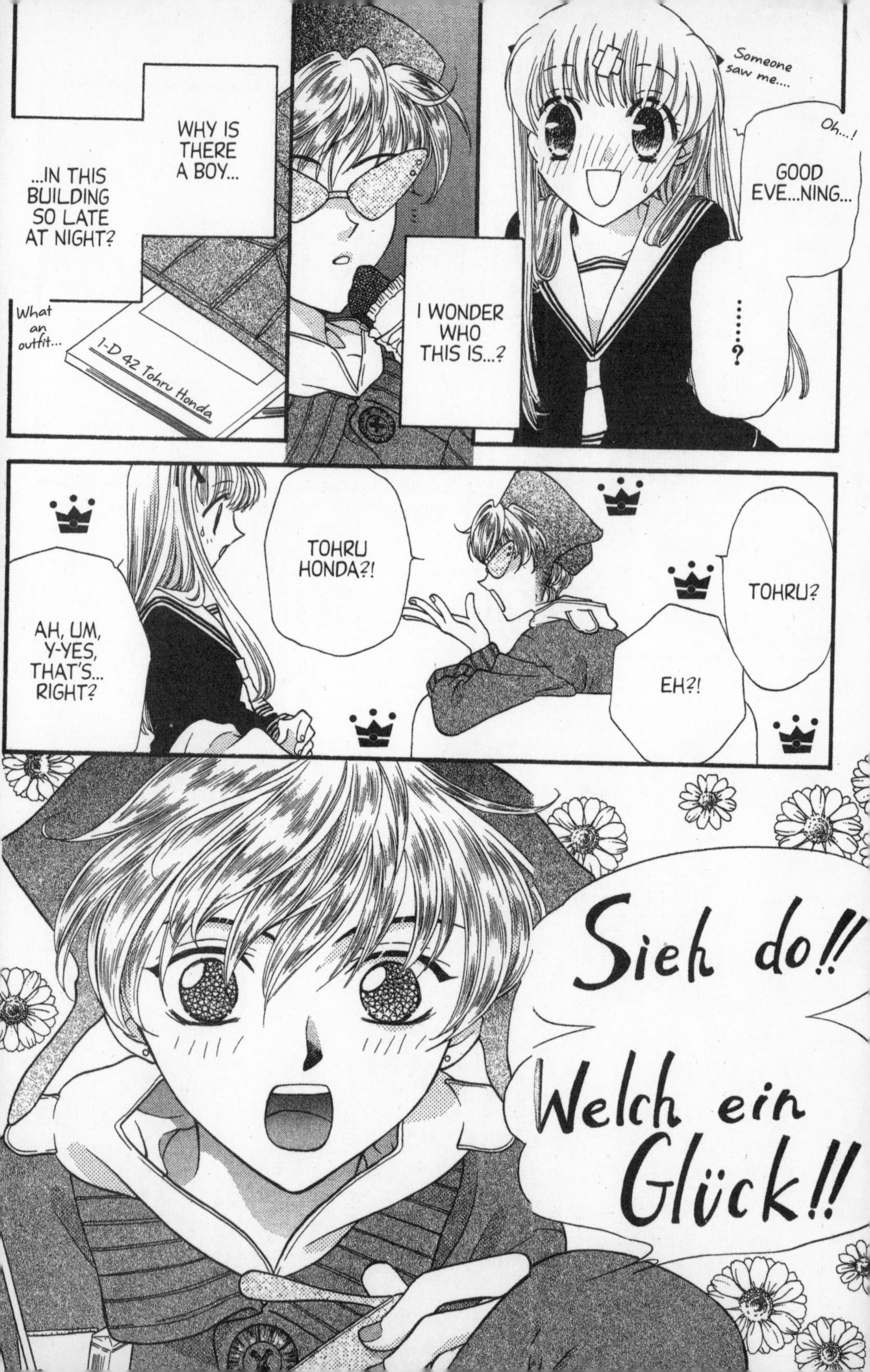
Someone saw me....
Oh...!
GOOD EVE...NING...
......?
I WONDER WHO THIS IS...?
WHY IS THERE A BOY...
...IN THIS BUILDING SO LATE AT NIGHT?
What an outfit...
1-D 42 Tohru Honda
TOHRU?
EH?!
TOHRU HONDA?!
AH, UM, Y-YES, THAT'S... RIGHT?
Sieh do!!
Welch ein Glück!!

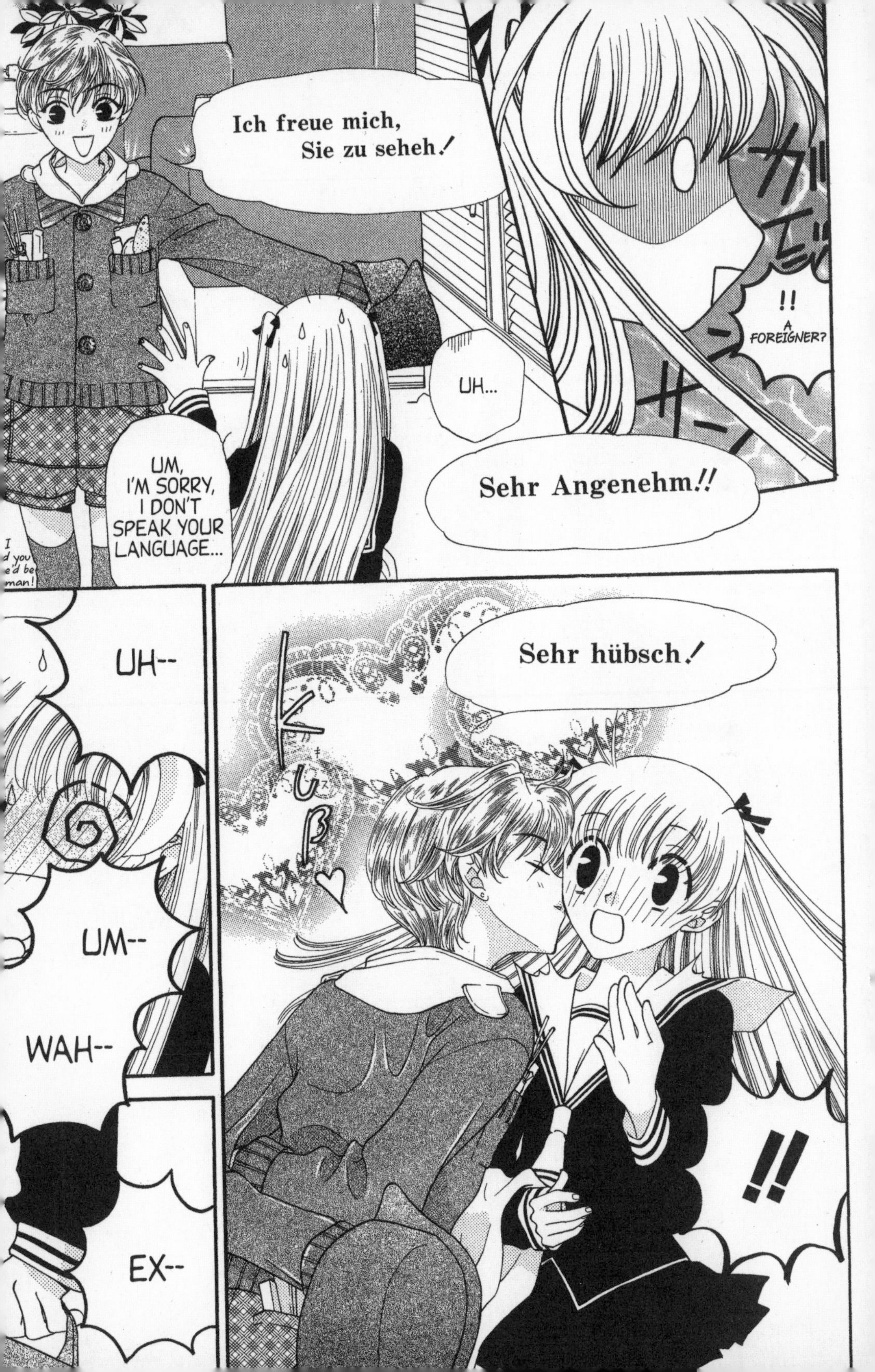
!!
A FOREIGNER?
Ich freue mich, Sie zu seheh!
UH...
Sehr Angenehm!!
UM, I'M SORRY, I DON'T SPEAK YOUR LANGUAGE...
Sehr hübsch!
!!
UH--
UM--
WAH--
EX--

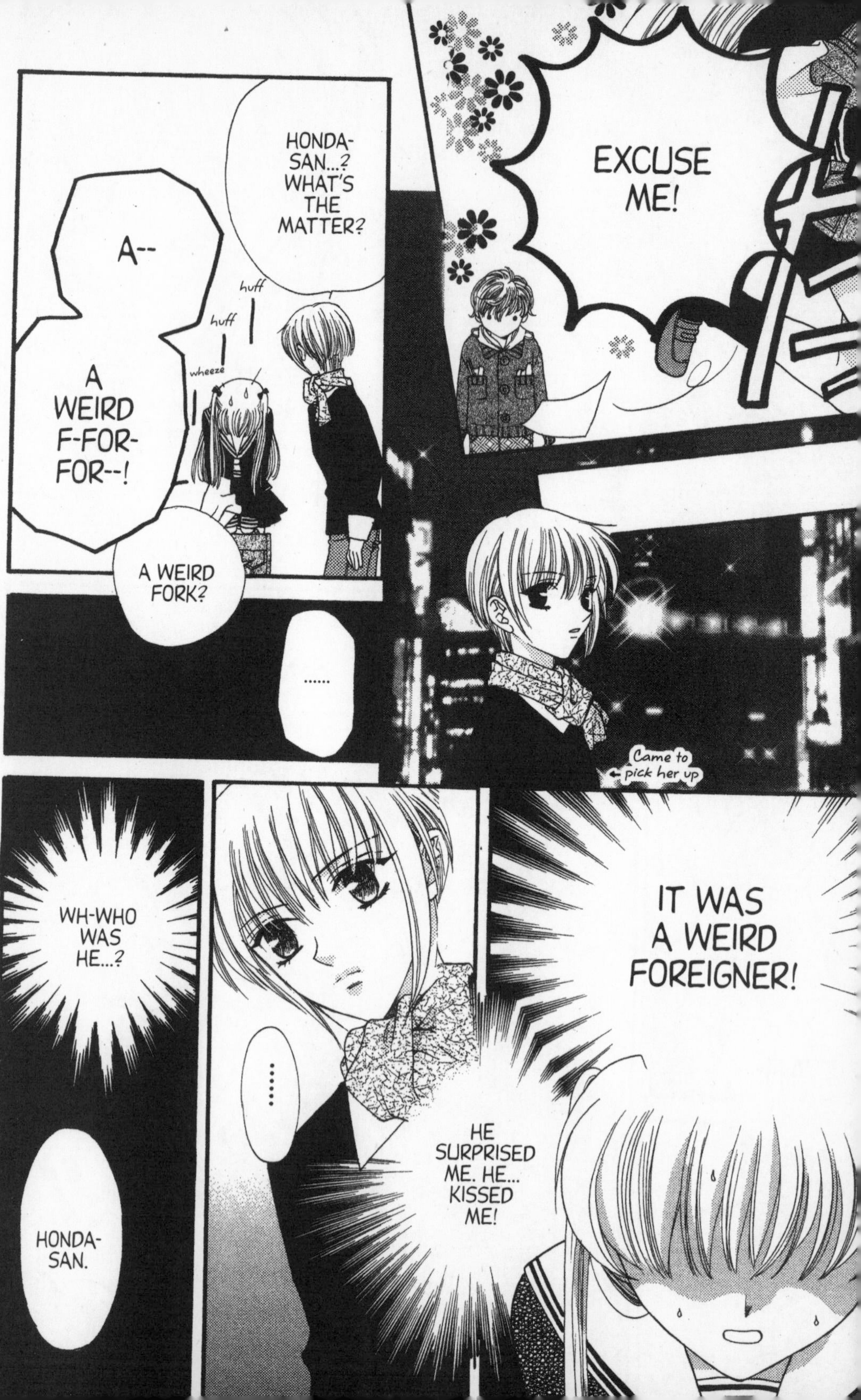
EXCUSE ME!
HONDA-SAN...? WHAT'S THE MATTER?
huff
huff
wheeze
A--
A WEIRD F-FOR-FOR--!
A WEIRD FORK?
Came to pick her up
......
IT WAS A WEIRD FOREIGNER!
HE SURPRISED ME. HE... KISSED ME!
......
WH-WHO WAS HE...?
HONDA-SAN.

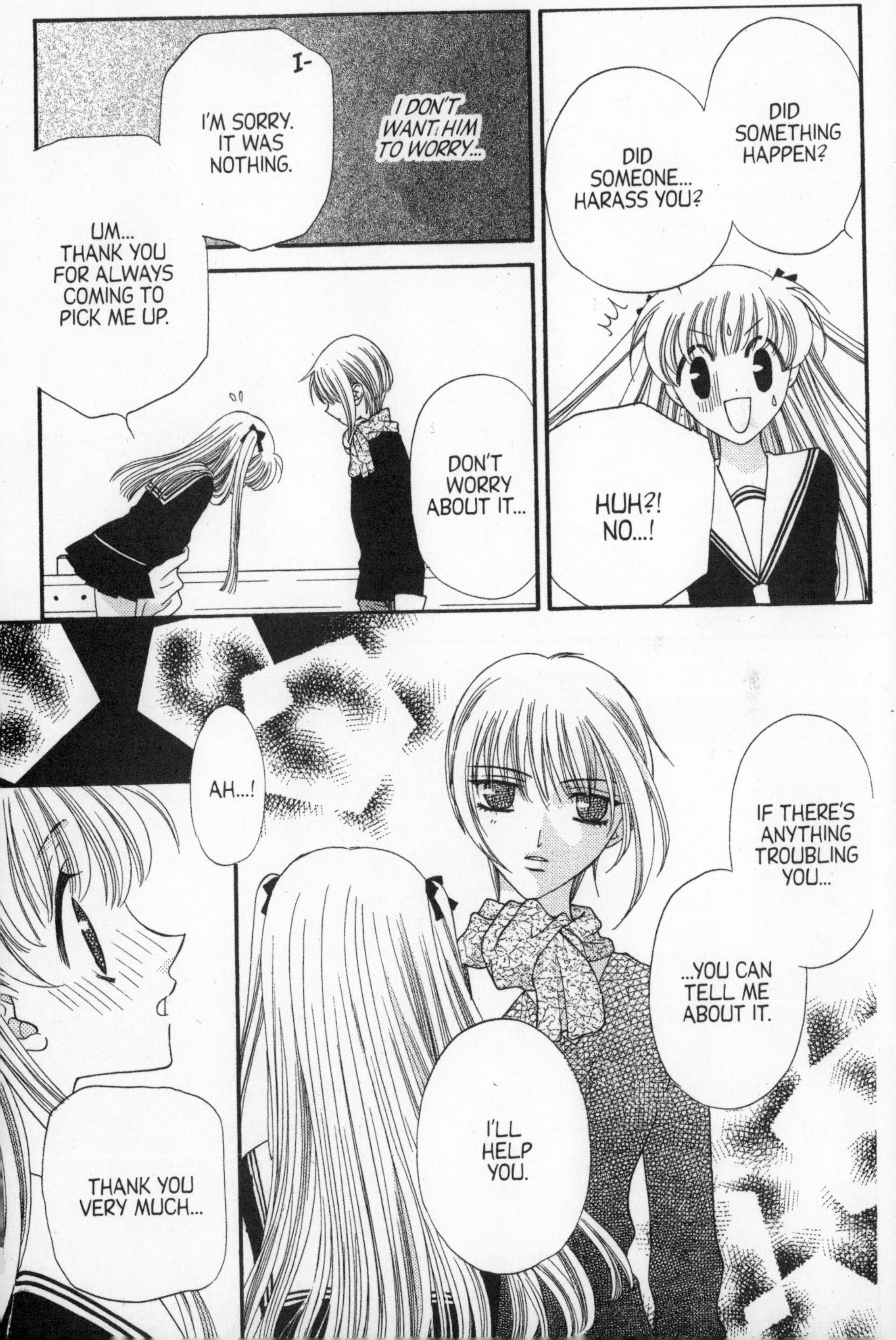
DID SOMETHING HAPPEN?
DID SOMEONE... HARASS YOU?
HUH?! NO...!
I-
I DON'T WANT HIM TO WORRY...
I'M SORRY. IT WAS NOTHING.
UM... THANK YOU FOR ALWAYS COMING TO PICK ME UP.
DON'T WORRY ABOUT IT...
IF THERE'S ANYTHING TROUBLING YOU...
...YOU CAN TELL ME ABOUT IT.
I'LL HELP YOU.
AH...!
THANK YOU VERY MUCH...

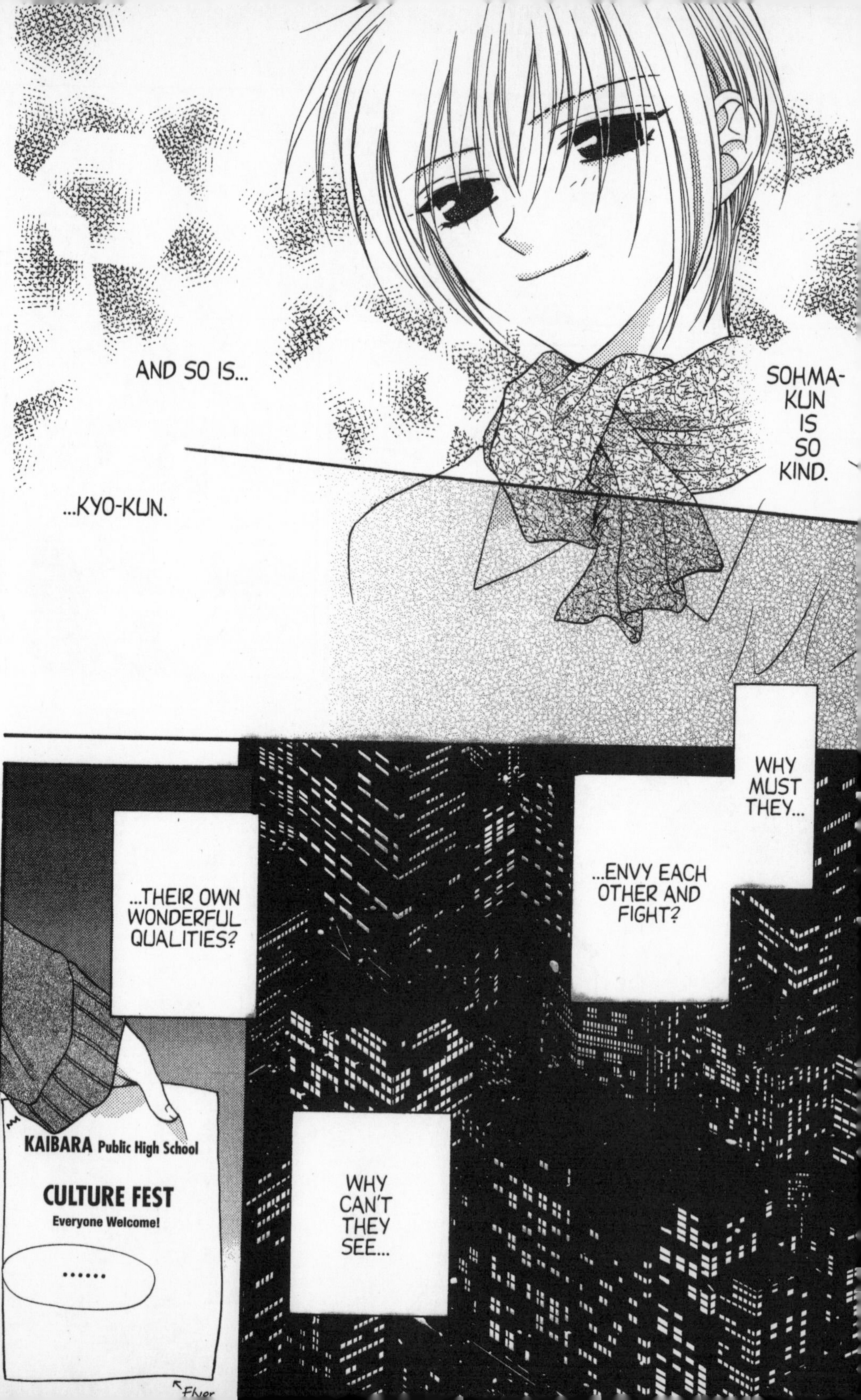
SOHMA-KUN IS SO KIND.
AND SO IS...
...KYO-KUN.
WHY MUST THEY...
...ENVY EACH OTHER AND FIGHT?
WHY CAN'T THEY SEE...
...THEIR OWN WONDERFUL QUALITIES?
KAIBARA Public High School
CULTURE FEST
Everyone Welcome!
......
Flyer

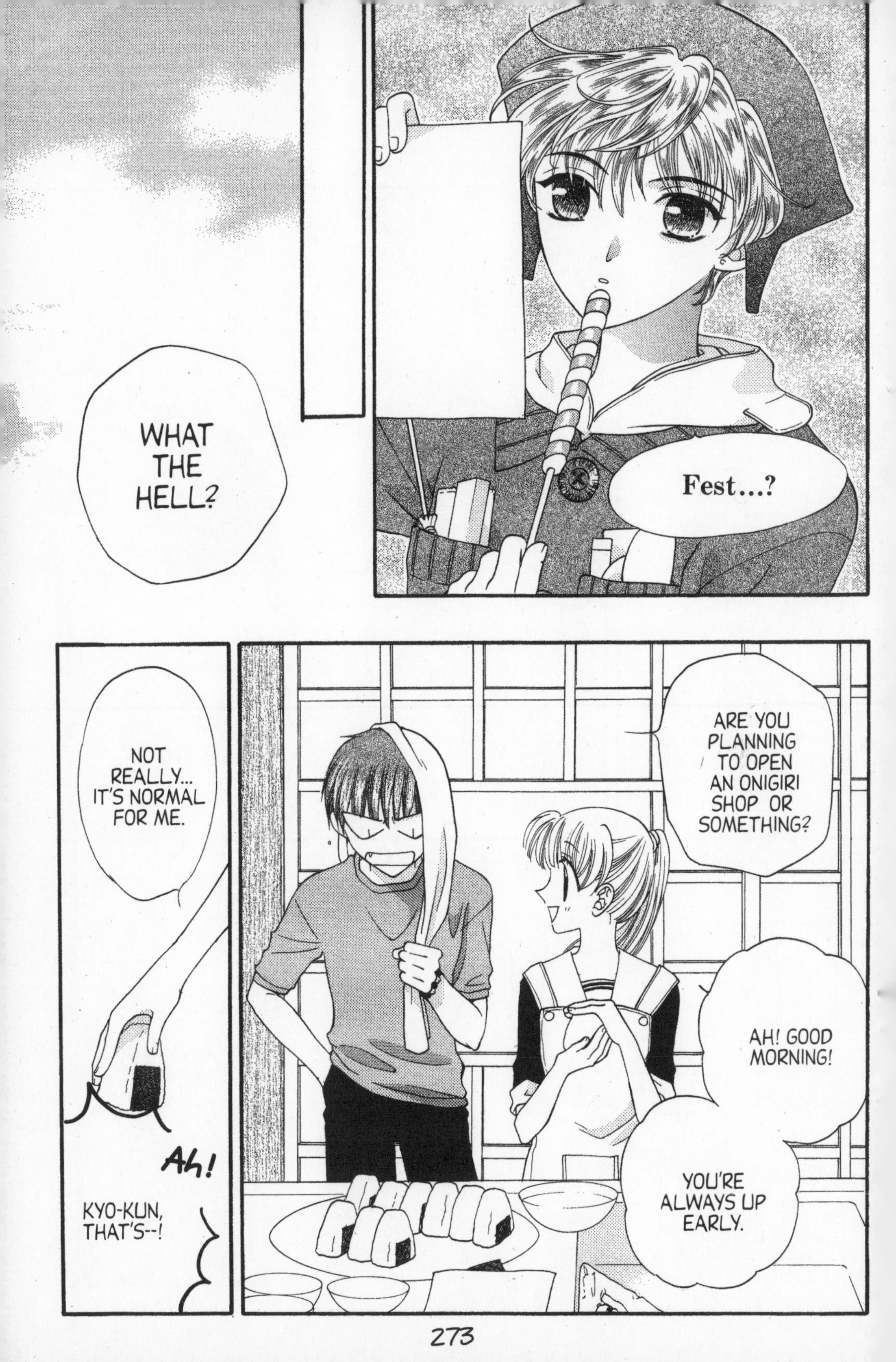
Fest...?
WHAT THE HELL?
ARE YOU PLANNING TO OPEN AN ONIGIRI SHOP OR SOMETHING?
AH! GOOD MORNING!
YOU'RE ALWAYS UP EARLY.
NOT REALLY... IT'S NORMAL FOR ME.
Ah!
KYO-KUN, THAT'S--!

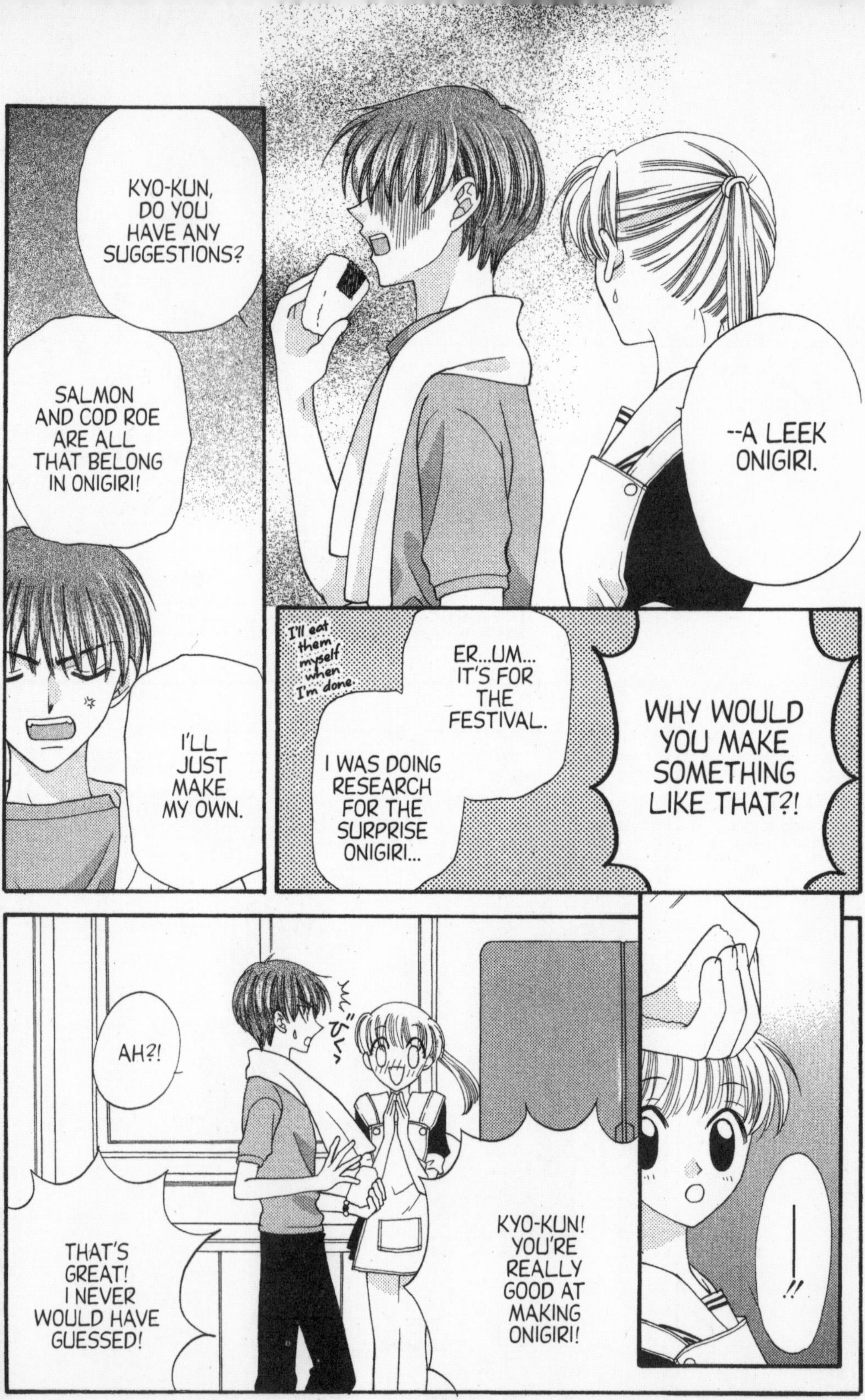
--A LEEK ONIGIRI.
WHY WOULD YOU MAKE SOMETHING LIKE THAT?!
ER...UM... IT'S FOR THE FESTIVAL.
I'll eat them myself when I'm done.
I WAS DOING RESEARCH FOR THE SURPRISE ONIGIRI...
KYO-KUN, DO YOU HAVE ANY SUGGESTIONS?
SALMON AND COD ROE ARE ALL THAT BELONG IN ONIGIRI!
I'LL JUST MAKE MY OWN.
—!!
KYO-KUN! YOU'RE REALLY GOOD AT MAKING ONIGIRI!
THAT'S GREAT! I NEVER WOULD HAVE GUESSED!
AH?!

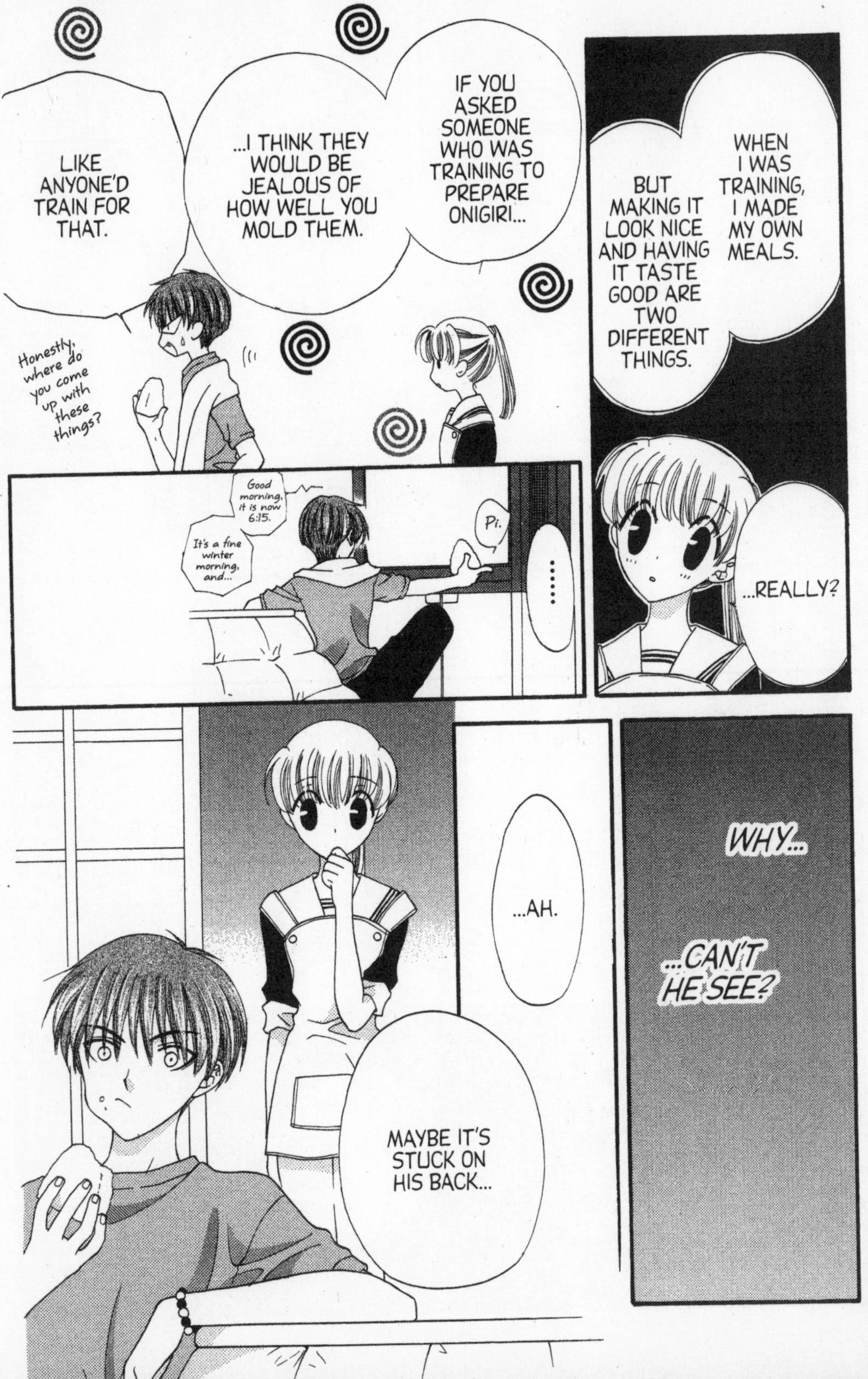
WHEN I WAS TRAINING, I MADE MY OWN MEALS.
BUT MAKING IT LOOK NICE AND HAVING IT TASTE GOOD ARE TWO DIFFERENT THINGS.
IF YOU ASKED SOMEONE WHO WAS TRAINING TO PREPARE ONIGIRI...
...I THINK THEY WOULD BE JEALOUS OF HOW WELL YOU MOLD THEM.
LIKE ANYONE'D TRAIN FOR THAT.
Honestly, where do you come up with these things?
...REALLY?
......
Pi.
Good morning, it is now 6:15.
It's a fine winter morning, and...
WHY...
...CAN'T HE SEE?
...AH.
MAYBE IT'S STUCK ON HIS BACK...

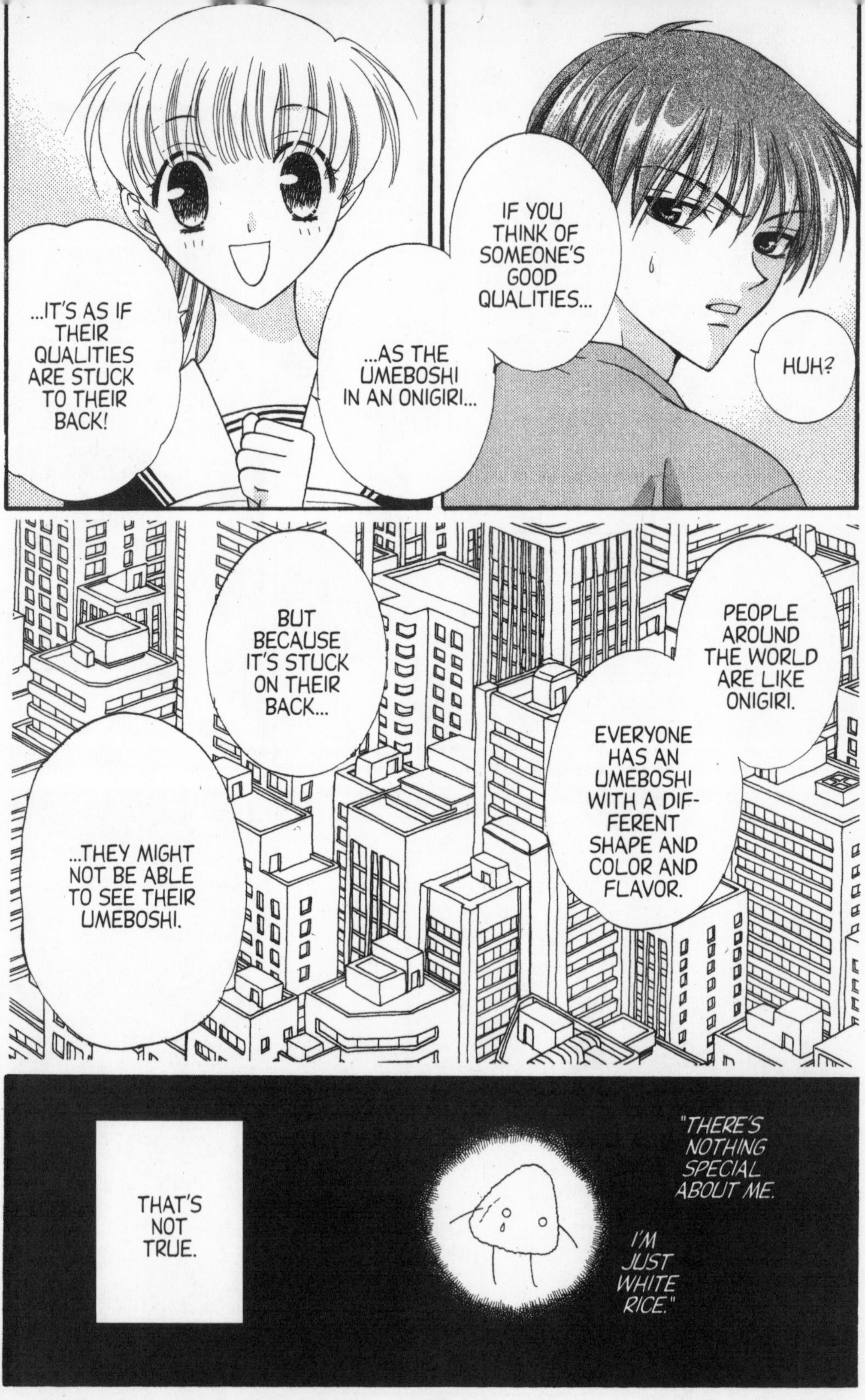
HUH?
IF YOU THINK OF SOMEONE'S GOOD QUALITIES...
...AS THE UMEBOSHI IN AN ONIGIRI...
...IT'S AS IF THEIR QUALITIES ARE STUCK TO THEIR BACK!
PEOPLE AROUND THE WORLD ARE LIKE ONIGIRI.
EVERYONE HAS AN UMEBOSHI WITH A DIF-FERENT SHAPE AND COLOR AND FLAVOR.
BUT BECAUSE IT'S STUCK ON THEIR BACK...
...THEY MIGHT NOT BE ABLE TO SEE THEIR UMEBOSHI.
"THERE'S NOTHING SPECIAL ABOUT ME.
I'M JUST WHITE RICE."
THAT'S NOT TRUE.

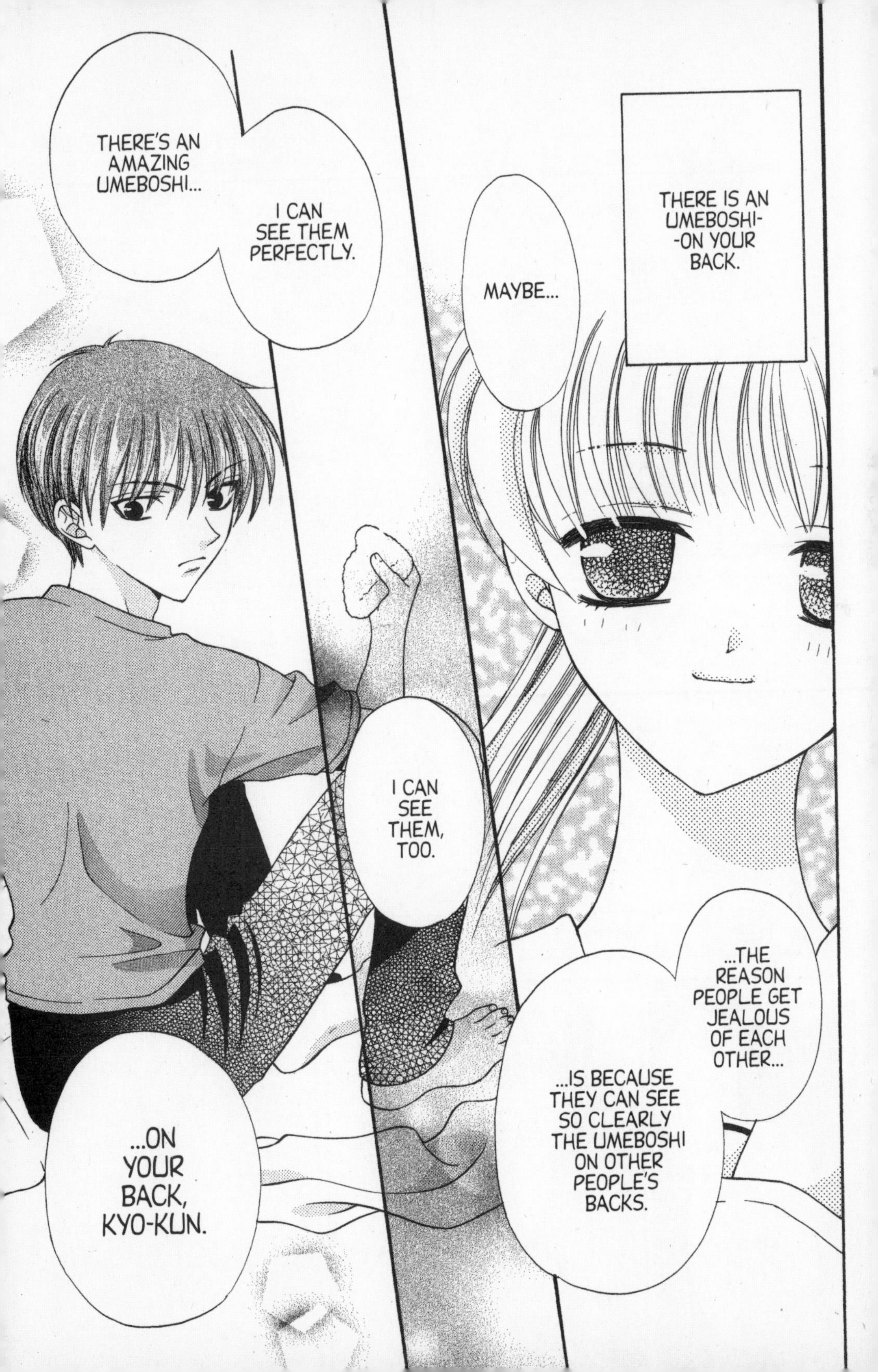
THERE IS AN UMEBOSHI- -ON YOUR BACK.
MAYBE...
...THE REASON PEOPLE GET JEALOUS OF EACH OTHER...
...IS BECAUSE THEY CAN SEE SO CLEARLY THE UMEBOSHI ON OTHER PEOPLE'S BACKS.
I CAN SEE THEM, TOO.
THERE'S AN AMAZING UMEBOSHI...
I CAN SEE THEM PERFECTLY.
...ON YOUR BACK, KYO-KUN.

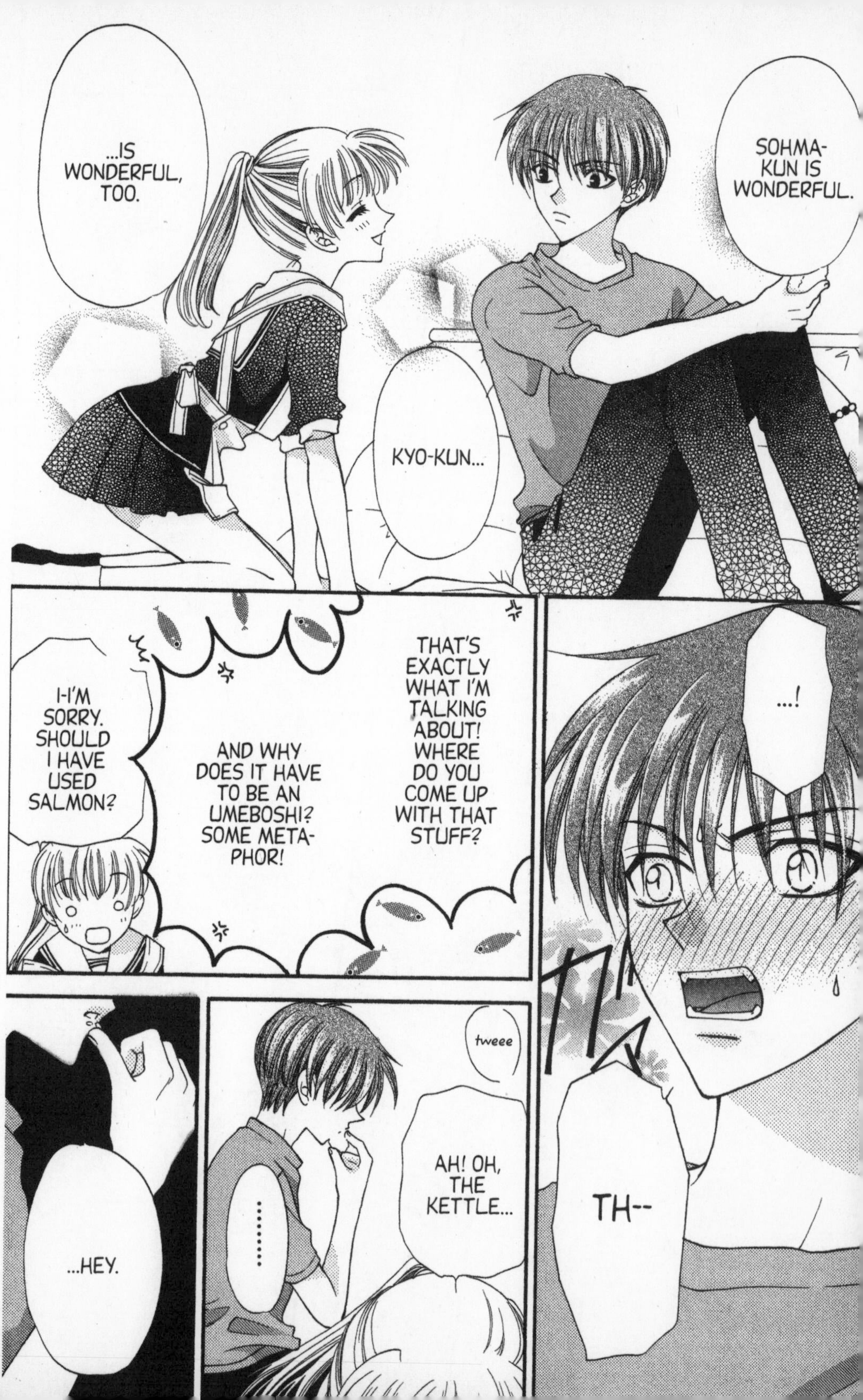
SOHMA-KUN IS WONDERFUL.
KYO-KUN...
...IS WONDERFUL, TOO.
...!
TH--
THAT'S EXACTLY WHAT I'M TALKING ABOUT! WHERE DO YOU COME UP WITH THAT STUFF?
AND WHY DOES IT HAVE TO BE AN UMEBOSHI? SOME METAPHOR!
I-I'M SORRY. SHOULD I HAVE USED SALMON?
tweee
AH! OH, THE KETTLE...
....
...HEY.

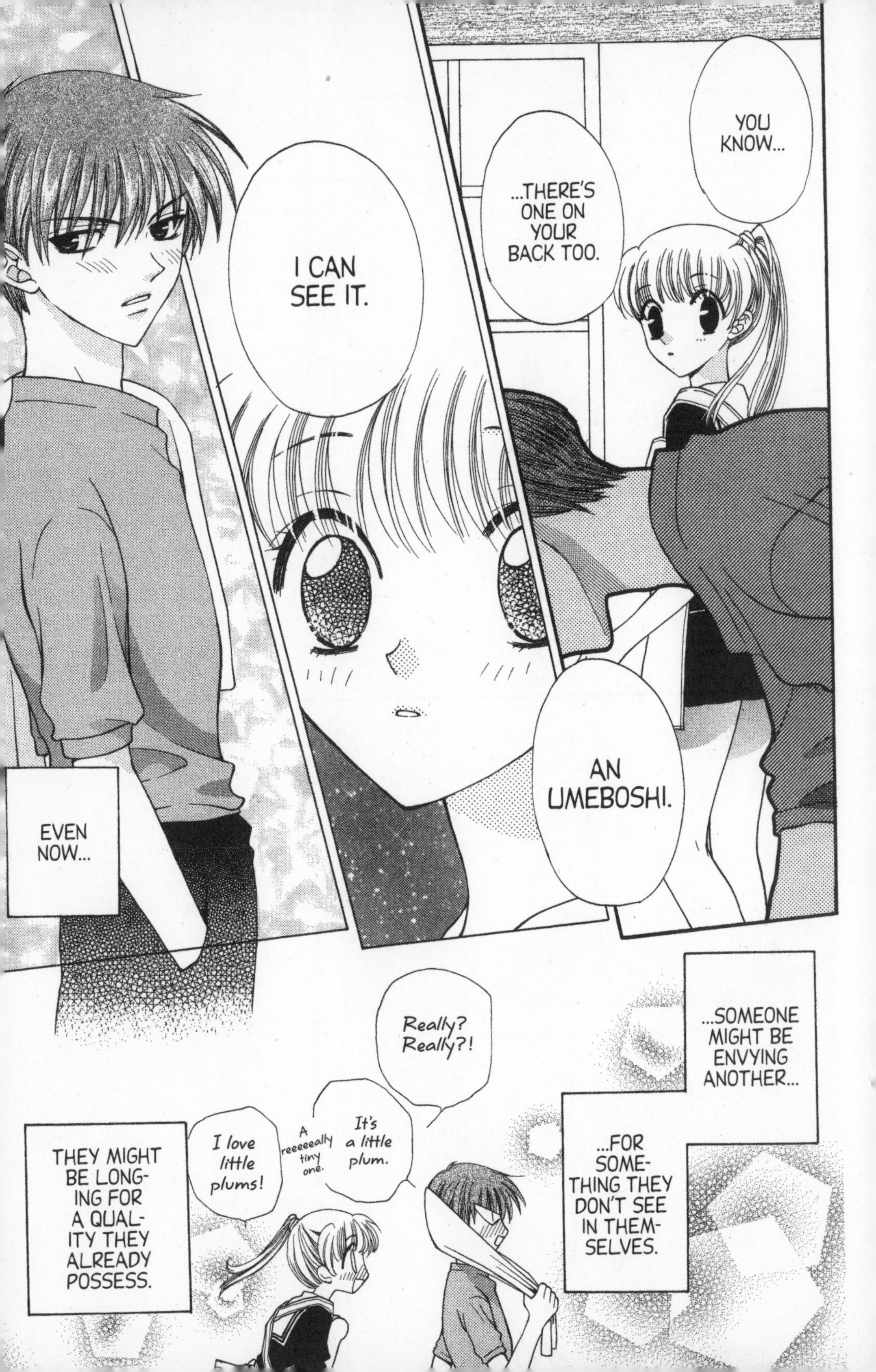
YOU KNOW...
...THERE'S ONE ON YOUR BACK TOO.
AN UMEBOSHI.
I CAN SEE IT.
EVEN NOW...
...SOMEONE MIGHT BE ENVYING ANOTHER...
...FOR SOME-THING THEY DON'T SEE IN THEM-SELVES.
Really? Really?!
It's a little plum.
A reeeeeeally tiny one.
I love little plums!
THEY MIGHT BE LONG-ING FOR A QUAL-ITY THEY ALREADY POSSESS.

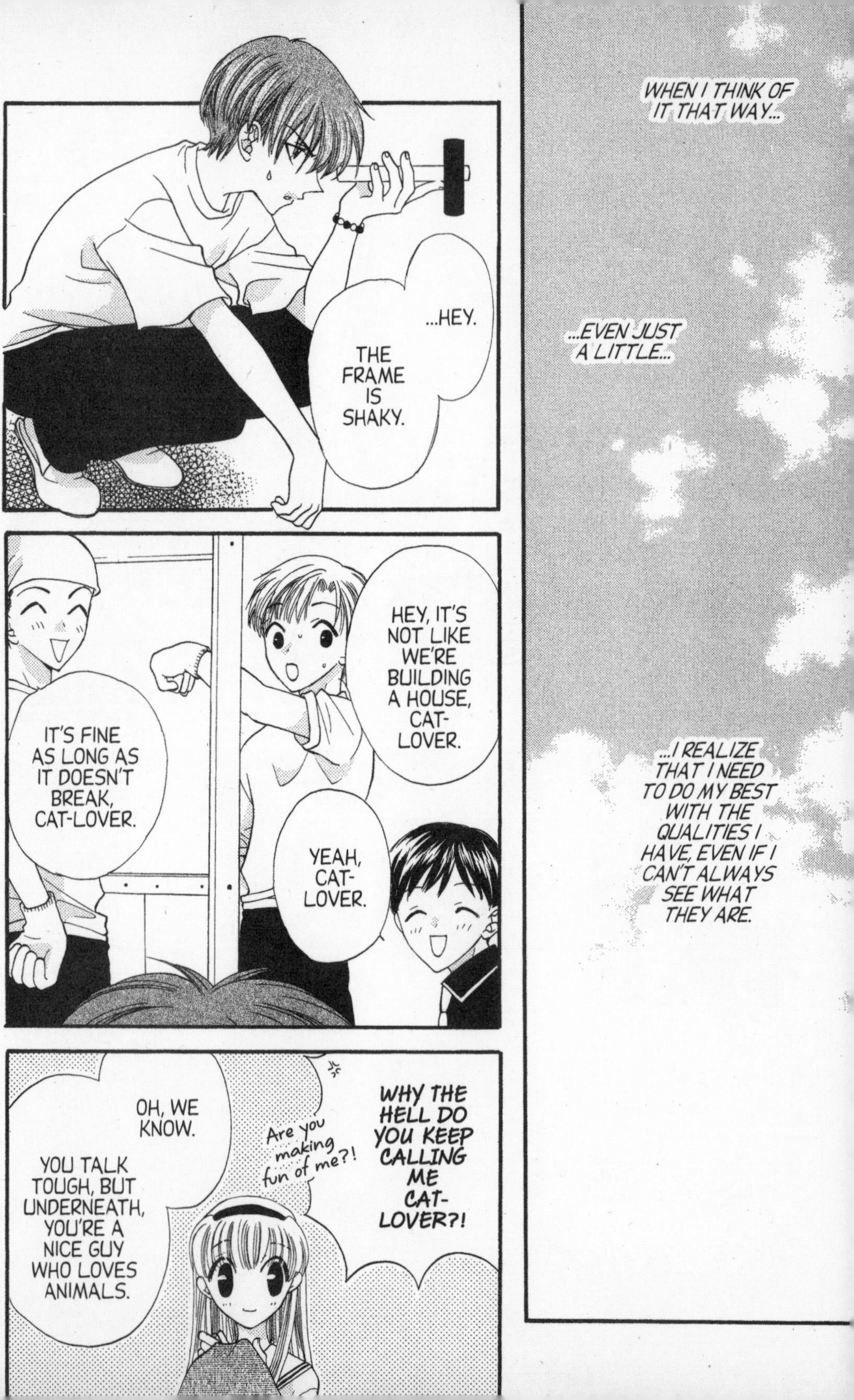
WHEN I THINK OF IT THAT WAY...
...EVEN JUST A LITTLE...
...I REALIZE THAT I NEED TO DO MY BEST WITH THE QUALITIES I HAVE, EVEN IF I CAN'T ALWAYS SEE WHAT THEY ARE.
...HEY.
THE FRAME IS SHAKY.
HEY, IT'S NOT LIKE WE'RE BUILDING A HOUSE, CAT-LOVER.
IT'S FINE AS LONG AS IT DOESN'T BREAK, CAT-LOVER.
YEAH, CAT-LOVER.
WHY THE HELL DO YOU KEEP CALLING ME CAT-LOVER?!
Are you making fun of me?!
OH, WE KNOW.
YOU TALK TOUGH, BUT UNDERNEATH, YOU'RE A NICE GUY WHO LOVES ANIMALS.

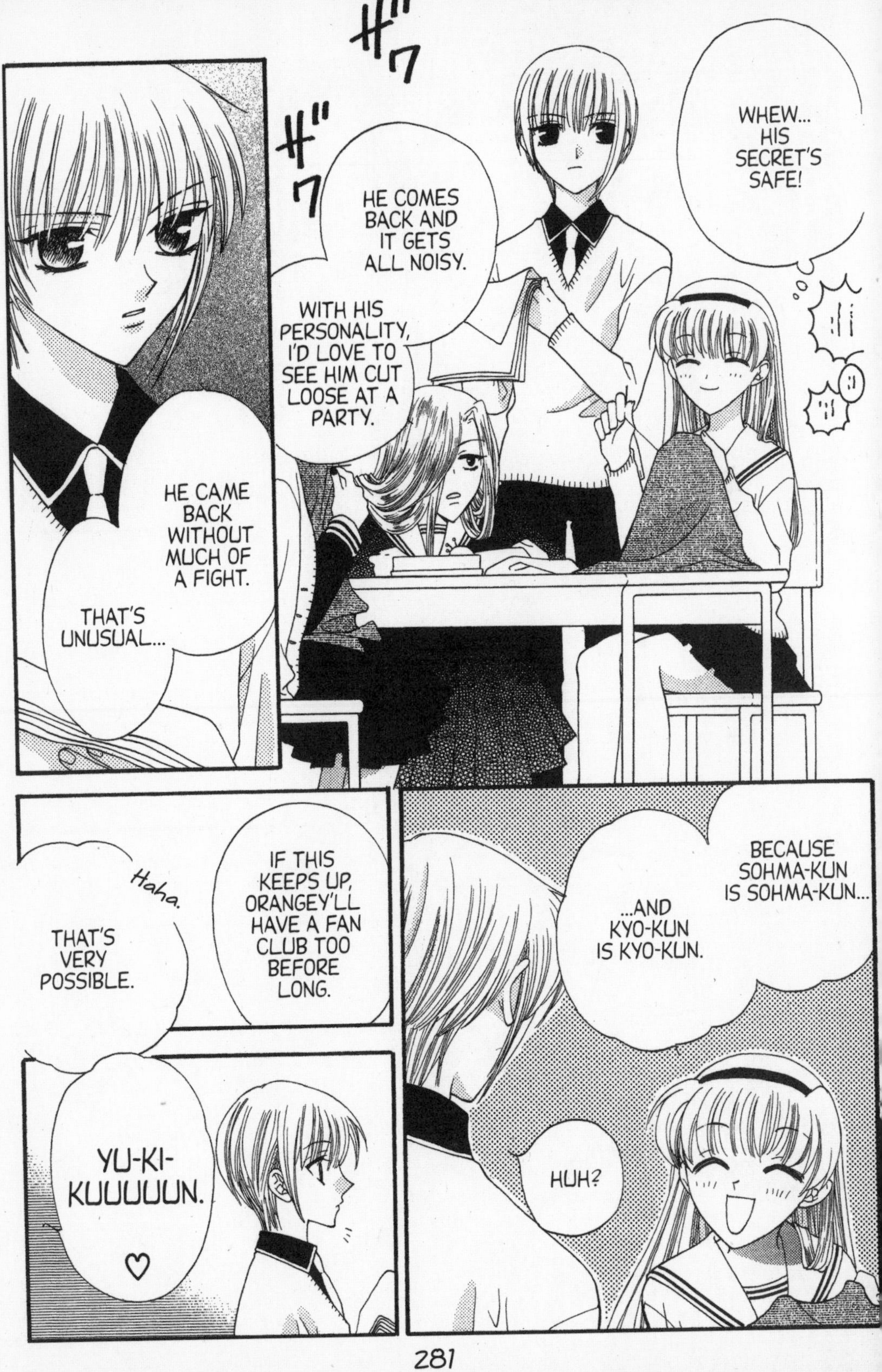
ザワ
ザワ
WHEW... HIS SECRET'S SAFE!
HE COMES BACK AND IT GETS ALL NOISY.
WITH HIS PERSONALITY, I'D LOVE TO SEE HIM CUT LOOSE AT A PARTY.
HE CAME BACK WITHOUT MUCH OF A FIGHT.
THAT'S UNUSUAL...
BECAUSE SOHMA-KUN IS SOHMA-KUN...
...AND KYO-KUN IS KYO-KUN.
HUH?
IF THIS KEEPS UP, ORANGEY'LL HAVE A FAN CLUB TOO BEFORE LONG.
Haha.
THAT'S VERY POSSIBLE.
YU-KI-KUUUUUN. ♡

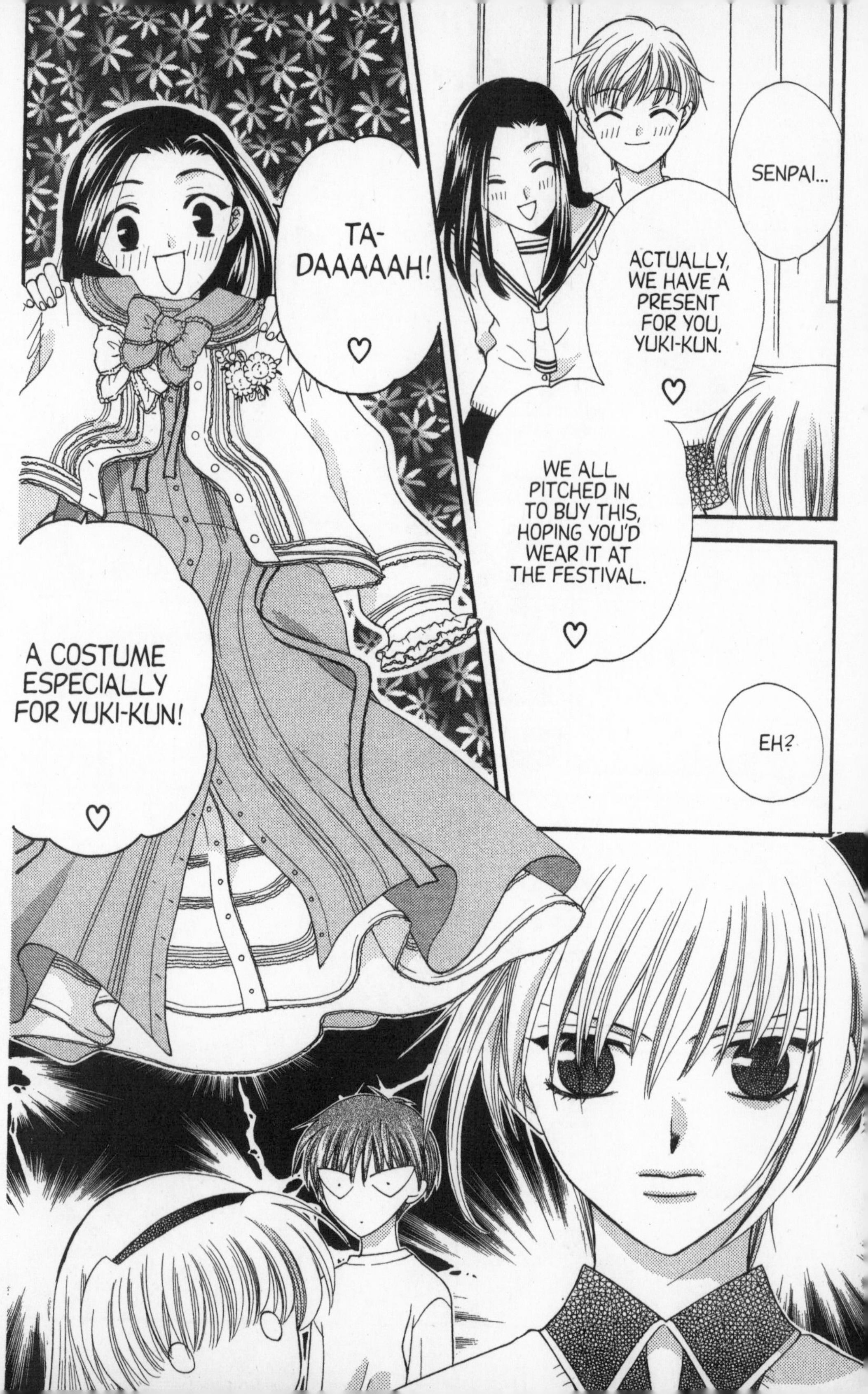
SENPAI...
ACTUALLY, WE HAVE A PRESENT FOR YOU, YUKI-KUN. ♡
WE ALL PITCHED IN TO BUY THIS, HOPING YOU'D WEAR IT AT THE FESTIVAL. ♡
EH?
TA-DAAAAAH! ♡
A COSTUME ESPECIALLY FOR YUKI-KUN! ♡

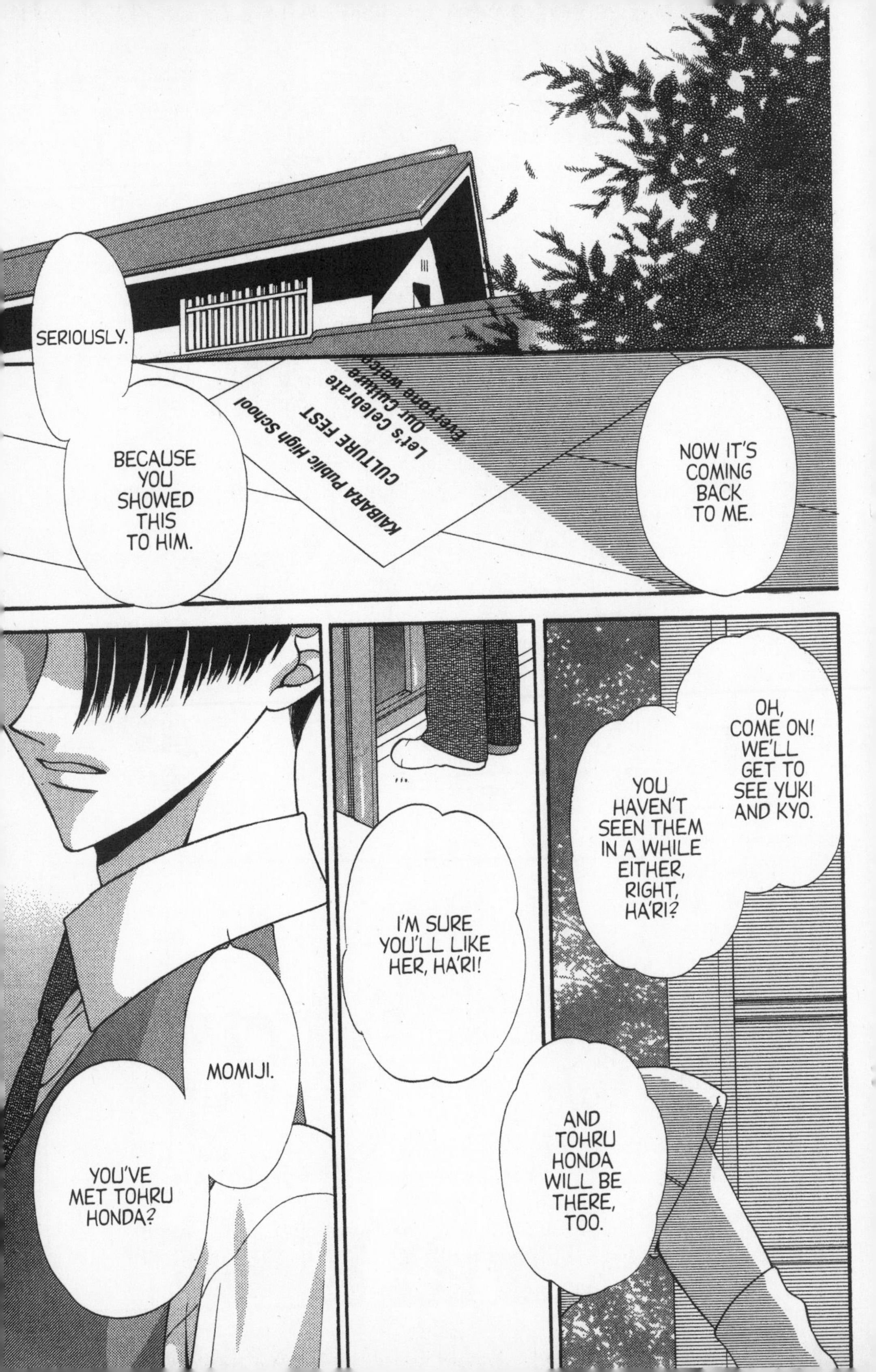
NOW IT'S COMING BACK TO ME.
KAIBARA Public High School
CULTURE FEST
Let's Celebrate
Our Culture
SERIOUSLY.
BECAUSE YOU SHOWED THIS TO HIM.
OH, COME ON! WE'LL GET TO SEE YUKI AND KYO.
YOU HAVEN'T SEEN THEM IN A WHILE EITHER, RIGHT, HA'RI?
AND TOHRU HONDA WILL BE THERE, TOO.
...
I'M SURE YOU'LL LIKE HER, HA'RI!
MOMIJI.
YOU'VE MET TOHRU HONDA?

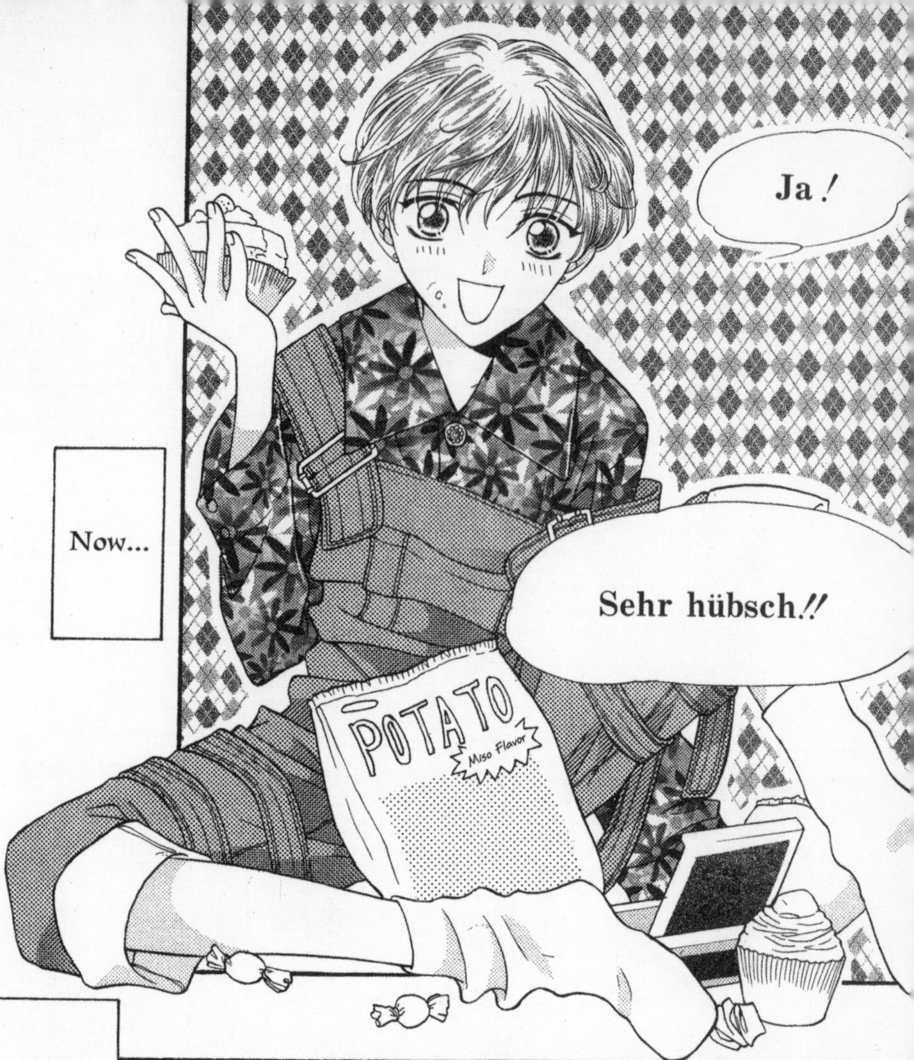
Ja!
Sehr hübsch!!
Now...
POTATO
Miso Flavor

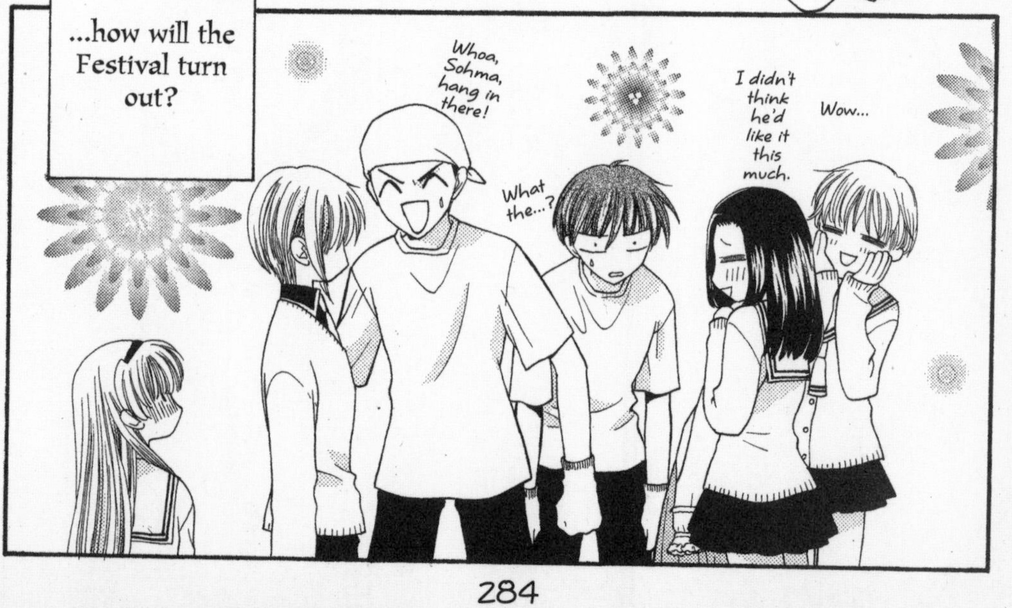
Wow...
I didn't think he'd like it this much.
What the...?
Whoa, Sohma, hang in there!
...how will the Festival turn out?

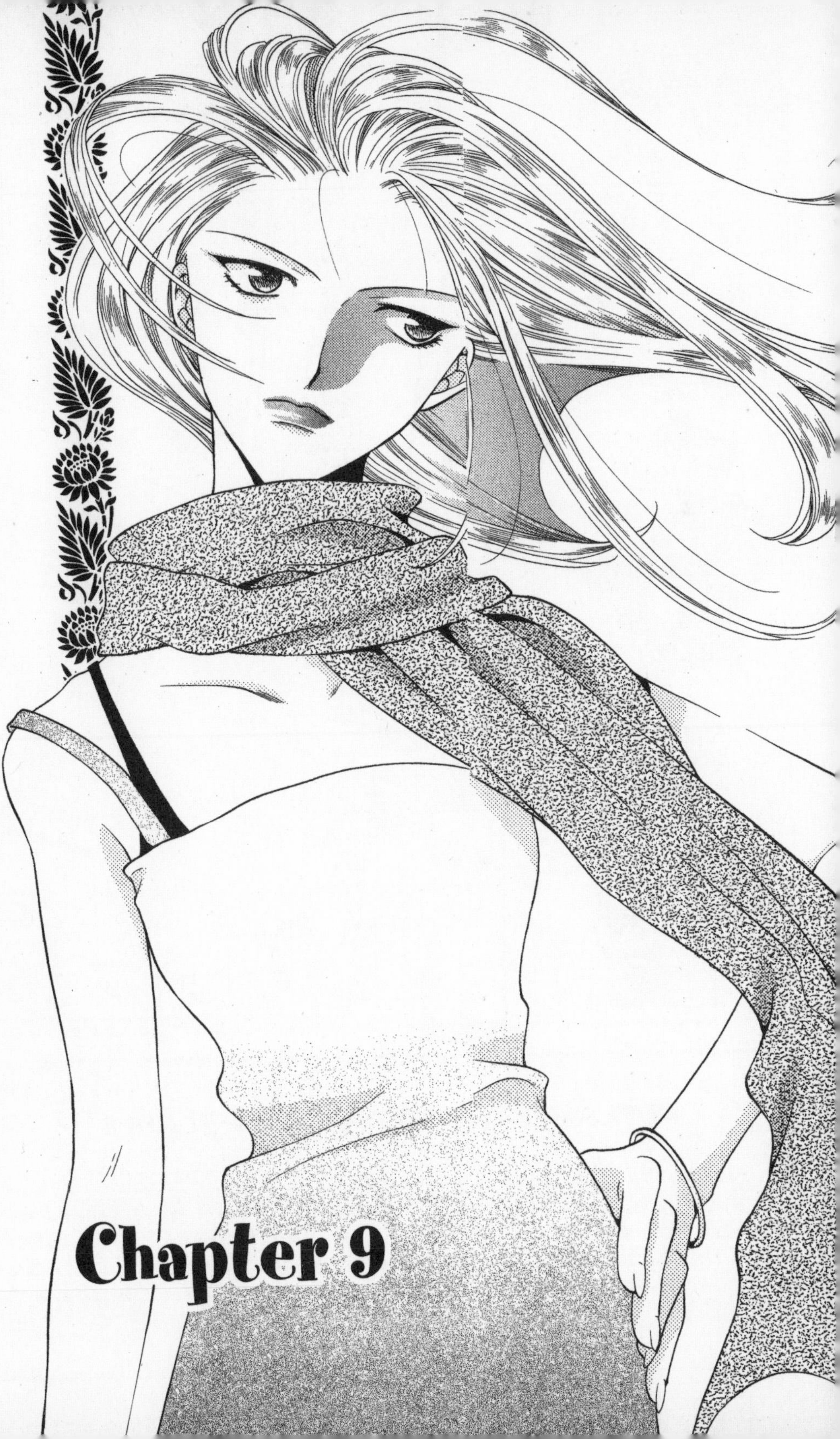
Chapter 9

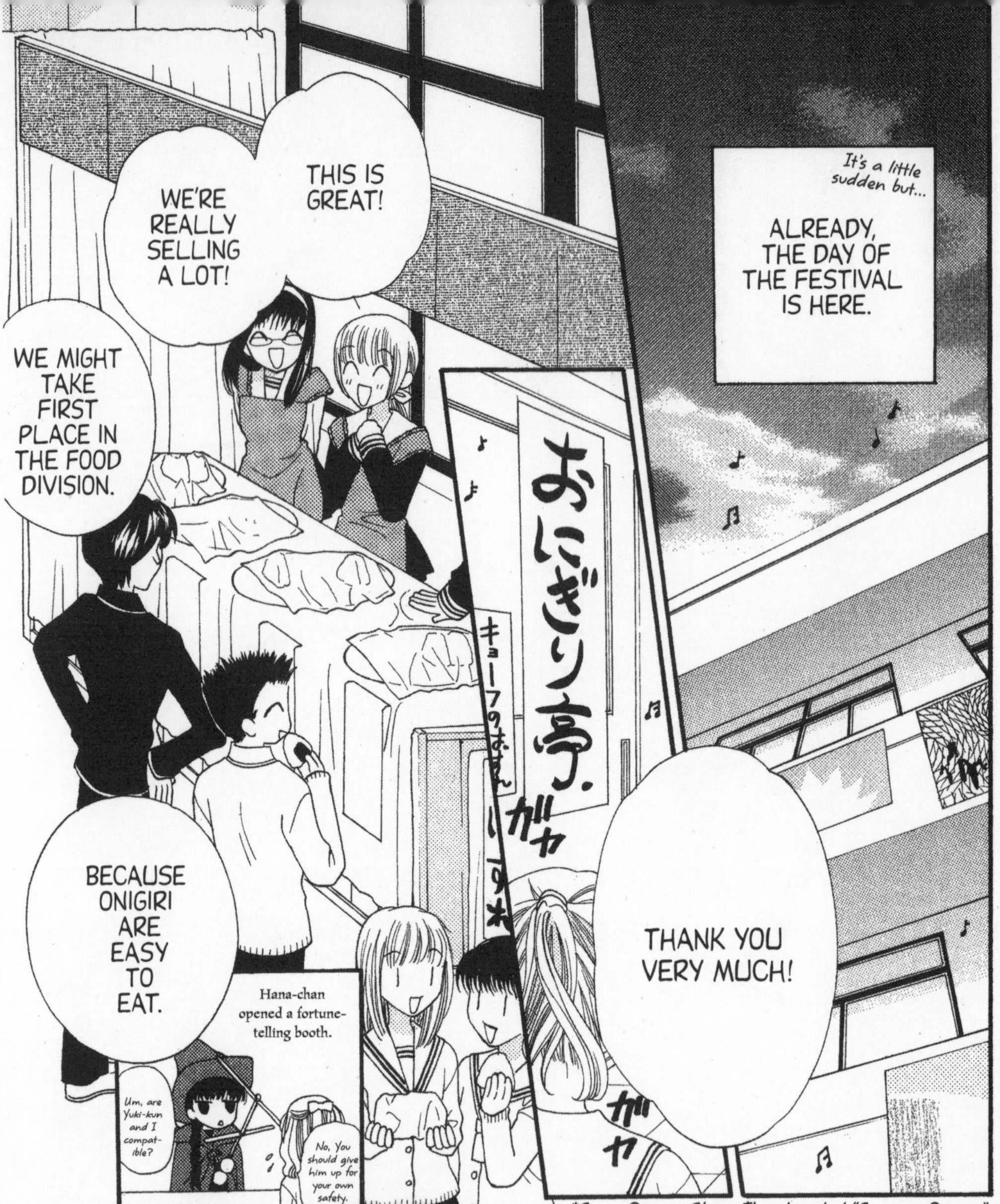
It's a little sudden but...
ALREADY, THE DAY OF THE FESTIVAL IS HERE.
THANK YOU VERY MUCH!
おにぎり亭
ガヤ
ガヤ
THIS IS GREAT!
WE'RE REALLY SELLING A LOT!
WE MIGHT TAKE FIRST PLACE IN THE FOOD DIVISION.
BECAUSE ONIGIRI ARE EASY TO EAT.
Hana-chan opened a fortune-telling booth.
Um, are Yuki-kun and I compatible?
No, You should give him up for your own safety.
*Sign: Onigiri Shop; The dreaded "Surprise Onigiri"

ULTRA SPECIAL BLAH BLAH BLAH 3

I've wanted to. I've wanted to do this. CROSS-DRESSING!! (ha ha) Until now, I've been drawing stories that don't have any room for it, so with Furuba, I thought, "You will do it, Yuki!" (Mind out of the gutter!) But boys with feminine faces are destined to cross-dress (or be made to)...think...if you asked him, I'm sure he'd hate me for it (ha ha).

Fruits Basket 2, Part 3:

It seemed like that feeling had almost disappeared. FF7 was too special. At least to me. Yes, yes, back to FF8. There are people who thought the Draw system was unending agony, but I enjoyed it. Anyway, if I didn't Draw, I felt unfulfilled. I would keep Drawing and not try to advance the story. Even when I was about to die, I would keep Drawing and Drawing. Oh, that was nice (ha ha). It's fun. Uh-huh, uh-huh. The cards were fun, too. Laguna-san was cute. I liked Irvine, too. Selphie is criminally adorable.... I really love her, Sel-Sel. Sensei enjoys eating monsters like there's no tomorrow (too bad they didn't animate it). The Devour command knocked me out. I love that type of command! And I hate Omega (ha ha)! Why is he hundreds of times harder than the last boss (ha ha)?! I had to keep casting Meltdown to do any damage (ha ha).

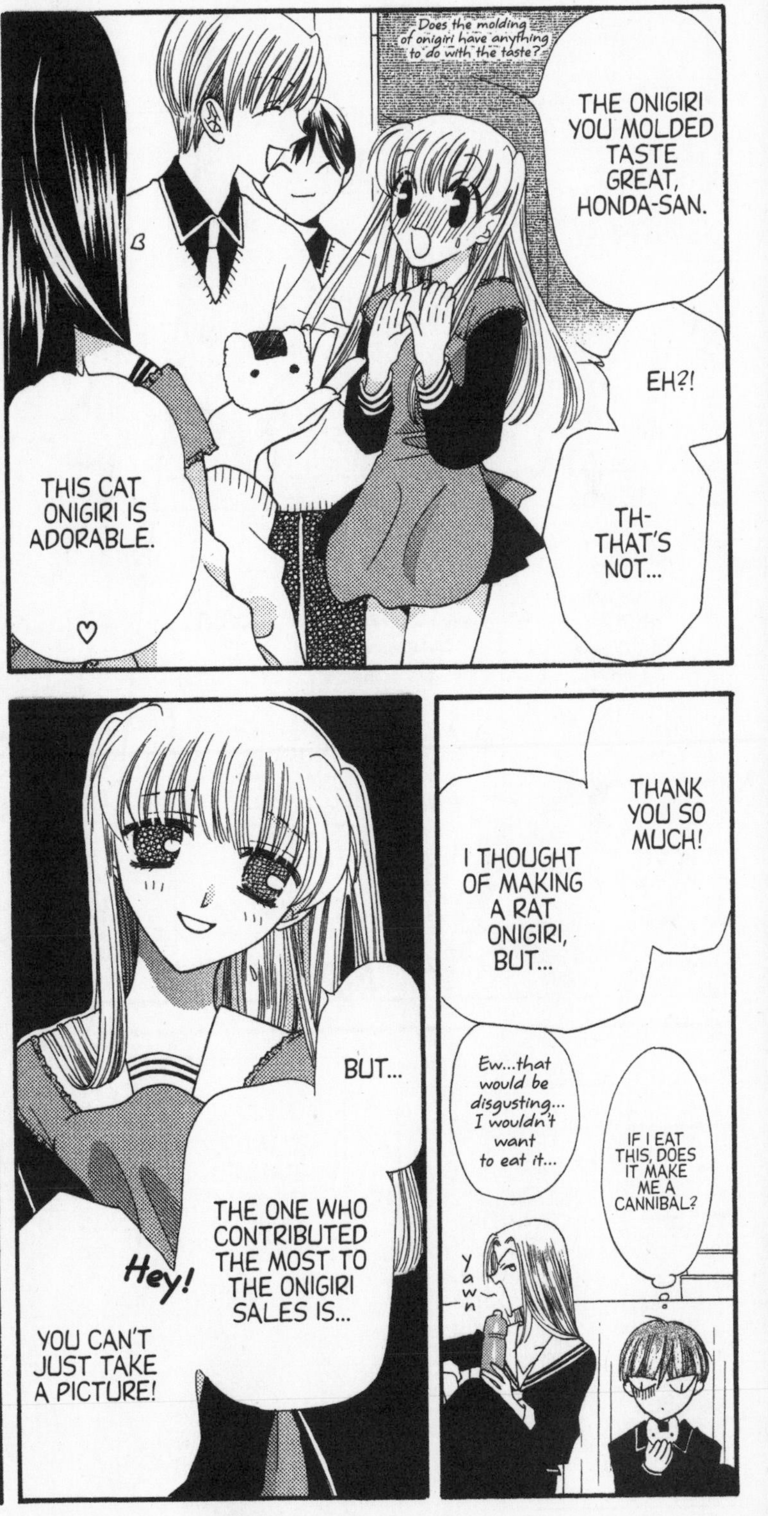
THE ONIGIRI YOU MOLDED TASTE GREAT, HONDA-SAN.
Does the molding of onigiri have anything to do with the taste?
EH?!
TH-THAT'S NOT...
THIS CAT ONIGIRI IS ADORABLE. ♡
THANK YOU SO MUCH!
I THOUGHT OF MAKING A RAT ONIGIRI, BUT...
IF I EAT THIS, DOES IT MAKE ME A CANNIBAL?
Ew...that would be disgusting... I wouldn't want to eat it...
yawn
BUT...
THE ONE WHO CONTRIBUTED THE MOST TO THE ONIGIRI SALES IS...
Hey!
YOU CAN'T JUST TAKE A PICTURE!

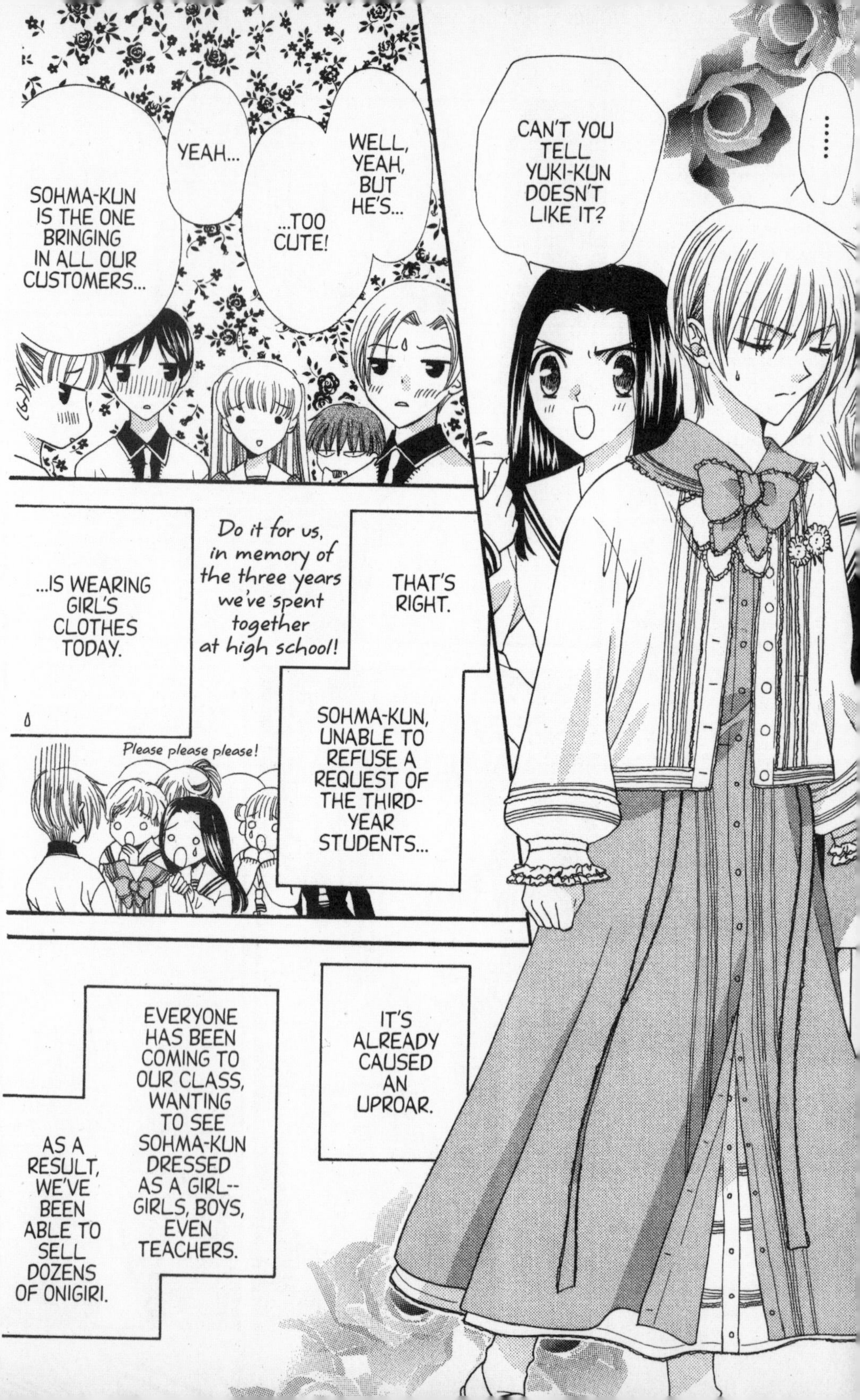
......
CAN'T YOU TELL YUKI-KUN DOESN'T LIKE IT?
WELL, YEAH, BUT HE'S...
...TOO CUTE!
YEAH...
SOHMA-KUN IS THE ONE BRINGING IN ALL OUR CUSTOMERS...
THAT'S RIGHT.
Do it for us, in memory of the three years we've spent together at high school!
SOHMA-KUN, UNABLE TO REFUSE A REQUEST OF THE THIRD-YEAR STUDENTS...
...IS WEARING GIRL'S CLOTHES TODAY.
Please please please!
IT'S ALREADY CAUSED AN UPROAR.
EVERYONE HAS BEEN COMING TO OUR CLASS, WANTING TO SEE SOHMA-KUN DRESSED AS A GIRL-- GIRLS, BOYS, EVEN TEACHERS.
AS A RESULT, WE'VE BEEN ABLE TO SELL DOZENS OF ONIGIRI.

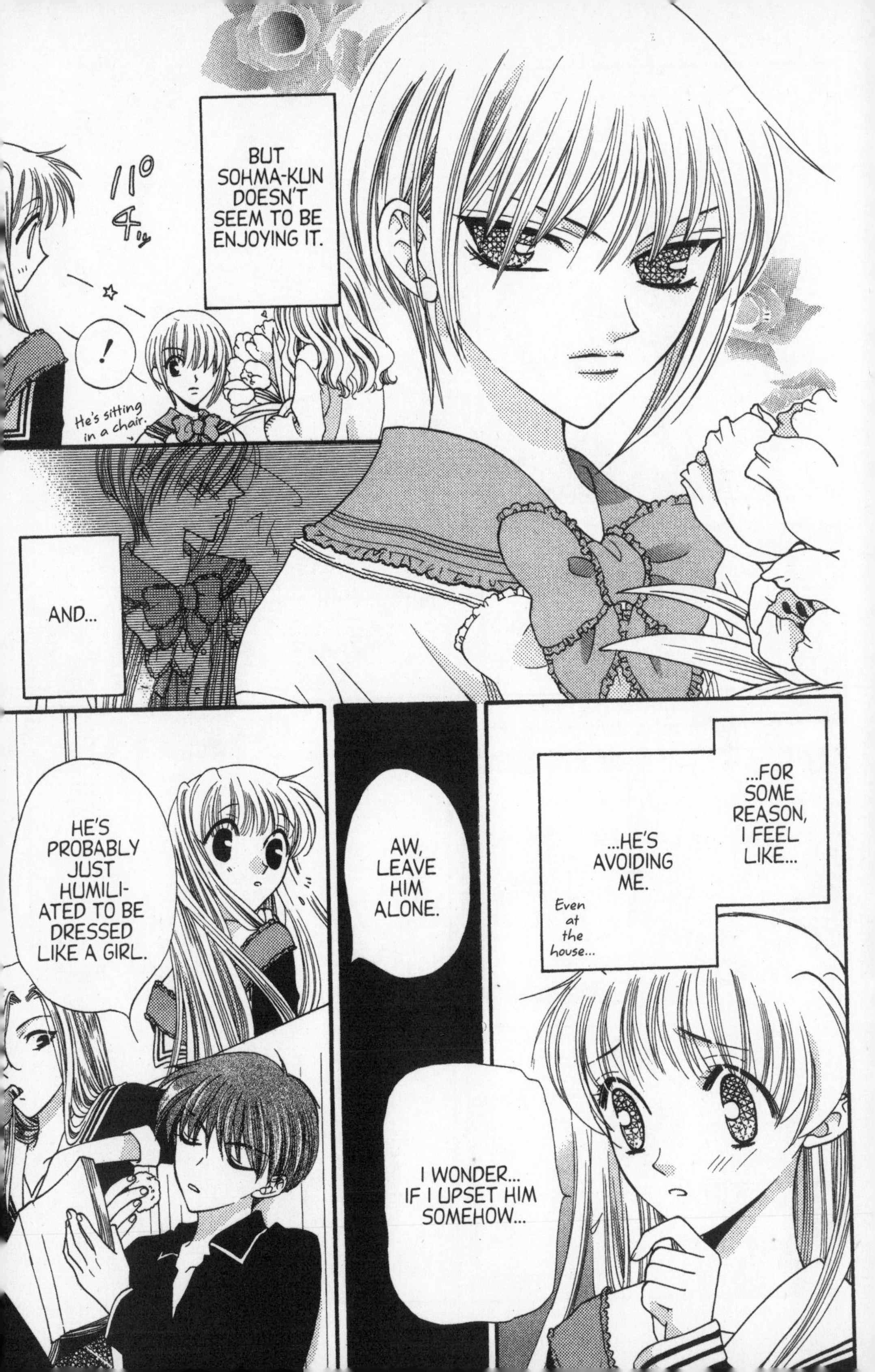
BUT SOHMA-KUN DOESN'T SEEM TO BE ENJOYING IT.
!
He's sitting in a chair.
AND...
...FOR SOME REASON, I FEEL LIKE...
...HE'S AVOIDING ME.
Even at the house...
I WONDER... IF I UPSET HIM SOMEHOW...
AW, LEAVE HIM ALONE.
HE'S PROBABLY JUST HUMILI-ATED TO BE DRESSED LIKE A GIRL.

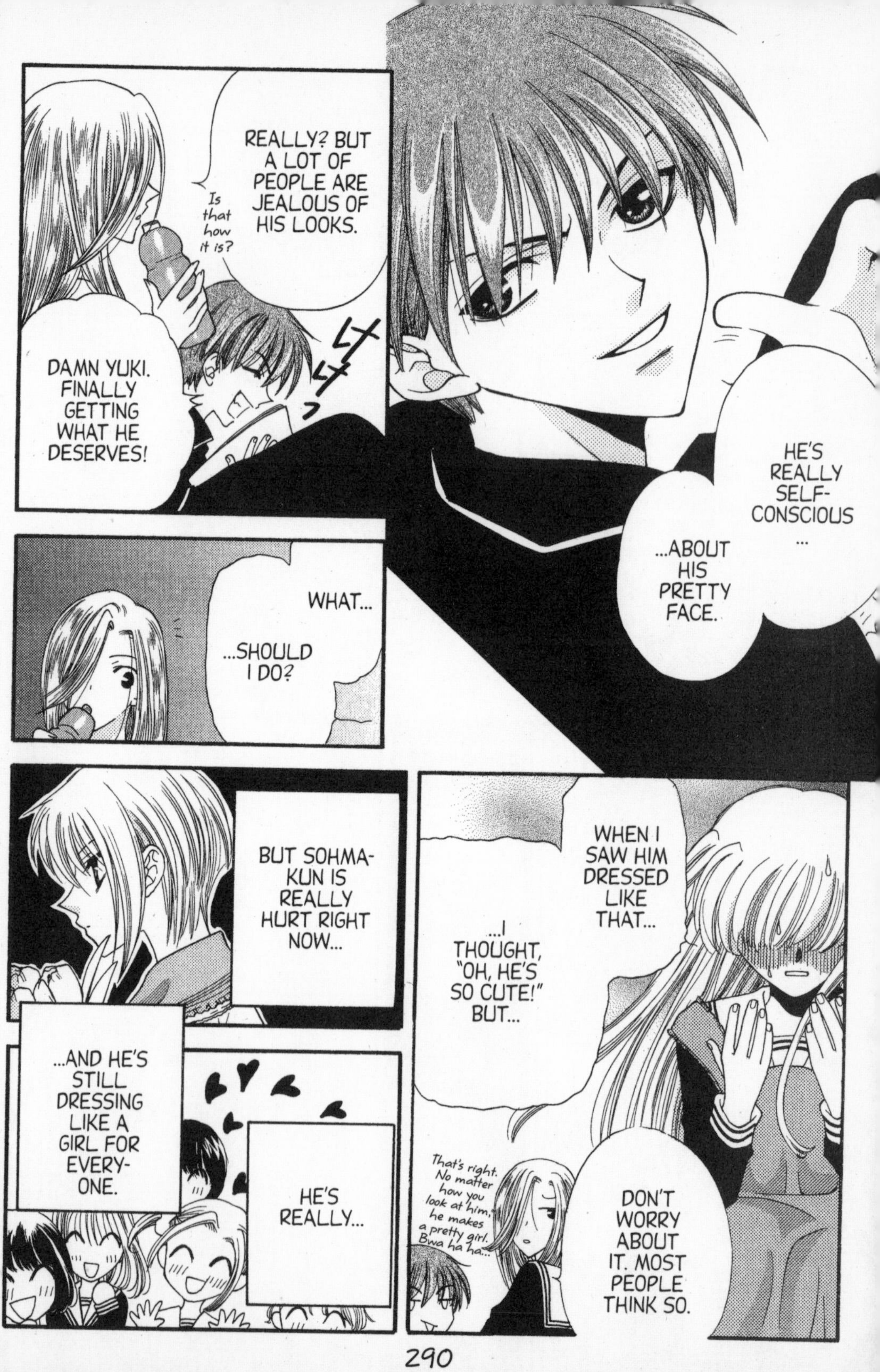
HE'S REALLY SELF-CONSCIOUS ...
...ABOUT HIS PRETTY FACE.
REALLY? BUT A LOT OF PEOPLE ARE JEALOUS OF HIS LOOKS.
Is that how it is?
DAMN YUKI. FINALLY GETTING WHAT HE DESERVES!
ケケッ
WHAT...
...SHOULD I DO?
WHEN I SAW HIM DRESSED LIKE THAT...
...I THOUGHT, "OH, HE'S SO CUTE!" BUT...
DON'T WORRY ABOUT IT. MOST PEOPLE THINK SO.
That's right. No matter how you look at him, he makes a pretty girl. Bwa ha ha...
BUT SOHMA-KUN IS REALLY HURT RIGHT NOW...
...AND HE'S STILL DRESSING LIKE A GIRL FOR EVERYONE.
HE'S REALLY...

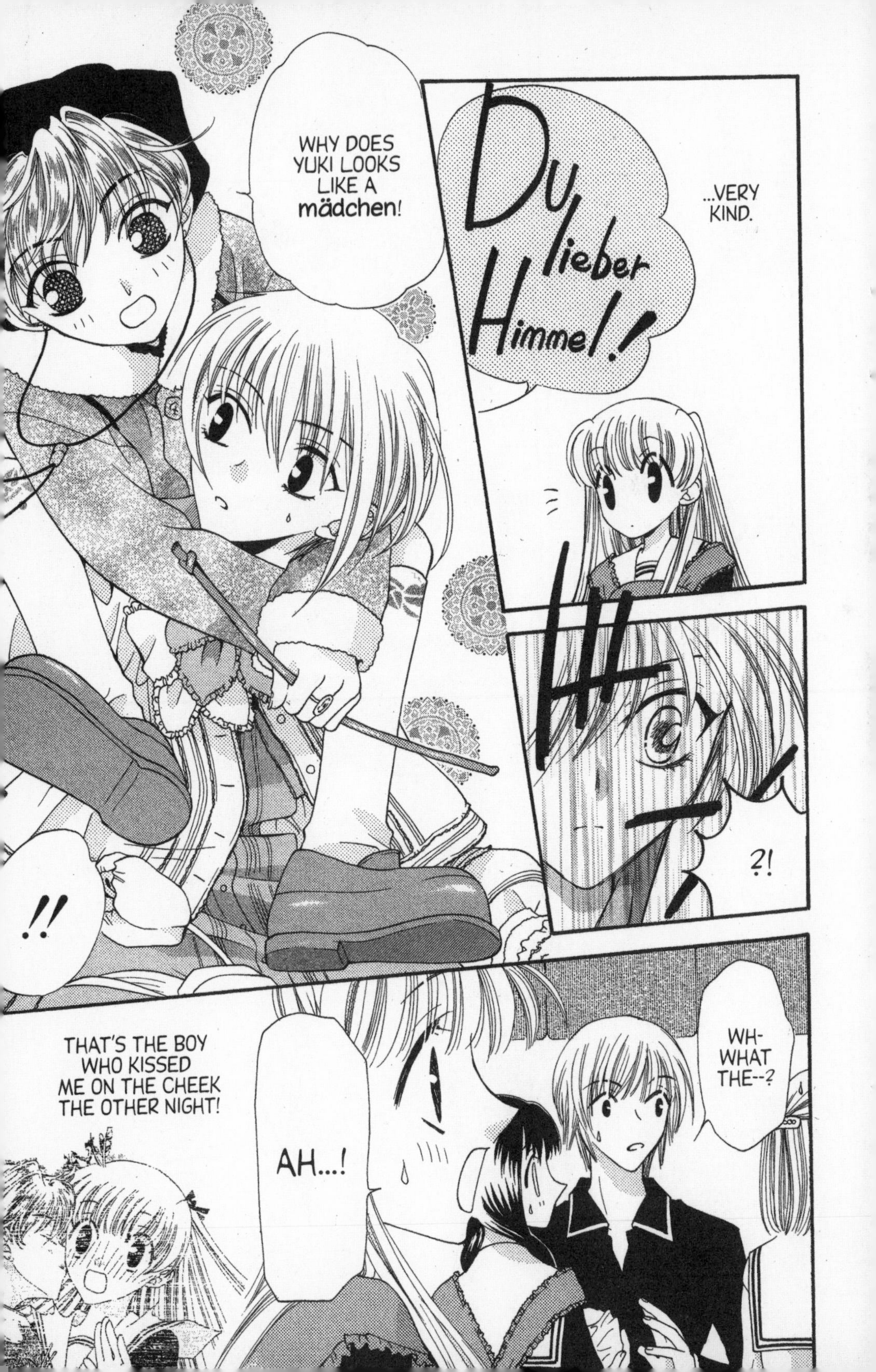
...VERY KIND.
Du lieber Himmel!!
?!
WHY DOES YUKI LOOKS LIKE A mädchen!
!!
WH- WHAT THE--?
AH...!
THAT'S THE BOY WHO KISSED ME ON THE CHEEK THE OTHER NIGHT!

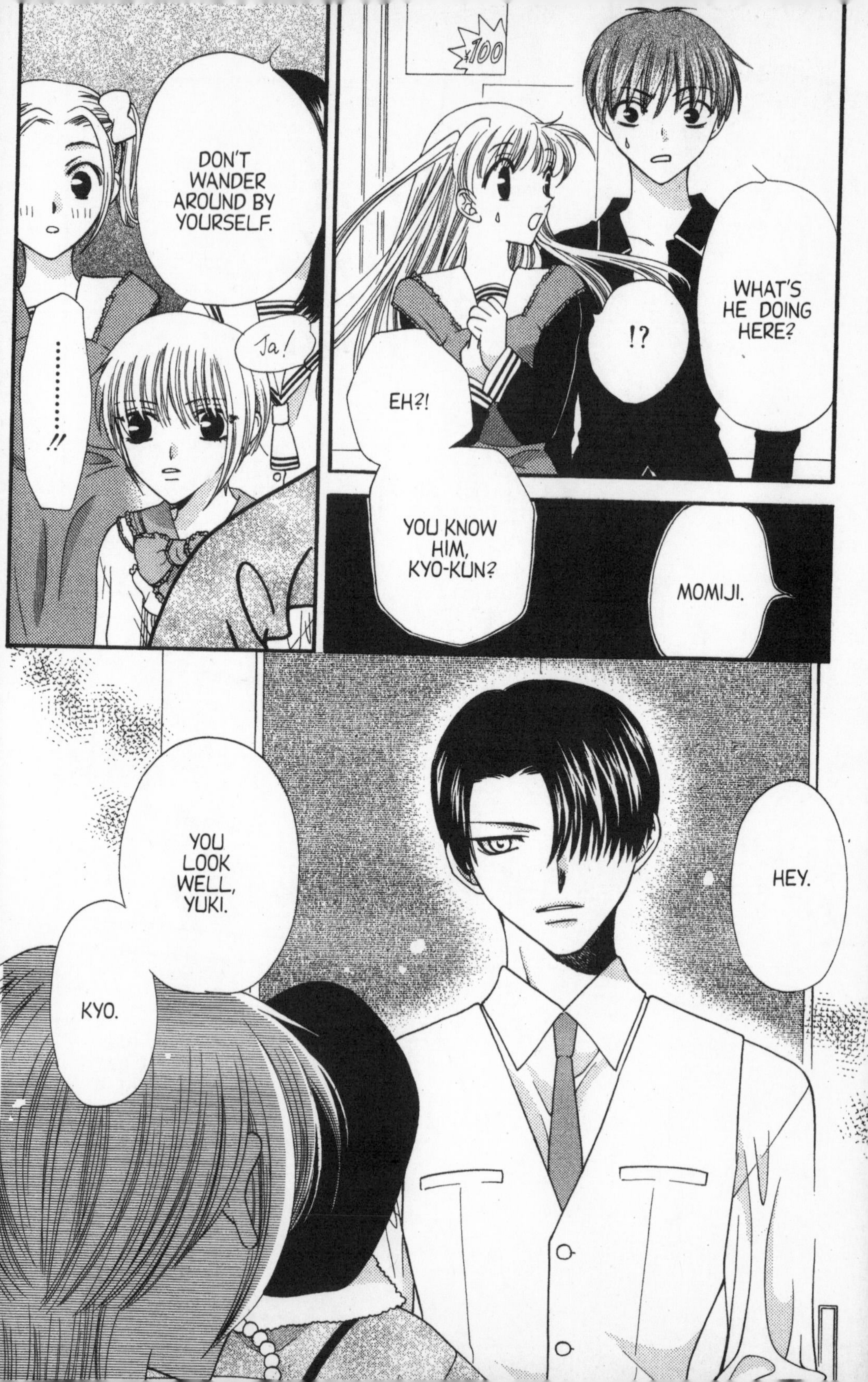
WHAT'S HE DOING HERE?
!?
EH?!
MOMIJI.
YOU KNOW HIM, KYO-KUN?
DON'T WANDER AROUND BY YOURSELF.
Ja!
......!!
HEY.
YOU LOOK WELL, YUKI.
KYO.

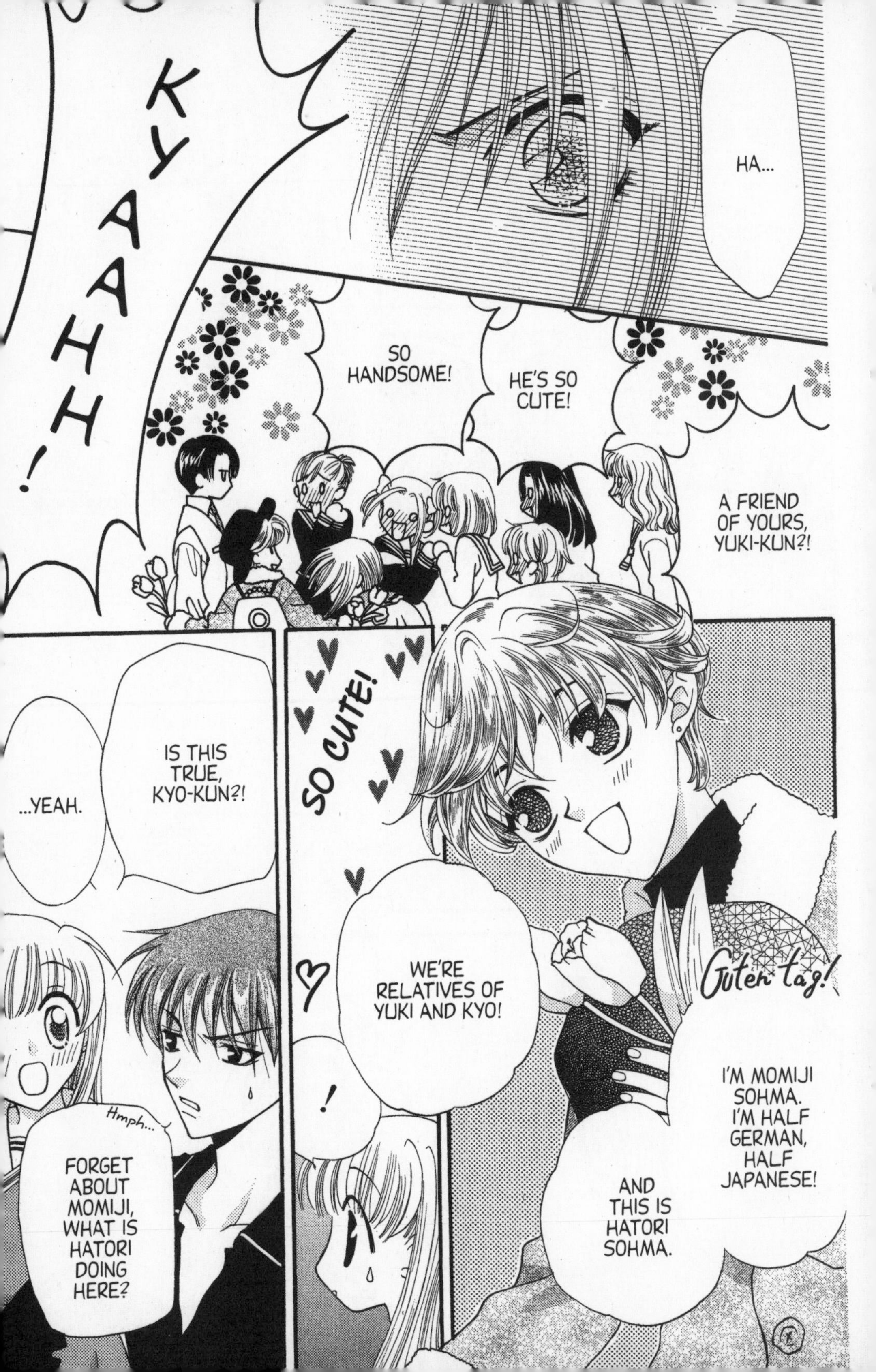
HA...
KYAAHH!
HE'S SO CUTE!
SO HANDSOME!
A FRIEND OF YOURS, YUKI-KUN?!
Guten tag!
I'M MOMIJI SOHMA. I'M HALF GERMAN, HALF JAPANESE!
AND THIS IS HATORI SOHMA.
SO CUTE!
WE'RE RELATIVES OF YUKI AND KYO!
!
IS THIS TRUE, KYO-KUN?!
...YEAH.
Hmph...
FORGET ABOUT MOMIJI, WHAT IS HATORI DOING HERE?

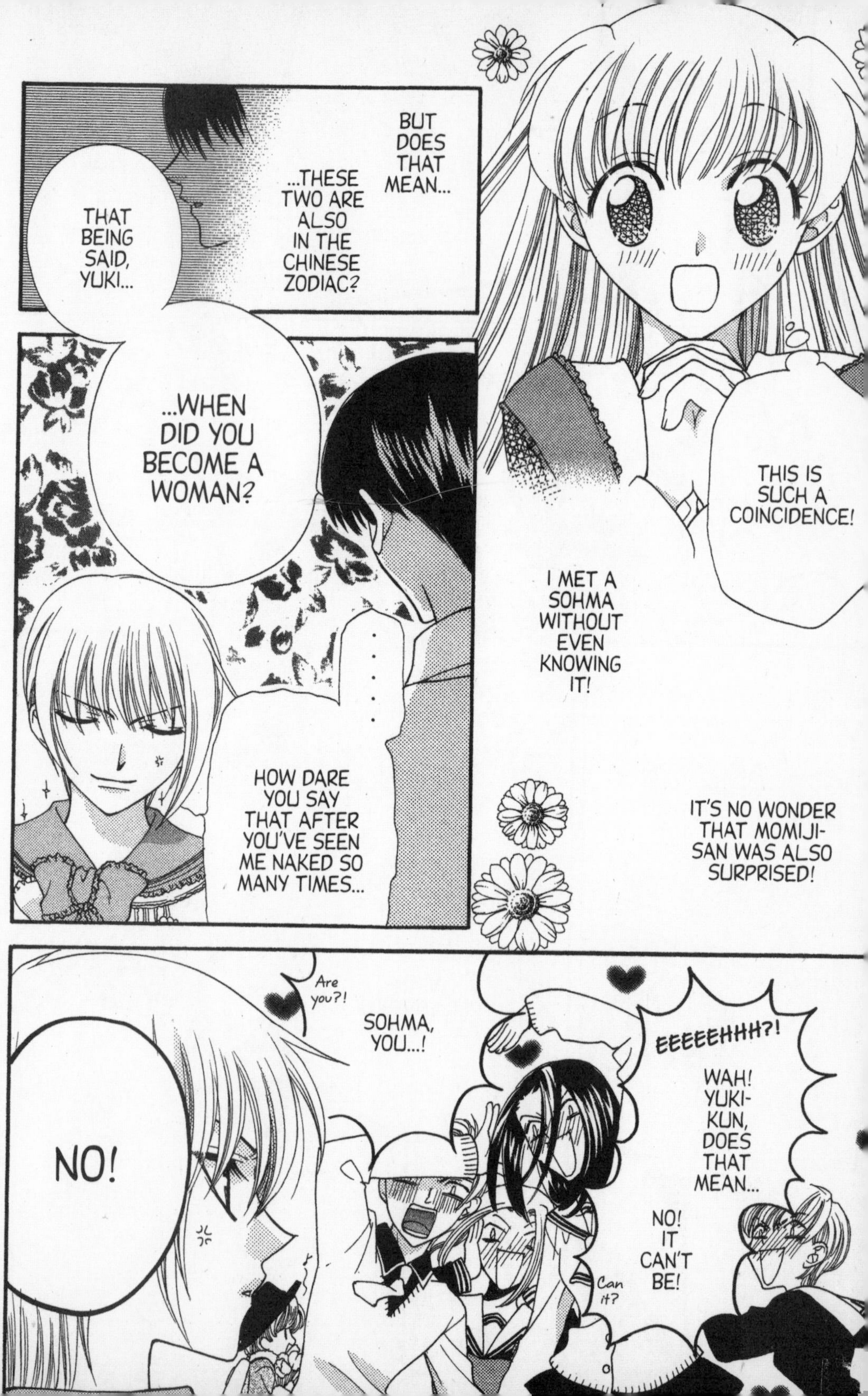
THIS IS SUCH A COINCIDENCE!
I MET A SOHMA WITHOUT EVEN KNOWING IT!
IT'S NO WONDER THAT MOMIJI-SAN WAS ALSO SURPRISED!
BUT DOES THAT MEAN...
...THESE TWO ARE ALSO IN THE CHINESE ZODIAC?
THAT BEING SAID, YUKI...
...WHEN DID YOU BECOME A WOMAN?
......
HOW DARE YOU SAY THAT AFTER YOU'VE SEEN ME NAKED SO MANY TIMES...
EEEEEHHH?!
WAH! YUKI-KUN, DOES THAT MEAN...
NO! IT CAN'T BE!
Can it?
SOHMA, YOU...!
Are you?!
NO!

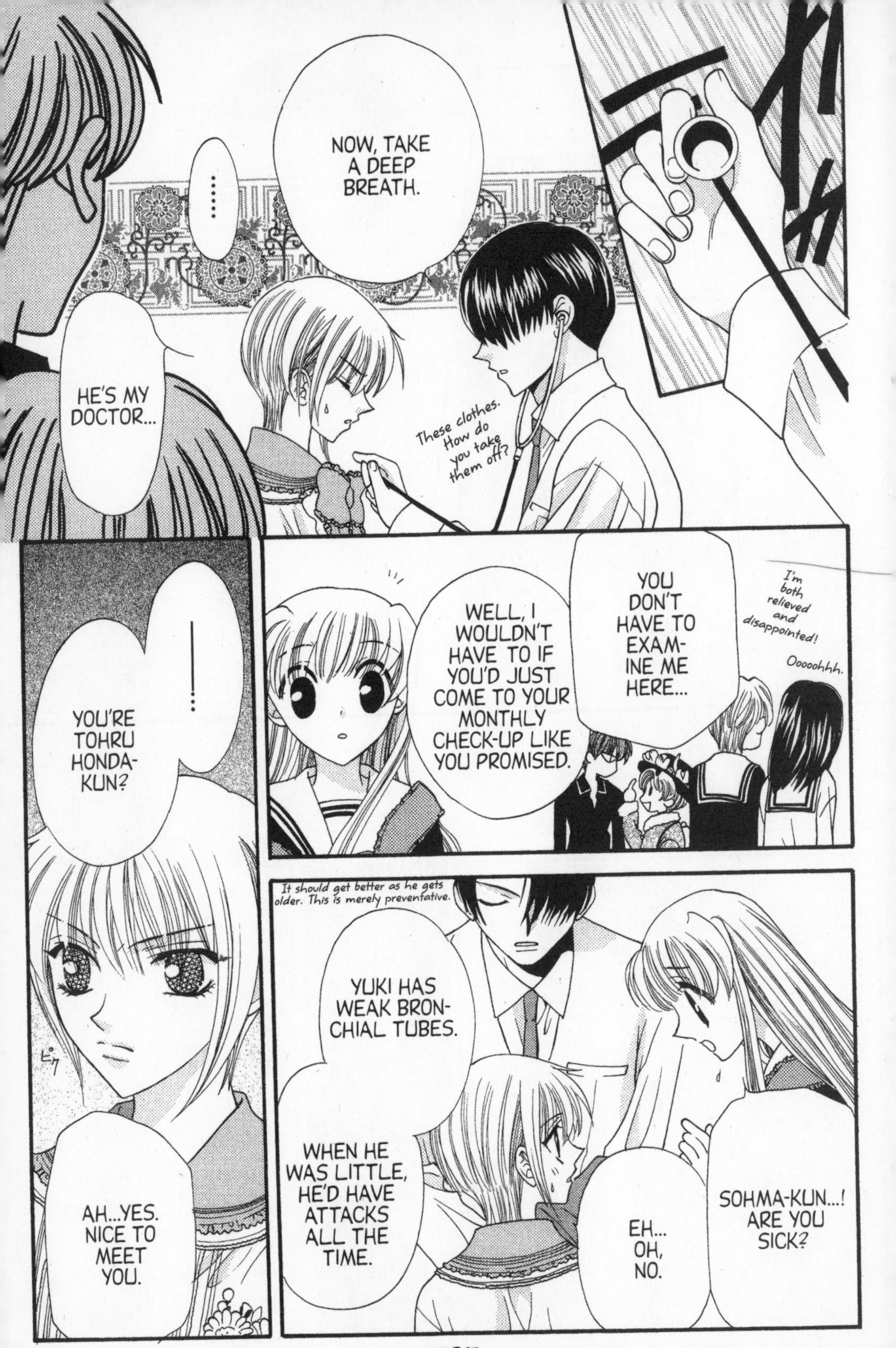
NOW, TAKE A DEEP BREATH.
......
These clothes. How do you take them off?
HE'S MY DOCTOR...
I'm both relieved and disappointed!
Oooohhh.
YOU DON'T HAVE TO EXAM- INE ME HERE...
WELL, I WOULDN'T HAVE TO IF YOU'D JUST COME TO YOUR MONTHLY CHECK-UP LIKE YOU PROMISED.
SOHMA-KUN...! ARE YOU SICK?
EH... OH, NO.
YUKI HAS WEAK BRON- CHIAL TUBES.
WHEN HE WAS LITTLE, HE'D HAVE ATTACKS ALL THE TIME.
It should get better as he gets older. This is merely preventative.
......!
YOU'RE TOHRU HONDA- KUN?
AH...YES. NICE TO MEET YOU.

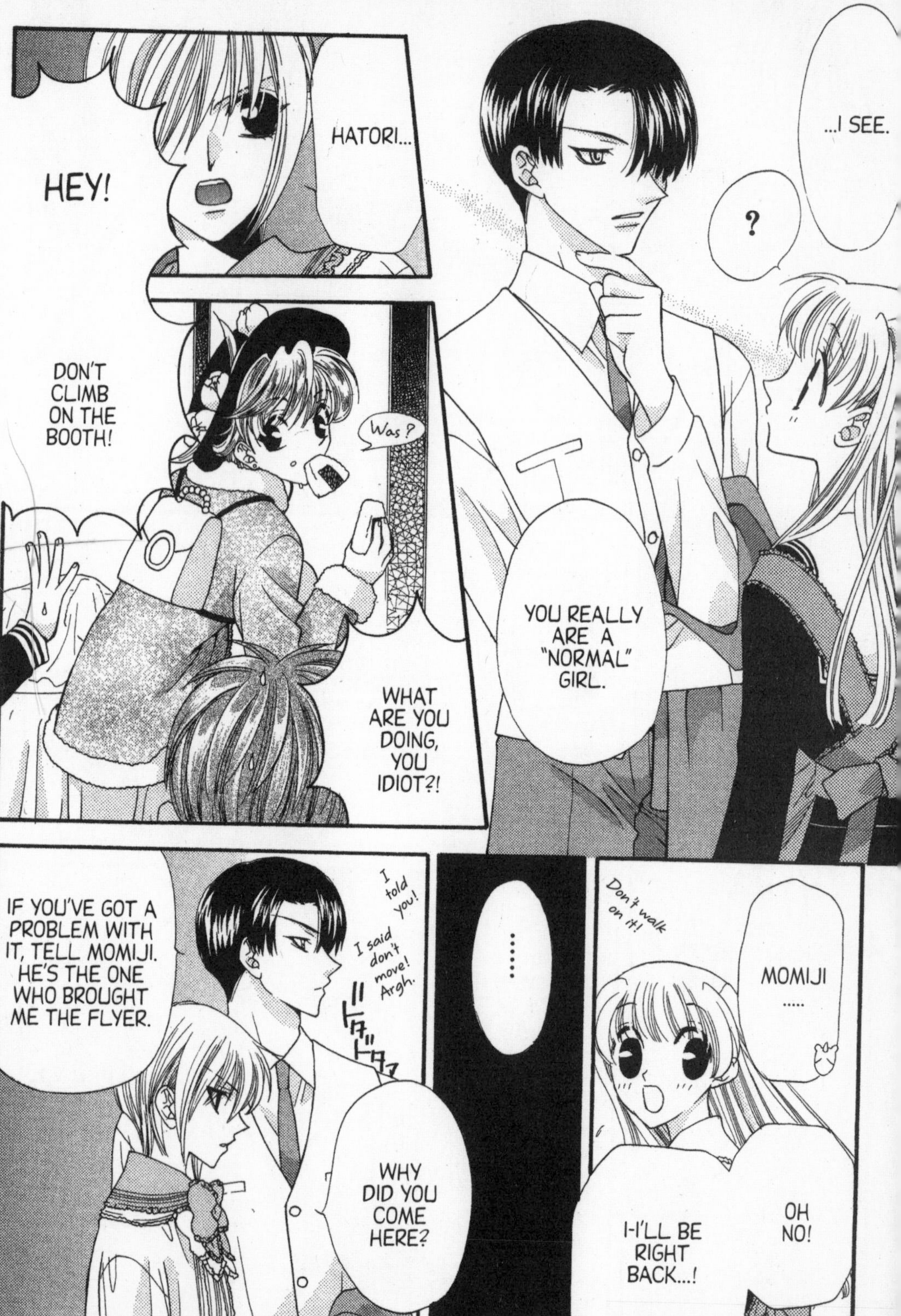
...I SEE.
?
YOU REALLY ARE A "NORMAL" GIRL.
HATORI...
HEY!
DON'T CLIMB ON THE BOOTH!
Was?
WHAT ARE YOU DOING, YOU IDIOT?!
Don't walk on it!
MOMIJI .....
OH NO!
I-I'LL BE RIGHT BACK...!
......
I told you!
I said don't move! Argh.
IF YOU'VE GOT A PROBLEM WITH IT, TELL MOMIJI. HE'S THE ONE WHO BROUGHT ME THE FLYER.
ドタドタ
WHY DID YOU COME HERE?

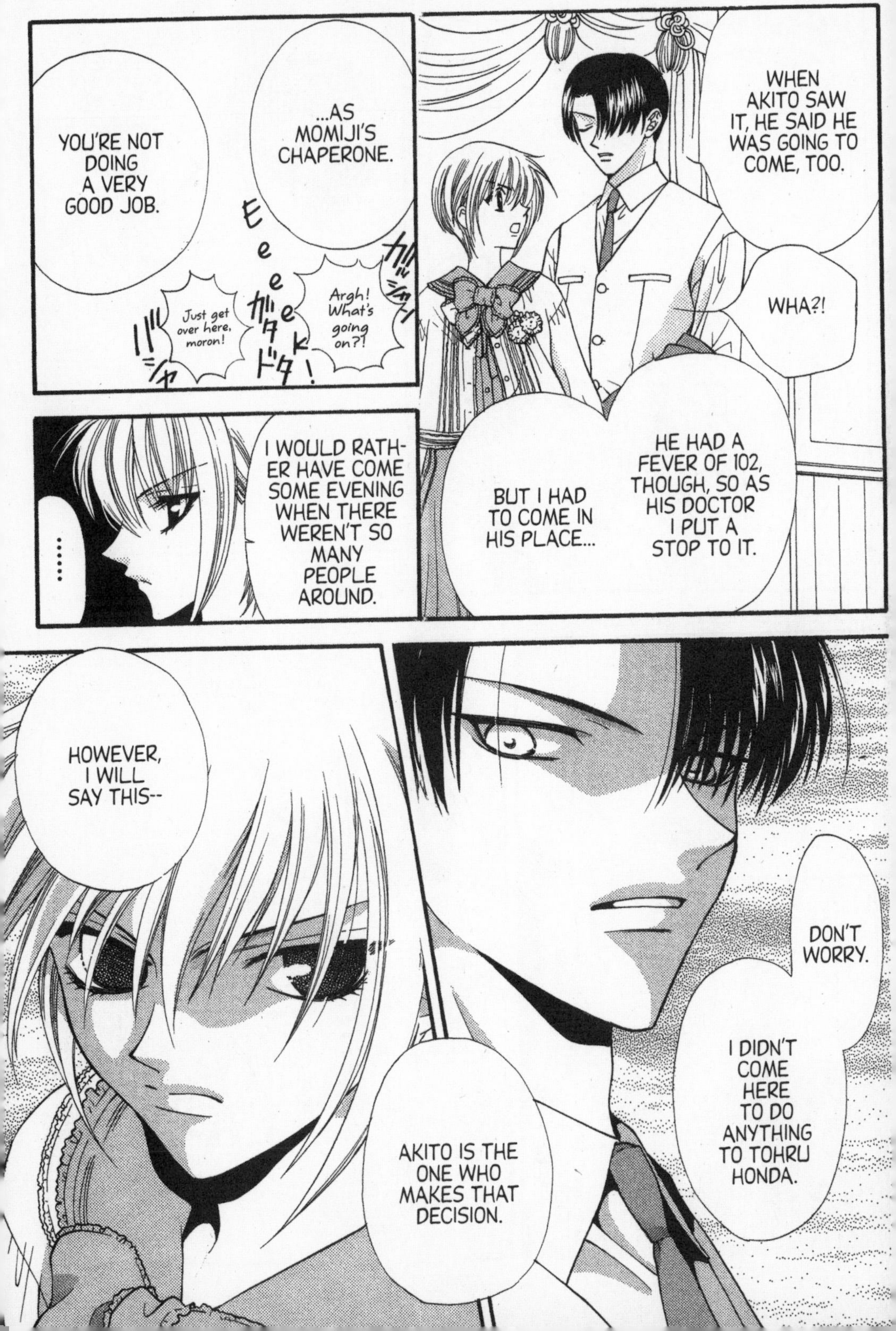
WHEN AKITO SAW IT, HE SAID HE WAS GOING TO COME, TOO.
WHA?!
HE HAD A FEVER OF 102, THOUGH, SO AS HIS DOCTOR I PUT A STOP TO IT.
BUT I HAD TO COME IN HIS PLACE...
...AS MOMIJI'S CHAPERONE.
YOU'RE NOT DOING A VERY GOOD JOB.
Argh! What's going on?!
Eeeek!
Just get over here, moron!
I WOULD RATHER HAVE COME SOME EVENING WHEN THERE WEREN'T SO MANY PEOPLE AROUND.
......
DON'T WORRY.
I DIDN'T COME HERE TO DO ANYTHING TO TOHRU HONDA.
AKITO IS THE ONE WHO MAKES THAT DECISION.
HOWEVER, I WILL SAY THIS--

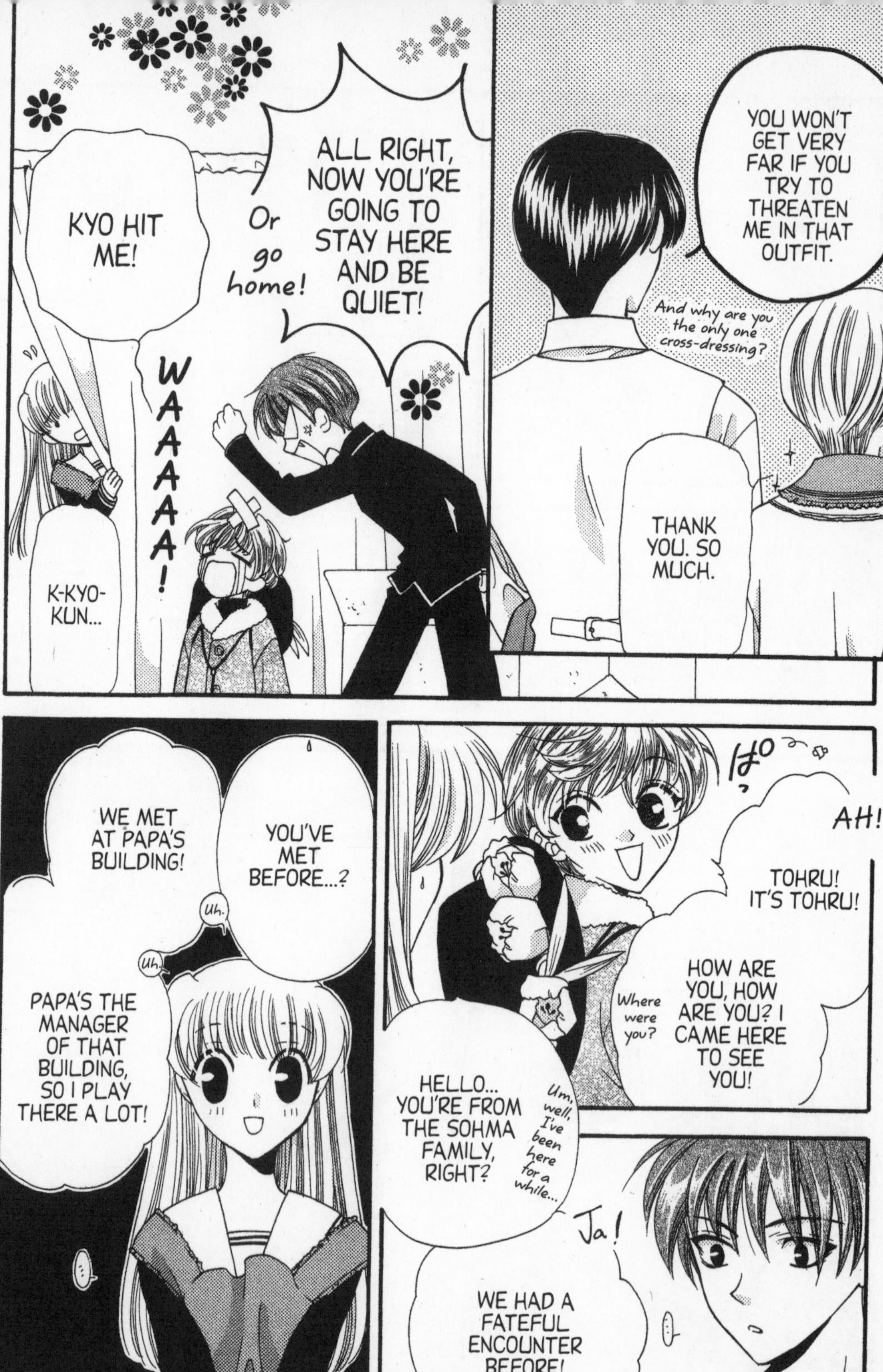
YOU WON'T GET VERY FAR IF YOU TRY TO THREATEN ME IN THAT OUTFIT.
And why are you the only one cross-dressing?
THANK YOU. SO MUCH.
ALL RIGHT, NOW YOU'RE GOING TO STAY HERE AND BE QUIET!
Or go home!
KYO HIT ME!
WAAAAAAA!
K-KYO-KUN...
ぱっ
AH!
TOHRU! IT'S TOHRU!
HOW ARE YOU, HOW ARE YOU? I CAME HERE TO SEE YOU!
Where were you?
HELLO... YOU'RE FROM THE SOHMA FAMILY, RIGHT?
Um, well, I've been here for a while...
Ja!
WE HAD A FATEFUL ENCOUNTER BEFORE!
YOU'VE MET BEFORE...?
WE MET AT PAPA'S BUILDING!
Uh.
Uh.
PAPA'S THE MANAGER OF THAT BUILDING, SO I PLAY THERE A LOT!

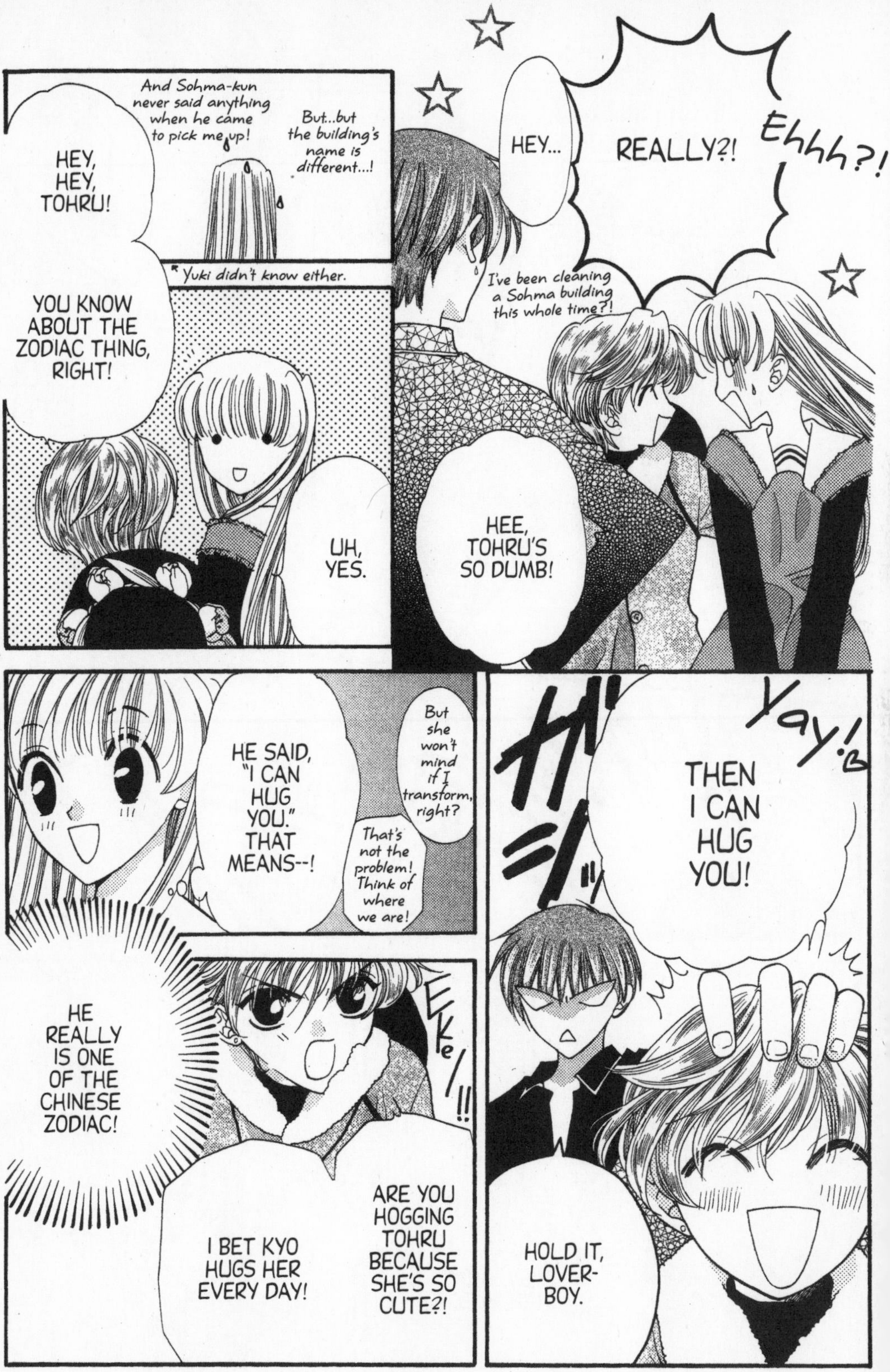
Ehhh?!
REALLY?!
HEY...
I've been cleaning a Sohma building this whole time?!
HEE, TOHRU'S SO DUMB!
But...but the building's name is different...!
And Sohma-kun never said anything when he came to pick me up!
HEY, HEY, TOHRU!
*Yuki didn't know either.
YOU KNOW ABOUT THE ZODIAC THING, RIGHT!
UH, YES.
Yay!♥
THEN I CAN HUG YOU!
HOLD IT, LOVER-BOY.
But she won't mind if I transform, right?
That's not the problem! Think of where we are!
HE SAID, "I CAN HUG YOU." THAT MEANS--!
Eeke!!
HE REALLY IS ONE OF THE CHINESE ZODIAC!
ARE YOU HOGGING TOHRU BECAUSE SHE'S SO CUTE?!
I BET KYO HUGS HER EVERY DAY!

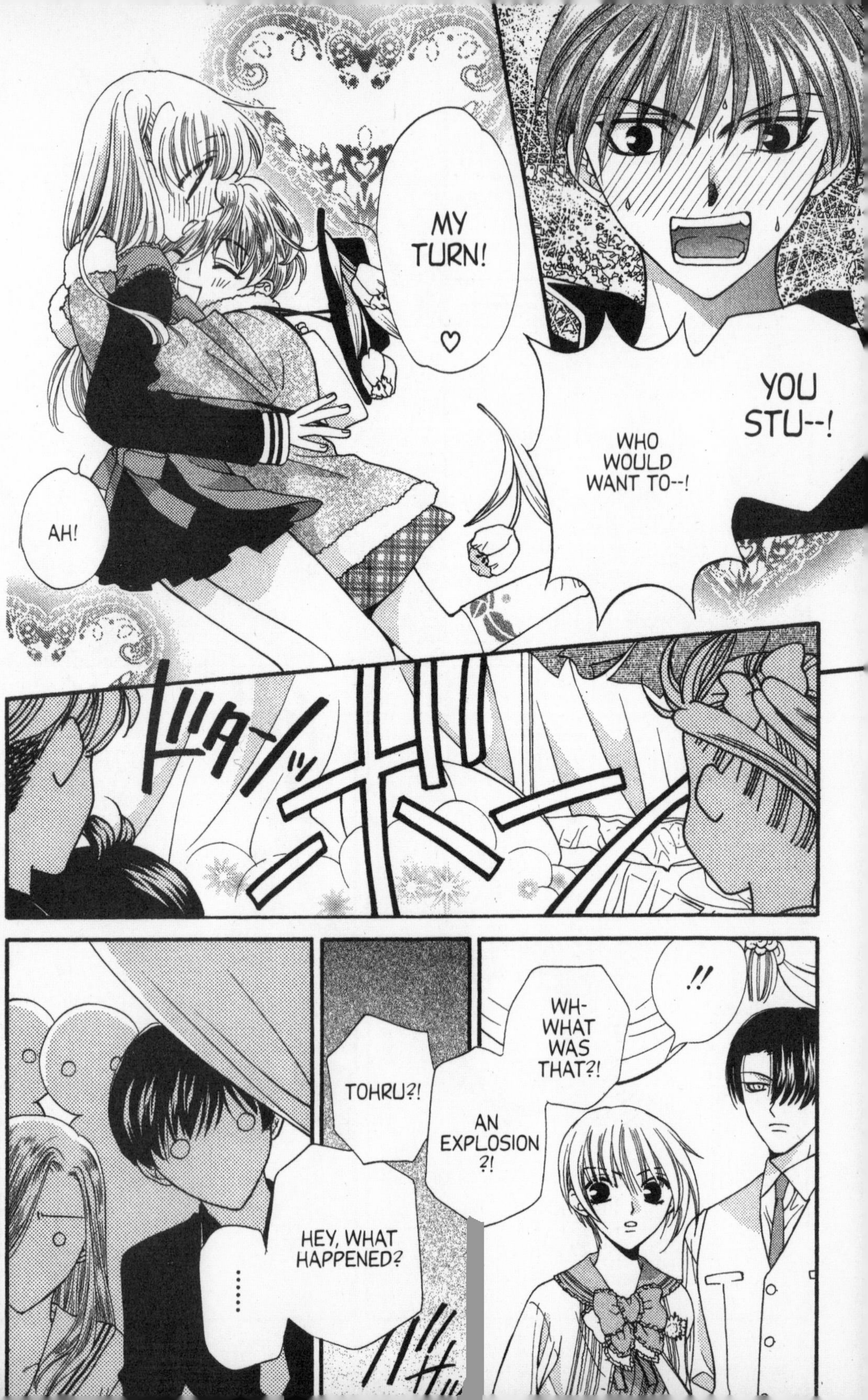
YOU STU--!
WHO WOULD WANT TO--!
MY TURN! ♡
AH!
!!
WH-WHAT WAS THAT?!
AN EXPLOSION?!
TOHRU?!
HEY, WHAT HAPPENED?
......

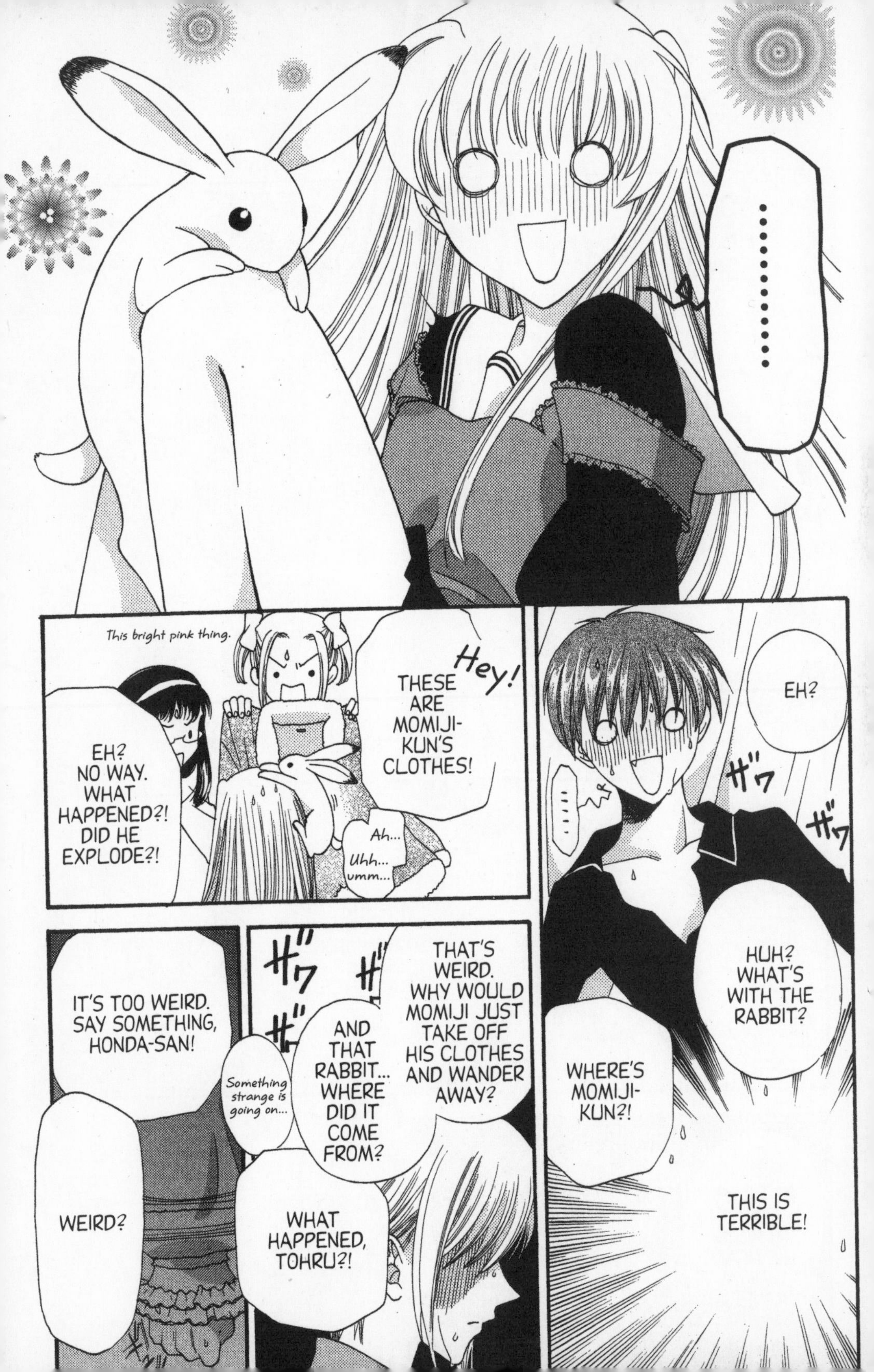
……
EH?
......
ザワ
ザワ
HUH? WHAT'S WITH THE RABBIT?
WHERE'S MOMIJI-KUN?!
THIS IS TERRIBLE!
Hey!
THESE ARE MOMIJI-KUN'S CLOTHES!
This bright pink thing.
EH? NO WAY. WHAT HAPPENED?! DID HE EXPLODE?!
Ah... Uhh... umm...
THAT'S WEIRD. WHY WOULD MOMIJI JUST TAKE OFF HIS CLOTHES AND WANDER AWAY?
ザワ
AND THAT RABBIT... WHERE DID IT COME FROM?
Something strange is going on...
WHAT HAPPENED, TOHRU?!
IT'S TOO WEIRD. SAY SOMETHING, HONDA-SAN!
WEIRD?

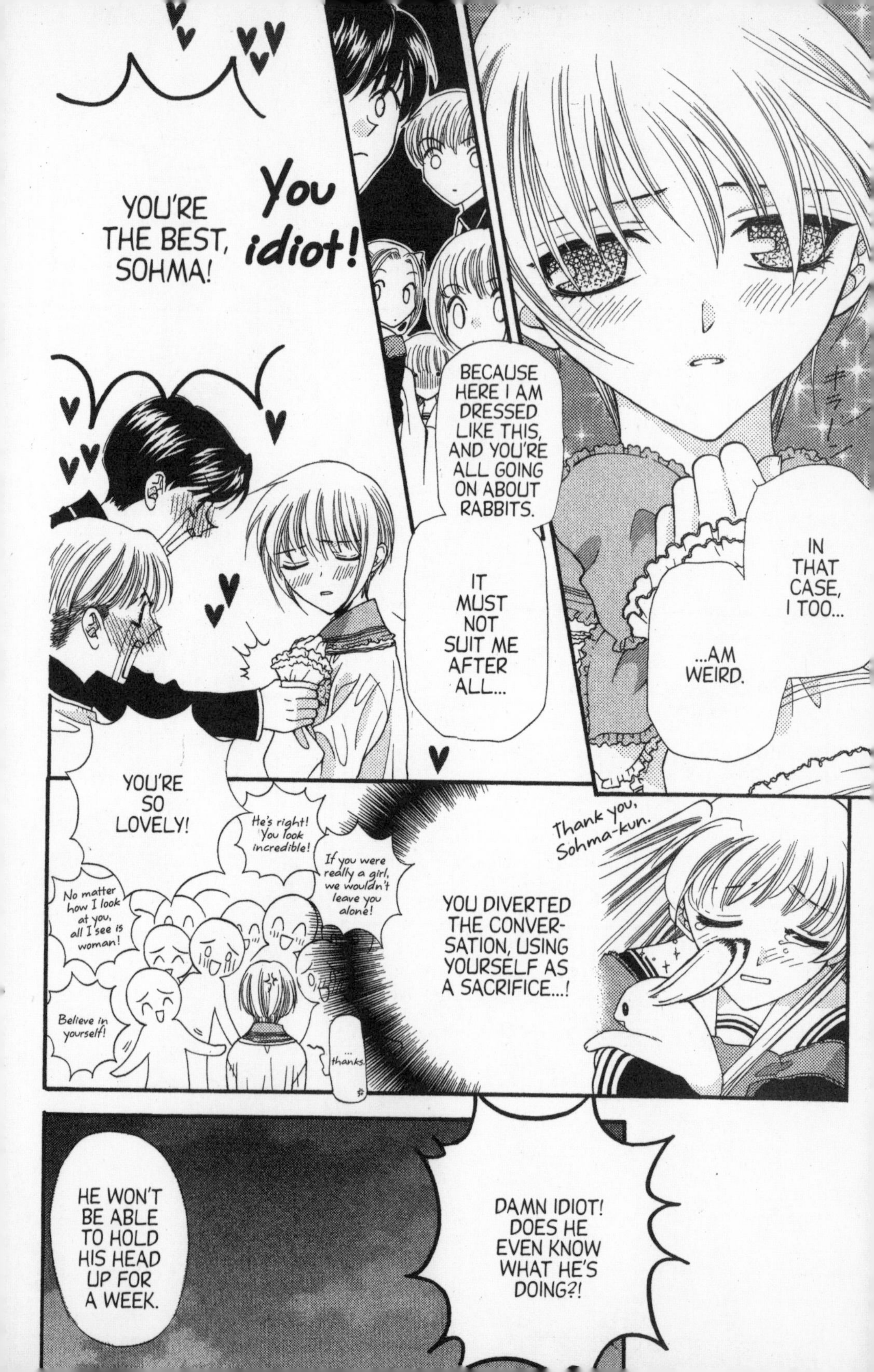
IN THAT CASE, I TOO...
...AM WEIRD.
BECAUSE HERE I AM DRESSED LIKE THIS, AND YOU'RE ALL GOING ON ABOUT RABBITS.
IT MUST NOT SUIT ME AFTER ALL...
You idiot!
YOU'RE THE BEST, SOHMA!
Thank you, Sohma-kun.
YOU DIVERTED THE CONVERSATION, USING YOURSELF AS A SACRIFICE...!
YOU'RE SO LOVELY!
He's right! You look incredible!
If you were really a girl, we wouldn't leave you alone!
No matter how I look at you, all I see is woman!
Believe in yourself!
...thanks.
DAMN IDIOT! DOES HE EVEN KNOW WHAT HE'S DOING?!
HE WON'T BE ABLE TO HOLD HIS HEAD UP FOR A WEEK.

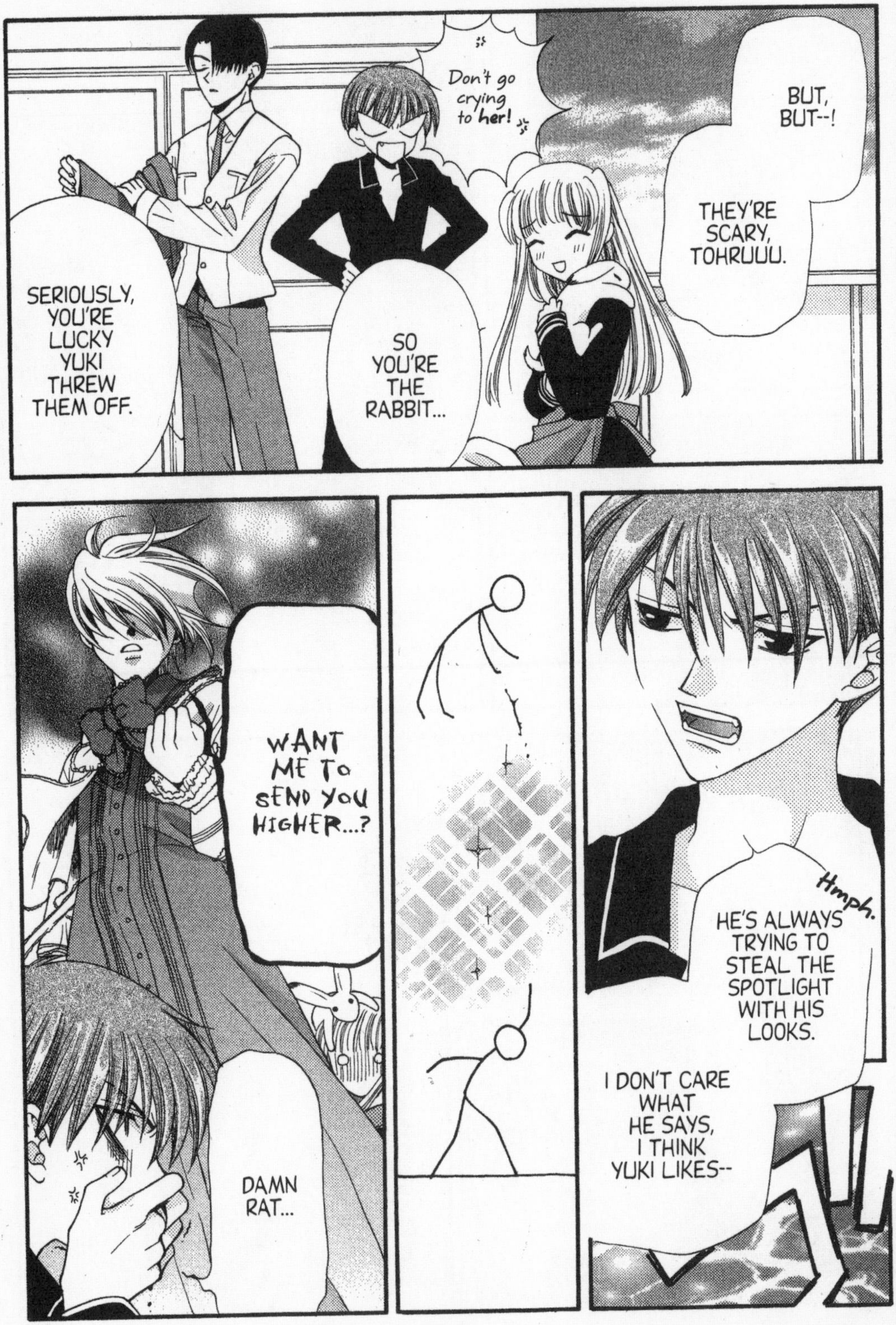
BUT, BUT--!
THEY'RE SCARY, TOHRUUU.
Don't go crying to her!
SO YOU'RE THE RABBIT...
SERIOUSLY, YOU'RE LUCKY YUKI THREW THEM OFF.
Hmph.
HE'S ALWAYS TRYING TO STEAL THE SPOTLIGHT WITH HIS LOOKS.
I DON'T CARE WHAT HE SAYS, I THINK YUKI LIKES--
WANT ME TO SEND YOU HIGHER...?
DAMN RAT...

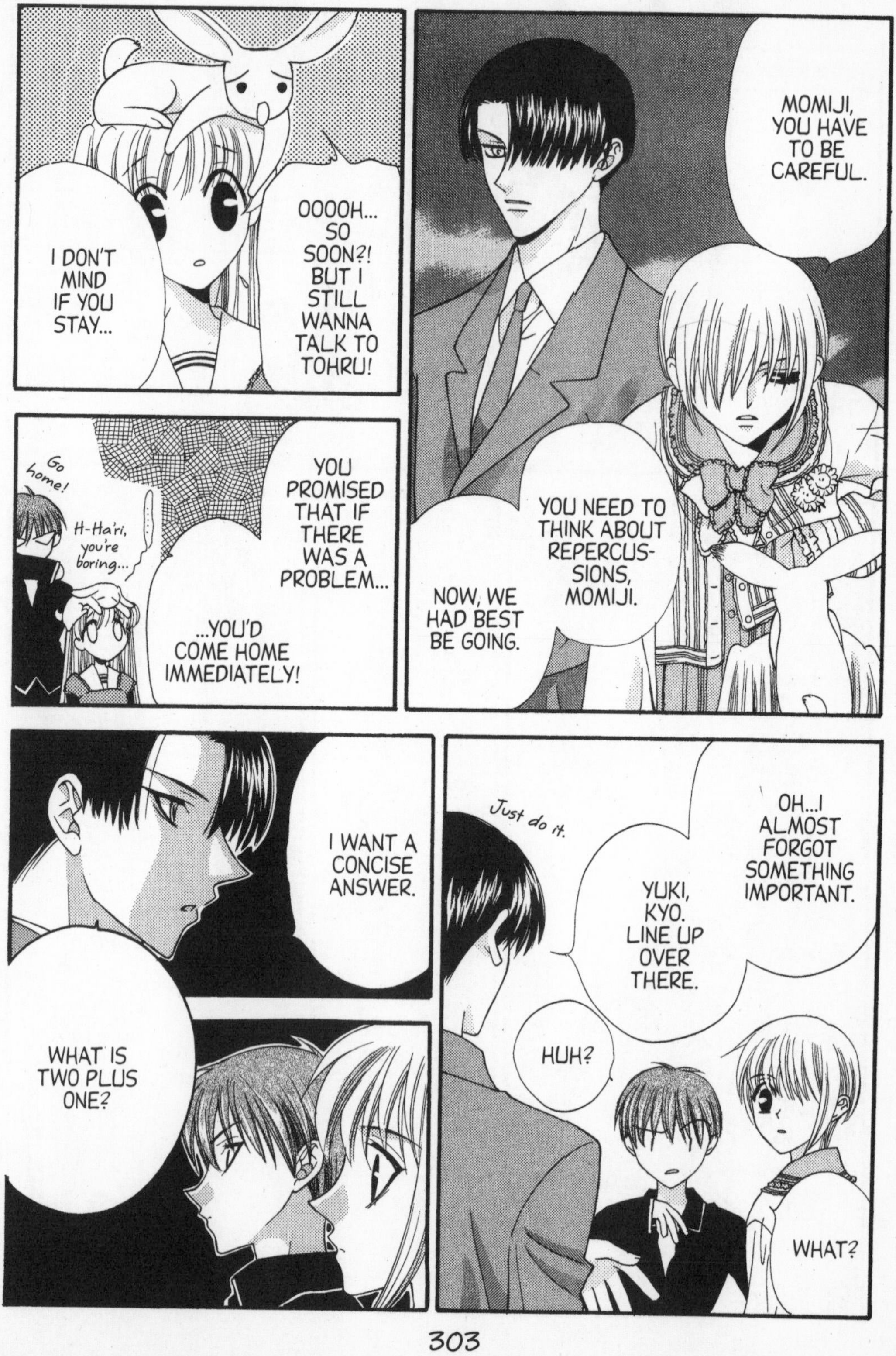
MOMIJI, YOU HAVE TO BE CAREFUL.
YOU NEED TO THINK ABOUT REPERCUSSIONS, MOMIJI.
NOW, WE HAD BEST BE GOING.
OOOOH... SO SOON?! BUT I STILL WANNA TALK TO TOHRU!
I DON'T MIND IF YOU STAY...
YOU PROMISED THAT IF THERE WAS A PROBLEM...
...YOU'D COME HOME IMMEDIATELY!
H-Ha'ri, you're boring...
Go home!
OH...I ALMOST FORGOT SOMETHING IMPORTANT.
Just do it.
YUKI, KYO. LINE UP OVER THERE.
HUH?
WHAT?
I WANT A CONCISE ANSWER.
WHAT IS TWO PLUS ONE?

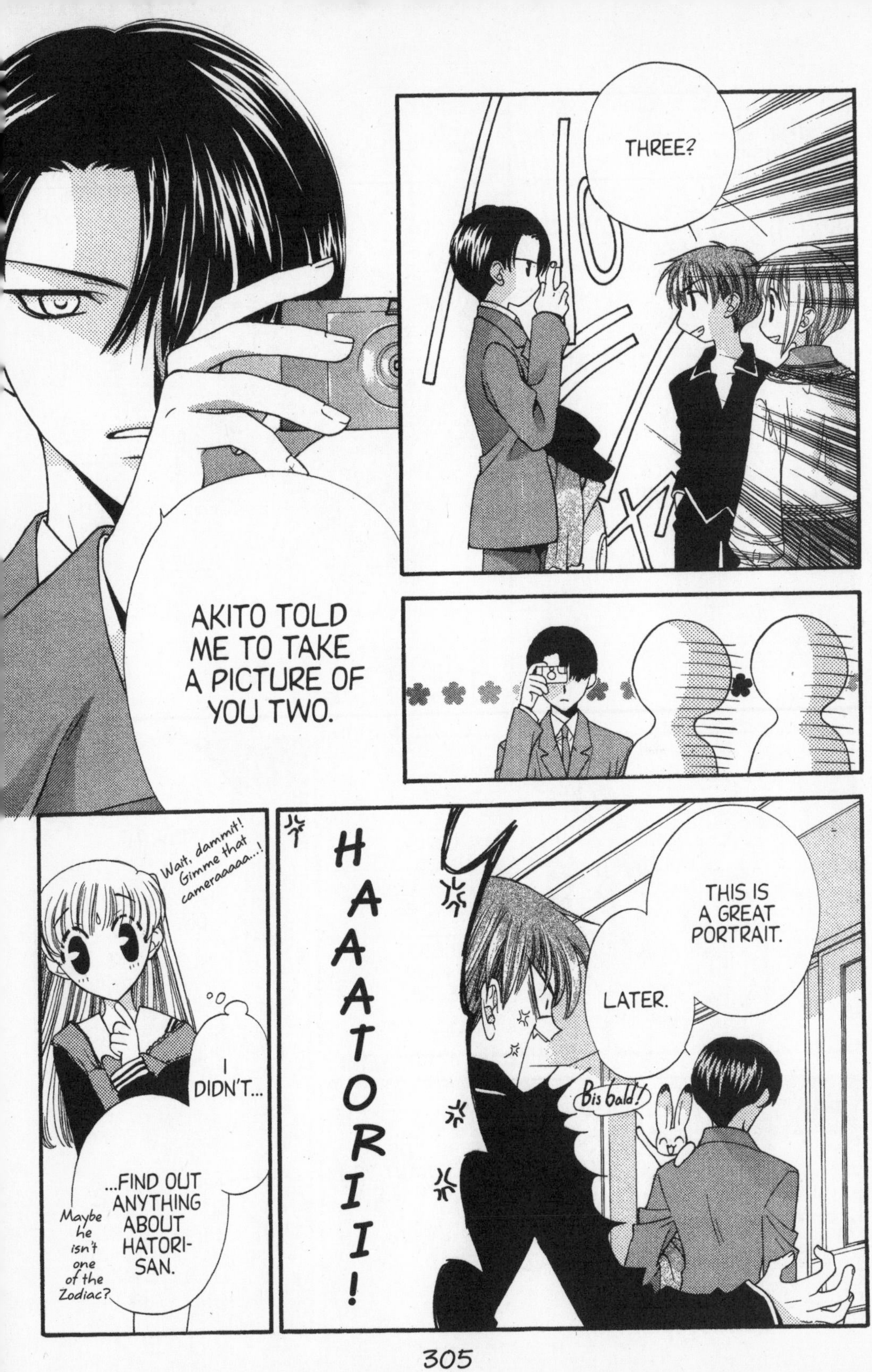

THREE?
AKITO TOLD ME TO TAKE A PICTURE OF YOU TWO.
THIS IS A GREAT PORTRAIT.
LATER.
HAAATORII!
Bis bald!
Wait, dammit! Gimme that cameraaaaa...!
I DIDN'T...
...FIND OUT ANYTHING ABOUT HATORI-SAN.
Maybe he isn't one of the Zodiac?

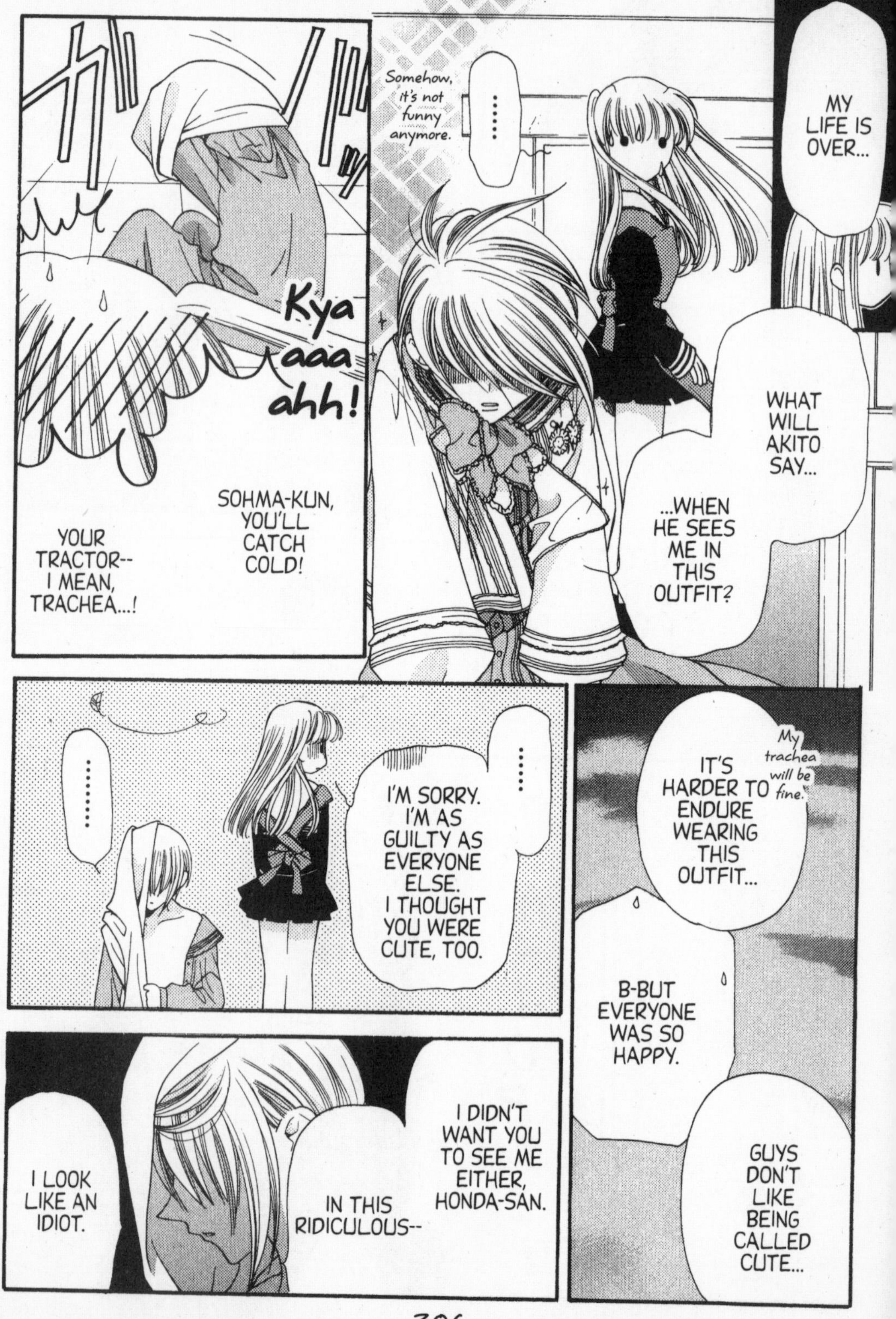
MY LIFE IS OVER...
WHAT WILL AKITO SAY...
...WHEN HE SEES ME IN THIS OUTFIT?
......
Somehow, it's not funny anymore.
Kya aaa ahh!
SOHMA-KUN, YOU'LL CATCH COLD!
YOUR TRACTOR-- I MEAN, TRACHEA...!
IT'S HARDER TO ENDURE WEARING THIS OUTFIT...
My trachea will be fine.
B-BUT EVERYONE WAS SO HAPPY.
GUYS DON'T LIKE BEING CALLED CUTE...
......
I'M SORRY. I'M AS GUILTY AS EVERYONE ELSE. I THOUGHT YOU WERE CUTE, TOO.
......
I DIDN'T WANT YOU TO SEE ME EITHER, HONDA-SAN.
IN THIS RIDICULOUS--
I LOOK LIKE AN IDIOT.

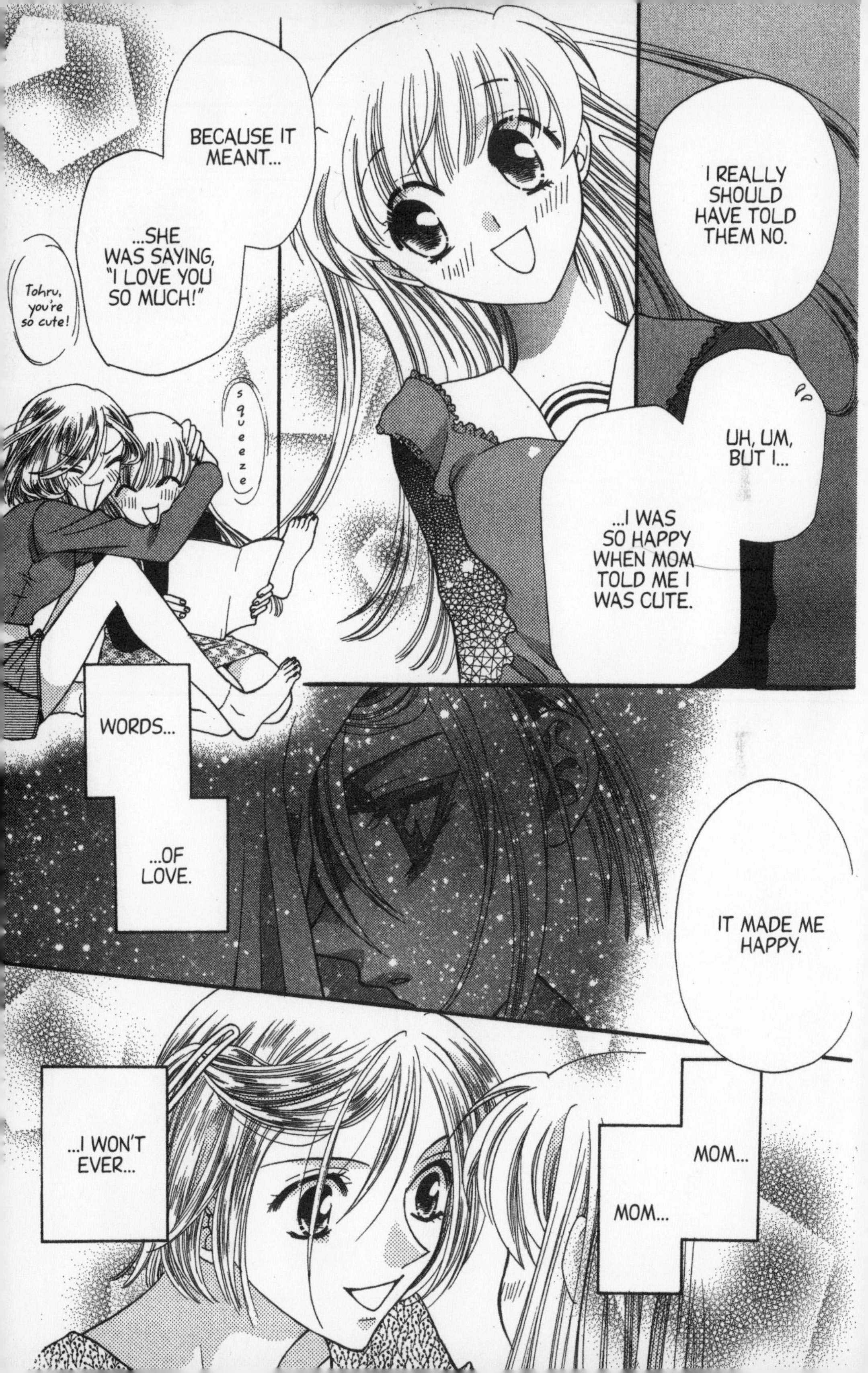
I REALLY SHOULD HAVE TOLD THEM NO.
UH, UM, BUT I...
...I WAS SO HAPPY WHEN MOM TOLD ME I WAS CUTE.
BECAUSE IT MEANT...
...SHE WAS SAYING, "I LOVE YOU SO MUCH!"
squeeze
Tohru, you're so cute!
IT MADE ME HAPPY.
WORDS...
...OF LOVE.
MOM...
MOM...
...I WON'T EVER...

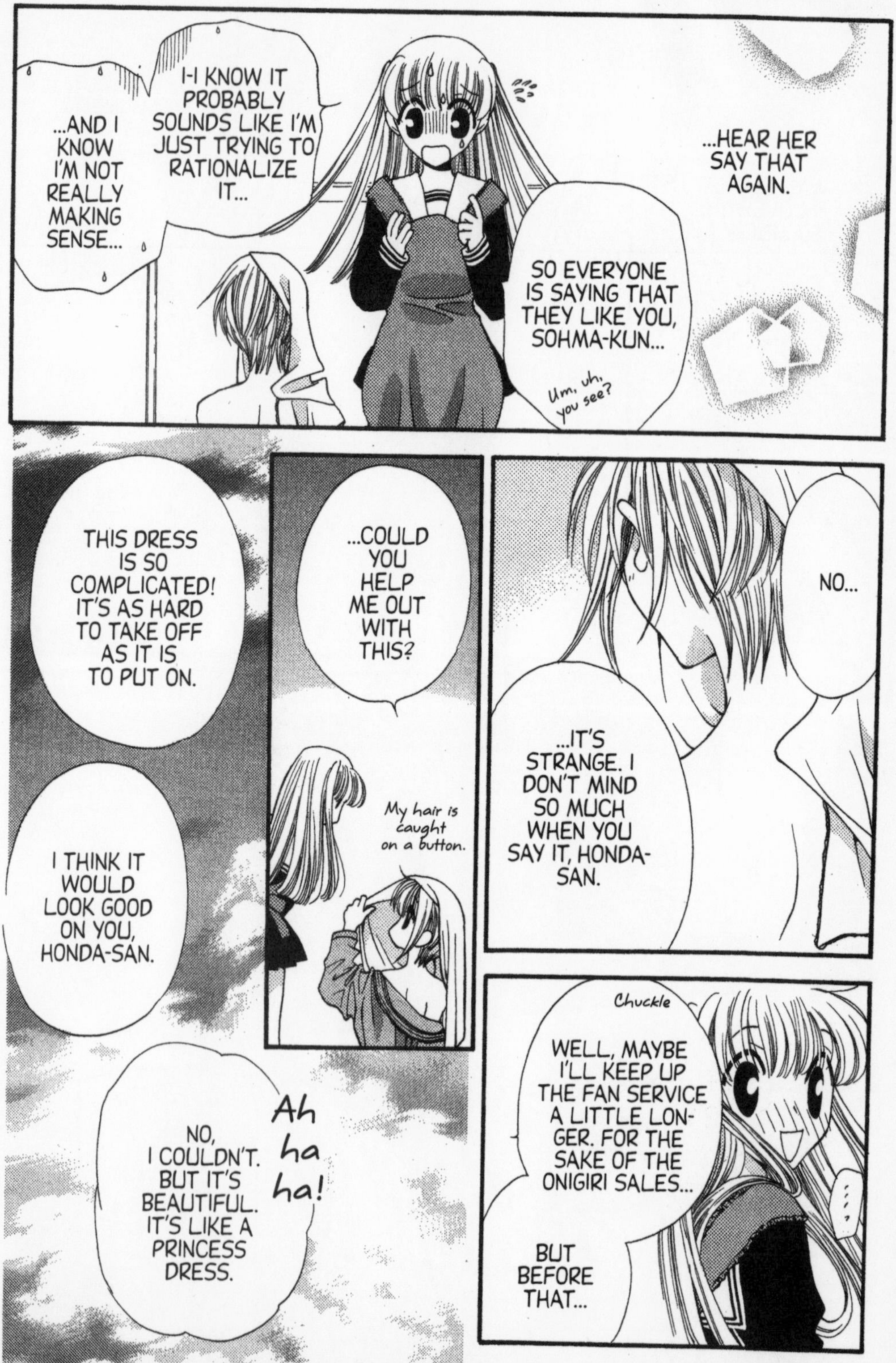
...HEAR HER SAY THAT AGAIN.
SO EVERYONE IS SAYING THAT THEY LIKE YOU, SOHMA-KUN...
Um, uh, you see?
I-I KNOW IT PROBABLY SOUNDS LIKE I'M JUST TRYING TO RATIONALIZE IT...
...AND I KNOW I'M NOT REALLY MAKING SENSE...
NO...
...IT'S STRANGE. I DON'T MIND SO MUCH WHEN YOU SAY IT, HONDA-SAN.
Chuckle
WELL, MAYBE I'LL KEEP UP THE FAN SERVICE A LITTLE LONGER. FOR THE SAKE OF THE ONIGIRI SALES...
BUT BEFORE THAT...
...COULD YOU HELP ME OUT WITH THIS?
My hair is caught on a button.
THIS DRESS IS SO COMPLICATED! IT'S AS HARD TO TAKE OFF AS IT IS TO PUT ON.
I THINK IT WOULD LOOK GOOD ON YOU, HONDA-SAN.
NO, I COULDN'T. BUT IT'S BEAUTIFUL. IT'S LIKE A PRINCESS DRESS.
Ah ha ha!

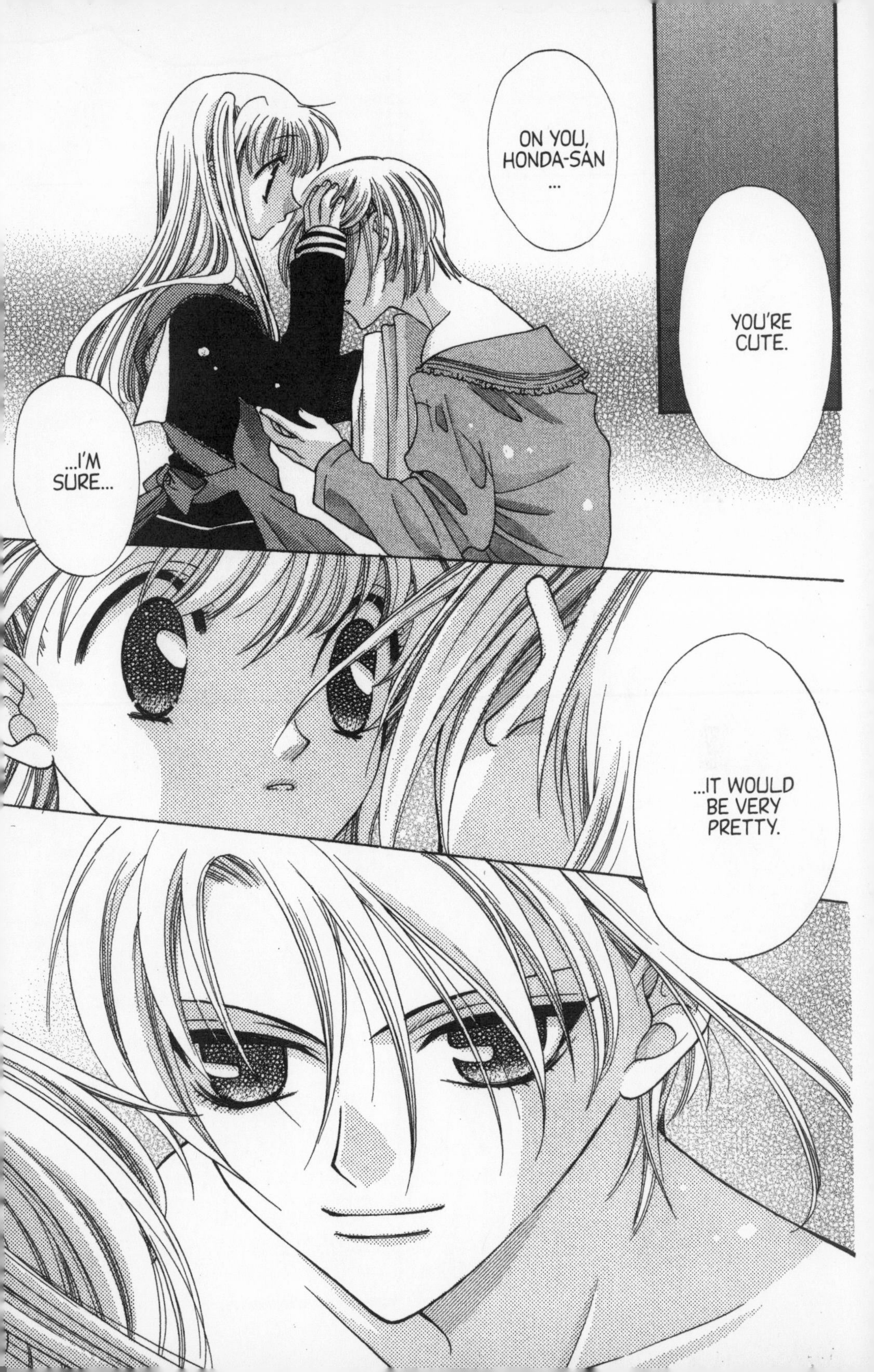
ON YOU, HONDA-SAN ...
YOU'RE CUTE.
...I'M SURE...
...IT WOULD BE VERY PRETTY.

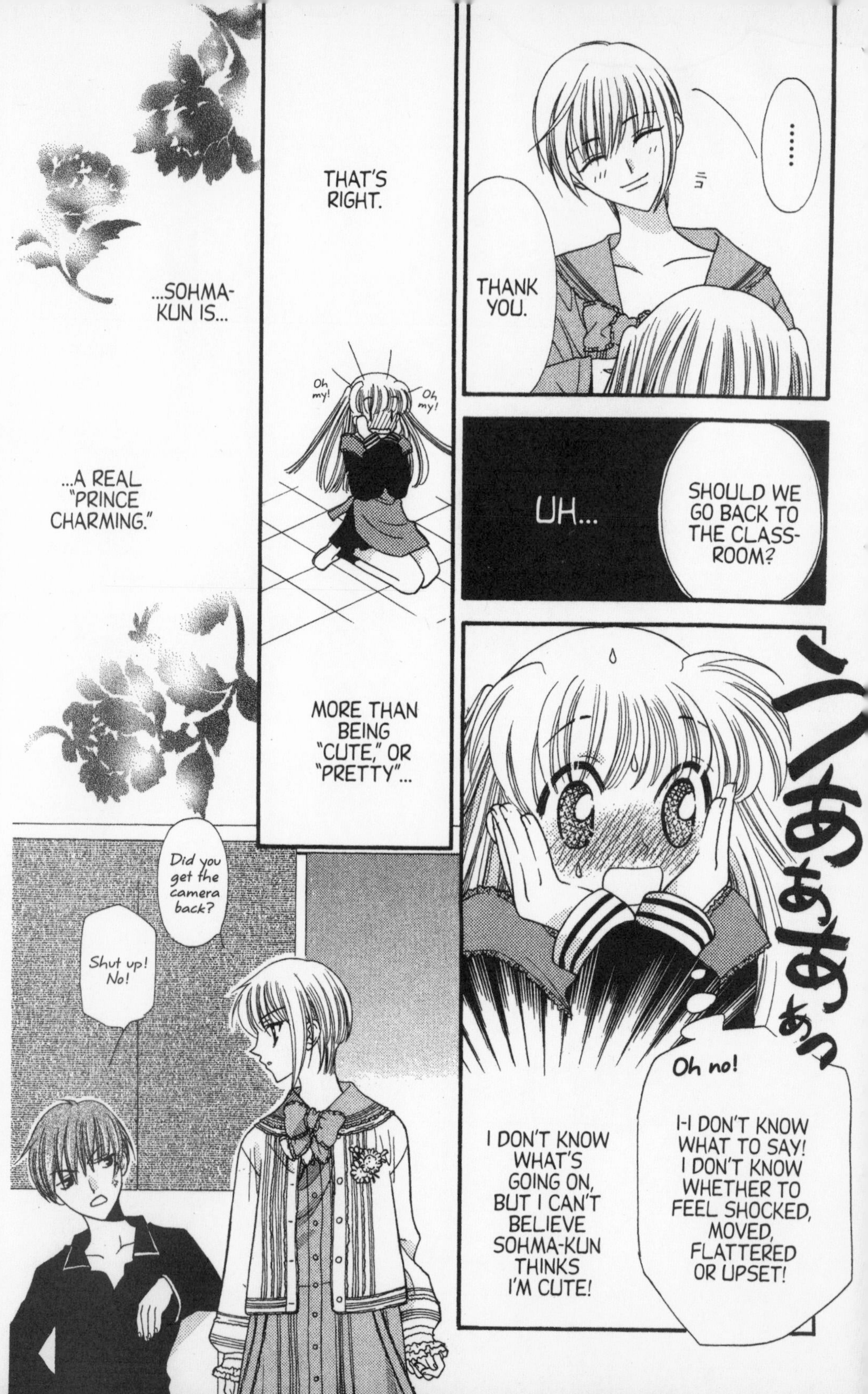

......
ニコ
THANK YOU.
SHOULD WE GO BACK TO THE CLASS-ROOM?
UH...
うあああっ
Oh no!
I-I DON'T KNOW WHAT TO SAY! I DON'T KNOW WHETHER TO FEEL SHOCKED, MOVED, FLATTERED OR UPSET!
I DON'T KNOW WHAT'S GOING ON, BUT I CAN'T BELIEVE SOHMA-KUN THINKS I'M CUTE!
THAT'S RIGHT.
Oh my!
Oh my!
MORE THAN BEING "CUTE," OR "PRETTY"...
...SOHMA-KUN IS...
...A REAL "PRINCE CHARMING."
Did you get the camera back?
Shut up! No!

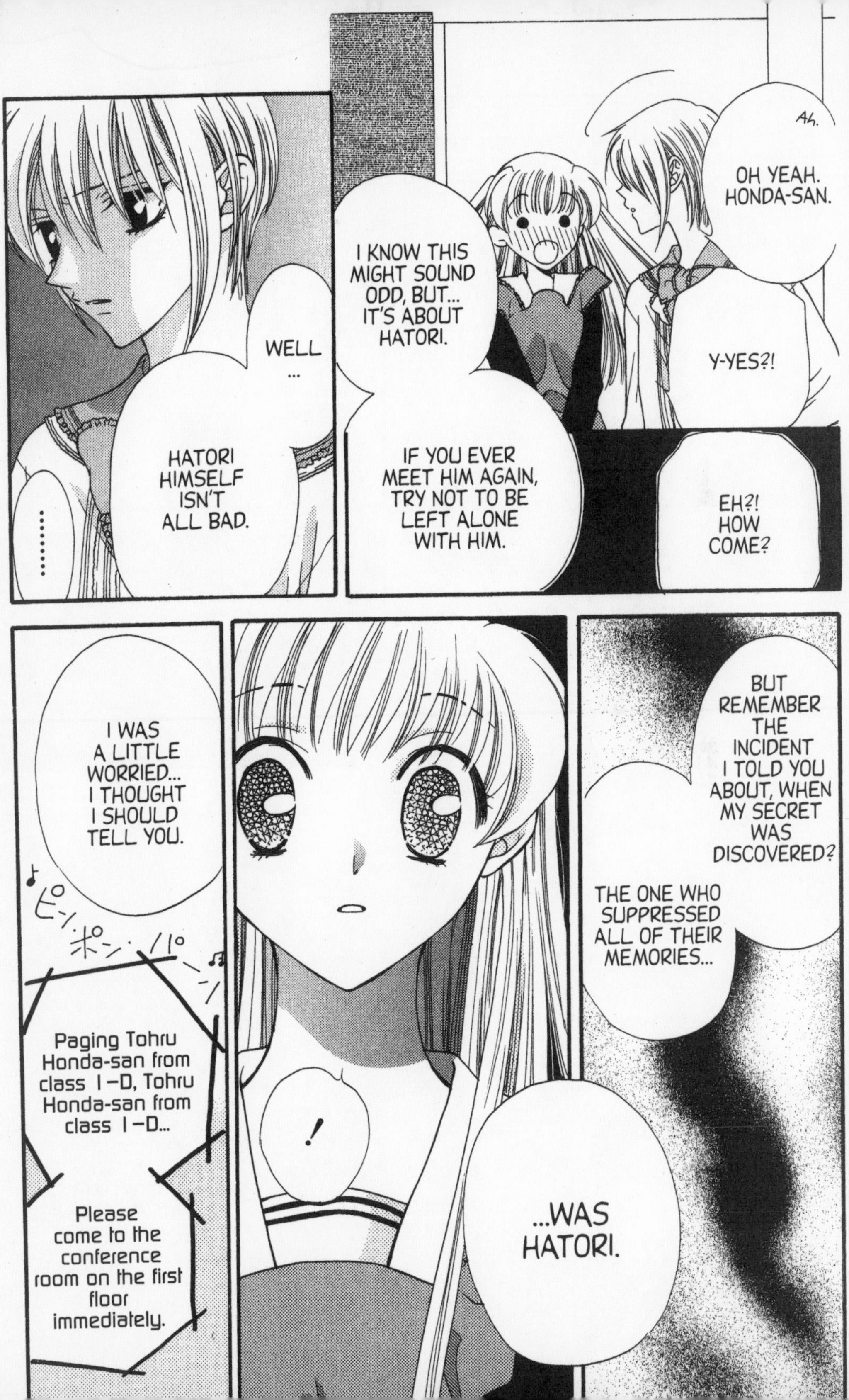
Ah.
OH YEAH. HONDA-SAN.
Y-YES?!
I KNOW THIS MIGHT SOUND ODD, BUT... IT'S ABOUT HATORI.
IF YOU EVER MEET HIM AGAIN, TRY NOT TO BE LEFT ALONE WITH HIM.
EH?! HOW COME?
WELL ...
HATORI HIMSELF ISN'T ALL BAD.
....
BUT REMEMBER THE INCIDENT I TOLD YOU ABOUT, WHEN MY SECRET WAS DISCOVERED?
THE ONE WHO SUPPRESSED ALL OF THEIR MEMORIES...
...WAS HATORI.
!
I WAS A LITTLE WORRIED... I THOUGHT I SHOULD TELL YOU.
Paging Tohru Honda-san from class 1-D, Tohru Honda-san from class 1-D...
Please come to the conference room on the first floor immediately.

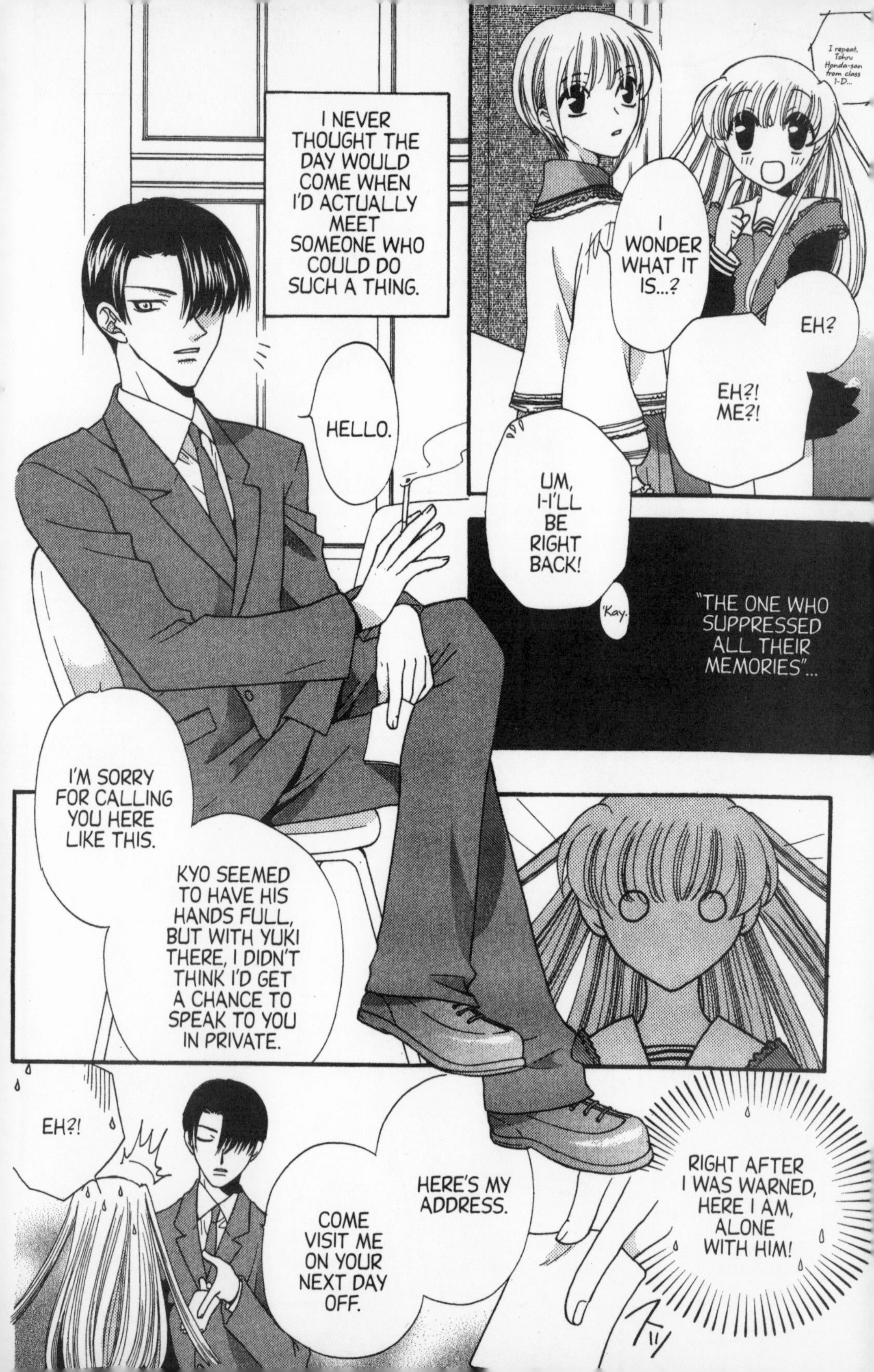
I repeat, Tohru Honda-san from class 1-D...
EH?
EH?! ME?!
I WONDER WHAT IT IS...?
UM, I-I'LL BE RIGHT BACK!
'Kay.
"THE ONE WHO SUPPRESSED ALL THEIR MEMORIES"...
I NEVER THOUGHT THE DAY WOULD COME WHEN I'D ACTUALLY MEET SOMEONE WHO COULD DO SUCH A THING.
HELLO.
I'M SORRY FOR CALLING YOU HERE LIKE THIS.
KYO SEEMED TO HAVE HIS HANDS FULL, BUT WITH YUKI THERE, I DIDN'T THINK I'D GET A CHANCE TO SPEAK TO YOU IN PRIVATE.
RIGHT AFTER I WAS WARNED, HERE I AM, ALONE WITH HIM!
HERE'S MY ADDRESS.
COME VISIT ME ON YOUR NEXT DAY OFF.
EH?!

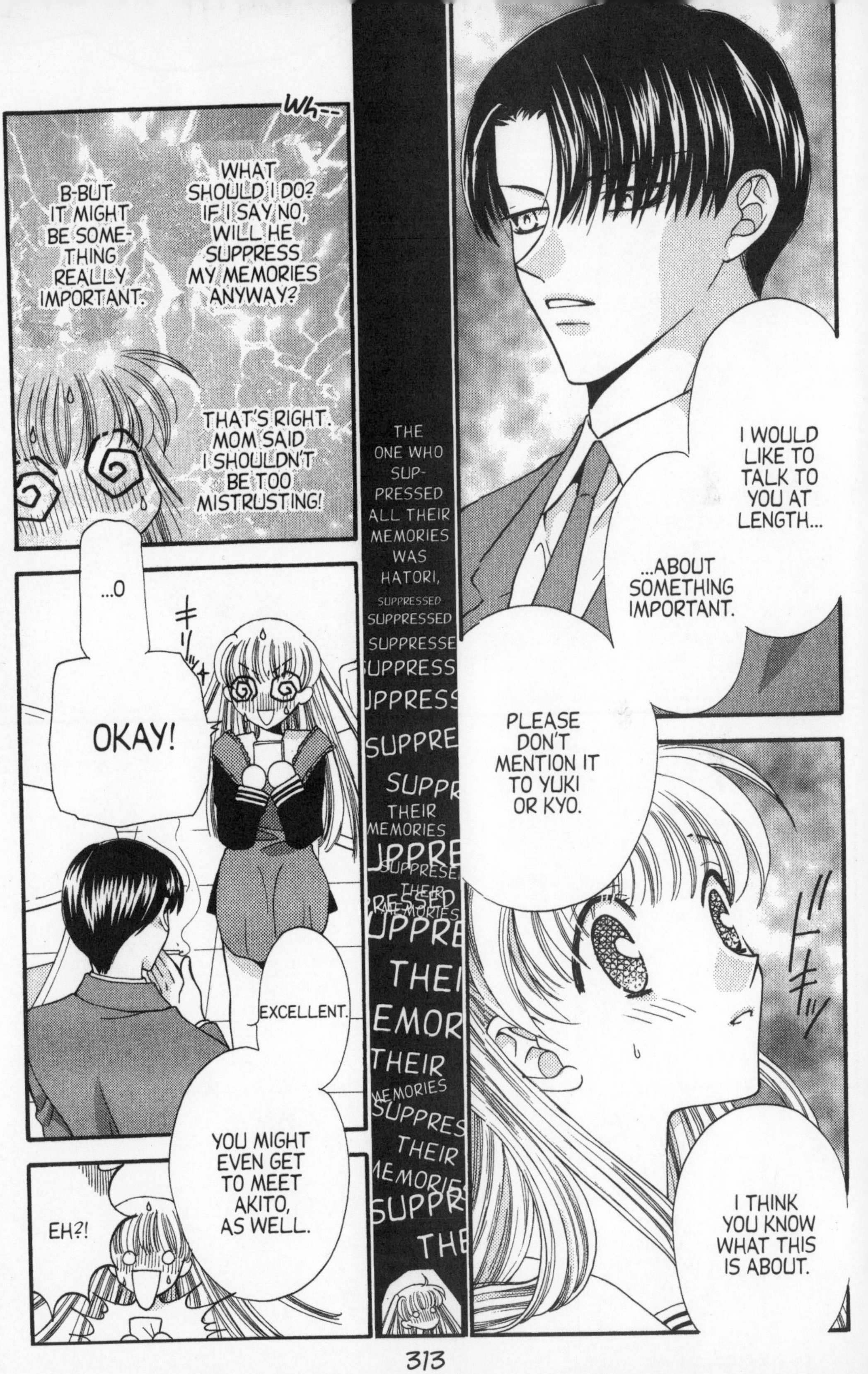
I WOULD LIKE TO TALK TO YOU AT LENGTH...
...ABOUT SOMETHING IMPORTANT.
PLEASE DON'T MENTION IT TO YUKI OR KYO.
I THINK YOU KNOW WHAT THIS IS ABOUT.
THE ONE WHO SUP-PRESSED ALL THEIR MEMORIES WAS HATORI,
SUPPRESSED
SUPPRESSED
SUPPRESSE
SUPPRESS
UPPRESS
SUPPRE
SUPPR
THEIR MEMORIES
UPPRE
SUPPRESE
THEIR
MEMORIES
PRESSED
UPPRE
THEI
EMOR
THEIR
MEMORIES
SUPPRES
THEIR
MEMORIES
SUPPR
THE
WH--
WHAT SHOULD I DO? IF I SAY NO, WILL HE SUPPRESS MY MEMORIES ANYWAY?
B-BUT IT MIGHT BE SOME-THING REALLY IMPORTANT.
THAT'S RIGHT. MOM SAID I SHOULDN'T BE TOO MISTRUSTING!
...O
OKAY!
EXCELLENT.
YOU MIGHT EVEN GET TO MEET AKITO, AS WELL.
EH?!

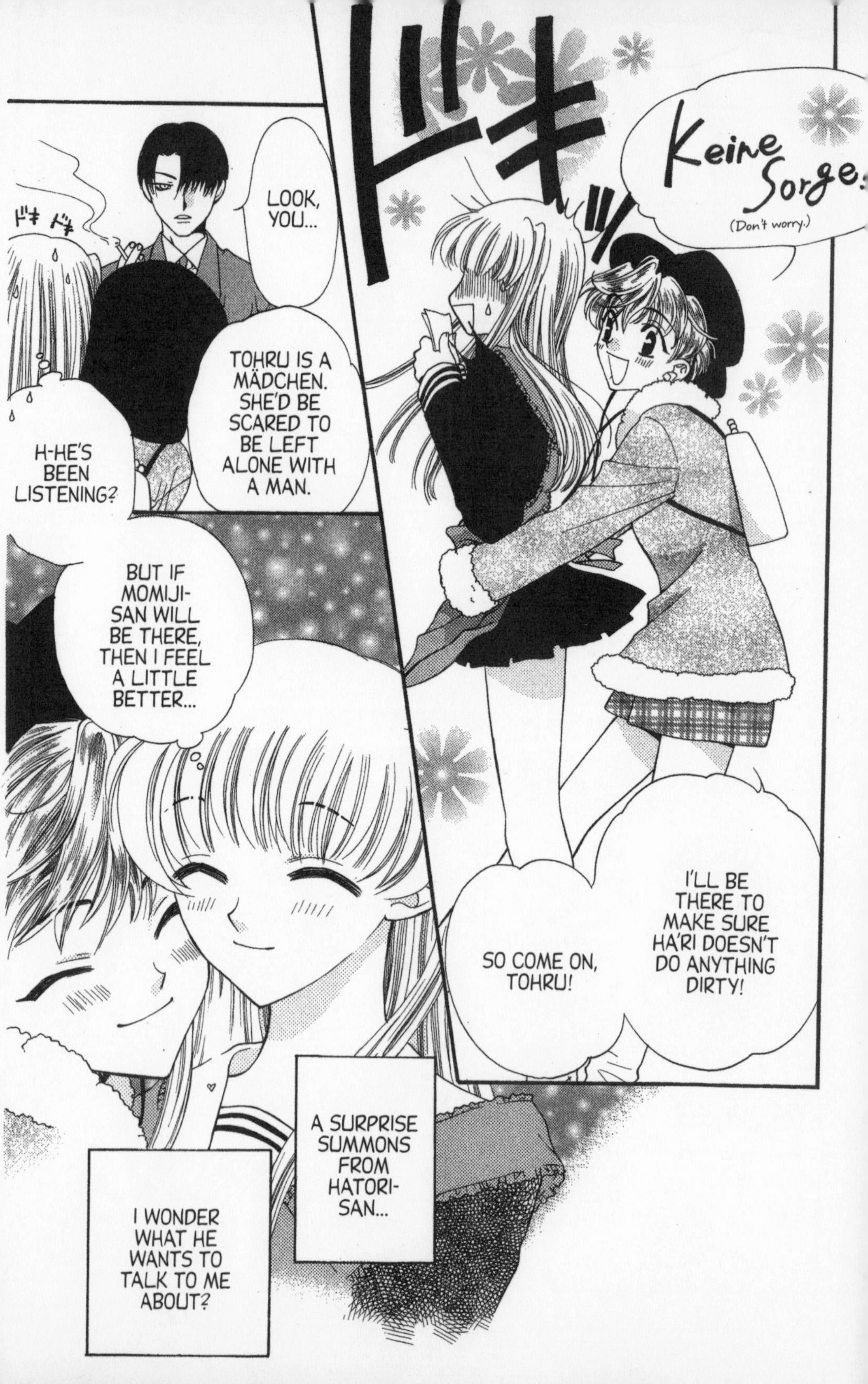
ドキッ
Keine Sorge! (Don't worry.)
I'LL BE THERE TO MAKE SURE HA'RI DOESN'T DO ANYTHING DIRTY!
SO COME ON, TOHRU!
LOOK, YOU...
TOHRU IS A MÄDCHEN. SHE'D BE SCARED TO BE LEFT ALONE WITH A MAN.
ドキ ドキ
H-HE'S BEEN LISTENING?
BUT IF MOMIJI-SAN WILL BE THERE, THEN I FEEL A LITTLE BETTER...
A SURPRISE SUMMONS FROM HATORI-SAN...
I WONDER WHAT HE WANTS TO TALK TO ME ABOUT?

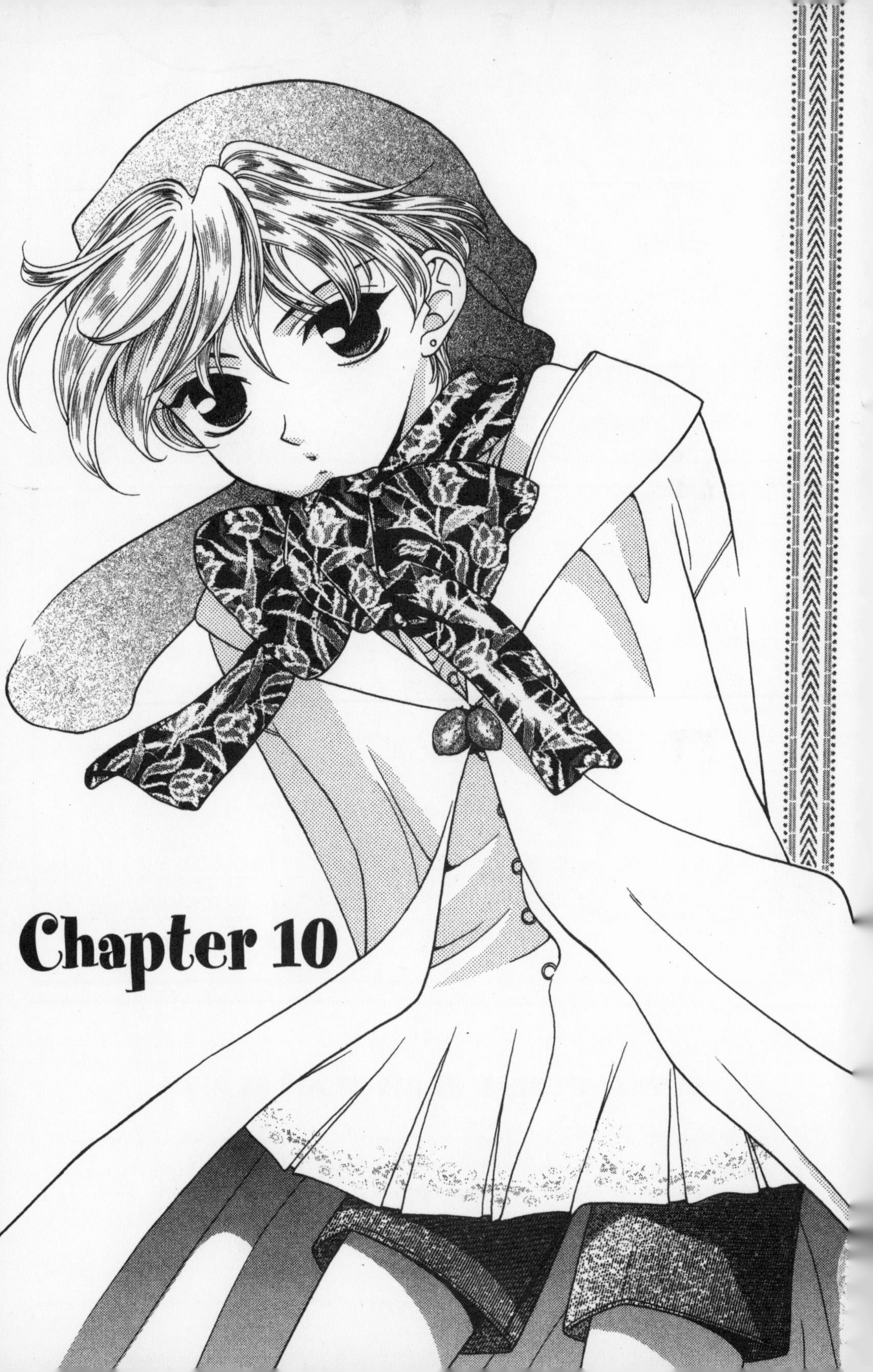
Chapter 10

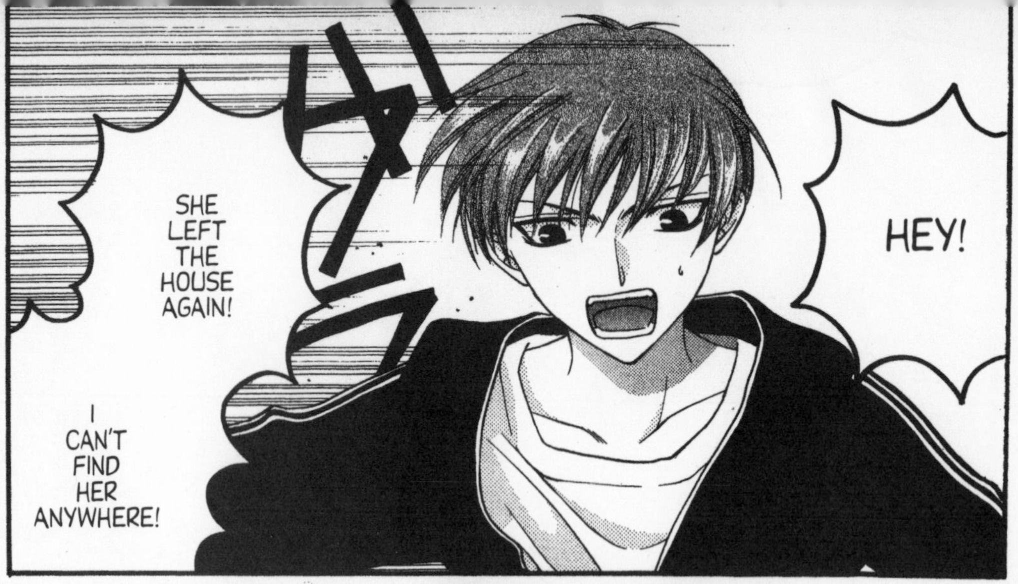
HEY!
SHE LEFT THE HOUSE AGAIN!
I CAN'T FIND HER ANYWHERE!

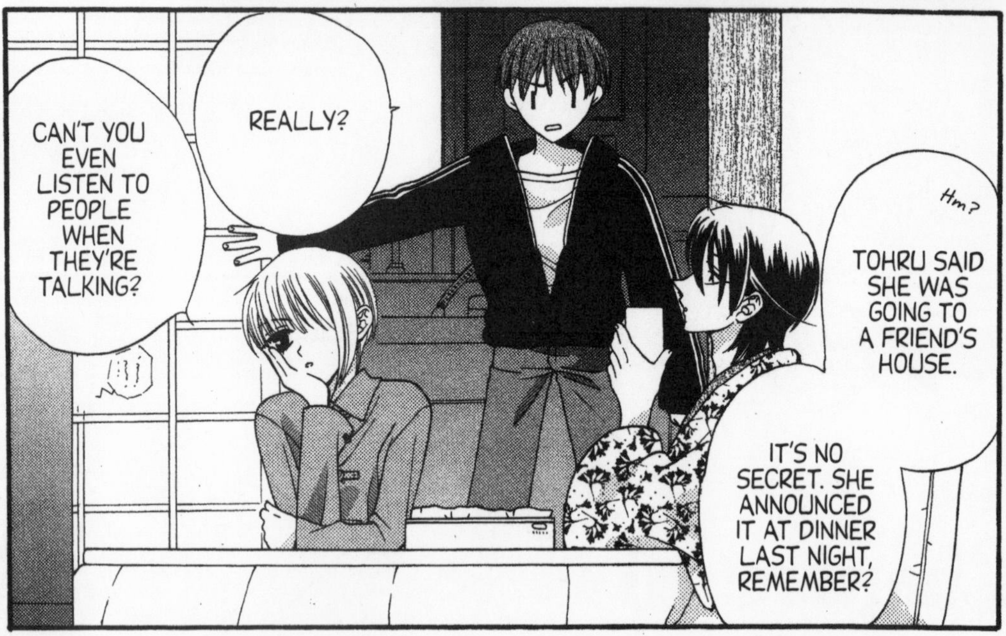
Hm?
TOHRU SAID SHE WAS GOING TO A FRIEND'S HOUSE.
IT'S NO SECRET. SHE ANNOUNCED IT AT DINNER LAST NIGHT, REMEMBER?
REALLY?
CAN'T YOU EVEN LISTEN TO PEOPLE WHEN THEY'RE TALKING?

ULTRA SPECIAL BLAH BLAH BLAH 4

Hatori stands out so much that I originally thought he would be on the cover of volume 2....his personality makes him easy to draw. I feel like he and Shigure are popular as a set. I wonder how Hatori feels about that (laugh).

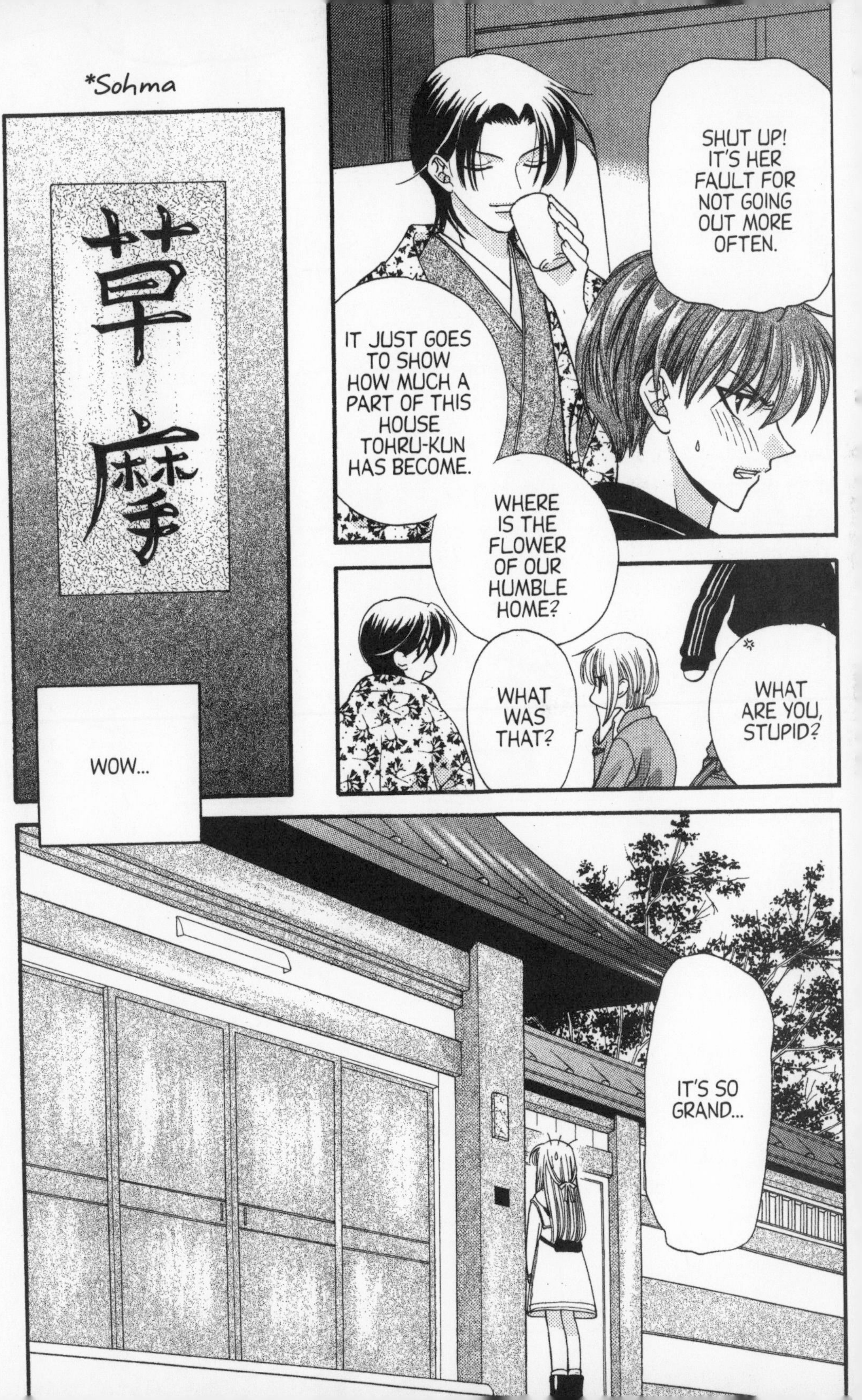

SHUT UP! IT'S HER FAULT FOR NOT GOING OUT MORE OFTEN.
IT JUST GOES TO SHOW HOW MUCH A PART OF THIS HOUSE TOHRU-KUN HAS BECOME.
WHERE IS THE FLOWER OF OUR HUMBLE HOME?
WHAT ARE YOU, STUPID?
WHAT WAS THAT?
草摩
*Sohma
WOW...
IT'S SO GRAND...

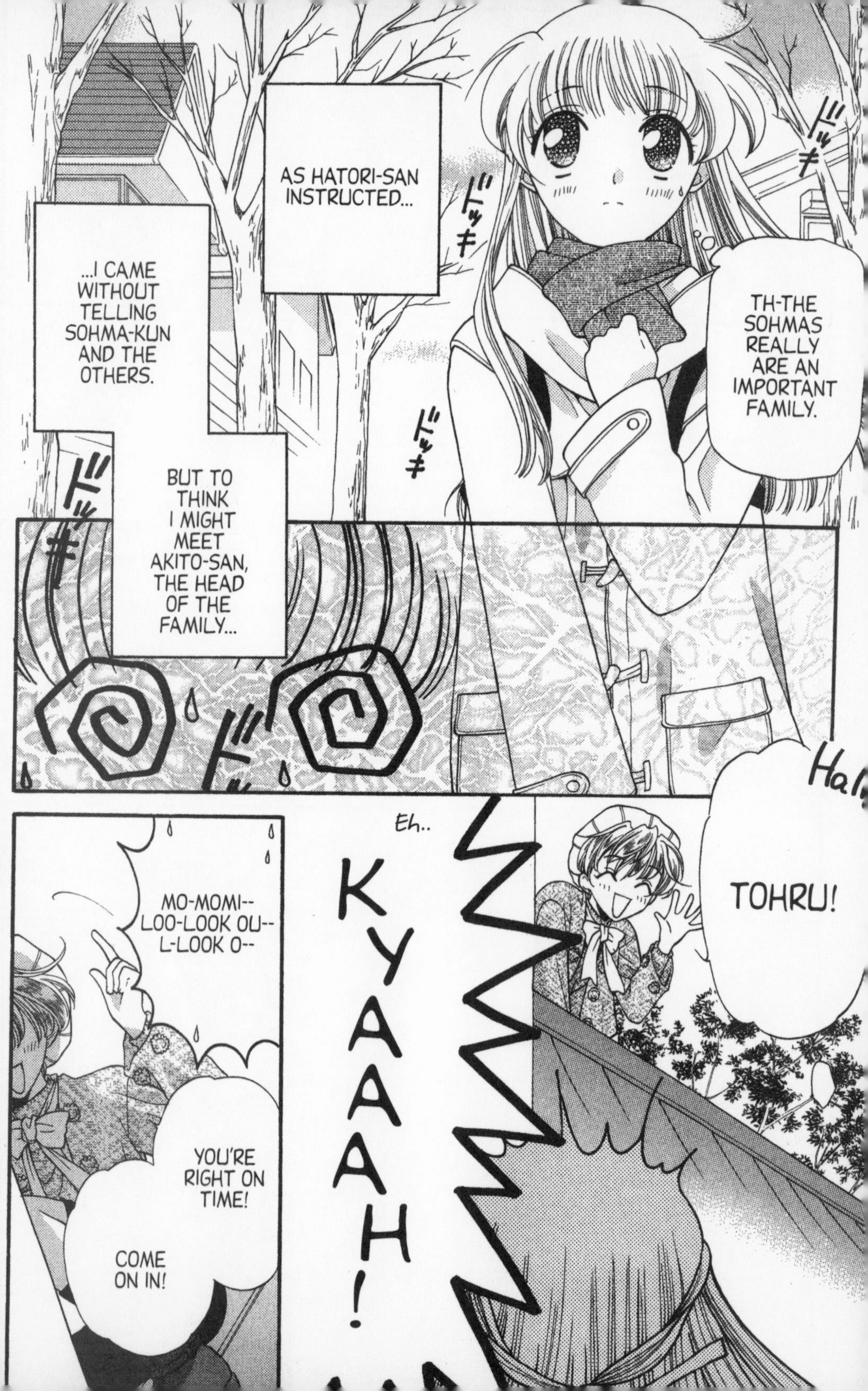
AS HATORI-SAN INSTRUCTED...
...I CAME WITHOUT TELLING SOHMA-KUN AND THE OTHERS.
ドッキ
ドッキ
TH-THE SOHMAS REALLY ARE AN IMPORTANT FAMILY.
ドッキ
BUT TO THINK I MIGHT MEET AKITO-SAN, THE HEAD OF THE FAMILY...
ドッキ
ド
Hal
TOHRU!
KYAAAH!
Eh..
MO-MOMI-- LOO-LOOK OU-- L-LOOK O--
YOU'RE RIGHT ON TIME!
COME ON IN!

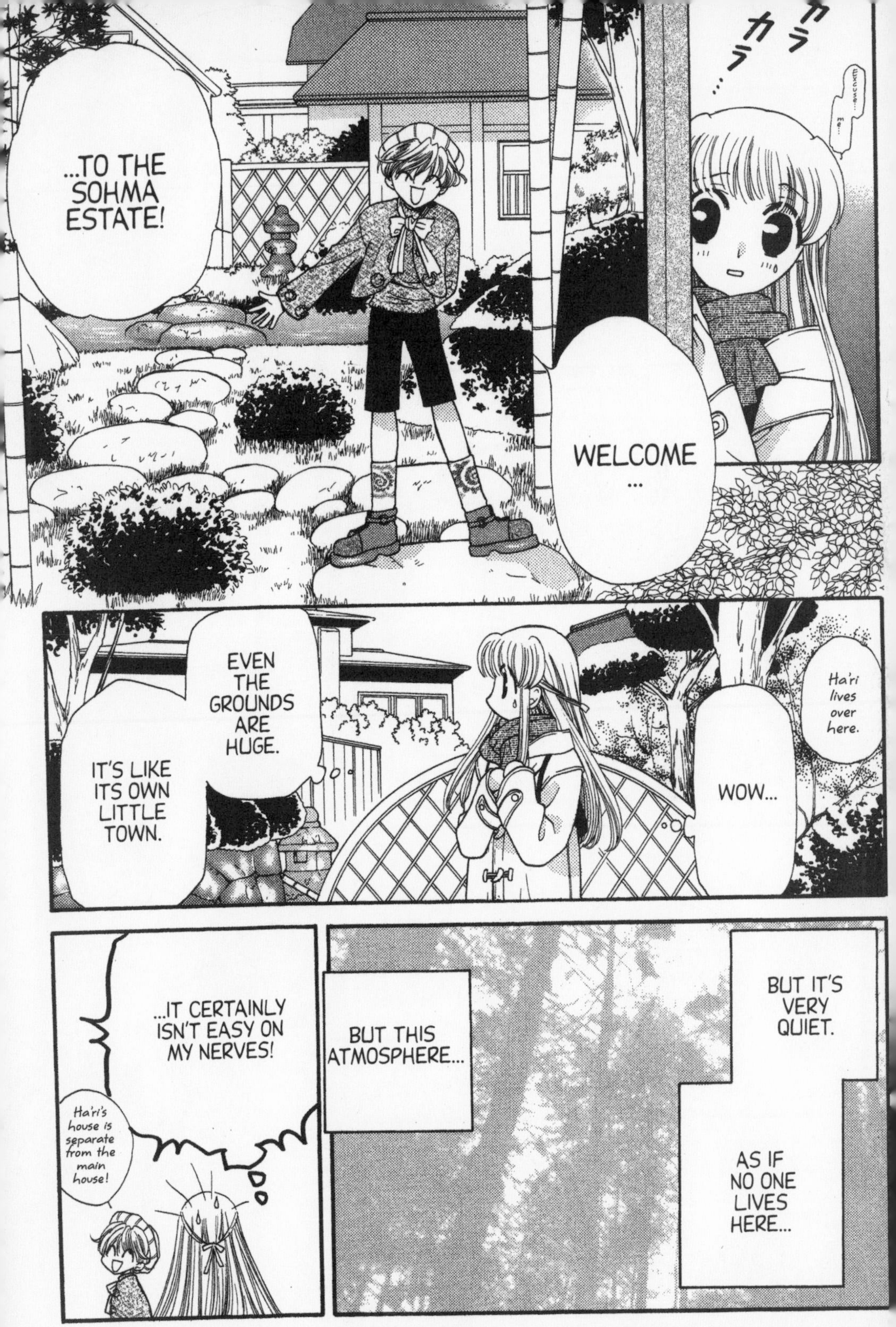
カラカラ…
Excuse me...
WELCOME ...
...TO THE SOHMA ESTATE!
Ha'ri lives over here.
WOW...
EVEN THE GROUNDS ARE HUGE.
IT'S LIKE ITS OWN LITTLE TOWN.
BUT IT'S VERY QUIET.
AS IF NO ONE LIVES HERE...
BUT THIS ATMOSPHERE...
...IT CERTAINLY ISN'T EASY ON MY NERVES!
Ha'ri's house is separate from the main house!

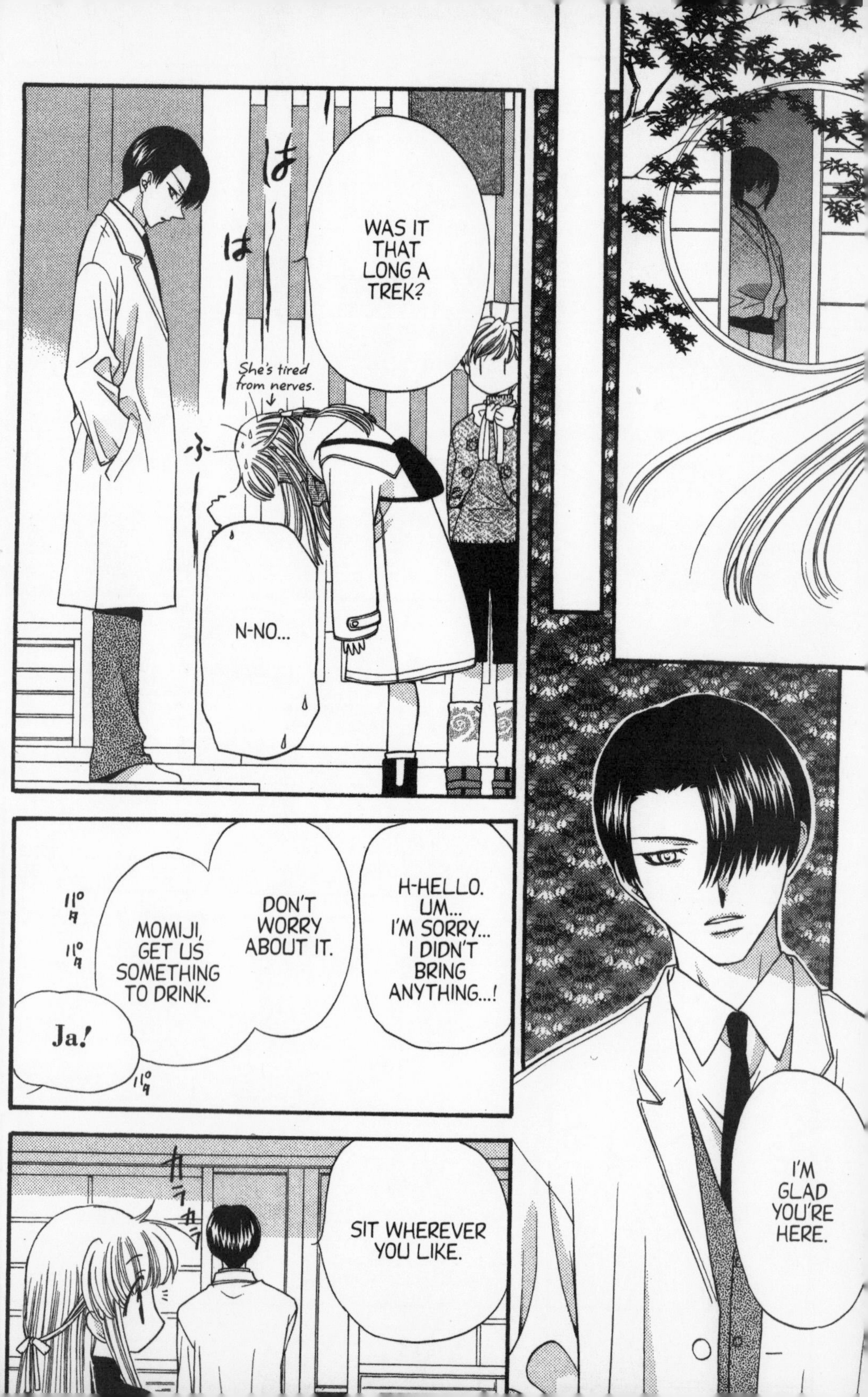
はーはーふー
WAS IT THAT LONG A TREK?
She's tired from nerves.
N-NO...
I'M GLAD YOU'RE HERE.
H-HELLO. UM... I'M SORRY... I DIDN'T BRING ANYTHING...!
DON'T WORRY ABOUT IT.
MOMIJI, GET US SOMETHING TO DRINK.
パタパタ
Ja!
パタ
カラカラ
SIT WHEREVER YOU LIKE.

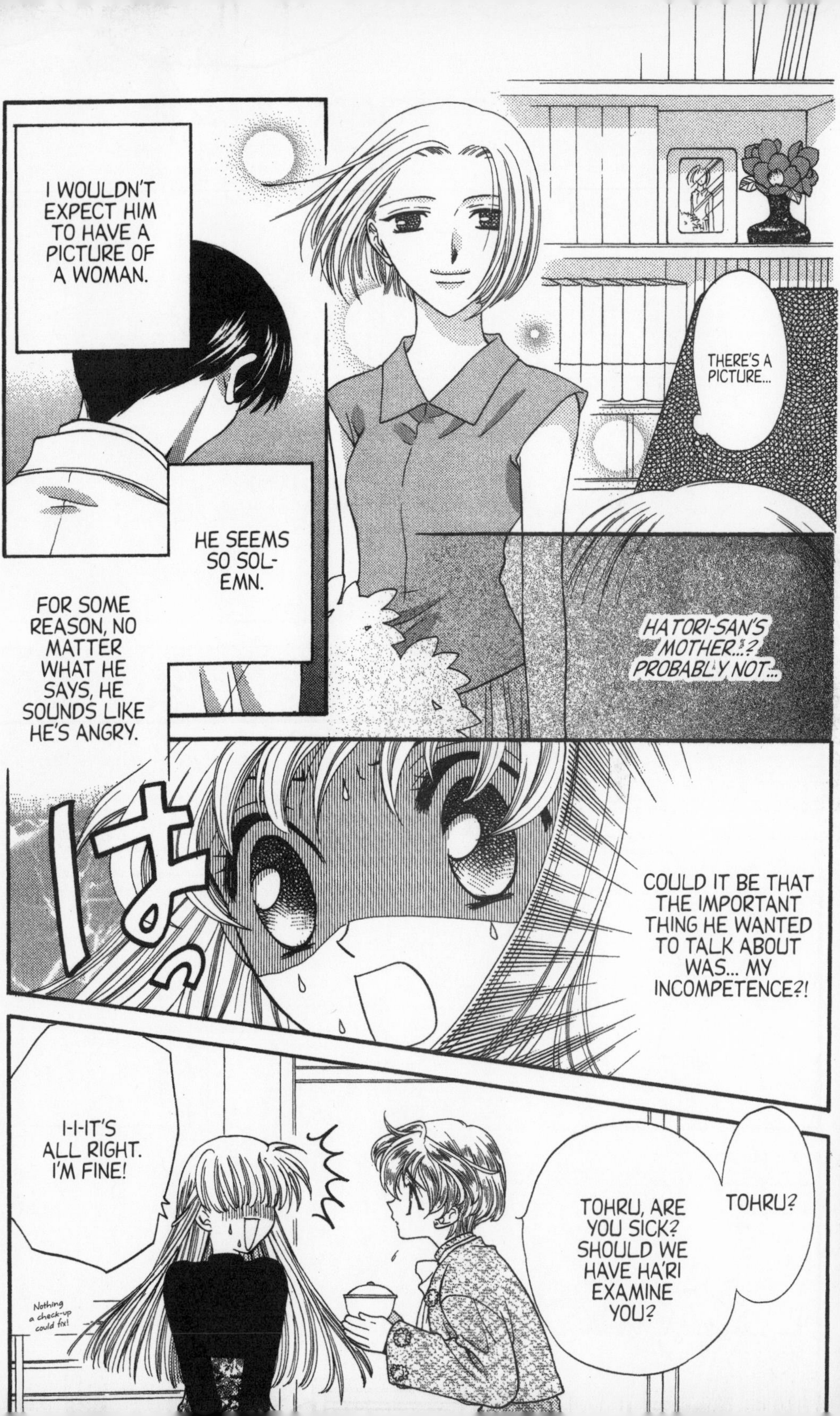
THERE'S A PICTURE...
I WOULDN'T EXPECT HIM TO HAVE A PICTURE OF A WOMAN.
HATORI-SAN'S MOTHER...?? PROBABLY NOT...
HE SEEMS SO SOL-EMN.
FOR SOME REASON, NO MATTER WHAT HE SAYS, HE SOUNDS LIKE HE'S ANGRY.
COULD IT BE THAT THE IMPORTANT THING HE WANTED TO TALK ABOUT WAS... MY INCOMPETENCE?!
はっ
TOHRU?
TOHRU, ARE YOU SICK? SHOULD WE HAVE HA'RI EXAMINE YOU?
I-I-IT'S ALL RIGHT. I'M FINE!
Nothing a check-up could fix!

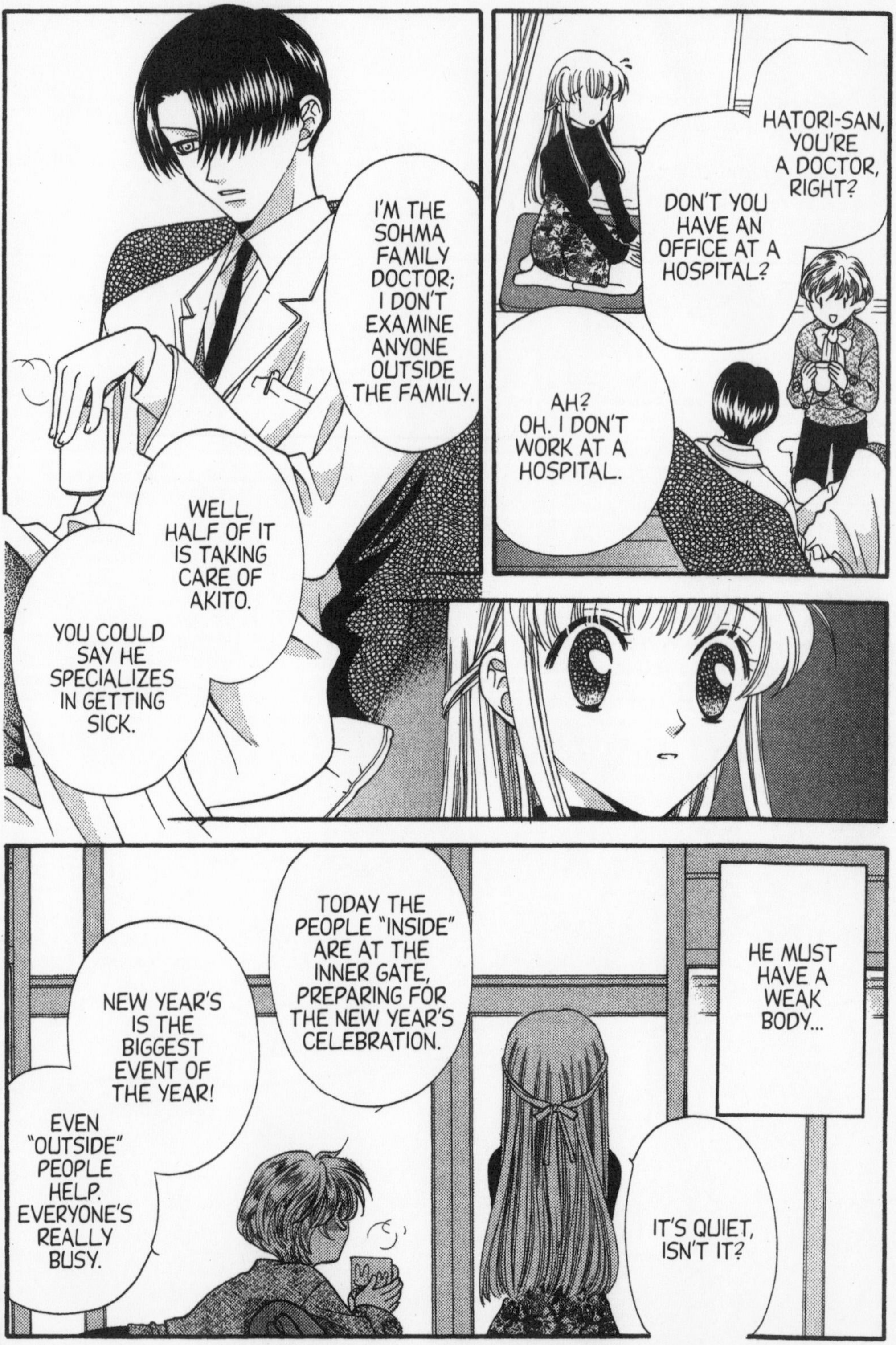
HATORI-SAN, YOU'RE A DOCTOR, RIGHT?
DON'T YOU HAVE AN OFFICE AT A HOSPITAL?
AH? OH. I DON'T WORK AT A HOSPITAL.
I'M THE SOHMA FAMILY DOCTOR; I DON'T EXAMINE ANYONE OUTSIDE THE FAMILY.
WELL, HALF OF IT IS TAKING CARE OF AKITO.
YOU COULD SAY HE SPECIALIZES IN GETTING SICK.
HE MUST HAVE A WEAK BODY...
IT'S QUIET, ISN'T IT?
TODAY THE PEOPLE "INSIDE" ARE AT THE INNER GATE, PREPARING FOR THE NEW YEAR'S CELEBRATION.
NEW YEAR'S IS THE BIGGEST EVENT OF THE YEAR!
EVEN "OUTSIDE" PEOPLE HELP. EVERYONE'S REALLY BUSY.

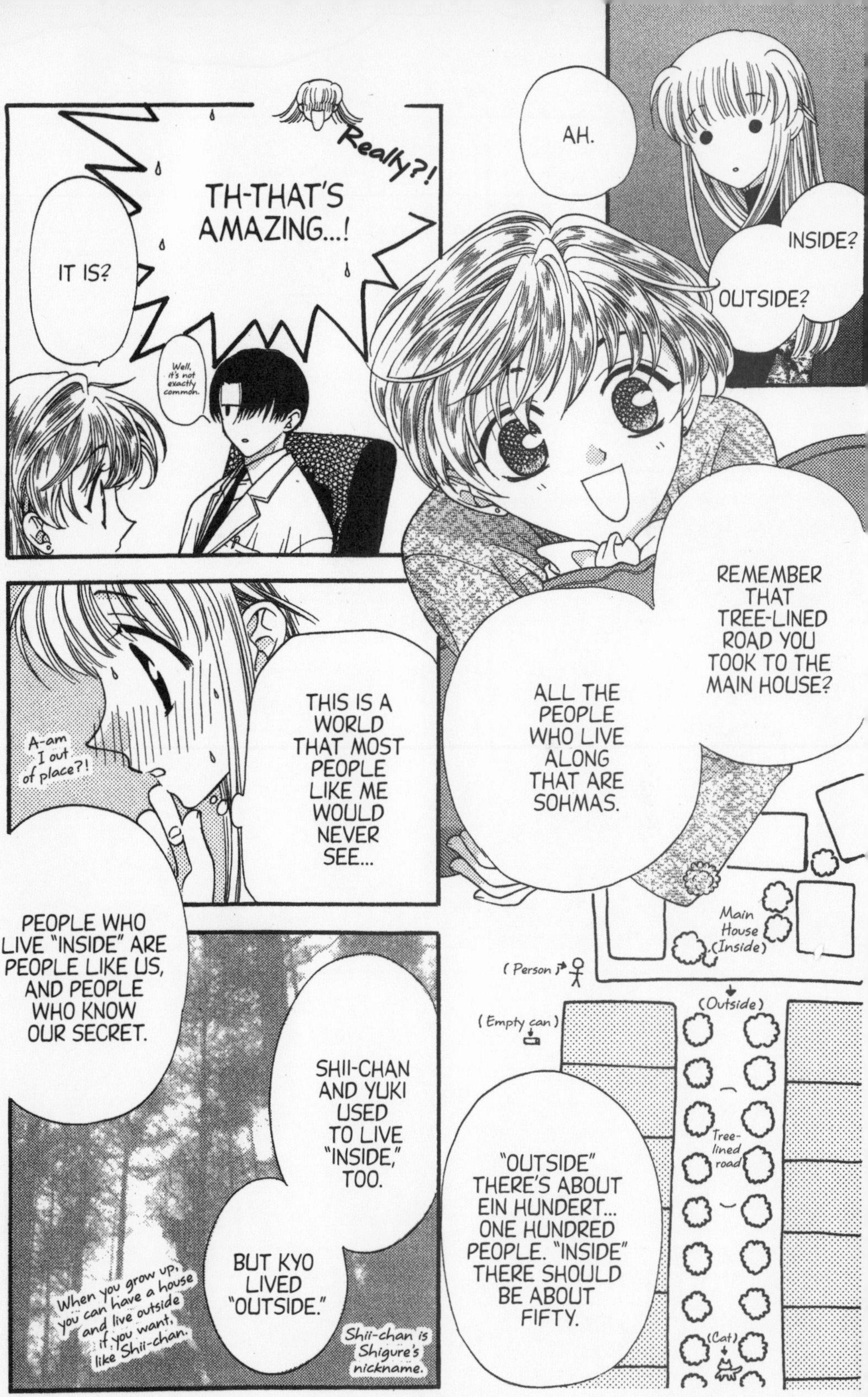
AH.
INSIDE?
OUTSIDE?
REMEMBER THAT TREE-LINED ROAD YOU TOOK TO THE MAIN HOUSE?
ALL THE PEOPLE WHO LIVE ALONG THAT ARE SOHMAS.
Main House (Inside)
(Person)
(Outside)
(Empty can)
Tree-lined road
(Cat)
"OUTSIDE" THERE'S ABOUT EIN HUNDERT... ONE HUNDRED PEOPLE. "INSIDE" THERE SHOULD BE ABOUT FIFTY.
Really?!
TH-THAT'S AMAZING...!
IT IS?
Well, it's not exactly common.
THIS IS A WORLD THAT MOST PEOPLE LIKE ME WOULD NEVER SEE...
A-am I out of place?!
PEOPLE WHO LIVE "INSIDE" ARE PEOPLE LIKE US, AND PEOPLE WHO KNOW OUR SECRET.
SHII-CHAN AND YUKI USED TO LIVE "INSIDE," TOO.
BUT KYO LIVED "OUTSIDE."
Shii-chan is Shigure's nickname.
When you grow up, you can have a house and live outside if you want, like Shii-chan.

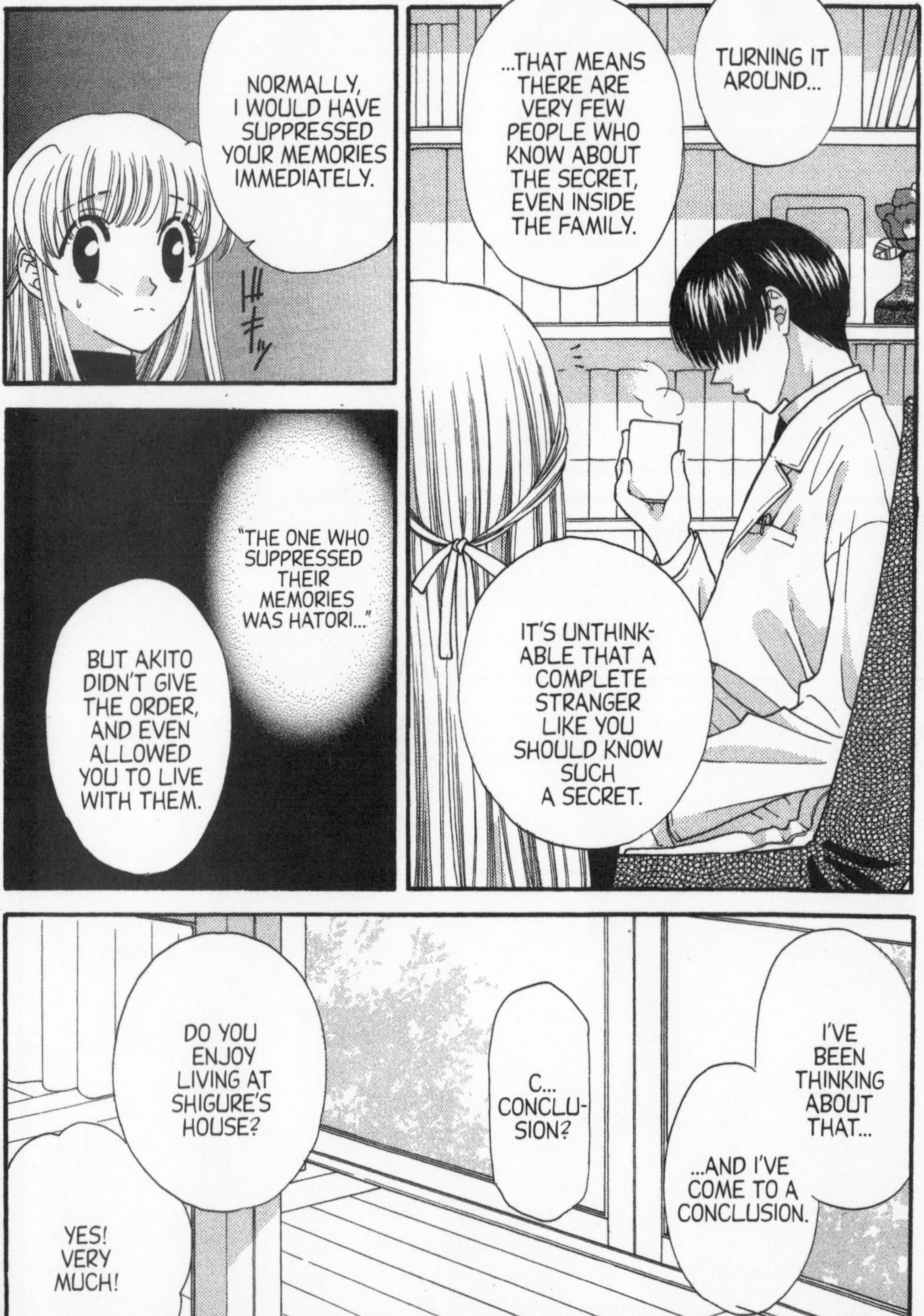
NORMALLY, I WOULD HAVE SUPPRESSED YOUR MEMORIES IMMEDIATELY.
"THE ONE WHO SUPPRESSED THEIR MEMORIES WAS HATORI..."
BUT AKITO DIDN'T GIVE THE ORDER, AND EVEN ALLOWED YOU TO LIVE WITH THEM.
TURNING IT AROUND...
...THAT MEANS THERE ARE VERY FEW PEOPLE WHO KNOW ABOUT THE SECRET, EVEN INSIDE THE FAMILY.
IT'S UNTHINKABLE THAT A COMPLETE STRANGER LIKE YOU SHOULD KNOW SUCH A SECRET.
I'VE BEEN THINKING ABOUT THAT...
...AND I'VE COME TO A CONCLUSION.
C... CONCLUSION?
DO YOU ENJOY LIVING AT SHIGURE'S HOUSE?
YES! VERY MUCH!

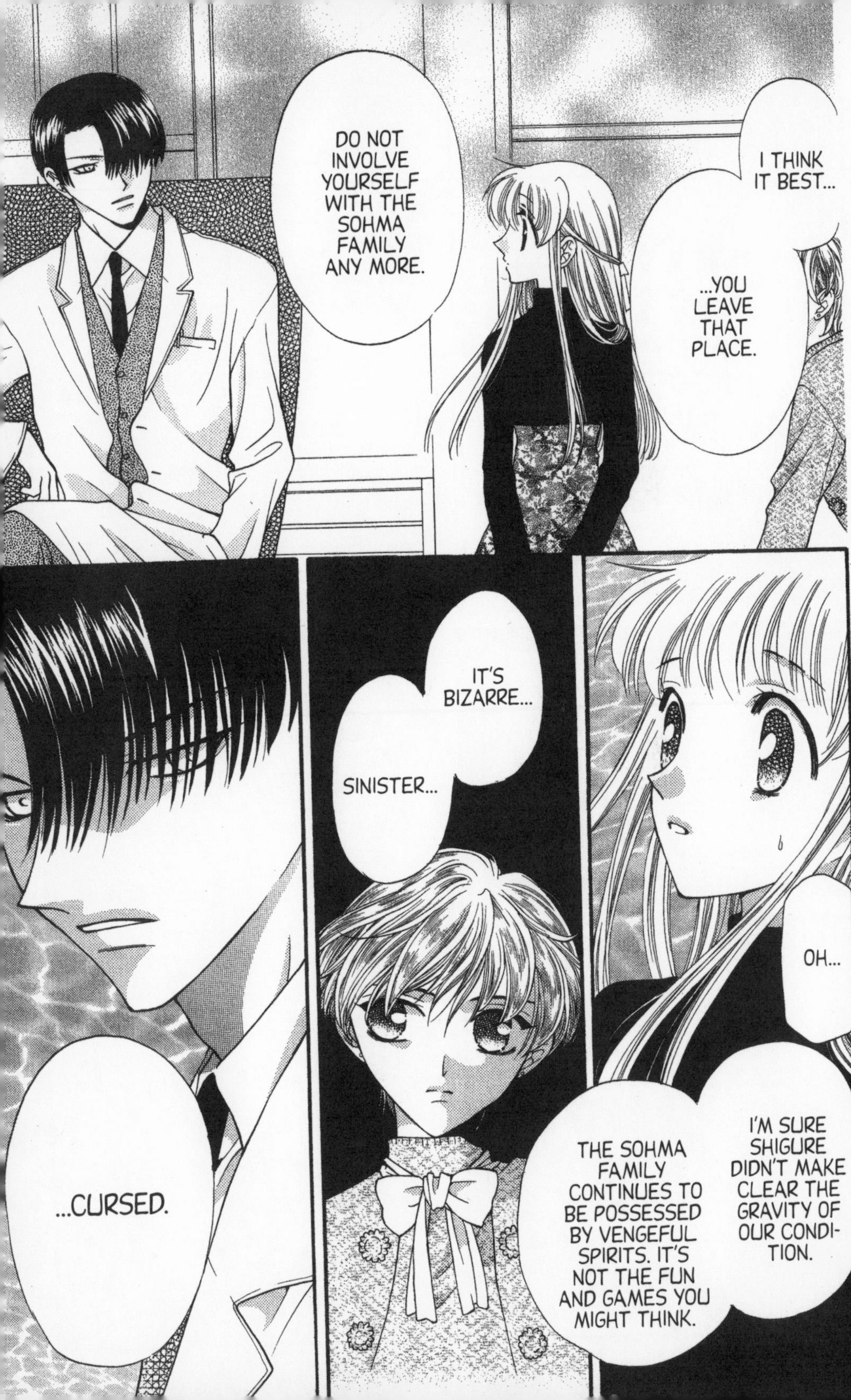
I THINK IT BEST...
...YOU LEAVE THAT PLACE.
DO NOT INVOLVE YOURSELF WITH THE SOHMA FAMILY ANY MORE.
OH...
I'M SURE SHIGURE DIDN'T MAKE CLEAR THE GRAVITY OF OUR CONDI-TION.
THE SOHMA FAMILY CONTINUES TO BE POSSESSED BY VENGEFUL SPIRITS. IT'S NOT THE FUN AND GAMES YOU MIGHT THINK.
IT'S BIZARRE...
SINISTER...
...CURSED.

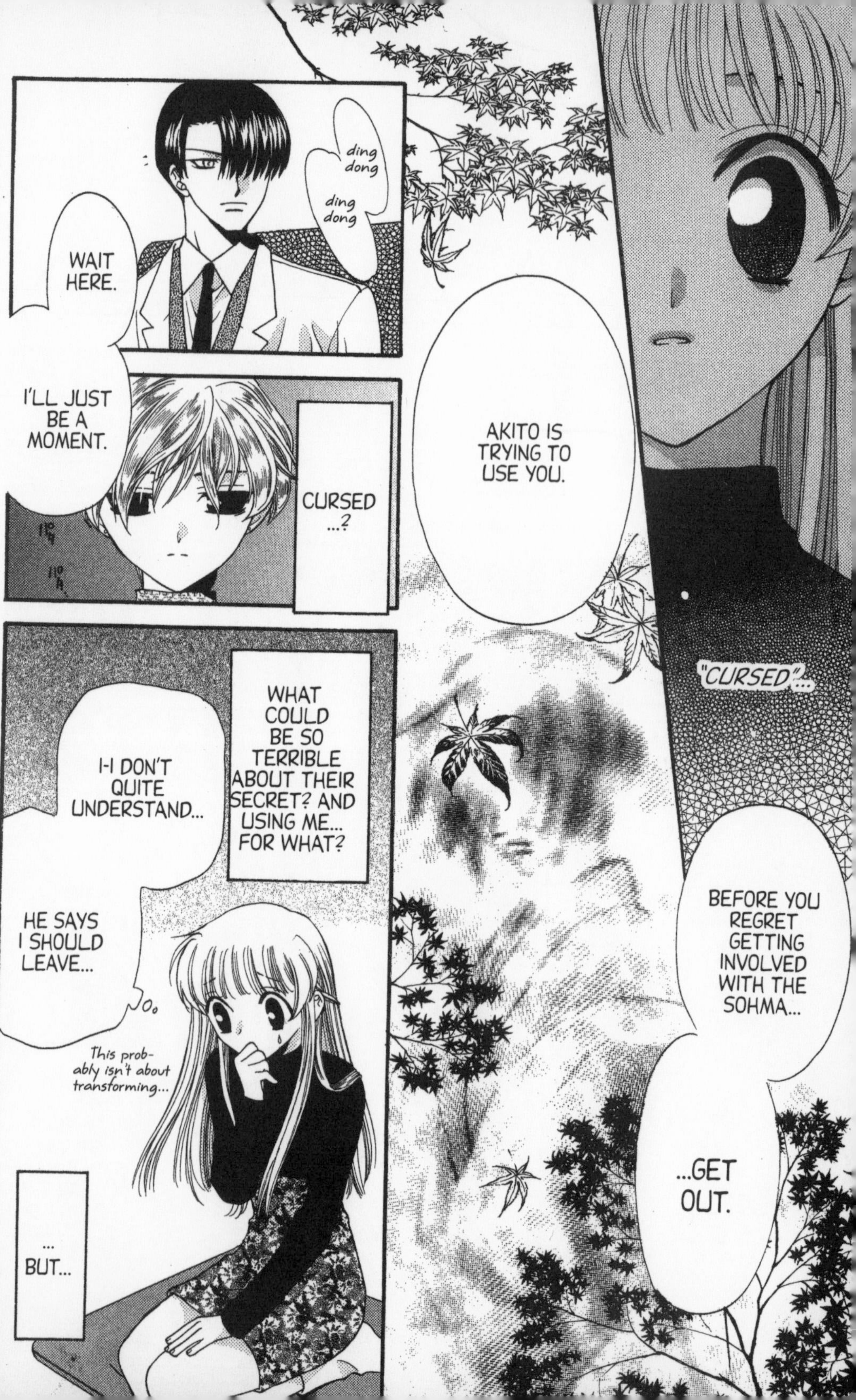
AKITO IS TRYING TO USE YOU.
"CURSED"...
BEFORE YOU REGRET GETTING INVOLVED WITH THE SOHMA...
...GET OUT.
ding dong
ding dong
WAIT HERE.
CURSED ...?
I'LL JUST BE A MOMENT.
WHAT COULD BE SO TERRIBLE ABOUT THEIR SECRET? AND USING ME... FOR WHAT?
I-I DON'T QUITE UNDERSTAND...
HE SAYS I SHOULD LEAVE...
This probably isn't about transforming...
... BUT...

Fruits Basket 2 Part 4:

I got the feeling that the last bosses in FF were getting weak.... Was it my imagination? I don't mind if they're weak! (Because then it's easier.) "End of Heart" gives me chills. While I was playing FF, I was playing Angelique. I like Sei-lan. And I like Oscar. Whenever Rachel starts dating one of them (especially Sei-lan) I reset the game. Even when she starts going after the other boys, I reset (laugh)! You're all like that too, right? I even played the RPG. Arios (cry). I wanted the two of us to be happy together... (What happened to Sei-lan?) And now I'm in the middle of Suikoden 2. Actually, I played 1, and I didn't like it much, but 2 is fun! As expected, I like Jowy... The name of my group is The Natsuki and Jowy Army!

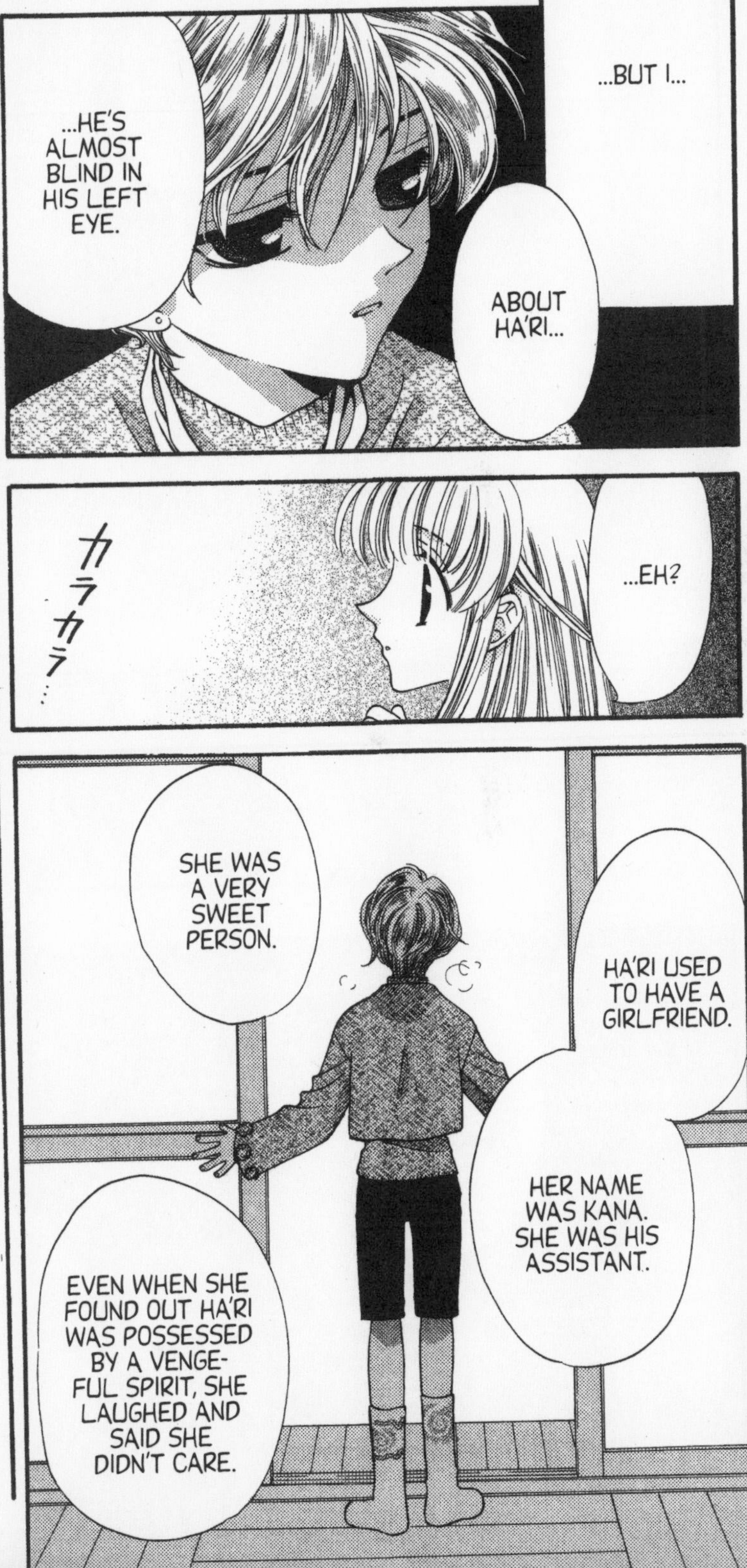

...BUT I...
ABOUT HA'RI...
...HE'S ALMOST BLIND IN HIS LEFT EYE.
...EH?
カラカラ...
HA'RI USED TO HAVE A GIRLFRIEND.
HER NAME WAS KANA. SHE WAS HIS ASSISTANT.
SHE WAS A VERY SWEET PERSON.
EVEN WHEN SHE FOUND OUT HA'RI WAS POSSESSED BY A VENGEFUL SPIRIT, SHE LAUGHED AND SAID SHE DIDN'T CARE.

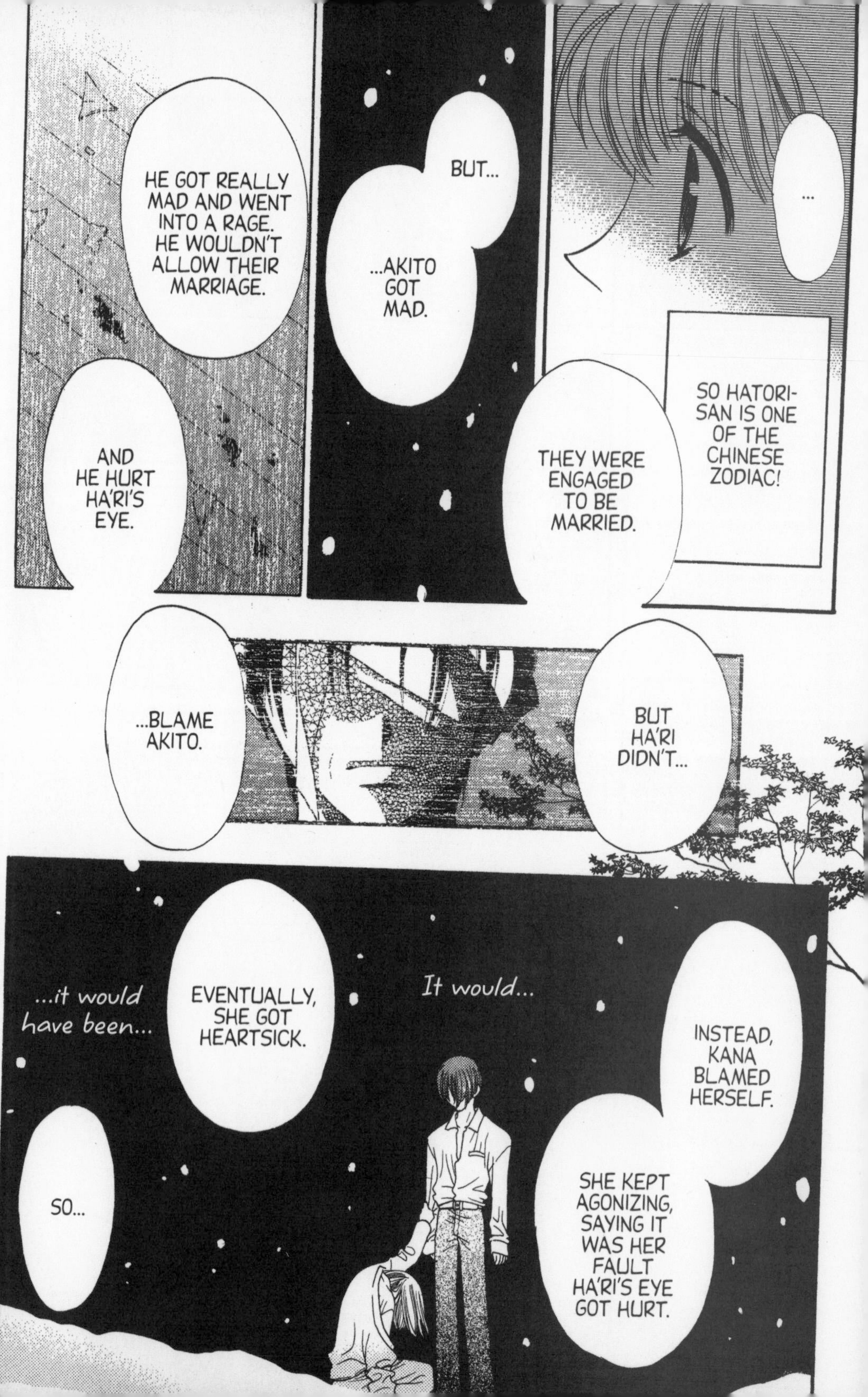
...
SO HATORI-SAN IS ONE OF THE CHINESE ZODIAC!
THEY WERE ENGAGED TO BE MARRIED.
BUT...
...AKITO GOT MAD.
HE GOT REALLY MAD AND WENT INTO A RAGE. HE WOULDN'T ALLOW THEIR MARRIAGE.
AND HE HURT HA'RI'S EYE.
BUT HA'RI DIDN'T...
...BLAME AKITO.
INSTEAD, KANA BLAMED HERSELF.
SHE KEPT AGONIZING, SAYING IT WAS HER FAULT HA'RI'S EYE GOT HURT.
It would...
EVENTUALLY, SHE GOT HEARTSICK.
...it would have been...
SO...

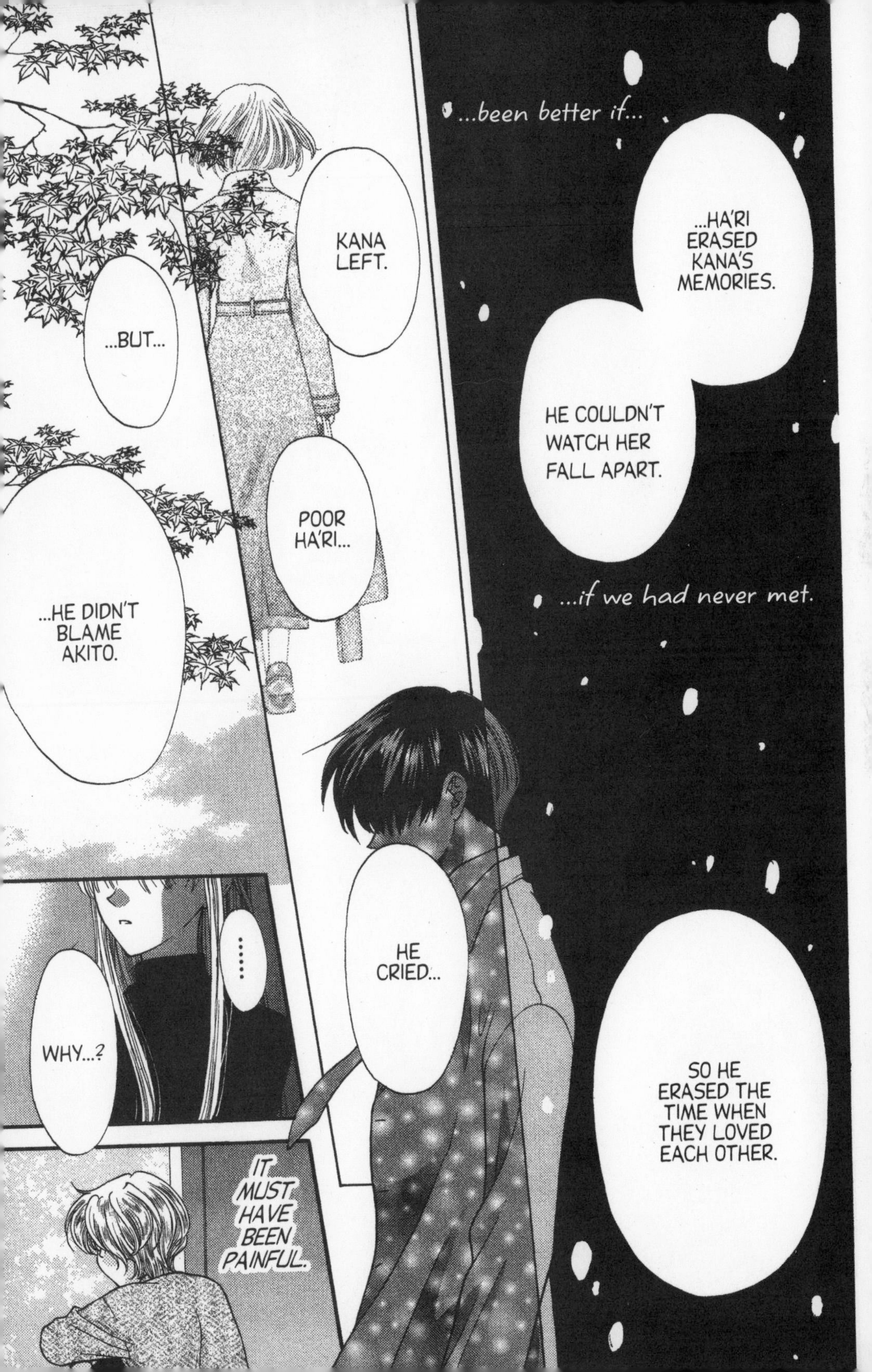

...been better if...
...HA'RI ERASED KANA'S MEMORIES.
HE COULDN'T WATCH HER FALL APART.
...if we had never met.
SO HE ERASED THE TIME WHEN THEY LOVED EACH OTHER.
KANA LEFT.
POOR HA'RI...
HE CRIED...
...BUT...
...HE DIDN'T BLAME AKITO.
......
WHY...?
IT MUST HAVE BEEN PAINFUL.

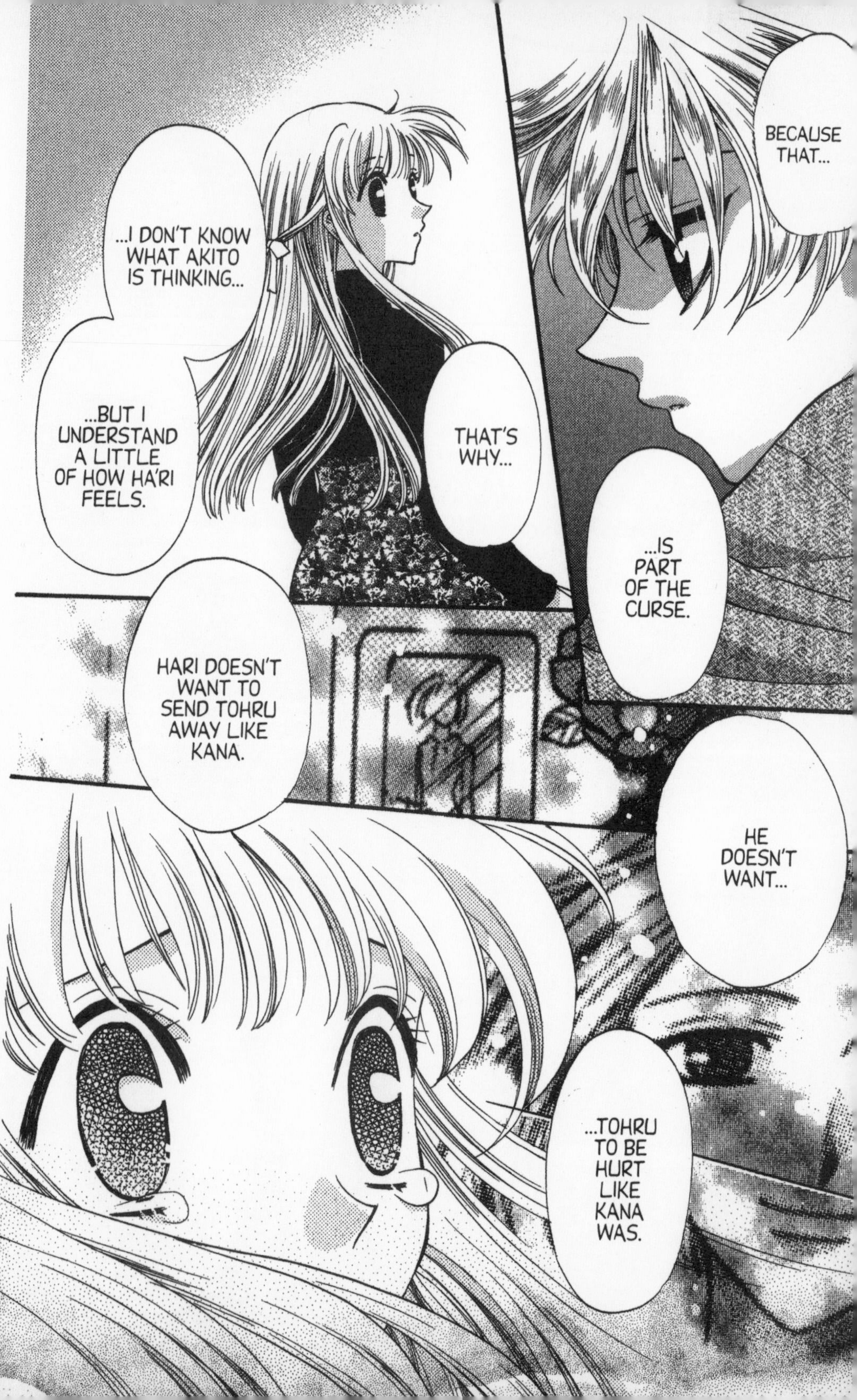
BECAUSE THAT...
...IS PART OF THE CURSE.
...I DON'T KNOW WHAT AKITO IS THINKING...
...BUT I UNDERSTAND A LITTLE OF HOW HA'RI FEELS.
THAT'S WHY...
HARI DOESN'T WANT TO SEND TOHRU AWAY LIKE KANA.
HE DOESN'T WANT...
...TOHRU TO BE HURT LIKE KANA WAS.

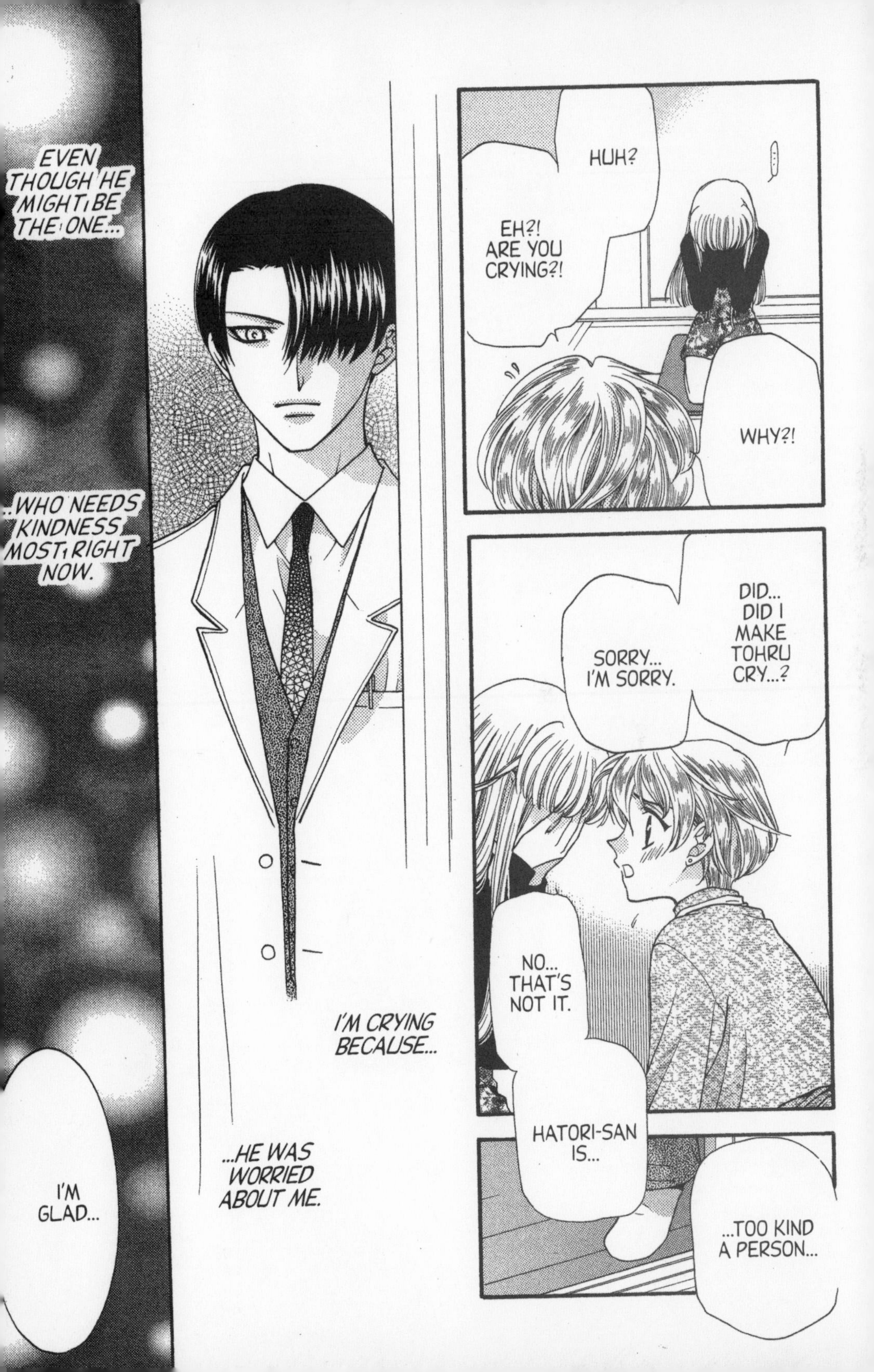
...
HUH?
EH?! ARE YOU CRYING?!
WHY?!
DID... DID I MAKE TOHRU CRY...?
SORRY... I'M SORRY.
NO... THAT'S NOT IT.
HATORI-SAN IS...
...TOO KIND A PERSON...
I'M CRYING BECAUSE...
...HE WAS WORRIED ABOUT ME.
EVEN THOUGH HE MIGHT BE THE ONE...
...WHO NEEDS KINDNESS MOST RIGHT NOW.
I'M GLAD...

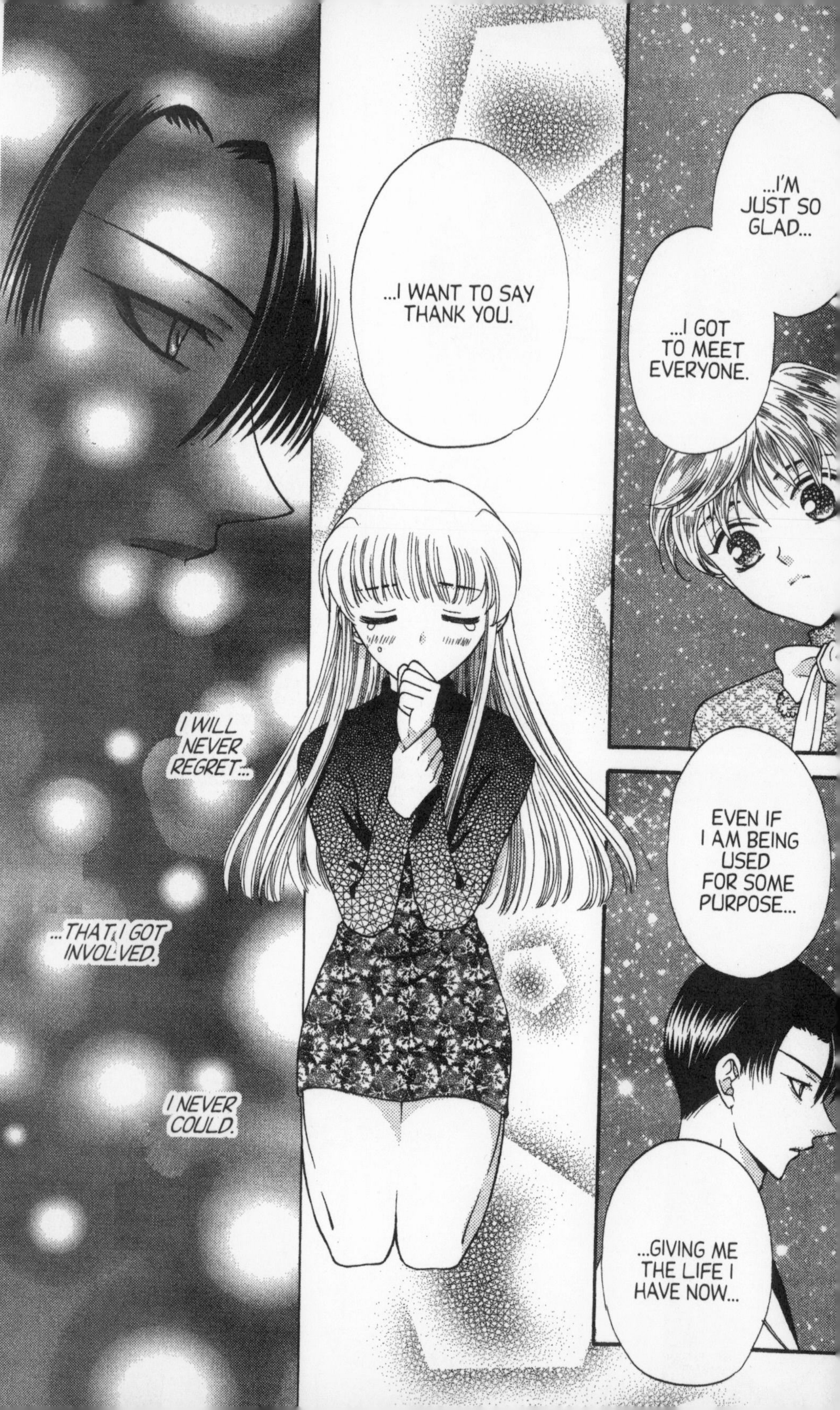
...I'M JUST SO GLAD...
...I GOT TO MEET EVERYONE.
EVEN IF I AM BEING USED FOR SOME PURPOSE...
...GIVING ME THE LIFE I HAVE NOW...
...I WANT TO SAY THANK YOU.
I WILL NEVER REGRET...
...THAT I GOT INVOLVED.
I NEVER COULD.

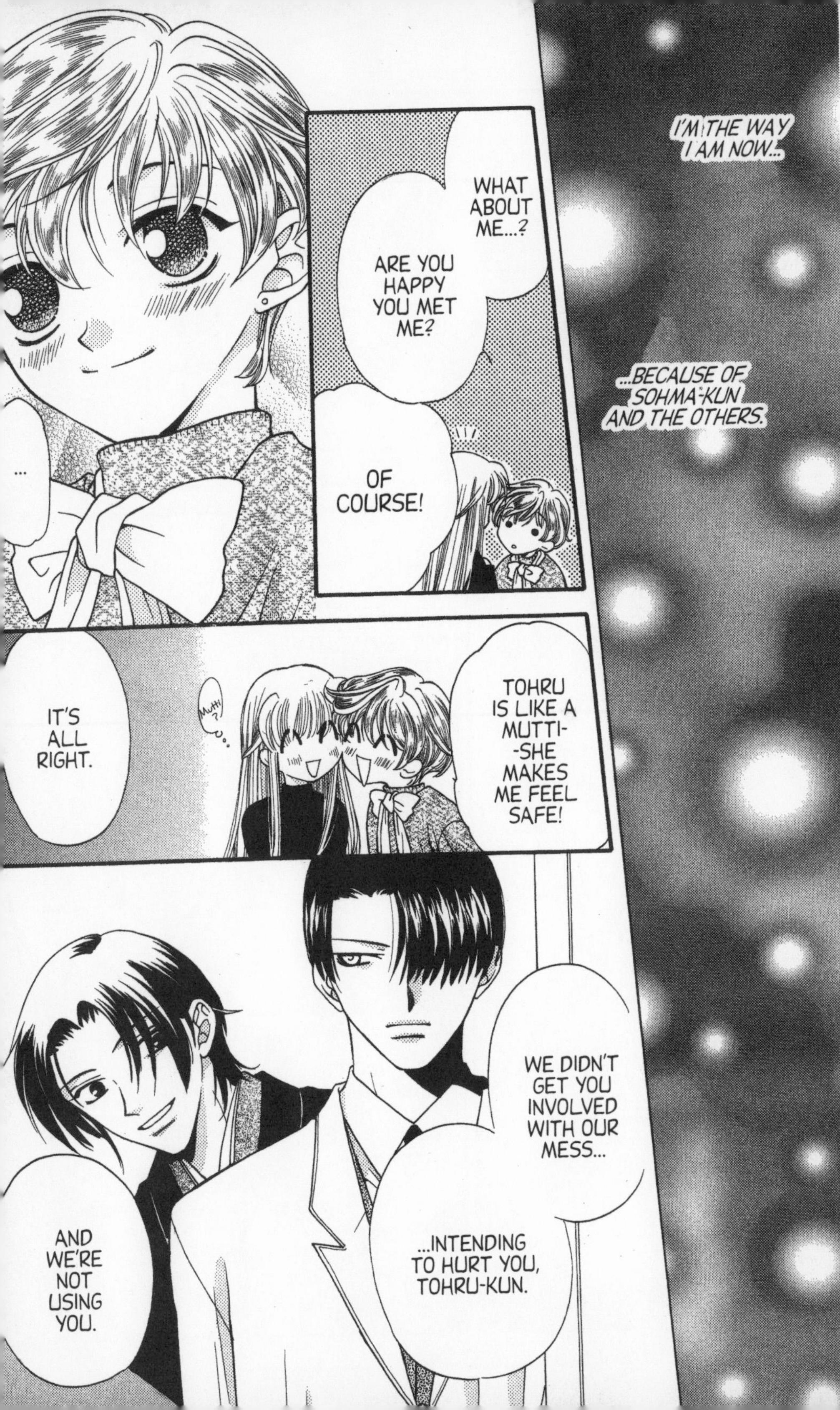
I'M THE WAY I AM NOW...
...BECAUSE OF SOHMA-KUN AND THE OTHERS.
WHAT ABOUT ME...?
ARE YOU HAPPY YOU MET ME?
OF COURSE!
...
TOHRU IS LIKE A MUTTI--SHE MAKES ME FEEL SAFE!
Mutti?
IT'S ALL RIGHT.
WE DIDN'T GET YOU INVOLVED WITH OUR MESS...
...INTENDING TO HURT YOU, TOHRU-KUN.
AND WE'RE NOT USING YOU.

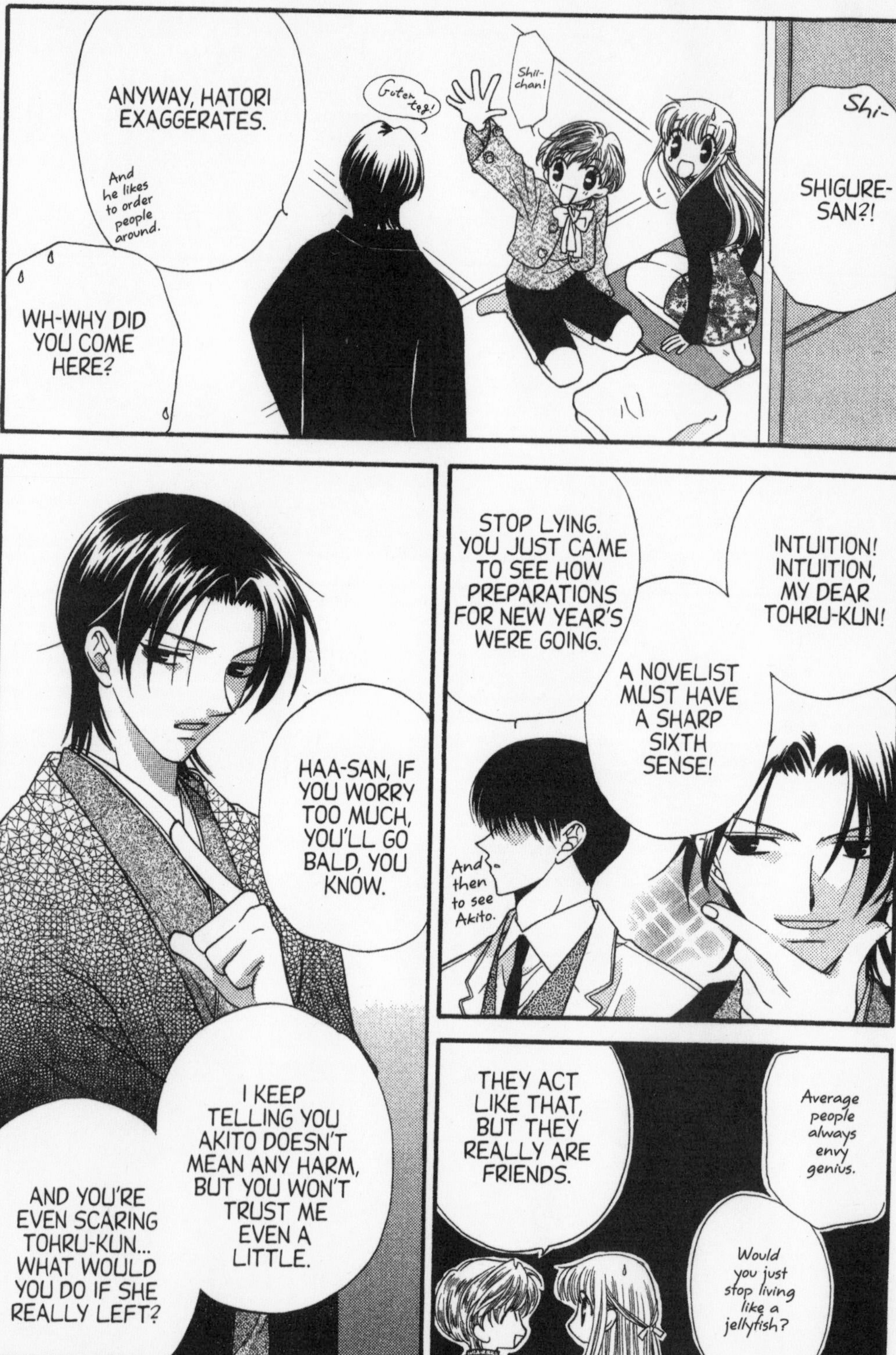
Shi-
SHIGURE-SAN?!
Shii-chan!
Guten tag!
ANYWAY, HATORI EXAGGERATES.
And he likes to order people around.
WH-WHY DID YOU COME HERE?
INTUITION! INTUITION, MY DEAR TOHRU-KUN!
STOP LYING. YOU JUST CAME TO SEE HOW PREPARATIONS FOR NEW YEAR'S WERE GOING.
A NOVELIST MUST HAVE A SHARP SIXTH SENSE!
And then to see Akito.
Average people always envy genius.
THEY ACT LIKE THAT, BUT THEY REALLY ARE FRIENDS.
Would you just stop living like a jellyfish?
HAA-SAN, IF YOU WORRY TOO MUCH, YOU'LL GO BALD, YOU KNOW.
I KEEP TELLING YOU AKITO DOESN'T MEAN ANY HARM, BUT YOU WON'T TRUST ME EVEN A LITTLE.
AND YOU'RE EVEN SCARING TOHRU-KUN... WHAT WOULD YOU DO IF SHE REALLY LEFT?

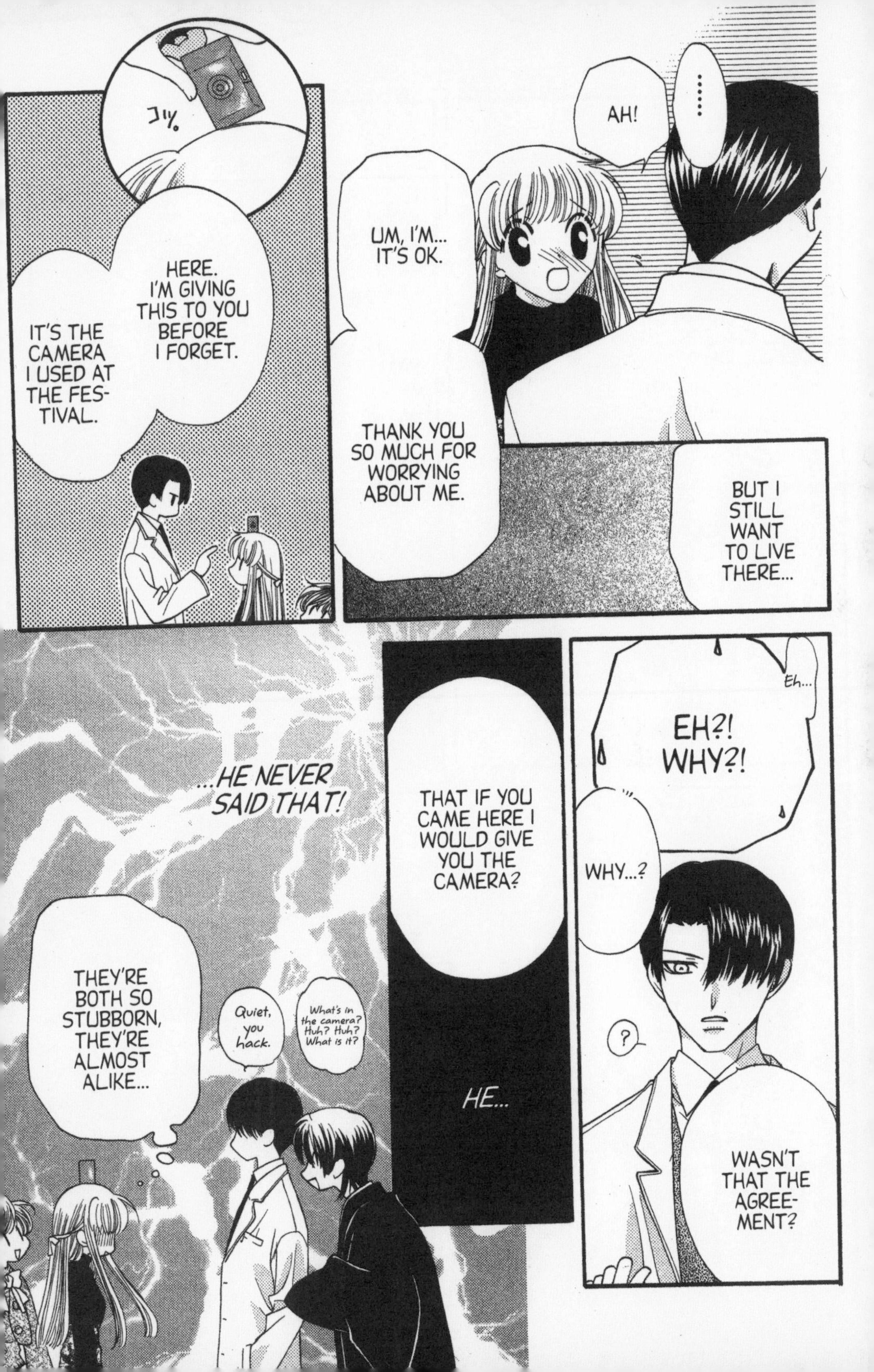
AH!
......
UM, I'M... IT'S OK.
THANK YOU SO MUCH FOR WORRYING ABOUT ME.
BUT I STILL WANT TO LIVE THERE...
コツ。
HERE. I'M GIVING THIS TO YOU BEFORE I FORGET.
IT'S THE CAMERA I USED AT THE FES-TIVAL.
Eh...
EH?! WHY?!
WHY...?
?
WASN'T THAT THE AGREE-MENT?
THAT IF YOU CAME HERE I WOULD GIVE YOU THE CAMERA?
HE...
...HE NEVER SAID THAT!
THEY'RE BOTH SO STUBBORN, THEY'RE ALMOST ALIKE...
What's in the camera? Huh? Huh? What is it?
Quiet, you hack.

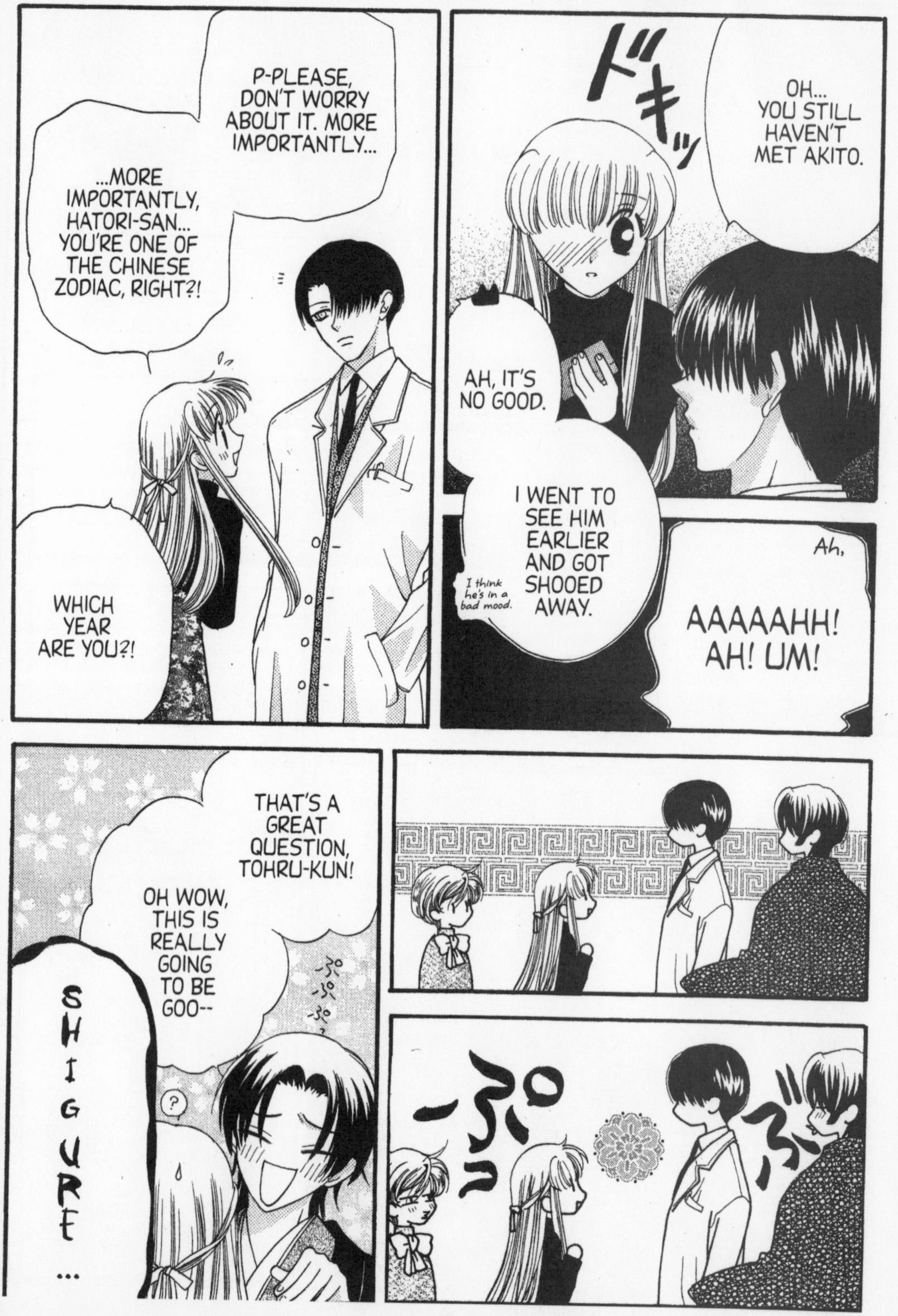
ドキッ
OH... YOU STILL HAVEN'T MET AKITO.
AH, IT'S NO GOOD.
I WENT TO SEE HIM EARLIER AND GOT SHOOED AWAY.
I think he's in a bad mood.
Ah,
AAAAAHH! AH! UM!
P-PLEASE, DON'T WORRY ABOUT IT. MORE IMPORTANTLY...
...MORE IMPORTANTLY, HATORI-SAN... YOU'RE ONE OF THE CHINESE ZODIAC, RIGHT?!
WHICH YEAR ARE YOU?!
ーぷっ
ふっ
THAT'S A GREAT QUESTION, TOHRU-KUN!
OH WOW, THIS IS REALLY GOING TO BE GOO--
-ぷっ -ぷっ -ぷっ
SHIGURE ...

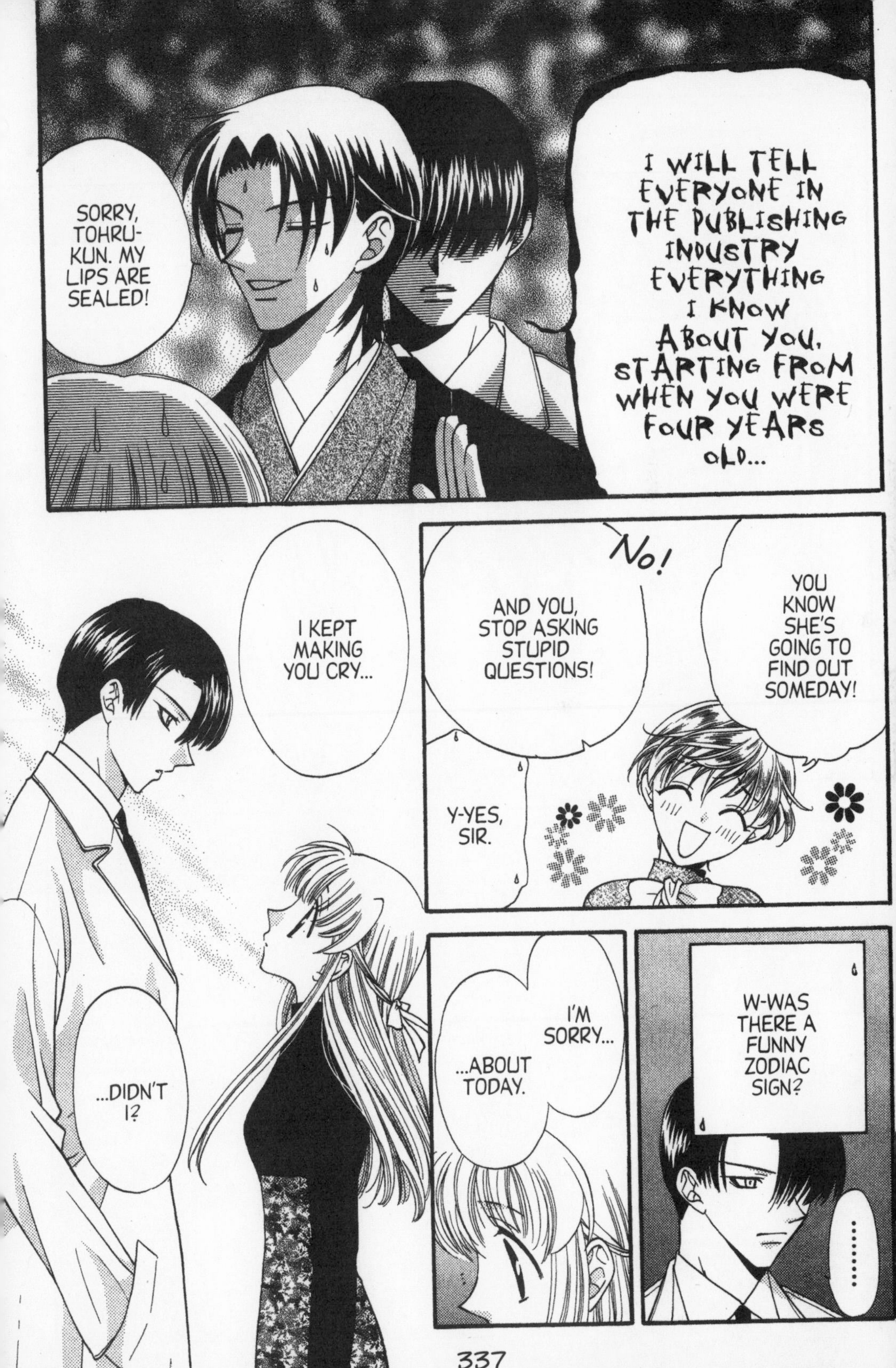

I WILL TELL EVERYONE IN THE PUBLISHING INDUSTRY EVERYTHING I KNOW ABOUT YOU, STARTING FROM WHEN YOU WERE FOUR YEARS OLD...
SORRY, TOHRU-KUN. MY LIPS ARE SEALED!
YOU KNOW SHE'S GOING TO FIND OUT SOMEDAY!
No!
AND YOU, STOP ASKING STUPID QUESTIONS!
Y-YES, SIR.
W-WAS THERE A FUNNY ZODIAC SIGN?
....
I'M SORRY...
...ABOUT TODAY.
I KEPT MAKING YOU CRY...
...DIDN'T I?

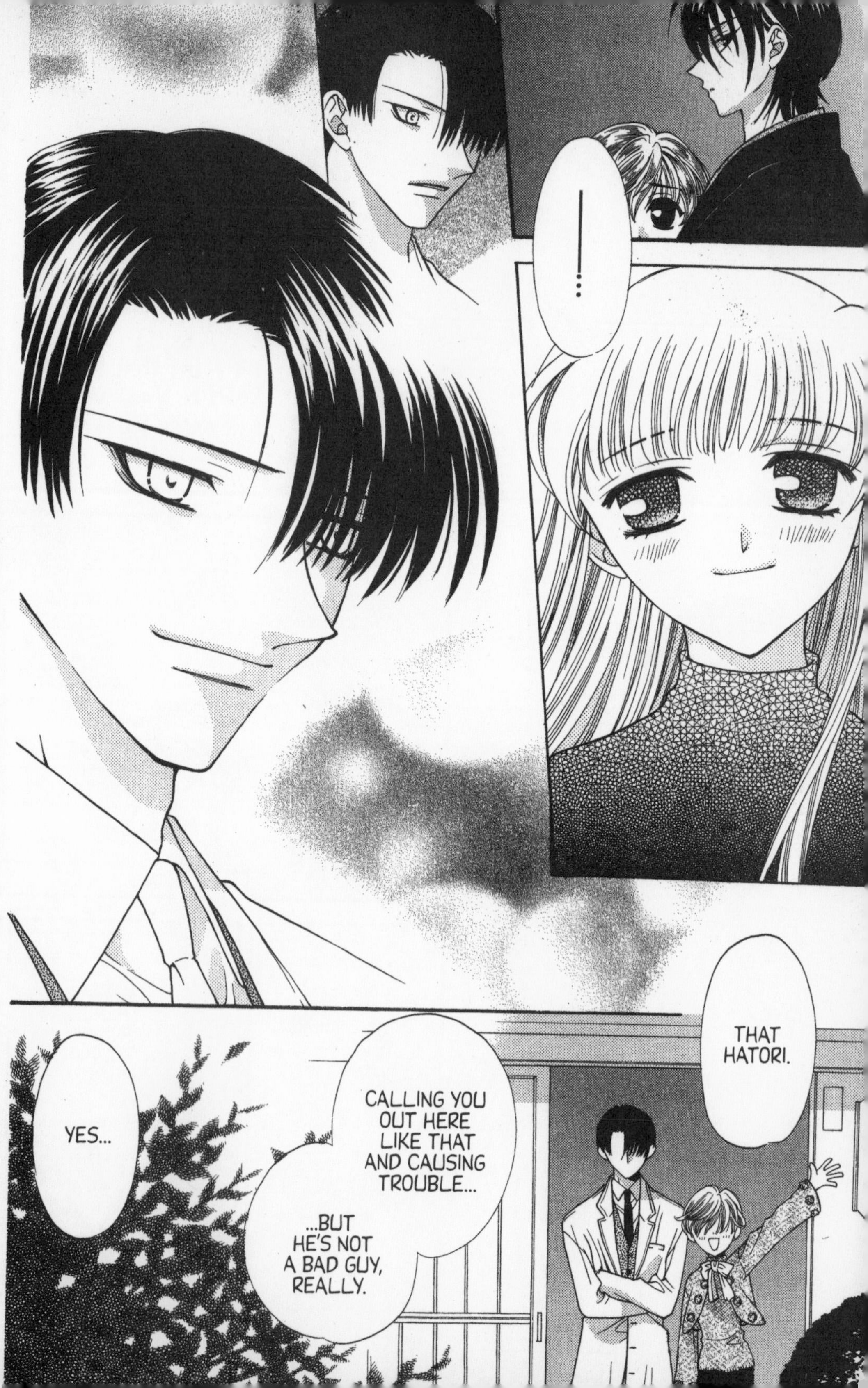
!....
THAT HATORI.
CALLING YOU OUT HERE LIKE THAT AND CAUSING TROUBLE...
...BUT HE'S NOT A BAD GUY, REALLY.
YES...

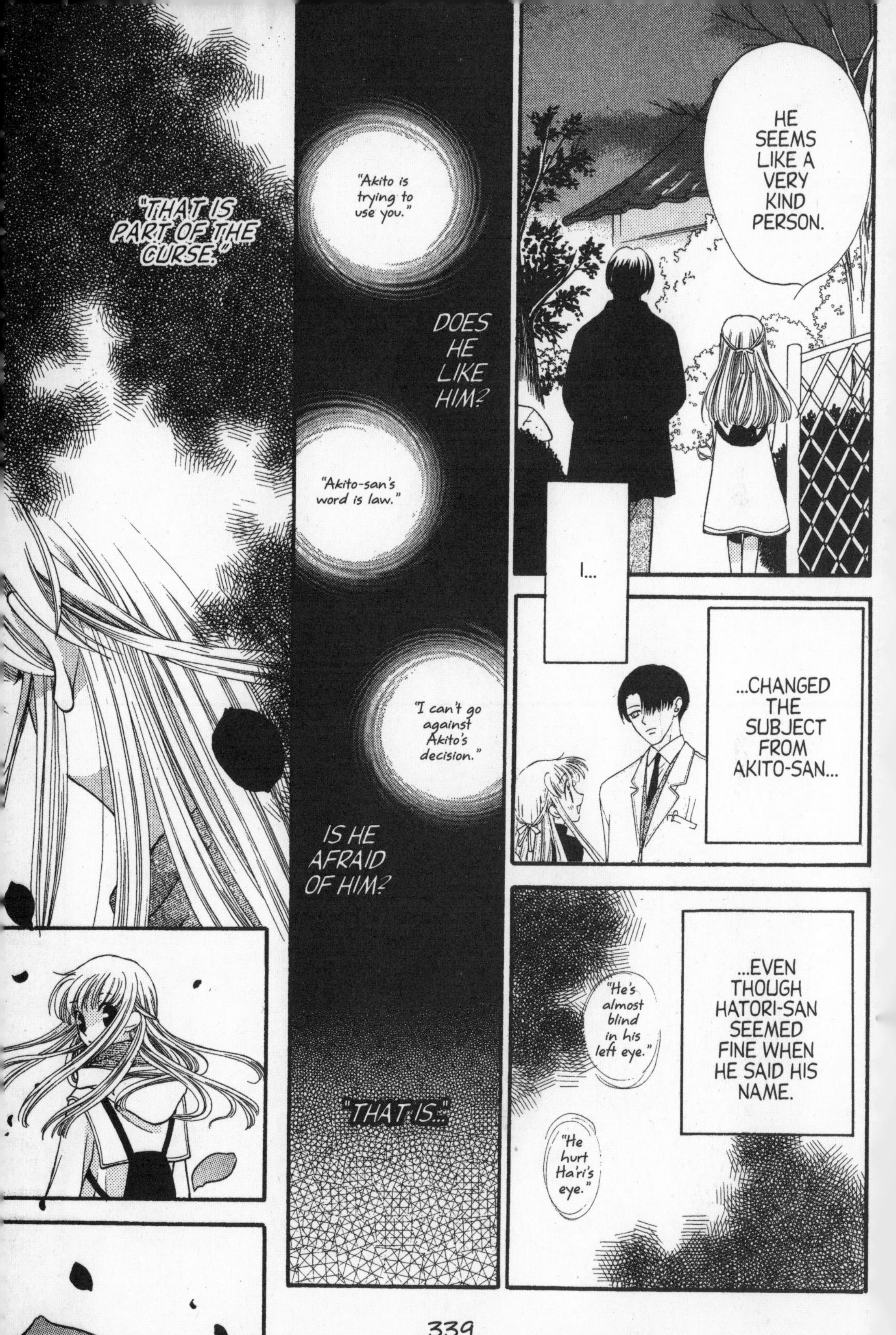
HE SEEMS LIKE A VERY KIND PERSON.
I...
...CHANGED THE SUBJECT FROM AKITO-SAN...
...EVEN THOUGH HATORI-SAN SEEMED FINE WHEN HE SAID HIS NAME.
"He's almost blind in his left eye."
"He hurt Ha'ri's eye."
"Akito is trying to use you."
DOES HE LIKE HIM?
"Akito-san's word is law."
"I can't go against Akito's decision."
IS HE AFRAID OF HIM?
"THAT IS..."
"THAT IS PART OF THE CURSE."

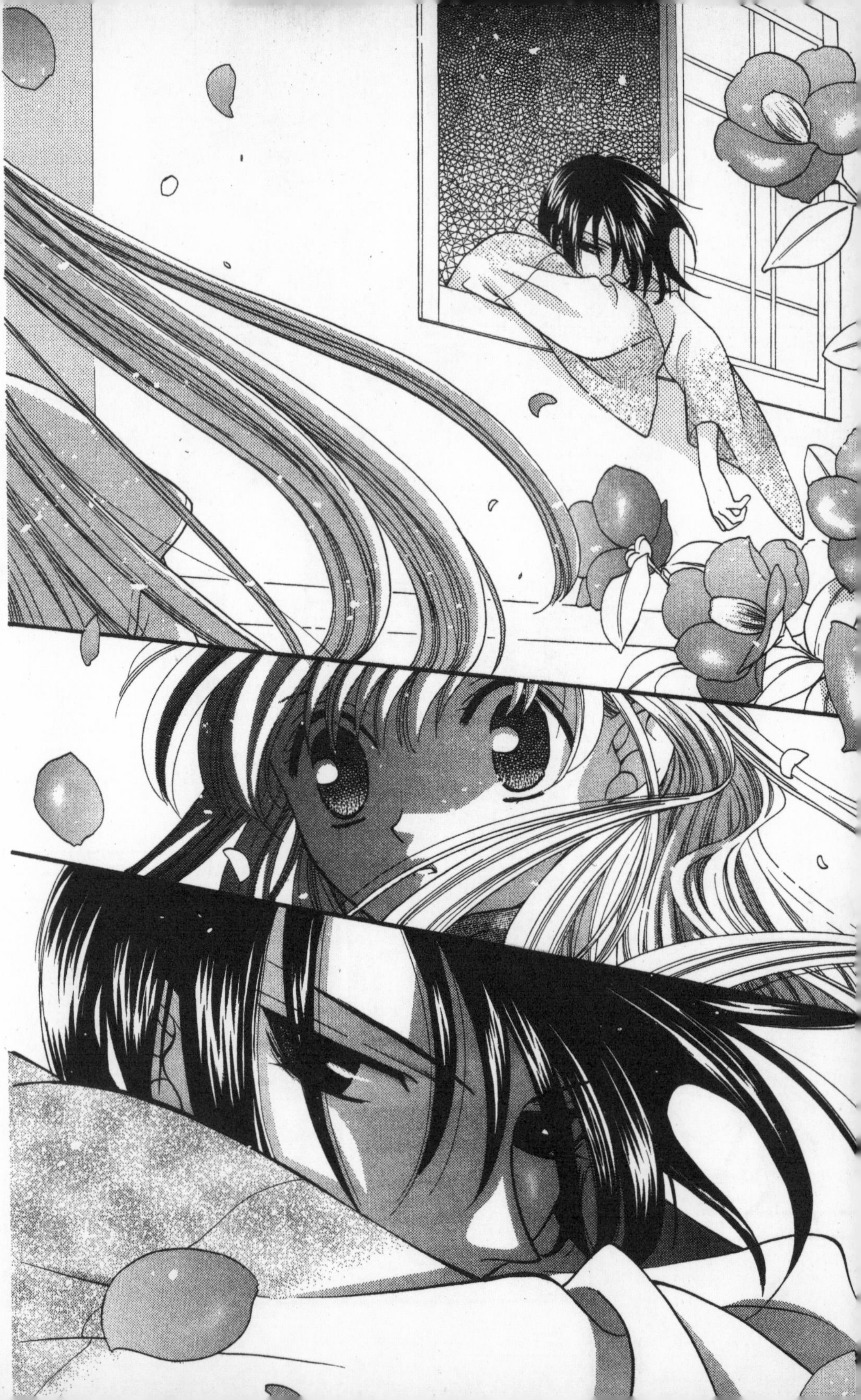

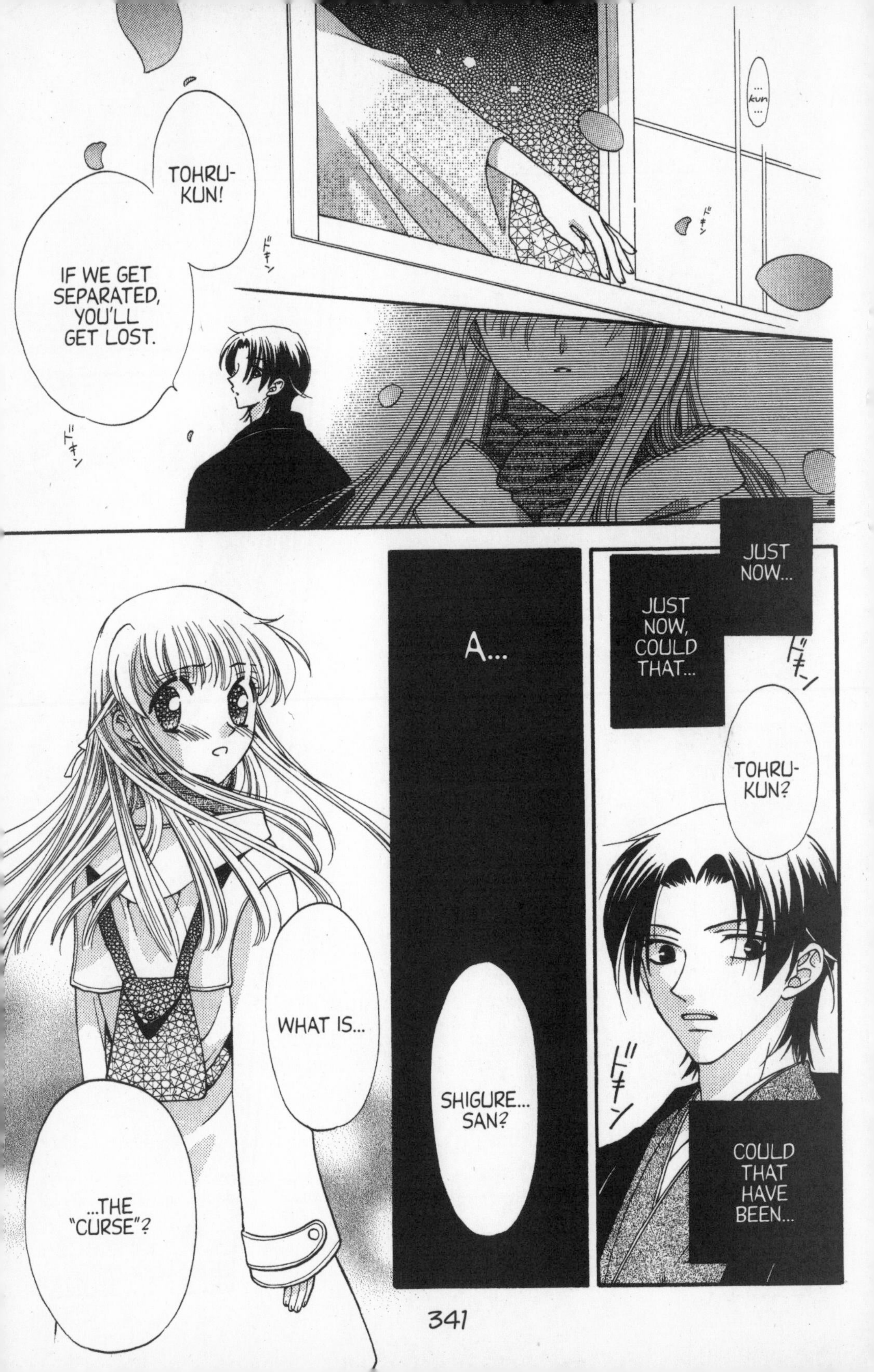
...kun...
ドキン
TOHRU-KUN!
IF WE GET SEPARATED, YOU'LL GET LOST.
ドキン
JUST NOW...
JUST NOW, COULD THAT...
ドキン
TOHRU-KUN?
ドキン
COULD THAT HAVE BEEN...
A...
SHIGURE... SAN?
WHAT IS...
...THE "CURSE"?

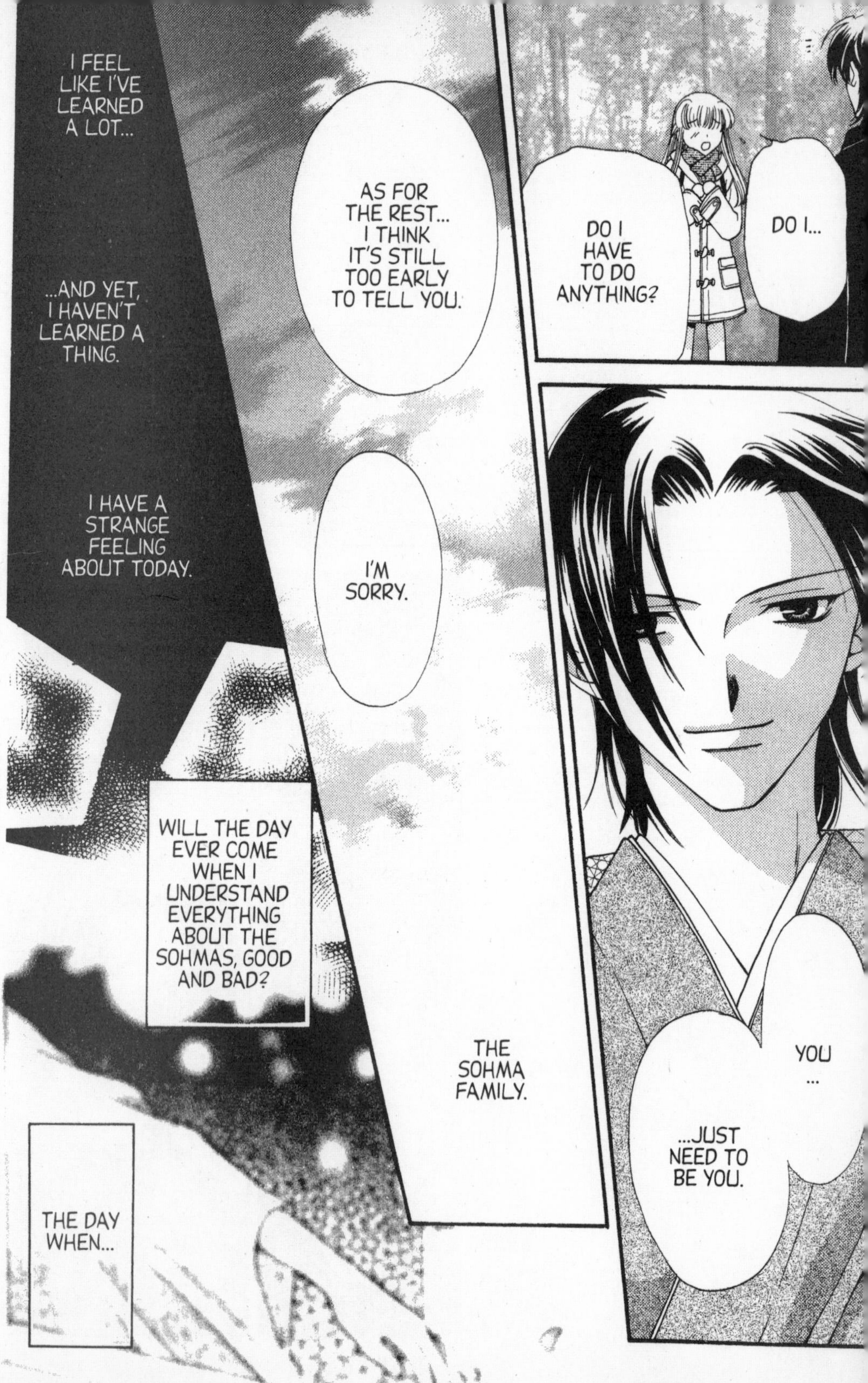
DO I...
DO I HAVE TO DO ANYTHING?
YOU ...
...JUST NEED TO BE YOU.
AS FOR THE REST... I THINK IT'S STILL TOO EARLY TO TELL YOU.
I'M SORRY.
THE SOHMA FAMILY.
I FEEL LIKE I'VE LEARNED A LOT...
...AND YET, I HAVEN'T LEARNED A THING.
I HAVE A STRANGE FEELING ABOUT TODAY.
WILL THE DAY EVER COME WHEN I UNDERSTAND EVERYTHING ABOUT THE SOHMAS, GOOD AND BAD?
THE DAY WHEN...

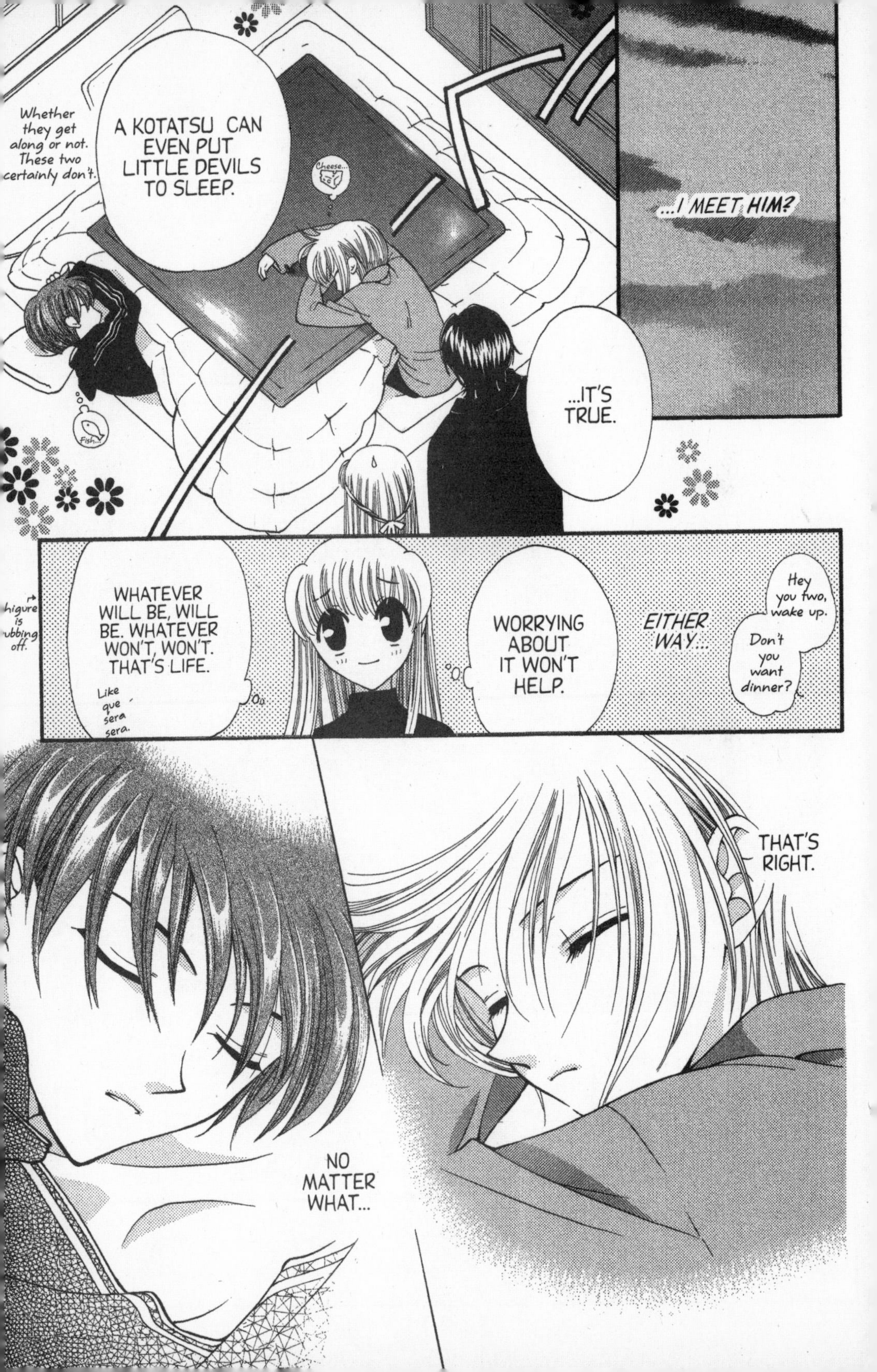
...I MEET HIM?
...IT'S TRUE.
A KOTATSU CAN EVEN PUT LITTLE DEVILS TO SLEEP.
Cheese...
Fish...
Whether they get along or not. These two certainly don't.
Hey you two, wake up.
Don't you want dinner?
EITHER WAY...
WORRYING ABOUT IT WON'T HELP.
WHATEVER WILL BE, WILL BE. WHATEVER WON'T, WON'T. THAT'S LIFE.
Like que sera sera.
higure is ubbing off.
THAT'S RIGHT.
NO MATTER WHAT...

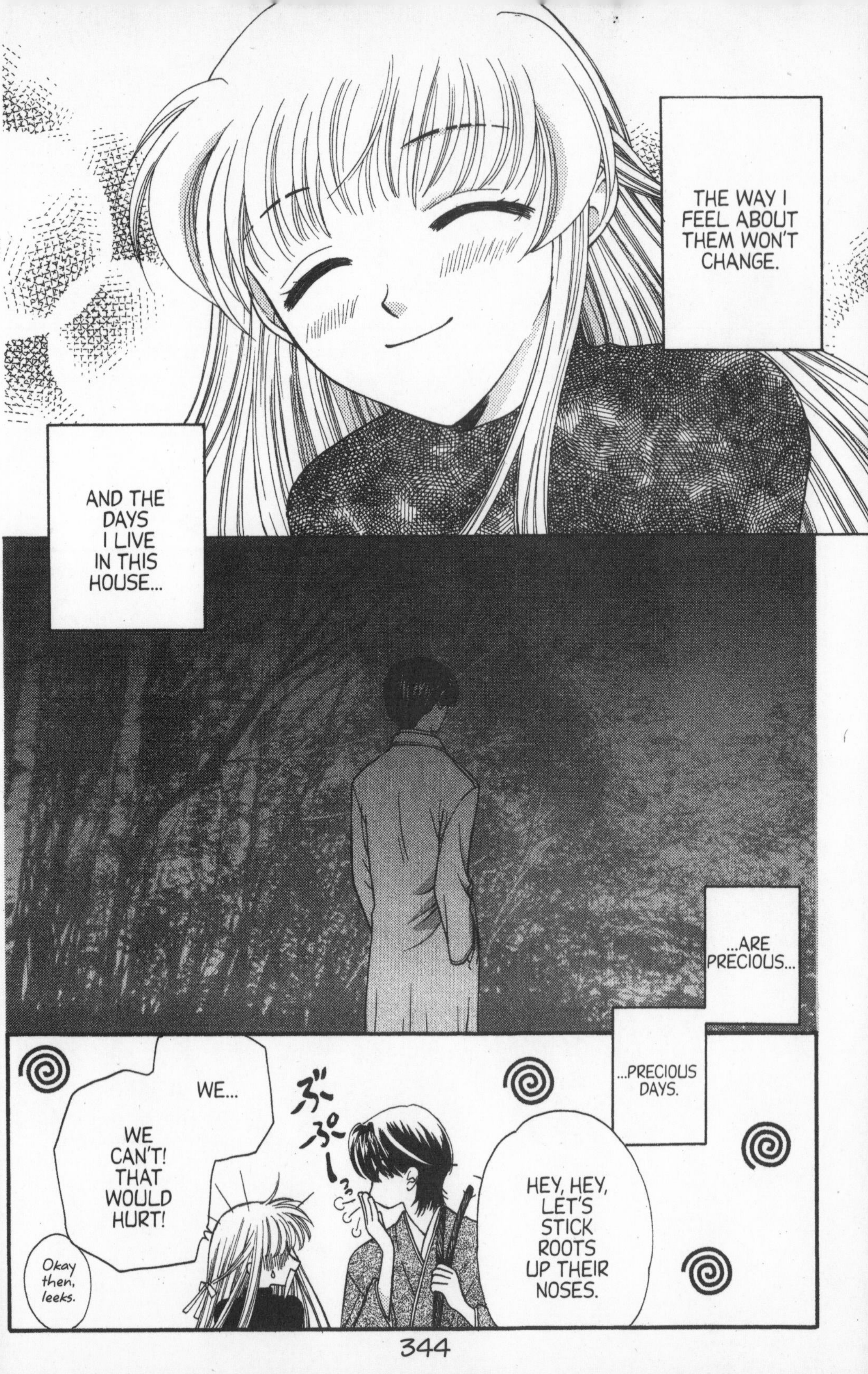
THE WAY I FEEL ABOUT THEM WON'T CHANGE.
AND THE DAYS I LIVE IN THIS HOUSE...
...ARE PRECIOUS...
...PRECIOUS DAYS.
HEY, HEY, LET'S STICK ROOTS UP THEIR NOSES.
WE...
WE CAN'T! THAT WOULD HURT!
Okay then, leeks.

Omake Theater: This has nothing to do with the manga, but right now I have a fever of 100.4F...

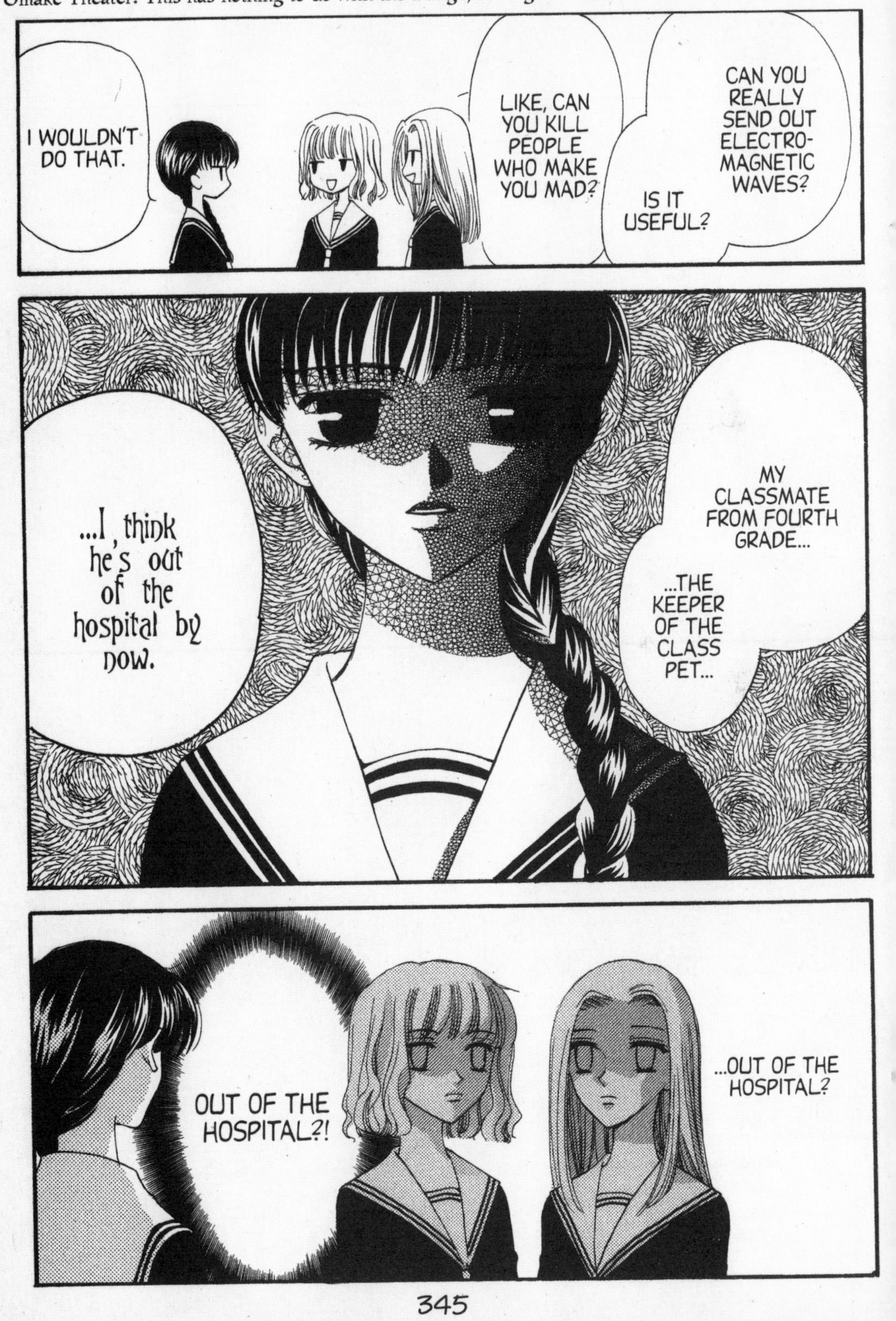
CAN YOU REALLY SEND OUT ELECTRO-MAGNETIC WAVES?
IS IT USEFUL?
LIKE, CAN YOU KILL PEOPLE WHO MAKE YOU MAD?
I WOULDN'T DO THAT.
MY CLASSMATE FROM FOURTH GRADE...
...THE KEEPER OF THE CLASS PET...
...I think he's out of the hospital by now.
...OUT OF THE HOSPITAL?
OUT OF THE HOSPITAL?!

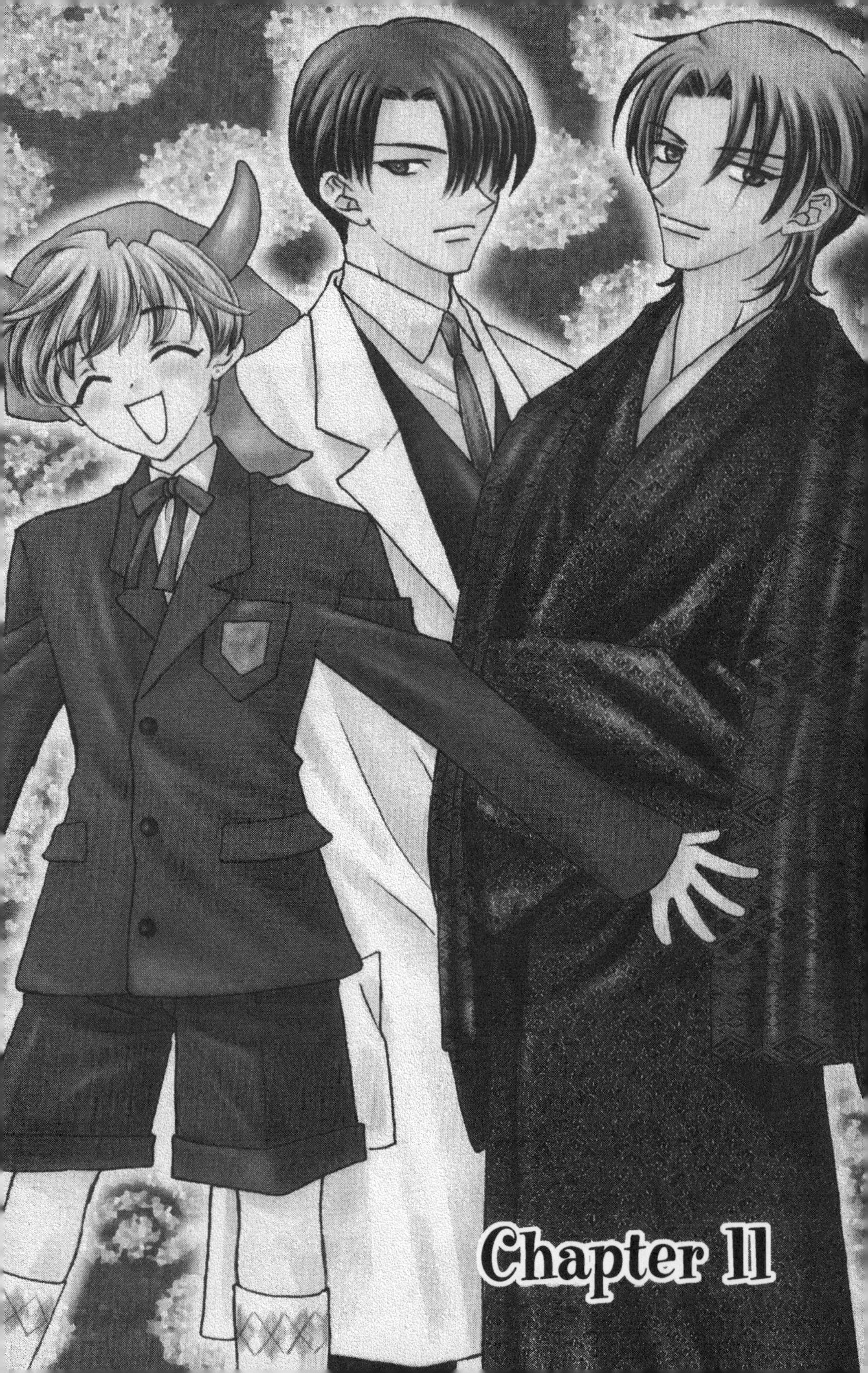
Chapter 11

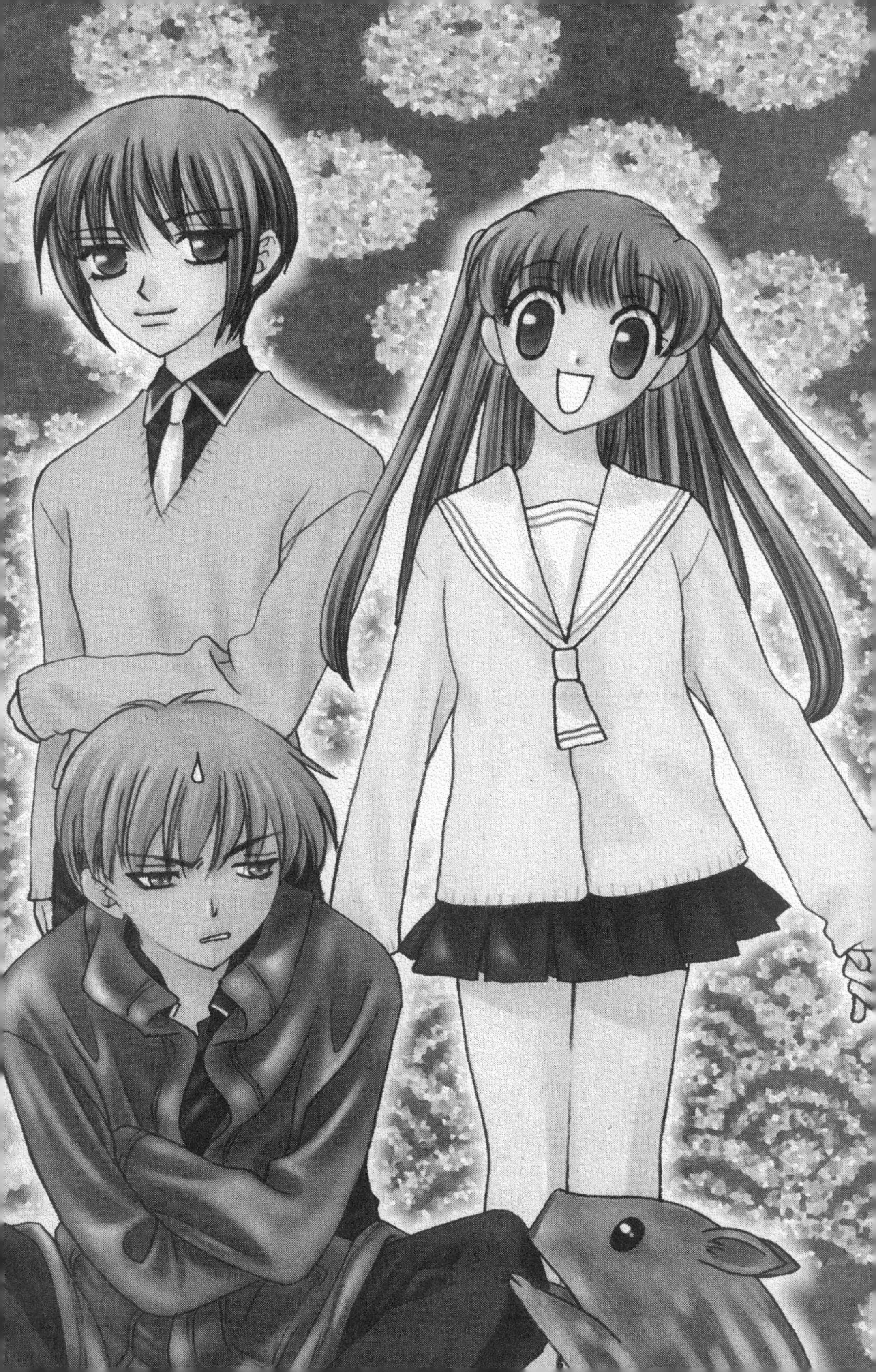

My thanks to...

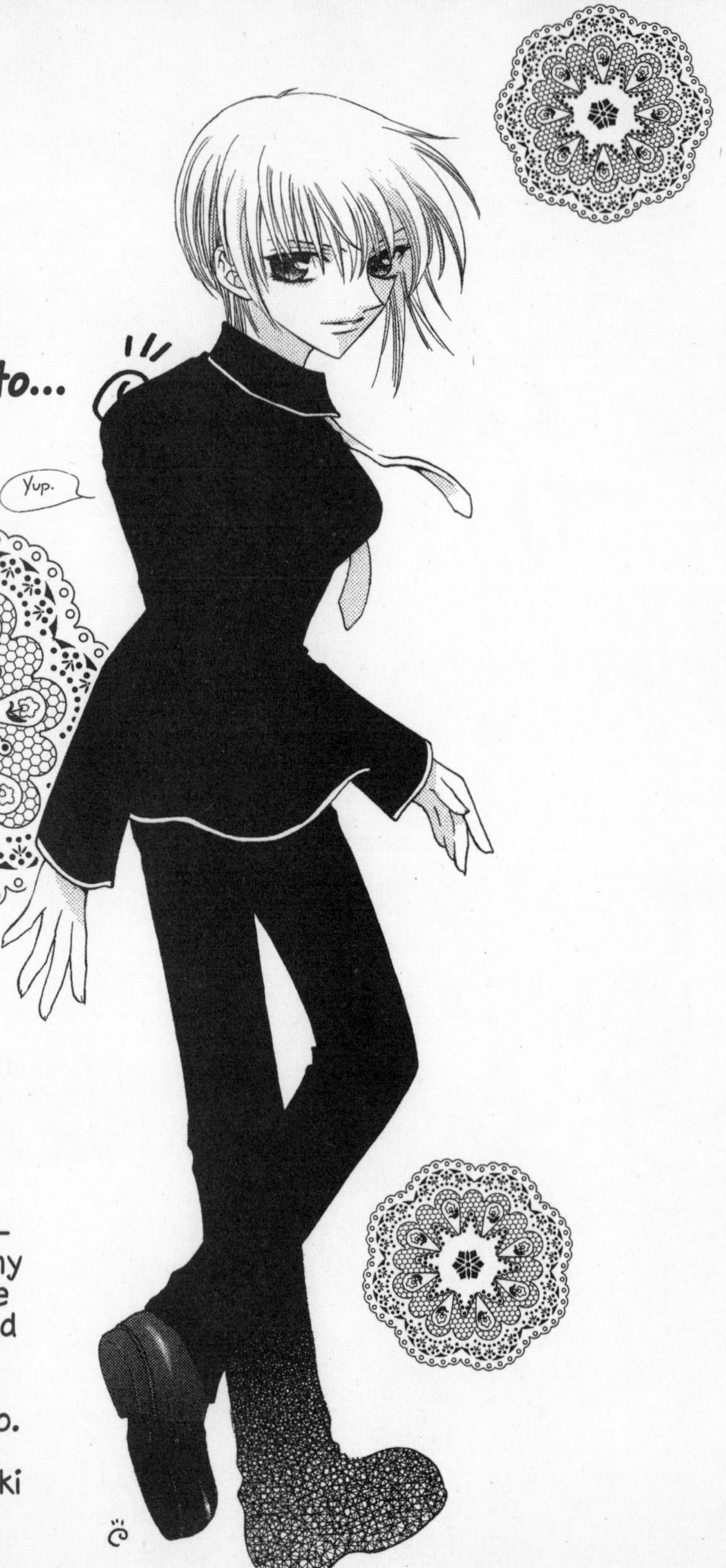
Yup.

Harada-sama, Araki-sama, my mother, my editor, and everyone who supports me and reads my work.

Next time it'll be Kyo.

This has been Natsuki Takaya.

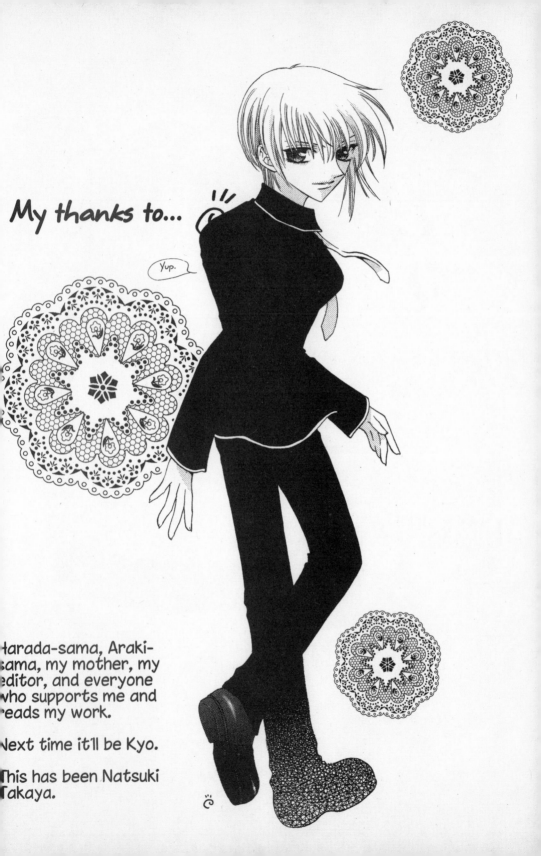

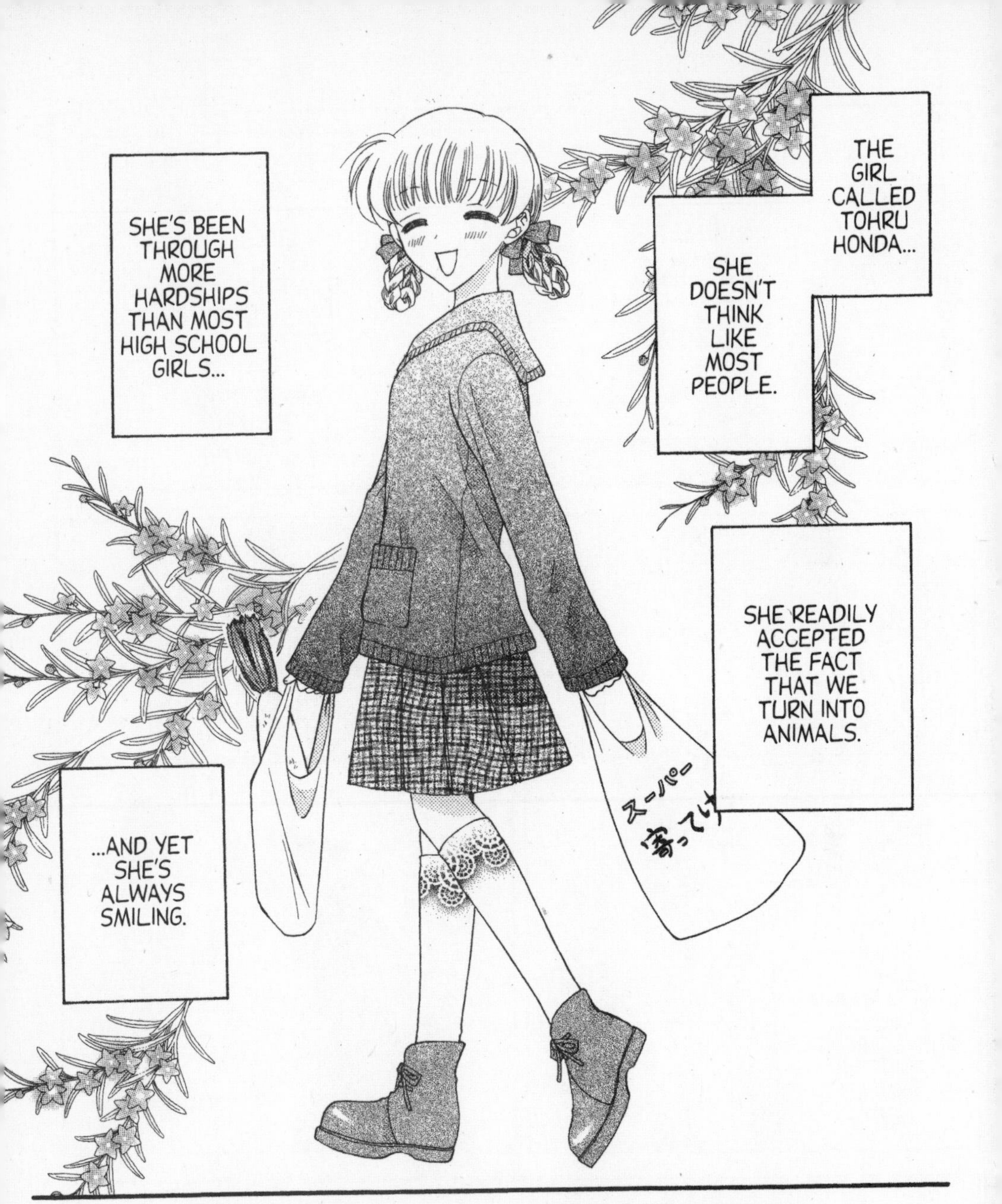
THE GIRL CALLED TOHRU HONDA...
SHE DOESN'T THINK LIKE MOST PEOPLE.
SHE'S BEEN THROUGH MORE HARDSHIPS THAN MOST HIGH SCHOOL GIRLS...
SHE READILY ACCEPTED THE FACT THAT WE TURN INTO ANIMALS.
...AND YET SHE'S ALWAYS SMILING.

ULTRA SPECIAL BLAH BLAH BLAH 5

In reality, the costume for the dance of the Chinese Zodiac is different every year. But here I have Momiji and Yuki wearing the same costume because I thought that if they had different costumes, it would be hard to understand. And on a completely different note, my older sister really liked Hana's line, "May you have good waves next year too..." (laugh). By the way, she seems to really like Kyo. She's a cat-lover.

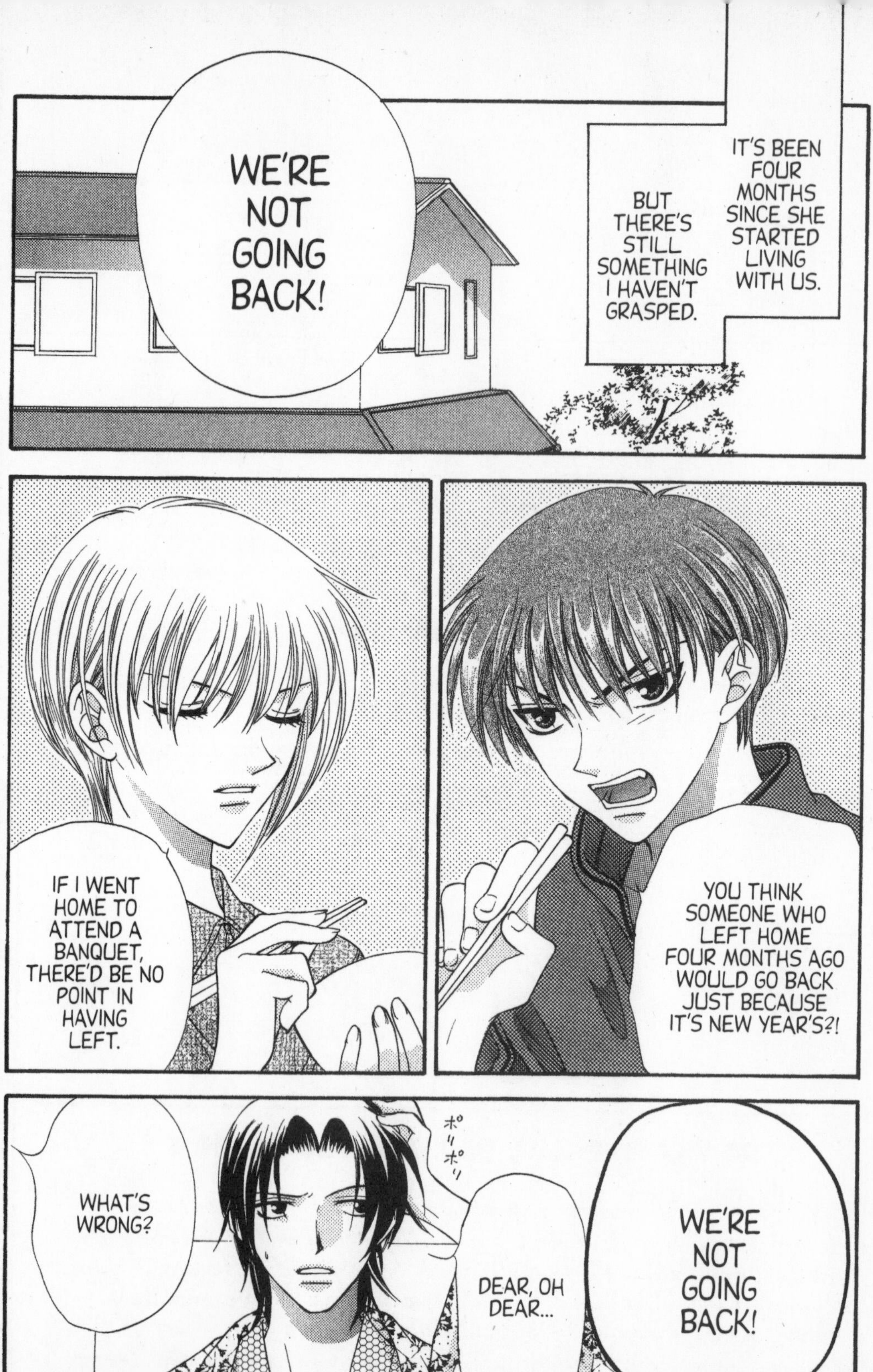
IT'S BEEN FOUR MONTHS SINCE SHE STARTED LIVING WITH US.
BUT THERE'S STILL SOMETHING I HAVEN'T GRASPED.
WE'RE NOT GOING BACK!
YOU THINK SOMEONE WHO LEFT HOME FOUR MONTHS AGO WOULD GO BACK JUST BECAUSE IT'S NEW YEAR'S?!
IF I WENT HOME TO ATTEND A BANQUET, THERE'D BE NO POINT IN HAVING LEFT.
WE'RE NOT GOING BACK!
DEAR, OH DEAR...
ポリポリ
WHAT'S WRONG?

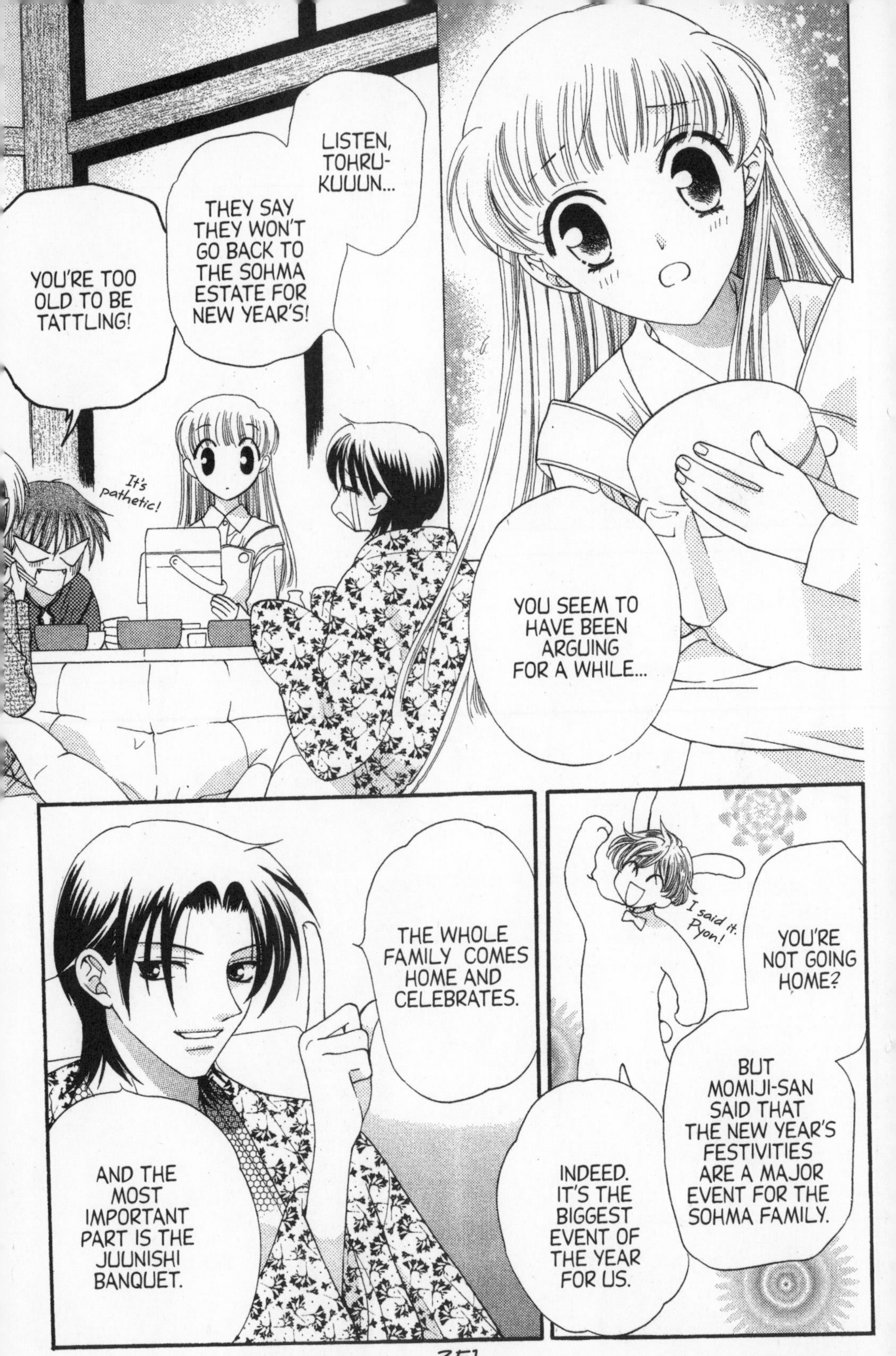
LISTEN, TOHRU-KUUUN...
THEY SAY THEY WON'T GO BACK TO THE SOHMA ESTATE FOR NEW YEAR'S!
YOU'RE TOO OLD TO BE TATTLING!
It's pathetic!
YOU SEEM TO HAVE BEEN ARGUING FOR A WHILE...
YOU'RE NOT GOING HOME?
I said it. Pyon!
BUT MOMIJI-SAN SAID THAT THE NEW YEAR'S FESTIVITIES ARE A MAJOR EVENT FOR THE SOHMA FAMILY.
INDEED. IT'S THE BIGGEST EVENT OF THE YEAR FOR US.
THE WHOLE FAMILY COMES HOME AND CELEBRATES.
AND THE MOST IMPORTANT PART IS THE JUUNISHI BANQUET.

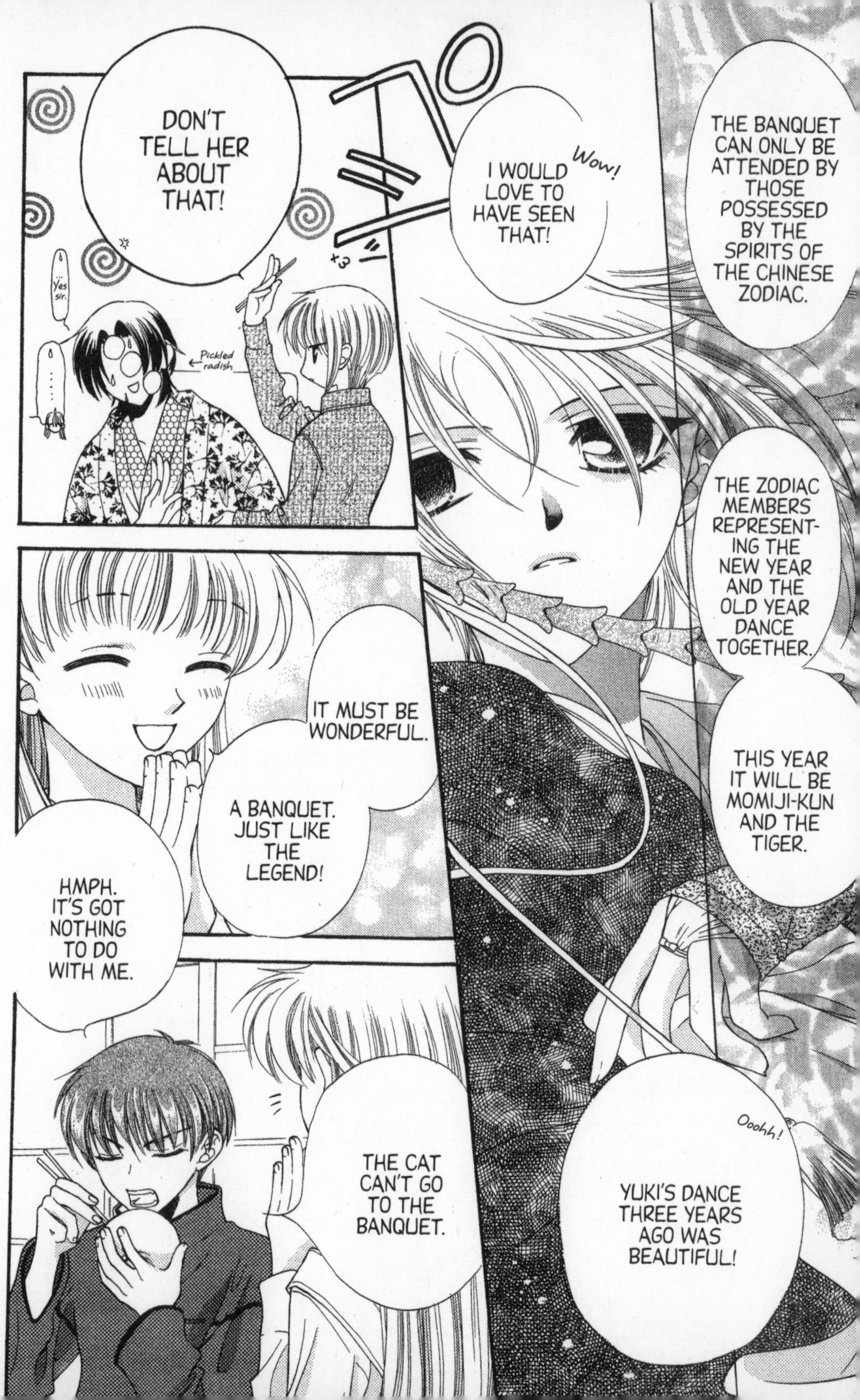
THE BANQUET CAN ONLY BE ATTENDED BY THOSE POSSESSED BY THE SPIRITS OF THE CHINESE ZODIAC.
THE ZODIAC MEMBERS REPRESENT-ING THE NEW YEAR AND THE OLD YEAR DANCE TOGETHER.
THIS YEAR IT WILL BE MOMIJI-KUN AND THE TIGER.
Ooohh!
YUKI'S DANCE THREE YEARS AGO WAS BEAUTIFUL!
Wow!
I WOULD LOVE TO HAVE SEEN THAT!
x3
DON'T TELL HER ABOUT THAT!
...Yes sir.
Pickled radish
IT MUST BE WONDERFUL.
A BANQUET. JUST LIKE THE LEGEND!
THE CAT CAN'T GO TO THE BANQUET.
HMPH. IT'S GOT NOTHING TO DO WITH ME.

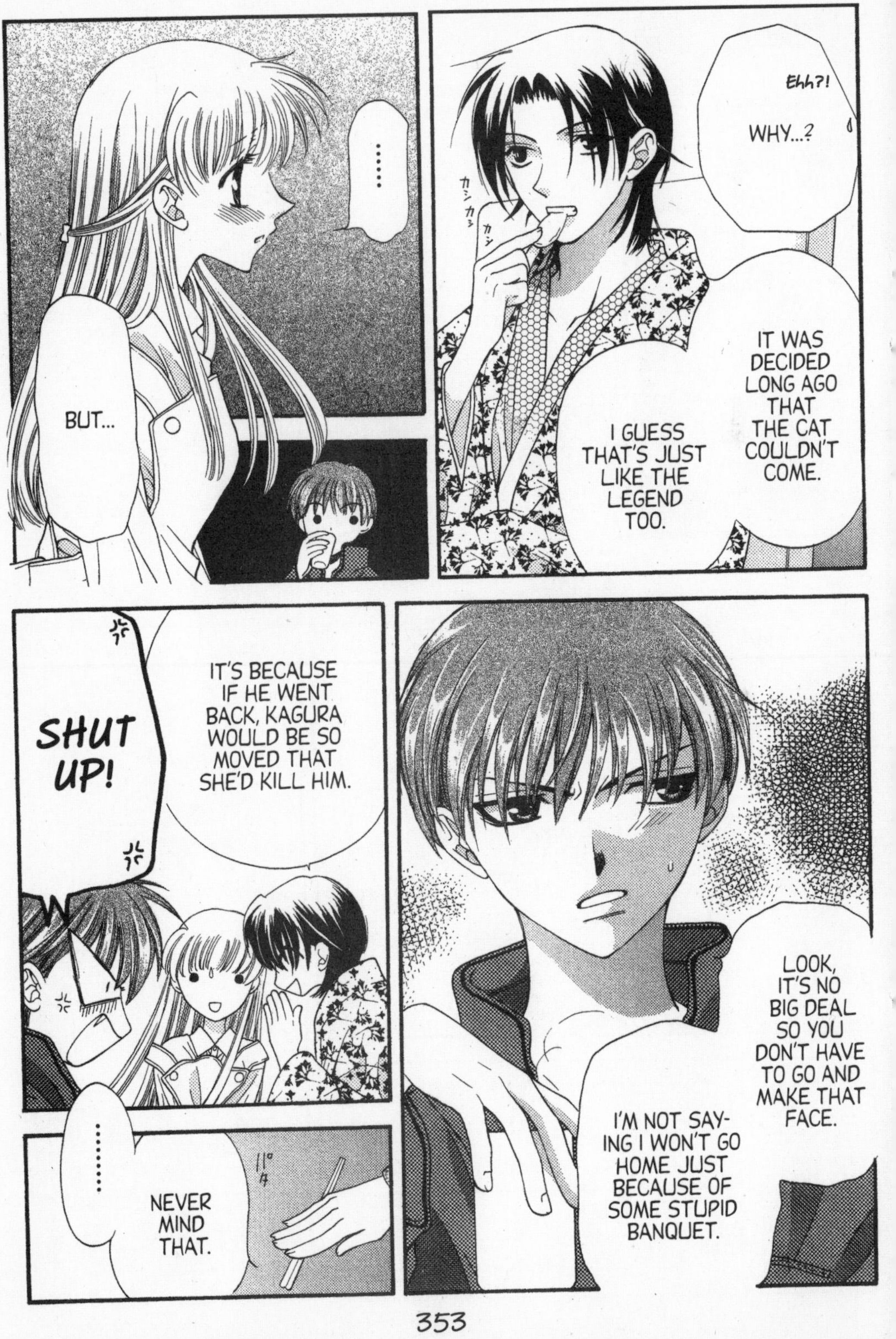
Ehh?!
WHY...?
IT WAS DECIDED LONG AGO THAT THE CAT COULDN'T COME.
I GUESS THAT'S JUST LIKE THE LEGEND TOO.
......
BUT...
LOOK, IT'S NO BIG DEAL SO YOU DON'T HAVE TO GO AND MAKE THAT FACE.
I'M NOT SAY-ING I WON'T GO HOME JUST BECAUSE OF SOME STUPID BANQUET.
IT'S BECAUSE IF HE WENT BACK, KAGURA WOULD BE SO MOVED THAT SHE'D KILL HIM.
SHUT UP!
......
NEVER MIND THAT.

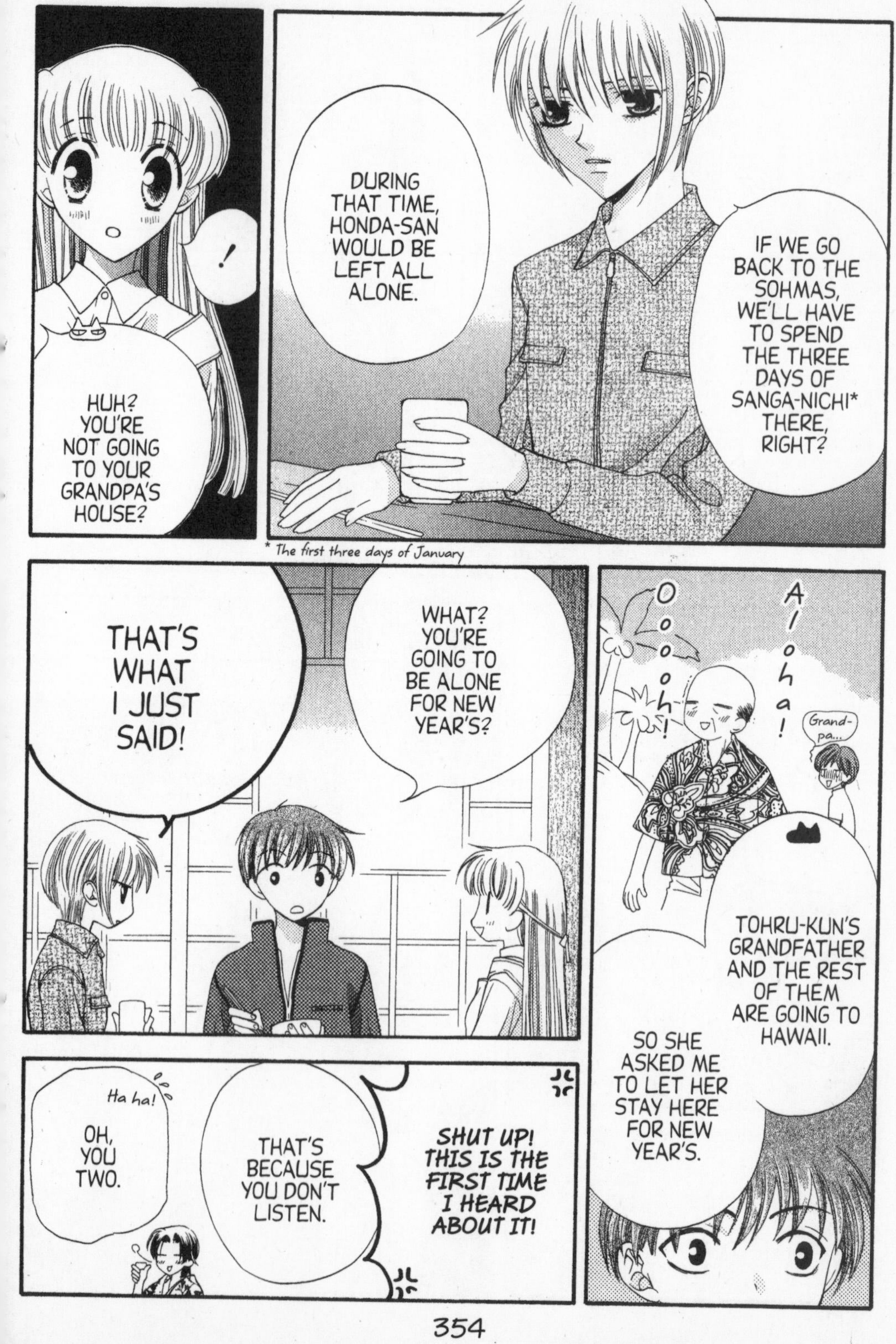
IF WE GO BACK TO THE SOHMAS, WE'LL HAVE TO SPEND THE THREE DAYS OF SANGA-NICHI* THERE, RIGHT?
DURING THAT TIME, HONDA-SAN WOULD BE LEFT ALL ALONE.
!
HUH? YOU'RE NOT GOING TO YOUR GRANDPA'S HOUSE?
Aloha!
Oooooh!
Grand-pa...
TOHRU-KUN'S GRANDFATHER AND THE REST OF THEM ARE GOING TO HAWAII.
SO SHE ASKED ME TO LET HER STAY HERE FOR NEW YEAR'S.
WHAT? YOU'RE GOING TO BE ALONE FOR NEW YEAR'S?
THAT'S WHAT I JUST SAID!
SHUT UP! THIS IS THE FIRST TIME I HEARD ABOUT IT!
THAT'S BECAUSE YOU DON'T LISTEN.
Ha ha!
OH, YOU TWO.

* The first three days of January

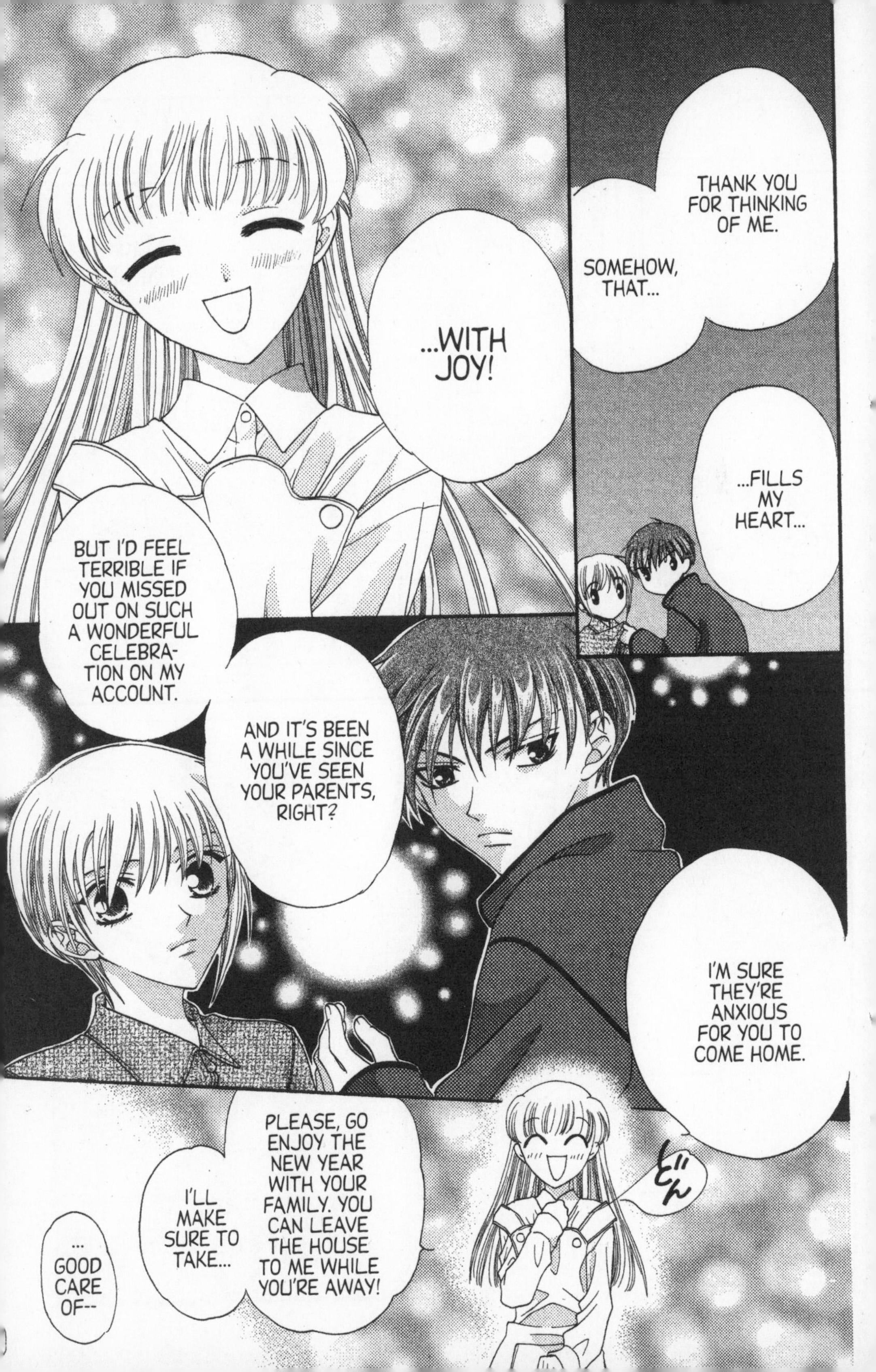
THANK YOU FOR THINKING OF ME.
SOMEHOW, THAT...
...FILLS MY HEART...
...WITH JOY!
BUT I'D FEEL TERRIBLE IF YOU MISSED OUT ON SUCH A WONDERFUL CELEBRA-TION ON MY ACCOUNT.
AND IT'S BEEN A WHILE SINCE YOU'VE SEEN YOUR PARENTS, RIGHT?
I'M SURE THEY'RE ANXIOUS FOR YOU TO COME HOME.
どん
PLEASE, GO ENJOY THE NEW YEAR WITH YOUR FAMILY. YOU CAN LEAVE THE HOUSE TO ME WHILE YOU'RE AWAY!
I'LL MAKE SURE TO TAKE...
... GOOD CARE OF--

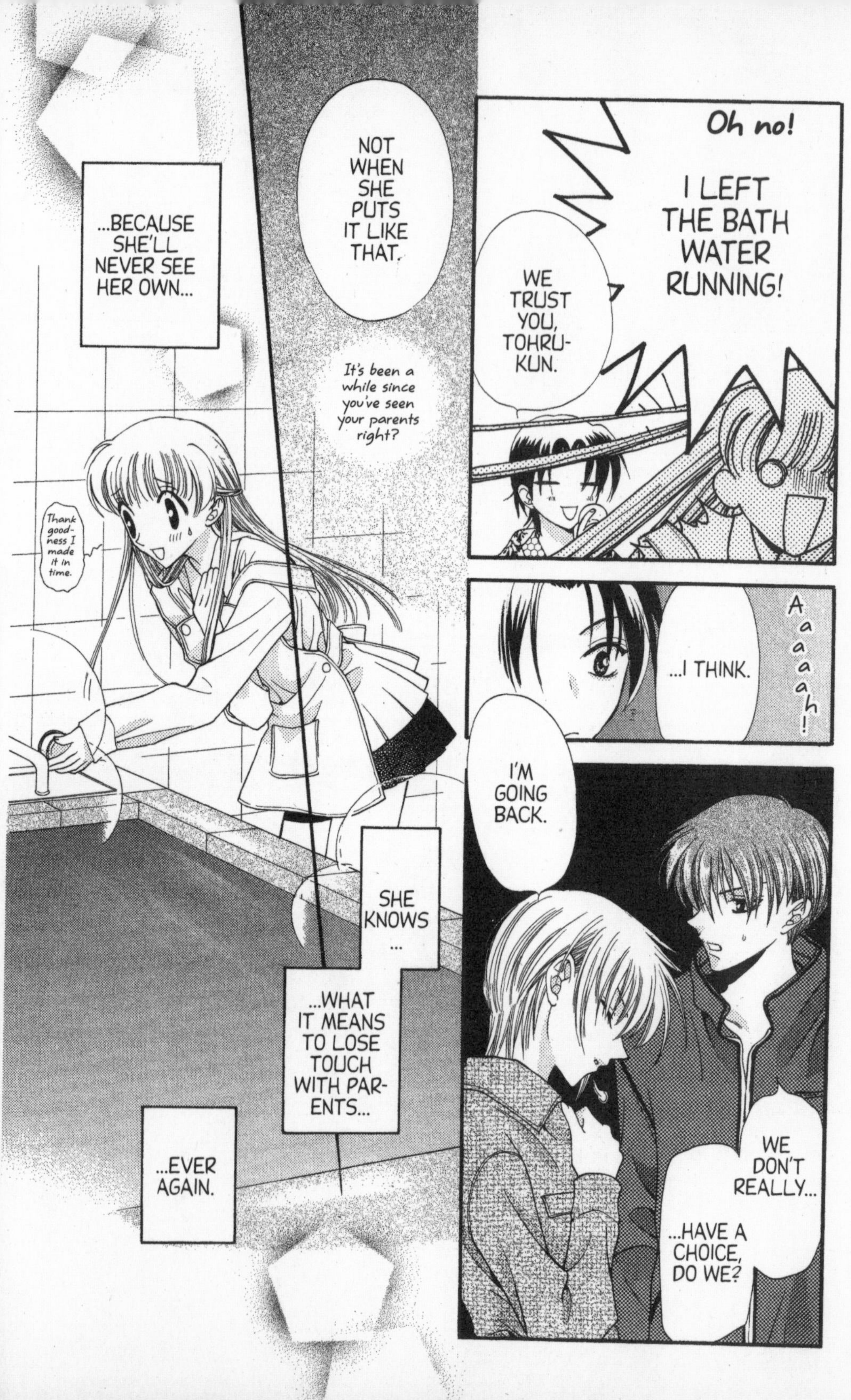
Oh no!
I LEFT THE BATH WATER RUNNING!
WE TRUST YOU, TOHRU-KUN.
Aaaaah!
...I THINK.
I'M GOING BACK.
WE DON'T REALLY...
...HAVE A CHOICE, DO WE?
NOT WHEN SHE PUTS IT LIKE THAT.
It's been a while since you've seen your parents right?
SHE KNOWS...
...WHAT IT MEANS TO LOSE TOUCH WITH PARENTS...
...BECAUSE SHE'LL NEVER SEE HER OWN...
Thank goodness I made it in time.
...EVER AGAIN.

Fruits Basket 2 Part 5:

The "Those with Wings" (Takaya-sensei's last manga series before Furuba) CD was released on June 5th. Did you buy it? Did you listen to it? It's a comedy and it's really funny, so I'd really like you to hear it. They got an amazing cast who all did a great job (of course) and I ended up laughing at my own jokes (laugh). When I went to the recording session, I was so nervous I was shaking. I was like, "Wow, the big time!" (laugh). I'm such a fan of Midorikawa-san that my friends often tell me, "We know already; you don't have to say it again," and when a certain anime was on and it turned out that he played the new character, my friend called and said, "You must be really happy, Takaya," and as soon as I got off the phone, I sent out a FAX that said that I really was very happy, but now I'm really, really happy! When I met him I shouted, "I love you! I adore you! I'm a huge fan!" (laugh)

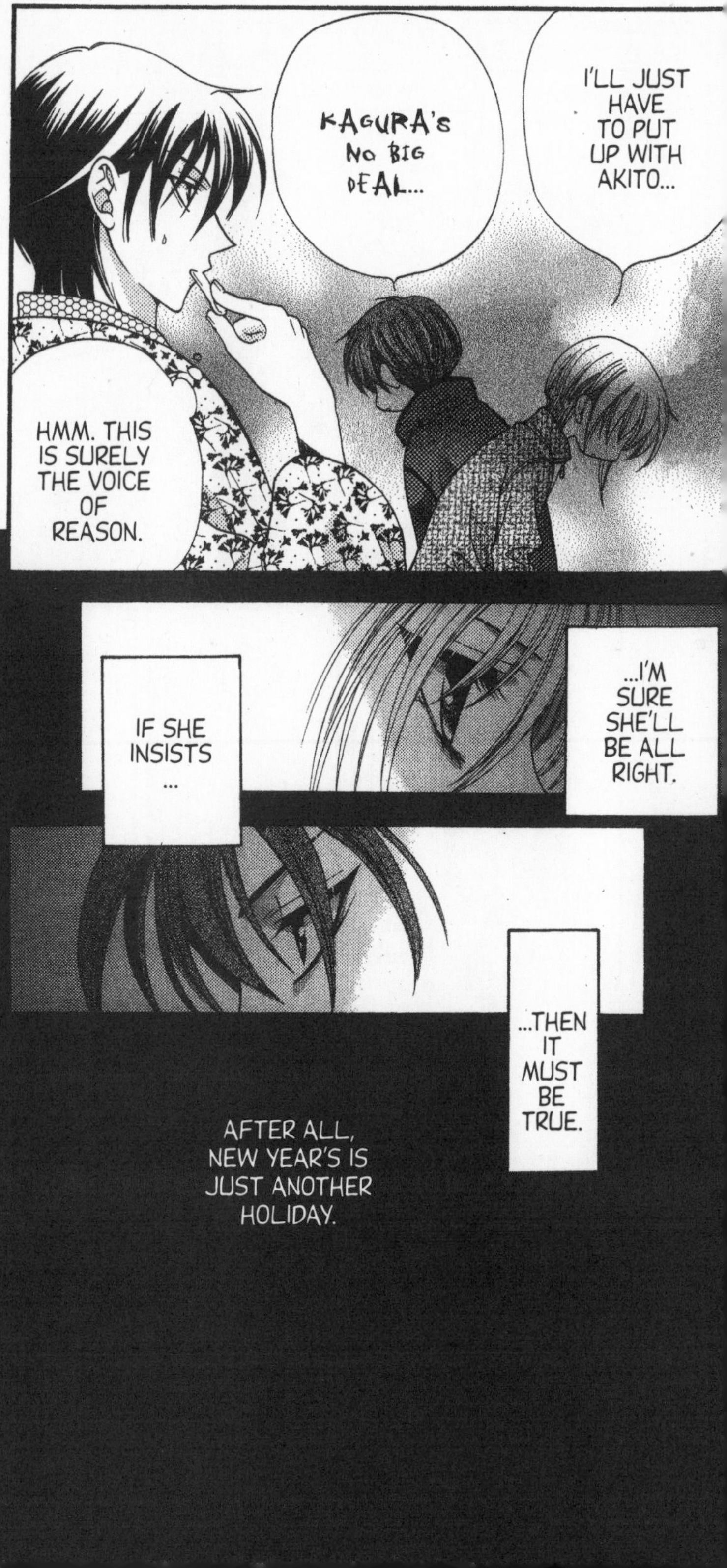
I'LL JUST HAVE TO PUT UP WITH AKITO...
KAGURA'S NO BIG DEAL...
HMM. THIS IS SURELY THE VOICE OF REASON.
...I'M SURE SHE'LL BE ALL RIGHT.
IF SHE INSISTS ...
...THEN IT MUST BE TRUE.
AFTER ALL, NEW YEAR'S IS JUST ANOTHER HOLIDAY.

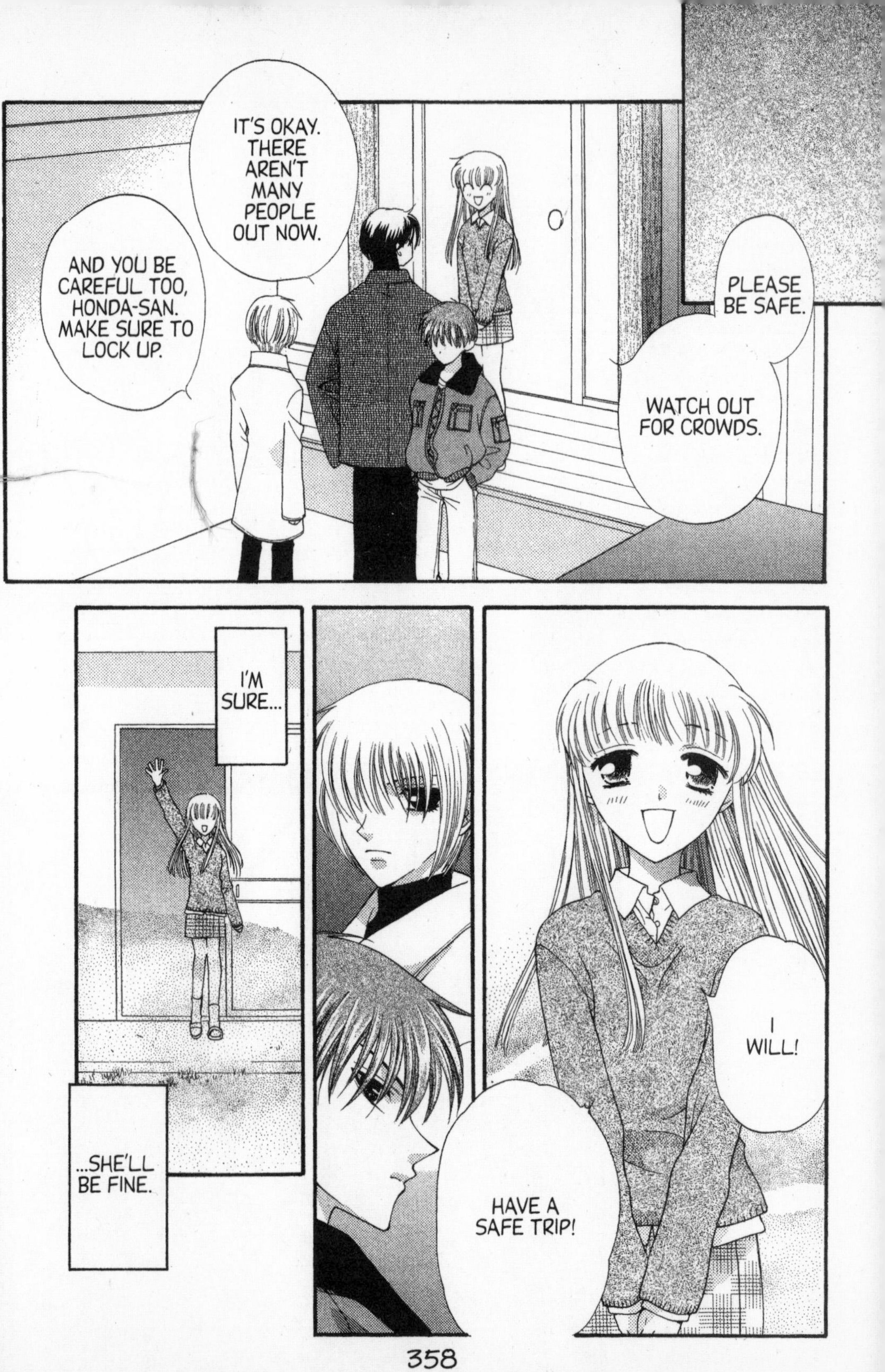
PLEASE BE SAFE.
WATCH OUT FOR CROWDS.
IT'S OKAY. THERE AREN'T MANY PEOPLE OUT NOW.
AND YOU BE CAREFUL TOO, HONDA-SAN. MAKE SURE TO LOCK UP.
I WILL!
HAVE A SAFE TRIP!
I'M SURE...
...SHE'LL BE FINE.

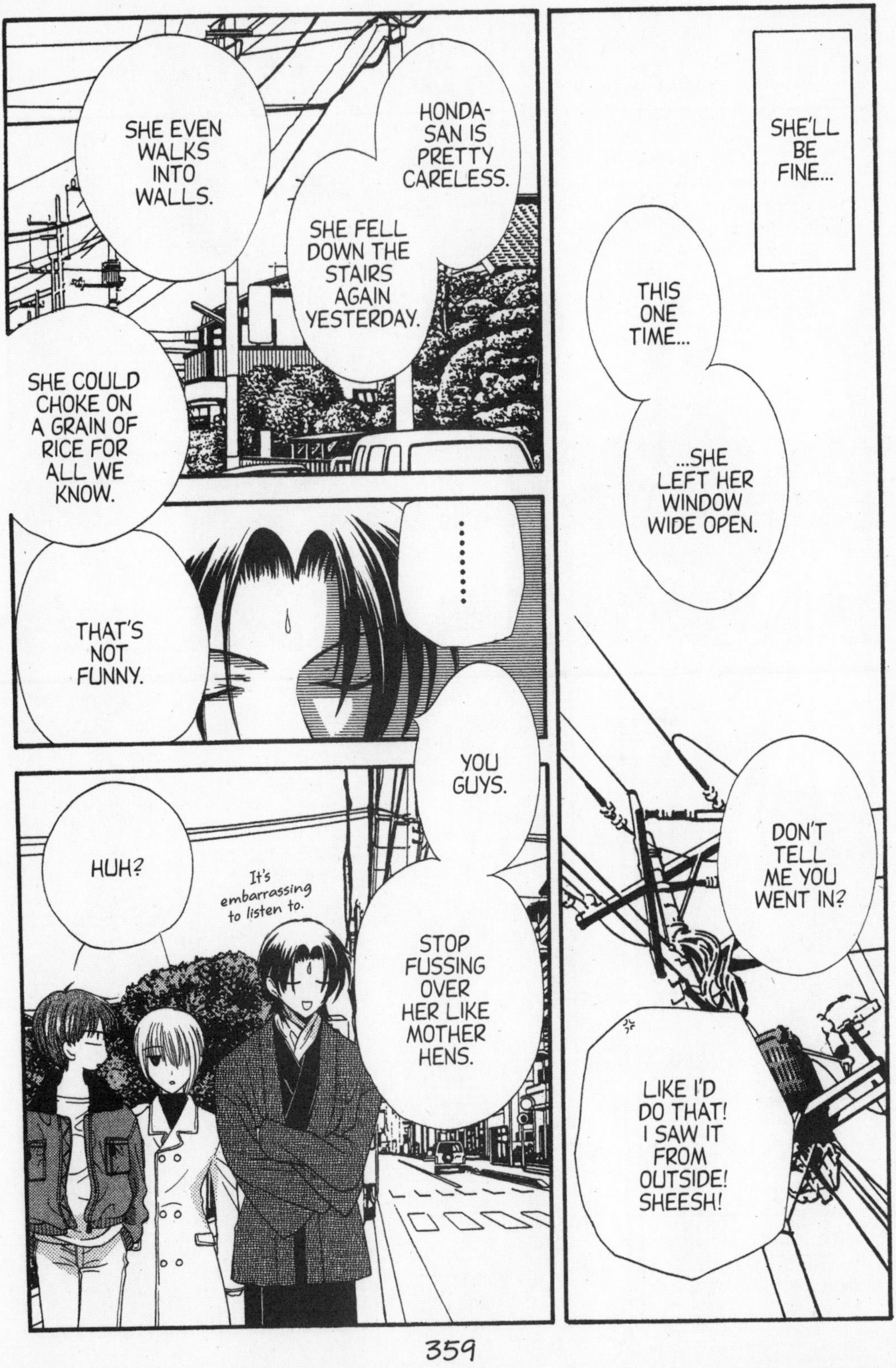
SHE'LL BE FINE...
THIS ONE TIME...
...SHE LEFT HER WINDOW WIDE OPEN.
DON'T TELL ME YOU WENT IN?
LIKE I'D DO THAT! I SAW IT FROM OUTSIDE! SHEESH!
HONDA-SAN IS PRETTY CARELESS.
SHE FELL DOWN THE STAIRS AGAIN YESTERDAY.
SHE EVEN WALKS INTO WALLS.
SHE COULD CHOKE ON A GRAIN OF RICE FOR ALL WE KNOW.
......
THAT'S NOT FUNNY.
YOU GUYS.
STOP FUSSING OVER HER LIKE MOTHER HENS.
It's embarrassing to listen to.
HUH?

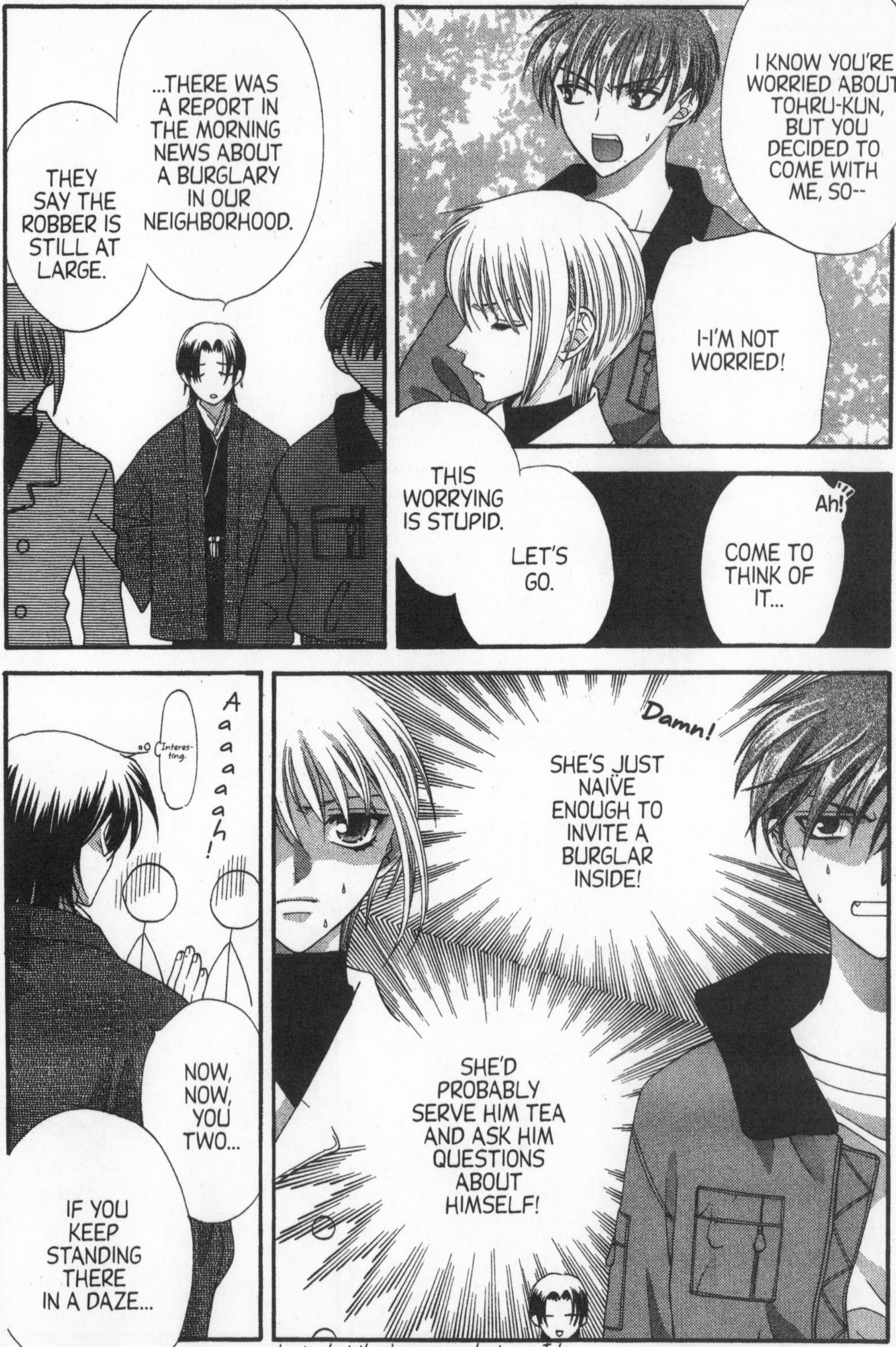
I KNOW YOU'RE WORRIED ABOUT TOHRU-KUN, BUT YOU DECIDED TO COME WITH ME, SO--
I-I'M NOT WORRIED!
THIS WORRYING IS STUPID.
LET'S GO.
Ah!
COME TO THINK OF IT...
...THERE WAS A REPORT IN THE MORNING NEWS ABOUT A BURGLARY IN OUR NEIGHBORHOOD.
THEY SAY THE ROBBER IS STILL AT LARGE.
Damn!
SHE'S JUST NAÏVE ENOUGH TO INVITE A BURGLAR INSIDE!
SHE'D PROBABLY SERVE HIM TEA AND ASK HIM QUESTIONS ABOUT HIMSELF!
Aaaaaah!
Interesting.
NOW, NOW, YOU TWO...
IF YOU KEEP STANDING THERE IN A DAZE...
Look what they're saying about you, Tohru.

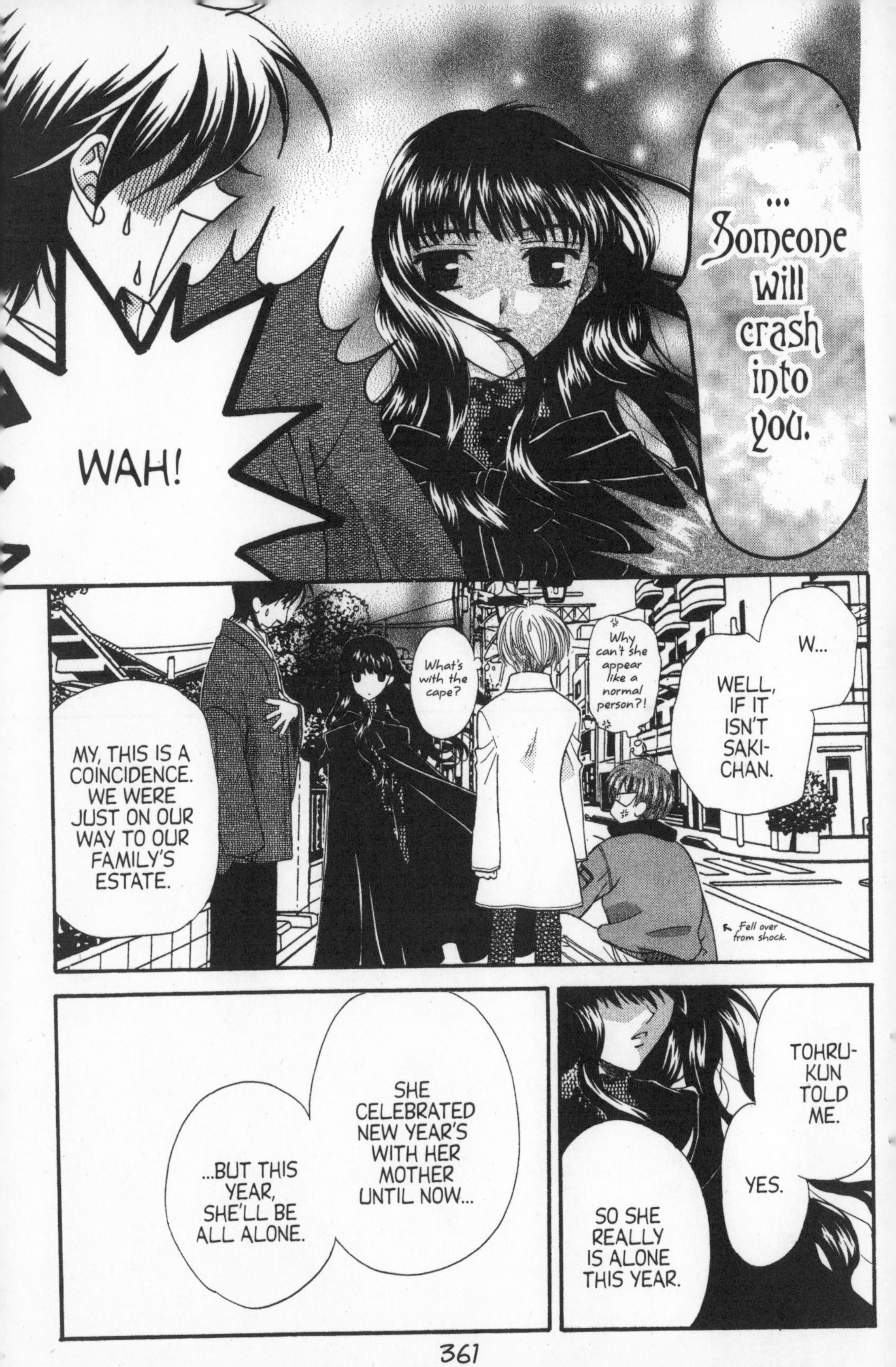
...Someone will crash into you.
WAH!
W...
WELL, IF IT ISN'T SAKI-CHAN.
Fell over from shock.
Why can't she appear like a normal person?!
What's with the cape?
MY, THIS IS A COINCIDENCE. WE WERE JUST ON OUR WAY TO OUR FAMILY'S ESTATE.
TOHRU-KUN TOLD ME.
YES.
SO SHE REALLY IS ALONE THIS YEAR.
SHE CELEBRATED NEW YEAR'S WITH HER MOTHER UNTIL NOW...
...BUT THIS YEAR, SHE'LL BE ALL ALONE.

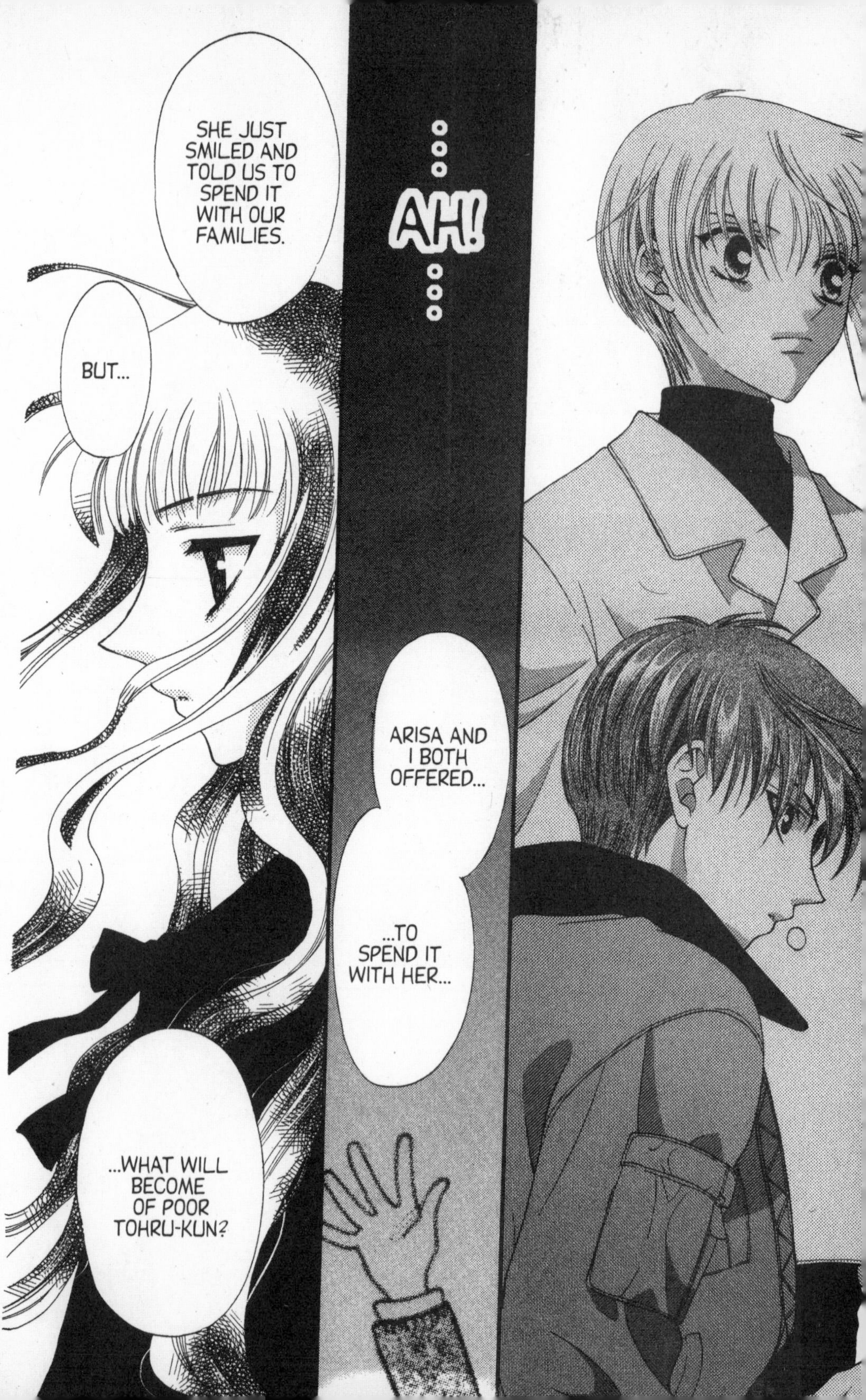
...AH!...
ARISA AND I BOTH OFFERED...
...TO SPEND IT WITH HER...
SHE JUST SMILED AND TOLD US TO SPEND IT WITH OUR FAMILIES.
BUT...
...WHAT WILL BECOME OF POOR TOHRU-KUN?

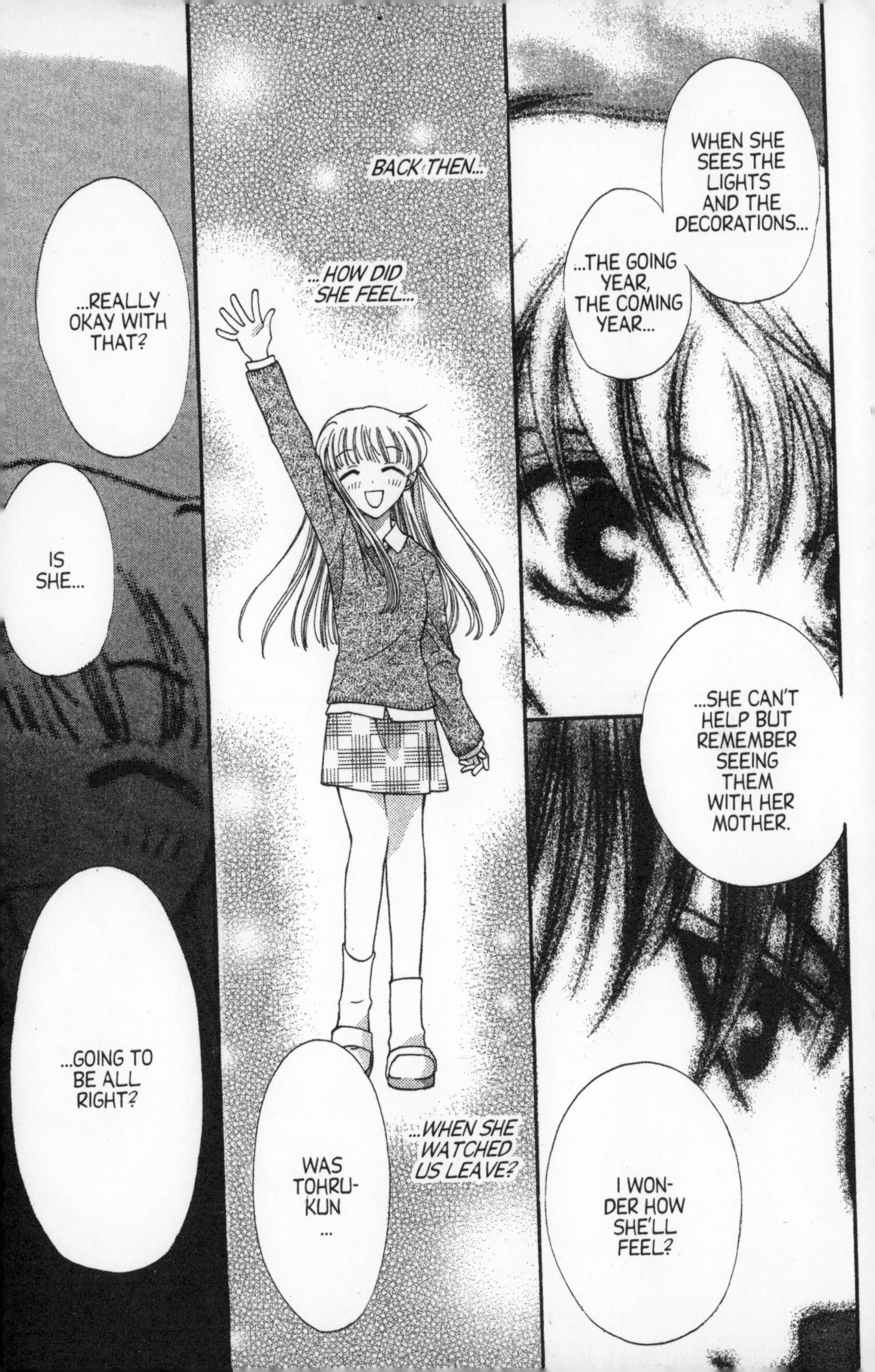
WHEN SHE SEES THE LIGHTS AND THE DECORATIONS...
...THE GOING YEAR, THE COMING YEAR...
...SHE CAN'T HELP BUT REMEMBER SEEING THEM WITH HER MOTHER.
I WON-DER HOW SHE'LL FEEL?
BACK THEN...
...HOW DID SHE FEEL...
...WHEN SHE WATCHED US LEAVE?
WAS TOHRU-KUN ...
...REALLY OKAY WITH THAT?
IS SHE...
...GOING TO BE ALL RIGHT?

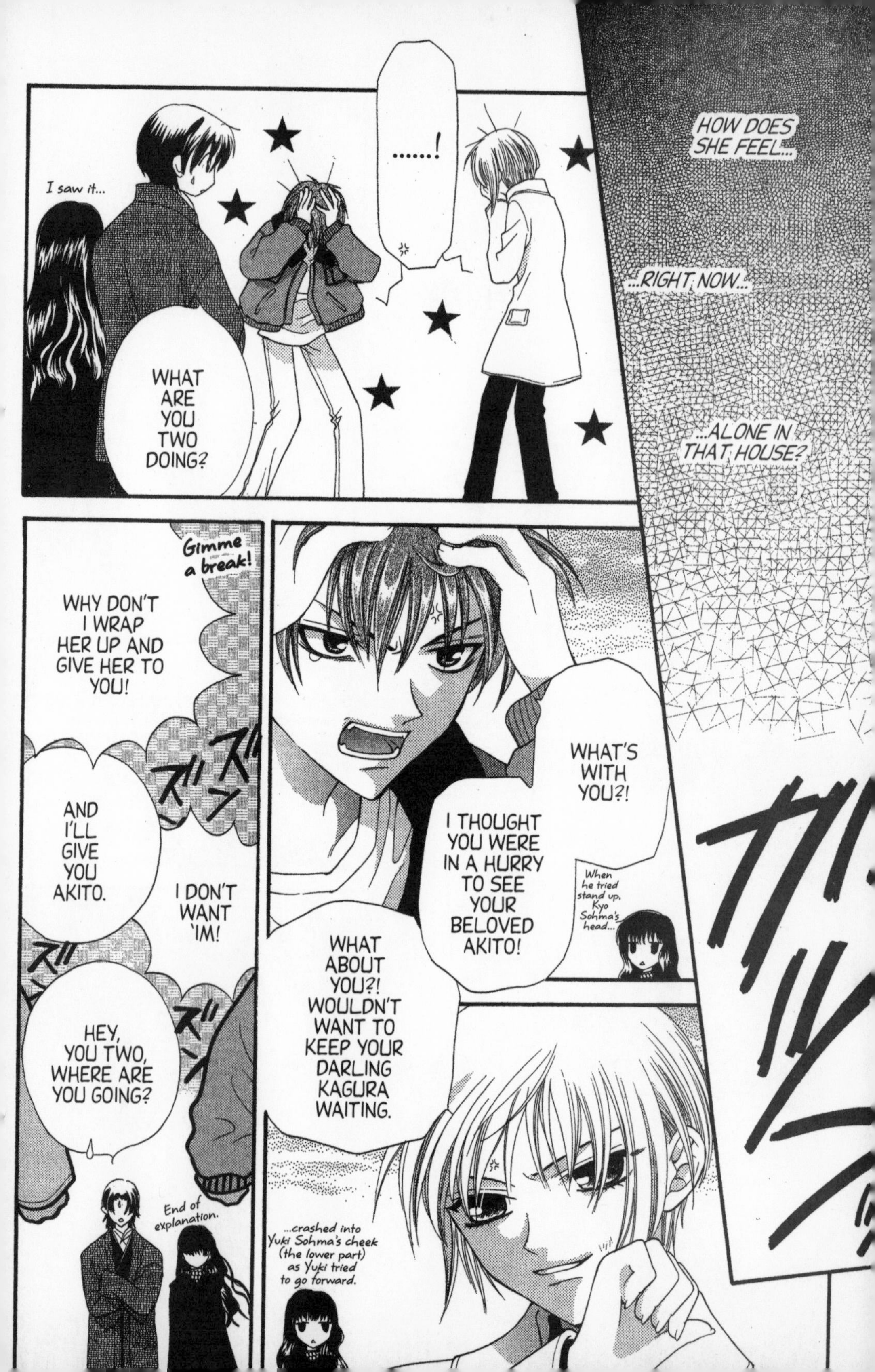
HOW DOES SHE FEEL...
...RIGHT NOW...
...ALONE IN THAT HOUSE?
......!
I saw it...
WHAT ARE YOU TWO DOING?
WHAT'S WITH YOU?!
I THOUGHT YOU WERE IN A HURRY TO SEE YOUR BELOVED AKITO!
When he tried stand up, Kyo Sohma's head...
WHAT ABOUT YOU?! WOULDN'T WANT TO KEEP YOUR DARLING KAGURA WAITING.
...crashed into Yuki Sohma's cheek (the lower part) as Yuki tried to go forward.
Gimme a break!
WHY DON'T I WRAP HER UP AND GIVE HER TO YOU!
AND I'LL GIVE YOU AKITO.
I DON'T WANT 'IM!
HEY, YOU TWO, WHERE ARE YOU GOING?
End of explanation.

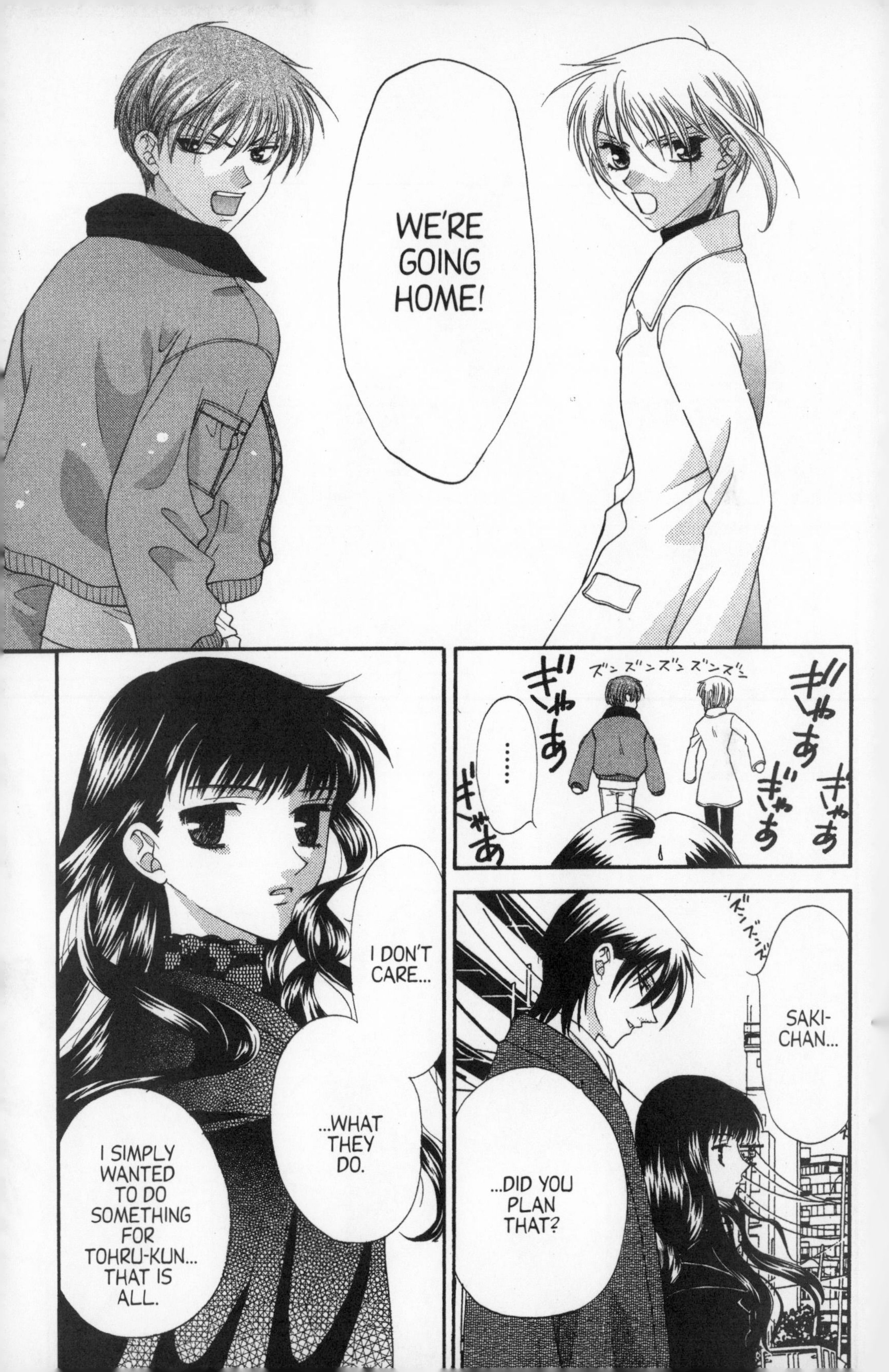
WE'RE GOING HOME!
ズンズンズンズンズン
ぎゃあ
ぎゃあ
ぎゃあ
ぎゃあ
......
SAKI-CHAN...
...DID YOU PLAN THAT?
I DON'T CARE...
...WHAT THEY DO.
I SIMPLY WANTED TO DO SOMETHING FOR TOHRU-KUN... THAT IS ALL.

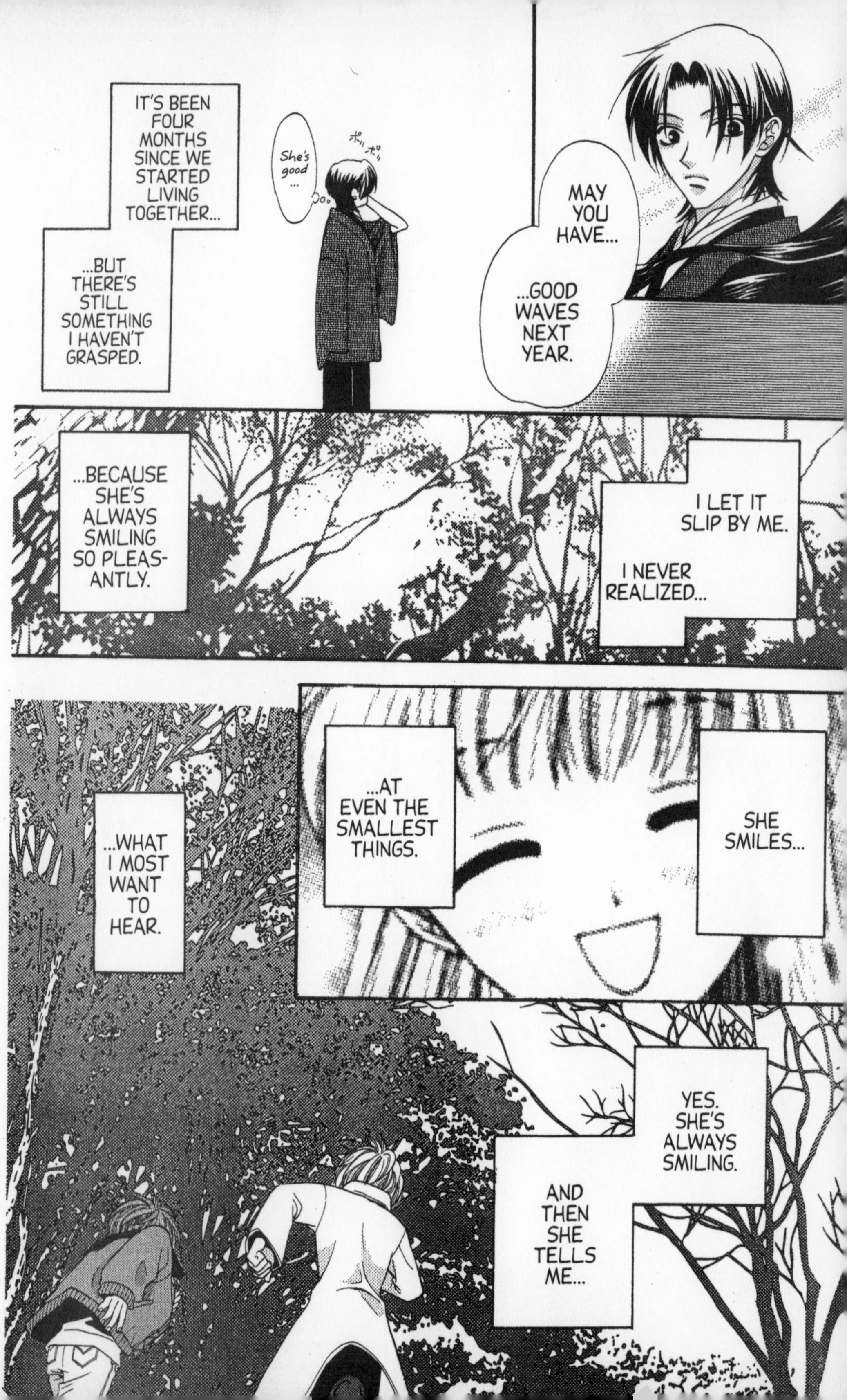
MAY YOU HAVE...
...GOOD WAVES NEXT YEAR.
She's good ...
IT'S BEEN FOUR MONTHS SINCE WE STARTED LIVING TOGETHER...
...BUT THERE'S STILL SOMETHING I HAVEN'T GRASPED.
I LET IT SLIP BY ME.
I NEVER REALIZED...
...BECAUSE SHE'S ALWAYS SMILING SO PLEAS-ANTLY.
SHE SMILES...
...AT EVEN THE SMALLEST THINGS.
YES. SHE'S ALWAYS SMILING.
AND THEN SHE TELLS ME...
...WHAT I MOST WANT TO HEAR.

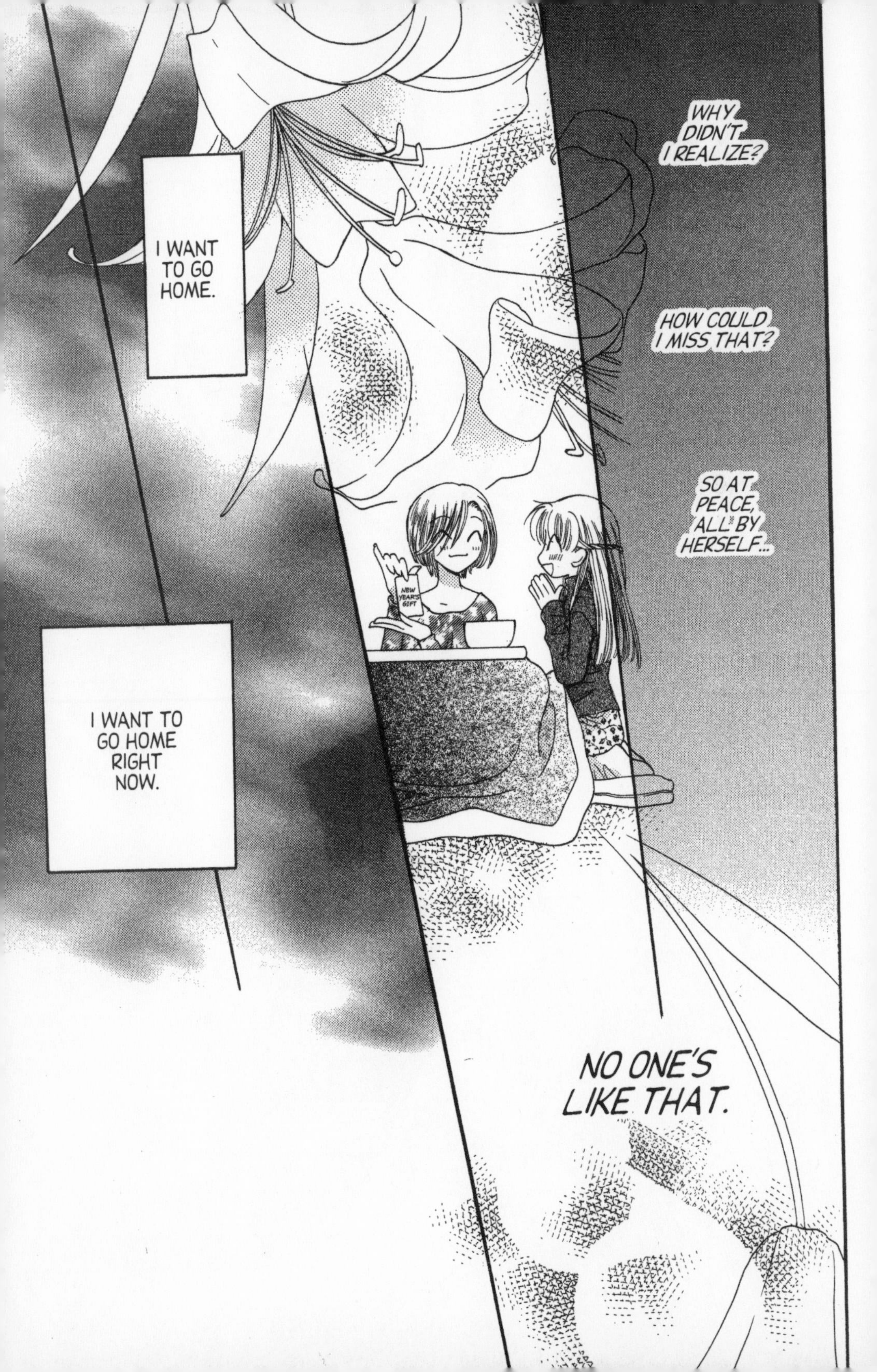
WHY DIDN'T I REALIZE?
HOW COULD I MISS THAT?
SO AT PEACE, ALL BY HERSELF...
NEW YEAR'S GIFT
NO ONE'S LIKE THAT.
I WANT TO GO HOME.
I WANT TO GO HOME RIGHT NOW.

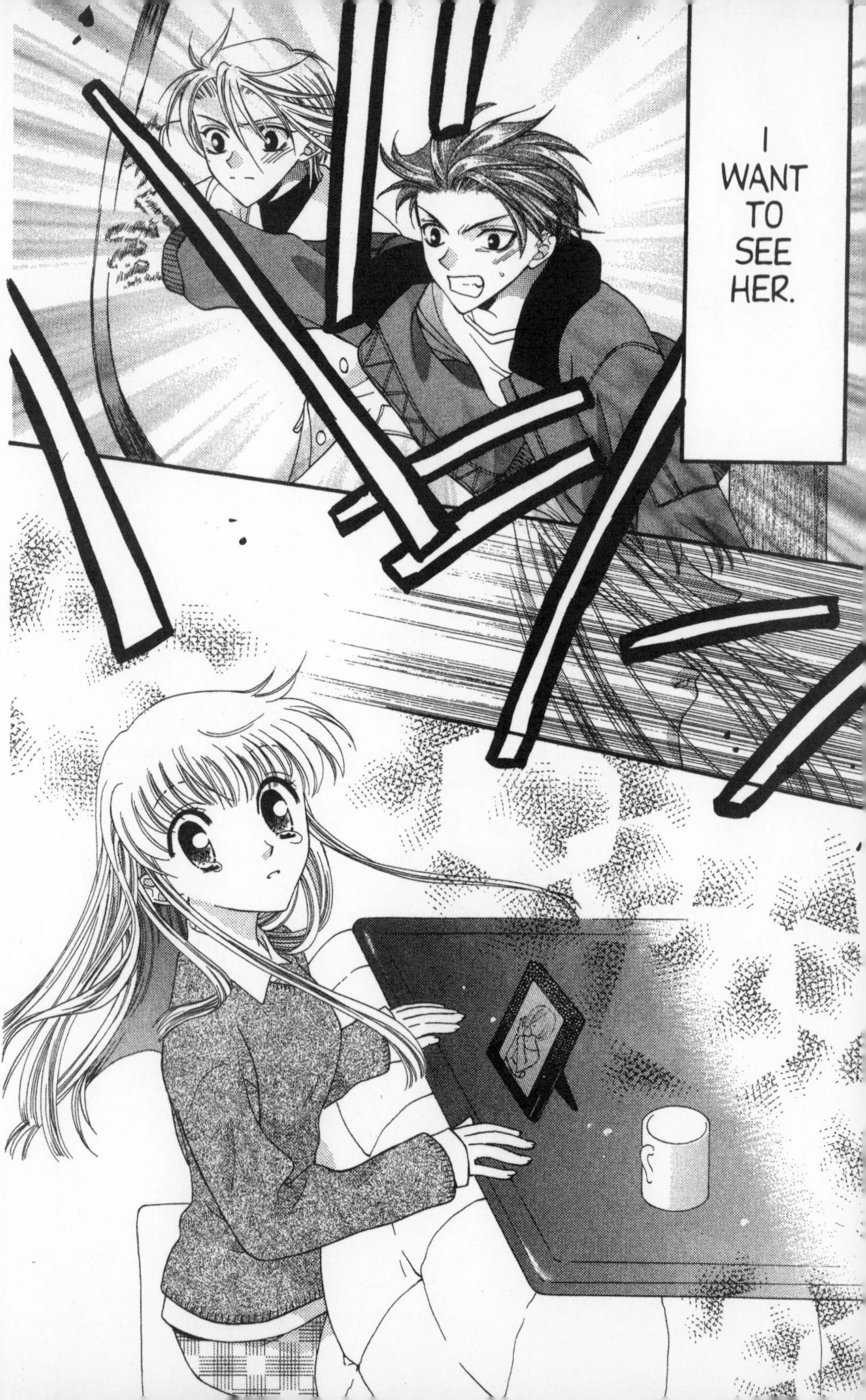
I WANT TO SEE HER.

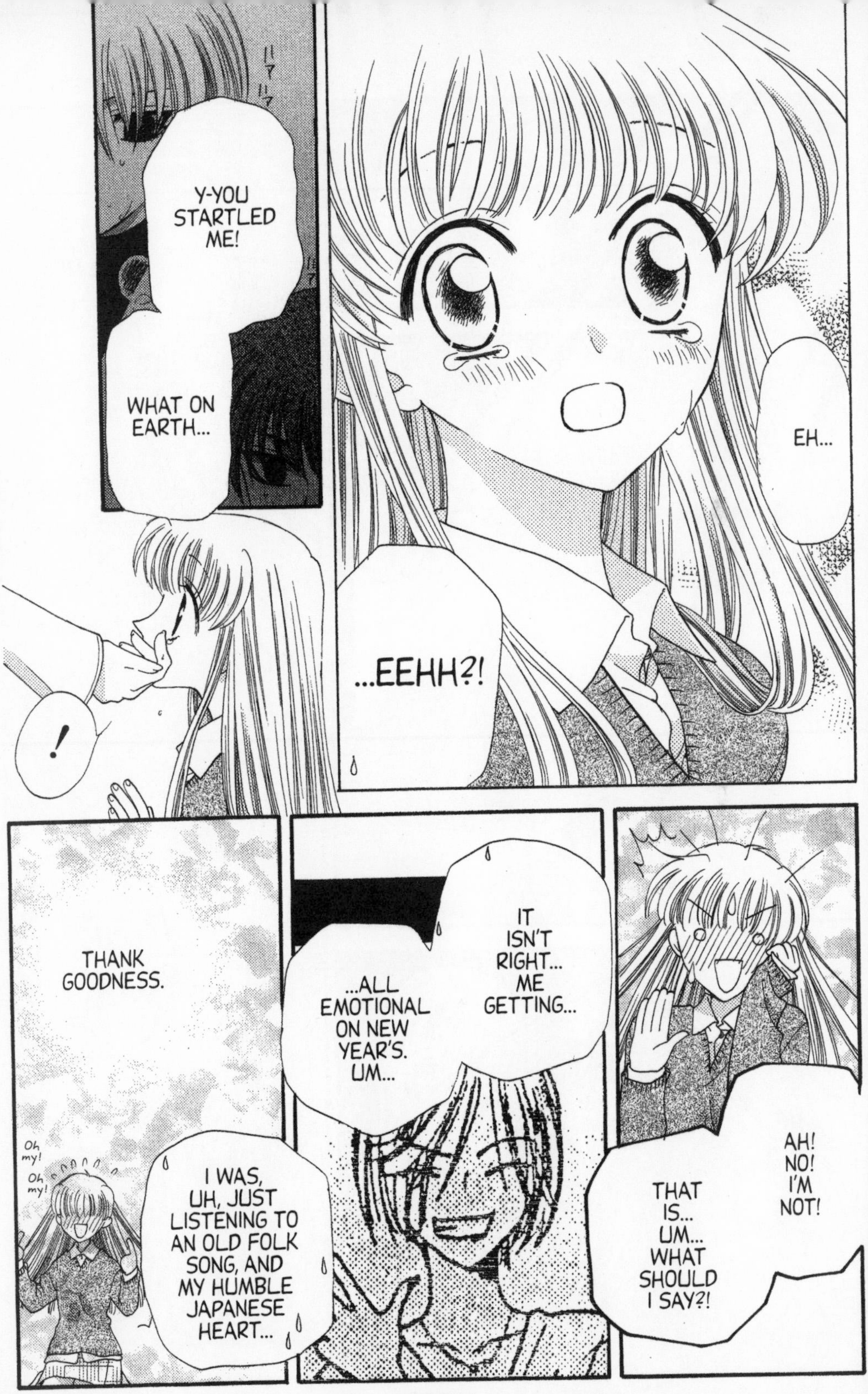
EH...
...EEHH?!
Y-YOU STARTLED ME!
WHAT ON EARTH...
!
AH! NO! I'M NOT!
THAT IS... UM... WHAT SHOULD I SAY?!
IT ISN'T RIGHT... ME GETTING...
...ALL EMOTIONAL ON NEW YEAR'S. UM...
THANK GOODNESS.
I WAS, UH, JUST LISTENING TO AN OLD FOLK SONG, AND MY HUMBLE JAPANESE HEART...
Oh my!
Oh my!

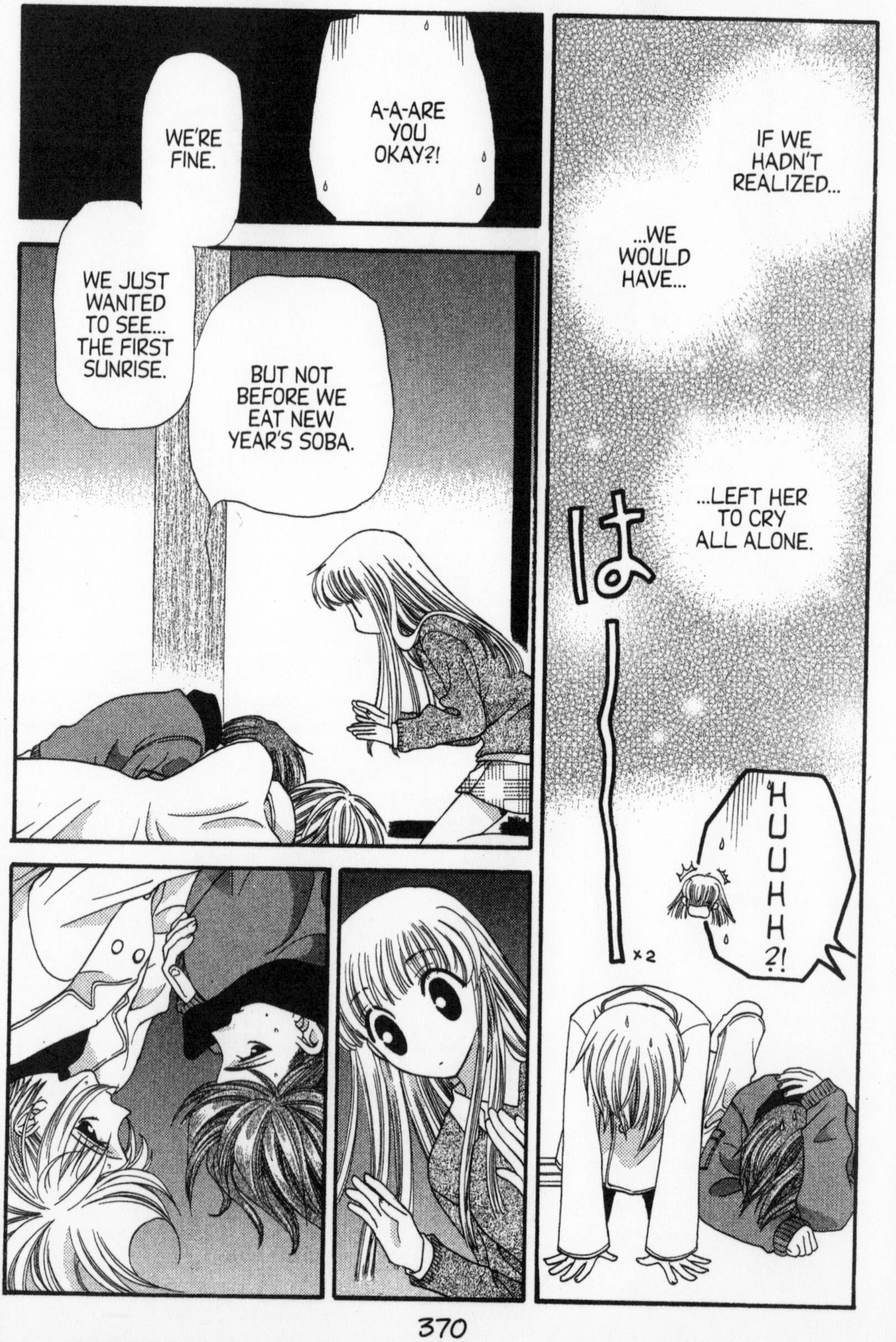
IF WE HADN'T REALIZED...
...WE WOULD HAVE...
...LEFT HER TO CRY ALL ALONE.
はー
×2
HUUUHH?!
A-A-ARE YOU OKAY?!
WE'RE FINE.
WE JUST WANTED TO SEE... THE FIRST SUNRISE.
BUT NOT BEFORE WE EAT NEW YEAR'S SOBA.

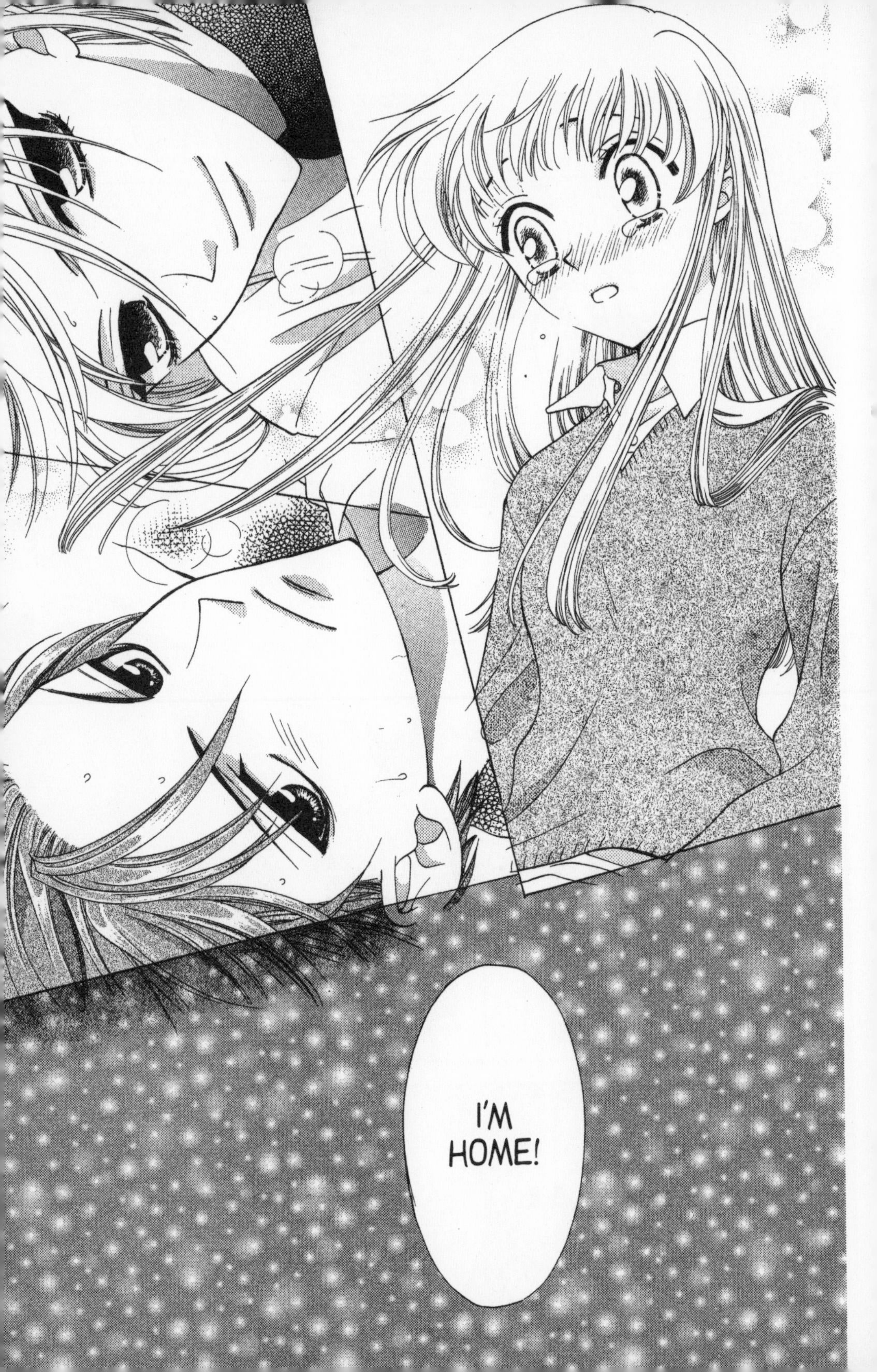
I'M HOME!

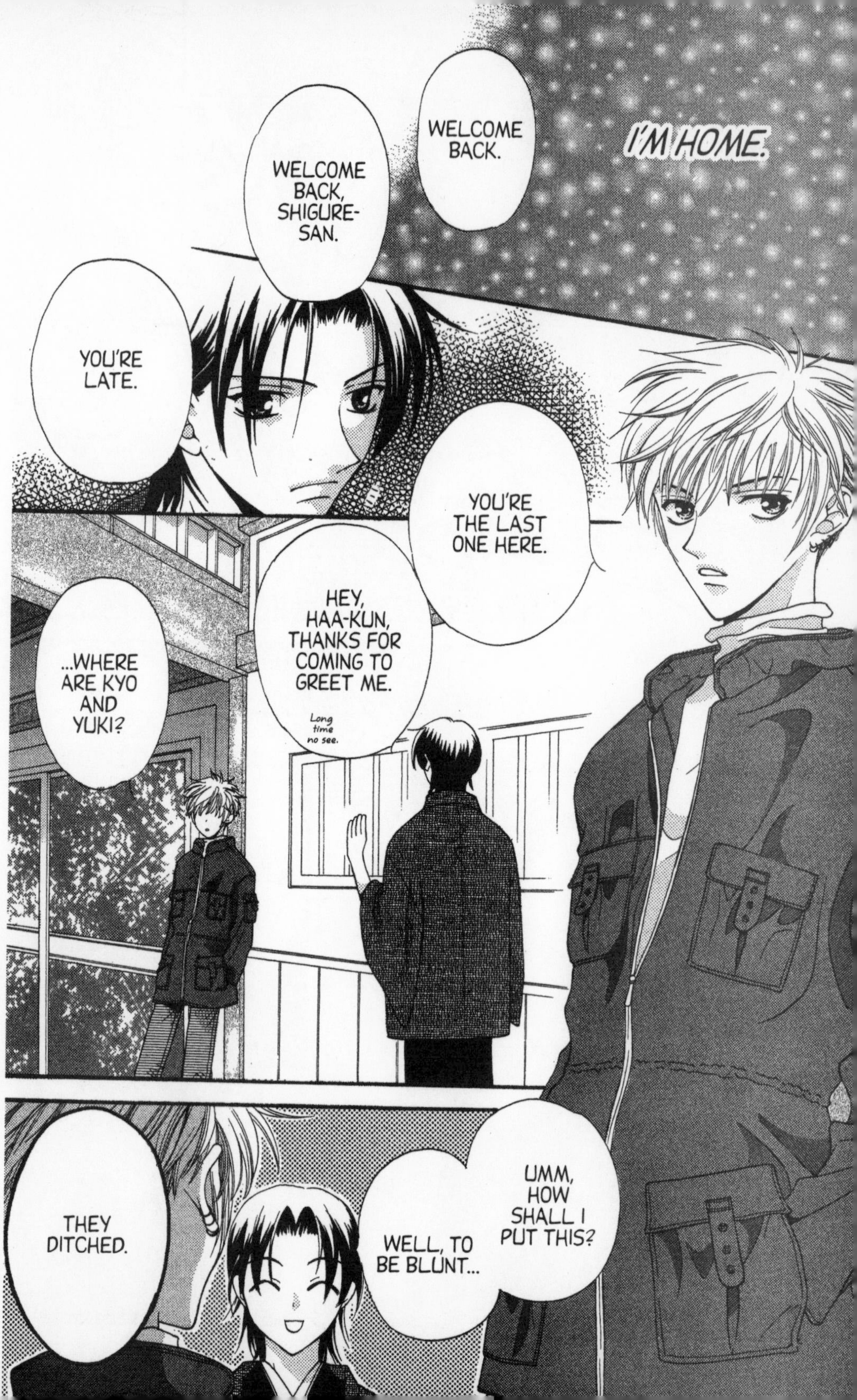
I'M HOME.
WELCOME BACK.
WELCOME BACK, SHIGURE-SAN.
YOU'RE LATE.
YOU'RE THE LAST ONE HERE.
HEY, HAA-KUN, THANKS FOR COMING TO GREET ME.
Long time no see.
...WHERE ARE KYO AND YUKI?
UMM, HOW SHALL I PUT THIS?
WELL, TO BE BLUNT...
THEY DITCHED.

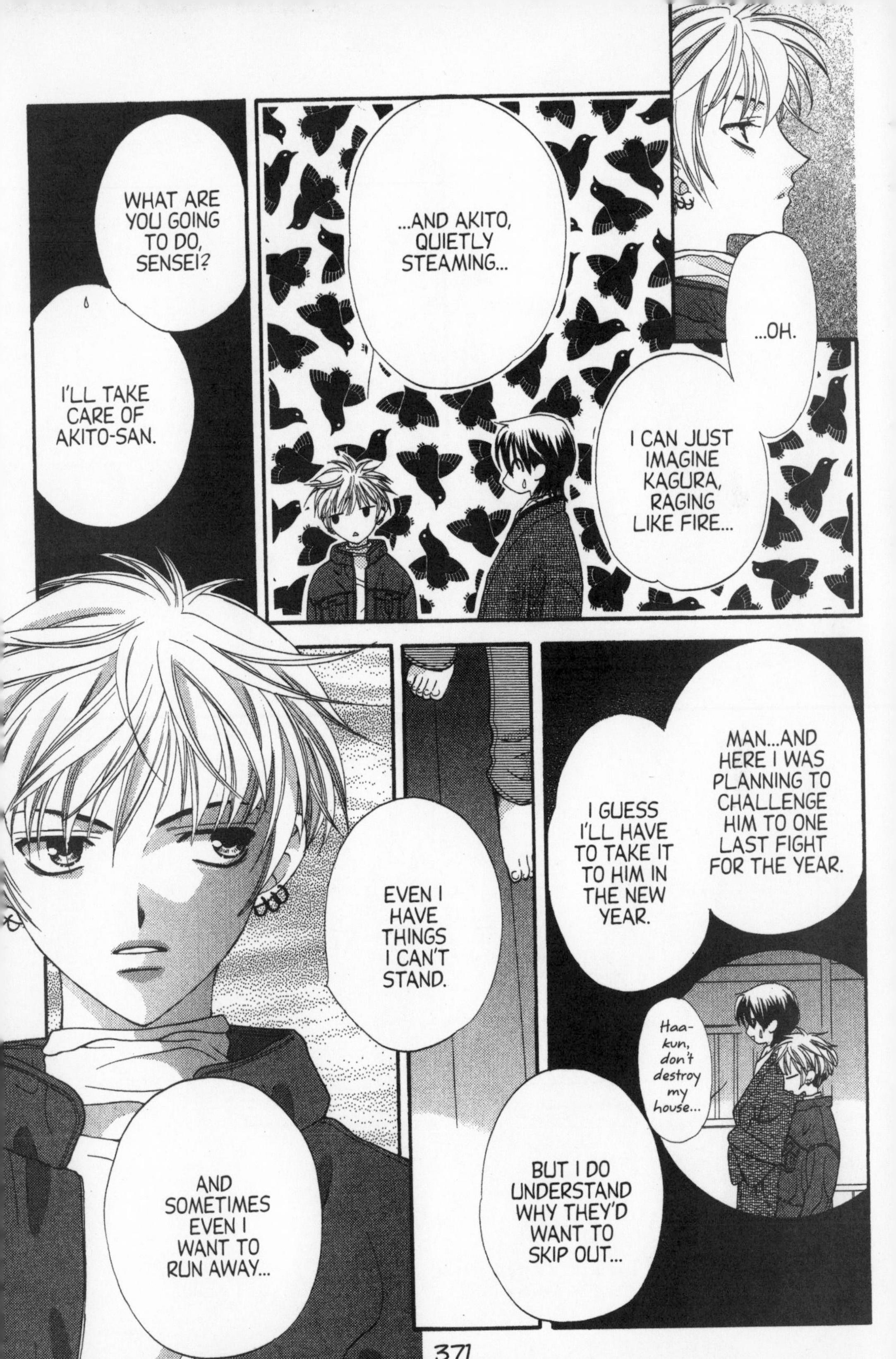
...OH.
I CAN JUST IMAGINE KAGURA, RAGING LIKE FIRE...
...AND AKITO, QUIETLY STEAMING...
WHAT ARE YOU GOING TO DO, SENSEI?
I'LL TAKE CARE OF AKITO-SAN.
MAN...AND HERE I WAS PLANNING TO CHALLENGE HIM TO ONE LAST FIGHT FOR THE YEAR.
I GUESS I'LL HAVE TO TAKE IT TO HIM IN THE NEW YEAR.
Haa-kun, don't destroy my house...
BUT I DO UNDERSTAND WHY THEY'D WANT TO SKIP OUT...
EVEN I HAVE THINGS I CAN'T STAND.
AND SOMETIMES EVEN I WANT TO RUN AWAY...

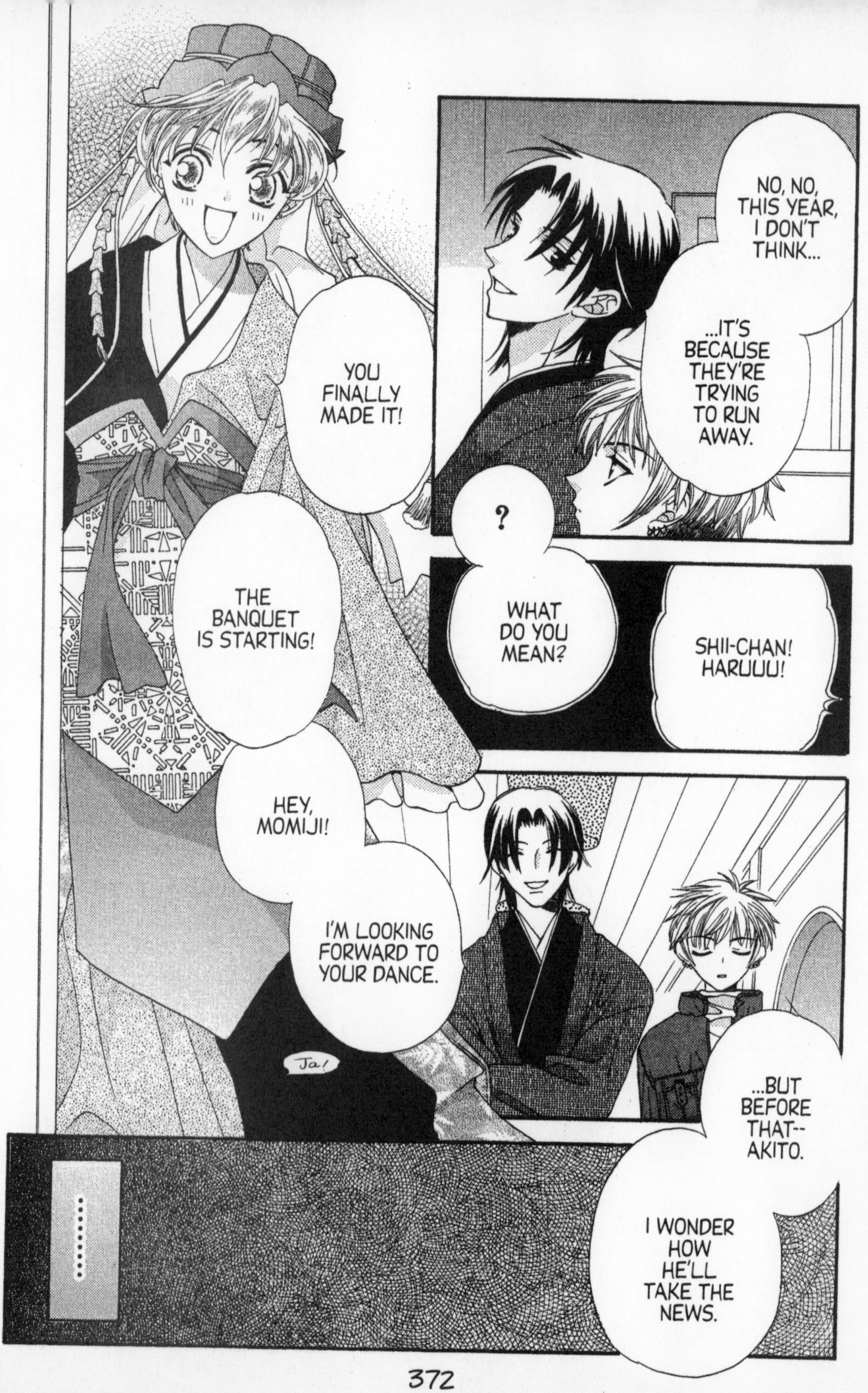
NO, NO, THIS YEAR, I DON'T THINK...
...IT'S BECAUSE THEY'RE TRYING TO RUN AWAY.
?
WHAT DO YOU MEAN?
SHII-CHAN! HARUUU!
YOU FINALLY MADE IT!
THE BANQUET IS STARTING!
HEY, MOMIJI!
I'M LOOKING FORWARD TO YOUR DANCE.
Ja!
...BUT BEFORE THAT-- AKITO.
I WONDER HOW HE'LL TAKE THE NEWS.
....

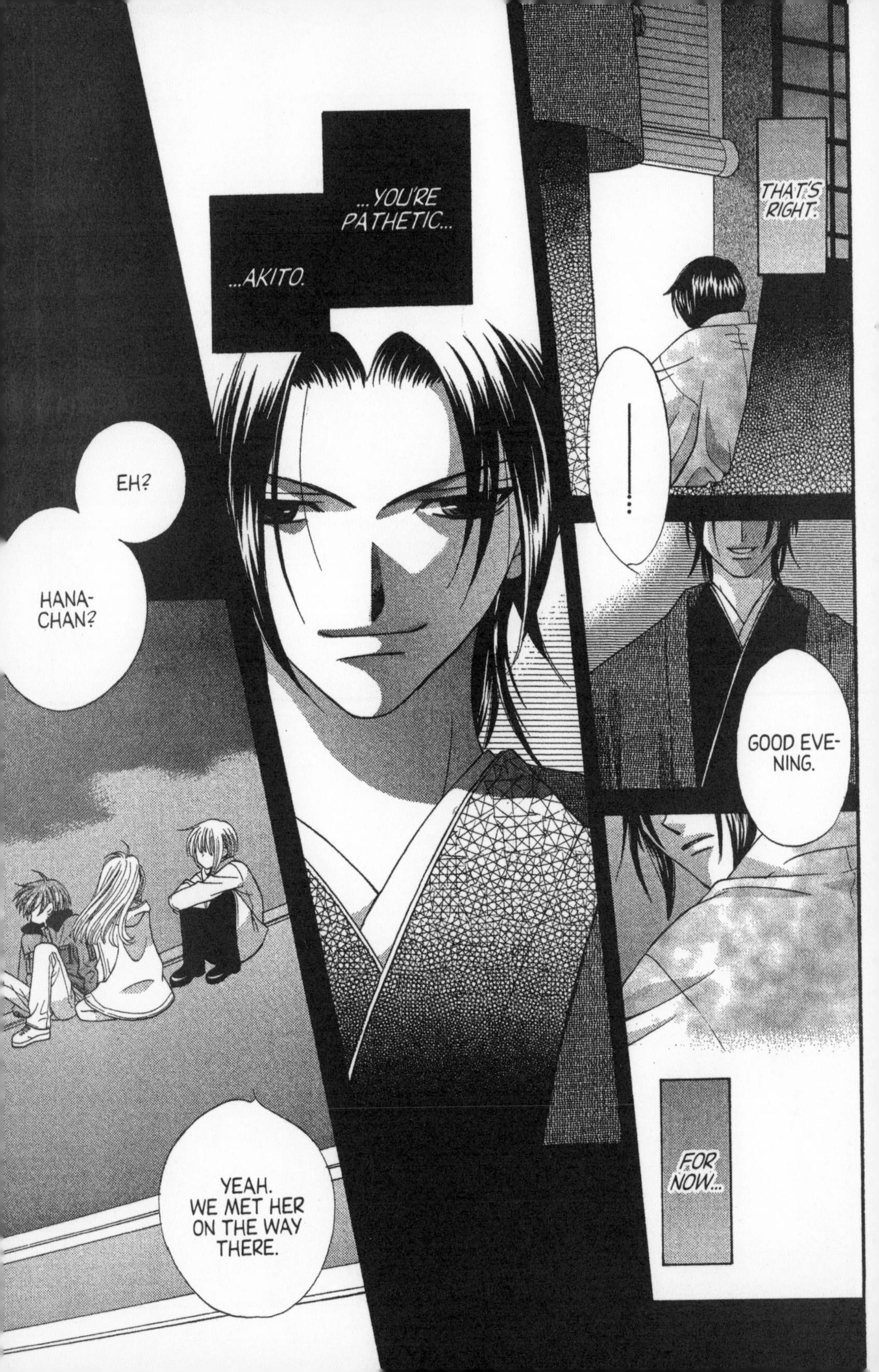
THAT'S RIGHT.
......
GOOD EVE-NING.
FOR NOW...
...YOU'RE PATHETIC...
...AKITO.
EH?
HANA-CHAN?
YEAH. WE MET HER ON THE WAY THERE.

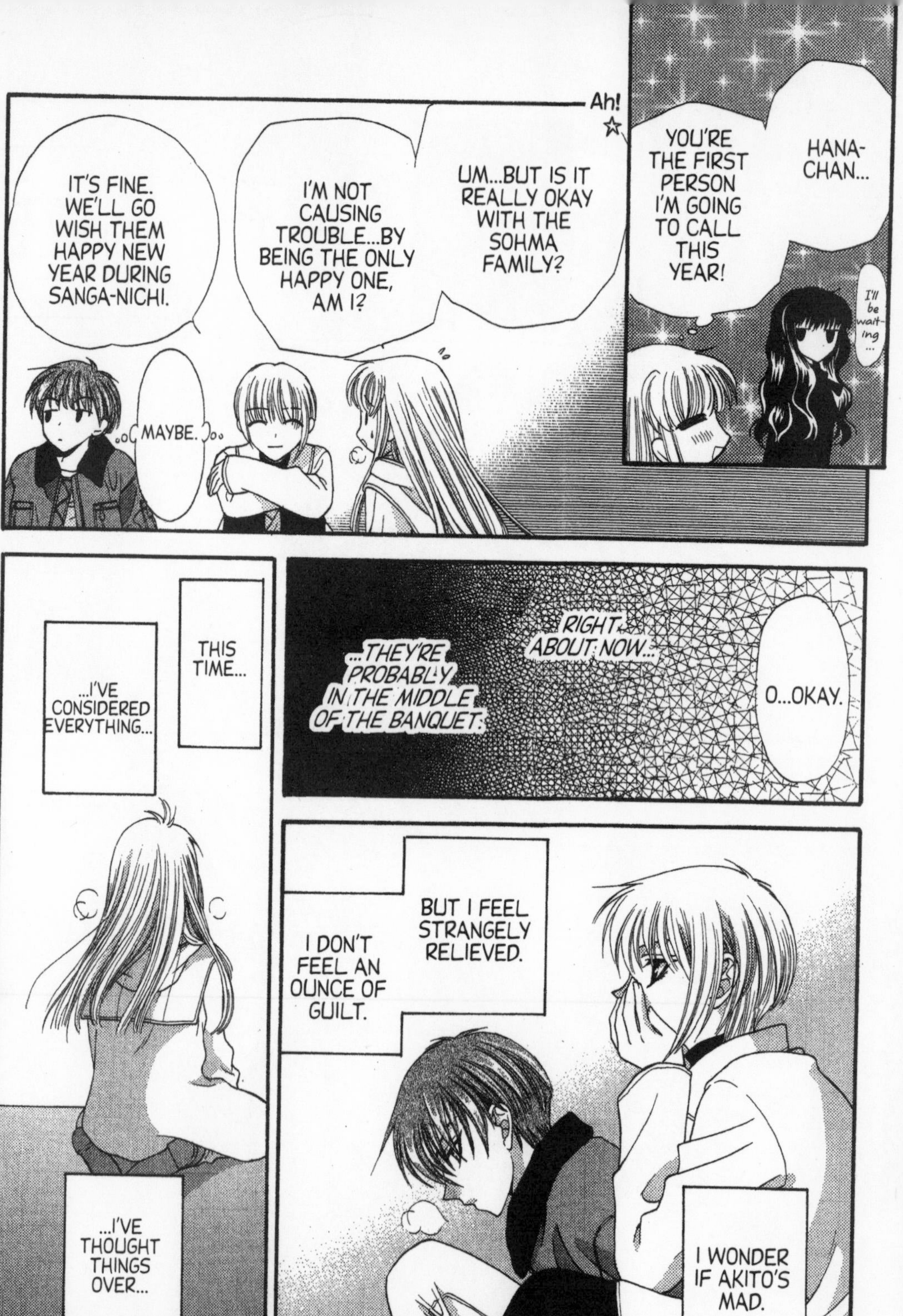
HANA-CHAN...
YOU'RE THE FIRST PERSON I'M GOING TO CALL THIS YEAR!
I'll be waiting...
Ah!
UM...BUT IS IT REALLY OKAY WITH THE SOHMA FAMILY?
I'M NOT CAUSING TROUBLE...BY BEING THE ONLY HAPPY ONE, AM I?
IT'S FINE. WE'LL GO WISH THEM HAPPY NEW YEAR DURING SANGA-NICHI.
MAYBE.
O...OKAY.
RIGHT ABOUT NOW...
...THEY'RE PROBABLY IN THE MIDDLE OF THE BANQUET.
I DON'T FEEL AN OUNCE OF GUILT.
BUT I FEEL STRANGELY RELIEVED.
I WONDER IF AKITO'S MAD.
THIS TIME...
...I'VE CONSIDERED EVERYTHING...
...I'VE THOUGHT THINGS OVER...

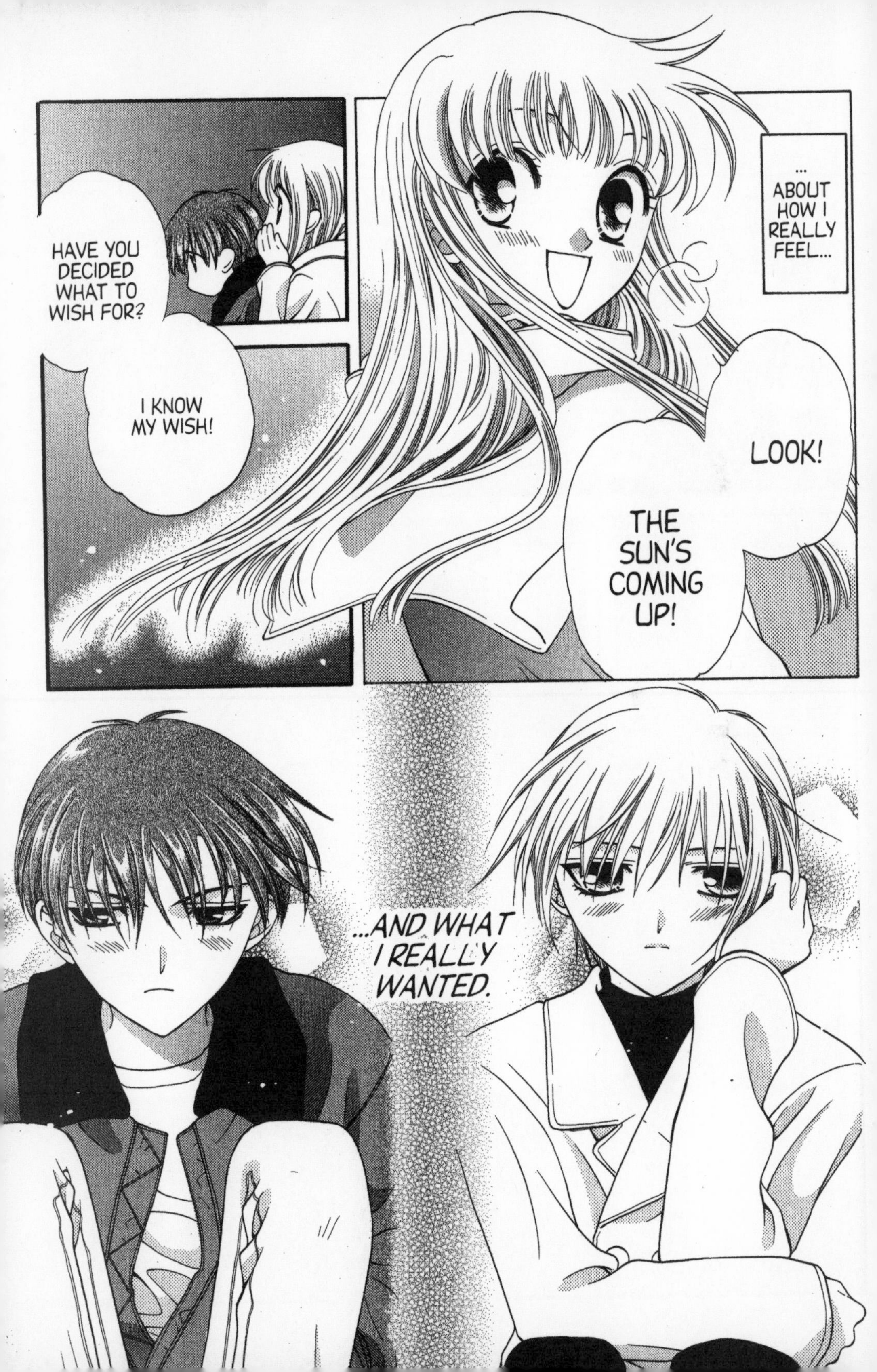
...
ABOUT HOW I REALLY FEEL...
LOOK!
THE SUN'S COMING UP!
HAVE YOU DECIDED WHAT TO WISH FOR?
I KNOW MY WISH!
...AND WHAT I REALLY WANTED.

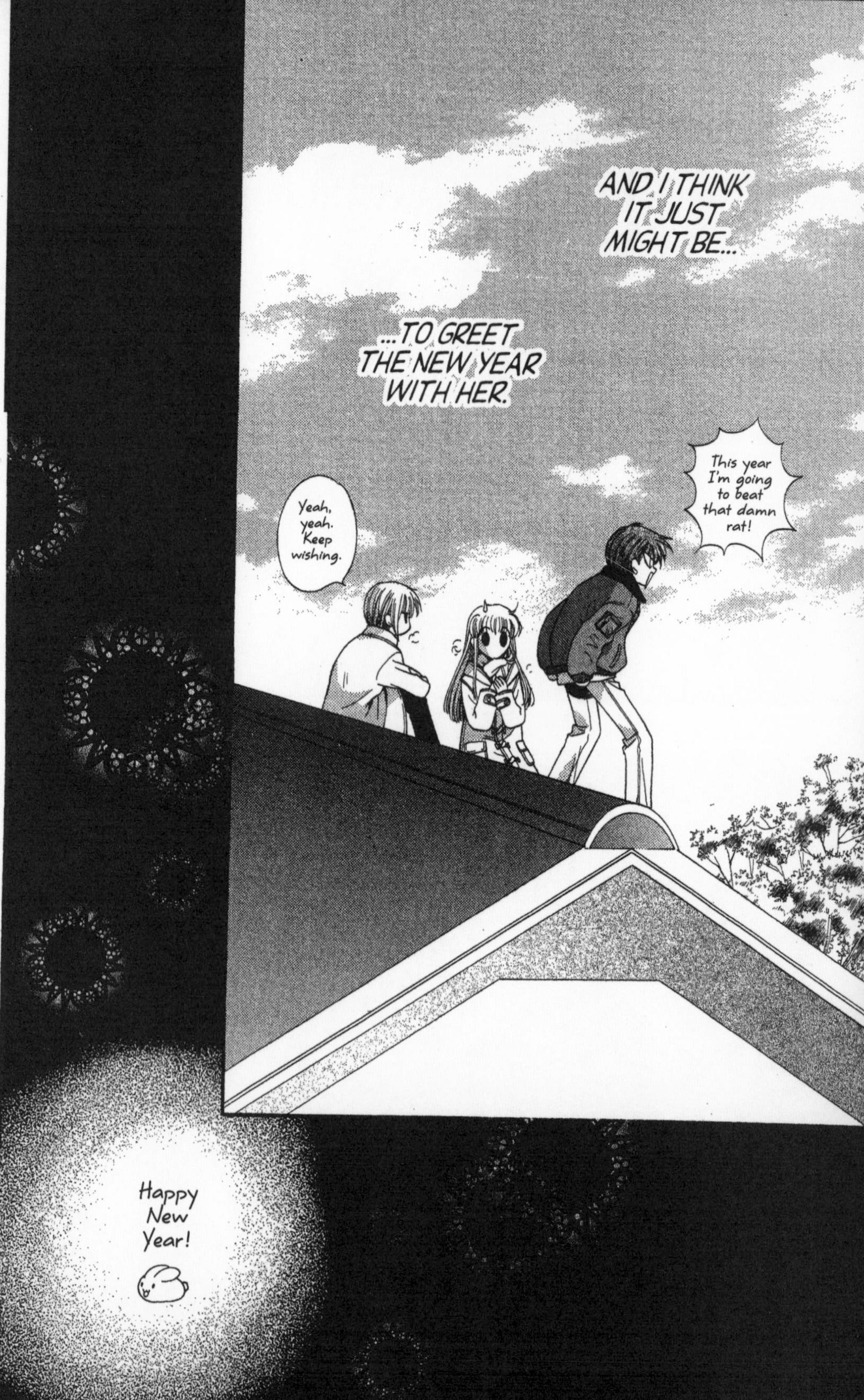
AND I THINK IT JUST MIGHT BE...
...TO GREET THE NEW YEAR WITH HER.
This year I'm going to beat that damn rat!
Yeah, yeah. Keep wishing.
Happy New Year!

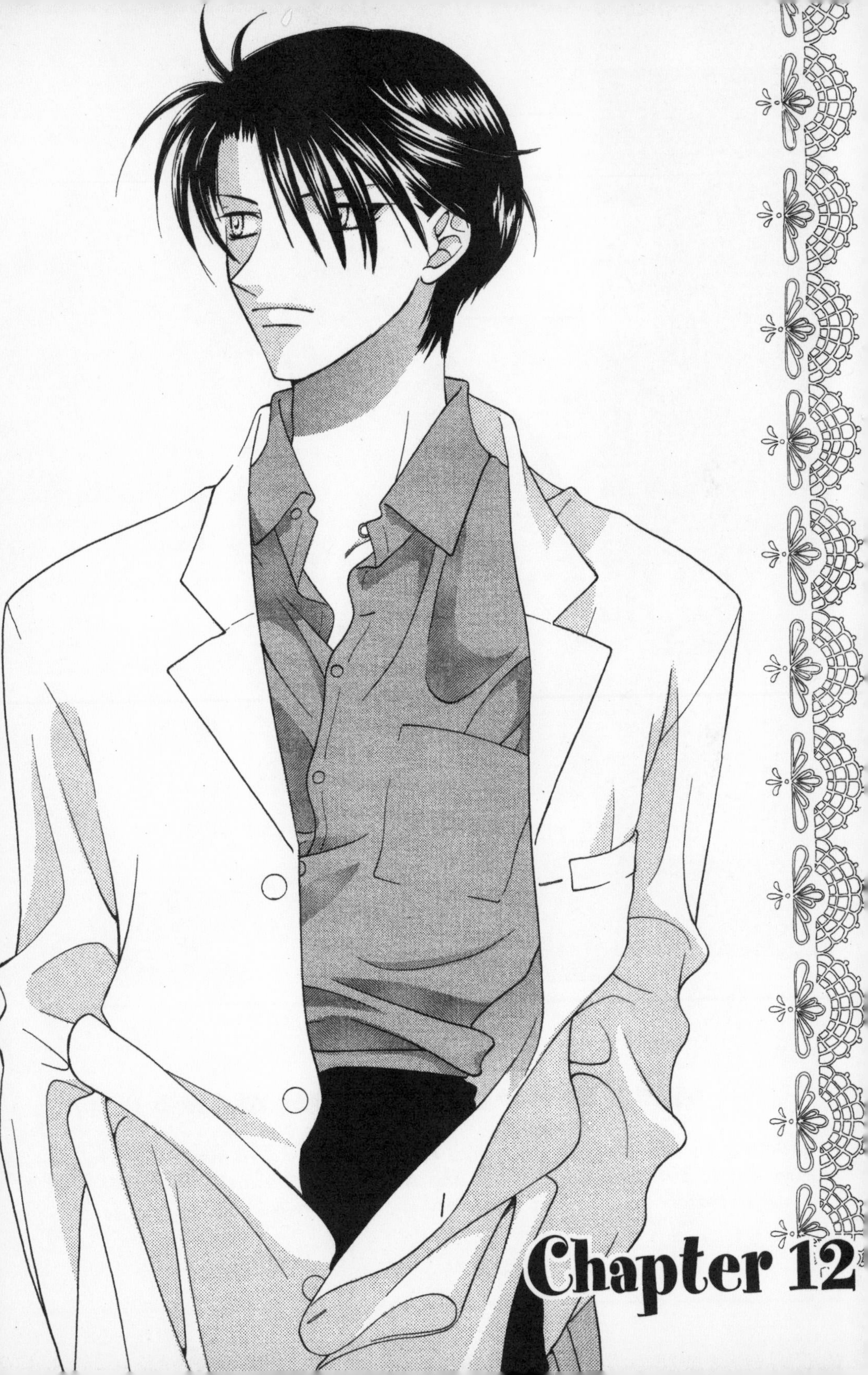

Chapter 12

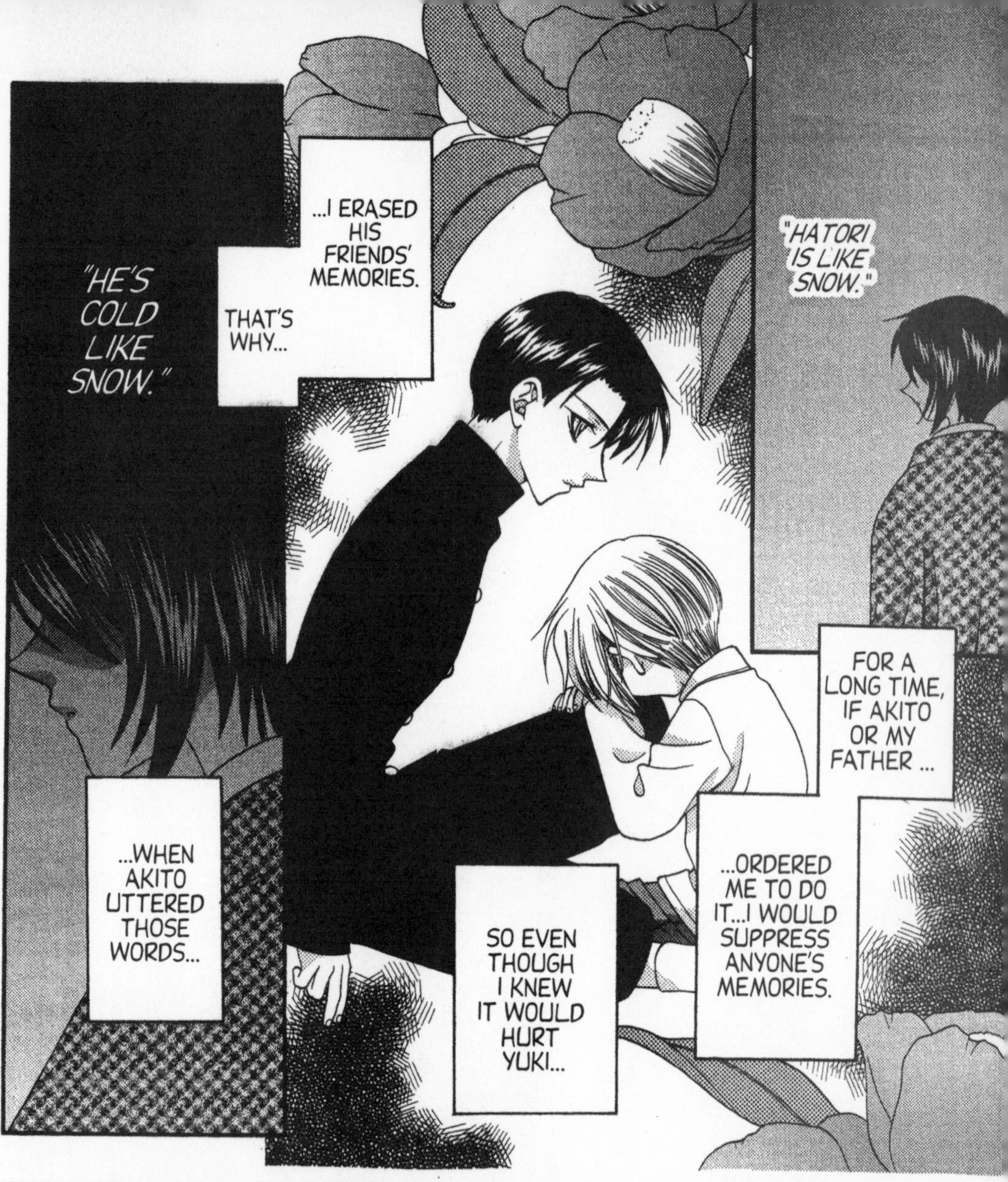
"HATORI IS LIKE SNOW."
...I ERASED HIS FRIENDS' MEMORIES.
THAT'S WHY...
"HE'S COLD LIKE SNOW."
FOR A LONG TIME, IF AKITO OR MY FATHER ...
...ORDERED ME TO DO IT...I WOULD SUPPRESS ANYONE'S MEMORIES.
SO EVEN THOUGH I KNEW IT WOULD HURT YUKI...
...WHEN AKITO UTTERED THOSE WORDS...

ULTRA SPECIAL BLAH BLAH BLAH 6

Starting in this chapter, Hatori's hair is longer...I'm sure Akito told him not to cut it...I don't think Hatori will meet Kana after this. Even if Hatori could meet her again, I don't think he'd want to.

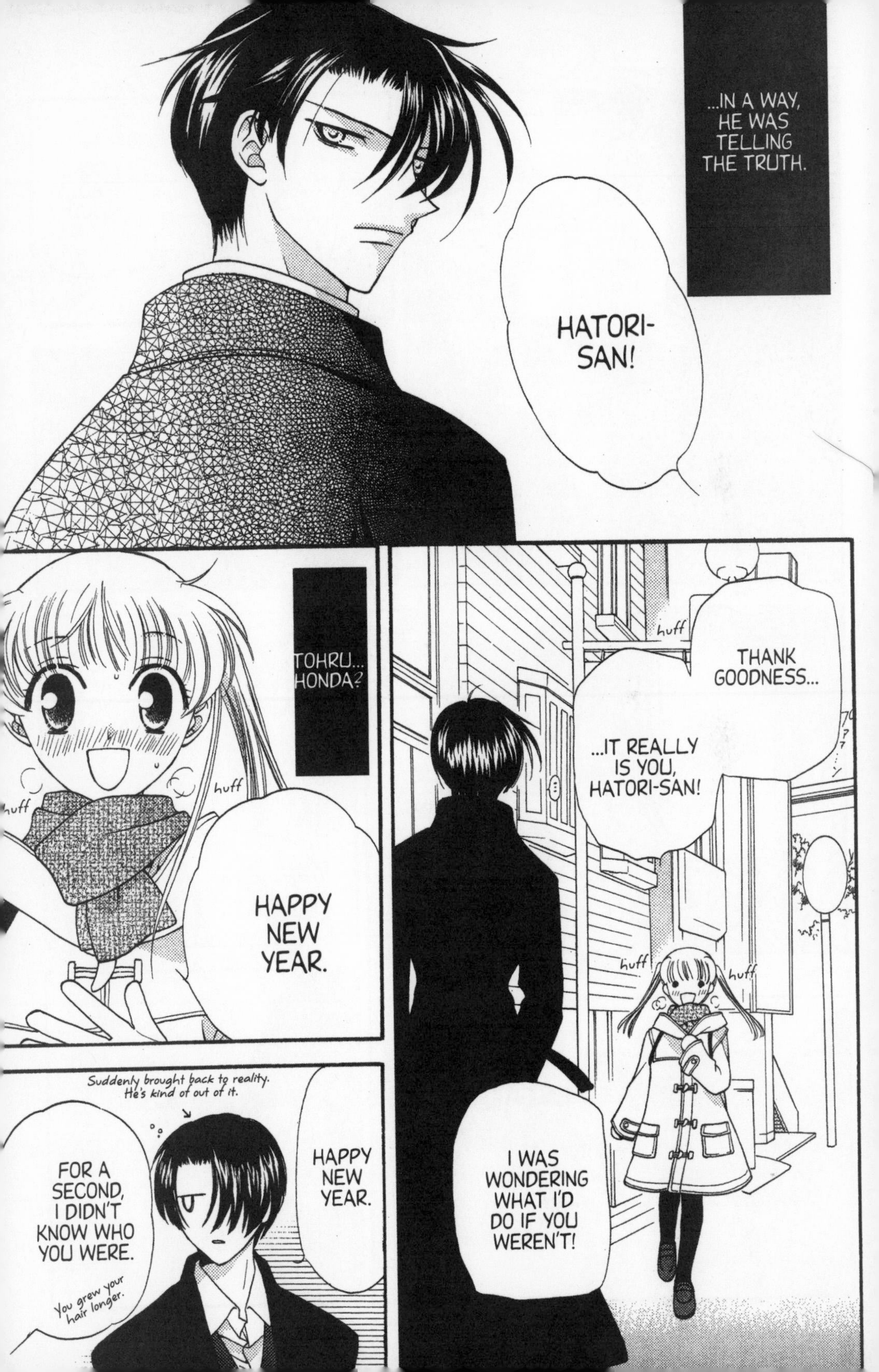
...IN A WAY, HE WAS TELLING THE TRUTH.
HATORI-SAN!
huff
THANK GOODNESS...
...IT REALLY IS YOU, HATORI-SAN!
huff
huff
I WAS WONDERING WHAT I'D DO IF YOU WEREN'T!
TOHRU... HONDA?
huff
huff
HAPPY NEW YEAR.
Suddenly brought back to reality. He's kind of out of it.
HAPPY NEW YEAR.
FOR A SECOND, I DIDN'T KNOW WHO YOU WERE.
You grew your hair longer.

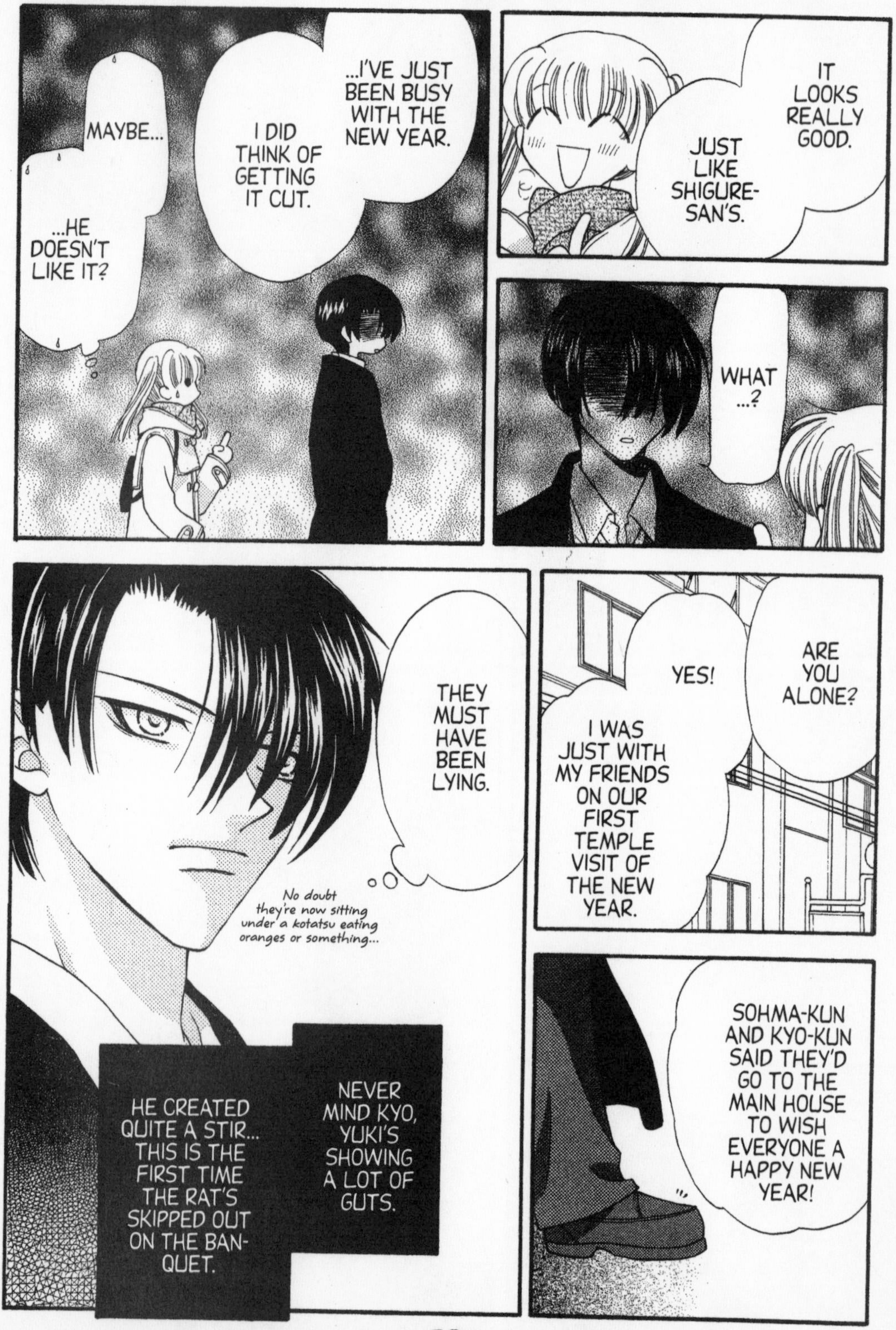
IT LOOKS REALLY GOOD.
JUST LIKE SHIGURE-SAN'S.
WHAT ...?
...I'VE JUST BEEN BUSY WITH THE NEW YEAR.
I DID THINK OF GETTING IT CUT.
MAYBE...
...HE DOESN'T LIKE IT?
ARE YOU ALONE?
YES!
I WAS JUST WITH MY FRIENDS ON OUR FIRST TEMPLE VISIT OF THE NEW YEAR.
SOHMA-KUN AND KYO-KUN SAID THEY'D GO TO THE MAIN HOUSE TO WISH EVERYONE A HAPPY NEW YEAR!
THEY MUST HAVE BEEN LYING.
No doubt they're now sitting under a kotatsu eating oranges or something...
NEVER MIND KYO, YUKI'S SHOWING A LOT OF GUTS.
HE CREATED QUITE A STIR... THIS IS THE FIRST TIME THE RAT'S SKIPPED OUT ON THE BAN-QUET.

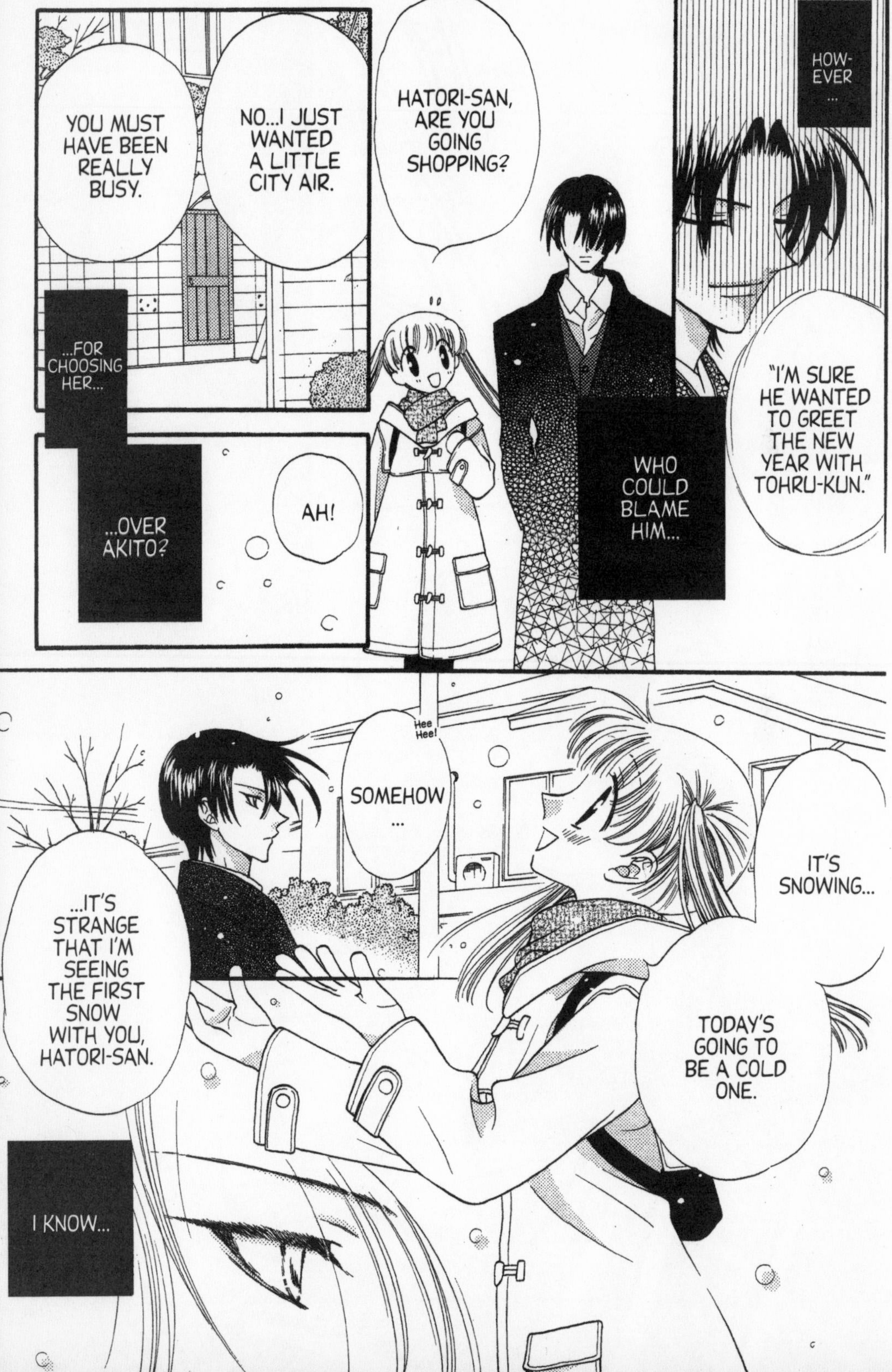
HOW-EVER...
"I'M SURE HE WANTED TO GREET THE NEW YEAR WITH TOHRU-KUN."
WHO COULD BLAME HIM...
HATORI-SAN, ARE YOU GOING SHOPPING?
NO...I JUST WANTED A LITTLE CITY AIR.
YOU MUST HAVE BEEN REALLY BUSY.
...FOR CHOOSING HER...
AH!
...OVER AKITO?
IT'S SNOWING...
Hee Hee!
SOMEHOW...
...IT'S STRANGE THAT I'M SEEING THE FIRST SNOW WITH YOU, HATORI-SAN.
TODAY'S GOING TO BE A COLD ONE.
I KNOW...

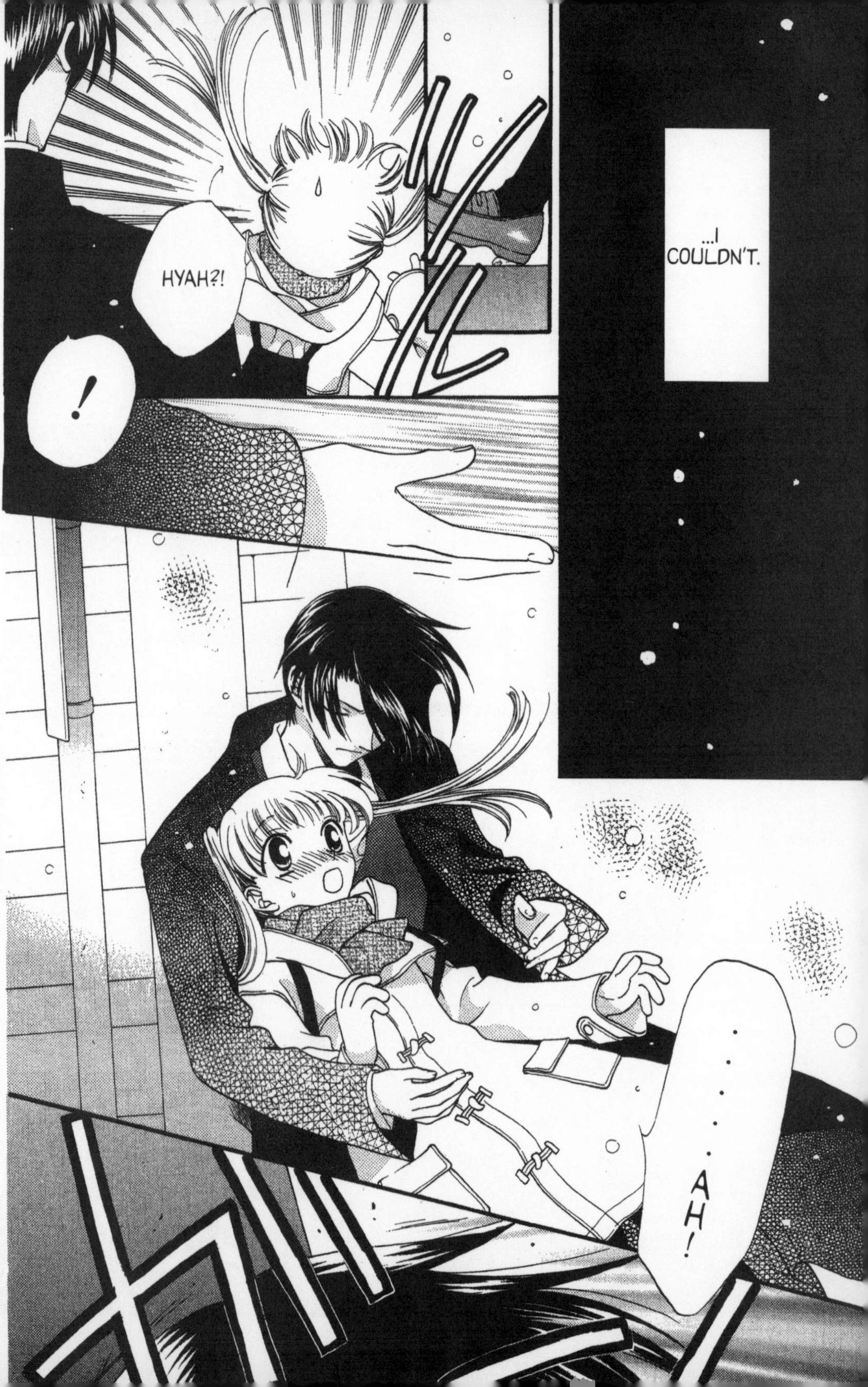
...I COULDN'T.
HYAH?!
!
.......AH!

Fruits Basket 2 Part 6:

I usually don't have a clear idea of characters' voices, and when I do, it's rare. I say that, but even from Chapter 1, I imagined Midorikawa-san's voice for Raimon in my head. I also imagined his voice for Tamaki in Gen'ei Muso...(laugh). I never thought I would hear it in real life...! <sob> (sparkle) As for Furuba...well, I think I've daydreamed enough and need to tell myself to wake up. Sorry... (There aren't any plans to.) But, but! Kouda-san as Kotobuki is explosively adorable! (More than the original Kotobuki.) Midorikawa-san as Raimon is wow...! Ok, I need to calm down... And Shouka and Yu and Hare and Rokuro and Addy and Yan and Fear and Tooya and Hilt fit the images perfectly, so I'm really happy!! I really, really want people to hear it! I'll be even more happy if people tell me they liked it. Thank you to all the voice-over actors who took time out of their busy schedules to be on this CD!

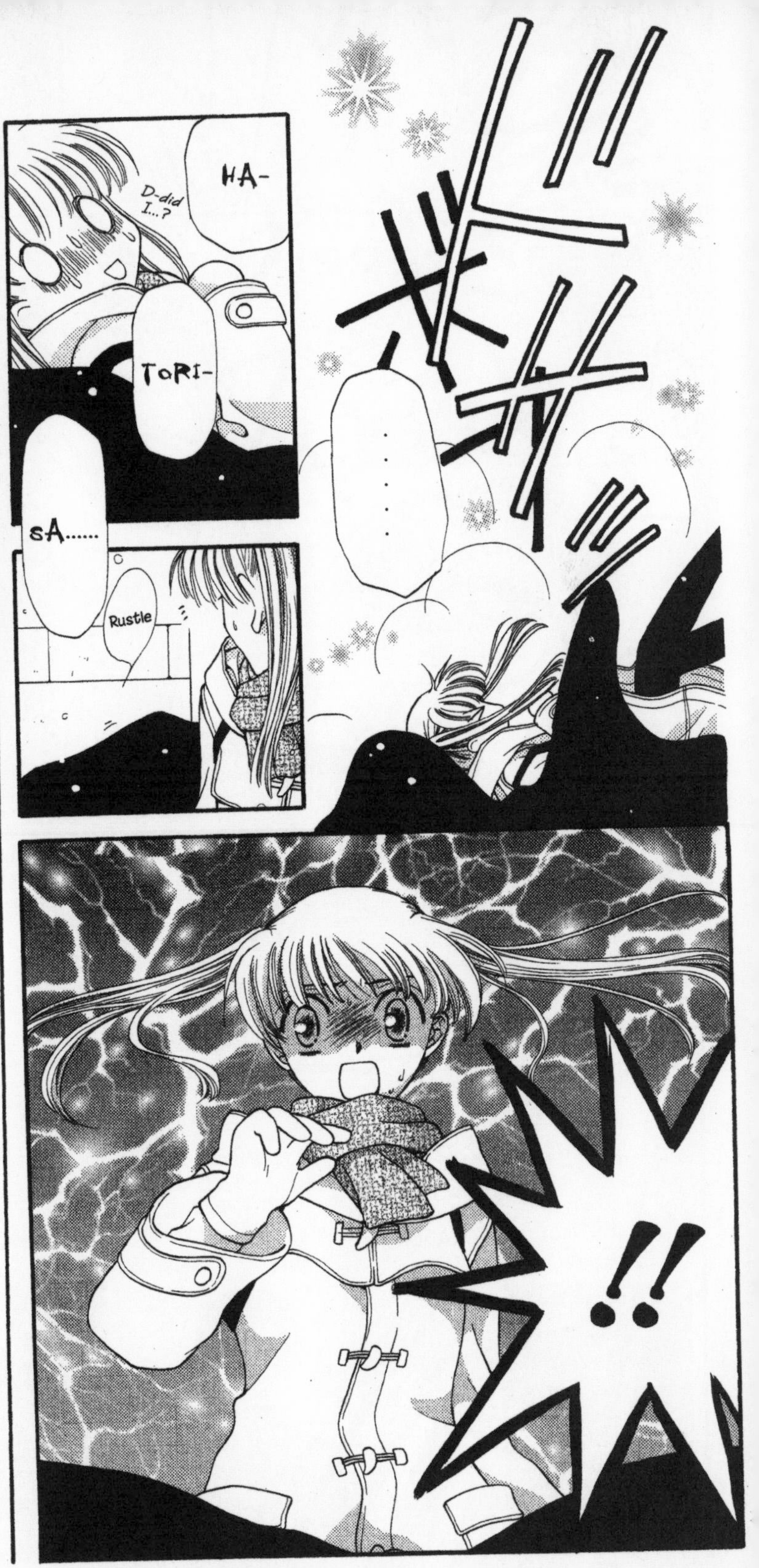
......
HA-
D-did I...?
TORI-
SA......
Rustle
!!

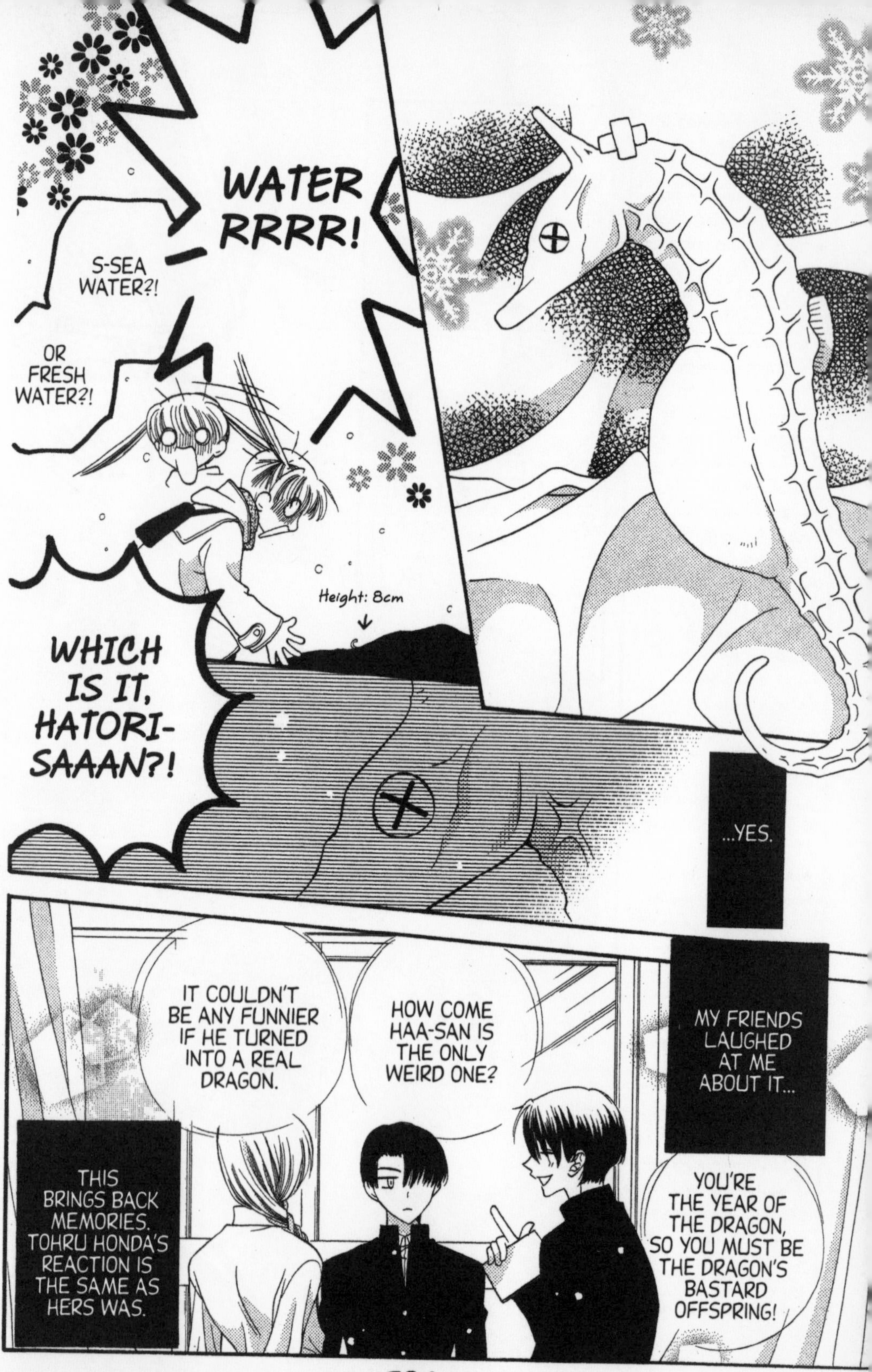
WATER RRRR!
S-SEA WATER?!
OR FRESH WATER?!
Height: 8cm
WHICH IS IT, HATORI-SAAAN?!
...YES.
MY FRIENDS LAUGHED AT ME ABOUT IT...
YOU'RE THE YEAR OF THE DRAGON, SO YOU MUST BE THE DRAGON'S BASTARD OFFSPRING!
HOW COME HAA-SAN IS THE ONLY WEIRD ONE?
IT COULDN'T BE ANY FUNNIER IF HE TURNED INTO A REAL DRAGON.
THIS BRINGS BACK MEMORIES. TOHRU HONDA'S REACTION IS THE SAME AS HERS WAS.

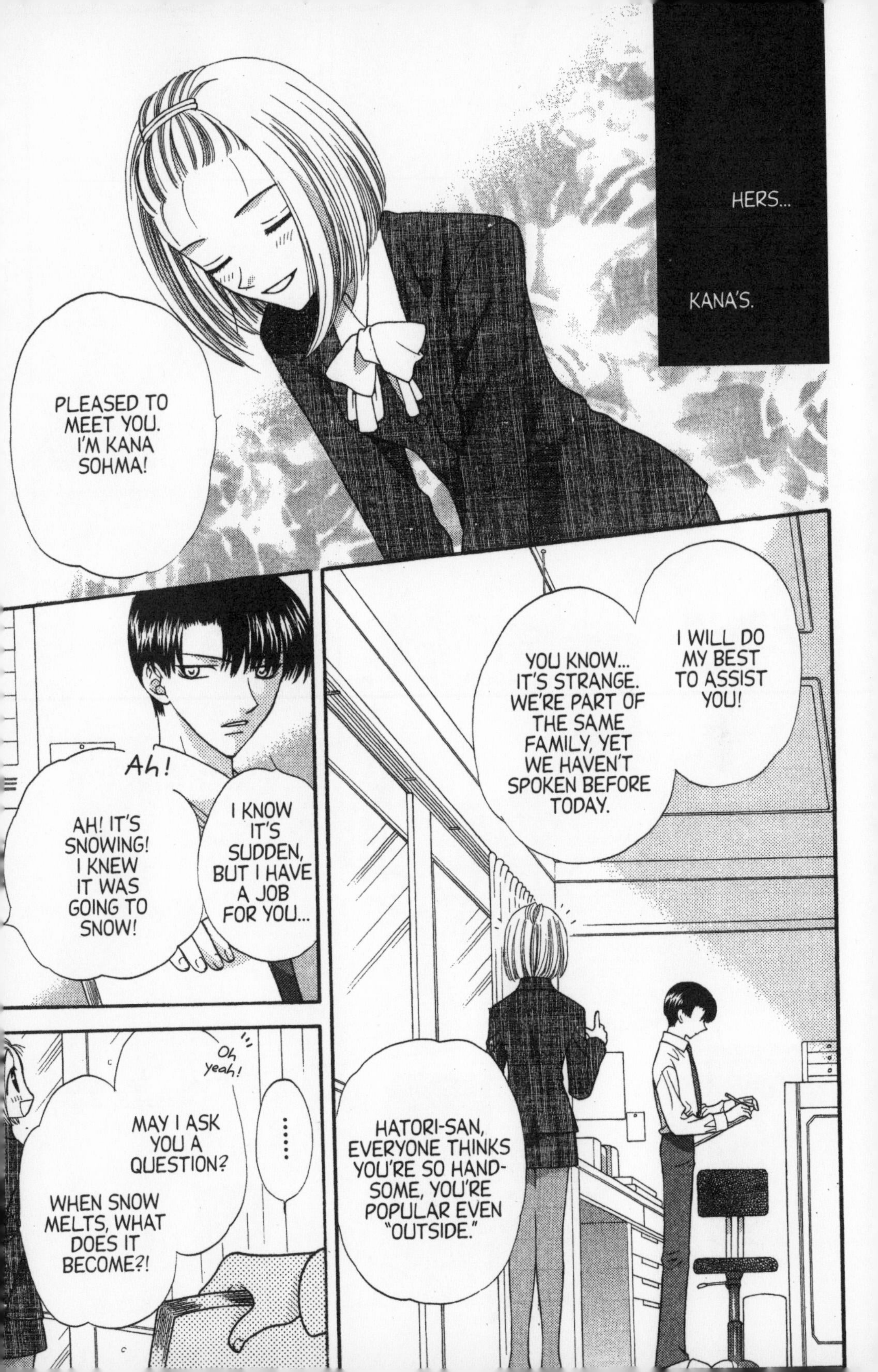

HERS...
KANA'S.
PLEASED TO MEET YOU. I'M KANA SOHMA!
I WILL DO MY BEST TO ASSIST YOU!
YOU KNOW... IT'S STRANGE. WE'RE PART OF THE SAME FAMILY, YET WE HAVEN'T SPOKEN BEFORE TODAY.
HATORI-SAN, EVERYONE THINKS YOU'RE SO HAND-SOME, YOU'RE POPULAR EVEN "OUTSIDE."
I KNOW IT'S SUDDEN, BUT I HAVE A JOB FOR YOU...
Ah!
AH! IT'S SNOWING! I KNEW IT WAS GOING TO SNOW!
Oh yeah!
......
MAY I ASK YOU A QUESTION?
WHEN SNOW MELTS, WHAT DOES IT BECOME?!

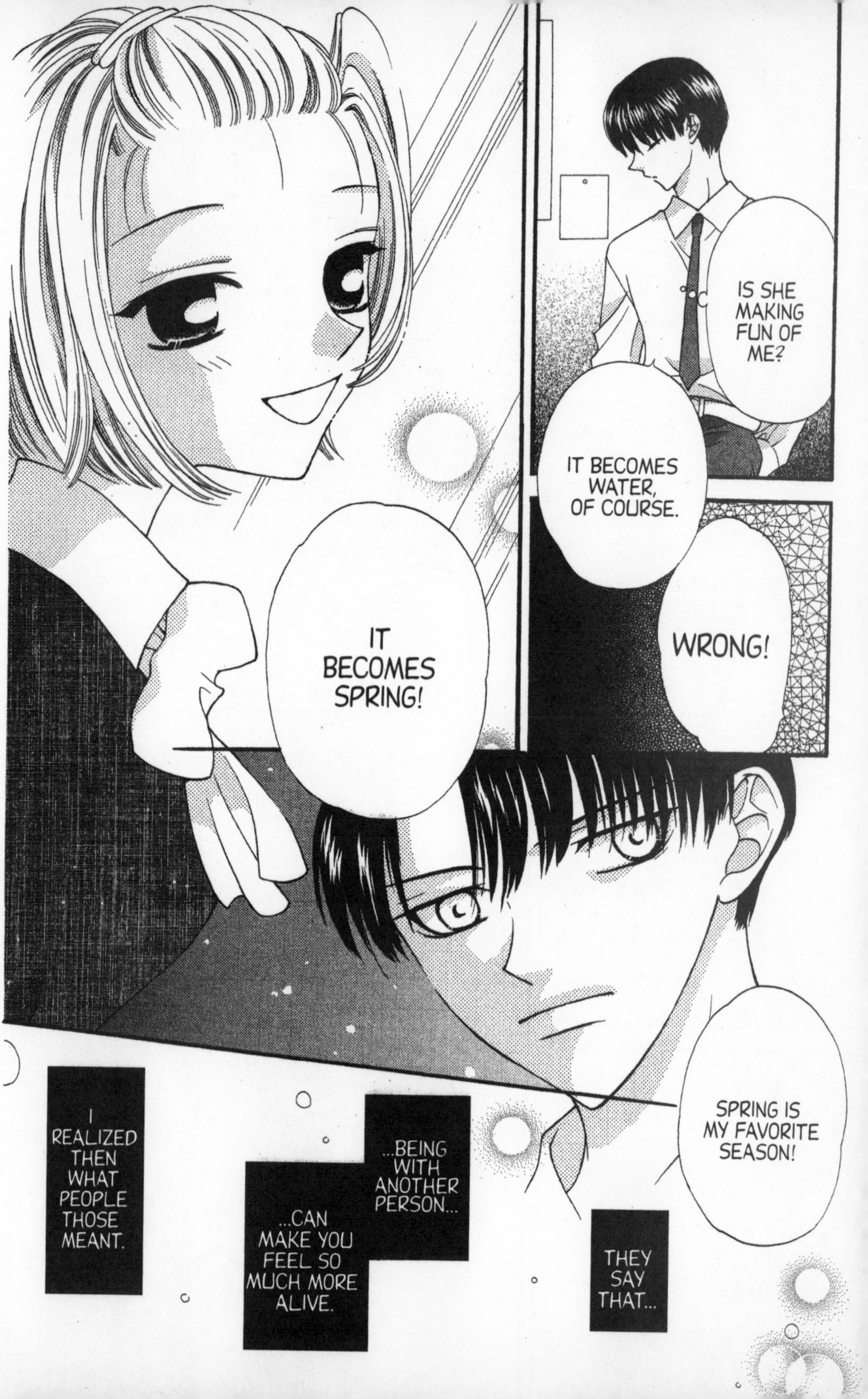
IS SHE MAKING FUN OF ME?
IT BECOMES WATER, OF COURSE.
WRONG!
IT BECOMES SPRING!
SPRING IS MY FAVORITE SEASON!
THEY SAY THAT...
...BEING WITH ANOTHER PERSON...
...CAN MAKE YOU FEEL SO MUCH MORE ALIVE.
I REALIZED THEN WHAT PEOPLE THOSE MEANT.

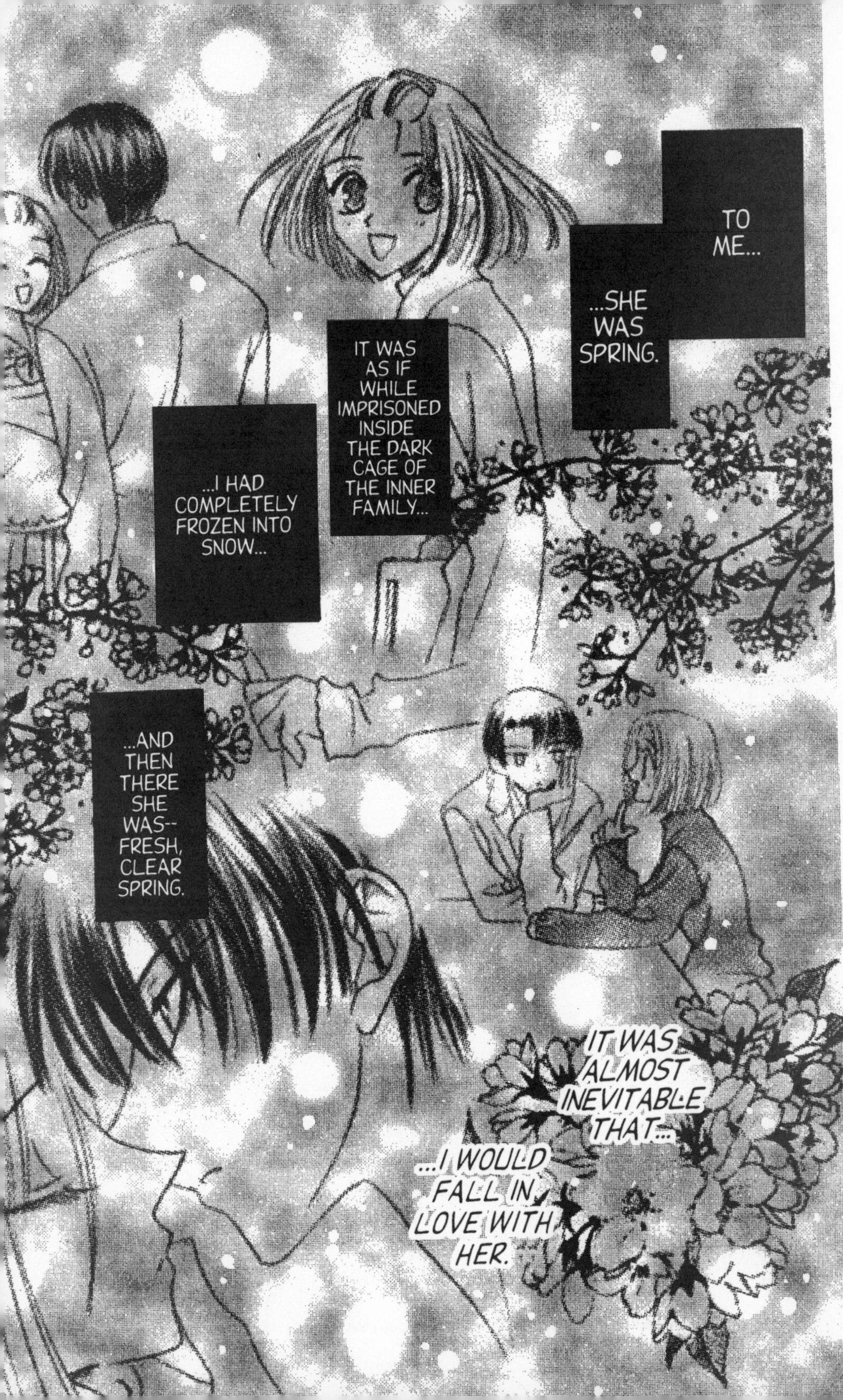
TO ME...
...SHE WAS SPRING.
IT WAS AS IF WHILE IMPRISONED INSIDE THE DARK CAGE OF THE INNER FAMILY...
...I HAD COMPLETELY FROZEN INTO SNOW...
...AND THEN THERE SHE WAS--FRESH, CLEAR SPRING.
IT WAS ALMOST INEVITABLE THAT...
...I WOULD FALL IN LOVE WITH HER.

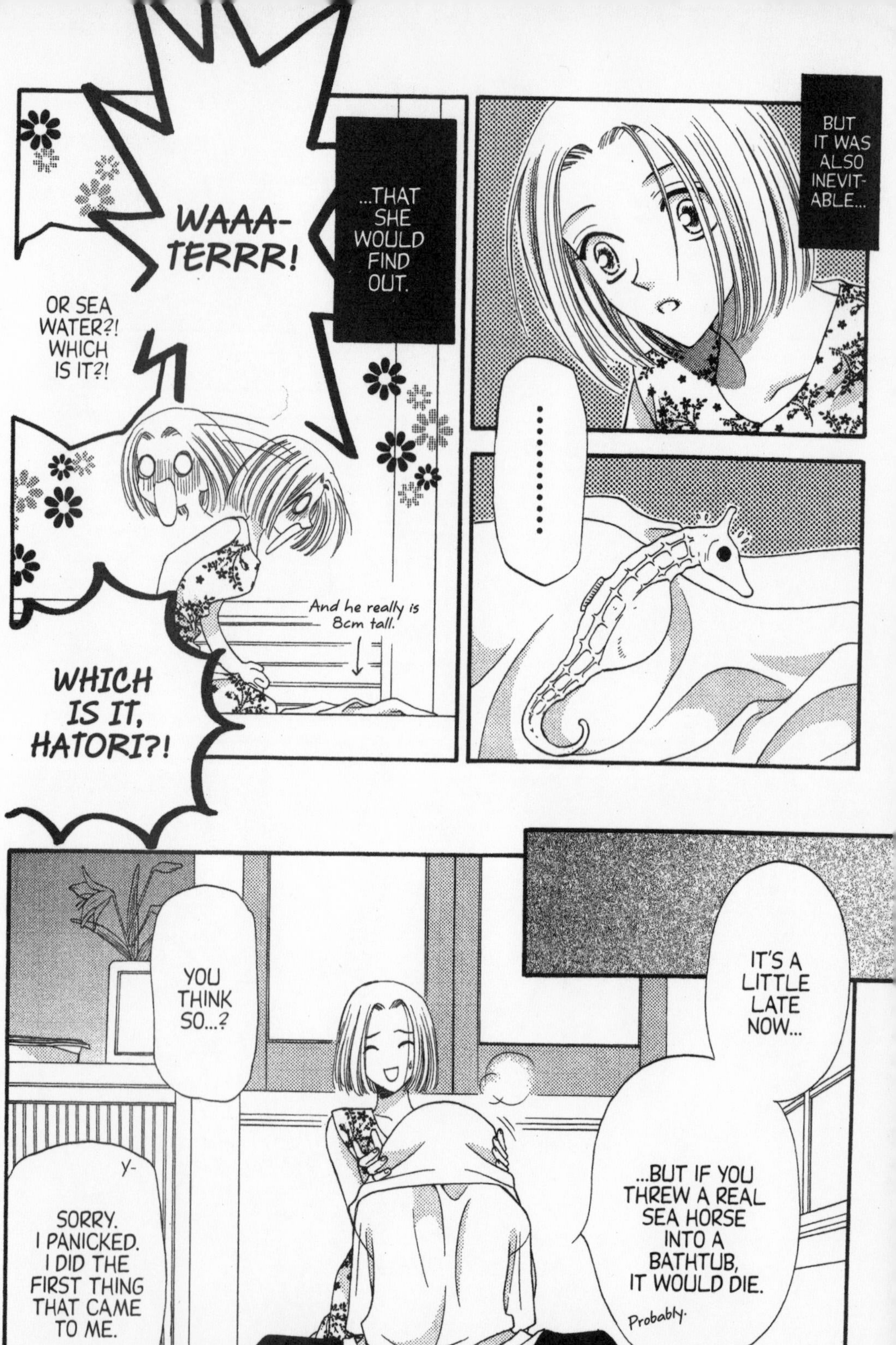
BUT IT WAS ALSO INEVITABLE...
......
...THAT SHE WOULD FIND OUT.
WAAA-TERRR!
OR SEA WATER?! WHICH IS IT?!
WHICH IS IT, HATORI?!
And he really is 8cm tall.
IT'S A LITTLE LATE NOW...
...BUT IF YOU THREW A REAL SEA HORSE INTO A BATHTUB, IT WOULD DIE.
Probably.
YOU THINK SO...?
Y-
SORRY. I PANICKED. I DID THE FIRST THING THAT CAME TO ME.

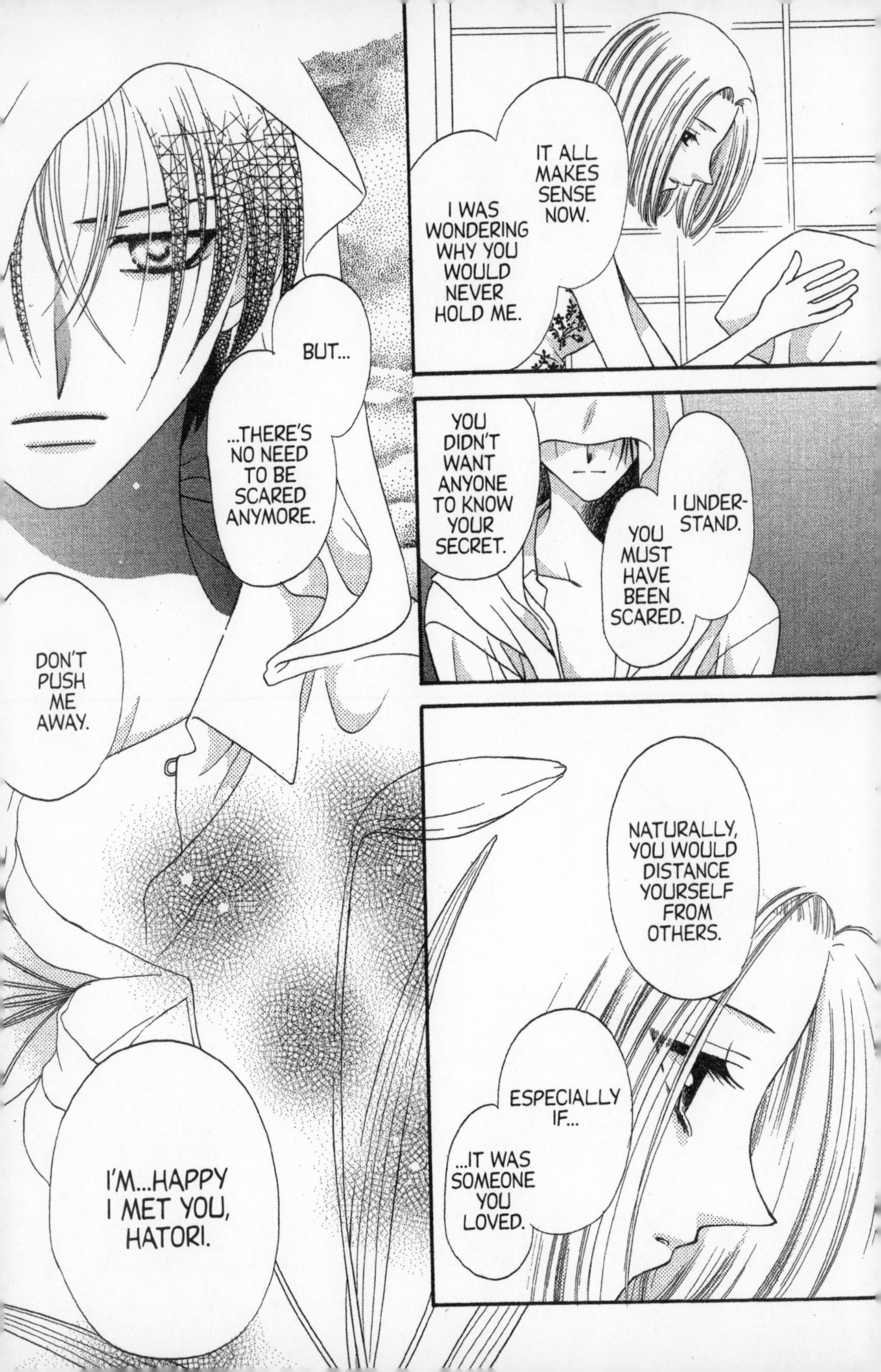
IT ALL MAKES SENSE NOW.
I WAS WONDERING WHY YOU WOULD NEVER HOLD ME.
I UNDER-STAND.
YOU MUST HAVE BEEN SCARED.
YOU DIDN'T WANT ANYONE TO KNOW YOUR SECRET.
NATURALLY, YOU WOULD DISTANCE YOURSELF FROM OTHERS.
ESPECIALLY IF...
...IT WAS SOMEONE YOU LOVED.
BUT...
...THERE'S NO NEED TO BE SCARED ANYMORE.
DON'T PUSH ME AWAY.
I'M...HAPPY I MET YOU, HATORI.

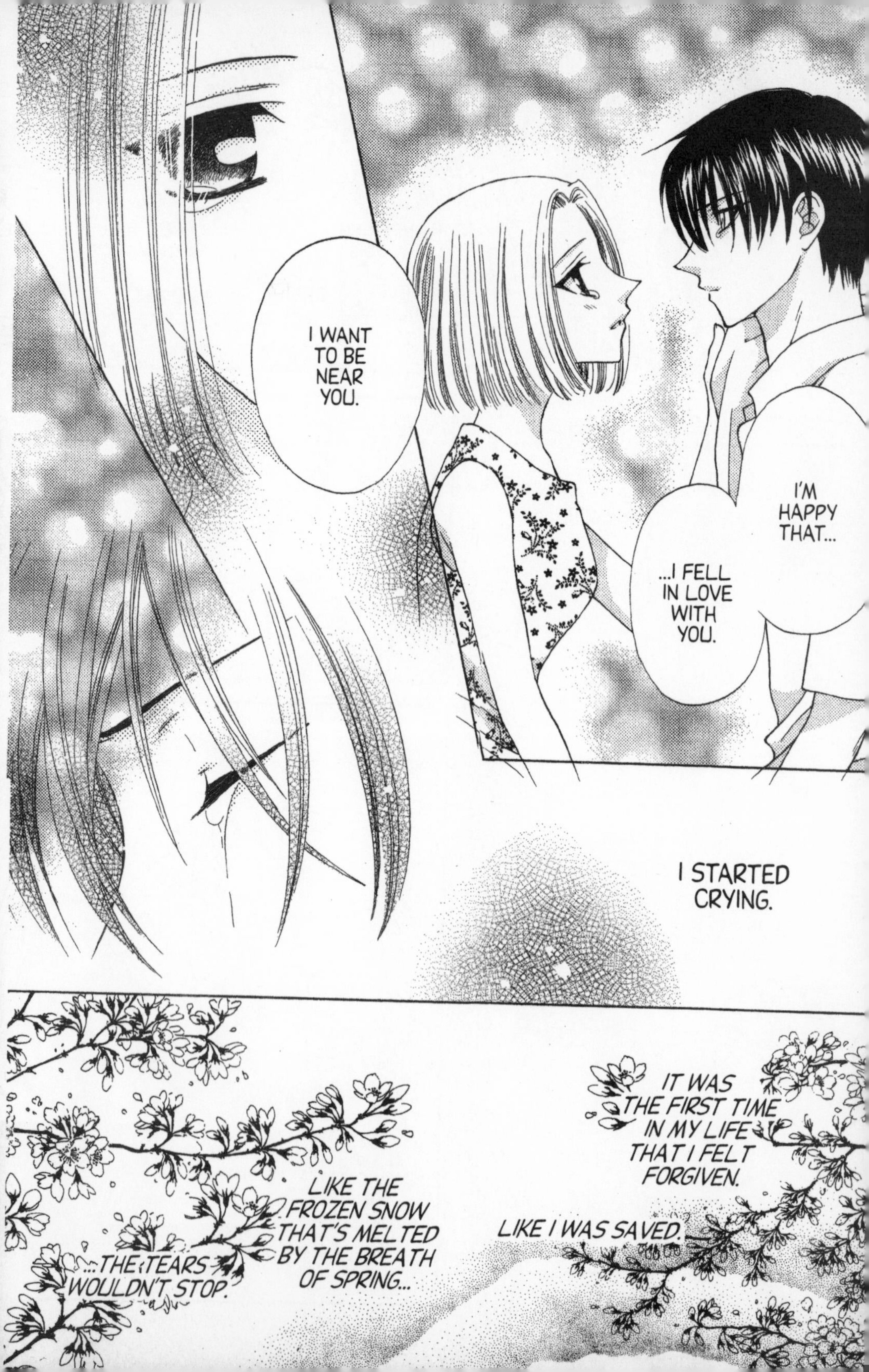
I'M HAPPY THAT...
...I FELL IN LOVE WITH YOU.
I WANT TO BE NEAR YOU.
I STARTED CRYING.
IT WAS THE FIRST TIME IN MY LIFE THAT I FELT FORGIVEN.
LIKE I WAS SAVED.
LIKE THE FROZEN SNOW THAT'S MELTED BY THE BREATH OF SPRING...
...THE TEARS WOULDN'T STOP.

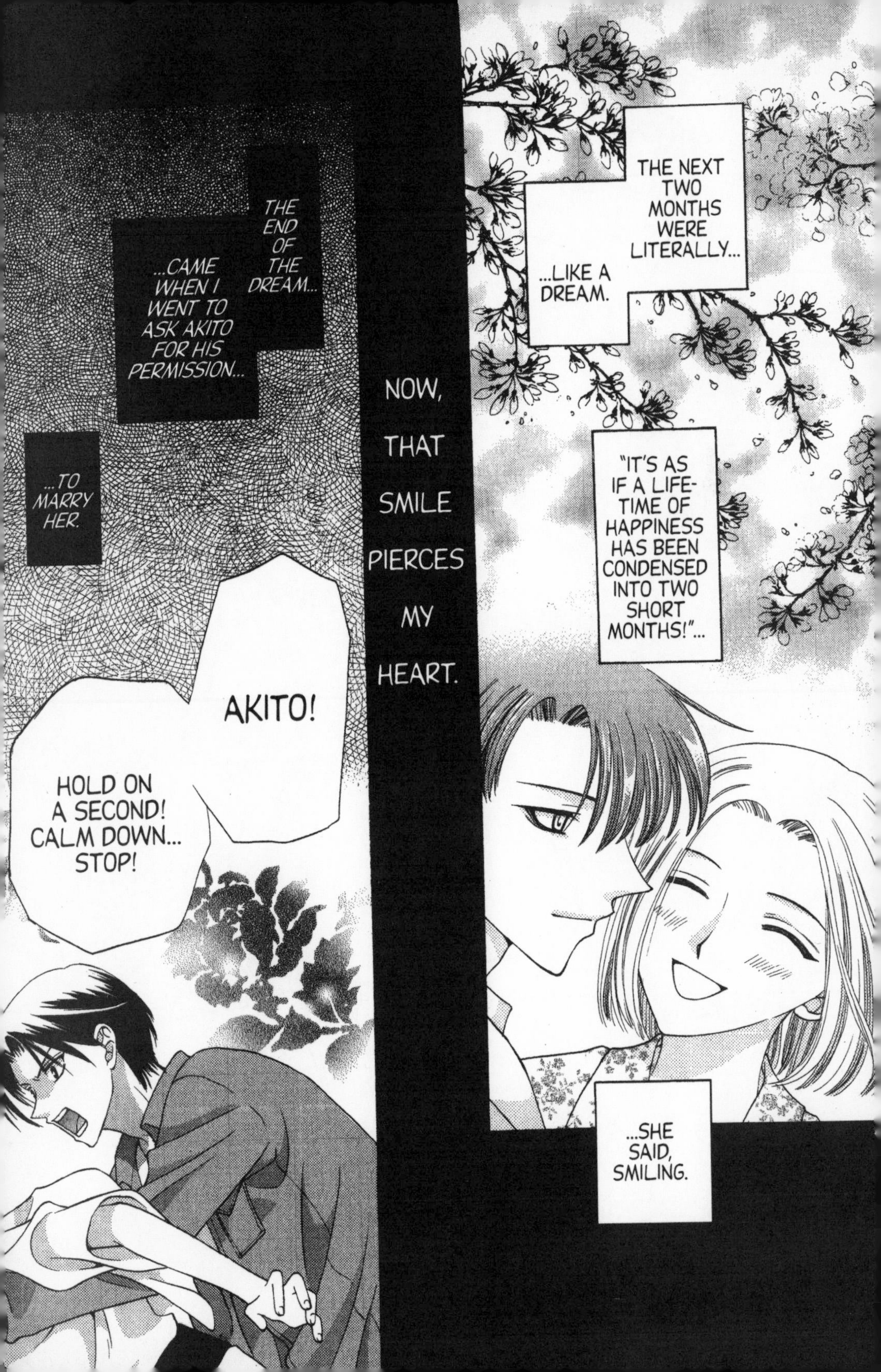
THE NEXT TWO MONTHS WERE LITERALLY...
...LIKE A DREAM.
"IT'S AS IF A LIFE-TIME OF HAPPINESS HAS BEEN CONDENSED INTO TWO SHORT MONTHS!"...
...SHE SAID, SMILING.
NOW, THAT SMILE PIERCES MY HEART.
THE END OF THE DREAM...
...CAME WHEN I WENT TO ASK AKITO FOR HIS PERMISSION...
...TO MARRY HER.
AKITO!
HOLD ON A SECOND! CALM DOWN... STOP!

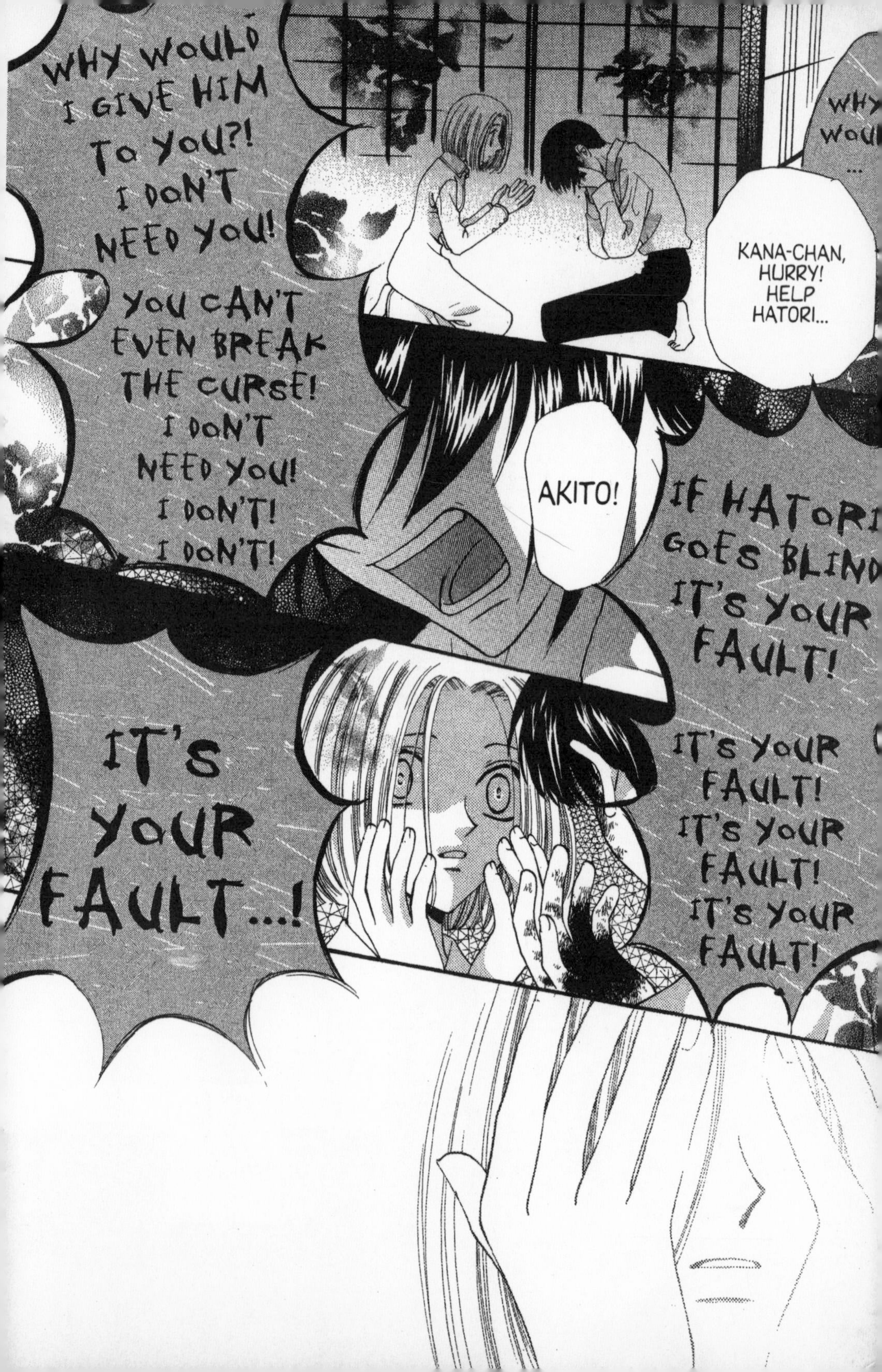
WHY WOUL ...
KANA-CHAN, HURRY! HELP HATORI...
WHY WOULD I GIVE HIM TO YOU?! I DON'T NEED YOU!
YOU CAN'T EVEN BREAK THE CURSE! I DON'T NEED YOU! I DON'T! I DON'T!
AKITO!
IF HATORI GOES BLIND IT'S YOUR FAULT!
IT'S YOUR FAULT! IT'S YOUR FAULT! IT'S YOUR FAULT!
IT'S YOUR FAULT...!

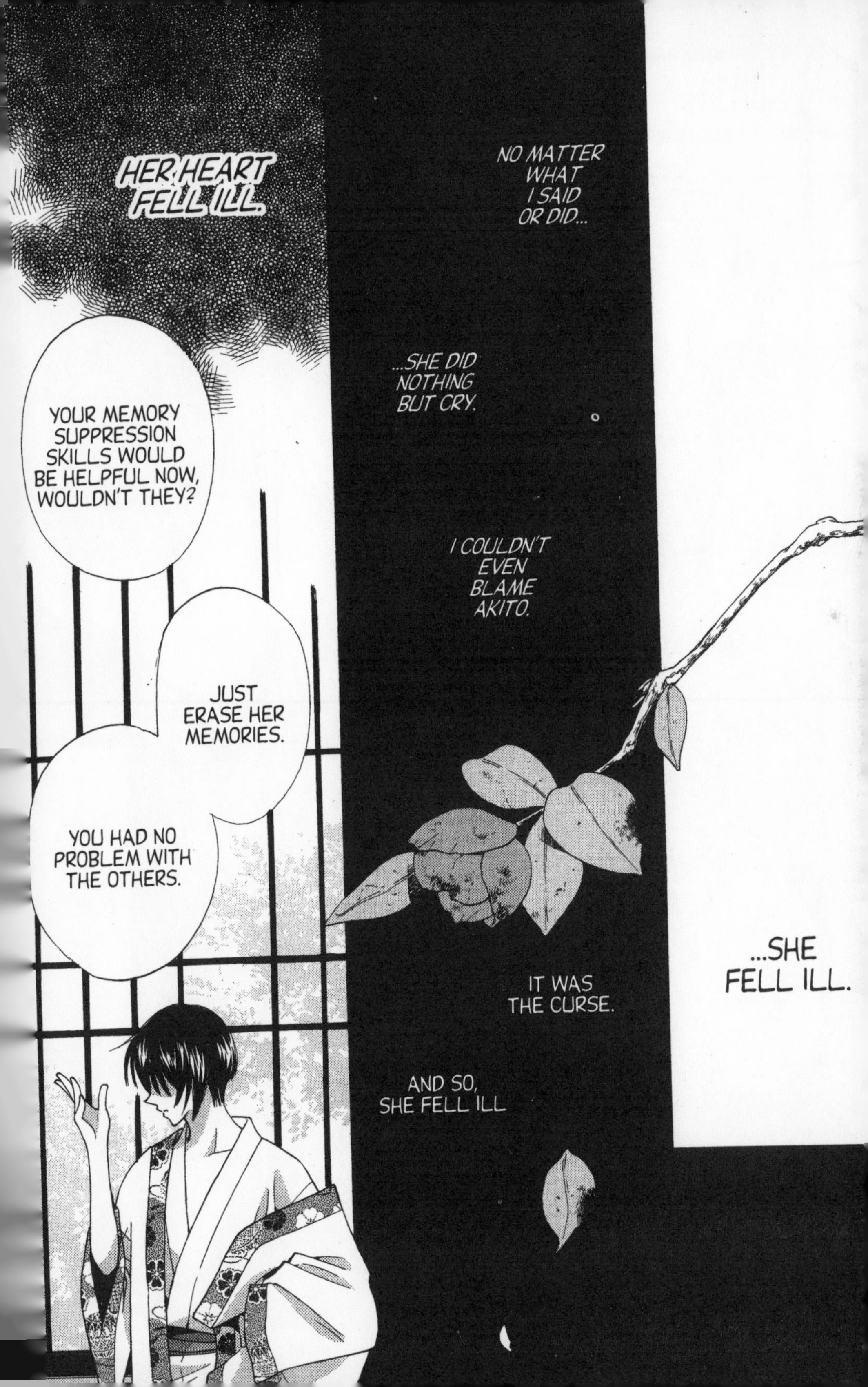

...SHE FELL ILL.
NO MATTER WHAT I SAID OR DID...
...SHE DID NOTHING BUT CRY.
I COULDN'T EVEN BLAME AKITO.
IT WAS THE CURSE.
AND SO, SHE FELL ILL
HER HEART FELL ILL.
YOUR MEMORY SUPPRESSION SKILLS WOULD BE HELPFUL NOW, WOULDN'T THEY?
JUST ERASE HER MEMORIES.
YOU HAD NO PROBLEM WITH THE OTHERS.

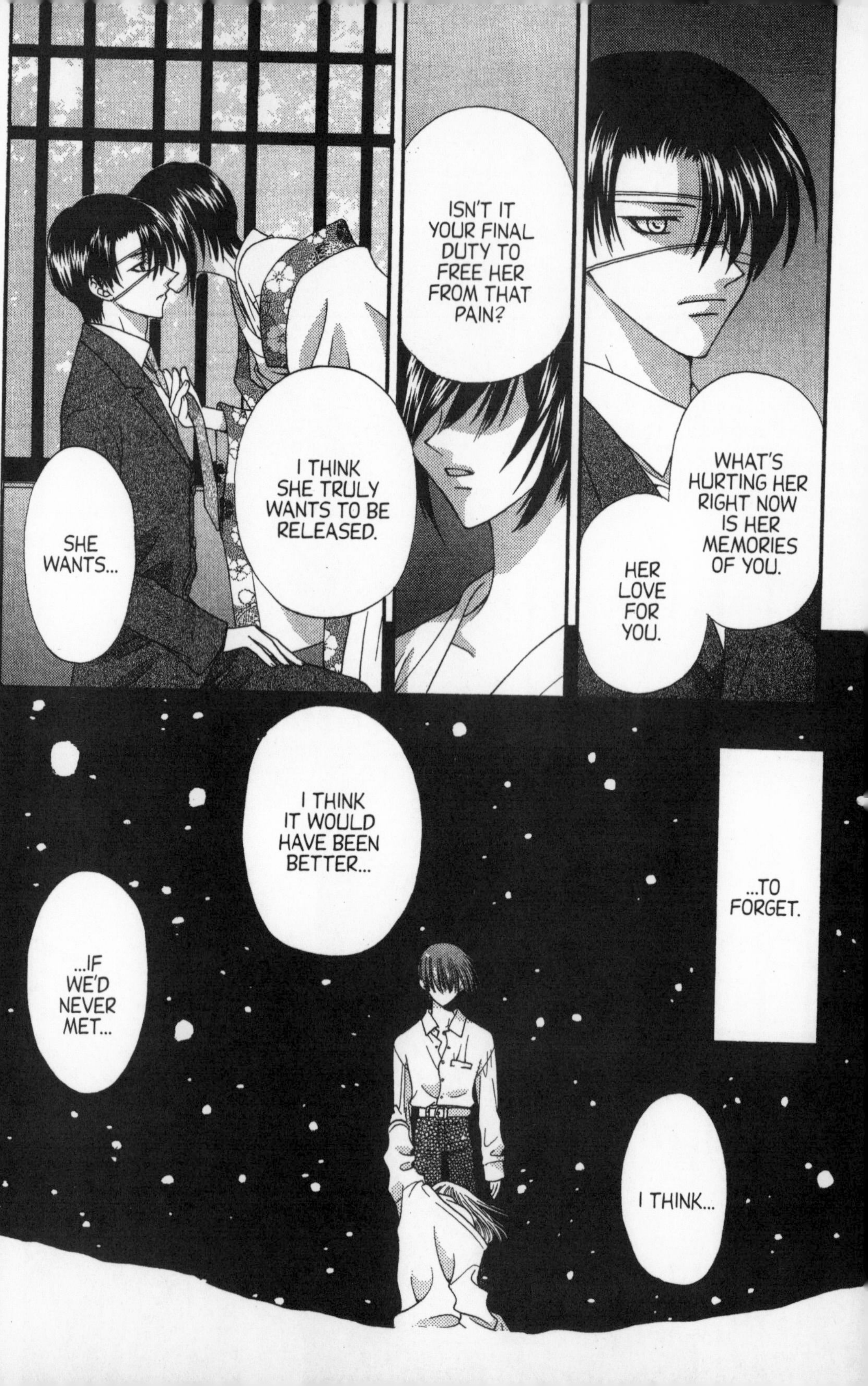
WHAT'S HURTING HER RIGHT NOW IS HER MEMORIES OF YOU.
HER LOVE FOR YOU.
ISN'T IT YOUR FINAL DUTY TO FREE HER FROM THAT PAIN?
I THINK SHE TRULY WANTS TO BE RELEASED.
SHE WANTS...
...TO FORGET.
I THINK...
I THINK IT WOULD HAVE BEEN BETTER...
...IF WE'D NEVER MET...

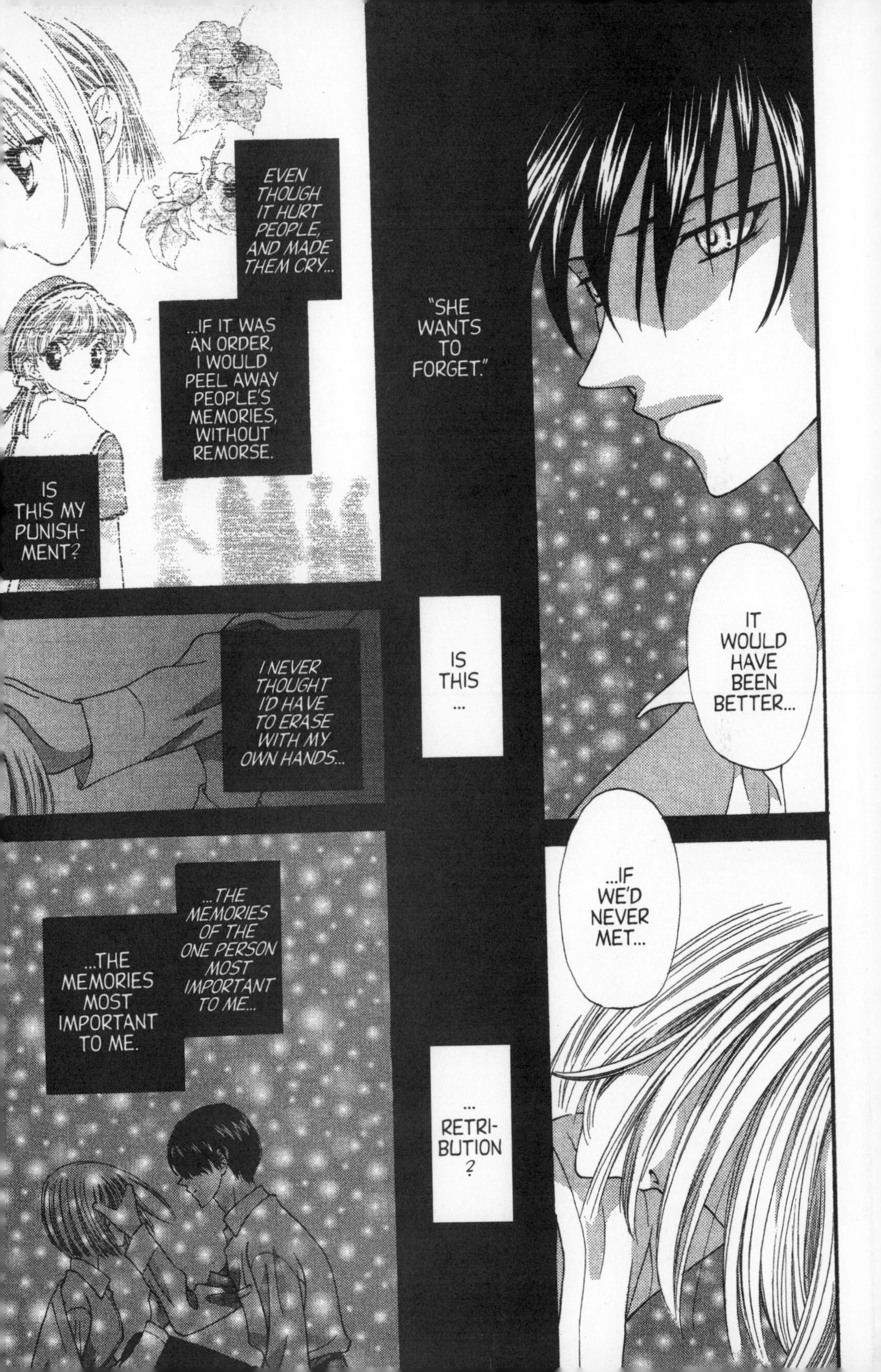
"SHE WANTS TO FORGET."
IT WOULD HAVE BEEN BETTER...
...IF WE'D NEVER MET...
IS THIS ...
... RETRIBUTION?
EVEN THOUGH IT HURT PEOPLE, AND MADE THEM CRY...
...IF IT WAS AN ORDER, I WOULD PEEL AWAY PEOPLE'S MEMORIES, WITHOUT REMORSE.
IS THIS MY PUNISHMENT?
I NEVER THOUGHT I'D HAVE TO ERASE WITH MY OWN HANDS...
...THE MEMORIES OF THE ONE PERSON MOST IMPORTANT TO ME...
...THE MEMORIES MOST IMPORTANT TO ME.

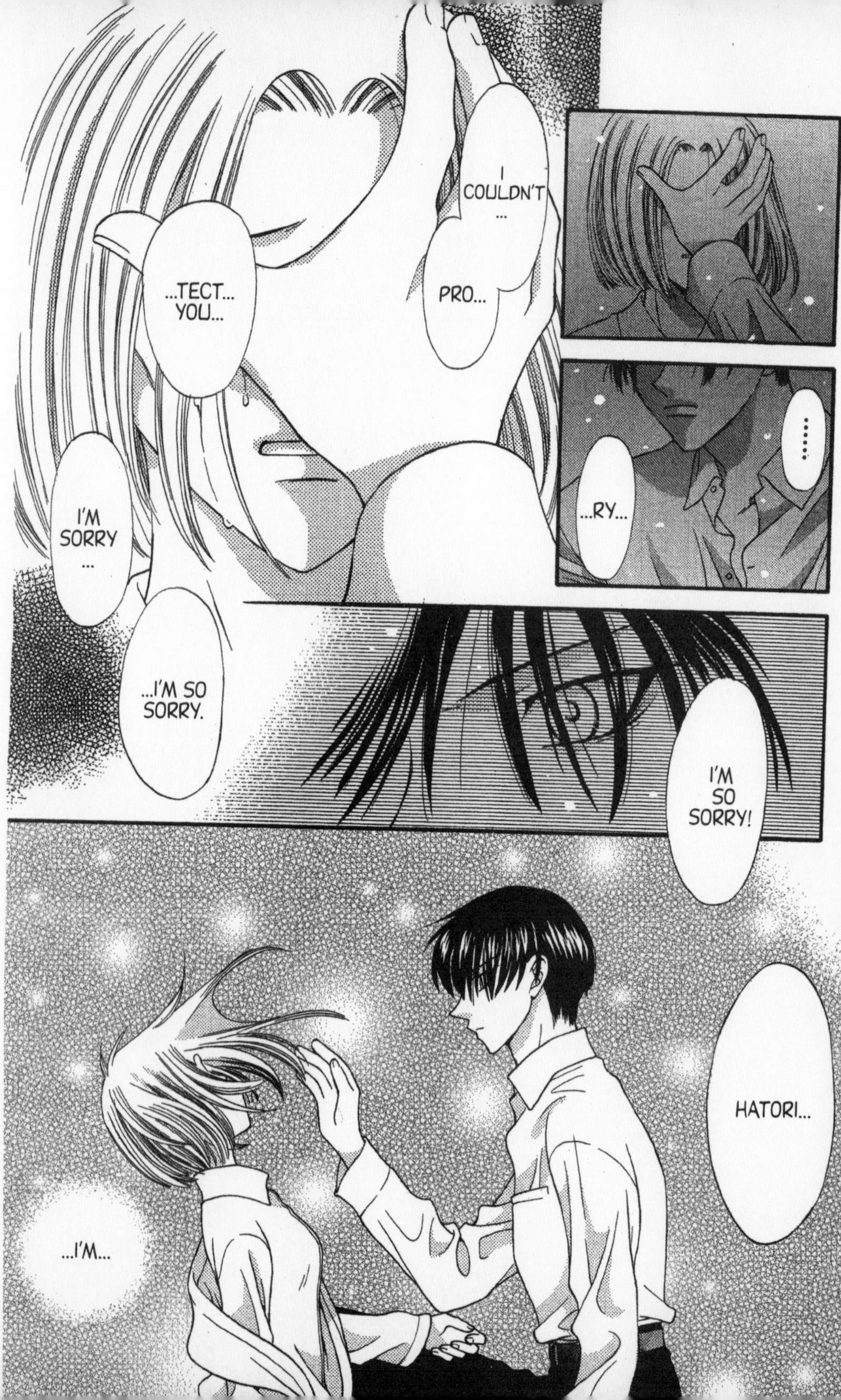
......
...RY...
I COULDN'T ...
PRO...
...TECT... YOU...
I'M SORRY ...
...I'M SO SORRY.
I'M SO SORRY!
HATORI...
...I'M...

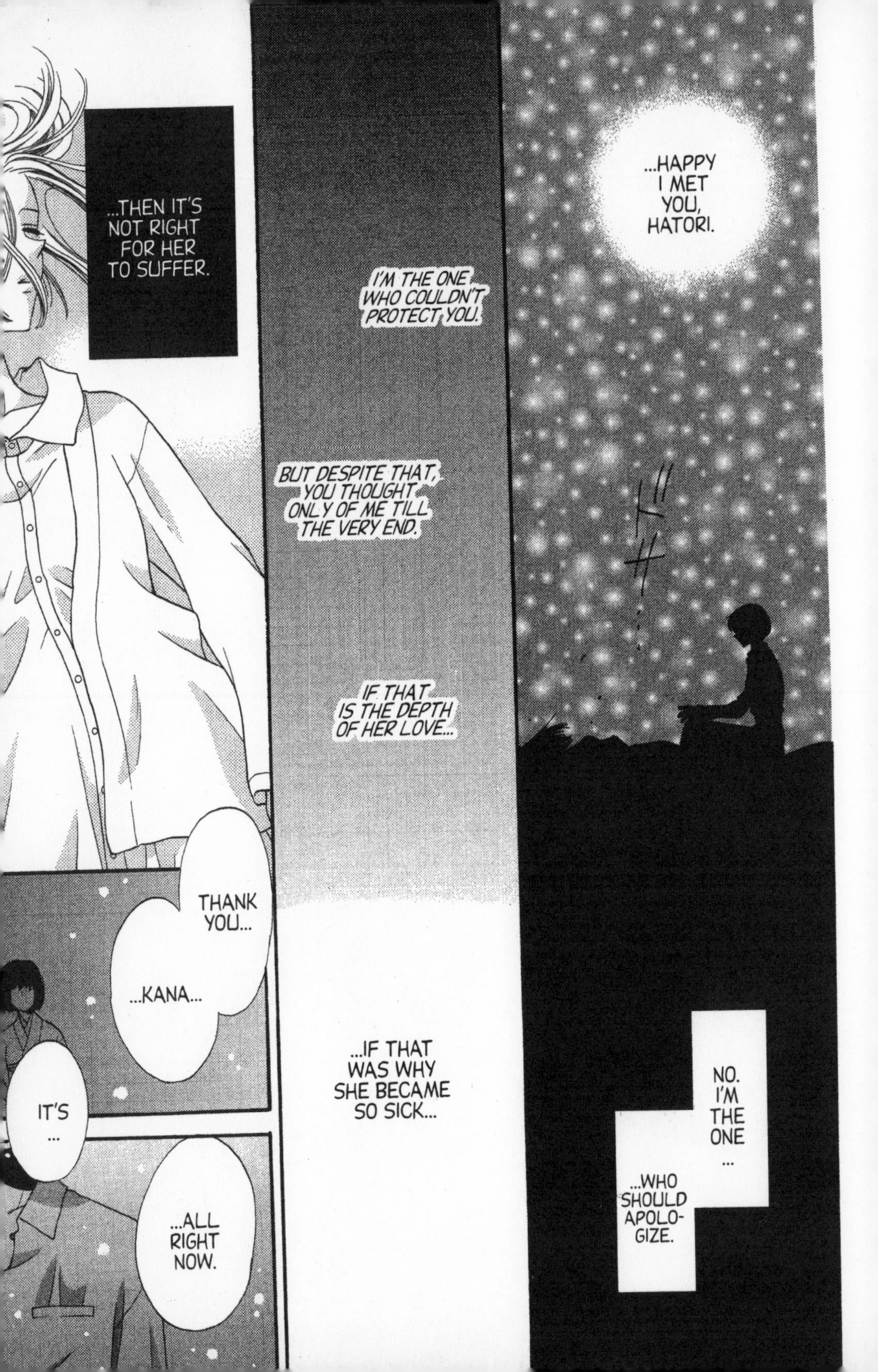
...HAPPY I MET YOU, HATORI.
NO. I'M THE ONE ...
...WHO SHOULD APOLO-GIZE.
I'M THE ONE WHO COULDN'T PROTECT YOU.
BUT DESPITE THAT, YOU THOUGHT ONLY OF ME TILL THE VERY END.
IF THAT IS THE DEPTH OF HER LOVE...
...IF THAT WAS WHY SHE BECAME SO SICK...
...THEN IT'S NOT RIGHT FOR HER TO SUFFER.
THANK YOU...
...KANA...
IT'S ...
...ALL RIGHT NOW.

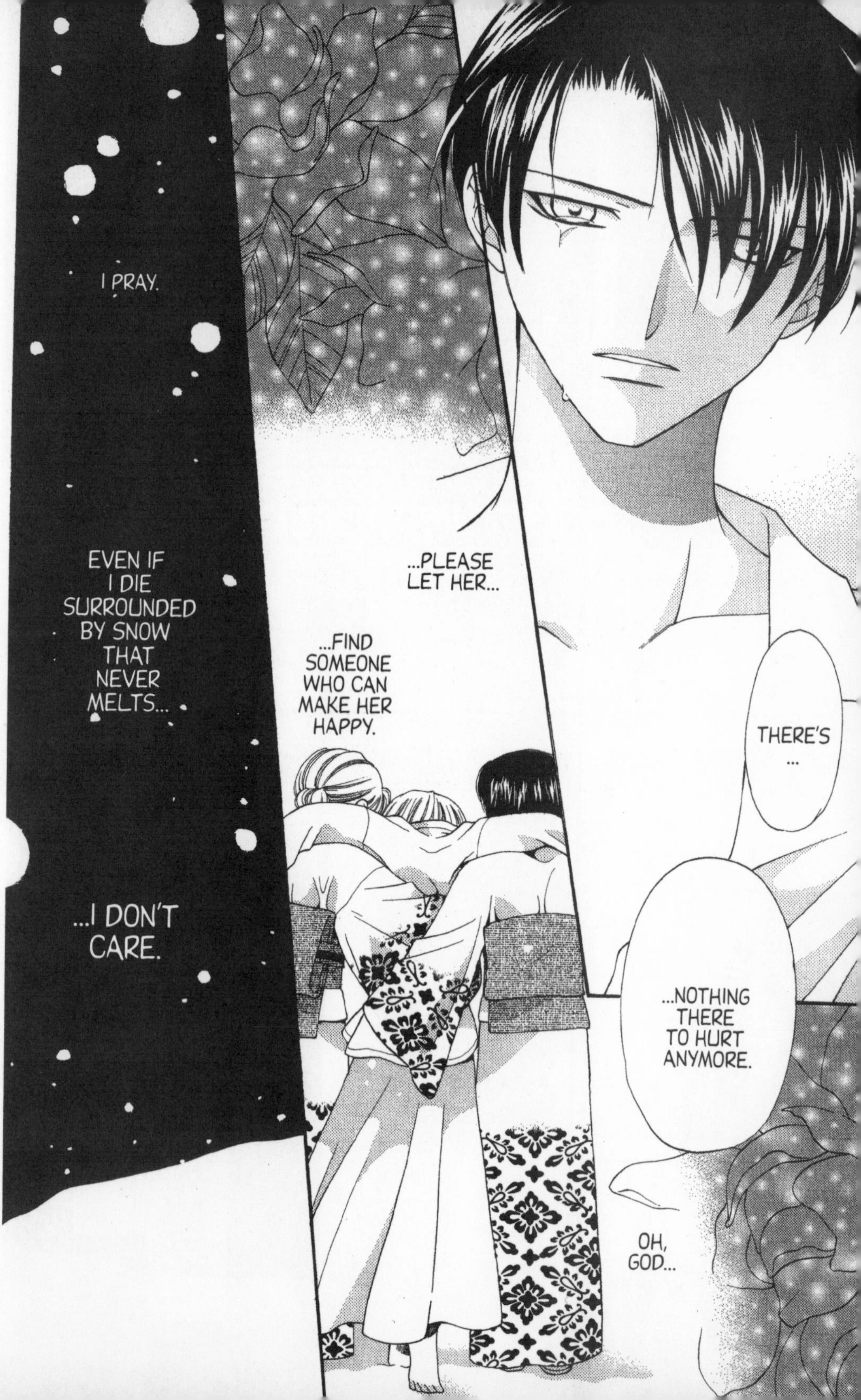
THERE'S ...
...NOTHING THERE TO HURT ANYMORE.
OH, GOD...
...PLEASE LET HER...
...FIND SOMEONE WHO CAN MAKE HER HAPPY.
I PRAY.
EVEN IF I DIE SURROUNDED BY SNOW THAT NEVER MELTS...
...I DON'T CARE.

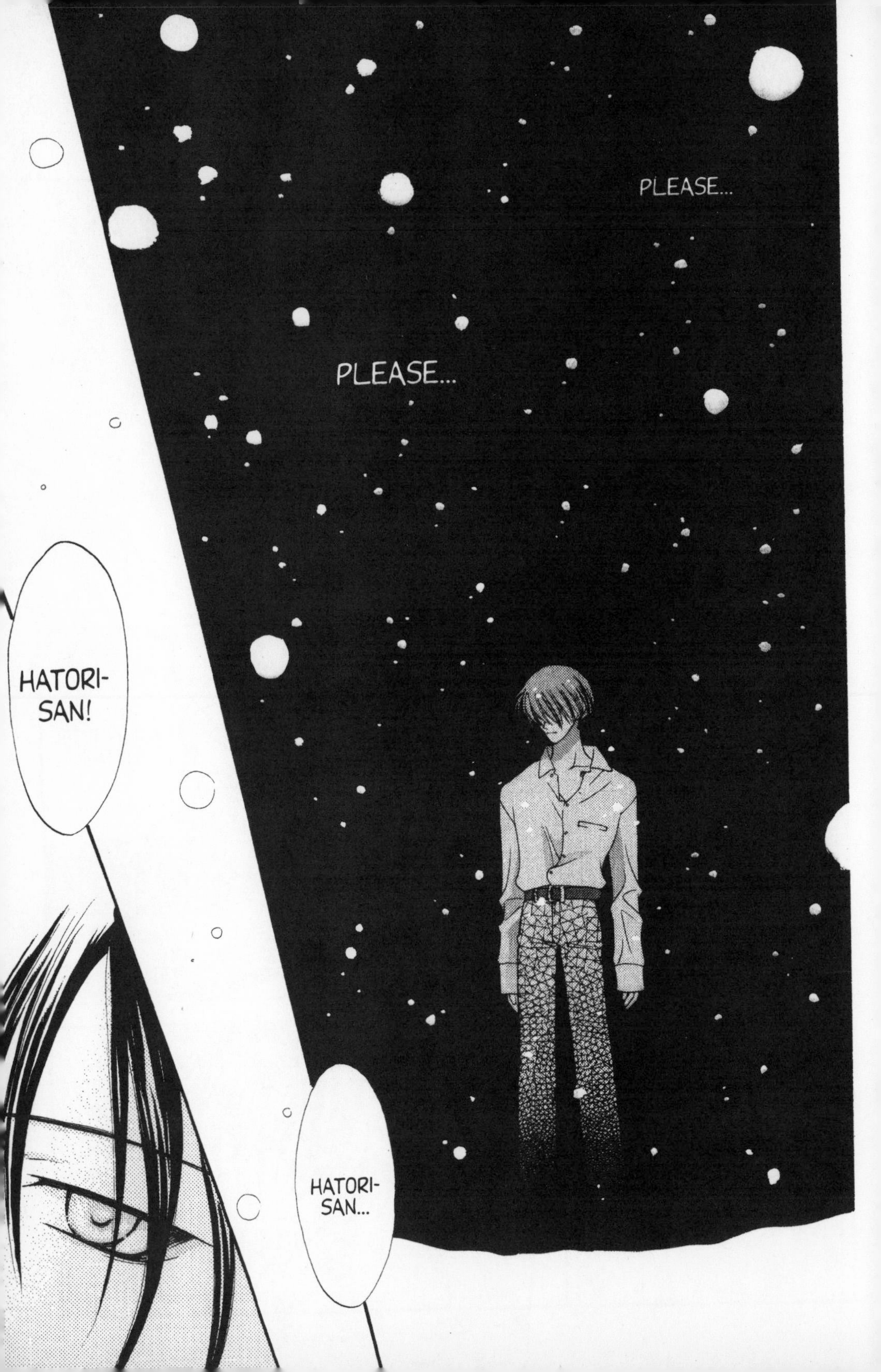
PLEASE...
PLEASE...
HATORI-SAN!
HATORI-SAN...

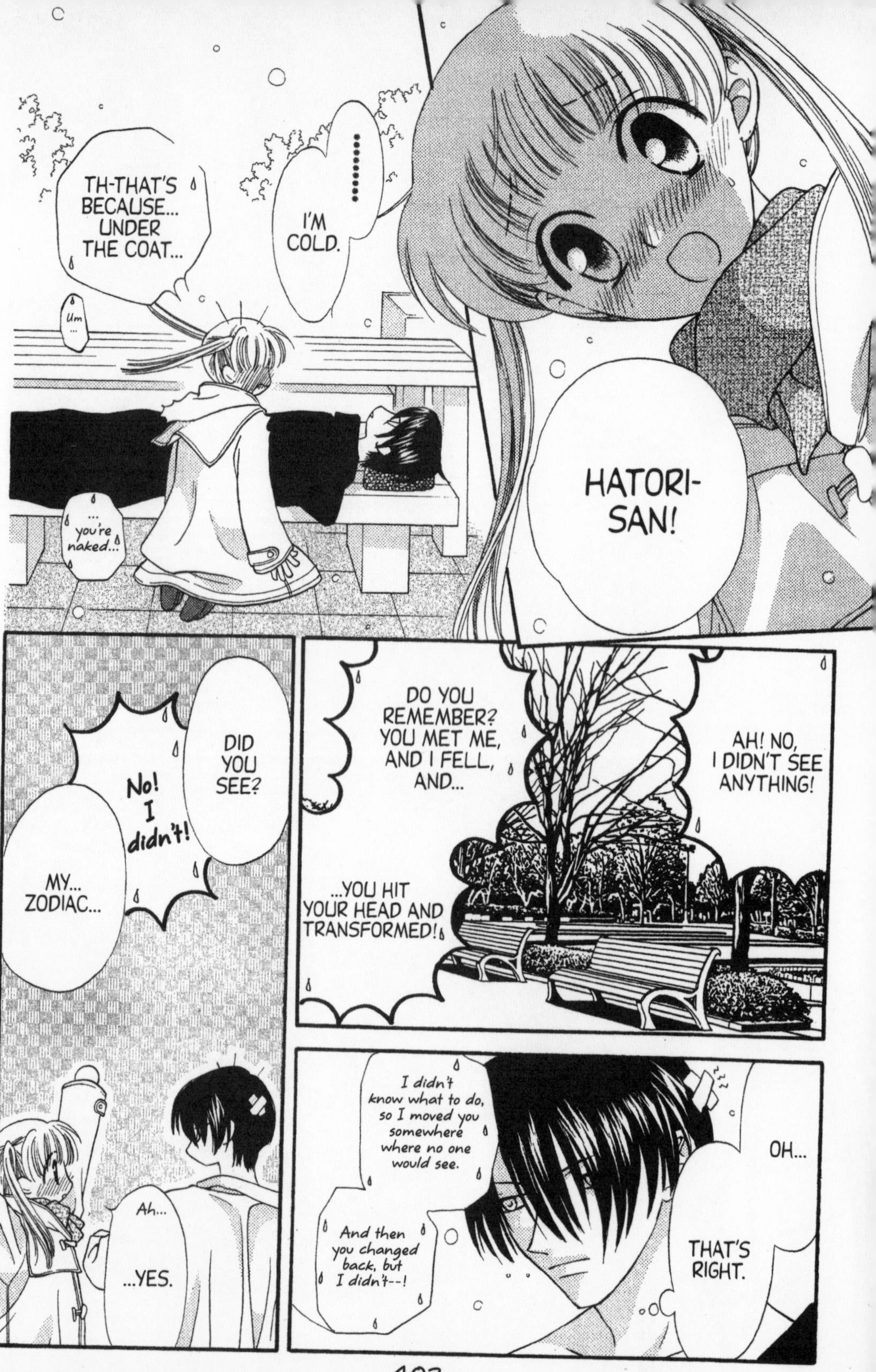
HATORI-SAN!
......
I'M COLD.
TH-THAT'S BECAUSE... UNDER THE COAT...
Um...
...you're naked...
AH! NO, I DIDN'T SEE ANYTHING!
DO YOU REMEMBER? YOU MET ME, AND I FELL, AND...
...YOU HIT YOUR HEAD AND TRANSFORMED!
OH...
THAT'S RIGHT.
I didn't know what to do, so I moved you somewhere where no one would see.
And then you changed back, but I didn't--!
DID YOU SEE?
No! I didn't!
MY... ZODIAC...
Ah...
...YES.

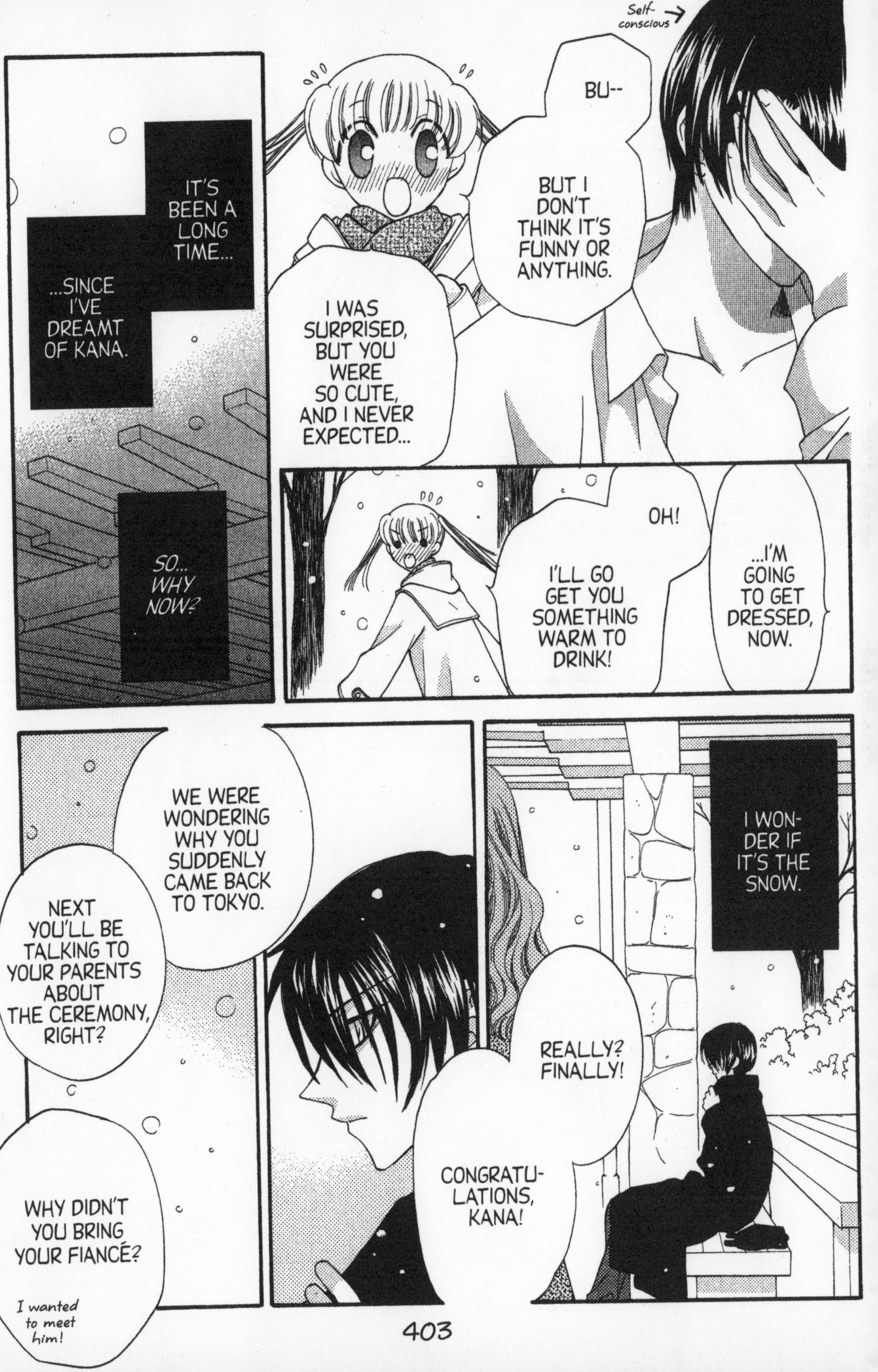
Self-conscious
BU--
BUT I DON'T THINK IT'S FUNNY OR ANYTHING.
I WAS SURPRISED, BUT YOU WERE SO CUTE, AND I NEVER EXPECTED...
...I'M GOING TO GET DRESSED, NOW.
OH!
I'LL GO GET YOU SOMETHING WARM TO DRINK!
IT'S BEEN A LONG TIME...
...SINCE I'VE DREAMT OF KANA.
SO... WHY NOW?
I WONDER IF IT'S THE SNOW.
REALLY? FINALLY!
CONGRATULATIONS, KANA!
WE WERE WONDERING WHY YOU SUDDENLY CAME BACK TO TOKYO.
NEXT YOU'LL BE TALKING TO YOUR PARENTS ABOUT THE CEREMONY, RIGHT?
WHY DIDN'T YOU BRING YOUR FIANCÉ?
I wanted to meet him!

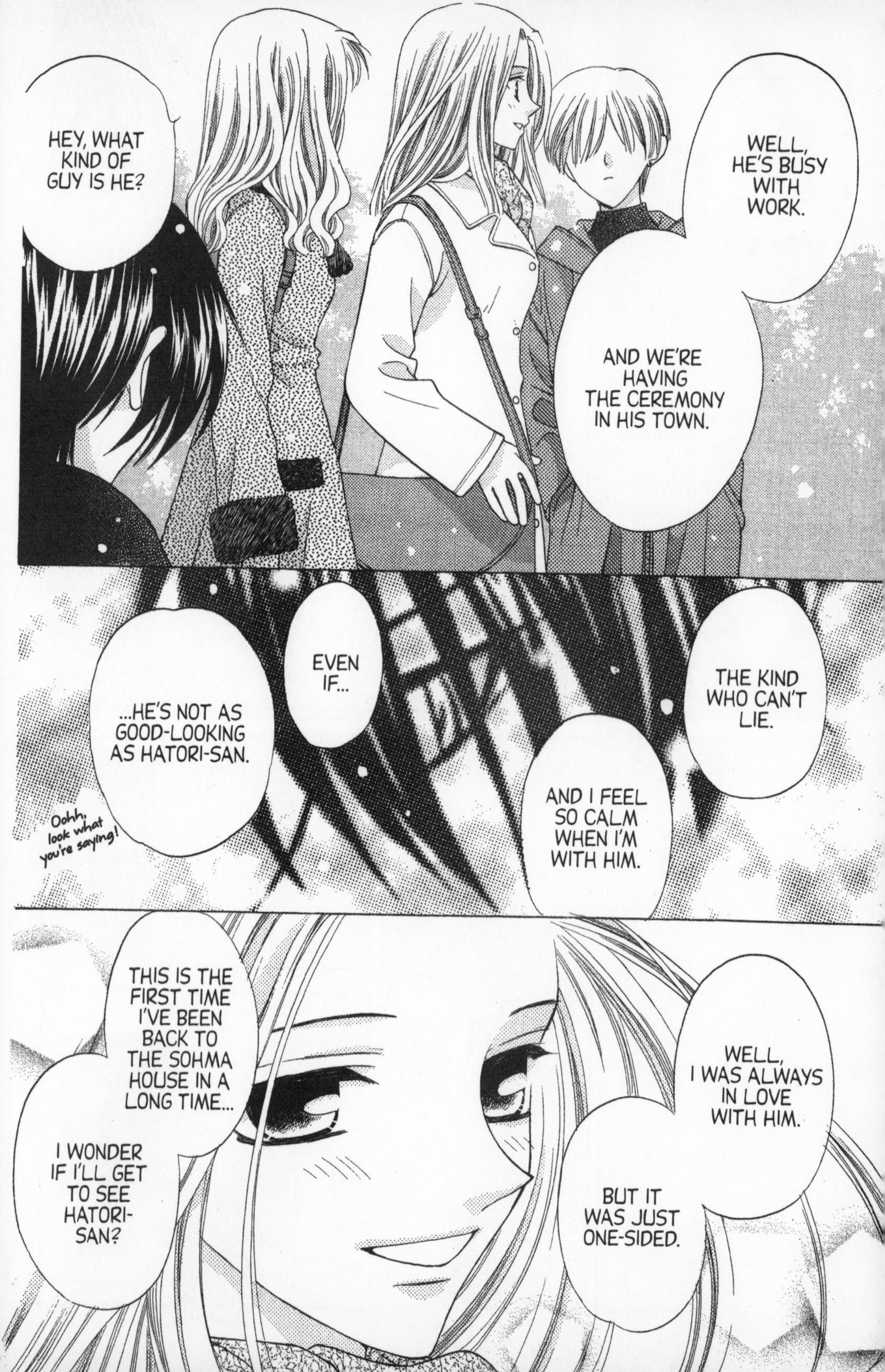
WELL, HE'S BUSY WITH WORK.
AND WE'RE HAVING THE CEREMONY IN HIS TOWN.
HEY, WHAT KIND OF GUY IS HE?
THE KIND WHO CAN'T LIE.
AND I FEEL SO CALM WHEN I'M WITH HIM.
EVEN IF...
...HE'S NOT AS GOOD-LOOKING AS HATORI-SAN.
Oohh, look what you're saying!
WELL, I WAS ALWAYS IN LOVE WITH HIM.
BUT IT WAS JUST ONE-SIDED.
THIS IS THE FIRST TIME I'VE BEEN BACK TO THE SOHMA HOUSE IN A LONG TIME...
I WONDER IF I'LL GET TO SEE HATORI-SAN?

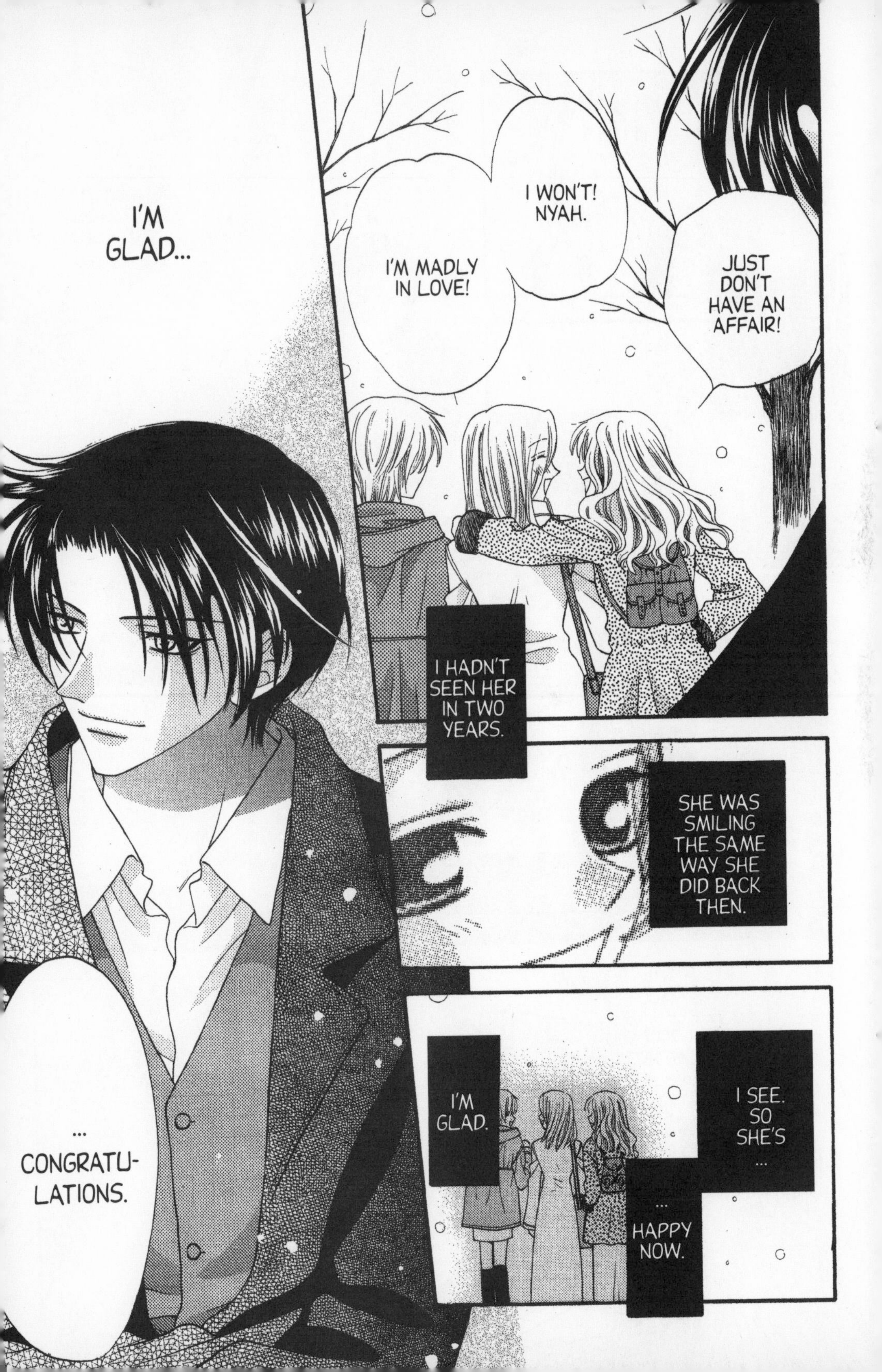
JUST DON'T HAVE AN AFFAIR!
I WON'T! NYAH.
I'M MADLY IN LOVE!
I HADN'T SEEN HER IN TWO YEARS.
SHE WAS SMILING THE SAME WAY SHE DID BACK THEN.
I SEE. SO SHE'S ...
... HAPPY NOW.
I'M GLAD.
I'M GLAD...
... CONGRATU-LATIONS.

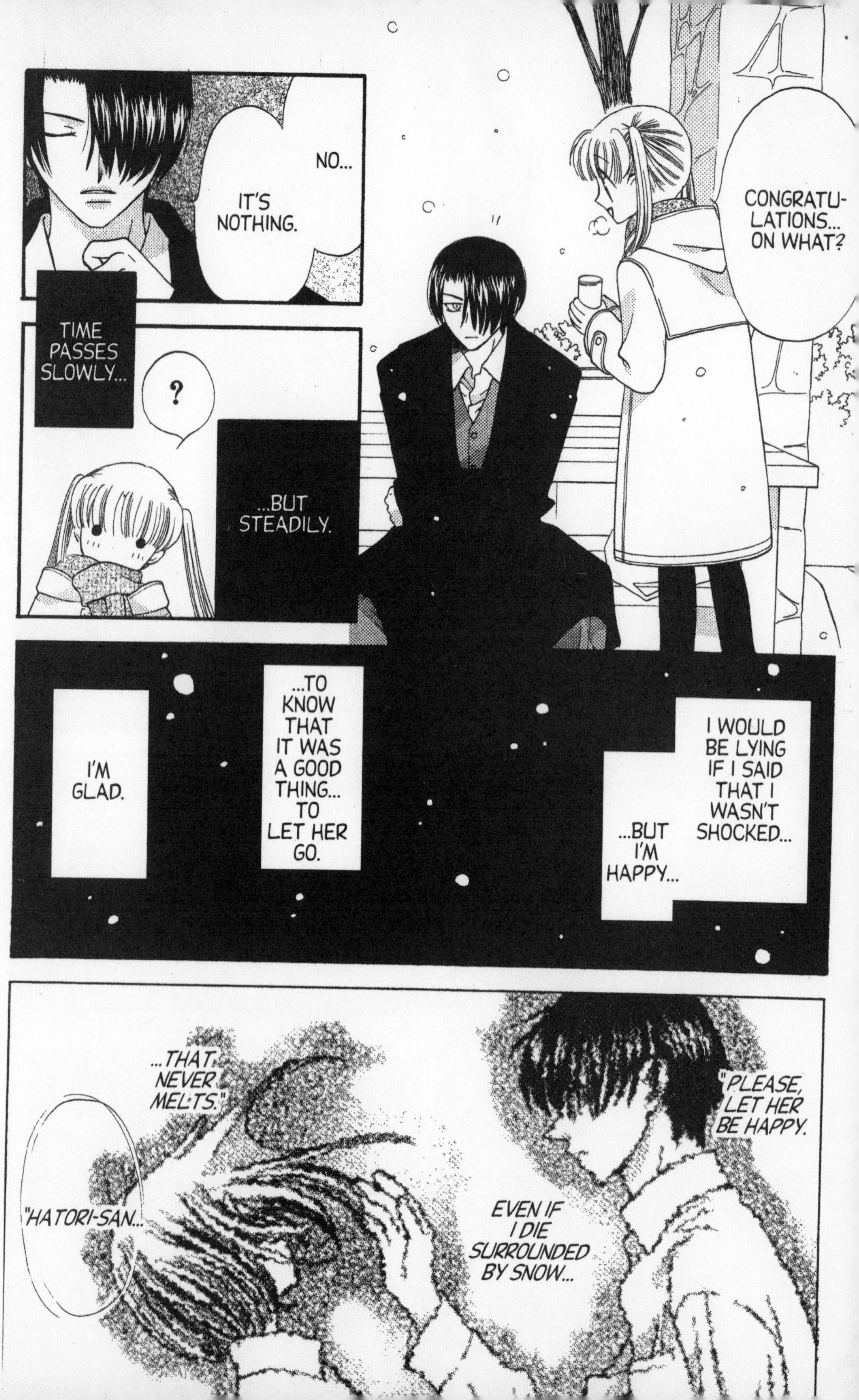
CONGRATULATIONS... ON WHAT?
NO...
IT'S NOTHING.
TIME PASSES SLOWLY...
?
...BUT STEADILY.
I WOULD BE LYING IF I SAID THAT I WASN'T SHOCKED...
...BUT I'M HAPPY...
...TO KNOW THAT IT WAS A GOOD THING... TO LET HER GO.
I'M GLAD.
"PLEASE, LET HER BE HAPPY.
EVEN IF I DIE SURROUNDED BY SNOW...
...THAT NEVER MELTS."
"HATORI-SAN...

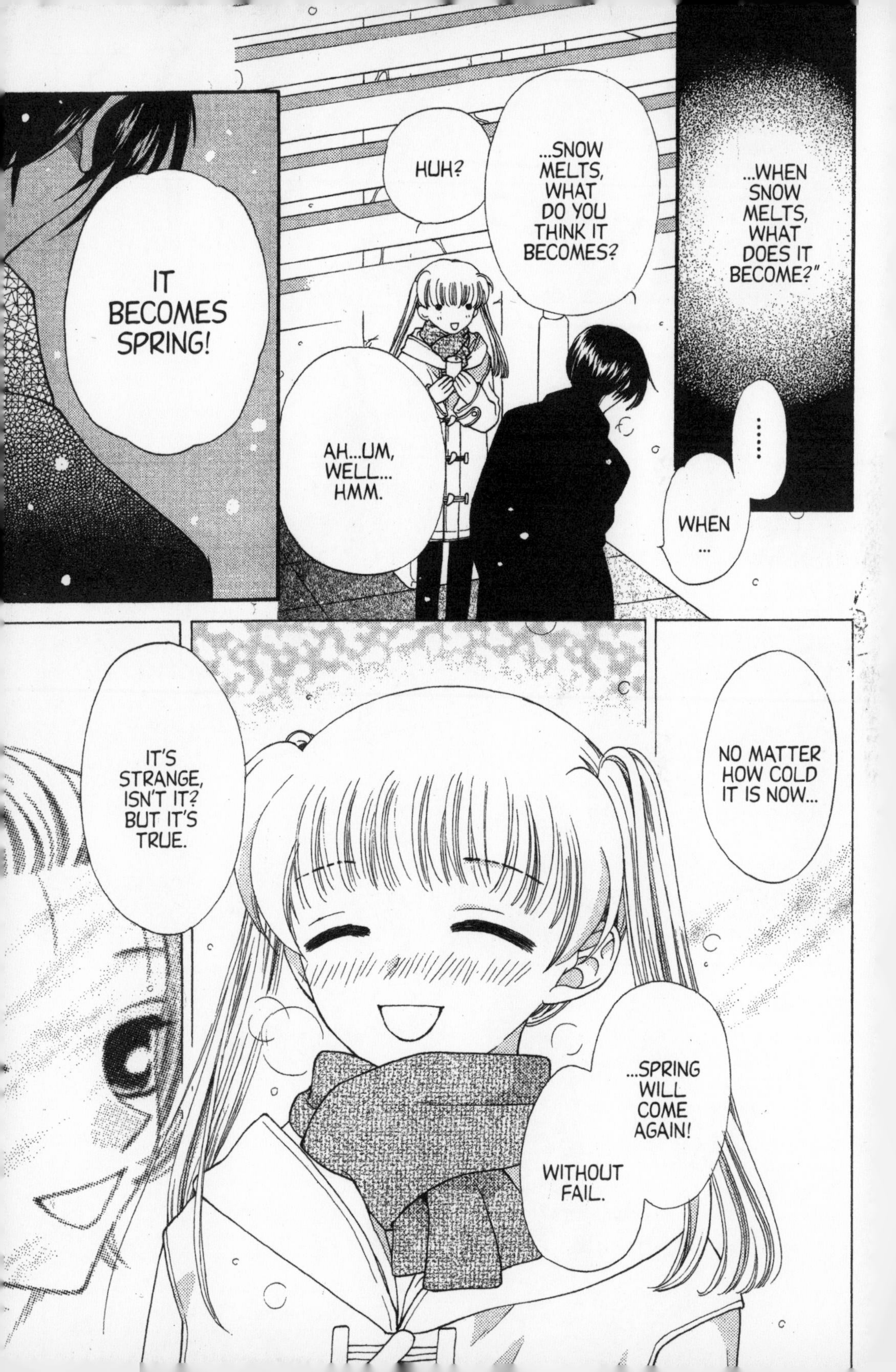

...WHEN SNOW MELTS, WHAT DOES IT BECOME?"
......
WHEN ...
...SNOW MELTS, WHAT DO YOU THINK IT BECOMES?
HUH?
AH...UM, WELL... HMM.
IT BECOMES SPRING!
NO MATTER HOW COLD IT IS NOW...
...SPRING WILL COME AGAIN!
WITHOUT FAIL.
IT'S STRANGE, ISN'T IT? BUT IT'S TRUE.

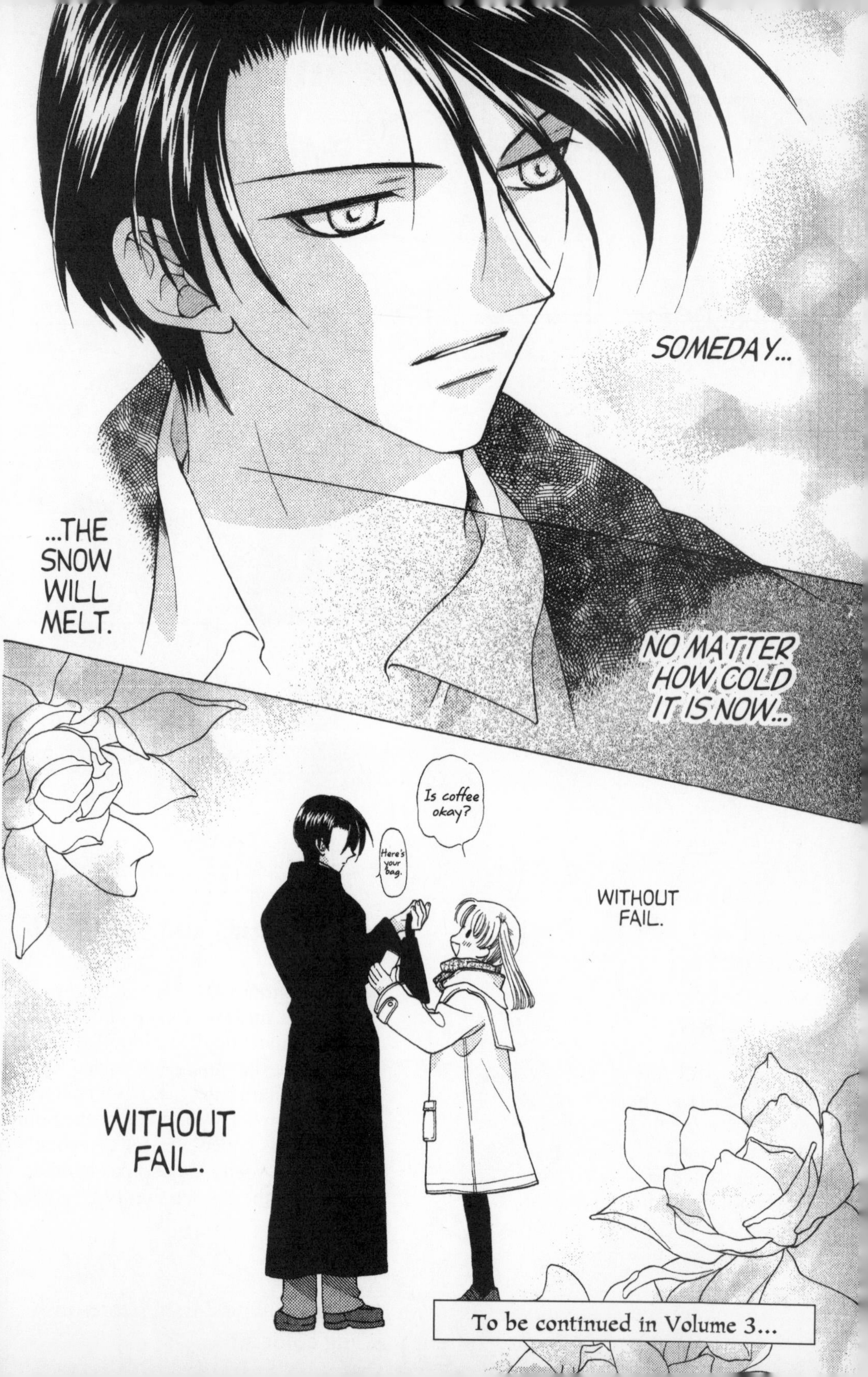
SOMEDAY...
...THE SNOW WILL MELT.
NO MATTER HOW COLD IT IS NOW...
Is coffee okay?
Here's your bag.
WITHOUT FAIL.
WITHOUT FAIL.
To be continued in Volume 3...

Next time in...

Fruits Basket Ultimate Edition

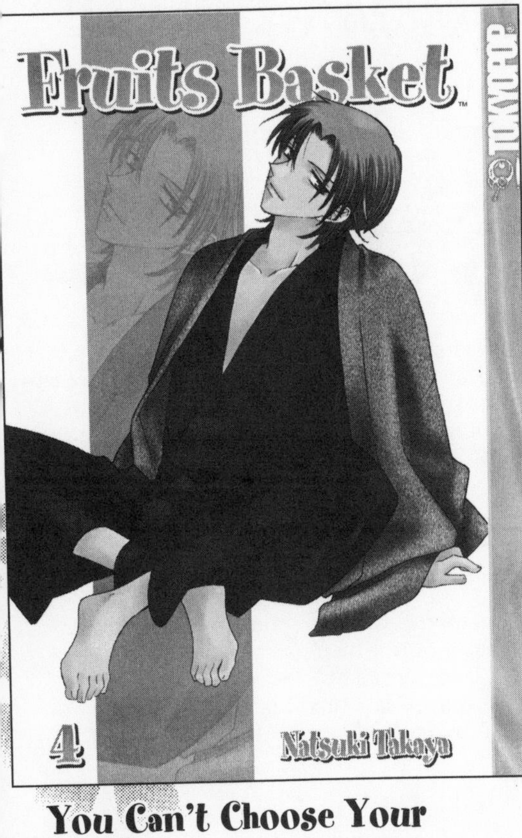

Fruits Basket
TOKYOPOP
4
Natsuki Takaya

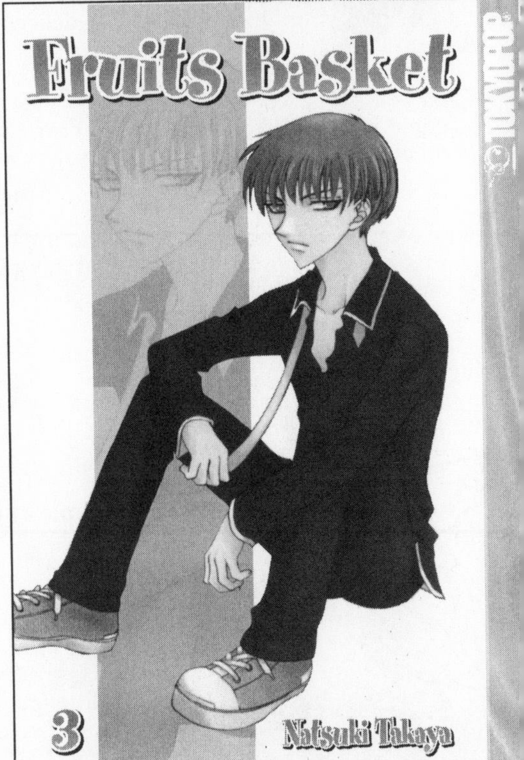

Fruits Basket
TOKYOPOP
3
Natsuki Takaya

You Can't Choose Your Family...

When the infamous Akito makes an in-class appearance at the start of the school year, the Sohma family worries that his arrival will be an uncensored exercise of show-and-tell about Yuki's past. Meanwhile, when Ayame vows to rekindle his brothers' lost friendship, he begins to realize that you can choose your friends but you can't choose your family--especially when they're acting like animals!

Hot Springs and Cold Feet

It's Valentines Day and you know what that means—lots of chocolates for the cutest boys at school! But who will score the most-- hotheaded Kyo or "prince charming" Yuki? Of course the kind-hearted Tohru, guest of the Sohma family, has chocolates for everyone! But when White Day comes around, what will the Sohma family give back?

Look for the *Fruits Basket Ultimate Edition* Volume 2 to hit stores in February 2008! Including color art!

How to Play Rich Man, Poor Man
(Dai Hin Min / Dai Fugo)

OBJECTIVE
The aim is to get rid of all your cards as soon as possible.

PLAYERS AND CARDS
About 4 to 7 people using a standard 54 card pack with jokers. The suits are irrelevant and the cards rank, from high to low with deuces high: 2 A K Q J 10 9 8 7 6 5 4 3. Jokers are wild.

DEAL
The game is played clockwise. All the cards are dealt out. Some players may have one more than others.

PLAY
The player to dealer's left starts by leading (face up) any single card or any set of cards of equal rank (for example, three fives). Each player in turn must then either pass (i.e. not play any cards), or play face up a card or set of cards which beats the previous play.

A single card is beaten by any higher single card. A set of cards can only be beaten by a higher set containing the same number of cards. So for example, if the previous player played two sixes, you can beat this with two kings, or two sevens, but not with a single king, and not with three sevens (though you could play two of them and hang onto the third).

It is not necessary to beat the previous play just because you can -- passing is always allowed. Also passing does not prevent you from playing the next time your turn comes round.

The play continues as many times around the table as necessary until someone makes a play which everyone else passes. All the cards played are then turned face down and put to one side, and the player who played last (and highest) in the previous "trick" starts again by leading any card or set of equal cards.

For example the play might go:
Tohru leads with a pair of fours. Kyo follows with a pair of sevens. Uo passes. Hanajima follows with a pair of Tens. Tohru passes. Kyo plays a pair of Jacks. Uo passes. Hanajima passes. Tohru passes. Kyo then starts again by leading any card or set.

When a player whose turn it is to play has no more cards left, the turn passes to the next player in rotation. Therefore in the example, if the two Jacks were Kyo's last two cards, he would sit out the rest of the round and it would then be Uo's turn to play anything.

Jokers are wild and are equal in rank to whatever card they are played with.

For scoring purposes, whoever goes out first gets 2 points. second out gets one point and

R
E
V
O
L
U
T
I
O
N

SOCIAL STATUS

The first player who is out of cards is dubbed the "Dai Fugo," or very rich man. Other variations on the rules call this person the President, King, or the Great Dalmuti. The last player to be left with any cards is known as the "Dai Hin Min," or very poor man. You can also use other derisive terms such as peon, beggar, scum, or a--hole.

While it's not part of the basic Dai Hin Min rules, many variations also give titles to the players based on their rank. So if you use "King" as your model, you might have King, Duke, Knight, Merchant, and Peon as your ranks. More importantly, the players of higher status are entitled to enjoy and generally abuse their power over the lower ranking players. You can also add to the fun by having players wear hats based on rank, with the leader wearing a crown and the loser wearing a dunce cap.

Between hands, players move seats based on ranks. The Dai Fugo selects the most comfortable chair; second place sits to the left, and so on around to the Dai Hin Min who sits to the Dai Fugo's right, probably on a crate or packing case.

The Dai Hin Min is responsible for shuffling, dealing and clearing away the cards when necessary. As the players are now seated clockwise in order of rank, the first card is dealt to the Dai Fugo, and so on down.

When the deal is complete, the Dai Hin Min must give his or her highest card to the Dai Fugo, and the Dai Fugo gives back in exchange any card that he or she does not want. Second place trades with second from last, etc. If there are an odd number of players, the middle player doesn't swap. (Variation: swap 2 cards per round)

The Dai Hin Min then leads any card or set of cards and the game continues as before.

END OF GAME

If scoring, set a target score (say 11 points). The game ends when someone reaches it.

VARIATIONS

Shibari

If a player follows a play with a card of the same suit, that player may declare "shibari," or "binding," which means that all other players must follow suit in order to play. For example, if Hanajima plays a seven of clubs and Tohru trumps it with a nine of clubs, she can declare shibari on clubs, and only clubs can be played. This variation can work with doubles and triples, too. Example—Kyo plays a six of clubs and a six of hearts. Uo trumps that with a eight of diamonds and an eight of hearts. She can declare shibari on hearts so that each subsequent play must have a heart plus any other. Double shibari or triple shibari can be declared if two or three suits match. Shibari's are only effective for the hand in which they are played.

Revolution!

If four of a kind are played, it is called a revolution. When this happens, the rank of cards is reversed. From that point on, lower values now trump higher values until there is another revolution.

Dai Fugo makes the rules!

Another fun variation is to let the Dai Fugo add an extra rule each round (or cancel an existing rule). The rules will likely make it easier for the Dai Fugo to keep winning or humiliating for the loser, but in Dai Hin Min, as in life, it's not always fair. But remember Karma—what comes around goes around, and you won't stay on top forever…

There are many other variations to Dai Hin Min and its Western equivalents, and the rules are slightly different depending on whoever you ask. For other variations, and rules on similar games, visit www.pagat.com, the web's leading resource for card games.

Year of the Rat: Behind the Whiskers

Rat

Years*: 1936, 1948, 1960, 1972, 1984, 1996, 2008, 2020, 2032
Positive Qualities: charming, imaginative, ambitious, sentimental, generous (to loved ones), frugal
Negative Qualities: hot-tempered, overly critical, prone to gossip, pack-rat
Suitable Jobs: sales, writing, publicity
Compatible With: Dragons, Monkeys, Oxen
Must Avoid: Horses (and cats)
Ruling Hours: 11 PM to 1 AM
Season: Winter
Ruling Month: December
Sign Direction: North
Fixed Element: Water
Corresponding Western Sign: Sagittarius

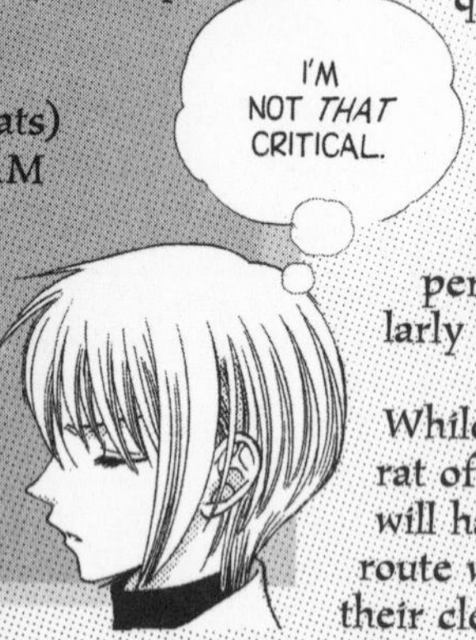
I'M NOT *THAT* CRITICAL.

The rat was at a disadvantage during the Zodiac race, but with his nimble abilities and smarts was able to land the coveted first place spot in the Chinese Zodiac. For people born in the year of the rat, this win spells some degree of financial freedom (if they don't marry a sheep), but their hearts will always remain true to family and friends. After all, friends are one thing that the rat can never have enough of.

Cheerful and always optimistic, Rats love living in groups and will gladly let a friend or relative crash for any amount of time, be it a night or ten years. Freeloading is not an issue because a rat can always find some kind of work that needs to be done. Even when someone swindles them, rats seldom hold a grudge. They simply just lock the bad memory away in their hearts. Keeping their loved ones close and happy is what matters most. Ironically though, rats also hold onto an exorbitant amount of trinkets and mementos from past experiences. This 'pack rat' mentality is detrimental though since rats often pick up or buy things they really never needed in the first place.

An interesting facet of the rat's personality is that they love to ask questions and have great memories, though they often single out the small nit-picky details and gloss over the other nicer points. It is a minor character flaw, but this cunning insight does tend make a person born in the rat year a particularly excellent writer.

While misfortune does not befall the rat often, whenever it does strike, a rat will have little to fear since an escape route was always carefully factored into their clever plans. Potential dangers are sized-up and quickly faced down with their fearless attitude, cool demeanor and quick wits. For the rat, perseverance is one of their keys to success. After all, no matter how fleeting success is...success is still success.

Celebrity Rats

Ben Affleck
Mandy Moore
Alice Cooper
Scarlett Johansson
Rizzo the Rat

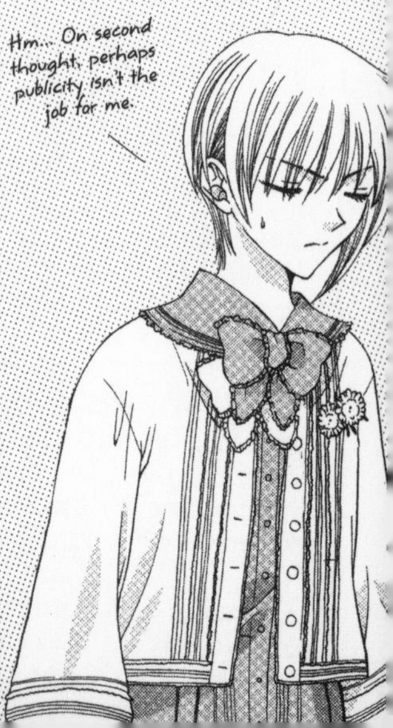
Hm... On second thought, perhaps publicity isn't the job for me.

* Note: If you were born in January or early February, then chances are you are probably the animal of the preceding year. The only way to know for certain is to know on which day Chinese New Year's was held. For example, this year (2004) the Chinese New Year began on January 22, so the first three weeks of January were still year of the sheep.

Do you want to share your love for Fruits Basket with fans around the world? "Fans Basket" is taking submissions of fan art, poetry, cosplay photos, or any other Furuaba fun you'd like to share!

How to submit:

1)Send your work via regular mail (NOT e-mail) to:

"Fans Basket"
c/o TOKYOPOP
5900 Wilshire Blvd.
Suite 2000
Los Angeles, CA 90036

2) All work should be in black and white and no larger than 8.5" x 11". (And try not to fold it too many times!)

3) Anything you send will not be returned. If you want to keep your original, it's fine to send us a copy.

4) Please include your full name, age, city and state for us to print with your work. If you'd rather us use a pen name, please include that too.

5) IMPORTANT: If you're under the age of 18, you must have your parent's permission in order for us to print your work. Any submissions without a signed note of parental consent cannot be used.

6) For full details, please check out our website.http://www.tokyopop.com/aboutus/fanart.php

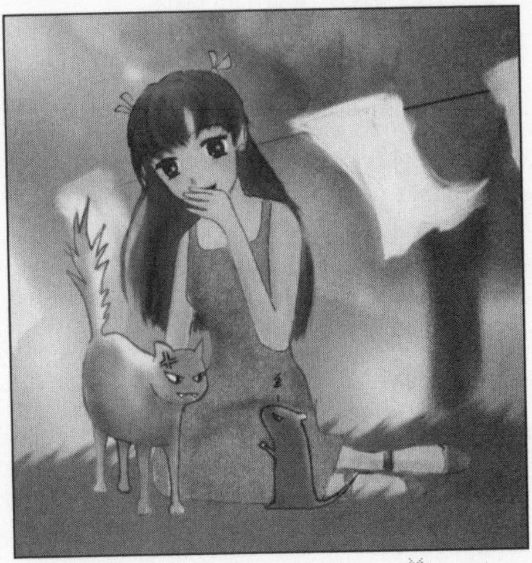

S-Girl,
Atlanta, GA

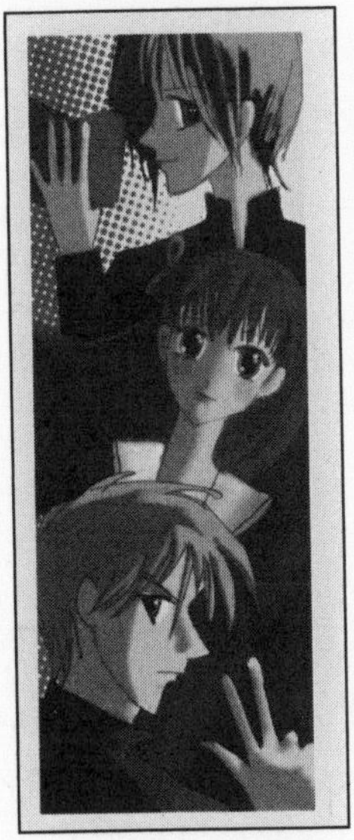

S-Girl

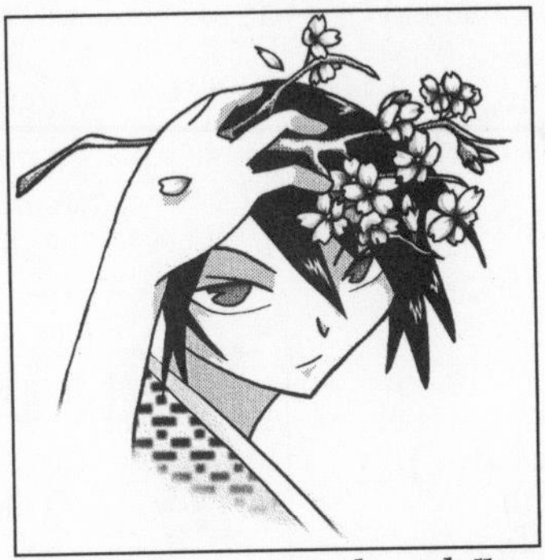

Kathy Schilling

And bonus art from TOKYOPOP's own Super Interns!

Chrissy Schilling

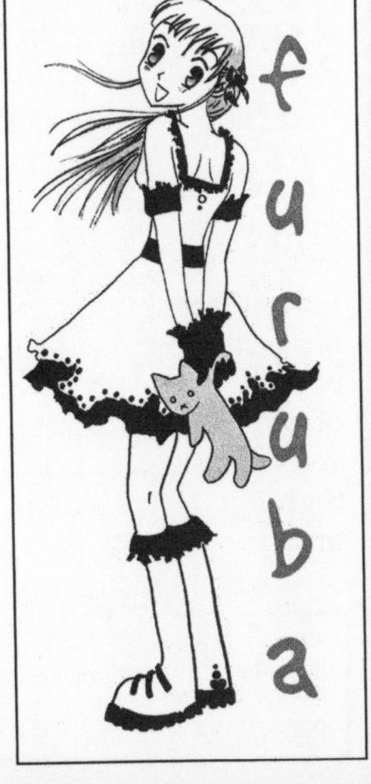
furuba

Here's a few haiku
I wrote about Fruits Basket
Print them if you can

Chinese Zodiac
Twelve there are but one left out
What of the poor cat?

Yuki or Kyo?
We don't know who Tohru picks
But I like the Rat

-Kathleen B.
West Hartford, CT

SOUND EFFECT INDEX

THE FOLLOWING IS A LIST OF THE SOUND EFFECTS USED IN FRUITS BASKET. EACH SOUND IS LABELED BY PAGE AND PANEL NUMBER, SEPARATED BY A PERIOD. THE FIRST DESCRIPTION IS THE PHONETIC READING OF THE JAPANESE, AND IS FOLLOWED BY THE EQUIVALENT ENGLISH SOUND OR A DESCRIPTION.

32.4	hiiiii: cringe
32.5	fura-fura: dazed
33.2	da-da-da-da-da: dash
33.3	dan: whack
34.3	dohki-dohki: badum-badum (pounding heartbeat)
35.4	jin: teary stare
40.1	zawa-zawa-zawa: chatter chatter
41.1	zawa-zawa: chatter chatter
41.3	gann: wham
42.4	mera-mera-mera: crackle crackle (burning rage)
45.3	gan: wham
45.4	zawa-zawa-zawa: chatter chatter
46.3	biku: eep!
46.4	doki-doki: badum-badum (heartbeat)
51.3a	zuruben: slip bam
51.3b	gann: wham
53.3	kiss (in german)
54.1	dah: dash
58.5	bikuu: eep!
62.2	gaa: blush
65.1	zawa-zawa: chatter chatter
70.2	gya-gya: chatter chatter
73.2	pachii: spark
73.3	fuii: turn
74.2	keke: cackle
75.2	don: bam
79.1	ninaka: shoop
79.5	piku: twitch
80.6	dota-dota: clatter-crash
81.2	gachan-tata-dota-bacha: bang-clatter-crash-bang
82.3	pah: pop
83.4	gashaa: grab

7.2a	basa-basa: tumble
7.2b	gonn: bonk
8.3	doko: dump
10.4	pata-pata: pitter patter
10.5	gara: clatter
12.4	bag: Crunchies
13.2	bari-bari; pari-pari: munch crunch
15.1	dohki-dohki: badum-badum (pounding heartbeat)
15.4	gotoh: clunk
16.4	ga-gan: (shock)
17.1	kandou: impressed
17.4	pata-pata: pitter patter

DOKI-DOKI

ド
キ

ONE OF THE MOST COMMON SOUND EFFECTS IN MANGA, "DOKI-DOKI" IS THE SOUND OF A POUNDING HEARTBEAT. IT'S USED TO INDICATE A TENSE, EMOTIONAL SITUATION.

18.1	patan: close (door)
20.4	gara: clatter
20.6	don: ta-da!
22.3	gyaa-gyaa: bicker
25.2	zusa: trip
25.3	gaba: (panic)
26.3	pasa: plop
31.3a	carton: You'll drink it all day long! Maibuum Milk. There's just not enough!
31.3b	patan: close (door)
32.3	GU: SNORE

128.3 pu-pu-pu: (stifled laughter)
133.1 bag: Supermarket- Come on by!
134.4 pori-pori: scratch-scratch
136.2 pashii x3: fwip x 3
137.1 kashi-kashi-kashi: munch munch munch

ANGER MARKS

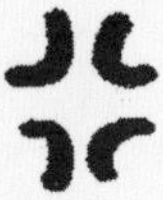

THESE LITTLE "PLUS SIGNS" ARE MEANT TO REPRESENT A THROBBING VEIN. OVER THE YEARS, THESE HAVE BECOME A VISUAL SHORT-CUT IN MANGA FOR ANGER. IN THE FRUITS BASKET ANIME, SHIGURE POKES FUN AT HIS EASY GOING PERSONALITY BY HOLDING AN ANGER MARK IN FRONT OF HIS FACE TO SHOW HIS RANGE.

137.6 pata: clack
139.4 don: thump
148.1 gashin: crash
148.5 zun-zun-zun-zun: stomp stomp
149.2a kya-kya-kya...: bicker bicker
149.2b zun-zun-zun-zun: stomp stomp
149.3 zun-zun-zun: stomp stomp
150.2 pori-pori: scratch-scratch
152.1 BASHIN: SLAM
154.1 HAx2: pantx2
168.2 tsuru: slip
168.5 gan: thunk
169.1a dosaa: thud
169.1b bon: poof
183.1 dosaa: thud

84.3a bon: poof
84.3b dotann: thump
84.5 basah: flutter
85.2 zawa-zawa: chatter chatter
85.3 zawa-zawa-zawa: chatter chatter
85.4 gyuu: clench
86.1 kiran: sparkle
87.2 go: punch
89.1 pasha: flash
90.3 gabaa: flop
95.5 pin-pon-pan: (intercom bell)
96.5 suu: fwip

ZAWA-ZAWA

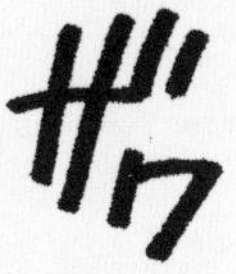

THE SOUND OF A CROWD. IF YOU SEE "ZAWA"S IN A CLASS-ROOM, IT PROBABLY MEANS THAT CLASS HASN'T STARTED YET. EITHER THAT, OR A TEACHER CAN'T CON-TROL HIS OR HER STUDENTS!

97.2 dokii: badum (heartbeat)
97.5 kirii: sparkle
98.1 dokii: badum (heartbeat)
98.2 doki-doki: badum-badum (heartbeat)
100.1 gara: clatter
102.1 dohki-dohki: badum-badum (pounding heartbeat)
102.2 dohki-dohki: badum-badum (pounding heartbeat)
103.1 kara-kara: rattle rattle
104.3 ha-ha-fu: huff-huff-pant
104.4 pata-pata: pitter patter
104.5 kara-kara: rattle rattle
105.4 hah: gasp
108.2 dokii: badum (heartbeat)
107.4 pata-pata: pitter patter
111.3 kara-kara: rattle rattle
119.3 kochi: plunk
120.1 dokii: badum (heartbeat)
120.5a "pu, bu: (stifled laughter)"
120.5b pu-pu-pu: (stifled laughter)
125.1 dokin: badum (heartbeat)
125.2 dokin: badum (heartbeat)
125.3 dokin-dokin: badum badum (heartbeat)
127.2 GU: SNORE

TOKYOPOP.com

Fruits Basket
By Natsuki Takaya
Volume 18

The next volume of the bestselling series is here!

Everyone knows Isuzu is in the hospital...or is she? While everyone is searching for her, Isuzu is hatching a scheme that may allow her to break the curse!

The #1 selling shojo manga in America!

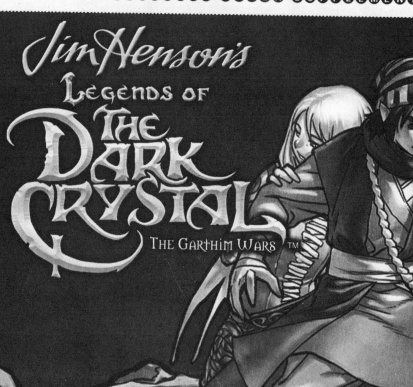

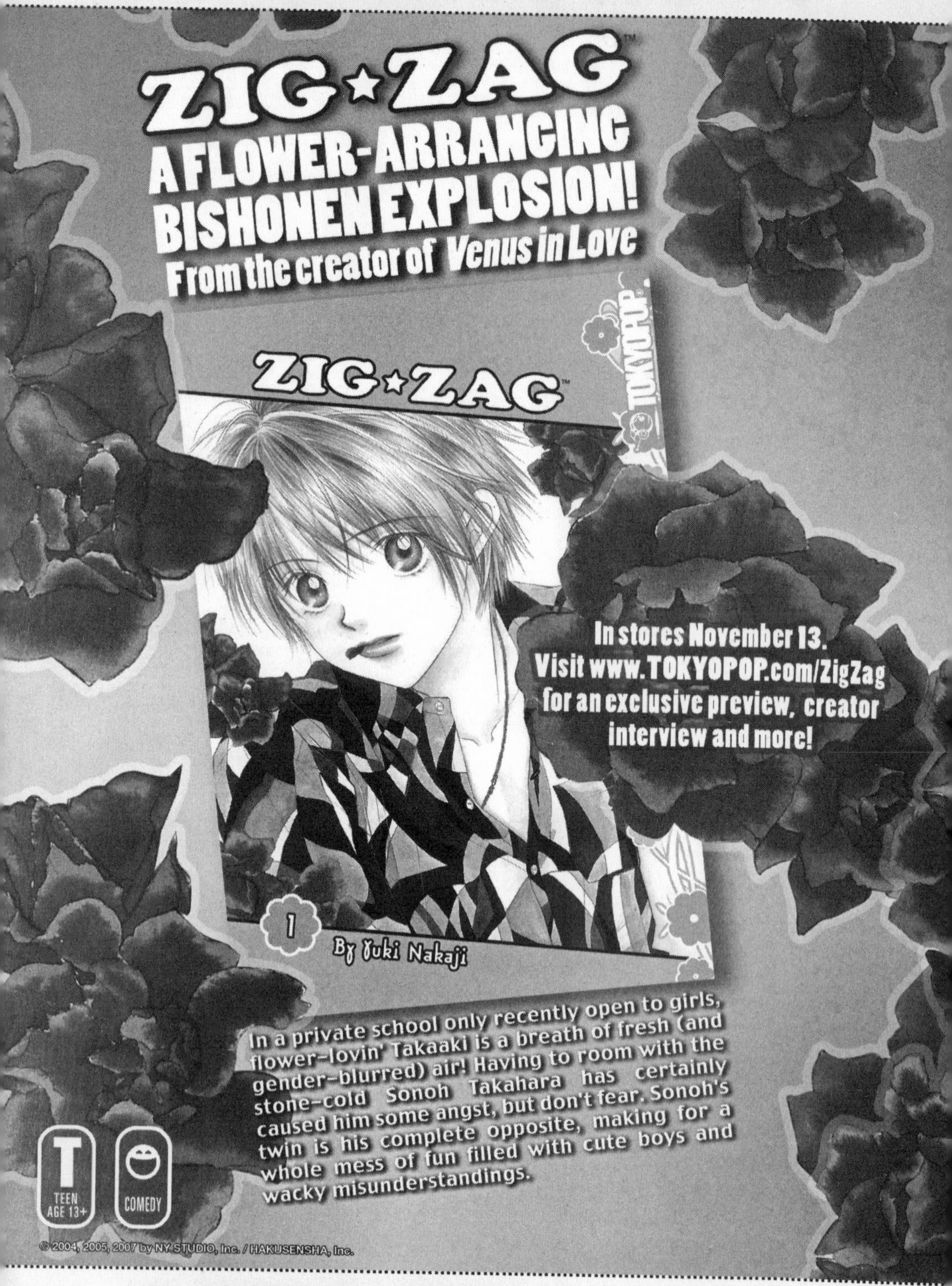
ZIG★ZAG™
A FLOWER-ARRANGING BISHONEN EXPLOSION!
From the creator of Venus in Love
ZIG★ZAG™
TOKYOPOP
1
By Yuki Nakaji
In stores November 13.
Visit www.TOKYOPOP.com/ZigZag for an exclusive preview, creator interview and more!
In a private school only recently open to girls, flower-lovin' Takaaki is a breath of fresh (and gender-blurred) air! Having to room with the stone-cold Sonoh Takahara has certainly caused him some angst, but don't fear. Sonoh's twin is his complete opposite, making for a whole mess of fun filled with cute boys and wacky misunderstandings.
T TEEN AGE 13+
COMEDY
© 2004, 2005, 2007 by NY STUDIO, Inc. / HAKUSENSHA, Inc.

Do you have the sixth sense?

6 7 8 7 5 2 . , 3 8 0 . , 9 9 0 . , 9 36 9 3

sixthsense@tokyopop.com

STOP!

This is the back of the book.
You wouldn't want to spoil a great ending!

This book is printed "manga-style," in the authentic Japanese right-to-left format. Since none of the artwork has been flipped or altered, readers get to experience the story just as the creator intended. You've been asking for it, so TOKYOPOP® delivered: authentic, hot-off-the-press, and far more fun!

DIRECTIONS

If this is your first time reading manga-style, here's a quick guide to help you understand how it works.

It's easy... just start in the top right panel and follow the numbers. Have fun, and look for more 100% authentic manga from TOKYOPOP®!